*Oxford Studies in Social History*
*General Editor: Keith Thomas*

# Oral and Literate
# Culture in England
## 1500—1700

# Oral and Literate
# Culture in England
## 1500–1700

ADAM FOX

**OXFORD**
UNIVERSITY PRESS

# OXFORD
### UNIVERSITY PRESS

Great Clarendon Street, Oxford OX2 6DP
Oxford University Press is a department of the University of Oxford.
It furthers the University's objective of excellence in research, scholarship,
and education by publishing worldwide in

Oxford New York

Auckland Bangkok Buenos Aires Cape Town
Chennai Dar es Salaam Delhi Hong Kong Istanbul Karachi
Kolkata Kuala Lumpur Madrid Melbourne Mexico City Mumbai Nairobi
São Paulo Shanghai Taipei Tokyo Toronto

Oxford is a registered trade mark of Oxford University Press
in the UK and in certain other countries

Published in the United States
by Oxford University Press Inc., New York

The moral rights of the author have been asserted
Database right Oxford University Press (maker)

First published 2000
First published in Paperback 2002

British Library Cataloguing in Publication Data
Data available

Library of Congress Cataloging in Publication Data
Data available

ISBN 0–19–820512–0 (hbk)
ISBN 0–19–925103–7 (pbk)

3 5 7 9 10 8 6 4 2

Typeset in Garamond MT
by Jayvee, Trivandrum, India
Printed in Great Britain
on acid-free paper by
Biddles Ltd. King's Lynn, Norfolk

*To Carolyn*

# ACKNOWLEDGEMENTS

I should like to acknowledge my debt to the many individuals and institutions from whose encouragement and assistance I have benefited in writing this book. My undergraduate tutors, Richard Tuck and Keith Wrightson, first introduced me to the intellectual and social life of early modern England and remain sources of inspiration and support. Keith Wrightson was an exemplary supervisor of research. I owe more to his guiding hand, as critic, mentor and friend, than can adequately be expressed here. Patrick Collinson and Sir Keith Thomas have given me generous help and advice over a number of years. I have profited greatly from their expertise, not least as rigorous Ph.D. examiners.

Among the many others who have taken the trouble to offer me counsel and support at various stages I wish to mention, in particular, Vic Gatrell, Olwen Hufton, Wallace MacCaffrey, Neil McKendrick, Bob Morris, Brian Outhwaite, and Margaret Spufford. A number of friends have kindly sent me references and been valued sources of stimulation during the course of work on this project. I should like to thank especially Alastair Bellany, Rich Connors, Alan Cromartie, Malcolm Gaskill, Paul Griffiths, Trevor Griffiths, Steve Hindle, Andrew McRae, Craig Muldrew, Steve Pincus, Tim Stretton, Naomi Tadmor, Helen Weinstein, and Andy Wood.

I am grateful to Jesus College, Cambridge for providing an academic home for so long; to the Kennedy Memorial Trust for enabling me to spend a year at Harvard as a Frank Knox Fellow; to the British Academy for awarding me a Postgraduate Studentship; to the Master and Fellows of Gonville and Caius College, Cambridge for electing me to a Research Fellowship; and to the University of Edinburgh for affording the most convivial of working environments.

Material from some of the following chapters has been published in other forms elsewhere. I wish to thank respectively the Past and Present Society, Macmillan Press Ltd., Cambridge University Press, and the Council of the Royal Historical Society for permission to reprint extracts from my essays: 'Ballads, Libels and Popular Ridicule in Jacobean England', *Past and Present*, 145 (1994), 47–83; 'Custom, Memory and the Authority of Writing', in Paul Griffiths, Adam Fox and Steve Hindle (eds.), *The Experience of Authority in Early Modern England* (Basingstoke,

1996), 89–116; 'Rumour, News and Popular Political Opinion in Elizabethan and Early Stuart England', *Historical Journal*, 40 (1997), 597–620; and 'Remembering the Past in Early Modern England: Oral and Written Tradition', *Transactions of the Royal Historical Society*, 6th ser., 9 (1999), 233–56.

Behind these efforts lies the unstinting support of my mother, Margaret, my brother, Richard, and my wife, Carolyn. Carolyn has helped me in innumerable ways, not least in reading successive drafts of the text, offering judicious opinion, and keeping my spirits up with unfailing kindness and patience. This book is dedicated to her with love.

# CONTENTS

# LIST OF ILLUSTRATIONS

# ABBREVIATIONS

| | |
|---|---|
| *APC* | *Acts of the Privy Council* |
| BL | British Library |
| Bod. Lib. | Bodleian Library |
| CRO | Cambridgeshire Record Office |
| *CSPD* | *Calendar of State Papers, Domestic* |
| CUL | Cambridge University Library |
| ERO | Essex Record Office |
| HMC | Historical Manuscripts Commission |
| *L&P* | *Letters and Papers* |
| *OED* | *Oxford English Dictionary* |
| ORO | Oxfordshire Record Office |
| PRO | Public Record Office |

As for orall traditions, what certaintie can there be in them? What foundation of truth can be layd vpon the breath of man?

Joseph Hall, *The Olde Religion* (London, 1628), 167.

Certainely hee that considereth these things in Gods peculiar people, will easily discerne how little of truth, there is in the wayes of the multitude; and though somtimes they are flattered with that aphorisme, will hardly beleeve the voyce of the people to bee the voyce of God.

Sir Thomas Browne, *Pseudodoxia Epidemica: or, Enquiries into Very Many Received Tenents, and Commonly Presumed Truths* (London, 1646), 10–11.

# Introduction: The Oral and the Literate

The invention of printing, though ingenious, compared with the invention of letters, is no great matter. But who was the first that found the use of letters, is not known . . . A profitable invention for continuing the memory of time past, and the conjunction of mankind, dispersed into so many, and distant regions of the earth . . . But the most noble and profitable invention of all other, was that of speech, consisting of names or appellations, and their connexion; whereby men register their thoughts; recall them when they are past; and also declare them one to another for mutuall utility and conversation . . .

> Thomas Hobbes, *Leviathan*, ed. Richard Tuck
> (Cambridge, 1991), 24.

Books may be helps to learning and knowledge, and make it more common and diffused; but I doubt whether they are necessary ones or no, or much advance any other science beyond the particular records of actions or registers of time; and these, perhaps, might be as long preserved without them, by the care and exactness of tradition in the long successions of certain races of men with whom they were intrusted.

> Sir William Temple, 'An Essay upon the Ancient and Modern
> Learning' (1690), in *Critical Essays of the Seventeenth Century*,
> ed. J. E. Spingarn (3 vols., Oxford, 1908), iii. 35.

CONSIDER the ballad of *Chevy Chase*. In sixteenth- and seventeenth-century England it was said to be the nation's favourite song. *The Hunting of the Cheviot* was its proper title and it told of a heroic battle fought in the Scottish marches between two great border chieftains, Henry Percy, the earl of Northumberland, and his rival, the earl of Douglas. On a field in Teviotdale two huge armies faced each other to settle a dispute over hunting rights. Percy and Douglas fought 'man for man' and toe to toe 'till blood a-downe their cheekes like raine' did fall. Then an English arrow struck Douglas 'a deepe and deadlye blow'. Taking the hand of his fallen foe Percy cried out, '"Erle dowglas! for thy sake wold I had lost my land!' But as he uttered forth his lament, a Scottish knight, Sir Hugh

Mountgomery, 'well mounted on a gallant steed', pierced the English
ranks 'and through Erle Percyes body then he thrust his hatfull spere'.
There these noble figures lay and with them the flower of their nations.
'Of 20 hundred Scottish speeres, scarce 55 did flye; of 1500 Englishmen,
went home but 53.' In the piteous strains of this, the greatest epic of our
popular poetry, could be heard all that was chivalrous, all that was honourable, all that was tragic, in days of yore.[1]

When this encounter took place, no one really knows. Perhaps the
ballad referred to the battle of Pepperden, fought in 1436 between Henry
Percy, third earl of Northumberland and William Douglas, earl of Angus.
A century later Hector Boethius described it as one 'fochtin cruelly with
gret slauchter on al sydis'. Songs in celebration of the slaughter, as of
other great border wars, probably circulated in manuscript and by word
of mouth soon after the event itself and by Boethius' day they were well
known on both sides of the border. Among the 'sueit melodius sangis of
natural music of the antiquite' which the shepherds sang to pass the time
until evening in a tract of 1549, *The Complaynt of Scotlande*, was 'The
Hunttis of Cheuet' in which 'the Perssee and the Mongumrye met, that
day, that day, that gentil day'. Soon afterwards, the poetical imagination of
the young Sir Philip Sidney was inflamed by what was already an 'olde
song' in the mouthes of blind fiddlers.

Certainly I must confesse my own barbarousnes: I neuer heard the olde song of
Percy and Duglas that I found not my heart mooued more then with a trumpet;
and yet is it sung by some blinde crouder, with no rougher voyce then rude stile;
which being so euill apparelled in the dust and cobwebbes of that vnciuill age,
what would it worke trymmed in the gorgeous eloquence of Pindar?[2]

One such crowder was Richard Sheale of Tamworth in Staffordshire
who toured the country singing in noblemen's houses and at fairs. It is to
him that we owe the first recorded version of this most famous of all
songs as it was transcribed into his working notebook sometime between
1557 and 1565. In common with almost all of the songs and ballads in the
book, 'The Hunting of the Cheviot' seems to have been taken down from
a printed broadside. It must, therefore, have been among that group of
great historical ballads of the later Middle Ages which was adopted by

---

[1] *Bishop Percy's Folio Manuscript*, ed. J. W. Hales and F. J. Furnivall (3 vols., London, 1867–8),
ii. 7–16.
[2] Hector Boethius, *The Hystory and Chroniklis of Scotland* (Edinburgh, 1540?), fo. 248ʳ; *The
Complaynt of Scotlande*, ed. J. A. H. Murray (Early English Text Society, extra ser., 17, London,
1872), 64–5; Sir Philip Sidney, *An Apology for Poetry* (1595), in *Elizabethan Critical Essays*, ed.
G. Gregory Smith (2 vols., Oxford, 1904), i. 178.

the new technology of print in the early sixteenth century.[3] Thus, by Sheale's day, *Chevy Chase* was already the product of a long series of inter-actions between oral, manuscript, and print culture. What probably began in manuscript form passed into oral circulation and eventually into print. From print it passed back again into manuscript and lived on in the mouths of minstrels and their audiences.

The first definite reference to the printed broadside is not until 1624 when *Chevie Chase* was entered in the register of the Stationers' Company of London. The silence before this is not surprising since only 65 per cent of the sixteenth-century ballads which have come down to us appear in the Stationers' register. This was probably not the version copied by Sheale but a revised and less antiquated rewriting for the expanding Jacobean market and it is this edition which became ubiquitous there-after. In the same year of 1624 Abraham Holland could invoke the image of 'north-villages' where 'o're the chymney they some ballad have of Chevy-Chase' pasted up. It was reprinted in 1675 as *A Memorable Song of the Unhappy Hunting in Chivey Chase* and many of the ballad collectors of the second half of the seventeenth century added this prize in one or more of its guises to their libraries. The Oxford antiquary Anthony Wood acquired two copies and quoted Sir Philip Sidney on the subject (see Plate 1).[4]

Meanwhile its place as the favourite of people in all walks of life was assured. As a youngster at the end of Elizabeth's reign the future bishop of Oxford and Norwich, Richard Corbet, sang it at the start of what would be a lifelong love affair with ballads. Reportedly 'Ben. Jonson used to say he had rather have been the author of it than of all his works'. After him, Joseph Addison, who grew up in rural Wiltshire in the 1670s, was 'so professed an admirer of this antiquated song' that he contributed a pair of essays on the subject. Henry Bold, a fellow of New College, Oxford, translated it into Latin verses in 1685 at the insistence of Henry Compton, the bishop of London. And yet for all this approval among the great and the good, the ballad was no less the darling of the people. 'The old song

---

[3] Bodleian Library (Bod. Lib.), MS Ashmole 48, fos. 15ʳ–18ʳ; *Songs and Ballads, with Other Short Poems, Chiefly of the Reign of Philip and Mary*, ed. Thomas Wright (London, 1860), 24–8; Hyder E. Rollins, 'Concerning Bodleian MS. Ashmole 48', *Modern Language Notes*, 34 (1919), 340–51; Tessa Watt, *Cheap Print and Popular Piety, 1550–1640* (Cambridge, 1991), 16–21.

[4] Watt, *Cheap Print and Popular Piety, 1550–1640*, 20 n., 39, 42; Hyder E. Rollins, 'An Analytical Index to the Ballad Entries (1557–1709) in the Register of the Company of Stationers of London', *Studies in Philology*, 21 (1924), 33, 148; Bod. Lib., Ballad Collection, Wood 401 (47), Wood 402 (30, 31), Harding B 2(41), Douce Ballads 3(99a); *The Roxburghe Ballads*, ed. W. Chappell and J. W. Ebsworth (9 vols., Ballad Society, London, 1871–99), vi. 738–43. See also National Library of Scotland, Crawford Collection of English Ballads, 430.

of Chevy Chase', thought Addison, 'is the favourite ballad of the common people of England.' When milkmaids chirped ballads at the churn, as famously they were wont to do, this was among their old favourites. When people in their villages sat and listened to 'the songs and fables that are common from father to son', this was their first delight.[5] And when crowds took to the urban streets to hoot political songs at their masters, this was the tune through which they commonly made their point.[6]

Nor did the ubiquity of the ballad in print and in oral circulation end its presence in manuscript. The new broadside version of *Chevy Chase* was transcribed into a folio scrapbook late in the reign of Charles I by a gentleman, probably from Lancashire, just as the old one had been copied for Richard Sheale almost a century before.[7] Such compilations illustrate the fact that despite the ever growing extent of the printed word in seventeenth-century England, this was still a society often most comfortable with manuscript, a world in which ownership was conferred by the labour of copying out above the expedient of pasting in. Perhaps the Lancastrian collector thought that careful transcription into a family ledger might better ensure the preservation of these ballads in an age when most broadsides ended up as lavatory paper. As it happened, he turned out to be right, but only by the very narrowest of margins.

In the middle years of the eighteenth century a young cleric paid a visit on a friend, Humphrey Pitt, at his house in Shifnal, Shropshire. While he was there he noticed an 'old manuscript . . . mutilated . . . unbound and sadly torn . . . lying dirty on the floor under a bureau in the parlour being used by the maids to light the fire'. He 'rescued [it] from destruction' and begged his host to let him keep it. A century on, and a long way from home, these tattered pages were what remained of the Lancashire gentle-

---

[5] *The Spectator*, ed. Donald F. Bond (5 vols., Oxford, 1965), i. 298, 297–303, and 315–22; W. Chappell, *Popular Music of the Olden Time* (London, 1859), 198; Izaak Walton, *The Complete Angler* (Everyman edn., London, 1906), 69, 168. Cf. *The Diary of Samuel Pepys*, ed. Robert Latham and William Matthews (11 vols., London, 1970–83), viii. 56.

[6] *The Life and Times of Anthony Wood, Antiquary, of Oxford, 1632–1695, described by Himself*, ed. Andrew Clark (5 vols., Oxford Historical Society, 19, 21, 26, 30, 40, Oxford, 1891–1900), i. 352; *The English Reports* (176 vols., Edinburgh, 1900–30), xc. 1132–3; *The Remains of Thomas Hearne*, ed. John Buchanan-Brown (London, 1966), 66; Natascha Wurzbach, *The Rise of the English Street Ballad, 1550–1650* (Cambridge, 1990), 284; *The Bagford Ballads*, ed. J. W. Ebsworth (Ballad Society, Hertford, 1878), 390–6, 736–40, 861–7. For the tune, which was named on around three dozen ballads before 1700, see Claude M. Simpson, *The British Broadside Ballad and its Music* (New Brunswick, NJ, 1966), 96–101.

[7] British Library (BL), Additional MS, 27879, fos. 94–5; *Bishop Percy's Folio Manuscript*, ed. Hales and Furnivall, i. xii–xiii, ii. 7–16. For another such commonplace book, see *The Shirburn Ballads, 1585–1616*, ed. Andrew Clark (Oxford, 1907).

man's ballad book. Some time later, in 1765, after inflicting not a little damage on the torn leaves himself, the cleric published forty-five of their contents, with *Chevy Chase* as the first, among three volumes of traditional ballads entitled *Reliques of Ancient English Poetry*. His name was Thomas Percy. The 'reliques' proved to be one of the foundation texts for the study of English folksong and, more than any other work, they stimulated the romantic 'rediscovery' of the people and the academic investigation of 'popular antiquities' in the later eighteenth century. As much as any other literary endeavour, they conjured up, in the historical imagination of the Enlightenment, the 'pleasing simplicity' of old England.[8]

The transmission of *Chevy Chase* vividly illustrates many of the themes with which this book is concerned. It is difficult to know whether to describe such a ballad as the product of oral, scribal, or print culture. First and foremost, it was a song, intended to be overheard, learned off by heart and carolled aloud. But it was probably the product of manuscript circulation in the first instance; certainly it is to this medium that it owes its first known recording and in this form that it came to the attention of its most famous publisher. Yet the immense popularity of the ballad was surely due to its dissemination in thousands of printed copies and the fact that people could also read it from the page, whether set above the fire-place at home or pasted on the alehouse wall.

England in the sixteenth and seventeenth centuries, therefore, was a society in which the three media of speech, script, and print infused and interacted with each other in a myriad ways. Then, as now, a song or a story, an expression or a piece of news, could migrate promiscuously between these three vehicles of transmission as it circulated around the country, throughout society and over time. There was no necessary antithesis between oral and literate forms of communication and preser-vation; the one did not have to destroy or undermine the other. If any-thing, the written word tended to augment the spoken, reinventing it and making it anew, propagating its contents, heightening its exposure, and ensuring its continued vitality, albeit sometimes in different forms.

The history of *Chevy Chase* demonstrates that England in this period was already a society profoundly influenced by the written word at every social level, not merely in legal and administrative contexts but down to the very fabric of its forms of entertainment and imaginative expression. Even those people who could not read the handwritten or printed word

---

[8] BL, Additional MS, 27879, fo. 1ʳ; *Bishop Percy's Folio Manuscript*, ed. Hales and Furnivall, i. lxxiv; Thomas Percy, *Reliques of Ancient English Poetry* (3 vols., London, 1765), i. xiii–xx, 1–17; Peter Burke, *Popular Culture in Early Modern Europe* (London, 1978), 5, 9, 18.

for themselves traded in forms which were derived from such sources. They, too, lived within an environment structured and fashioned by text. Any crude binary opposition between 'oral' and 'literate' culture fails to accommodate the reciprocity between the different media by this time; just as any crude dichotomy between 'elite' and 'popular' fails to illuminate a spectrum of participation which extended from the Latin verse of Oxford dons to the rude style of blind crowders.

But these dichotomies go back to the days of Bishop Percy himself. When ancient songs and popular traditions first started to become the subject of retrospective analysis and antiquarian interest in the late eighteenth century, due in part to the publication of his 'reliques', enthusiasts failed to appreciate the centuries of mutual transaction between oral, scribal, and printed sources which by then lay behind the evolution of their materials. The sensibilities of the Romantic era needed to believe in the idea of a pure oral tradition of the folk which had perpetuated itself since time immemorial, untainted by the influence of the written word and unsuspected in the drawing rooms of the polite reading classes. This was the spirit in which John Brand published his collection of 'popular antiquities' in 1777, a work which became one of the seminal texts of English folklore.

Tradition has in no instance so clearly evinced her faithfulness, as in the transmitting of vulgar rites and popular opinions . . . These, consecrated to the fancies of men, by usage from time immemorial, though erazed by public authority from the written word, were committed as a venerable deposit to the keeping of oral tradition . . .[9]

It was the same spirit which inspired the sense of national identity in men like Oliver Goldsmith.

Every country has it traditions, which, either too minute or not sufficiently authentic to receive historical sanction, are handed down among the vulgar, and serve at once to instruct and amuse them. Of this number, the adventures of Robin Hood, the hunting of Chevy Chace, and the bravery of Johnny Armstrong, among the English . . .[10]

In the nineteenth century, the idea that popular tradition was the product of unmediated oral transmission and that it bore little relationship to the culture of the literate classes was the first principle from which the developing study of folklore began. Thus old regional dialects were said to have been transmitted by 'passing through the mouths of uneducated people, speaking an inherited language', being 'the ordinary medium of

---

[9]  John Brand, *Observations on Popular Antiquities* (Newcastle, 1777), iii–iv.
[10]  Oliver Goldsmith, *The Bee and Other Essays* (Oxford, 1914), 30.

communication between peasant and peasant' oblivious to the norms
and standards of written language. Equally, it was believed that old
proverbs existed before the written word and 'like the oral traditions of
the Jews, they floated down from age to age on the lips of successive generations'. Only now have they 'ceased to be studied, or employed in conversation, since the time we have derived our knowledge from books'. As
for 'customs, rights and beliefs', they too, in G. L. Gomme's conventional
opinion, had been 'mostly kept alive by tradition' among the masses who
played no part in the 'civilisation which towers over them'. Meanwhile,
lack of contact with the written word had always kept the majority ignorant of current affairs. In the late seventeenth century, thought the historian Macaulay, 'scarce any of the clowns who came to the parish church
ever saw a Gazette or a political pamphlet', and this was a prevailing image
of country folk even in his own day.[11]

From this view it followed that the forward march of literacy and the
civilizing process of education in the modern era were destroying the
popular lore of ages. Reading and writing were necessarily the antithesis
and the nemesis of oral tradition; the advance of the one inevitably
entailed the dissipation of the other. The mood was generally elegiac
about the death knell of a plebeian culture which, until that time, was
thought to have been unchanged for centuries. In the country towns of
East Anglia, the old dialect was fading fast, thought Robert Forby in 1830,
due to the 'many and various schools, circulating or subscription libraries,
book clubs, reading-rooms, and other appliances and means of literary
proficiency, adapted to the different ranks of a numerous population'.
North of the border, William Motherwell lamented that 'not many years
ago, it was a common country pastime of a winter's night to while time
away by repeating proverbs, telling tales, and reciting songs and ballads;
but these old fashions are fast disappearing since the schoolmaster and
politics were let loose upon the country'. Thomas Hardy was able to confirm the nostalgic sensibilites of the late Victorian middle class in his
depictions of an imagined Wessex.

Mrs Durbeyfield habitually spoke the dialect; her daughter, who had passed the
Sixth Standard in the National School under a London-trained mistress, spoke
two languages; the dialect at home, more or less; ordinary English abroad and to
persons of quality . . . Between the mother, with her fast-perishing lumber of

---

[11] A. J. Ellis, *On Early English Pronunciation* (5 vols., London, 1869–89), v. 1; Isaac D'Israeli,
'The Philosophy of Proverbs', in *A Second Series of Curiosities of Literature* (3 vols., London, 1823),
i. 417, 479; Gomme quoted in Bob Bushaway, *By Rite: Custom, Ceremony and Community in England,
1700–1880* (London, 1982), 10; T. B. Macaulay, *The History of England*, ed. Hugh Trevor-Roper
(Harmondsworth, 1979), 68.

superstitions, folk-lore, dialect, and orally transmitted ballads, and the daughter, with her trained National teachings and Standard knowledge under an infinitely Revised Code, there was a gap of two hundred years as ordinarily understood. When they were together the Jacobean and the Victorian ages were juxtaposed.[12]

But this popular repertoire was by no means as purely oral or a suddenly vulnerable as Hardy made out. A recent study has shown that at least ninety-one of the English folksongs which were circulating in Mrs Durbeyfield's day derived from broadsides printed before 1700.[13] Characteristic of the folkloric imagination of the nineteenth century, therefore, was a 'failure to appreciate the partial nature of the "oral tradition" to be found in a society with writing, anyhow one with long and extensive literacy'.[14] This failure has never been completely rectified, and vestiges of the misconceptions to which it has given rise remain even today. It is still quite common for historians to regard certain sections of the labouring population, especially in the countryside, as being essentially cut off from contact with the written word, not only in the sixteenth and seventeenth centuries, but also in subsequent periods.[15]

In the last two decades, however, there has been a number of detailed investigations of the popular literature which was printed in early modern England. It was produced in vast quantities and sold for a few pence throughout the country. The implication of this work is that cheap printed matter was circulating widely and penetrating deeply in society even in the Tudor period.[16] Perhaps a majority of people may not yet have been able to read it for themselves, but it was also the case that the vernacular repertoire was being structured and determined by this print,

[12] Robert Forby, *The Vocabulary of East Anglia* (2 vols., London, 1830), i. 69; William Motherwell, 'Preface', in Andrew Henderson, *Scottish Proverbs* (Edinburgh, 1832), xxix; Thomas Hardy, *Tess of the d'Urbervilles* (1891; New Wessex edn., London, 1974), 48, 50–1.

[13] R. S. Thomson, 'The Development of the Broadside Ballad Trade and its Influence upon the Transmission of English Folksongs' (unpublished Cambridge University Ph.D. thesis, 1974), 312–14.

[14] Jack Goody, *The Interface between the Written and the Oral* (Cambridge, 1987), xv.

[15] See the comments in R. S. Schofield, 'The Measurement of Literacy in Pre-Industrial England', in Jack Goody (ed.), *Literacy in Traditional Societies* (Cambridge, 1968), 313; Peter Laslett, *The World We Have Lost—Further Explored* (London, 1983), 233–4; R. W. Malcolmson, *Life and Labour in England, 1700–1780* (London, 1981), 99, and quoted in Barry Reay, 'Introduction', in Reay (ed.), *Popular Culture in Seventeenth-Century England* (London, 1985), 5.

[16] Bernard Capp, *Astrology and the Popular Press: English Almanacs, 1500–1800* (London, 1979); Margaret Spufford, *Small Books and Pleasant Histories: Popular Fiction and its Readership in Seventeenth-Century England* (London, 1981); Bernard Capp, 'Popular Literature', in Reay (ed.), *Popular Culture in Seventeenth-Century England*, 198–243; Wurzbach, *The Rise of the English Street Ballad, 1550–1650*; Watt, *Cheap Print and Popular Piety, 1550–1640*; Margaret Spufford (ed.), *The World of Rural Dissenters, 1520–1725* (Cambridge, 1995), 64–85, 235–72, 273–87.

and a multitude of other written materials, in fundamental ways. As early as the mid-sixteenth century, the Scottish shepherds on their hillside, the people of Penshurst who may have overheard the same blind crowder as Sir Philip Sidney, the folk gathered in Tamworth market listening to Richard Sheale strum on his harp, were all learning a ballad which began with the written word and owed its popularity to print.

Nor is it possible any longer to think, as the perceptions which we have inherited from the late eighteenth and nineteenth centuries still encourage us to do, that the written word was the natural antidote to oral tradition. Well before the early modern period, the popular repertoire had ceased to be purely oral. Centuries of manuscript transmission, sermon exempla, minstrelsy, and drama had seen to it that the folklore of the village contained elements which came down from learned and literate culture. By the sixteenth century the pace of this infusion was quickened enormously by the advent of printed texts which almost from the first were highly accessible. All manner of information and entertainment was soon produced in broadside and broadsheet format; it was cheap to buy, posted in public places, and distributed throughout the nation in town and country alike. The contents of this print did not destroy circulation by word of mouth. Sometimes it enshrined material picked up from the oral realm; certainly it fed back into it. The written word helped instruct people in what to sing, what to retell, and how to express themselves in ways which greatly enhanced and enriched their cultural world.

The reality of this was appreciated even at the time. The Elizabethan preacher Nicholas Bownd observed the way in which the common people bought broadside ballads and set them up in their cottages and shops even if they themselves could not read. He believed that after the Reformation of the 1530s 'the singing of ballads (that was rife in poperie) began to cease, and in time was cleane banished away in many places'. By the 1590s, however, 'and indeed I know not how it commeth to passe, (but you may obserue it) that the singing of ballades is very lately renewed, and commeth on a fresh againe, so that in euery faire and market almost you shall haue one or two singing and selling of ballades, and they are brought vp a pace . . .'. In other words, far from undermining oral circulation, print had greatly reinvigorated and refreshed something which was in danger of disappearing.[17]

What was true of ballads was true of much else in the vernacular stock. In the case of all the forms of oral culture discussed in this book, even

---

[17] Nicholas Bownd, *The Doctrine of the Sabbath Plainely Layde Forth* (London, 1595), 242.

those which were largely the preserve of the unlettered majority, each was profoundly influenced on some level by the fruits of the written and printed word. Thus the language itself was enormously augmented and enriched both by new coinages and the huge infusion of loan words imported from ancient and modern European languages over the sixteenth and seventeenth centuries. Thanks to the exchange of ideas and texts facilitated by Renaissance humanism, thousands of new terms were naturalized into English, especially in the Elizabethan and early Stuart period.[18] At the same time much of the common proverbial wisdom which became the platitudes of the nation first entered the vernacular via the same channels. The ten editions of *Adages* which Erasmus published in the first four decades of the sixteenth century were alone responsible for the dissemination of over 4,000 sayings and aphorisms in England, many of which were soon adopted and remain household favourites today.[19]

At the same time, few superstitions or common beliefs on almost any subject in this period cannot be traced back to some written source, very often the classical writers on natural history such as Pliny the Elder whose works were also disseminated afresh during the Renaissance. Few popular traditions about the past in early modern England cannot be found in the pages of the medieval chroniclers or preachers who set so much legend on foot. So many of the very wildest rumours and fantastic fears which convulsed the nation under the Tudors and Stuarts and regularly sent it into panic owed their origin to a written letter or a printed newsbook. In short, almost every context confirms the wisdom of Sir Thomas Browne's observation in the 1640s, that 'there is scare any tradition or popular error but stands also delivered by some good author'.[20]

No one was immune from the influences wrought by the written word. Everyone who spoke the language, uttered its habitual sayings, sang its popular songs, inherited its commonplace assumptions and adhered to its normative beliefs, was absorbed in a world governed by text.

---

[18] Charles Barber, *Early Modern English* (London, 1976), ch. 6; Manfred Görlach, *Introduction to Early Modern English* (Cambridge, 1991), 136–9, 166–9.

[19] Margaret Mann Phillips, *The 'Adages' of Erasmus: A Study with Translations* (Cambridge, 1964), 3.

[20] Sir Thomas Browne, *Pseudodoxia Epidemica* (1646), in *The Works of Sir Thomas Browne*, ed. Geoffrey Keynes (4 vols., London, 1964), ii. 52. The derivation of many popular superstitions from ancient writers is made clear in Thomas Lupton, *A Thousand Notable Things, of Sundry Sortes* (London, 1579).

## THE CONTEXT

A large body of work by anthropologists and pychologists, linguists and historians, has now been devoted to assessing the impact which the spread of literacy has had in various societies past and present. The influence of the written word on oral communication and mental processes is regarded as being one of the key questions in the human and social sciences. The implications of reading and writing for intellectual and cultural life, social structure and economic development, political participation, and religious belief, have become the focus of intensive study. Some scholars have identified fundamental differences between societies which are largely oral and those with long traditions of written culture. Literacy has been claimed to transform the way in which people think and act. It has been linked to the rise of more 'rational' modes of belief and the onset of secularization; it has been invoked to account for industrial growth and the spread of democracy; it has been regarded as a sign of progress and a mark of civilization.[21] Alternatively, there are those who see little fundamental difference between the conceptual categories of literates and illiterates, or between the frames of reference in largely oral and heavily textual societies. They would deny that the ability to read and transmit information through writing is a necessary condition for any of these broader developments and transformations.[22]

In practice, most societies are characterized by a dynamic series of interactions between spoken and written forms of communication and record. At the same time, literacy is most often regarded not as an autonomous agent of change or a monolithic technology the effects of which are always and everywhere the same. Instead, the implications of reading and writing are recognized to vary between societies and over time, and to depend upon the particular circumstances of their dissemination and use. General theories, therefore, always require qualification: only by the detailed investigation of specific contexts can the effects of this most important aspect of social and historical change be assessed with any precision.

[21] See, for example, Richard D. Altick, *The English Common Reader: A Social History of the Mass Reading Public, 1800–1900* (Chicago, 1957); Marshall McLuhan, *The Gutenberg Galaxy* (London, 1962); Jack Goody and Ian Watt, 'The Consequences of Literacy', in Goody (ed.), *Literacy in Traditional Societies*, 27–68; Jack Goody, *The Domestication of the Savage Mind* (Cambridge, 1977); Walter J. Ong, *Orality and Literacy: The Technologizing of the Word* (London, 1982).

[22] Ruth Finnegan, 'Literacy Versus Non-Literacy: The Great Divide?', in Robin Horton and Ruth Finnegan (eds.), *Modes of Thought: Essays on Thinking in Western and Non-Western Societies* (London, 1973), 112–44; B. V. Street, *Literacy in Theory and Practice* (Cambridge, 1984); Harvey J. Graff, *The Legacies of Literacy* (Bloomington, 1987), 381–90; Ruth Finnegan, *Literacy and Orality: Studies in the Technology of Communication* (Oxford, 1988).

This book sets out to explore the interaction between the different media, oral, scribal, and printed, in sixteenth- and seventeenth-century England. Its particular focus is the way in which an increasingly literate and print-based culture influenced both the means and the content of communication throughout society, and especially among that majority of the population least familiar with the written word. As a case study for examining the relationship between oral and written forms, these centuries are particularly fascinating and important. On the one hand oral exchange remained the primary mode of receiving and transmitting cultural capital for most people. On the other hand this was a period in which significant advances were made in popular literacy and the new technology of print first made a real impact on society.

The formative nature of the early modern period must not be exaggerated, however. For generations before the sixteenth century, written documents had been recording, defining, and prescribing many aspects of political, legal, and religious life. Something like 2,000 charters and writs survive from Anglo-Saxon England as testimony to the fact that writing was already an important feature of administrative life. The great transition 'from memory to written record', however, took place in the centuries after the Norman Conquest. Tens of thousands of charters and writs are extant from the thirteenth century as evidence of the huge increase in bureaucracy at this time. In the reign of Edward I property rights were being enshrined in written title and warrants and deeds replaced the memory of elders as proof of ownership. The pipe rolls of the Exchequer begin in the early twelfth century; borough court records survive from the late twelfth and early thirteenth centuries; the earliest manor court rolls date from the 1240s. The statute of Exeter of 1285 required local bailiffs to record all villages and hamlets within each franchise of the kingdom, meaning that every community must have been familiar with official documents by this time at least.[23]

In the later Middle Ages the written word extended further into almost every aspect of economic, social, and cultural life. The precedents set in the thirteenth century for collecting documents in local and central archives and for reporting legal cases in yearbooks developed a cumulative momentum. The superiority of written evidence in court was firmly established while local society became ever more used to conveying land in the form of written indentures.[24] At the same time, the late medieval

---

[23] M. T. Clanchy, *From Memory to Written Record: England, 1066–1307* (2nd edn., Oxford, 1993), 1–3, 28, 46–51, 68, 96–8, 104.

[24] Ibid. 98–9, 149–72; W. S. Holdsworth, *A History of English Law* (17 vols., London, 1903–72), ii; J. H. Baker, *An Introduction to English Legal History* (3rd edn., London, 1990), 204–7,

Church had become thoroughly accustomed to disseminating its message through text. The Bible itself was widely dispersed, even in the vernacular: over 250 manuscripts of the Wycliffite translation of the Scriptures have survived. Meanwhile, thousands of primers, lives of saints, accounts of visions, and moralistic fables circulated in the same form.[25] The expansion of literary expression was also manifest in many other spheres. Written texts of the great miracle plays and mysteries which survive from the fourteenth century, together with innumerable collections of poems, carols, and songs, all bear witness to the ever greater tendency to record the fruits of imaginative and artistic achievement. Romances detailing the exploits of legendary heroes are extant from this time and earlier, while the fifteenth century witnessed a renaissance in the writing of historical chronicles.[26] These texts circulated widely thanks to a brisk trade in scribal copying and they reached the widest audiences via the common practice of reading aloud.[27]

This proliferation of written texts cannot be dissociated from the commensurate increase in the ability to read throughout the lay population. In part this was a function of the expansion of formal education in the form of elementary and endowed grammar schools from the late fourteenth century, and it may also have been a consequence of the enduring but much less easily detectable presence of mothers teaching their children basic reading skills within the home.[28] Between 40 and 50 per cent of the

211–12; R H Britnell, *The Commercialisation of English Society, 1000–1500* (2nd edn., Manchester, 1996), 80, 116–17, 139–40, 142–4, 231.

[25] Margaret Aston, 'Lollardy and Literacy', in her *Lollards and Reformers: Images and Literacy in Late Medieval Religion* (London, 1984), 193–217; Anne Hudson, *The Premature Reformation: Wycliffite Texts and Lollard History* (Oxford, 1988), 200–17, 231–68; Eamon Duffy, *The Stripping of the Altars: Traditional Religion in England, c.1400–c.1580* (New Haven, 1992), 7–8, 68–77, 210–32.

[26] E. K. Chambers, *The Mediaeval Stage* (2 vols., Oxford, 1903), ii. 1–176; E. K. Chambers, *English Literature at the Close of the Middle Ages* (Oxford, 1945); M. B. Parkes, 'The Literacy of the Laity', in David Daiches and Anthony Thorlby (eds.), *Literature and Western Civilisation: The Mediaeval World* (London, 1973), 555–77; *Fragments of an Early Fourteenth-Century Guy of Warwick*, ed. Maldwyn Mills and Daniel Huws (Medium Aevum Monographs, new ser., 4, Oxford, 1974); P. R. Coss, 'Aspects of Cultural Diffusion in Medieval England: The Early Romances, Local Society and Robin Hood', *Past and Present*, 108 (1985), 35–79; C. L. Kingsford, *English Historical Literature in the Fifteenth Century* (Oxford, 1913).

[27] Lucien Febvre and Henri-Jean Martin, *The Coming of the Book: The Impact of Printing, 1450–1800*, trans. David Gerard (London, 1976), 15–28; Clanchy, *From Memory to Written Record*, 189, 207, 255, 266–72, 285; Ruth Crosby, 'Oral Delivery in the Middle Ages', *Speculum*, 11 (1936), 94–100; H. J. Chaytor, *From Script to Print: An Introduction to Medieval Vernacular Literature* (Cambridge, 1945), 10–21; Aston, 'Lollardy and Literacy', 195.

[28] Nicholas Orme, *English Schools in the Middle Ages* (London, 1973), chs. 6–7; id., *Education and Society in Medieval and Renaissance England* (London, 1989), chs. 1–2; J. Hoeppner Moran, *The Growth of English Schooling, 1340–1548: Learning, Literacy and Laicization in Pre-Reformation York Diocese* (Princeton, 1985); Hudson, *The Premature Reformation*, 180–200; M. T. Clanchy, 'Learning

lay population of London appear to have been able to sign their names in the 1470s and reading ability may have been even more widespread. Moreover, evidence from Norfolk at the same time and from Glastonbury in the previous century confirming exactly these literacy levels, suggests that the capital was by no means exceptional in this respect. An analysis of wills witnessed in the diocese of York during the early Tudor period indicates that 15 per cent of people could make a signature, a consequence in part, no doubt, of the rapid growth of grammar, song, and reading schools in the region during the fifteenth century.[29]

By the beginning of the Tudor period, therefore, England had long been a highly documentary society in which the ability to read the hand-written word in the vernacular, and in some cases in Latin too, was dispersed quite widely in society. In the sixteenth and seventeenth centuries, however, there were a number of significant developments which greatly accelerated these trends. The first was the spread of printing. Print was no more than an extension of the already well-developed culture of scribal copying, but it increased enormously the quantity of the texts in circulation and, in due course, their variety as well.[30] Forty-six titles were published in England in the year 1500; by 1530, this figure had risen to 214; 259 books were printed in 1600, and 577 in 1640. Given print runs of about 1,000 copies per title, it has been estimated that there were, on average, around 300,000 volumes published every year between 1576 and 1640. When control of the press lapsed in the middle decades of the seventeenth century some years saw up to 2,000 titles appearing.[31]

to Read in the Middle Ages and the Role of Mothers', in Greg Brooks and A. K. Pugh (eds.), *Studies in the History of Reading* (Reading, 1984), 33–9; Clanchy, *From Memory to Written Record*, 13–14, 111–12, 251–2.

[29] Sylvia L. Thrupp, *The Merchant Class of Medieval London, 1300–1500* (Chicago, 1948), 156–8; R. W. Kaeuper, 'Two Early Lists of Literates in England: 1334, 1373', *English Historical Review*, 99 (1984), 363–9; J. Hoeppner Moran, 'Literacy and Education in Northern England, 1350–1550: A Methodological Inquiry', *Northern History*, 17 (1981), 14–16, 17; Hoeppner Moran, *The Growth of English Schooling*, 178–82. See also, F. R. H. Du Boulay, *An Age of Ambition: English Society in the Late Middle Ages* (London, 1970), 118–19; L. R. Poos, *A Rural Society after the Black Death: Essex, 1350–1525* (Cambridge, 1991), 280–8.

[30] Febvre and Martin, *The Coming of the Book*; Elizabeth L. Eisenstein, *The Printing Press as an Agent of Change: Communications and Cultural Transformations in Early-Modern Europe* (2 vols., Cambridge, 1979); Roger Chartier (ed.), *The Culture of Print: Power and the Uses of Print in Early Modern Europe*, trans. L. G. Cochrane (Cambridge, 1989).

[31] A. W. Pollard and G. R. Redgrave, *A Short-Title Catalogue of Books Printed in England, Scotland, and Ireland and of English Books Printed Abroad, 1475–1640* (rev. edn., 3 vols., London, 1976–91); Donald Wing, *Short-Title Catalogue of Books Printed in England, Scotland, Ireland, Wales and British America and of English Books Printed in Other Countries, 1641–1700* (rev. edn., 3 vols., New York 1982–94). See H. S. Bennett, *English Books and Readers, 1475 to 1640* (3 vols., Cambridge, 1965–70); J. A. Sharpe, *Early Modern England: A Social History, 1550–1760* (2nd edn., London, 1997), 263.

Printed literature on every subject and in every format grew progressively larger over the course of the early modern period. It has been calculated, for example, that there had already been 57,000 Latin primers printed in England before the Reformation of the 1530s. At least 60,000 catechisms were published in the period 1580–1640 and perhaps half a million bibles, if not many more, had come from the presses by the end of the seventeenth century. Medical advice in the vernacular accounted for only 3 per cent of total book production between 1485 and 1603, and yet there were probably some 392,000 copies of such works produced in that period. It is a reasonable estimate that three or four million broadside ballads were printed in the second half of the sixteenth century alone. By the 1620s these were being complemented by the 'small book', or cheap octavo pamphlet, containing a similar diet of material, and by the Restoration the scale of this 'chapbook' production was probably similar to that of printed almanacs, with about 400,000 copies being produced annually. Newspapers proliferated when censorship lapsed in the 1640s and 1650s: in 1644 a dozen were appearing in London every week selling anything between 200 and 1,000 copies each.[32]

The inventories of various booksellers over these two centuries reveal just how dispersed was the market for printed works from the first and how diverse was the range of tastes for which it catered. In a period of less than ten months during 1520, the Oxford bookseller John Dorne sold 1,850 items. Over 150 of these were works by Erasmus and many others were theological and classical texts in Latin. But he also sold ABCs 'for to lerne rede', a number of the great prose romances familiar in manuscript circulation during the late Middle Ages, as well as 170 ballads at a halfpenny each. In 1585 the Shrewsbury bookseller, Roger Ward, had an inventory of some 546 different items covering all aspects of the publishing spectrum, and his stock was not dissimilar to that which John Foster carried in Jacobean York. In 1644 John Awdley of Hull had a list of 832 volumes offered for sale, including numerous 'small books' which suggest that he was supplying a wide popular readership. The proliferation of printed works during the political breakdown of the mid-seventeenth century is revealed by the surviving collection of the London stationer,

---

[32] Duffy, *The Stripping of the Altars*, 212; T. W. Laqueur, 'The Cultural Origins of Popular Literacy in England, 1500–1850', *Oxford Review of Education*, 2 (1976), 262; Paul Slack, 'Mirrors of Health and Treasures of Poor Men: The Uses of the Vernacular Medical Literature of Tudor England', in Charles Webster (ed.), *Health, Medicine and Mortality in the Sixteenth Century* (Cambridge, 1979), 239–40; Watt, *Cheap Print and Popular Piety*, 11; Capp, *Astrology and the Popular Press*, 44; Spufford, *Small Books and Pleasant Histories*, 118; G. A. Cranfield, *The Press and Society from Caxton to Northcliffe* (London, 1978), 11.

George Thomason, which amounted to a huge 14,942 pamphlets and 7,216 newspapers by the early 1660s. At the end of the seventeenth century a small provincial bookseller such as Roger Williams of Hereford was catering for the pocket and tastes of a wide reading public: his stock in 1695 contained 120 volumes or parcels of books in handy octavo size, chiefly vernacular works on religion and history, together with school-texts, as against only forty-two in folio and eight in quarto.[33]

Another crucial development of the period in this respect was the Reformation. It is by no means clear how much of an influence the new religion had on promoting educational advance or increasing literacy levels in the sixteenth and seventeenth centuries. The foundation of schools and the growth of reading and writing ability may well have progressed in this period regardless of doctrinal change. But the Protestant emphasis on 'the word', and its insistence on individual believers experiencing the Scriptures for themselves as a necessary condition for salvation, may have been an added stimulus in this direction. Whatever its motivation, there was clearly a considerable expansion in the provision of formal education at every level under the Tudors and Stuarts. The universities at Oxford and Cambridge witnessed a steady increase in the number of their entrants between the mid-sixteenth and mid-seventeenth centuries with over 2 per cent of 17-year-olds attending in the 1630s, a higher percentage than at any stage before recent times. Meanwhile, the grammar schools, devoted to the teaching of classical languages, were also experiencing significant growth: they doubled their numbers between the reigns of Elizabeth I and Charles II and a survey of 1673 revealed a total of 704 nationwide, or one for every urban centre in the country.[34] At the elementary level there appears to have been similar development. Of the 398

---

[33] F. Madan, 'Day-Book of John Dorne, Bookseller in Oxford, A.D. 1520', *Collectanea* (Oxford Historical Society, 1st ser., Oxford, 1885), 71–177; Alexander Roger, 'Roger Ward's Shrewbury Stock: An Inventory of 1585', *Library*, 5th ser., 13 (1958), 247–68; Robert Davies, *A Memoir of the York Press* (Westminster, 1868), 342–71; C. W. Chilton, 'The Inventory of a Provincial Bookseller's Stock of 1644', *Library*, 6th ser., 1 (1979), 126–43; George Thomason, *Catalogue of the Pamphlets, Books, Newspapers, and Manuscripts Relating to the Civil War, the Commonwealth, and Restoration, Collected by George Thomason, 1640–1661* (2 vols., London, 1908), i. p. xxi; Historical Manuscripts Commission (HMC), *Thirteenth Report, Appendix, Part IV* (London, 1892), 352.

[34] Lawrence Stone, 'The Educational Revolution in England, 1560–1640', *Past and Present*, 28 (1964), 41–80; id., 'The Size and Composition of the Oxford Student Body 1580–1910', in Stone (ed.), *The University in Society* (2 vols., Princeton, 1975), i. 3–110; Joan Simon, *Education and Society in Tudor England* (Cambridge, 1966); Foster Watson, *The Grammar Schools to 1660: Their Curriculum and Practice* (Cambridge, 1908); W. A. L. Vincent, *The Grammar Schools: Their Continuing Tradition, 1660–1714* (London, 1969); Rosemary O'Day, *Education and Society, 1500–1800: The Social Foundations of Education in Early Modern Britain* (London, 1982).

parishes in Essex, 258 had some form of school during the Elizabethan period, while forty-four out of fifty-three Hertfordshire parishes had a petty school. At the same time, sporadic evidence suggests the repeated incidence of unlicensed teachers instructing the children of the poor in basic reading, and even writing and 'cyphering'.[35] Perhaps more important still, in terms of these elementary skills, Protestantism re-emphasized the educational responsibilities of the Christian mother within the home.[36]

Clearly, there is no necessary correlation between the increase in printed matter, or the provision of formal education, and the growth of literacy, but this period also witnessed significant increases in reading and writing ability. Quantitative estimates have been arrived at on the basis of calculating the number of people able to put their name to census-like documents such as the Protestation Oath of 1642, or by counting the signatures appended to marriage registers or depositions given before courts. Since reading was generally taught before writing, it is believed by some that the ability to write a signature, as opposed to making a mark or drawing a symbol, constitutes evidence of the ability to read relatively well. This method assumes that the ability to sign is commensurate with fluent reading ability. At the same time, it recognizes that far fewer people than can sign their name will be able to write fluently, but that far more will be able to read at a very faltering level. Surveys undertaken in the early nineteenth century suggested that any figure for 'literacy' levels based on the counting of signatures would need to be increased by 50 per cent in order to give a roughly accurate estimate of the ability to read in this most basic way.[37]

---

[35] Margaret Spufford, *Contrasting Communities: English Villagers in the Sixteenth and Seventeenth Centuries* (Cambridge, 1974), chs. 6–8; A. J. Fletcher, 'The Expansion of Education in Berkshire and Oxfordshire, 1500–1670', *British Journal of Educational Studies*, 15 (1967), 51–9; W. R. Feyerharm, 'The Status of the Schoolmaster and the Continuity of Education in Elizabethan East Anglia', *History of Education*, 5 (1976), 103–15; Alan Smith, 'Private Schools and Schoolmasters in the Diocese of Lichfield and Coventry in the Seventeenth Century', *History of Education*, 5 (1976), 117–26; J. P. Anglin, 'The Expansion of Literacy: Opportunities for the Study of the Three Rs in the London Diocese of Elizabeth I', *Guildhall Studies in London History*, 4 (1980), 63–74; M. K. McIntosh, *A Community Transformed: The Manor and Liberty of Havering, 1500–1620* (Cambridge, 1991), 206, 228, 260–5.

[36] Margaret Spufford, 'First Steps in Literacy: The Reading and Writing Experiences of the Humblest Seventeenth-Century Spiritual Autobiographers', *Social History*, 4 (1979), 407–35; ead., 'Women Teaching Reading to Poor Children in the Sixteenth and Seventeenth Centuries', in Mary Hilton, Morag Styles, and Victor Watson (eds.), *Opening the Nursery Door: Reading, Writing and Childhood, 1600–1900* (London, 1997), 47–62; Kenneth Charlton, '"Not Publike onely but also Private and Domesticall": Mothers and Familial Education in Pre-Industrial England', *History of Education*, 17 (1988), 1–20; id., 'Mothers as Educative Agents in Pre-Industrial England', *History of Education*, 23 (1994), 129–56.

[37] Schofield, 'The Measurement of Literacy in Pre-Industrial England', in Goody (ed.), *Literacy in Traditional Societies*, 323–4.

On this basis, it has been calculated that in 1500 an aggregate of perhaps 5 per cent of adult males and 1 per cent of adult females could sign their names in England. By the accession of Elizabeth I in 1558 these figures had risen quite substantially, with 20 per cent of men and 5 per cent of women then being able to sign; at the outbreak of the Civil War in 1642, there had been a further increase to 30 per cent and 10 per cent respectively; and by the time George I came to the throne in 1714 a total of 45 per cent of men and 25 per cent of women had attained this level of writing competence. In addition to this discrepancy between male and female signing, these statistics also confirm considerable variation according to social status. By the turn of the seventeenth century, those from the gentle and professional classes were universally 'literate' in these terms, but the ability to sign decreased down through society, being far greater among merchants and specialist craftsmen than among husbandmen and labourers. The figures imply some very broad regional disparities so that, for example, yeomen in Essex and Hertfordshire were significantly more likely to be literate than yeomen in Durham and Northumberland over the period 1560–1730. But in general there appears to have been no distinctive geographical pattern, with huge variation existing within counties and even between adjacent parishes. Urban areas seem to have been more 'literate' than rural ones, with London in particular displaying very high levels by contemporary standards: in the 1640s, about two-thirds of adults in the capital could sign their name.[38]

The impression given by these statistics, however, is that an inflation of 50 per cent is not sufficient to give a realistic idea of those able to read in some form. In the light of the variety of evidence which confirms already high levels of lay literacy in the fourteenth and fifteenth centuries, the figures derived for the early modern period appear to be very substantial underestimates of the extent of basic reading capacity. Whereas in the nineteenth century, when the method of counting signatures was first proposed, there may have been some correlation between the ability to write and the ability to read, this assumption is clearly not relevant for the medieval and early modern periods when the two skills were quite separate. In the case of women particularly, the common inability to sign, or the

[38] David Cressy, *Literacy and the Social Order: Reading and Writing in Tudor and Stuart England* (Cambridge, 1980), 176–7, 136, 150–1, 72–4. For other evidence based upon signatures, see Keith Wrightson and David Levine, *Poverty and Piety in an English Village: Terling, 1525–1700* (2nd edn., Oxford, 1995), 145–51; R. A. Houston, *Scottish Literacy and the Scottish Identity: Illiteracy and Society in Scotland and Northern England, 1600–1800* (Cambridge, 1985), chs. 2–3; McIntosh, *A Community Transformed: The Manor and Liberty of Havering, 1500–1620*, 236–7, 265–71.

impression of such given in formal and legal documents, disguises what was clearly a widespread ability to read print.[39]

Despite their significant underestimation of reading ability, the statistics for literacy levels in the sixteenth and seventeenth centuries do at least point to a trend of steady, if uneven, growth over the period. By 1700 it may reasonably be assumed that England was a society in which at least half the adult population could read print. This likelihood, combined with the increase in written materials of all kinds, contributed to the creation of a substantially 'literate culture' in England. Over the course of time, this was a society ever more accustomed to communicating information, disseminating opinion, and enshrining ideas in text. If the high Middle Ages witnessed the fundamental transition from memory to written record in the administrative and legal sense, and the late medieval centuries saw manuscript becoming a normal medium of artistic expression, intellectual exchange, and religious instruction, then the early modern period may be said to have experienced the literary restructuring of popular culture.

## THE WORLD OF THE UNLETTERED

In early modern England, therefore, no one lived beyond the reach of the written and printed word. It was scarcely possible to function in society without some reference to records and even unconsciously people imbibed cultural influences from textual sources. At the same time however, those at different social levels encountered literature to varying extents and in different ways. In the lower and least literate ranks of society its influence might be more oblique and tangential, something received through the mediation of others or at several removes. At the same time, there continued to be many aspects of life in which writing was irrelevant or unavailable, and elements of communication and exchange which always remained purely oral. In the small communities in which most people lived, what was important was the seasonal cycle of work, the operation of local custom, the lore and tradition of the neighbourhood, and the gossip about its inhabitants. These were the things most immediate, most relevant to their experience, most salient in the construction of their mental world, and none of them were written down. Even in highly

---

[39] Spufford, 'First Steps in Literacy', 414; T. C. Smout, 'Born Again in Cambuslang: New Evidence on Popular Religion and Literacy in Eighteenth-Century Scotland', *Past and Present*, 97 (1982), 121–3; Hoeppner Moran, 'Literacy and Education in Northern England, 1350–1550', 8; Keith Thomas, 'The Meaning of Literacy in Early Modern England', in Gerd Baumann (ed.), *The Written Word: Literacy in Transition* (Oxford, 1986), 102–3.

literate societies this can be so; in this partially literate one it is crucial to an understanding of how people perceived their world.

It is for this reason that many contemporaries never felt the need of learning to read, still less of learning to write. At best these skills were often seen as irrelevant, and at worst they could be regarded as a waste of time. No one was held 'in more disesteem among the common vulgar' than the schoolmaster, observed Henry Peacham, for 'the greater part of the multitude being ignorant, they are desirous that their children should be so likewise'. As Richard Baxter put it at the end of the seventeenth century, 'when poverty and custome have trained up the people in so happy a way, they usually grow into contempt, and thence into a malignant scorne and hatred, of that which they want'. The dictates of the agricultural year and the needs of the family economy clearly cut short the formal education of many children and the prejudice against learning choked off the opportunities of others. In the 1630s, relatives of the yeoman father of Adam Martindale, a future Lancashire clergyman, urged him to dissuade his son from scholarship 'alledging too many instances of such as made no advantage of their learning, though they had been brought up so long to it as to be fit for nothing else'.[40]

In the day-to-day tasks of most occupations reading and writing were of little practical benefit. There were 'many poore servants and labourers' and 'many that are of trades and manuall sciences' among those who 'never learned so much as to reade', lamented the Jacobean preacher Francis Inman. Such people often had neither the occasion nor the need. In the agricultural world in which most earned their living, the attitude of Nicholas Breton's 'countryman' was probably common. 'Farmers know their cattle by their heads, and sheepheards know their sheepe by the brand, what more learning haue we need of, but that experience will teach vs without booke?' 'Servants in husbandrie', agreed Gervase Markham in 1635, had no need of literacy, 'for these vertues of writing and reading, it is not much materiall whether they are acquainted therewith I or no, for there is more trust in an honest score chaulkt on a trencher, then in a cunning written scrowle, how well so ever painted on the best parchment.'[41]

   [40] Henry Peacham, *The Truth of Our Times* (1638), ed. Virgil B. Heltzel (Ithaca, NY, 1962), 185; 'The Reverend Richard Baxter's Last Treatise', ed. Frederick J. Powicke, *Bulletin of the John Rylands Library*, 10 (1926), 182; *The Life of Adam Martindale Written by Himself*, ed. Richard Parkinson (Chetham Society, vi, London, 1845), 24. For other examples of such attitudes, see John Ferne, *The Blazon of Gentrie* (London, 1586), ii. 23; Spufford, *Contrasting Communities*, 172–3; Keith Wrightson, *English Society, 1580–1680* (London, 1982), 187–9; *John Clare's Autobiographical Writings*, ed. Eric Robinson (Oxford, 1983), 5.

   [41] Francis Inman, *A Light vnto the Vnlearned* (London, 1622), sig. A2ʳ; Nicholas Breton,

Throughout this period and beyond honest scores chalked on trenchers continued to act as a perfectly serviceable means of recording, counting, and reckoning time, as they had done since the early Middle Ages. At the end of the seventeenth century, for example, the people of Grasmere in Westmorland were observed to have 'a peculiar way of making their bills—not with paper and ink, but a stick and a knife . . . and let him that despises their rural simplicity read this if they can; for any child or illiterate person in the parish can read it'. The stick and the knife were used by shepherds to tally their flocks and by shopkeepers to do their accounts. It remained common among poultry farmers to reckon their accounts on wooden tallies, notched and split down the centre. Still used in Staffordshire in the 1680s 'amongst the meaner sort of people' were an 'ancient sort of almanacks they call cloggs', or wooden calendars on which there were symbols and notches indicating full moons and movable feasts: some were small for the pocket, others larger 'which hang commonly here at one end of the mantletree of their chimneys, for the use of the whole family'. In mid-eighteenth-century Yorkshire the same devices were found 'used by the common people in the moor lands at this day'. Well into the Victorian period, the court leet of Pamber, near Basingstoke in Hampshire, was recording its proceedings in the old way 'on a piece of wood called a tally, about three feet long and an inch and a half square'.[42]

Even without tallies it was possible to do basic addition without the notion of figures on a page or, indeed, without any sense of numbers at all. Oral tradition has preserved from the Middle Ages right into this century various sets of counting words, extending up to twenty. They were used by shepherds on the north country hills to tally their flocks, by fishermen on the East Anglian coast to reckon their catches, and by knitting women

*The Court and the Country* (1618), in *The Works in Verse and Prose of Nicholas Breton*, ed. Alexander B. Grosart (2 vols., Edinburgh, 1879), ii, u, 10; Gervase Markham, *The English Husbandman* (London, 1635), 8–9.

[42] *Antiquary on Horseback. The First Publication of the Collections of the Rev. Thos. Machell Chaplain to King Charles II towards a History of the Barony of Kendal*, ed. Jane M. Ewbank (Cumberland and Westmorland Antiquarian and Archaeological Society, extra ser., 19, Kendal, 1963), 144; *The Farming and Memorandum Books of Henry Best of Elmswell, 1642*, ed. Donald Woodward (British Academy, Records of Social and Economic History, new ser., 8, London, 1984), 87; *Wiltshire: The Topographical Collections of John Aubrey, F. R. S., A.D. 1659–70*, ed. J. E. Jackson (Devizes, 1862), 15; Keith Thomas, 'Numeracy in Early Modern England', *Transactions of the Royal Historical Society*, fifth ser., 37 (1987), 119–20; Alan Everitt, 'The Marketing of Agricultural Produce', in Joan Thirsk (ed.), *The Agrarian History of England and Wales*, iv: *1500–1640* (Cambridge, 1967), 565; Robert Plot, *The Natural History of Stafford-Shire* (Oxford, 1686), 418–20; *The Travels through England of Dr Richard Pococke*, ed. J. J. Cartwright (2 vols., Camden Society, new ser., 42–4, London, 1888–9), i. 66; W. C. Hazlitt, *Tenures of Land and Customs of Manors* (London, 1874), 238.

in many regions to count their stitches. Thus the fisherfolk of Yarmouth would incant: 'ina, mina, tethera, methera, pin, sithera, lithera, cothra, hothra, dic'. A different series was common throughout Cornwall. 'In numbring they say, wonnen, deaw, tre, pidder, pimp, whey, zith, eath, naw, deg, ednack, dowthack, tarnack, puzwarthack, punthack, wheytack, zitack, itack, nannzack, eygganz'. In the north-west of England they would remember the order of feast days over Easter with the jingle: 'Tid, Mid, Misera | Carl, Paum, good Pase-day'. Thus, 'the vulgar', it was observed, add up 'by the remembrance only of the sounds of the names of numbers' rather than by any conception of written figures.[43]

There is also evidence to suggest that those people who could not rely on writing as a means of storing information or as an aid to memory developed quite considerable mnemonic powers in compensation. 'I haue observed', wrote the surveyor John Norden, 'that many vnlearned men haue better and more retentiue memories than haue some schollers', for 'such as haue not the use of the pen, must use the memory only, which being fed by continuall pondering the things they delight in, becomes as a calender of their accounts.' Even people holding public office could apparently manage perfectly well without being able to read or write, as long as they had the help of a good memory. In 1584 the mayor of Chester, Robert Brerewood, needed the clerk to write his Christmas Eve speech for him which was then 'learned by hart and by him pronounced: for although he could nether write nor read, yet was of excelent memory and very braue and gentile partes otherways'. It is not uncommon to find evidence from this period of people with excellent knowledge of the Bible even if they could not actually read it for themselves. In the early eighteenth century, for example, the antiquary William Stukeley came across a Worcester man who, although 'otherwise his capacity is very weak', was of 'prodigious memory'. 'If we name any passage in the whole Bible, he will immediately tell you what book, chapter and verse it is in: a truely living concordance.'[44]

Being unable to read or write in no way restricted people's capacity to perform skilfully and dexterously in most aspects of their daily lives,

[43] Iona and Peter Opie, *The Oxford Dictionary of Nursery Rhymes* (Oxford, 1951), 13–14; Richard Carew, *The Survey of Cornwall* (London, 1602), fo. 55ᵛ; BL, Lansdowne MS, 1033, fo. 290ᶠ; *Aubrey on Education*, ed. J. E. Stephens (London, 1972), 100.

[44] John Norden, *The Surveyors Dialogue* (London, 1610), 173; *Records of Early English Drama: Chester*, ed. Lawrence M. Clopper (Toronto, 1979), 142; William Stukeley, *Itinerarium Curiosum* (London, 1724), 65. On the tradition of memorizing sermons and passages from Scripture, see Hudson, *The Premature Reformation*, 190–2; Patrick Collinson, 'The English Conventicle', in W. J. Sheils and Diana Wood (eds.), *Voluntary Religion* (Studies in Church History, 23, Oxford, 1986), 239–43.

therefore. It was quite possible for 'mechanicall men and countrey fellowes' to 'measure a peece of land, and though illiterate', to 'account the quantity by the parts of money'. Sometimes the most simple folk, observed Robert Plot in the 1680s, 'can perform things scarce attainable by the quickest parts or most solid understandings'. He related the story of 'a certain fool' who was able, without the aid of a clock, to judge precisely when an hour had elapsed. It was even possible to encounter figures such as the 'ordinary countryman' who could 'neither read nor write, yet has a most wonderful strength of mind and memory'. He was able to multiply any two four-figure numbers together in his head and he 'used his fingers by way of counting, on his knee, in some particular method of his own'.[45]

Nor was the ability to read necessary for intellectual subtlety or abstract reasoning. At the end of Elizabeth's reign Sir William Cornwallis claimed to have come away from a conversation with a husbandman who, from 'his experience, his learning of tradition, and his naturall witte hath enformed mee of many things. I haue picked out of him good philosophy and astronomy and other obseruations of time and of the worlde . . .'. Similarly, in 1648 Meric Casaubon met a remarkable horse-courser from Somerset who could tame wild dogs, bulls, and other animals merely by playing his pipe. Moreover, he explained 'that all creatures were made by God for the use of man, and to be subject unto him; and that if men did use their power rightly, any man might do what he did'. Casaubon was surprised 'to hear a man, whom by his profession and his countenance, you would hardly have thought able to read (and whether he was, I do not know) to speak so philosophically'.[46]

Although unlettered, many people clearly had highly developed skills which were relevant to the circumstances of their own lives and at which the book-learned might only wonder. Martin Martin's observation on the inhabitants of the Western Isles of Scotland in the 1690s may have been made of the population in much of rural England: they 'for the most part labour under the want of knowledge of letters and other useful arts and sciences; notwithstanding which defect, they seem to be better versed in the book of nature than many that have greater opportunities of improvement'. A good example was the 'illiterate empiric', Neil Beaton of Skye, who was totally 'without the advantage of education'. Yet he could exactly

[45] Norden, *The Surveyors Dialogue*, 15; Plot, *Natural History of Stafford-Shire*, 303; *The Family Memoirs of the Rev. William Stukeley, M.D.*, ed. W. C. Lukis (3 vols., Surtees Society, 73, 76, 80, Durham, 1882–7), iii. 467.

[46] Sir William Cornwallis, *Essayes*, ed. D. C. Allen (Baltimore, 1946), 50; Meric Casaubon, *A Treatise Proving Spirits, Witches and Supernatural Operations* (London, 1672), 107–11.

judge the various qualities of plants and roots by their taste, assess their 'astringent and loosening qualities' merely from the colour of their flowers, and extract their juice with a special technique which left 'little or no damage'.[47] Country folk in England might not have been able to read and write but they could tell you that if animals licked their hoofs or certain flowers closed their leaves, rain would follow, and if oak-apples were full of worms or birds flocked unusally into towns, pestilence was near at hand. They knew that abnormal numbers of fry fish presaged scarcity of corn or death of cattle, and that if the breast bone of duck was red it signified a long winter ahead, but, if white, then a brief one. In short, they read fluently in the book of nature, in face of which many learned scholars were illiterate.[48]

For those who could not rely on storing information on paper or remembering useful knowledge through written memoranda, there were many alternatives available. Rhyming was one device which provided an aid to memory in innumerable contexts. Prayers, for example, were often couched in verse for this reason. Sir William Temple remembered of his youth, spent in Kent before the Civil War, 'some persons of our country to have said grace in rhymes, and others their constant prayers'. Alternatively, spells and charms were often delivered in some hobbling verse, easily repeated by cunning folk and their customers alike. More generally, moral advice and practical guidance of all kinds was enshrined in a huge wealth of proverbial lore, much of which was rhymed and alliterative to be kept easily in mind. 'Because verses are easier got by heart, and stick faster in the memory than prose', it was said in the early eighteenth century, 'and because the ordinary people use to be much taken with the clinking of syllables, many of our proverbs are so form'd, and often put into false rhymes; as, "A Stitch in time, may save nine"; "Many a little will make a mickle".'[49]

Many trades or occupations had their own rhymes as a way of remembering their duties. Thus gentlemen's servants had such mnemonics to

[47] Martin Martin, *A Description of the Western Islands of Scotland, circa 1695* (Glasgow, 1884), xiv, 197.

[48] Francis Bacon, *Sylva Sylvarum: Or A Natural History* (1627), in *The Works of Francis Bacon*, ed. James Spedding, Robert Leslie Ellis, and Douglas Denon Heath (7 vols., London, 1857–9), ii. 516, 576, 603–9; Markham, *The English Husbandman*, 9, 11–12, 20; John Worlidge, *Systema Agriculturae: The Mystery of Husbandry Discovered* (London, 1669), 219–64.

[49] Sir William Temple, 'Of Poetry' (1690), in *Critical Essays of the Seventeenth Century*, ed. J. E. Spingarn (3 vols., Oxford, 1908), iii. 98; Keith Thomas, *Religion and the Decline of Magic: Studies in Popular Beliefs in Sixteenth- and Seventeenth-Century England* (London, 1971), 180–1; Thomas Fuller, *Gnomologia: Adagies and Proverbs, Wise Sentences and Witty Sayings, Ancient and Modern, Foreign and British* (London, 1732), ix.

prevent them forgetting the long list of items needed by their masters on long journeys. By the same token, no journeyman shoemaker worth his salt could not 'readily reckon by his tooles in rime'. Farmers, meanwhile, had innumerable 'short remembrances' in verse available to them in preparing their equipment at each stage of the agricultural year.[50] There seems to have been scarcely a subject on which there were not a couplet or a verse to be of assistance. Thus, countrymen wanting to acquire a new greyhound might think upon this 'old rime, left by our forefathers', for 'the better helpe ... of memory': 'If you will have a good tike | Of which there are few like | He must be headed like a snake | Neckt like a drake | Backt like a beame | Tailed like a batt | And footed like a cat'. Housewives wanting to summon up the knowledge of herbs and simples by which they were expected to preserve the family's health, needed only to recall a series of distichs: 'Vervain and dill | Hinders witches from their will'; 'They that will have their heale | Must put setwall in their keale'; 'He that would live for aye | Must eat sage in May'.[51]

One antiquary thought that the roads around the country should have signposts which would teach 'the country people to read'. In lieu of these, various rhymes came to their aid such as the one in Somerset which advised, 'Stanton Drew | a mile from Pensford | another from Chew', or that on the north Norfolk coast which ran 'Gimingham, Trimingham, Knapton and Trunch | Northrepps and Southrepps, are all of a bunch'. On a different theme, one could hear 'among the vulgar' along the East Lothian coast, verses which enabled them to remember the names of the rare seabirds inhabiting Bass Rock. 'The scout, the scart, the cattiwake | The soland goose sits on the lack | Yearly in the spring', jingled one of them. The people of Hereford were prompted to start mending their nets by watching the alder tree and recalling that 'When the bud of aul is as big as the trout's eye | Then that fish is in season in the river Wye'.[52]

---

[50] Sir Anthony Fitzherbert, *The Book of Husbandry*, ed. W. W. Skeat (English Dialect Society, 37, London, 1882), 93; Thomas Deloney, *The Gentle Craft* (London, 1637), sig. C4ᵛ; Thomas Tusser, *Five Hundred Points of Good Husbandry*, ed. Geoffrey Grigson (Oxford, 1984), 31–3.

[51] Gervase Markham, *Countrey Contentments, in Two Bookes* (London, 1615), i. 100; *John Aubrey: Three Prose Works*, ed. John Buchanan-Brown (Fontwell, 1972), 88, 231; John Gerard, *The Herball or General Historie of Plantes*, ed. Thomas Johnson (London, 1633), 1078; John Ray, *A Collection of English Proverbs* (2nd edn., Cambridge, 1678), 36. Cf. Thomas Cogan, *The Haven of Health* (London, 1612), 32, 41.

[52] Stukeley, *Itinerarium Curiosum*, 78–9, and (2nd edn., 2 vols., London, 1776), ii. 169; Francis Grose, *A Provincial Glossary with a Collection of Local Proverbs and Popular Superstitions* (London, 1787), sig. Q2ᵛ; *Early Travellers in Scotland*, ed. P. Hume Brown (Edinburgh, 1891), 233; J. O. Halliwell, *Popular Rhymes and Nursery Tales* (London, 1849), 180. For later recordings of directional rhymes, see G. F. Northall, *English Folk-Rhymes* (London, 1892), 8, 42.

People also carried around their sense of the past in this form, preserving in it a perception of the heroes and villains, victories and defeats, of history. 'Henricus Octavus | Took more than he gave us', ran one strand of opinion in the seventeenth century. In the area around Chippenham, or Pewsham, Forest in Wiltshire, 'the poor people' kept alive their bitter memories of the disafforestation begun in 1619 with a little rhyme. 'When Chipnam stood in Pewsham's wood | Before it was destroy'd | A cow might have gone for a groat a yeare | But now it is denyed'. 'The metre is lamentable', conceded John Aubrey who recorded this after the Restoration, 'but the cry of the poor was more lamentable'. Many communities, it seems, enshrined some remembered incident in a rhyme which informed an important part of their collective identity. Thus, around Cadbury Castle in Devonshire 'the neighbour dwellers have this hobbling rhyme frequent in their discourses: "If Cadbury castle, and Dolberry hill, down delved were | Then Denshire might plow with a golden coulter | And eare with a gilded shere".'[53]

Such jingles emerged from a culture in which the inventing and retaining of rhymes was commonplace at all social levels. Versifying not only preserved a variety of useful knowledge, but also provided a standard form of entertainment. This was a society in which it was quite normal to sit around the fire or the workbench improvising and extemporizing on a theme in such a way. Such habits have been all but forgotten in subsequent centuries when people have become accustomed to receiving their entertainment from commercial forms. But at this time, London fish-wives would meet in taverns 'when they haue done their faire', and while 'singing, dancing' and drinking, did 'vse to take and put vp words, and end not till either their money or wit, or credit bee cleane spent out'. Countrymen might have been heard 'on a holiday, dancing lubberly, and upbraiding one another, in *ex tempore* doggerel, with their defects and vices'. It was a world in which figures such as John Stukeley, who lived at Uffington, Lincolnshire, in the mid-seventeenth century, were not uncommon in being 'mighty fond of making extempore jokes and verses upon company'. Or one might meet, as did some travellers in Derbyshire two

---

[53] Machell, *Antiquary on Horseback*, ed. Ewbank, 64–5; John Aubrey, *The Natural History of Wiltshire*, ed. John Britton (London, 1847), 58; Tristram Risdon, *The Chorographical Description or Survey of the County of Devon* (London, 1811), 78. Among many other examples, see Roger Dodsworth, *Yorkshire Church Notes, 1619–1631*, ed. J. W. Clay (Yorkshire Archaeological Society, record ser., 34, 1904), 15; Richard Hollingworth, *Mancuniensis; Or, an History of the Towne of Manchester* (Manchester, 1839), 27; John Morton, *The Natural History of Northamptonshire* (London, 1712), 542; Halliwell, *Popular Rhymes and Nursery Tales*, 188–206.

generations later, 'a country fellow, who seem'd to be more of a plowman than a poet' but pressed upon them some verses he had made 'for his neighbour, who married for love without acquainting any of his relations'.[54]

Such extemporization was a stock-in-trade of professional minstrels, of course, and much of their invention passed into common circulation. In the early seventeenth century, it was still common to find medieval-style entertainers travelling the country, 'rymers, (who perhaps were fidlers too) that upon any subject given, would versifie extempore halfe an hower together'. They performed for the crowds at fairs and festivals while 'every gentleman almost kept a harper in his house; and some of them could versifiie'. An example of the type was the 'Scotch bagpiper' who on being asked when he intended to pay for some hay he had received on credit 'spoke . . . rhymes ex tempore, at Durham, many gent[lemen] being present, to whome the piper was playing and rhyming, particularly on each man'. They concluded: 'When sowters they can cloat na shane | Than yee's ha payment for yor hay.' Many minstrels clearly worked from texts or even had notebooks like that of Richard Sheale in which to write their repertoire, but their ranks must also have been swelled by illiterate extemporizers, 'blind harpers or such like tauerne minstrels that giue a fit of mirth for a groat', as George Puttenham described them around 1570. The 'doggrel rhymer, who makes songs to tunes, and sings them for a livelihood', was still going strong when John Dryden referred to him disparagingly more than a century later.[55]

But people did not need professional performers to provide their songs. Rhyming and singing were a ubiquitous and natural accompaniment to almost every aspect of work and leisure. No domestic chore, no toil or task, was without its doleful ditty or soothing song. In the 1530s Miles Coverdale could evoke the image of 'carters and plow men' whistling while they worked and 'women syttynge at theyr rockes, or spynnyng at the wheles', singing 'hey nony nony, hey troly loly, and such

[54] Donald Lupton, *London and the Countrey Carbonadoed and Quartred into Severall Characters* (London, 1632), 93; John Dryden, 'A Discourse Concerning the Original and Progress of Satire', in *Essays of John Dryden*, ed. W. P. Ker (2 vols., Oxford, 1900), ii. 56; *The Family Memoirs of the Rev. William Stukeley*, ed. Lukis, i. 2, and cf. 9; Joseph Taylor, *A Journey to Edenborough in Scotland*, ed. William Cowan (Edinburgh, 1903), 23–4.

[55] *John Aubrey: Three Prose Works*, ed. Buchanan-Brown, 284; Bod. Lib., MS Ashmole 36–37, fo. 312ᵛ; George Puttenham, *The Arte of English Poesie* (London, 1589), 69; John Dryden, 'Preface to Albion and Albanius', in *Essays of John Dryden*, ed. Ker, i. 278. For another example of a minstrel who could write, see Peter Roberts, 'Elizabethan Players and Minstrels and the Legislation of 1572 against Retainers and Vagabonds', in Anthony Fletcher and Peter Roberts (eds.), *Religion, Culture and Society in Early Modern Britain* (Cambridge, 1994), 50–1.

lyke fantasies'. Two generations later Shakespeare probably heard their voices undiminished.

> Sing no more ditties, sing no mo
>     Of dumps so dull and heavy;
> The fraud of men was ever so,
>     Since summer first was leavy.
>         Then sigh not so,
>         But let them go,
> And be you blithe and bonny,
> Converting all your sounds of woe
>     Into Hey nonny, nonny.

So, too, the Jacobean bishop, Martin Fotherby, who observed from 'plaine experience; how countrymen doe use to lighten their toyling; old-wives, their spinning; mariners, their labours; soldiers, their dangers; by their severall musicall harmonies', while crying babies were quickly 'stilled with their nurses singing'.[56]

Everyone agreed with him that there was no better means of easing the burdens of labour, of overcoming fear, or conquering melancholy, than with a merry tune. 'Labouring men that sing to their work can tell as much, and so can soldiers when they go to fight . . .', affirmed Robert Burton. '"It makes the child quiet", the nurse's song; and many times the sound of a trumpet on a sudden, bells ringing, a carman's whistle, a boy singing some ballad tune early in the street, alters, revives, recreates a restless patient that cannot sleep in the night.' As one Elizabethan commentator had put it, 'euen the ploughma[n] and cartar, are by the instinct of their harmonicall soules co[m]pelled to frame their breath into a whistle, thereby not only pleasing the[m]selues, but also diminishing the tediousnes of their labors'.

And hence it is, that wayfaring men, solace the[m]selues with songs, and ease the wearisomnes of their iourney, co[n]sidering that musick as a pleasant companion, is vnto the[m] in steed of a wago[n] on the way. And hence it is, that manual labourers, and mechanicall artificers of all sorts, keepe such a chaunting and singing in their shoppes, the tailor on his bulk, the shomaker at his last, the mason at his wal, the shipboy at his oare, the tinker at his pan, and the tylor on the house top.[57]

---

[56] Miles Coverdale, *Goostly Psalmes and Spirituall Songes Drawen out of the Holy Scripture* (London, 1535?), preface; William Shakespeare, *Much Ado about Nothing*, ii. iii. 65–82; Martin Fotherby, *Atheomastix: Clearing Foure Truthes, against Atheists and Infidels* (London, 1622), 337–8.

[57] Robert Burton, *The Anatomy of Melancholy*, ed. Holbrook Jackson (3 vols., Everyman, edn., London, 1932), ii. 116; [John Case?], *The Praise of Mvsicke* (Oxford, 1586), 43, 44.

Women knew that the best way of calming children was with a lullaby, 'for euen the litle babes lacking the vse of reason', noticed Roger Ascham, 'are scarse so well stilled in suckyng theyr mothers pap, as in hearynge theyr mother syng'. It was just as commonplace for housewives 'washing at the river' to break into song, and 'young wenches' keeping 'sheep and cows' in the summer meadows to 'sitt in the shade singing of ballads'. In the cities, every street resounded to the noise of a carman whistling his 'vile tunes'. In the countryside, farm servants were 'oftenest painfull and good, that sing in their labour', thought Thomas Tusser. Every phase of the agricultural year was accompanied by its own particular chants and refrains. At harvest-home the whole community gathered to work with one purpose and sing with one voice. A foreign visitor to England in the reign of James I noticed 'the country people bringing home, in a cart from the harvest field, a figure made of corn, round which men and women were promiscuously singing, preceeded by a piper and drum'. In 1600 Thomas Nashe quoted a harvest-home song in *Summers Last Will and Testament* which was still familiar to farm labourers in the nineteenth century. 'Hooky, hooky, we haue shorne | And we haue bound | And we haue brought haruest | Home to towne'.[58]

In communal labour such as this, the singing of rounds, or catches, was a habitual practice. Not only those gathering the harvest, but also tailors and blacksmiths in their shops, weavers at their looms, and groups of tinkers on the road, were all renowned for this part-singing. 'Never trust a tailor that does not sing at his work', says one of Beaumont and Fletcher's characters. In 1604 Samuel Harsnet alluded to the 'catches, or rounds, used to be sung by tinkers as they sit by the fire, with a pot of good ale between their legs'. At the same time, it was possible to come down with a cold 'sitting up late and singing catches with cloth-workers'. Sailors were already famed for the shanties with which they incanted the rhythm of tasks aboard ship. In the mid-sixteenth century, the men aboard a vessel off the Scottish coast were heard chanting words to keep time as they weighed anchor and unfurled the sails.

than ane of the marynalis began to hail and to cry, and al the marynalis ansuert of that samyn sound. hou hou. pulpela pulpela. boulena boulena. darta darta. hard out steif, hard out steif. afoir the vynd, afoir the vynd. god send, god send, fayr

---

[58] Roger Ascham, *Toxophilus: The Schole of Shootinge* (London, 1545), i, fo. 11ʳ; *John Aubrey: Three Prose Works*, ed. Buchanan-Brown, 284; Dorothy Osborne, *Letters to Sir William Temple*, ed. Kenneth Parker (Harmondsworth, 1987), 89; Chappell, *Popular Music of the Olden Time*, 138, 579–84; Tusser, *Five Hundred Points of Good Husbandry*, ed. Grigson, 166; Thomas Nashe, *Summers Last Will and Testament* (1600), in *The Works of Thomas Nashe*, ed. R. B. McKerrow, rev. F. P. Wilson (5 vols., Oxford, 1958), iii. 259.

vedthir, fayr vedthir. mony pricis, mony pricis. god foir lend, god foir lend. stou, stou. mak fast and belay.

Over 200 years later John Brand noticed that the seamen of Newcastle heaved up their anchors with a rhythmical song which he thought very similar to those of harvest home.[59]

Songs were not only a help in passing the hours at work, of course, but also a staple component of recreation. Every 'poore countrie man and his familie', it was said in the 1580s, who were wont to ask 'what shall we doe in the long winter nights, how shall we passe away the time on Sundays, what wold you have us doe in the Christmas holydayes? . . . are naturally given to sing'.[60] Indeed, the winter fireside was the focal point of much oral tradition, as well as a hub of social life now all but forgotten. In the dark of a world without artificial light and the chill of a dwelling without alternative heat, the fire had a crucial and symbolic place. During the winter especially, when the nights drew in, recourse to the burning hearth was both a necessity and a diversion. Women sat and span, men mended their tools, children played games. The sense of familial or communal collectivity which this occasion inspired, and the skills of singing and storytelling which it engendered, now require an effort of imagination to conjure up.

But contemporaries were in no doubt of its importance. In the 1620s Robert Burton casually set down a list of the 'ordinary recreations which we have in winter', which amounted to a compendium of the oral tradition around the family hearth. It included 'jests, riddles, catches, purposes, questions and commands, merry tales and errant knights, queenes, lovers, lords, ladies, giants, dwarfes, theeves, cheaters, witches, fayries, goblins, friers, &c'. There was not quite, perhaps, an English equivalent of the Irish 'tale-tellers' who could recount 'a story of a king, or a gyant, a dwarf and a damosel, and such rambling stuff, and continue it all night long', but this was still a culture rich in storytelling. Burton might also have added to his catalogue the repeating of prophecies, which Francis Bacon thought should serve for none other than 'winter talk by the fireside', or the earnest discussion of spiritual matters between neighbours. Above all, people just sat and talked. How often, reflected Michael Drayton, had he and Henry Reynolds spent 'winter evenings' together by

[59] Chappell, *Popular Music of the Olden Time*, 108–10, 78, 291–2, 597–8, 729, 742–3; Burke, *Popular Culture in Early Modern Europe*, 43–4; *The Complaynt of Scotlande*, ed. Murray, 40–1; John Brand, *Observations on the Popular Antiquities of Great Britain*, ed. Sir Henry Ellis (3 vols., London, 1849), ii. 27.

[60] John Rhodes, *The Countrie Mans Comfort or Religious Recreations, Fitte for all Well-Disposed Persons* (1588; rev. edn., London, 1637), 'To the Christian Reader'.

the fire, passing 'the howres contentedly with chat, now talk'd of this, and then discours'd of that'.[61]

At the same time, people recounted those parochial traditions and historical anecdotes which neighbourhoods treasured as part of their imagined heritage. William Camden heard on his travels many such tales of local heroes and their 'great exploits, which for certain are fitter for tattling gossips in a winter night, than a grave historian'. Among similar stories which Thomas Westcote collected from the people of Devonshire in the reign of Charles I were those he thought worth a 'good fire in a winter's cold night', or 'not unfit . . . for winter nights when you roast crabs by the fire'. In Northumberland, Thomas Bewick would remember much later how 'the winter evenings were often spent in listning to the traditionary tales and songs, relating to men who had been eminent for their prowess and bravery in the border wars, and of others who had been esteemed for better and milder qualities . . .'.[62]

Many such stories and songs clearly had meaning only within a specific community. Despite the illusion created by the popular printed literature which has come down to us, much anecdote and tradition was as likely to revolve around events and individuals who were obscure and irrelevant beyond this purely parochial context as it was to involve the famous exploits and legendary figures of chivalric romance or epic balladry. These memorials of the microcosm had little chance of ever being written down, still less of finding their way into print. So many of the cultural influences which structured people's mental horizons, even more so then than now, were highly localized: it was this which gave them their immediacy and their appeal, but it also ensured that they were scarcely recorded in their day and are barely recoverable by posterity.

Occasionally it is possible to catch glimpses of their transmission and their content. In the parish of Myddle, Shropshire, for example, tales were still told at the end of the seventeenth century of one William Preece who back in the reign of Elizabeth had been famed as a great storyteller. He had spent some time fighting in the Low Countries during the 1590s.

<hr />

[61] Burton, *The Anatomy of Melancholy*, ed. Jackson, ii. 81; Temple, 'Of Poetry', in *Critical Essays of the Seventeenth Century*, ed. Spingarn, iii. 98; Francis Bacon, *The Essayes or Counsels, Civill and Morall* (1625), in *The Works of Francis Bacon*, ed. Spedding, Ellis, and Heath, vi. 465; John Goodman, *Winter-Evening Conference between Neighbours* (2nd edn., London, 1684); Michael Drayton, 'To My Most Dearely-Loved Friend Henery Reynolds Esquire', in *The Works of Michael Drayton*, ed. J. William Hebel (5 vols., Oxford, 1931–41), iii. 226.

[62] William Camden, *Britannia*, ed. Edmund Gibson (London, 1695), 471; Thomas Westcote, *A View of Devonshire in 1630*, ed. George Oliver and Pitman Jones (Exeter, 1845), 221, 302; *A Memoir of Thomas Bewick Written by Himself*, ed. Iain Bain (Oxford, 1975), 8.

After his return from the wars he told so many romanticke storyes, of his strange adventures, that people gave him the name of Scoggan, by which name (at last) hee was better known than by the name of William Preece. But amongst the rest of the storyes that were told of him, or by him, one was, that hee had killed a monstrouse boar, of soe large a size that the bristles on his back were as big as pikeeavell grains [pitchfork prongs].

Many towns and villages must have had 'Scoggins' in their midst, christened after Edward IV's famous jester, who had exotic experiences to relate and whose exploits grew larger and larger in the telling. Two generations later Myddle had another hero in Vincent Jukes, a local lad who went off to fight the Turks in Tangier. He was captured but managed to contrive a miraculous escape with another man. After winning the trust of their captors by becoming Muslims, they seized the opportunity to hijack a vessel, lock up its crew and 'hoisted up saile for England'. By the time the valiant Jukes returned to Shropshire, 'they were singing ballads abroad in markett townes of this adventure'. After that he went off to sea again 'and was heard of noe more'.[63]

Another local hero was 'The Pedlar of Swaffham' of whom the inhabitants of this Norfolk village were said in the seventeenth century to have a 'constant tradition'. It told of how a neighbourhood pedlar was informed in a dream that if he went to London Bridge he would hear 'joyful newse'. At the bridge he met a shopkeeper who said, "'I'll tell thee country fellow, last night I dream'd that I was at Sopham, in Norfolk, a place utterly unknown to me, where, methought behind a pedlar's house, in a certain orchard, and under a great oak tree, if I digged, I should find a vast treasure! Now think you", says he, "that I am such a fool to take such a long jorney upon me upon the instigation of a silly dream?"' Thus the pedlar rushed home, excavated the hoard, and became a rich man. This is the earliest known English version of the folktale 'The Treasure of Home' which has been recorded all over central Europe and beyond. It is not clear how it found its way to Norfolk, but other versions of it recorded later elsewhere in Britain suggest that it may have been a familiar motif adapted to fit local circumstances. What fuelled the legend in Swaffham was the statue of a pedlar in the parish church 'cut in stone, with his pack at his back, and his dogg at his heels; and his memory is also preserved by the same form or picture in most of the old glass windows, taverns, and alehouses of that town, unto this day'. These figures were actually representations of John Chapman, a local merchant whose generous benefactions had helped to rebuild the church in the mid-fifteenth century, but

[63] Richard Gough, *The History of Myddle*, ed. David Hey (Harmondsworth, 1981), 32–3, 115.

they had been conveniently reinvented in the popular mind to ratify this classic rags-to-riches story.[64]

As the traditions of Swaffham suggest, iconography and visual imagery of all sorts could be an extremely powerful medium of communication, aid to memory, and stimulus to cultural invention in early modern England. As in all societies in which literacy is limited, pictures, signs, and symbolic objects served an important function in conveying meanings and messages to the majority. Contemporaries may have been more 'visually literate' than those in subsequent centuries whose dependence on the written word has dulled their capacity to 'read' and interpret the subtleties and significances of graphic representation. Since the Middle Ages, stained glass, wall paintings, and statues had been regarded as the 'books of the illiterate'. 'According to the maxime, "pictures are the books,"' wrote Thomas Fuller in 1662, 'painted windows were in the time of popery the library of lay men.'[65]

For many people, this notion remained no less valid in the sixteenth and seventeenth centuries. During this period, however, religious imagery in particular became the focus of heated polemic and zealous activism. The iconoclasm perpetrated in the wake of the Reformation and again during the civil wars of the mid-seventeenth century, destroyed an enormous amount of sacred art and denuded churches of their visual messages. Iconophobia remained a defining characteristic of the radical Protestant tradition. In the 1660s the antiquary Philip Kinder even refused to illustrate his history of Derbyshire with 'pictures of churches and monuments', preferring only to describe them in words 'for I'me verily persuaded that a vocall expression will far more satisfy the phansie, then any dead letter or figure, vulgarly called the books of the ignorant'.[66]

Such attitudes, however, may have been to the cost of those not able to read the biblical 'sentences' which now appeared on church walls, or fully to comprehend the teachings of the book. A Catholic priest, Lewis Bennett, was making a political point but perhaps speaking from experience when he protested at Barkham, Sussex, in April 1603, that 'images were more availeable for . . . ignorant unlearned men then sermons were, for

---

[64] W[illiam] W[instanley], *The New Help to Discourse* (London, 1669), 74–6; *The Diary of Abraham de la Pryme, the Yorkshire Antiquary*, ed. Charles Jackson (Surtees Society, 54, Durham, 1869–70), 219–20; Jennifer Westwood, *Albion: A Guide to Legendary England* (London, 1985), 161–4.

[65] Thomas Fuller, *The History of the Worthies of England* (London, 1662), ii. 97. On this subject, see Margaret Aston, *England's Iconoclasts* (Oxford, 1988); Patrick Collinson, *The Birthpangs of Protestant England: Religious and Cultural Change in the Sixteenth and Seventeenth Centuries* (Basingstoke, 1988), ch. 4.

[66] Philip Kinder, 'Historie of Darby-Shire', ed. W. G. D. Fletcher, *Reliquary*, 23 (1882–3), 10.

that sermons went in att one eare and out att another, but images would
be better kept in mynde'. The ability of visual representations to communicate and to inspire was appreciated no less by moderate Protestants,
such as the historian of Cumberland, Edmund Sandford. In the reign of
James I he had visited Kirkoswald Castle and in one of the chapels there
was a picture of the crucifixion. A 'substantiall subsidy yeoman man' who
was present asked him what it was. On being told, 'he said that he never
knew so much of Christs crucifying and his dolorous death and sufferings
and passion'. Thus 'we may hereby see', Sandford later wrote, 'that pictures is most proper for contemplation' and above 'the puritanicall and
jesuiticall practice of mentall prayer: for we be more taken, and sensibly
feeling with the sight of any mans sufferings . . . then with either hearing
or reading therof'.[67]

It was not only in the spiritual sphere, of course, that pictures performed this kind of service. As at Swaffham, much local tradition was
kept in mind, or invented, by images and icons around the community,
both in homes and in public. In common with many of the more substantial inhabitants of Elizabethan England, Thomas Shouncke of Pyrgo
Street in Havering, Essex, 'had a painted cloth of Robin Hood that
hangeth in the hall'; his contemporary, John Wood, a mercer from Earls
Colne in the same county, had a number of 'stained cloths' draped behind
his 'old cupboard' with 'a little story of Tobias' represented on them.
Meanwhile, a cottage in the high street of Amersham, Buckinghamshire,
proudly displayed a large wall painting of Julius Caesar; another mural at a
farmhouse in Fenny Stratford celebrated that famous pair, the cat and the
fiddle. Inns, taverns, and alehouses were similarly bedecked with famous
figures and chivalric heroes. The ubiquitous King Arthur was everywhere
'abused', in the eyes of one contemporary, by 'monkish verses' and 'vile
painting in an alehouse'.[68] Sometimes their signs outside kept alive
parochial tradition which might otherwise have faded: at Marlborough,
for example, 'the memorye of the ruined castle is preserved in the signe of

---

[67] *Calendar of Assize Records: Sussex Indictments James I*, ed. J. S. Cockburn (London, 1975), 1;
Edmund Sandford, *A Cursory Relation of all the Antiquities and Familyes in Cumberland*, ed. R. S.
Ferguson (Cumberland and Westmorland Antiquarian and Archaeological Society, 4, Kendal,
1890), 45. For examples of such art, see M. B. Merback, *The Thief, the Cross and the Wheel: Pain and
the Spectacle of Punishment in Medieval and Renaissance Europe* (London, 1999).

[68] F. G. Emmison, *Elizabethan Life: Home, Work and Land* (Chelmsford, 1976), 22, and cf. 7, 9,
13, 78; F. W. Reader, 'Tudor Mural Paintings in the Lesser Houses in Bucks', *Archaeological
Journal*, 89 (1932), 140 and plate IX, 167 and plate XXII; John Aubrey, *Monumenta Britannica*, ed.
John Fowles and Rodney Legg (Sherborne, 1980–2), 542. See also Lupton, *London and the Countrey Carbonadoed*, 127; F. W. Reader, 'Tudor Domestic Wall-Paintings', *Archaeological Journal*, 92
(1935), 243–86, and 93 (1936), 220–62; Watt, *Cheap Print and Popular Piety*, ch. 5.

the castle at an inn thereby'. On other occasions, they cashed in on local claims to fame: thus, around Robin Hood's Bay on the Yorkshire coast the famous outlaw provided 'a sign to most publick houses in this country' by the end of the seventeenth century.[69]

Townscapes offered a gallery of such signboards, graphically advertising at a glance the services offered by the people who lived 'at the sign' of their occupation. They were designed to communicate immediately to a non-reading public in their symbolic depictions of function. Thus, the red lion and the green dragon, adapted from heraldry, represented food and shelter and so were often hung outside taverns and inns. Tradesmen displayed images of their tools or materials: a pair of scissors for a tailor, a hand for a glover, a bunch of grapes for a vintner. Barbers were already identifiable by the red and white striped pole outside their doors, signifying a bandaged limb and advertising the surgical services which they then provided. They also hung teeth on strings at their windows, denoting their skill in remedial dentistry. The surnames of some tradesmen lent themselves to depiction in a rebus which might easily be interpreted by the unlettered. Thus a hare and bottle stood for Harebottle, and a pair of cocks stood for Cox. As a result there was little need for writing. 'They seldom write upon the sign the name of the thing represented in it', commented a French resident in England in the late seventeenth century, which was a difficulty for foreigners, 'because for want of the things being so nam'd, they have not an opportunity of learning their names in English, as they strole along the streets.'[70]

Another important aspect of visual communication to the unlettered was simply the example of others. The 'vulgar', observed Sir Thomas Browne, are 'led rather by example, than precept: receiving perswasions from visible inducements, before intellectual instructions'. Much of the useful knowledge which sustained the majority in their daily round was not learned by reading but by emulation, not copied from books but from people. In the countryside, 'the rude, simple, and ignorant clowne, who onely knoweth how to doe his labour, but cannot give a reason why he doth . . .', picked up his skills not from agricultural writers like Gervase

---

[69] BL, Sloane MS, 241, fo. 54ᵛ; Taylor, *A Journey to Edenborough*, ed. Cowan, 69. Cf. Jacob Larwood and John Camden Hotten, *The History of Signboards, from the Earliest Times to the Present Day* (2nd edn., London, 1866), ch. 2.

[70] Larwood and Hotten, *The History of Signboards*, 5, 26; Chappell, *Popular Music of the Olden Time*, 104; *M. Misson's Memoirs and Observations in his Travels over England: With some Account of Scotland and Ireland*, trans. John Ozell (London, 1719), 302. See also Brand, *Observations on the Popular Antiquities of Great Britain*, ed. Ellis, ii. 351–8; Ambrose Heal, *The Sign-Boards of Old London Shops* (London, 1947); Ronald Paulson, *The Art of Hogarth* (London, 1975), 64, 65.

Markham, but from 'the instruction of his parents, or the custome of the country' in which he lived. Custom, ceremony, and ritual often made far deeper and more lasting impressions on people's minds than anything which they might read. And, in any case, so much of what they needed to know was unwritten. In most instances, for example, it was only possible to learn the bounds of manor or parish from the old men who pointed them out at the annual perambulations. It was only possible to absorb the customary law which dictated the workings of the community by listening to the accounts of these same ancient inhabitants. Then, as now, so much of the social knowledge which was necessary to function in a locality was nowhere to be found in text: it was preserved in the memories and enacted in the lives of the inhabitants themselves.[71]

## A LITERATE CULTURE

This was the environment, therefore, in which most people operated in sixteenth- and seventeenth-century England. It was one in which there was a variety of perfectly functional alternatives to making records and keeping accounts with pen and paper, in which much entertainment was extemporized and spontaneous, and in which most essential knowledge was passed on by example and emulation. Many could not read, nor did the inability much matter to them. Despite this, however, even the world of the unlettered was not immune from the influence of the written and printed word. To some extent this had been so even before the early modern period, but in these centuries the increased use of writing in almost every sphere of life, coupled with the impact made by print, enormously accelerated the process of literary infusion.

The consequences of illiteracy were substantially mitigated by the fact that no one in sixteenth-century England lived very far away from someone who could read a manuscript writing or a printed work for them. This was a time in which reading was habitually done out loud and it was necessary only to be in the presence of someone working through a text to be privy to its contents.[72] Far from it being the case, as was once assumed, that some people lived out their lives without ever encountering documents

---

[71] Browne, *Pseudodoxia Epidemica*, in *The Works of Sir Thomas Browne*, ed. Keynes, ii. 26; Markham, *The English Husbandman*, 95; E. P. Thompson, *Customs in Common* (London, 1991), 7–8, 98, 100.

[72] See the comments in Wrightson, *English Society, 1580–1680*, 194–6; Houston, *Scottish Literacy and the Scottish Identity*, ch. 6; Thomas, 'The Meaning of Literacy', 106–7; Jonathan Barry, 'Literacy and Literature in Popular Culture: Reading and Writing in Historical Perspective', in Tim Harris (ed.), *Popular Culture in England, c.1500–1850* (Basingstoke, 1995), 82–3.

or books, letters or broadsides, this was a period in which nobody could avoid them in one context or another. Reader or not, no one who participated in the culture could help but repeat material and articulate forms which derived from these sources. Early modern England may not have been a wholly literate society, but it comprised a fundamentally literate environment.

Reading aloud helped to draw everyone into the ambit of the written word. In the sixteenth century, particularly, prose style had a very 'oral' quality, a high degree of colloquialism and formularity, which facilitated its spoken delivery. Even the format and the punctuation of printed works was often designed to that end.[73] Many readers, particularly the less expert, were probably incapable of performing the function in silence. This seems to have applied to Arthur Chapman, a blacksmith from Wolsingham in County Durham. He disturbed the congregation in church on St Matthew's Day 1570 by his 'redinge of an ynglish boke, or prymer, while as the preist was sayinge of his servic, no myndynge what the preist redd, but tendynge his own boke and praier. Mary, he redd not allowde to the hynderenc of the preist, to his knowledg; but the preist, after the first lesson, wyllyd him ... to reid mor softly.' Such reading aloud can be found throughout society, giving texts a public and communal dimension. When in November 1638, for example, an illiterate Essex man was shown the will which had been drawn up for him, he asked the writer, since he was also 'thicke of hearing, to reade it aloude in his eare that he might the better hear it'. The Yorkshire yeoman, Adam Eyre, was habitually performing such services for his friends and neighbours in the mid-years of the seventeenth century. So was the apprentice shopkeeper of Ashton-in-Makerfield, Lancashire, Roger Lowe. Typically, he comforted the dying wife of old William Hasleden one night in December 1666 by reading to her from Lewis Bayly's *The Practice of Piety*.[74]

Even if people could not read themselves, they bought printed texts and books in the expectation that they would be read aloud to them when the opportunity arose. The Bible was the supreme example of this. From the time when Henry VIII first appointed the vernacular Scriptures to be

[73] Walter J. Ong, 'Oral Residue in Tudor Prose Style', *Publications of the Modern Language Association*, 80 (1965), 145–54; Ong, *Orality and Literacy*, 120–1; A. C. Partridge, *Orthography in Shakespeare and Elizabethan Drama* (London, 1964), 182, 186–7, 192–4.

[74] *Depositions and Other Ecclesiastical Proceedings from the Courts of Durham, Extending from 1311 to the Reign of Elizabeth*, ed. James Raine (Surtees Society, 21, London, 1845), 231; Bod. Lib., MS Eng. Lang. e. 6. fo. 7ᵛ; Adam Eyre, *A Dyurnall, or Catalogue of all my Accions and Expences from the 1st of January, 1646[7]*, ed. H. J. Morehouse (Surtees Society, 65, Durham, 1877), 2, 56, 92, 114; *The Diary of Roger Lowe of Ashton-in-Makerfield, Lancashire, 1663–74*, ed. William L. Sachse (London, 1938), 109.

read in churches, those who were able stepped in to perform the service
for all. Thus at Chelmsford around 1540 'divers poor men in the town'
could be found on Sundays 'reading in [the] lower end of the church, and
many would flock about them to hear their reading'. In London, meanwhile, the tailor John Porter, was to be heard at St Paul's reading the Bible,
in a 'very audible' voice, to the assembled crowds. It was the duty of all
Christian heads of households to read aloud to their families, and as formal education expanded the possibility that children might do this
for their parents became ever more likely. 'And hereof we have (God be
thanked) many examples in England', wrote Archbishop Whitgift in
Elizabeth's reign, 'of those which, being not able to read themselves, by
means of their children reading to them at home, receive instruction and
edifying.' Given the scale of production, the family Bible was becoming a
more common possession by the end of the seventeenth century and, as
Richard Baxter observed, 'some few that cannot read get others to read to
them, and get a good measure of saying knowledge'. The same was true
of the catechisms containing the basic articles of faith which clergymen
like Baxter read to their unlearned parishioners who would learn them
by rote.[75]

It was not only spiritual works, of course, which enjoyed this kind of
oral dissemination. Broadside ballads provide a conspicuous example of
material which was intended to be sung despite the expedient of transmitting it through text. Not being able to understand print by no means
dissuaded people from buying such publications, for as Nicholas Bownd
observed in the 1590s, there were many who, 'though they cannot reade
themselues, nor any of theirs, yet will haue many ballades set vp in their
houses, that so they might learne them, as they shall haue occasion'.
Alternatively they might follow the example of the tailor's servant from
Hereford who discovered 'a popish ballett' as he was opening his master's
stall one morning in October 1600, and took it to William Cowper, a
stationer and book-binder of the town, to have it read for him. When such
material was posted up in public places, as it frequently was, there would
always be at least one reader in the crowd who could speak up for all to
hear. In a comic tale of 1607 a scurrilous ballad was set above the door of
a Durham townsman and 'no man passed by' without 'reading the verses',
if he was able, while 'others that had no skill in letters, got them perused
by such as could'. Many printed broadsides began with an opening refrain

[75] A. G. Dickens, *The English Reformation* (London, 1964), 190–1; Aston, 'Lollardy and
Literacy', 195; Spufford, *Contrasting Communities*, 210–11; 'The Reverend Richard Baxter's Last
Treatise', ed. Powicke, 190; Ian Green, *The Christian's ABC: Catechisms and Catechizing in England,
c.1530–1740* (Oxford, 1996).

which demonstrated their purpose to be read or sung out loud. 'Listen to my dity country man'; 'Come grant me, come lend me, your listning eares'; 'And if you please to stay a while, you shall heare how . . .'.

> Give eare, my loving countrey-men,
>   that still desire newes,
> Nor passe not while you heare it sung,
>   or else the song peruse.[76]

In all cases, non-readers were able to seek out a skilled person such as a clergyman or a tradesman, an apprentice or a schoolboy, who would be able to help them. Barbers provide one example of a group who seem often to have been readers: their shops acted both as centres of news and gossip and as places where newsletters or pamphlets might be seen. One London barber in the 1660s was clearly unusual in that he 'could not read' and amusing stories were told of the time when he 'flung a letter in the kennel when one came to desire him to read the superscripcion, saying, "Do you think I stand here to read letters?" ' By this time coffee houses were emerging as a feature of the urban landscape and they offered a tremendous supplement to this aspect of a barber's services. The coffee-master himself, the scriveners who plied their trade on his premises, or any number of his customers would have been ready readers of a document or pamphlet. A play of 1667 contains a scene in which a coffee-master produces a *Gazette* which is read aloud to those present at the suggestion that 'one read for all'.[77]

In addition to reading aloud, another factor which ensured that the written word permeated the fabric of popular culture was the essential reciprocity between the substance of the 'oral' and 'literate' realms. On the one hand, both manuscript and printed works enshrined material gathered from circulation by word of mouth and, on the other, they fed back into it. The boundaries between speech and text, hearing and reading, were thoroughly permeable and constantly shifting so that the dichotomy is difficult to identify and impossible to sustain. In the case of an essentially spoken form such as jokes, for example, their vitality derived from being told, one to another. And yet it was common for gentlemen of the period to keep a notebook in which they jotted down jests and anecdotes heard in taverns and alehouses, from watermen or market

---

[76] Bownd, *The Doctrine of the Sabbath*, 241; HMC, *13th Report, Appendix, Part IV,* 338; *Dobsons Drie Bobbes,* ed. E. A. Horsman (Oxford, 1955), 22; Wurzbach, *The Rise of the English Street Ballad,* 44.

[77] *The Diary of Samuel Pepys,* ed. Latham and Matthews, iii. 180; Harold Love, *Scribal Publication in Seventeenth-Century England* (Oxford, 1993), 206.

women, and this provided them with material which could then be reused in conversation.[78] At the same time, printed jestbooks were becoming a popular genre and many of them claimed to be compiled from the fruits of eavesdropping. Typically, John Taylor's *Wit and Mirth* (1626) contained material said to have been 'chargeably collected out of tavernes, ordinaries, innes, bowling-greenes and alleys, ale-houses, tabacco-shops, highwaies and water-passages'.[79] But such pamphlets also made it clear that they were intended merely to nourish common discourse, to be an aid to facetious chat around the fireside or in the field. As the author of *The Cobler of Caunterburie* (1590) insisted:

Here is a gallimaufre of all sorts, the gentlemen may finde Salem, to sauour their eares with iestes: and clownes plaine Dunstable dogrell to make them laugh, while their leather buttons flie off. When the farmer is set in his chaire turning (in a winters euening) the crabbe in the fier, heere may hee heare how his sonne can reade, and when he hath done laugh while his belly akes. The olde wiues that wedded themselues to the profound histories of Robin Hood, Clim of the Clough, and worthy Syr Isenbras, may here learne a tale to tell amongst their gossippes.[80]

Equally, in the case of news or information about current affairs, the promiscuous exchange between the oral, scribal, and printed realms thoroughly undermines the extent to which a story can be assigned to any one medium. What began as gossip could easily be taken up and enshrined in text, before passing back again into oral circulation. In April 1670, for example, one of the periodic rumours about an impending uprising by London apprentices was at large in the city. It was being fermented at the Red Cow alehouse near Little Old Bailey where a tailor from Nottinghamshire decided to write it down, read it aloud, and then distribute copies. One of the patrons picked up a flysheet but since he was unable to

[78] For examples, see BL, Sloane MS, 384; BL, Sloane MS, 1489; '*Merry Passages and Jeasts': A Manuscript Jestbook of Sir Nicholas Le Strange (1603–1655)*, ed. H. F. Lippincott (Salzburg, 1974); *The Diary of Samuel Pepys*, ed. Latham and Matthews, iv. 346, 406, viii. 95 (untraced); Alan Macfarlane, *The Justice and the Mare's Ale* (Oxford, 1981), 42 (I am grateful to Alan Macfarlane for lending me his notes on the manuscript jestbook of Sir Daniel Fleming).

[79] John Taylor, *Wit and Mirth* (1626; London, 1628), title-page. For a depiction of jests being collected from eavesdropping on tavern banter and then put into a play, see Thomas Heywood, *The Fayre Mayde of the Exchange* (1607), iii. ii, in *The Dramatic Works of Thomas Heywood* (6 vols., London, 1874), ii. 46–7. For printed jestbooks, see *Shakespeare Jest-Books*, ed. W. C. Hazlitt (3 vols., London, 1864); F. P. Wilson, 'The English Jest-Books of the Sixteenth and Early Seventeenth Centuries', repr. in his *Shakespearian and Other Studies*, ed. Helen Gardner (Oxford, 1969), 285–324.

[80] *The Cobler of Caunterburie* (London, 1590), sig. A3. For depictions of the reading of *A Hundred Merry Tales* (1526) on winter nights by the fire, see *Cyuile and Vncyuile Life* (1579), in *Inedited Tracts*, ed. W. C. Hazlitt (Roxburghe Library, London, 1868), 56–7; John Lyly, *Pappe with Hatchet* (1589), in *The Complete Works of John Lyly*, ed. R. W. Bond (3 vols., Oxford, 1902), iii. 400.

read the handwriting himself, took it home to his wife who apparently could. It was precisely such stories which also found their way into the newletters sent out by London's professional journalists to their subscribers in the provinces.[81] Equally, news could migrate in the other direction, from written to spoken. Government statutes and proclamations were printed, for example, but they were intended to be read aloud to the crowds assembled in market squares. What was heard then spread around on the grapevine, radiating out from urban centres into the surrounding countryside from mouth to mouth. A typical instance occurred when two royal proclamations were announced in the market-place at Newbury, Berkshire, one Thursday early in July 1683. One of them informed the traders of a new excise tax to be levied by the king. The 'market women' clearly needed this explaining and 'when the proclamacions were reading' they 'askt "what matter?"' of some of the 'understanding men of Newbury' there gathered. Once understood, the news 'presently was in the country . . . and spread amongst the country people at some distance, and come too confirm'd from the other side of the country'.[82]

In the case of songs, it might be imagined that the ditties of women at their spinning and the lullabies of the nursery fire, or the catches of tinkers and the harmonies of harvesters, were the stuff of unmediated oral tradition, but here too the evidence suggests the permeating influence of print. By the Elizabethan period, at least, the printed page was informing the songs of work when Nicholas Bownd found broadside ballads in 'the shops of artificers, and cottages of poore husbandmen'. It was also providing the rounds sung by shepherd girls and milkmaids: the ballad which Shakespeare's Autolycus famously sells to Mopsa and Dorcas, 'there's scarce a maid westward but she sings it', is just one of these catches, 'in three parts'. Printed entertainment had thus been an accompaniment to labour for a least a century by the time the assize judge, Francis North, on his way back from Lancaster in the 1680s, noticed the chimneys 'where ballads are pasted round, and the folk sit about it working or merrymaking'.[83]

The songs of merrymaking were also being determined quite fundamentally in this way. By the early seventeenth century, if not before, every country alehouse had its 'painted cloath, with a row of balletts pasted on it', or its 'cleanly room' with 'twenty ballads stuck about the walls'. Print was also providing a stimulus to the soothing strains of childcare. The fact

---

[81]  Public Record Office (PRO), SP29/274/205–6. On this subject, see Chapter 7 below.

[82]  PRO, SP29/428/52.

[83]  Bownd, *The Doctrine of the Sabbath*, 242; Shakespeare, *The Winter's Tale*, IV. iii. 292–7; Roger North, *The Lives of the Norths*, ed. Augustus Jessopp (3 vols., London, 1890), i. 184.

that in 1614 Ben Jonson can have the esquire of Harrow, Bartholomew
Cokes, remember his childhood with 'the ballads ouer the nursery-
chimney at home o' my owne pasting vp', suggests that such things were
a feature, at least of gentry households, in Elizabeth's reign. William
Stukeley was, therefore, heir to a well-established tradition of print-
inspired songs for children when, as a young boy in the 1690s, he
delighted in the entertainment of one of his father's servants: he 'had got
the collection of old songs made on Robin Hood . . . which he usd to sing
over to us in a winter's evening'.[84]

The printed ballad also came to have a profound effect on the local
folklore which was spun around the winter fireside. Thus, it was clearly
thanks to the many published songs and plays about Robin Hood that
numerous landmarks around the country began to be associated with his
legend from the mid-sixteenth century. Similarly, *The Blind Beggar of Bethnal
Green*, a tale set in the reign of Henry III, was responsible for inventing
the tradition in that village east of London by the seventeenth century,
that the great house, actually of mainly Elizabethan construction, had
been built by their local hero 'so much talked of and sung in ballets'. The
small town of Mansfield in Nottinghamshire earned its reputation in the
popular mind and was 'made famous amongst country people by means
of that ballad or song called *Gelding of the Devil*'. As for *Chevy Chase*, the
tourist around England after the Restoration could visit the church at
Beverley in Yorkshire where the clerk would tell that there lay interred
'the so famed earl Percy, who as the ballad sings was met in Chevy Chace
by Douglas a Scottish earl'; or call at the Heugh Head in Wooler where the
locals could boast 'a true notion' of the famous encounter, 'not like what
is represented in the ballad of *Chevy Chase* which has turn'd the whole
story into a fable', and claim to show the very spot where the two pro-
tagonists had fallen.[85]

Even those verses and rhymes which people loved to extemporize as a
staple form of entertainment and a memorable means of communication, benefited from the inspiration provided by printed broadsides.
The pieces of doggerel which ordinary men and women regularly concocted in local alehouses to ridicule the antics of their neighbours were

---

[84] Watt, *Cheap Print and Popular Piety*, 194; Ben Jonson, *Bartholomew Fayre* (1631), III. v. 49–50,
in *The Works of Ben Jonson*, ed. C. H. Herford and Percy Simpson (11 vols., Oxford, 1925–52), vi.
74; *The Family Memoirs of the Rev. William Stukeley*, ed. Lukis, i. 16.

[85] Westwood, *Albion: A Guide to Legendary Britain*, 119, 207; *The Diary of Samuel Pepys*, ed.
Latham and Matthews, iv. 200; 'Thomas Baskerville's Journeys in England, temp. Charles II', in
HMC, *Thirteenth Report, Appendix, Part II* (London, 1893), 309, 313; Daniel Defoe, *A Tour thro' the
Whole Island of Great Britain*, ed. G. D. H. Cole (London, 1927), 662, 768–9.

beginning, by the later sixteenth century at least, to draw on some of the forms, characters, and tunes popularized by the commercial ballad. What is even more remarkable, perhaps, is that such people, even if they could not read or write themselves, frequently wanted to have these crude jingles written down. Despite the fact that this was a world in which a writer needed to be sought out, in which paper was expensive, and fewer people could read handwriting than could manage print, they still went to strenuous efforts to have manuscript copies of these 'libels' distributed around the community and displayed in public. Very occasionally such material was even printed itself, after being expanded and improved by a professional balladeer. Thus, this most basic of oral forms felt the impact of the written word, both drawing from and feeding into script and print. Once again, the transactions between the three media, first in one direction, and then in the other, were multiple.[86]

Another oral form which was deeply influenced by the written word was local customary law. This vital part of the economic and social life of most communities had always been essentially unwritten, being perpetuated in practice and handed down the generations in the remembrances of ancient inhabitants. But increasingly during the sixteenth and seventeenth centuries these customs were being written down as they became subject to new pressures and disputed before courts outside the locality. So the very rhythms of work and the access to resources in both agricultural and industrial environments, town and country, were gradually bound by the formulations of written codes.[87]

The reciprocities, therefore, between oral culture and literate were widespread and deep-seated. Although transmission by word of mouth may have remained the most common and most immediate medium through which people imbibed their information and received their stimulation, much of that spoken repertoire was structured, determined, or fed by the written word. Even those many contexts in which script or print had once played little part began to be influenced by its contents. The non-reading ranks of society were to find, as well as others, that the jokes they told and the news they spread, the songs they sang and the

---

[86] See Chapter 6 below. Cf. C. J. Sisson, *Lost Plays of Shakespeare's Age* (Cambridge, 1936); Martin Ingram, 'Ridings, Rough Music and Mocking Rhymes in Early Modern England', in Reay (ed.), *Popular Culture in Seventeenth-Century England*, 166–97.

[87] See Chapter 5 below. For examples, see Thompson, *Customs in Common*, 99–101, 158–9; Michael Zell, 'Fixing the Custom of the Manor: Slindon, West Sussex, 1568', *Sussex Archaeolgical Collections*, 122 (1984), 101–6; Andy Wood, 'Custom, Identity and Resistance: English Free Miners and their Law, *c.*1550–1800', in Paul Griffiths, Adam Fox, and Steve Hindle (eds.), *The Experience of Authority in Early Modern England* (Basingstoke, 1996), 266–72.

sayings they repeated, the traditions they remembered and the customs they enacted, were being derived, directly or indirectly, from textual sources. Since the Middle Ages, of course, manuscript had been infusing the content of oral circulation. Even the repertoire of the unlettered peasantry was not uninfluenced by the imaginative productions which entered the common stock via the pulpit and the stage, through minstrelsy or from reading aloud. But the advent of print greatly increased both the quantity and range of such material available, helping to ensure this thoroughgoing penetration of popular culture by the end of the sixteenth century.

In this environment it was perhaps inevitable that popular attitudes towards reading would gradually change. Although, very clearly, the inability to read represented no barrier to participation in scribal and print culture, the enormous volume of written material in almost every context must have done something to develop the sense that to be incapable of understanding it at first hand was in some way to be missing out. In a world where literature is scarce and few people can read, little importance is naturally attached to the skill. Far from there being any stigma associated with the inability to read, a stigma tended to be attached to the ability. Many folk referred to literates disparagingly as 'scholars', just as they were liable to call anyone with some skill in mathematics a 'conjuror'. But in the circumstances in which people found themselves over the course of time, such attitudes were likely to soften. The evidence of popular education and of growing literacy levels suggests an ever increasing awareness of the benefits which reading might bring.

Not being able to read something like a broadside ballad may not have mattered much since its contents were intended to be sung and it was more likely to be learned by hearing than by any other means. But in the case of certain texts, the inability to understand them for oneself could be disadvantageous. To recall the women in the market-place at Newbury in 1683: the 'understanding men' there chose only to explain the first of the two proclamations to them and apparently they remained ignorant of the second since 'no body talks of [it]'. Moreover, the men clearly glossed its contents, telling them only 'as much as one of the countrey folk could carry away at once'. Many of the popular misconceptions and wild rumours which bedevilled governments in this period arose out of misunderstandings which might have been avoided in a more literate society. As for the people themselves, misinformation was only one form of ignorance which could cost them their livelihoods and even their lives. The observation of a correspondent to the *Gentleman's Magazine* in 1757 was scarcely less relevant to former centuries. 'The persons most likely to offend against the laws, more especially in criminal matters, are the low and illiterate part of the people. Among these, many cannot read at all; and to several who can, the antiquated type of an act of parliament is nevertheless as illegible as an arrangement of Chinese characters.' They could not be blamed, in other words, for being unaware of changes in the law which were merely posted in public. But this was of little consequence since, as everyone knew, 'ignorance of the law excuses no one'.[88]

In a society in which so much was coming to be communicated through texts and structured by the written word, the cost of illiteracy was ever rising. In cities such as York and Exeter, for example, proclamations and statutes were already less likely to be announced in the streets by the 'bellman' during the course of the sixteenth century and were posted up instead 'where they might best be seen and redd of all men'. At York in 1574 the charges for hiring labourers were displayed on 'tables' around the city so that even this least literate of groups could not legitimately claim ignorance of them.[89] With the development of the market economy at this time, the use of written instruments of credit and of paper receipts, bills, and accounts in business dealings gradually increased. By the same token, no person who became embroiled in the legal process, as unprecedented numbers were to do in the late sixteenth and early seventeenth centuries, can have felt comfortable operating in a world dominated by the written word as precedent, procedure, and proof. No landholder with a written copy of his or her terms of tenancy, carefully preserved with other 'evidences' in the family chest at home, can have been insensible to the benefits of reading (see Plate 11).[90]

Even the afterlife was envisioned as a kind of ethereal courtroom dominated by written evidence and proof. 'Can you by a fine, answer your faults in the Star-Chamber of heauen?' the Jacobean preacher Thomas Adams asked his congregation at St Benet's, near Paul's Wharf, in London. Since the Middle Ages, iconography had depicted the devil with pen in hand, like the clerk of some ecclesiastical court writing down people's

---

[88] PRO, SP29/428/52; *Gentleman's Magazine*, 27 (Oct. 1757), 453–4; M. P. Tilley, *A Dictionary of the Proverbs in England in the Sixteenth and Seventeenth Centuries* (Ann Arbor, Mich., 1950), 337.

[89] D. M. Palliser, 'Civic Mentality and the Environment in Tudor York', *Northern History*, 18 (1982), 102; John Hooker, *The Description of the Citie of Excester*, ed. W. J. Harte, J. W. Schopp, and H. Tapley-Soper (Devon and Cornwall Record Society, Exeter, 1919), 804, 846, 866, 887–8. Cf. HMC, *Fourteenth Report, Appendix, Part VIII* (London, 1895), 56.

[90] See, for example, Craig Muldrew, *The Economy of Obligation: The Culture of Credit and Social Relations in Early Modern England* (Basingstoke, 1998); C. W. Brooks, *Pettyfoggers and Vipers of the Commonwealth: The 'Lower Branch' of the Legal Profession in Early Modern England* (Cambridge, 1986), chs. 4–5; Mildred Campbell, *The English Yeoman under Elizabeth and the Early Stuarts* (London, 1960), 106–7, 264–5.

sins in the register. Near the entrance to heaven was imagined a man, like the official by the gates of an earthly city, sitting 'at a table side, with a book, and his inkhorn before him, to take the name of him that should enter therein', and somewhere 'a record kept the names' of all those who had passed successfully that way before. Only by reading the Bible, the Protestant clergy repeatedly insisted, could souls come to enter the celestial kingdom, and it was this motivation which inspired people, perhaps above all others, to go in search of learning. This was the imperative goading the Christian mother, the performance of whose duty in the home gave children their first, and often their only, instruction in letters. This was the call inspiring those many 'honest, sober and godly matrons' who crop up in the records supervising youngsters in village schools. Thus the unrepentant Grace Coates of Basford in Nottinghamshire, presented in July 1625 for teaching children without a licence, who 'sayeth that all such as cannot read are damned'.[91]

So far as the social and educated elite were concerned, lack of proficiency in letters came to be regarded as another particular characterisic of the 'vulgar'. Again, in a situation in which illiteracy is common throughout society, it is unlikely to carry any special social connotations or stigmas. With the attainment of reading by all of the upper and many of the middle ranks in this period, however, lack of the skill came to be confined to the lower orders and, in due course, to define them in altogether new ways. Significantly, the very meanings of 'literate' and 'illiterate' were changing. In the high Middle Ages the term 'literatus' had denoted a cleric, or else someone 'scholarly' or 'learned' in the classics; 'illiteratus', meanwhile, generally meant either a layman or someone without knowledge of ancient authors. All of these senses lingered throughout the early modern period. A Kentish timber merchant described himself, or was described by a lawyer, in Elizabeth's reign as 'being a mere layman and illiterate'; even in the eighteenth century learned gentlemen continued to regard anyone who could not read Latin as 'illiterate'. But by the end of the fourteenth century the modern usages, denoting basic ability to read and write in the vernacular, were becoming widespread. In the sixteenth century they were normal. At the end of Elizabeth's reign George Owen could refer to witnesses being able to sign title deeds in Henrician Pembrokeshire 'if they were literate'; Shakespeare's 'clownish servant',

---

[91] Thomas Adams, *The Workes of Tho: Adams* (London, 1629), 58; Clanchy, *From Memory to Written Record*, 187–8, 193; John Bunyan, *The Pilgrim's Progress*, ed. J. B. Wharey and R. Sharrock (Oxford, 1960), 33, 38, 304; Thomas, 'The Meaning of Literacy', 111–12; Nottinghamshire Record Office, M463, 429.

Speed, is described as an 'illiterate loiterer' when it is thought that he 'canst not read' a 'paper'.[92]

Thus, vernacular 'illiteracy' came increasingly to be regarded as a deficiency and a defect in various contexts. By the later seventeenth century it was thought of as a serious impediment to holding public office or performing any kind of official function. Whereas the inability of the mayor of Chester, Robert Brerewood, to read and write had attracted no adverse comment in Elizabeth's reign, by the 1660s the mayor of Bristol who tried to read a pass while holding it upside down became a joke in the taverns of London.[93] Whereas there are plenty of examples from the sixteenth and early seventeenth centuries of local officials, such as churchwardens and petty constables, who could not read, this would be far less acceptable in due course. Richard Gough thought the parish clerk of Myddle, Thomas Highway, 'a person alltogeather unfitt for such an imployment. Hee can read but litle; hee can sing but one tune of the psalmes. Hee can scarce write his owne name, or read any written hand...'.[94] Whereas it was not unusual in the Tudor period to have illiterates as executors of wills, the Yorkshire gentlewoman Alice Thornton refused to let a neighbour perform this function on behalf of her dead husband in 1668 because he could neither read nor write.[95]

Inevitably, then, the selective distribution of literacy skills in a way which to some extent, although by no means absolutely, mirrored the hierarchy of wealth and status generally, was bound to have implications for social distinctions and social relations. Up to a point, level of competence in this respect became a reflection of place and rank, the variegation of the one running alongside the gradations of the other. The vast range of capacities and competencies which lay behind the term 'literacy' were as stratified as the social order itself. Many more people could read than could write, while among readers there were some who could manage the printed word but could not always decipher one, or any, of the variety of scripts which characterized contemporary handwriting. So there were those, like some followers of the mid-seventeenth-century religious

---

[92] Clanchy, *From Memory to Written Record*, 226–31; Everitt, 'The Marketing of Agricultural Produce', 566; Thomas, 'The Meaning of Literacy', 101; Hoeppner Moran, 'Literacy and Education in Northern England, 1350–1550', 3–4; George Owen, *The Description of Pembrokeshire*, ed. Dillwyn Miles (Llandysul, 1994), 170; Shakespeare, *The Two Gentlemen of Verona*, III. i. 298–302.

[93] *Records of Early English Drama: Chester*, ed. Clopper, 142 (as above); *The Diary of Samuel Pepys*, ed. Latham and Matthews, iii. 180.

[94] Thomas, 'The Meaning of Literacy', 110; Gough, *The History of Myddle*, ed. Hey, 45.

[95] Wrightson and Levine, *Poverty and Piety in an English Village*, 152; *The Autobiography of Mrs Alice Thornton, of East Newton, Co. York*, ed. Charles Jackson (Surtees Society, 62, Durham, 1875), 241.

radical Lodowick Muggleton, who were said not even to be able to read 'print-hand'. There were others, meanwhile, like the wife of Edward Duffield, a yeoman of Jacobean Suffolk, who, in common with Thomas Highway of Myddle, could 'not write or reade a written hande' and yet may have been capable of understanding a printed page from the Bible or the contents of a broadside. Another such was clearly Francis Barrett, a poor seaman from Dover, who claimed in 1633 that he could not 'writte or reade anie other hande then printed hande'. A Yorkshire woman, born in the 1620s, was obviously noteworthy because 'she reads also written-hand as well as print'.[96]

It is possible to observe this range of abilities encountering the hand-written and the printed word in its many forms. Those who struggled with 'print hand' may have been becoming rarer by the end of the seventeenth century but they were still common. It is not unusual, therefore, to find people like William Kirkby, sexton of the parish church at Dalton in Lancashire, who, one Saturday night in February 1685, 'did see a paper and a Bible leafe … both fixed to the church doore with balme', but 'being illiterate' he left them there and only later took them to the vicar. Even the two constables who found the culprit in John Bowes, a carrier with some pages torn from his Bible, could only identify the missing leaf by reckoning that it 'seemes to bee of the same character and bignesse with the other leafes in that Bible'. For most, the handwritten word would have appeared as to Hopeful, or else perhaps to Christian, meeting the monument by the side of the road. 'At last Hopeful espied written above upon the head thereof, a writing in an unusual hand; but he being no scholar, called to Christian (for he was learned) to see if he could pick out the meaning: so he came, and after a little laying of letters together, he found the same to be this, "*Remember Lot's Wife*".'[97]

At the other end of the spectrum, however, practised readers and learned scholars used books with facility and fluency, dipping in and out as they wished, moving from one to another, here glancing through, there attending with care. 'Some books are to be tasted, others to be swallowed, and some few to be chewed and digested', reflected Francis Bacon, 'that is, some books are to be read only in parts; others to be read, but not

---

[96] Christopher Hill, Barry Reay, and William Lamont, *The World of the Muggletonians* (London, 1983), 48; Campbell, *The English Yeoman under Elizabeth and the Early Stuarts*, 274; PRO, SP16/252/67ii; Ralph Thoresby, *Ducatus Leodiensis: Or, the Topography of the Ancient and Populous Town and Parish of Leedes* (London, 1715), 621. On the various forms of the written and printed word at this time, see Thomas, 'The Meaning of Literacy', 99–100.

[97] PRO, PL27/1 (*Kirkby* v. *Bowes*, 1685); Bunyan, *The Pilgrim's Progress*, ed. Wharey and Sharrock, 108.

curiously; and some few to be read wholly, and with diligence and attention'. Thus the very skilled might simultaneously compare and cross-
reference texts, as did the Renaissance scholars whose book wheels
revolved a dozen or more large volumes before them at a sitting. Others
might browse casually in a variety of different works, as did Samuel Pepys
who, on a pay day in December 1663, rushed down to his bookseller in
Paul's churchyard and spent two or three hours leafing through twenty
diverse volumes trying to decide what to add to his library. And which
modern academic would not envy the skill of the Elizabethan divine
William Perkins?

He had a rare felicity in speedy reading of books, and as it were by turning them
over would give an exact account of all considerables therein. So that as it were
riding post thorow an authour, he took strick notice of all passages, as if he had
dwelt on them particularly; perusing books so speedily, one would think he read
nothing; so accurately, one would think he read all.[98]

This is the background, therefore, against which the growth of literacy
and the spread of the written word in sixteenth- and seventeenth-century
England must be viewed. So far as most people were concerned, it did not
profoundly alter their access to information or the content of their cultural repertoire since much of what appeared on the page both drew from
and fed into oral circulation. There was, of course, as large a spectrum in
the intellectual sophistication of reading matter as there was in the readers themselves. Manuscript and print met with different receptions at different social levels; they had more impact in certain walks of life than in
others. But no one was immune from their pervasive influence; few
aspects of economy, society, and culture remained untouched by their
implications. Even the 'illiterate' were quite used to receiving the words of
others, as well as to expressing their own, through the medium of text.

This book sets out to explore certain key aspects of the oral culture of six-
teenth- and seventeenth-century England and to assess the influence
which the written and printed word had upon them. This was an environment in which oral traditions and cultural forms of all sorts remained vital
and highly developed. It was a partially literate society in which many
could not read and even those who could received much of their information and knowledge, edification and entertainment, by listening to the

[98] Bacon, *The Essayes*, in *The Works of Francis Bacon*, ed. Spedding, Ellis, and Heath, vi. 498;
Lisa Jardine and Anthony Grafton, '"Studied for Action": How Gabriel Harvey Read his Livy',
*Past and Present*, 129 (1990), 46–51; *The Diary of Samuel Pepys*, ed. Latham and Matthews, iv. 410–11;
Thomas Fuller, *The Holy State* (Cambridge, 1642), 91.

spoken word. In many ways it is impossible to penetrate the mental world of the majority of the English population at this time, without approaching the subject at this level of verbal exchange and face-to-face transmission.

What makes the early modern period such a fascinating case study in this context, however, is the extent to which this oral culture was structured and determined by the enormous expansion in manuscript texts and the new technology of print which are essential defining characteristics of this age. The degree to which the unwritten repertoire fed into the written, and then drew again from it, at a time of rapid intellectual and social change, is one of the compelling issues of historical study. In the following chapters, specific investigations of the spoken language, the use of proverbial wisdom, the telling of tales and the singing of songs, the transmission of local custom and the spreading of news, explore this relationship between oral, scribal, and printed culture from different perspectives, all of which were crucial to the experience of contemporaries.

The argument advanced in these pages is that while the spoken word remained the principal vehicle of communication and information for most people at this time, England was far from being an oral culture in any meaningful sense. Even in the early sixteenth century, and certainly by the later seventeenth, the world of those at the lowest and least literate levels was fundamentally permeated by the written word. Contrary to long-cherished views about society at this time, held in one form or another since the history of its popular culture began to be written in the late eighteenth century, this was not an environment in which the unlettered majority lived without reference to the printed word or used oral forms which were not at some level influenced by it. Moreover, the growth of literacy and the spread of print did not destroy or weaken the force of communication by word of mouth. Instead it reinvigorated it, providing new material and fresh inspiration for the vernacular repertoire. Written sources fed into the popular mind providing it with a stock of images and themes to fashion in terms relevant to its own experience. Words and sayings, storylines and tunes, traditions and news stories were all taken up from print and recycled or reapplied in specific communities as the property of local people. 'Oral' and 'literate' are rarely discrete entities or inversely related, an increase in the one necessarily entailing a corresponding retreat in the other. Instead they form a dynamic continuum, each feeding in and out of the other to the development and nourishment of both. The case of England in the sixteenth and seventeenth centuries demonstrates this process at work.

# I

# Popular Speech

Language most shewes a man: speake that I may see thee.

> Ben Jonson, *Timber: or, Discoveries* (1641), in *The Works of
> Ben Jonson*, ed. C. H. Herford and Percy Simpson
> (11 vols., Oxford, 1925–52), viii. 625.

Q: What makes languages change so often, so that scarce any
nation understands what their ancestors spoke or writ 2 or 300 years
ago?
A: The same that makes the fashion of cloaths alter. When the
vulgar are got into the fashion, the gentry invent somthing new to
diversifie and distinguish themselves from them.

> Cumbria Record Office, D Lons/W1/14, 135 (Sir John
> Lowther's Memorandum Book, 1677–89).

THE starting point for a discussion of the oral culture of any society must
be the very language itself. The spoken word, in particular, provides a
more immediate and sensitive insight into the mental world of a people
than perhaps all other forms of expression. Language is a product of the
environment in which it evolves, a reflection of its social constructs, an
articulation of its beliefs and values. It is also a powerful determinant of
that environment, helping to structure its individual relationships and
give vent to its group identities.[1]

In early modern England there was far greater linguistic diversity than
today. One of the most striking aspects of life in 'the world we have have
lost', though one of the least recognized by social historians, is the rich
and variegated nature of popular speech. The varieties of English were
so copious that it is scarcely possible to speak of a national language or
native tongue. There was instead a multiplicity of different dialects, based
upon geographical, occupational, and social allegiances, which divided

---

[1] For remarks on the relationship between language and society, see Peter Burke,
'Introduction', in Peter Burke and Roy Porter (eds.), *The Social History of Language* (Cambridge,
1987), 1–20; Peter Trudgill, *Sociolinguistics: An Introduction* (Harmondsworth, 1974); useful studies
are also collected in Pier Paolo Giglioli (ed.), *Language and Social Context* (Harmondsworth, 1972)
and J. B. Pride and J. Holmes (eds.), *Sociolinguistics* (Harmondsworth, 1972).

up the country into a complex configuration of overlapping 'speech communities'. They could be markedly different in vocabulary, grammar, and phonology, each one expressing and encompassing quite distinct cultural contexts, the variety of the one reflecting the variety of the other.

Commentators on the language in the sixteenth and seventeenth centuries were fond of quoting the classical dictum that 'speech is the picture of the mind'.[2] As such, the spoken word, in so far as it can be retrieved from written sources, promises to reveal much about the normative values and basic assumptions of contemporaries. For students of popular culture, the dialects of the period offer a point of entry into the frame of reference of that majority of people whose words are usually hardest to recover. In some of their now opaque terms and obscure phrases, they suggest alien world views, ways of perceiving and behaving now lost, the ideas and practices they conveyed as redundant as the means by which they were then expressed. Dialect speech was, as E. P. Thompson once remarked, 'studded with words which point not only towards forgotten tools, measures, things, but also towards forgotten modes of thought and habits of work'.[3]

For those concerned with the relationship between oral and literate forms of culture, the linguistic change of this period affords equally revealing insights. Thanks to the influence of print culture and the cross-fertilization in European intellectual life during the Renaissance, English was enormously enriched and expanded by the infusion of words and phrases from other languages. There are few better examples of the stimulation and invigoration of oral communication by written forms than the transformation of the vernacular vocabulary at this time. In parallel with this process, the early modern period also witnessed the consolidation of something like a standard or authorized version of the mother tongue. This had the effect of throwing into relief the idiom of the majority who remained less effected by the rapidly changing influences which informed the 'best speech'. What came to be known by the later sixteenth century as 'dialects', or alternative and subordinate strains of the language, were relatively untouched by the rules and conventions shaping the literary and courtly variant. Instead, dialects continued to express and

[2] See, for example, James Sanforde, *The Garden of Pleasure* (London, 1573), fo. 56ᵛ; John Hoskyns, 'Direccons for Speech and Style', in *The Life, Letters, and Writings of John Hoskyns, 1566–1638*, ed. L. B. Osborn (New Haven, 1937), 111; Henry Peacham, *The Complete Gentleman* (1634), ed. Virgil B. Heltzel (Ithaca, NY, 1962), 54; George Granville, *An Essay upon Unnatural Flights in Poetry* (1701), in *Critical Essays of the Seventeenth Century*, ed. J. E. Spingarn (3 vols., Oxford, 1908), iii. 292.

[3] E. P. Thompson, 'Anthropology and the Discipline of Historical Context', *Midland History*, 1/3 (1972), 53.

reflect a popular culture in which literate habits of mind and national processes of incorporation had scarcely undermined oral traditions or subsumed local identities.

The dominance of a single variety of spoken English also had significant implications for social relations more broadly. For 'received speech' became not only the medium of the learned elite but also of the social elite. In this period, to a much greater extent than ever before, language came to underpin social hierarchies, to provide a litmus of rank and degree, and a vehicle for status differentiation. In this context as in others, the unevenness of cultural change was a function of the inequalities of wealth and power within society. The way in which people spoke was not merely determined by their place in the order of things, but it came to ratify and confirm it in new and subtly pervasive ways. On the one hand, vowel sounds and vocabulary might facilitate a common identity and interest among certain individuals and groups; on the other hand, they might serve as an agent of exclusion and social differentiation. 'Language', it has justly been said, 'is an instrument of both communication and excommunication'.[4]

## THE KING'S ENGLISH

The rise of a 'standard' form of written English has been much discussed by historians of the language. It appears that in the late fourteenth and early fifteenth centuries the variety of Middle English then commonly used in London began to gain ascendancy over the other forms. In 1417 it was this strain of the vernacular which replaced Latin and French as the usual medium of government business and by 1430 a clearly identifiable 'chancery standard' had emerged. Crucially, this was the form of English adopted by Caxton for the printing press introduced to London in 1476.[5] Meanwhile, the fragmentary evidence suggests that a standard spoken English can be traced back at least as early. At the end of the fourteenth century Chaucer was imitating some unspecified northern dialect to comic effect in *The Reeve's Tale*, while the affectation of a southern dialect

---

[4] P. J. Waller, 'Democracy and Dialect, Speech and Class', in Waller (ed.), *Politics and Social Change in Modern Britain* (Brighton, 1987), 2.

[5] Basil Cottle, *The Triumph of English, 1350–1400* (London, 1969); John H. Fisher, 'Chancery English and the Emergence of Standard Written English in the Fifteenth Century', *Speculum*, 52 (1977), 870–99; id., 'Caxton and Chancery English', in Robert F. Yeager (ed.), *Fifteenth-Century Studies* (Hamden, Conn., 1984), 161–85; Margaret Shaklee, 'The Rise of Standard English', in Timothy Shopen and Joseph M. Williams (eds.), *Standards and Dialects in English* (Cambridge, Mass., 1980), 33–62.

by the shepherd Mak in one of the Wakefield mystery plays, indicates that this form may already have been regarded as superior.[6]

It is likely, therefore, that the idea of 'the King's English' to denote a single standard, authorized by the court in London, was applied to both the written and the spoken language in the late Middle Ages. The phrase itself does not appear to have been used until the mid-sixteenth century, however. 'These fine English clerkes will say, they speake in their mother tongue, if a man should charge them for counterfeiting the kings English,' wrote Thomas Wilson in 1553. 'Still he must be running on the letter', commented Thomas Nashe in Elizabeth's reign, 'and abusing the queenes English without pittie or mercie'. In *The Merry Wives of Windsor*, Mistress Quickly accuses her master, the French physician Doctor Caius, of 'abusing of God's patience and the king's English'.[7]

At the same time it became common for writers on the state of the language to uphold the English of the court as the model for all writers and speakers to follow. There were those, John Hart commented, of the 'farre west, or north countryes, which vse differing English termes from those of the court, and London, where the flower of the English tongue is vsed'. Wilson contrasted 'court talke' with 'countrey speech', the one 'learned' the other 'rude'. 'Wee haue court and wee haue countrey English, wee haue northerne and southerne, grosse and ordinarie', agreed Richard Carew in the 1590s. Famously, George Puttenham, counselled authors not to copy

the termes of northern-men, such as they vse in dayly talke, whether they be noble men or gentlemen, or of their best clarkes, all is a matter: nor in effect any speach vsed beyond the riuer of Trent, though no man can deny that theirs is the purer English Saxon at this day, yet it is not so courtly nor so currant as our Southerne English is, no more is the far westerne mans speach: ye shall therefore take the vsuall speach of the court, and that of London and the shires lying about London within lx. myles, and not much aboue.[8]

---

[6] J. R. R. Tolkien, 'Chaucer as a Philologist: The Reeve's Tale', *Transactions of the Philological Society* (1934), 1–70; E. J. Dobson, 'Early Modern Standard English', *Transactions of the Philological Society* (1955), 25; Martyn F. Wakelin, *English Dialects: An Introduction* (rev. edn., London, 1977), 34–5.

[7] Thomas Wilson, *The Arte of Rhetorique*, ed. G. H. Mair (Oxford, 1909), 162; Thomas Nashe, *Strange News* (1592), in *The Works of Thomas Nashe*, ed. R. B. McKerrow, rev. F. P. Wilson (5 vols., Oxford, 1958), i. 261; Shakespeare, *The Merry Wives of Windsor*, i. iv. 5–6.

[8] John Hart, *A Methode or Comfortable Beginning* (London, 1570), sig. A3ʳ; Wilson, *The Arte of Rhetorique*, ed. Mair, 164; Richard Carew, 'The Excellencie of the English Tongue', in William Camden, *Remaines, Concerning Britaine* (2nd edn., London, 1614), 42; George Puttenham, *The Arte of English Poesie* (London, 1589), 120–1. Cf. William Harrison, *The Description of England*, ed. Georges Edelen (Ithaca, NY, 1968), 416–17.

By this time, and probably long before, there was an apparent homo-geneity in the language of the courtly and learned elite, a 'usual speech' which passed for a standard English. 'Among people of learned and civil upringing, there is one ubiquitous speech and pronuncing, and meaning', confirmed Alexander Gil, the Highmaster of St Paul's school in the reign of James I. The idea of a 'received English' in terms of vocabulary, gram-mar, and pronuciation was already a commonplace in the mid-sixteenth century when Thomas Wilson advised of the necessity to 'speake as is commonly receiued'. It was essential for public speakers, in particular, Robert Cawdrey later affirmed 'to speake so as is commonly receiued . . . vsing their speech as most men doe'.[9]

There always remained disagreement, however, as to what exactly con-stituted received English and controversy was fuelled by the fact the lan-guage was subject to considerable change over the course of the early modern period. In 1490 Caxton had commented on the way in which 'our langage now vsed varyeth ferre from that whiche was vsed and spoken whan I was borne', in the Weald of Kent seventy years before. Thereafter, the pace of change may have been even quicker. In terms of vocabulary the English language was enormously expanded, particularly in the period 1570–1630, and over 30,000 new words were either coined or bor-rowed from Latin and modern European languages during the sixteenth and seventeenth centuries. Pronunciation also developed significantly at the same time, undergoing a 'great vowel shift', or the shortening of most of the long vowel sounds implied by late medieval script. Thus by the end of the sixteenth century William Camden could observe how 'our sparke-full youth laugh at their great grandfathers English, who had more care to do wel, than to speake minion-like, and left more glory to vs by their exploiting of great acts, than we shall do by our forging a-new words, and vncouth phrases'.[10]

In due course, the spoken and written language of Caroline England differed in many respects from that of Camden's day. In 1633 Charles Butler observed that 'wee have generally, or in the more civil parts (as the universities and citties) forsaken the old pronunciation', by which he meant that evidenced by the spellings in *The Book of Homilies* printed in 1562.

[9] Alexander Gil, *Logonomia Anglica: Qua Gentis Sermo Facilius Addiscitur* (London, 1619), 18 (my trans.); Wilson, *The Arte of Rhetorique*, ed. Mair, 162; Robert Cawdrey, *A Table Alphabeticall* (London, 1604), sig. A3ʳ.

[10] *The Prologues and Epilogues of William Caxton*, ed. W. J. B. Crotch (Early English Text Society, orig. ser., 176, London, 1928), 108; Manfred Görlach, *Introduction to Early Modern English* (Cambridge, 1991), 136–9, 166–9; E. J. Dobson, *English Pronunciation, 1500–1700* (2 vols., 2nd edn., Oxford, 1968); Camden, *Remaines, Concerning Britaine*, 25.

Vowel sounds had been altered since that time, he believed, and accordingly 'wee conform our writing to the nue sound', although not in the north of England. A generation later, John Dryden was among those to analyse the way in which the language of Restoration England differed so markedly from that of Shakespeare, Fletcher, and Jonson. Part of the reason, as a chorus of commentators which included John Evelyn lamented, was the way in which religious zealots and mechanic preachers of the Civil War years had corrupted the mother tongue with cant jargon and provincial pronunciation. With predictable circularity, Jonathan Swift would later sum up the view of the early eighteenth century when he condemned the 'licentiousness which entered with the Restoration, and from infecting our religion and morals fell to corrupt our language'.[11]

It was in an effort to keep pace with this linguistic change that the first English dictionaries began to appear in the seventeenth century. Robert Cawdrey published his *Table Alphabeticall* in 1604 in order to help interpret the many difficult and uncertain new words as well as to demonstrate their true orthography. He was followed in this project by John Bullokar, Henry Cockeram, Thomas Blount, Edward Phillips, and Elisha Coles. Even many London tradesmen 'have new dialects' full of imported terms, noted Blount in the 1650s. Not until John Kersey's *New English Dictionary* of 1702 was there an attempt made to define not just 'hard words' but the full range of vocabulary in the mother tongue.[12]

As the dictionaries explained 'hard words', a number of works appeared suggesting the way in which they might best be written and articulated. In the mid-sixteenth century Thomas Smith, John Hart, and William Bullokar were among the first to offer proposals for the reform of orthography, not only in an attempt to achieve a more phonetic written language, but also because of the effect which it was thought to have on speech. In 1586 George Whetstone anticipated a popular eighteenth-century genre when he published one of the first pronouncing manuals,

---

[11] Charles Butler, *The English Grammar* (Oxford, 1633), 3; John Dryden, 'Defence of the Epilogue', and 'Preface to Troilus and Cressida', in *Essays of John Dryden*, ed. W. P. Ker (2 vols., Oxford, 1900), i. 164–5, 203; John Evelyn, 'Letter to Sir Peter Wyche', in *Critical Essays of the Seventeenth Century*, ed. Spingarn, ii. 310; Jonathan Swift, *A Proposal for Correcting, Improving and Ascertaining the English Tongue* (London, 1712), 18–20. Cf. Thomas Sprat, *The History of the Royal Society of London* (London, 1667), 41–2.

[12] Cawdrey, *A Table Alphabeticall*, sig. A2ʳ; John Bullokar, *An English Expositor* (London, 1616), sig. A3ᵛ; Henry Cockeram, *The English Dictionarie* (London, 1623); Thomas Blount, *Glossographia: Or a Dictionary Interpreting All Such Hard Words* (London, 1656), sigs. A2ᵛ–A3ʳ; Edward Phillips, *The New World of English Words* (London, 1658), sig. B4ᵛ; Elisha Coles, *An English Dictionary* (London, 1676); *Gazophylacium Anglicanum: Containing the Derivation of English Words* (London, 1689); J[ohn] K[ersey], *New English Dictionary* (London, 1702). See De Witt T. Starnes and Gertrude E. Noyes, *The English Dictionary from Cawdrey to Johnson, 1604–1755* (Chapel Hill, NC, 1946).

and in the early seventeenth century Robert Robinson continued the attempt to achieve greater conformity between the spelling and sounding of words in the *The Art of Pronunciation* (1617), considered to be the first scientific treatise on phonetics in English. In 1633, Charles Butler could claim that considerable progress had already been made in this respect since the beginning of Elizabeth's reign.[13] All of these proposals for reform of vocabulary, pronunciation, and orthography preceded the most radical suggestion of all, in the middle decades of the seventeenth century, for the creation of a universal language, derived logically from first principles and the 'primitive roots' of Hebrew.[14]

Whatever the changes in 'received speech' which took place over the sixteenth and seventeenth centuries and the ongoing debate about what constituted best practice, the creation of a more or less uniform standard had the effect of exposing a contrast between it and all other varieties. The term 'dialect' emerged in the last quarter of the sixteenth century to refer to those subordinate variations of the vernacular which did not conform to 'pure', 'common', or 'usual' English.[15] In parallel with these developments, it became one of the priorities of formal education to expunge non-standard vocabulary and usage from both writing and speech and to inculcate the 'received' pronunciation of the social and learned elite. The best schoolmasters appreciated, with Roger Ascham, that 'all languages' are 'gotten onelie by imitation' and that 'if yow be borne or brought vp in a rude contrie, ye shall not chose but speake rudelie'. Charles Hoole later advised that 'the sweet and natural pronunciation' of letters 'is gotten rather by imitation then precept, and therefore the teacher must be careful to give every letter its distinct and clear sound, that the childe may get it from his voice . . .'. The 'speech of the master authoriseth the childs imitation', confirmed Obadiah Walker in the 1670s.[16]

[13] Sir Thomas Smith, *De Recta et Emendata Lingvae Anglicae Scriptione, Dialogus* (London, 1568); John Hart, *An Orthographie* (London, 1569); William Bullokar, *Bullokars Booke at Large, for the Amendment of Orthographie for English Speech* (London, 1580), 1–2; George Whetstone, 'English Pronvnciation: Or a Shorte Introdvction and Waye to the English Speache', in his *The Honovrable Repvtation of a Sovldier* (Leyden, 1586), 73–103; Robert Robinson, *The Art of Pronunciation* (London, 1617), sig. A5ʳ; Butler, *The English Grammar*, 3.

[14] Vivian Salmon, 'Language-Planning in Seventeenth-Century England; Its Context and Aims', in C. E. Bazell et al. (eds.), *In Memory of J. R. Firth* (London, 1966), 370–97; ead. 'John Wilkins' *Essay*: Critics and Continuators', in her *The Study of Language in Seventeenth-Century England* (Amsterdam, 1979), 191–206; ead., 'Nathaniel Chamberlain and his *Tractatus De Letteris Et Lingua Philosophica* (1679)', in her *Language and Society in Early Modern England* (Amsterdam, 1984), 131–40.

[15] *OED*, s.v. 'dialect'; Paula Blank, *Broken English: Dialects and the Politics of Language in Renaissance Writings* (London, 1996), 7–8.

[16] Roger Ascham, *The Scholemaster* (London, 1570), fo. 46ʳ; Charles Hoole, *A New Discovery of*

Educationalists often lamented the way in which either the poor example set by the unlearned women who acted as nurses, or else the unconscious emulation of provincial custom at an impressionable age, formed habits of speech which were very difficult to break later on. As early as 1531 the courtier, Sir Thomas Elyot, advised the nurses of gentle children to 'speke none englisshe but that whiche is cleane, polite, perfectly and articulately pronounced, omittinge no lettre or sillable, as folisshe women often times do of a wantonnesse, wherby diuers noble men and gentilmennes chyldren (as I do at this daye knowe) haue attained corrupte and foule pronuntiation'. In the 1580s the master of Merchant Taylors' school in London, Richard Mulcaster, pitied the poor infants who 'moile themselues sore, with the maners and conditions of the nurse, with the sines or rudenes of her speeche'. William Kempe warned parents against employing 'barbarous nursses' and using 'any rude or barbarous speach' themselves in front of their children, since even a 'small diuersitie of speach . . . being admitted at the first, will hardly afterwards euer ware out of use'. So it was, lamented Thomas Tryon at the end of the seventeenth century, that 'many children have reason to condemn their governors and nurses, all the days of their life, for those manifold inconveniences they are expos'd to by an uncomfortable imperfection in the utterance of their speech'.[17]

It was also such ill-bred people, 'poor women, or others, whose necessities compel them to undertake it, as a meer shelter from beggery', in Charles Hoole's words, who often presided over the parochial schools in which many children received their first, or sometimes their only, instruction. It was for this reason that Edmund Coote, the headmaster of Bury St Edmunds grammar school during Elizabeth's reign, urged 'all carefull ministers, that as they tender the good education of the youth of the parishes, they would sometimes repayre vnto the schools of such teachers as are not grammarians, to heare their children pronounce . . .'. Too often, however, the advice went unheeded or else the task proved simply too difficult and by the time a boy reached the grammar school the die had been cast. Try 'to preuent the griefe and wearisomnesse of teaching them to forget euill customes in pronouncing, which they tooke vp in their first ill

the *Old Art of Teaching Schoole* (London, 1660), 3; Obadiah Walker, *Of Education, Especially of Young Gentlemen* (London, 1673), 26–7.

[17] Sir Thomas Elyot, *The Boke Named the Gouernour* (London, 1531), fo. 19ᵛ; Richard Mulcaster, *Positions wherein those Primitive Circumstances be Examined, which are Necessarie for the Training up of Children* (London, 1581), 15; William Kempe, *The Education of Children in Learning* (London, 1588), sigs. E3ᵛ–E4ʳ; Thomas Tryon, *A New Method of Educating Children* (London, 1695), 38. Cf. Richard Mulcaster, *The First Part of the Elementarie* (London, 1582), 84.

learning', John Brinsley encouraged grammar school masters in 1612.
'And so euer in teaching to read, the teachers are to continue the like care
of sweete and naturall pronuntiation.'[18]

This method of inculcating correct pronunciation through listening to
a child read aloud was a standard pedagogic technique. In the early sixteenth century a Mr Southwell was instructing Gregory Cromwell, the
son of Henry VIII's first minister, 'dailie hering him to reade sumwhatt in
thenglishe tongue, and advertisenge hime of the naturell and true kynde
of pronuntiation thereof'. At the grammar schools this was a principal
means of cultivating the best articulation both of the classical and vulgar
tongues. The statutes of the King Edward VI school in Morpeth,
Northumberland, for example, enjoined the master and ushers to 'take
great care that all their scholars read and pronounce articulately with due
sound and accent'. The first visitors of Merchant Taylors', London, in
1562 were compelled to upbraid the Cumberland-bred Richard Mulcaster
and his ushers for negligence in this respect, 'that being northern men
born, they had not taught the children to speak distinctly, or to pronounce
their words as well as they ought'.[19]

Just as reading aloud was believed to aid good pronunciation, it was
generally agreed that only by speaking properly could youngsters learn to
write 'true' English. In the 1560s John Hart asserted the commonplace
that people wrote as they spoke, and spoke as they wrote. Thus 'if any one
were minded at Newcastle uppon Tine, or Bodman in Cornewale, to
write or print his minde there, who could lustly blame him for his
orthographie, to serue hys neyghbours according to their mother
speach...'. For those aspiring to the best pronunciation of London, however, the phonetic spelling of such local dialects had to be reformed. The
aim of the English–Latin dictionary published in 1570 by Peter Levins, a
product of Beverley grammar school, was 'that as wel children and ruder
schoolers, as also the barbarous countries and ruder writers, may not a
little . . . well and easily correct and amend, both their pen and speache'.
Francis Clement advised Elizabethan petty school teachers that in order
for a child to be able to 'write truely' it was necessary for him 'to know at
the least rightly to pronounce his word'. To grammar school masters,
Brinsley offered this example: 'aske the child how he spells a "strea" (as

[18] Hoole, *A New Discovery of the Old Art of Teaching Schoole*, 28; Edmund Coote, *The English Schoole-Maister* (London, 1596), sig. A4; John Brinsley, *Ludus Literarius: Or, The Grammar Schoole* (London, 1612), 15.

[19] H. C. Wyld, *A History of Modern Colloquial English* (3rd edn., Oxford, 1936), 103; *The Antiquarian Repertory*, ed. Francis Grose (4 vols., London, 1775–84), i. 206; Dobson, 'Early Modern Standard English', 40–1.

in many places the country manner is to pronounce it), he will spell
"strea" or "stre": but ask him how hee spels a "strawe" and so pronounce
it and he will spell "strawe".[20]

A number of schoolmasters published spelling-books during the
seventeenth century which were as much guides to correct forms of
pronunciation as they were textbooks on orthography. Simon Daines
urged his pupils in Suffolk during the reign of Charles I to make their
writing and speaking conform and to 'follow the custome of the learned'
in this, although he accepted that a logical method of doing so had yet
to be devised. The schoolmaster at Salisbury and later of St Dunstan's-
in-the-East, London, Thomas Hunt, produced another example of
this genre in 1661, unusually in the form of a dialogue. He was followed
by Elisha Coles whose *Compleat English Schoolmaster* (1674) was based on
the premiss that 'all words must so be spell'd, as they are afterwards to be
pronounc'd'. And just before the Glorious Revolution, Christopher
Cooper, the headmaster of Bishop's Stortford grammar school,
Hertfordshire, published an equally influential textbook in this vein: 'He
that would write more exactly, must avoid barbarous pronunciation', he
reaffirmed, considering that 'many words are not sounded after the best
dialect.'[21]

Throughout the sixteenth and seventeenth centuries, therefore, the
expurgation of traces of local dialects in both writing and speaking was an
imperative of formal education. The enormous expansion of grammar
schools clearly had a significant effect in helping to homogenize the
speech of the social elite and in organizing a self-conscious attempt to distance the language of the learned gentility from that of the lower orders.
At Bury St Edmunds, Edmund Coote told his Elizabethan pupils to avoid
'imitating the barbarous speech of your countrie people' and held up
many of their 'absurdities' to ridicule. Similar warnings were later offered
by Alexander Gil at St Paul's, who disparaged by example the various
regional dialects, including that of his native Lincolnshire and those of the
West Country which he considered to be particularly 'barbarous'. Simon
Daines was to concur in condemning 'the absurdities used among the

---

[20] Hart, *An Orthographie*, fos. 20ᵛ–21ʳ; Peter Levins, *Manipulus Vocabulorum* (London, 1570),
preface; Francis Clement, *The Petie Schole* (London, 1587), 18; Brinsley, *Ludus Literarius*, 17.

[21] Simon Daines, *Orthoepia Anglicana* (London, 1640), 80; Thomas Hunt, *Libellus Orthographicus:
Or, the Diligent School Boy's Directory* (London, 1661); Elisha Coles, *The Compleat English Schoolmaster*
(London, 1674), sig. A2ʳ; Christopher Cooper, *The English Teacher* (London, 1687), 77. Among
other examples, see Thomas Lye, *The Childs Delight* (London, 1671); Henry Care, *The Tutor to True
English* (London, 1687), esp. 22–3; Thomas Dyche, *A Guide to the English Tongue in Two Parts*
(London, 1707).

vulgar in Somerset-shire, and other remote places, as not worth the nominating, so much by way of reprehension'.[22]

The evidence offered by the letters and private papers of the educated classes suggests that certainly by the seventeenth century this pedagogic effort had been reasonably successful in removing any grammar or vocabulary derived from local or regional speech. Standard written and spoken English was clearly normal among the social elite by this time and probably before. As for pronunciation, or accents, there seems to have been much more variety of practice.[23] Many products of provincial schools were never able to shed the cadences of home, no matter how they widened their horizons subsequently. Famously, it was said of Sir Walter Ralegh, a product of local schools around Budleigh Salterton in the mid-sixteenth century, that 'notwithstanding his great travells, conversation, learning, etc. yet he spake broade Devonshire to his dyeing day'. Thomas Hobbes began his academic career at the small village school in Westport, Wiltshire, and 'though he left his native countrey at 14, and lived so long, yet sometimes one might find a little touch of our pronunciation'. Sir Isaac Newton, who received his first formal education at Grantham grammar school, always betrayed his Lincolnshire origins in this respect. Even Samuel Johnson, that seminal figure in English lexicography, had to guard against lapsing into the pure Staffordshire which must still have been common at Lichfield grammar school early in the eighteenth century.[24]

The problem which teachers faced is no more graphically illustrated than in the remarkable account given by Daniel Defoe of his tour through Somerset during Johnson's youth. He paid a visit on a relation who was the schoolmaster at Martock and,

coming into the school, I observ'd one of the lowest scholars was reading his lesson to the usher, which lesson it seems was a chapter in the Bible, so I sat down by the master, till the boy had read out his chapter: I observ'd the boy read a little oddly in the tone of the country, which made me the more attentive, because on enquiry, I found that the words were the same, and the orthography the same as in all our Bibles. I observ'd also the boy read it out with eyes still on the book, and his head like a meer boy, moving from side to side, as the lines

[22] Coote, *The English Schoole-Maister*, 30–1; Gil, *Logonomia Anglica*, 15, 17; Daines, *Orthoepia Anglicana*, 80.

[23] Wyld, *A History of Modern Colloquial English*, 103, 112, 162–7; Constance Davies, *English Pronunciation from the Fifteenth to the Eighteenth Century* (London, 1934), xii n. and 112–49.

[24] John Aubrey, *Brief Lives*, ed. Andrew Clark (2 vols., Oxford, 1898), i. 354, ii. 182; R. W. V. Elliott, 'Isaac Newton as Phonetician', *Modern Language Review*, 49 (1954), 5–12; James Boswell, *The Life of Samuel Johnson* (2 vols., Everyman edn., London, 1906), i. 417.

reach'd cross the columns of the book; his lesson was in the cant. 5. 3. of which the words are these,

> 'I have put off my coat, how shall I put it on,
> I have wash'd my feet, how shall I defile them?'

The boy read thus, with his eyes, as I say full on the text.

> 'Chav a doffed my cooat, how shall I don't,
> Chav a wash'd my veet, how shall I moil 'em?'

How the dexterous dunce could form his mouth to express so readily the words (which stood right printed in the book) in his country jargon, I could not but admire.[25]

As this striking example of the simultaneous adaptation of orthodox vocabulary and orthography into dialect in the very act of reading a printed book reveals, the standardization of written English during the seventeenth century was by no means sufficient in itself to effect similar changes in the spoken language.

The continued failure of much grammar school education to reform the accents of boys remained conspicuous throughout this period, therefore. An Englishman travelling in Scotland in 1689 commented on the 'misrepresentations in words' and the 'unhappy tone' in pronunciation 'which the gentry and nobles cannot overcome, tho' educated in our schools, or never so conversant with us'. At the same time, he admitted, 'our northern and remote English have the same imperfection'. This is one of the reasons why the socially self-conscious provincial gentry were beginning to abandon such institutions by Defoe's day in favour of the tutelage increasingly on offer elsewhere. In March 1714, for example, Henry Liddell of Ravensworth, County Durham, advised a friend against the grammar school in Newcastle as a suitable place for his son. 'For a polite education I dislike the place intirely', he opined, and the boy was subsequently transferred to Sedbergh school.[26]

This inadequacy in the grammar schools is also evident in the traits of many of those pupils who went on to the universities. In 1540 John Palsgrave commented that certain students, 'partly bycause of the rude language vsed in their natyue countreyes, where they were borne and firste

[25] Daniel Defoe, *A Tour thro' the Whole Island of Great Britain*, ed. G. D. H. Cole (London, 1927), 219. The grammar school at Martock was founded in 1662: W. A. L. Vincent, *The Grammar Schools: Their Continuing Tradition, 1660–1714* (London, 1969), 81.

[26] Thomas Morer, *A Short Account of Scotland* (1715), in *Early Travellers in Scotland*, ed. P. Hume Brown (Edinburgh, 1891), 272–3; *The Letters of Henry Liddell to William Cotesworth*, ed. J. M. Ellis (Surtees Society, 197, Durham, 1987), 120. For similar examples from the same region later in the century, see Edward Hughes, *North Country Life in the Eighteenth Century: The North East, 1700–1750* (Oxford, 1952), 364–6.

lerned . . . their grammer rules, and partely bycause that commyng streyght from thense, vnto some of [the] vniuersities, they haue not had occasions to be conuersaunte in suche places . . . as the pureste englysshe is spoken, they be not able to expresse theyr conceyte in theyr vulgar tonge . . .'. The enduring regional affiliations of many colleges in Oxford and Cambridge were probably due, in some measure, to the need to find a tutor familiar with a boy's manner of speech. This is certainly suggested in the novella *Dobsons Drie Bobbes* (1607), the fictional tale of George Dobson, a known resident of Elizabethan Durham. He was a country boy, who 'was so rustike like, that he could not cover his clownish and wayward manners with the habite of civility', and proceeded from the local grammar school to Christ's College, Cambridge, which then took six of its twelve fellows and twenty-three of its forty-seven scholars from the nine English counties north of the Trent. While at Cambridge, Dobson engaged in university debates with both a Welshman and a Kentishman whose regional origins were just as evident as his own.[27]

Over in Oxford, meanwhile, the same situation prevailed. According to John Aubrey, the Exeter College men were conspicuous during debates in the mid-seventeenth century: 'when they allege, "Causae causae est causae causati", they pronounce it, "Caza caza est caza cazati", very un-gracefully'. By the same token, the Welshmen of Jesus College provided the butt of innumerable jokes throughout this period for their manner of speech, among other alleged foibles. Even fellows of colleges were not immune from comment in this respect. The unforgiving Anthony Wood suggested that Dr Robert Morison, the Professor of Botany, spoke better Latin than he did English, the latter 'being much spoyled by his Scottish tone'. It was presumably in order to avoid such censure that John North, a product of Bury St Edmund's grammar school and a future professor of greek, would, as a fellow of Jesus College, Cambridge, in the late 1660s, seek out in his spare moments 'the best penned English books and read them aloud; which he said he did to form and improve his English style and pronunciation'.[28]

---

[27] *The Comedy of Acolastus Translated from the Latin of Fullonius by John Palsgrave*, ed. P. L. Carver (Early English Text Society, orig. ser., 202, London, 1937), 6; Richard Tuck, 'Civil Conflict in School and Town, 1500–1700', in Brian Mains and Anthony Tuck (eds.), *Royal Grammar School Newcastle upon Tyne: A History of the School in its Community* (Stocksfield, 1986), 25–6; *Dobsons Drie Bobbes: A Story of Sixteenth-Century Durham*, ed. E. A. Horsman (Oxford, 1955), xv–xvi, 13, 86–91.

[28] Bod. Lib., MS Aubrey 1, fo. 23$^v$; John Cotgrave, *The English Treasury of Wit and Language* (London, 1655), 255; *The Life and Times of Anthony Wood, Antiquary, of Oxford, 1632–1695, Described by Himself*, ed. Andrew Clark (5 vols., Oxford Historical Society, 19, 21, 26, 30, 40, Oxford, 1891–1900), iii. 49–50; Roger North, *The Lives of the Norths*, ed. Augustus Jessopp (3 vols., London, 1890), ii. 283.

During the sixteenth and seventeenth centuries, therefore, something like a received English, in terms of vocabulary and grammar, although to a much lesser extent in terms of orthography and pronunciation, spread through the higher ranks of society. Although this 'usual' or 'common' form was constantly developing and changing over the course of the period, it provided, nevertheless, a shifting standard against which to judge all other 'dialects' as illegitimate and inferior. This process of linguistic incorporation cannot be divorced from the wider trends of political centralization and educational advance which are such prominent features of life in Tudor and Stuart England. The dominance of 'the King's English' is inseparable from the growth of the nation state, the development of national identity, and the fabrication of something like a common culture.

### DIALECTS

One consequence of the spread and domination of a linguistic standard was to render alternative varieties of English the objects of curiosity and academic interest. As features of dialect speech were abandoned in some circles, they ceased to form part of a living language and became instead the focus of antiquarian research. The tremendous flowering of historical and topographical scholarship in the sixteenth and seventeenth centuries stimulated interest in archaic vocabulary and the etymology of place names which would shed light on the origins and development of particular counties or the nation as a whole.

Thus it was in the course of compiling what was the first dictionary of Anglo-Saxon, in the 1560s, that Laurence Nowell made comparative reference to 173 of the dialect words still current in his native Lancashire, in addition to a small number from elsewhere. The Kentish antiquary William Lambarde contributed a few more examples when he inherited Nowell's manuscript. Equally, while writing his history of Ireland in the 1570s, Richard Stanihurst was interested to find that English speakers in that country still preserved 'the dregs of the old ancient Chaucer English',

as they terme a spider, an 'attercop'; a wisp, a 'wad'; a lumpe of bread, a 'pocket', or a 'pucket'; a sillibucke, a 'copprous'; a faggot, a 'blease', or a 'blaze' ... a phisicion, a 'leache'; a gap, a 'shard'; a base court or quadrangle, a 'bawen' ... a dunghill, a 'mizen' ...

A little later, the antiquary Richard Carew noted down a variety of unintelligible words and phrases in use among his Cornish neighbours. '"'Tis not bezibd (that is, fortuned) to me", "Thou hast no road (ayme)", "He wil neuer scrip (escape) it", "He is nothing pridy (handsome)", as also "boobish" (lubberly), "dule" (comfort), "lidden" (by-word), "shune" (strange), "thew" (threaten), "shew" (shun), "hoase" (forbear)."[29]

By the seventeenth century, this interest in the dialect words of particular regions was a common feature of antiquarian scholarship. Thus the physician, Sir Thomas Browne, noted some of the 'many words of no general reception in England but of common use in Norfolk, or peculiar to the East Angle countries'. They included:

baund, bunny, thurck, enemmis, sammodithee, manther, kedge, seele, straft, clever, matchly, deve, nicked, stingy, noneare, feft, thepes, gosgod, kamp, sibrit, fangast, sap, cothish, thokish, bide ore, paxwax.

Browne was followed by the incumbent of Rougham Hall, Roger North, who jotted down various local words such as 'hogg', the term for a yearling sheep, or 'gostsbrad' the name for a corn mower. He also commented on peculiarities of East Anglian pronunciation, such as 'raabin' for 'robin', 'seld' for 'sold', 'ago' for 'ague', and 'undernean' for 'underneath' among others. At the same time, the then vicar of Ambrosden, White Kennett, annexed a list of 428 archaic words to his account of the antiquities of his parish and 'adjacent parts'. Kennett's contemporary, John Aubrey, also recorded 'some peculiar words used by the vulgar in Surrey' when writing the history of the county. They included 'yarrow' or 'yare' (shye), 'eve' (modest, or weak), 'nott' (sheere), 'druxen at heart' (rotten at heart), 'stover' (in a fret or rage), 'to foreflowe the time' (to be remiss or backward), 'pre' (plank or bridge), 'gill' (narrow valley).[30]

Aubrey was unusual among antiquaries of his generation in a research method which relied heavily on oral sources. In his fragmentary play, *The Countrey Revell*, the character of Sowgelder expresses what was Aubrey's own practice and belief. 'Oh, sir, I ride up and downe the country, and observe things: I have made it my businesse to study mankind these . . . yeares', for so much may be learned 'from the *puris naturalibus* [pure

---

[29] Albert H. Marckwardt, 'An Unnoted Source of English Dialect Vocabulary', *Journal of English and Germanic Philology*, 46 (1947), 177–82; *Laurence Nowell's Vocabularium Saxonicum*, ed. Albert H. Marckwardt (Ann Arbor, Mich., 1952); Richard Stanihurst, 'A Treatise Conteining a Plaine and Perfect Description of Ireland', in *Holinshed's Chronicles of England, Scotland and Ireland* (6 vols., London, 1807–8), vi. 4; Richard Carew, *The Survey of Cornwall* (London, 1602), fo. 56ᵛ.

[30] Sir Thomas Browne, 'Of Languages and Particularly of the Saxon Tongue', in *The Works of Sir Thomas Browne*, ed. Geoffrey Keynes (4 vols., London, 1964), iii. 80; BL, Additional MS, 32530, fos. 147ᵛ–149ʳ; White Kennett, *Parochial Antiquities Attempted in the History of Ambrosden, Burcester, and Other Adjacent Parts in the Counties of Oxford and Bucks* (Oxford, 1695), glossary; John Aubrey, *The Natural History and Antiquities of the County of Surrey: Begun in the Year 1673* (5 vols., London, 1718–19), v. 402–3.

natural things] which I dayly converse with'. The result was that Aubrey's accounts of antiquities in his native Wiltshire are full of the dialect words and peculiar pronunciations gleaned in conversation with local men and women. Thus, in various towns, he commented, 'the poore people, &c. gather the cow-shorne [dung] in the meadows and pastures and mix it with hay or strawe, clap it against the walles for ollit; they say 'tis good ollit, i.e. fuell: they call it compas, they meane I suppose compost'. Equally, he heard people say 'shillin' for shed, and use the letter 'a' in place of 'she'. They would pronounce St Oswald 'St Twosole', and Silbury Hill 'Zelbury Hill', while Avebury was 'vulgarly called Abury'. Aubrey was also sensitive to recent linguistic change, noting that 'I trow', which had still been used by Archbishop Laud, was by the later seventeenth century, in north Wiltshire, only to be heard on the lips of old folk.[31]

By this time the first dialect dictionary had been put in print. In 1674 the botanist from Essex, John Ray, published *A Collection of English Words, Not Generally Used*. As he travelled around England after the Restoration, collecting material for his scientific research, he had been struck by 'the difference of dialect, and variety of local words' in the places which he visited 'such as are not of general use'. He decided to make a list for his own benefit but since this amounted to such 'an inconsiderable part of what were in use among the vulgar' he solicited friends in a number of different counties to send him 'what they had observed each of their own countrey words, or should afterwards gather up out of the mouths of the people'. Even then, he realized that the resulting collection did not contain 'more than one moiety of the local words used in all the several counties of England'. Following the publication of the first edition, however, various correspondents sent him lists of vocabulary from several parts of the country and on the basis of this he was able to complete a much expanded second edition in 1691. As late as 1703 the Leeds antiquary Ralph Thoresby responded to a request from Ray with a list of 531 Yorkshire words, which suggests that he may have had a third edition in mind before his death.[32]

The same method of gathering information from friends and correspondents around the country was employed by White Kennett for his

---

[31] Michael Hunter, *John Aubrey and the Realm of Learning* (London, 1975), 228, 170; *Wiltshire: The Topographical Collections of John Aubrey, F.R.S., A.D. 1659–70*, ed. J. E. Jackson (Devizes, 1862), 192, 332, 417; John Aubrey, *Monumenta Britannica*, ed. John Fowles and Rodney Legg (Sherborne, 1980–2), 44, 477, 683, 41; Bod. Lib., MS Aubrey 5, fo. 91ʳ.

[32] John Ray, *A Collection of English Words, Not Generally Used* (London, 1674), sigs. A1–A4; (2nd edn., London, 1691), sig. A5ʳ–A6ʳ; *The Diary of Ralph Thoresby, F.R.S.*, ed. Joseph Hunter (2 vols., London, 1830), i. 421; *The Correspondence of John Ray*, ed. Edwin Lankester (London, 1848), 418–30. See also C. E. Raven, *John Ray: Naturalist* (2nd edn., Cambridge, 1950), 169–71, 271–3.

'Etymologia Anglicana', or 'Etymological Collections of English Words and Phrases', a substantial dialect dictionary compiled in the 1690s. It remained in manuscript on his death in 1728 and has never been printed. Kennett drew on a variety of written and printed sources, including Ray's dictionary, as well as the experience of his own childhood in Kent and pastoral work in Oxfordshire. He endorsed the view common among antiquaries and philologists of the period that 'the parts of England most remote from London retain most the purity of the langua[ge]'.[33] The contribution of early dialect lexicographers such as Ray and Kennett is rendered all the more significant since it appears that no other dialect dictionary purporting to cover the whole country was attempted during the eighteenth century, until Francis Grose published his limited and derivative *Provincial Glossary* in 1787.[34] A variety of antiquaries left collections of local words in manuscript, however.[35] Meanwhile, many of the printed parochial and county histories of the period continued to include small collections of regional vocabulary.[36]

Antiquaries were interested in both vocabulary and pronunciation as they tended to believe that uneducated country folk were caught in a kind of time warp, immune from the linguistic change which had made the received English of the learned elite so different from that of their ancestors. They were thought to preserve in oral tradition words and forms of enunciation which were otherwise obsolete and might contain valuable clues as to the origin of place names or the meaning of ancient terms.

[33] BL, Lansdowne MS, 1033: quotation at fo. 3ʳ; for correspondence, fos. 4, 453–84. On Kennett, see *John Aubrey: Three Prose Works*, ed. John Buchanan-Brown (Fontwell, 1972), 404–7. The method of gathering information by correspondence was common among antiquaries and scientists of the late seventeenth century: see, for example, BL, Egerton MS, 2231 (early nineteenth-century copies of John Aubrey's letters, from the Bodleian originals); *The Correspondence of John Ray*, ed. Lankester; *The Works of the Honourable Robert Boyle*, ed. Thomas Birch (6 vols., London, 1772), vi; vol. xiv of *Early Science in Oxford*, ed. R. T. Gunther, *Life and Letters of Edward Lhwyd* (Oxford, 1945).

[34] Francis Grose, *A Provincial Glossary Glossary with a Collection of Local Proverbs and Popular Superstitions* (London, 1787), sigs. B1–K4.

[35] Among such collections, see Samuel Pegge, 'Kenticisms' (1735–6) and 'Derbycisms' (1740s), in Bod. Lib., MS Eng. Lang. e. 4, 1–120, 121–50; Ralph Bigland, 'Lincolnshire Dialect' (1780s), in BL, Additional MS, 34141, fos. 51ᵛ–53ʳ; Joseph Hunter, 'An Alphabetical Catalogue of Uncommon Words and Forms of Expression found in the Vernacular Language of Hallamshire' (1790–1810), in BL, Additional MS, 24539. Other examples are listed in Wakelin, *English Dialects*, 43.

[36] See, for example, John Lewis, *The History and Antiquities Ecclesiastical and Civil of the Isle of Tenet in Kent* (London, 1723), 22–3; John Watson, *The History and Antiquities of the Parish of Halifax, in Yorkshire* (London, 1775), 531–48; Sir John Cullum, *The History and Antiquities of Hawsted, and Hardwick, in the County of Suffolk* (2nd edn., London, 1813), 199–204; *Reprinted Glossaries*, ed. W. W. Skeat (4 vols., English Dialect Society, 1–4, London, 1873–9).

Thus in 1610 John Denton thought the etymological origins of Sedbergh in the West Riding were to be explained by its location on a hillside partly 'covered with rushes which the country people call seives, and thereupon the place was called Seevy-Bergh'. Sir Peter Leycester later found confirmation of his theory that Poosey chapel near Runcorn in Cheshire derived its name from the Anglo-Saxon, meaning by a river and pool, in the fact that 'our common language anciently, as the country people at this day, did call pool a "poo"; and thence it was denominated "Poo's-ey-chappel"'. Aubrey discovered that in Herefordshire,

the common people (whose dialect and pronunciation antiquaries are not to slight) still say, 'Hariford', with a full 'a'; which (leaving out the aspirate 'h') is 'ariford', i.[e.], 'ar wiford'; which is the very description of the situation of the city, upon the way over the river Wye. So Ariconium.[37]

There were others, however, who blamed the false pronunciation of 'the vulgar' for obscuring etymological origins. The provenance of many place names and occupational surnames had been lost, thought Camden, 'by corruption of speech' among the common people 'which sway all in names'. Opinion from around the country endorsed this view. In Kent William Lambarde complained about the laziness of the local vernacular which had contracted 'Medweys Towne' to Maidstone, and 'Eglesford' to Aylesford, among others, so that most people had lost sight of their original derivation. 'Neyther hath this, our manner of abbreuiation, corrupted the names of townes and places only', he lamented, 'but infected (as it were with a certain contagion) almoste our whole speache and language . . .'. In Warwickshire Sir William Dugdale later noted some other victims of the 'corrupt pronunciation of the vulgar', although he thought that Henley 'ought to have been written Heanley, as the ordinary sort of people doe still pronounce it'. In Hertfordshire, meanwhile, Sir Henry Chauncy regretted the way in which the county town was now pronounced 'Hartford', 'by reason of the broad dialect, and ill speaking of the vulgar sort of people, which oftentimes thro' usage changed the true names of divers places'.[38]

---

[37] John Denton, *An Accompt of the Most Considerable Estates and Families in the County of Cumberland*, ed. R. S. Ferguson (Cumberland and Westmorland Antiquarian and Archaeological Society, 2, Kendal, 1887), 95; Sir Peter Leycester, *Historical Antiquities, in Two Books* (London, 1673), 249; Aubrey, *Monumenta Britannica*, ed. Fowles and Legg, 443; and cf. Bod. Lib., MS Aubrey 5. For other examples, see Thomas Gerard, *The Description of the County of Somerset*, ed. E. H. Bates (Somerset Record Society, 15, London, 1900), 147; *Antiquary on Horseback: The First Publication of the Collections of the Rev. Thos. Machell Chaplain to King Charles II towards a History of the Barony of Kendal*, ed. Jane M. Ewbank (Cumberland and Westmorland Antiquarian and Archaeological Society, extra ser., 19, Kendal, 1963), 116; N[athaniel] Salmon, *The History of Hertfordshire* (London, 1728), 93–4, 136.

[38] Camden, *Remaines, Concerning Britaine*, 122, 147; William Lambarde, *A Perambulation of Kent:*

As they travelled the country in the course of their research, antiquaries were naturally struck by differences in pronunciation in the various
regions. In 1605 Richard Verstegan observed that with 'so many different
countries and regions . . . we see that in some several partes of England it
self, both the names of things and pronountiations of woords are somewhat different, and that among the countrey people that never borrow
any woords out of the Latin or French'. He attempted to render the principal regional characteristics.

For pronouncing according as one would say at London, 'I would eat more
cheese yf I had it' | the northern man saith, 'Ay sud eat mare cheese gin ay hadet'
| and the western man saith: 'Chud eat more cheese an chad it'. Lo heer three dif-
ferent pronountiations in our own country in one thing, and thereof many the
lyke examples might be alleaged.

Later in the century John Aubrey also attempted to convey some of the
broad regional differences.

The northern parts of England speake gutturally: and in Yorkshire and the
Bishoprick of Durham, they have more of the cadance, or Scotish tone than they
have at Edinborough: in like manner, in Herefordshire, they have more of the
Welsh cadence, than they have in Wales. The Wisterne people cannot open their
mouthes, to speak *ore rotundo*: we pronounce 'paal', 'pale', &c: and especially
in Devonshire . . . One may observe, that the speech (twang or accent) of the
vulgar begins to alter something towards the Herefordshire manner, even at
Cyrencester.[39]

The antiquarian interest in regional and local language during this
period was also paralleled by the emergence of 'dialect literature' as a
genre of writing. The first evidence of it appeared in the mid-sixteenth
century from which time a variety of dramatic works, jestbooks and
ephemeral writings began to contain snatches of verse or dialogue imitative of broadly 'southern', 'western', or 'northern' speech, and sometimes
more specifically attributed. In 1542, for example, the physician Andrew
Borde included twenty-six lines of doggerel intended to represent the
Cornish dialect in his *Fyrst Boke of the Introduction of Knowledge*. Borde may
also have been the author of *Scoggin's Jests* which contains an anecdote

*Conteining the Description, Historie, and Customes of that Shyre* (London, 1576), 205–6; Sir William
Dugdale, *The Antiquities of Warwickshire* (London, 1656), 60, 451, 597; Sir Henry Chauncy, *The
Historical Antiquities of Hertfordshire* (London, 1700), 231. For other examples, see William
Stukeley, *Itinerarium Curiosum* (London, 1724), 60, 85, 136; William Hutchinson, *A View of
Northumberland* (2 vols., Newcastle, 1778), i. 183.

[39] Richard Verstegan, *A Restitution of Decayed Intelligence* (Antwerp, 1605), 195; Bod. Lib., MS
Aubrey 1, fo. 23ᵛ.

about an ignorant and 'slovenly boy' who is given a vaguely southern dialect. In the same vein, the *Merie Tales of Master Skelton* contains a tale which
has a 'Kendalman' and his phonetically rendered speech as the butt of its
joke. Characters in plays of the mid-Tudor period, such as 'Ignorance'
in John Redford's *Wit and Science* (*c.*1550) or 'People' in Nicholas Udall's
*Respublica* (1553), are also made to speak dialogue in a stylized literary
dialect intended to represent the language of humble provincial folk.[40]

Thereafter, the poem or dialogue entirely devoted to recreating on
paper the popular speech of particular regions developed into a literary
form in its own right. Several wooing ballads made up of exchanges
between country lovers rendered in broad dialect were included in the
early seventeenth-century song-books intended for genteel audiences
such as Corkine's *First Book of Airs* (1610) and Ravenscroft's *Briefe Discourse*
(1614). For wider audiences, meanwhile, there were innumerable
broadside ballads involving conversations in dialect between 'Tom and
Dick', 'a countryman and a citizen', 'Dick Downright', 'Wat' the West
Country clown, 'the northern-man' or 'Tom Hoyden of Taunton Dean'.
Some were on the theme of love, such as 'The Merry Wooing of Robin
and Joan', and others in the 'clown's journey to see London' vein. Ballad
characters even provided material for the stage when Tom Hoyden of
Taunton Dean appeared in Richard Brome's *Sparagus Garden* (1635) and in
the Epilogue of *The Court Beggar* (1653). At the same time, Brome's *The
Northern Lass* (1632) revolved around the dialect of a north country girl,
while Jonson's *A Tale of a Tub* (1640), set in 'Finnesbury hundred', attempted
to recreate the speech of the 'clowns and constables' of Middlesex.[41]

Typical of the phonetically stylized nature of such representations of
dialect are the verses transcribed in the commonplace book of John
Davies, compiled between 1618 and 1630, and entitled 'The Somerset
shire man's complaint'. It begins:

> Gods boddkins, 'chill worke no more
> Dost thinke 'chill labor to be poore?
>   No, no, ich haue a doe.
> If this be how the world and trade
> That I must breake and rogues be made,
>   Ich will a plundring too.[42]

[40] Andrew Borde, *The Fyrst Boke of the Introduction of Knowledge* (1542; London, 1555?), sig. B2; Blank, *Broken English*, 80–1, 83, 85, 105.

[41] C. R. Baskervill, *The Elizabethan Jig and Related Song Drama* (Chicago, 1929), 188–98, 316–19, 417–19, 420–2, 428–31, 473–90; *The Bagford Ballads*, ed. J. W. Ebsworth (Ballad Society, Hertford, 1878), 22–3; Blank, *Broken English*, 94–9, 111–12.

[42] BL, Lansdowne MS, 674, fo. 20ᵛ. The whole poem is printed together with two other

At about the same time, the Devonshire gentleman William Stoude transcribed a 'sonnett' in the dialect of his native county which took the form of a dialogue between two rustic neighbours, Tom and Tan.

> Ruddle, ruddle, nebour Tan
>> Whare ich a late a benn a.
> Why ich a benn to Plymouth man,
>> The lik wah neuer zeene a.
> Zutch streates, zutch men, zutch hougeous zeas,
>> Zutch gunns wth things ther tumblinge.
> Thy zul wth me woudst blest to zee,
>> Zuth bomination rumblinge.[43]

None of these examples, however, represented anything more than the stylized literary rendering of different varieties of regional English which was already familiar in the mid-sixteenth century. They were all intended to be more or less comprehensible to more than merely local audiences and as such, they contained little in the way of genuine dialect vocabulary and repeated the phonetic spellings characteristic of the genre. By the second half of the seventeenth century, however, examples of dialect literature were beginning to emerge which went beyond these constraints. Several specimens of dialect poetry were transcribed by an anonymous author of the later seventeenth century and never printed. One was 'A Lancashire Tale', consisting of 110 lines and beginning:

> Feeuy me gentles, an inny wun tarry,
> I'll tell o how Gilbert Scott sowd is mere berry.
> He sowd is mere berry at Warritt'n fere,
> Baw coud naw tell whether it be pede ere or nere.
> Baw when he coom whom, and toud is weif Greace,
> Hoo up wuth a kibboo, an swattim o'rth fece.
> He towd her soe monny a mad farrant tele,
> At hoo sweer he was madder in tum-a good-ele.
> Baw when i' good yornst, hoo see noo munny coome,
> Ten hoo lede abawt uppaw Gilbert soon.
> Hoo thrutt im tuth' hillock wo sicke a thwark,
> At he hed welly brokken his back.

In the same manuscript is a dialogue in a Yorkshire dialect which is followed by a 'Clavis' explaining pronunciation and listing a glossary of 436 words.[44]

seventeenth-century examples of Somerset verse in *A Collection of Pieces in the Dialect of Zummerzet*, ed. J. O. Halliwell (London, 1843), 3–12.

[43] BL, Sloane MS, 542, fo. 18ᵛ.
[44] Folger Library MS, Va. 308 (I am grateful to Steve Pincus for this reference).

Another Yorkshire dialogue was printed in 1683 by George Meriton, a lawyer and antiquary from Northallerton in the North Riding, to which he also appended a guide to pronunciation and later a glossary. This pamphlet, printed in York, purported to recreate the popular speech, 'in its pure natural dialect, as it is now commonly spoken in the north parts of Yorkshire'. Together with 'The Lancashire Tale', it represents a seminal contribution to English dialect literature, being the effort of a native speaker to render the specifics of local vocabulary and pronunciation, rather than merely the stylized parody of an outsider written for comic effect.

> D[aughter]. Mother our crockey's canven fine't grew dark,
> And ise flaid to come nar, she macks sicke narke, tee.
> M[other]. Seaun, seaun barne, bring my skeel and late my.
> Mack hast and high thee ore to'th laer to me:
> Weese git a battin and a burden rape,
> Though it be mirke, weese late it out by grape
> Then wee'l to'th field and give the cow some hay
> And see her cleen before she come away:
> And flaid she git some watter before she cleen
> And mar her milk, ise greet out bath my neen.[45]

These last examples anticipate the more accurate and faithful attempts to transcribe local speech which came to characterize dialect literature in the eighteenth century and beyond.[46]

### LOCAL LANGUAGE, LOCAL IDENTITY

Meriton's evocation of the speech of the North Riding began to approach the level of local specificity necessary to register the real complexity of early modern speech patterns. England at this time comprised a network of variegated and interlocking speech communities which provided very

---

[45] George Meriton, *The Praise of York-Shire Ale* (3rd edn., York, 1697), 35.

[46] For some examples, see 'Exmoor Courtship' and 'An Exmoor Scolding', in *Gentleman's Magazine*, 16 (1746), 297–300, 352–5; Josiah Relph, *A Miscellany of Poems* (Glasgow, 1747); John Collier, *The Miscellaneous Works of Tim Bobbin, Esq. Containing his View of the Lancashire Dialect* (London, 1775); Ann Wheeler, *The Westmorland Dialect, in Three Familiar Dialogues* (Kendal, 1790); Joshua Larwood, 'A Norfolk Dialogue', in *Nine Specimens of English Dialects*, ed. W. W. Skeat (English Dialect Society, 76, London, 1896), 117. Nineteenth-century examples are discussed in Martha Vicinus, *The Industrial Muse: A Study of Nineteenth-Century British Working Class Literature* (London, 1974), ch. 5; John Langton, 'The Industrial Revolution and the Regional Geography of England', *Transactions of the Institute of British Geographers*, new ser., 11 (1984), 145–67; Patrick Joyce, *Visions of the People: Industrial England and the Question of Class, 1840–1914* (Cambridge, 1991), chs. 8, 11, 12.

significant boundaries of inclusion and exclusion for those who experienced them. The first comprehensive survey of English pronunciation in the nineteenth century distinguished six major linguistic regions within England and Lowland Scotland. These could be divided more accurately into forty-two districts, twenty-one of which could further be divided into varieties and eight of these into sub-varieties.[47] It is probable that something like this pattern, if not one even more diverse, had existed for many centuries by this time. The microcosmic nature of speech communities in the early modern period was captured in 1551 by John Hart when he commented that if people 'heare their neyghbour borne of their next citie, or d[w]elling not past one or two dais [j]orney from theim, speaking some other word then is (in that place) emongest theim used, yt so litell contenteth their eare, that . . . they seem the stranger were therfore worthie to be derided, and skorned'.[48]

Sometimes these speech communities might conform to the artificial demarcations imposed by county boundaries, administrative units, or urban developments, but they were just as likely to be determined by topographical features and ecological systems. In the early modern period, the locality to which people thought of themselves as belonging, their 'country', was very often defined by the physical divisions emerging from changes in soil type and landscape or the natural barriers constituted by hills and valleys. These features delineated the limits of belonging for most people, enclosing habitats in which agricultural practices and economic structures, social relations and cultural norms might be quite distinct from those outside.[49]

Patterns of speech appear to have mirrored quite sensitively these regions or 'countries' as prescribed either by natural or man-made borders. In Elizabethan Pembrokeshire, for example, George Owen recorded the way in which 'half the shire is mere English, both in speech

[47] Alexander J. Ellis, *On Early English Pronunciation* (5 vols., London, 1869–89), v; Wakelin, *English Dialects*, 51. See now, Harold Orton et al. (eds.), *Survey of English Dialects* (4 vols., Leeds, 1962–71); Harold Orton, Stewart Sanderson, and John Widdowson, *The Linguistic Atlas of England* (London, 1978).

[48] Quoted in Joseph M. Williams, '"O! When Degree is Shak'd": Sixteenth-Century Anticipations of Some Modern Attitudes toward Usage', in T. W. Machan and C. T. Scott (eds.), *English in its Social Contexts: Essays in Historical Sociolinguistics* (New York, 1992), 73.

[49] On the concept of 'countries', see Alan Everitt, 'River and Wold: Reflections on the Historical Origin of Regions and Pays', *Journal of Historical Geography*, 3 (1977), 1–19; id., 'Country, County and Town: Patterns of Regional Evolution in England', *Transactions of the Royal Historical Society*, 5th ser., 29 (1979), 78–108; Peter Clark, *English Provincial Society from the Reformation to the Revolution: Religion, Politics and Society in Kent, 1500–1640* (Hassocks, 1977), 120–1; Charles Phythian-Adams, *Re-thinking English Local History* (Occasional Papers in English Local History, Leicester, 1987).

and manners', while 'the other half speaks the Welsh tongue'. Even within the confines of one parish a thoroughfare might divide English from Welsh speakers. The 'meaner sort of people' from one side would not marry those from the other; they would not buy and sell from one another; they differed 'in tilling and in measuring of their land and divers other matters'. This 'diversity of speech breeds some inconveniences', he confessed, 'so that often times is found at the assizes that in a jury of twelve men there will be one half that cannot understand the other's words . . .'. This difference between the English and Welsh languages described by Owen may have been an extreme example, but it very graphically illustrates the presence of linguistic boundaries which could cut across parochial or county borders.[50]

The same situation was described in seventeenth-century Wiltshire by John Aubrey. He appreciated the importance in cultural terms of the distinction between the two ecologically distinct halves of the county. The people of the chalk downlands in the south, where '`tis all upon tillage', were very different from the dairying folk of the clay-based wood-pasture country to the north. The northerners 'speake drawling'; they were more phlegmatic, 'more apt to be fanatiques' in religion, and more litigious than their southern neighbours.[51] In the eighteenth century, the agricultural writer William Marshall would be impressed by the 'strikingly various' nature of popular speech even within the North Riding of Yorkshire and he described a level of variegation which can have been scarcely less pronounced in former centuries.

The provincial language of Cleveland differs more widely, in some respects, from that of the Vale of Pickering, though situated only twelve or fifteen miles from each other, than the dialect of the Vale does from that of Devonshire, which is situated at an opposite extreme of the kingdom. The eastern morelands are a barrier which formerly cut off all communication between the two districts. But this cannot be the only cause of difference: the language and the manners of their respective inhabitants appear to have no natural affinity: they are, to present appearance, as distinct races of people as if they were descended from different roots. The pronunciation of the Vale bears a strong analogy to the Scotch; while that of Cleveland, which lies immediately between the Vale and Scotland, has little or no affintiy to the Scotch pronunciation.

Moreover, he found that the speech around Leeds varied still further,

[50] George Owen, *The Description of Pembrokeshire*, ed. Dillwyn Miles (Llandysul, 1994), 13–14, 36, 39–40, 41–3.

[51] John Aubrey, *The Natural History of Wiltshire*, ed. John Britton (London, 1847), 11–12. For a discussion of these cultural differences, see David Underdown, *Revel, Riot and Rebellion: Popular Politics and Culture in England, 1603–1660* (Oxford, 1985), ch. 4.

while over in 'the more extreme parts of West Yorkshire' it was very different again from that in the rest of the county. Thus, 'the language even of Wakefield and that of Leeds, though these two places are situated within twenty miles of each other, are in many particulars less analogous than those of Scotland and the Vale of Pickering'.[52]

Such divisions, cultural and linguistic as well as socio-economic, were found to exist within the boundaries of all English counties when subsequent research began to investigate such matters. In Suffolk, for example, there was a significant difference between the 'high' dialect to be heard in just six parishes in the east of the county and the 'low' dialect common elsewhere. In Lancashire a great distinction existed between the area around Rochdale, 'the centre of the genuine Lancashire dialect', and the speech of Furness, bordering on Cumberland and Westmorland to the north, or that of the Rosendale valley, abutting Yorkshire to the west. Equally, England's most northerly county could be divided in dialect terms, as in others, into at least four regions: north Northumberland, south Northumberland, Tyneside, and west Tyne.[53]

Some dialectical peculiarities were even more highly localized than this, being specific to individual communities by virtue, perhaps, of their geographical isolation or economic speciality. Thus, in the course of his antiquarian investigations at the beginning of the seventeenth century, Sir Robert Cotton happened upon Combe Martin, 5 miles from Ilfracombe on the north Devon coast, where 'the people have a dialect differing from the very next villages'.[54] It was William Camden who first remarked on the strangely idiosyncratic speech of the village of Carlton, near Market Bosworth in Leicestershire, where most of the natives 'either from some peculiar quality of the soil, or water, or other unknown cause in nature, have a harsh and ungrateful manner of speech, with a guttural and difficult pronunciation, and a strange wharling in the utterence of their words'.[55] In parts of north Northumberland, locals were 'distinguished by a shibboleth upon their tongues, namely, a difficulty in pronouncing the letter R, which they cannot deliver from their tongues without a

[52] William Marshall, *The Rural Economy of Yorkshire* (2 vols., London, 1788), ii. 303–4.

[53] Historical Manuscripts Commission, *10th Report, Appendix, Part IV* (London, 1885), 513–14; Robert Forby, *The Vocabulary of East Anglia* (2 vols., London, 1830), i. 83; John Aikin, *A Description of the Country from Thirty to Forty Miles Round Manchester* (London, 1795), 250; Oliver Heslop, *Northumberland Words: A Glossary of Words Used in the County of Northumberland and on Tyneside* (2 vols., English Dialect Society, 66, London, 1892), i. xvi–xxi, 1.

[54] BL, Sloane MS, 241, fo. 48[r].

[55] William Camden, *Britannia*, ed. Edmund Gibson (London, 1695), 443, 450; William Burton, *The Description of Leicester Shire* (London, 1622), 67; James Brome, *Travels over England, Scotland and Wales* (London, 1700), 77.

hollow jarring in the throat . . . and the natives value themselves upon that imperfection, because, forsooth, it shews the antiquity of their blood'.[56]

The observation that people prided themselves on their highly particular modes of expression exposes the significance which dialect speech could have as an integral part of local identity and a fundamental contribution to parochial consciousness. There was no more immediate or powerful agent of identification with neighbours, and no more palpable or abrupt manifestion of difference from 'foreigners', than in patterns of speech. The language of their 'country' bound people to the soil, not only in an emotional and instinctive sense, but also in a practical one, since to stray beyond the borders of the dialect boundary was to enter a foreign environment in which the inhabitants often spoke and behaved very differently. As much as any other factor, language both defined the sense and prescribed the limits of belonging.

The significance of dialect boundaries in early modern England and the importance of local speech to the self-perception of its users is no more graphically captured than in the description of the hundred of Berkeley, Gloucestershire, written by John Smyth of Nibley in 1639. Smyth's account is of particular value since, although he spent much time in London, he was a native, estate steward to the earls of Berkeley and a churchwarden of North Nibley, who wrote with the benefit of intimate local knowledge. His account demonstrates an acute sense of place, a great awareness of the physical extent of his neighbourhood and the particular characteristics which defined the inhabitants locked within it. The vale of Berkeley was a clearly demarcated agrarian 'country', bounded by solid natural barriers in the form of the river Severn to the west and the Cotswold edge to the east, and tributaries of the Severn marking the border with Somerset to the south and the vale of Gloucester to the north. Even when William Marshall rode down the Severn valley a century and a half after Smyth wrote his account, he was struck by the 'natural insection, which divides it into two districts, very different in produce and rural management', being the vales of Gloucester and Berkeley.[57]

---

[56] Defoe, *A Tour thro' the Whole Island of Great Britain*, ed. Cole, 662. Cf. Richard Dawes, *The Origin of the Newcastle Burr* (2nd edn., 1767), repr. in *Reprints of Rare Tracts and Imprints of Antient Manuscripts*, ed. M. A. Richardson (7 vols, Newcastle, 1843–9), iii. 18. As youngsters, the present author and his brother were much amused at the somewhat unorthodox rendition of a favourite nursery rhyme by an old shepherd of their acquaintance in Embleton, Northumberland: 'Marrry had a little lamb, she kept it in the shrrrubberrry | Aloung came a gust of wind, and blew it aull to buggerrry'.

[57] John Smyth, *The Berkeley Manuscripts*, ed. Sir John Maclean (3 vols., Gloucester, 1883–5), iii; William Marshall, *The Rural Economy of Gloucestershire* (2 vols., London, 1789), i. 8, and see

Smyth was concerned to explore the impact of these natural divisions in cultural terms, to express the pyschological meaning of country and neighbourhood. He discussed the sports and traditions of the hundred; he detailed the particular customary laws and even mentioned the unique currency, all of which contributed to a sense of distinct identity among its inhabitants. Above all, Smyth believed, what captured the very essence of the hundreders, what epitomized them more than anything else, was the way in which they spoke.

In this hundred of Berkeley are frequently vsed certaine words, proverbs and phrases of speach, which wee hundreders conceive, (as we doe of certaine market moneyes), to bee not only native but confined to the soile bounds and territory therof; which if found in the mouthes of any forraigners, wee deeme them as leapt over our wall, or as strayed from their proper pasture and dwellinge place: And doubtles, in the handsome mouthinge of them, the dialect seemes borne of our owne bodies and naturall vnto vs from the breasts of our nurses . . .

The dialect was not, therefore, something of which to be ashamed, as contemporary educationalists would have insisted, but a linguistic inher-itance of which to be proud, and to be mouthed handsomely as a celebra-tion of local origin. The vernacular of the hundreders, in preserving various archaic forms now expunged from the 'civilized' language of London and the court, was the purer English, boasted Smyth. We account 'our selves by such manner of speach to bee true patryots, and true pre-servers of the honored memory of our old forefathers, Gower, Chauser, Lidgate, Robert de Glouc[ester], and others of those and former ages'.[58]

He went on to offer various illustrations of this. Thus, 'a native hun-dreder, beinge asked where hee was borne, answereth, "Where shu'd y bee y bore, but at Berkeley hurns, and there, begis, each was y bore." Or thus, "Each was 'geboren at Berkeley hurns"'. As Smyth explained, 'so naturall is the dialect of pronouncinge the l[ett]re "y" betweene words endinge and beginninge with consonants, that it seemes droppinge from the aire into our mouthes', as in the case of 'each ha kild a ferry vat y hogg', 'watt y ge Tom y some nin y wel y din'd', or 'th'art my pretty dick y'. At the same time, local speech frequently replaced the letter 'v' with the letter 'f' and vice-versa, as in 'fewed for viewed' or 'fenison for venison', and 'vethers for feathers' or 'vire for fire'. Equally, 'g' was often used for 'c', as in 'guckowe for cuckowe; grabs for crabs; a guckold for a cuckold, and the like'.

323–6. For a discussion of Smyth in this context, see David Rollison, *The Local Origins of Modern Society: Gloucestershire, 1500–1800* (London, 1992), ch. 3.

[58] Smyth, *The Berkeley Manuscripts*, ed. Maclean, iii. 22–3.

The hundreders had various other distinctive usages. For example, 'thicke and thucke, for this and that, rush out with vs at every breath'. They would say 'putton vp, for put it up', or 'cutton of, for cut it of', and 'many the like'. They often omitted the possessive pronoun 'your', as in 'howe fare fader and moder', 'when sawe you fader and moder', or 'fader and moder will bee heere to morrowe'. They used either 'gay' or 'goe', depending on the circumstance: 'gaye, is let vs goe, when my selfe goes as one of the company: but, goe, is the sendinge of others when my selfe staies behinde'. Certain words could change their meaning according to context. Thus 'hild' might be employed in the sense of 'I wou'd it was hild', meaning 'I would it were flead, or the skyn of', or else as 'y w'ood t'wert hild', meaning 'I would thou were hanged'. The word 'tyd' could mean 'wanton', or if used in the sense of 'a tyd bit', it would signify 'a speciall morsell reserved to eat at last'.

Smyth managed to convey, about as well as is possible on paper, the sound of local pronunciation. Thus hundreders would pronounce neighbourhood 'neighboriden', wenches 'wenchen', and ashes 'axen'; or they would say 'harroust' for harvest, 'meese' for moss, and 'meeve' for move, as in 'meeve them a lich, i.e. move them a like'. Certain familiar sayings and phrases give some idea of the way in which these people must have sounded. 'What? wil't y pisse a bed, i.e. what will you pisse your bed?'; 'y wud al y cud, i.e. I would doe it if I could'; 'each ha'nnot wel y din'd, i.e. I have not well dyned'; 'ga'as zo'm of thuck bread, i.e. give mee some of that bread'; 'ch'am w'oodly agreezd, i.e. I am wonderfully agreived'; 'thuck vire don't y bran, i.e. this fire doth not burne'; 'Gyn y com y and tyff y the windowes, i.[e]. Jone, come, and trim vp the windowes, (meaninge with flowers)'.

Finally, Smyth recorded a variety of the dialect words which were commonly used in the hundred. A sample of verbs would include: 'to veize' meaning to chase, 'to loxe' or 'to vocket', meaning to purloin, and 'to songe' meaning to receive. Common adjectives were 'camplinge, i.e. brawlinge, chidinge'; 'flippant, i.e. slippery, quick, nimble'; and 'an angry or crosse natur'd wench' would be described as 'an attery, or thwartover wench'. Out in the fields would be heard words such as 'a shard, i.e. a gapp or broken place in an hedge'; 'a loppertage, i.e. a lowe place where a hedge is trodden downe'; 'the pugg, i.e. the refuse corne left at winnowinge'; 'a grible, i.e. a crabstocke to grast vpon'; 'hurts, i.e. bilbaries'; 'pilsteers, i.e. pillow beers'; and phrases such as 'beanes thick yeare are orribly hang'd, i.e. beanes this yeare are horribly codded'; and 'this hay did well y henton, i.e. dry or wither well'. Other vocabulary and its use included, 'you speake dwelth, i.e. you talke you know not what'; 'each ha songd to a childe, i.e. I have byn godfather at a childes christeninge'; 'hee wants boot a beame, i.e. hee wants money to spend'; 'hur is dothered, i.e. shee is amazed, astonished'; 'hur ha's well y tund her geer to day, i.e. shee hath applied her booke to day'; and 'hur goes too blive for mee, i.e. shee goes too fast for mee'.[59]

The hundred of Berkeley does not appear to have been unusual in the way its speech registered the ways of local life and expressed the contours of parochial identity. For scores of other communities around the country it was language which articulated their relationship with their environment and organized the understanding of their experience. It was language which bound their members together, and distinguished them from others, at the most basic and fundamental level.

### THE CONFUSION OF TONGUES

Given the often highly localized nature of spoken English in the myriad speech communities which made up the nation, it is hardly surprising that communication between them could be very difficult. To those from outside a district or region the vocabulary and pronunciation of native inhabitants could be as opaque as any other foreign language. Contemporaries often noted that people from different parts of the country simply found it difficult to understand each other. Given the inflection and intonation, together with the rapid speed of delivery and the colloquial devices which characterize real speech, the practical business of comprehension could be even greater than might be conveyed on paper. As Daniel Defoe acknowledged when he tried to render the dialect of Somerset, 'it is not possible to explain this fully by writing, because the difference is not so much in the orthography of words, as in the tone, and diction'.[60]

Thus, one commentator explained in 1530, the language was 'so dyuerse in yt selfe that the commen maner of spekynge in Englysshe of some contre can skante be vnderstondid in some other contre of the same londe'. Little had changed at the beginning of the seventeenth century when Richard Verstegan could concur '(as by often experience is found), that some Englishmen discoursing together, others being present and of our own nation, and that naturally speak the English toung, are not able to vnderstand what the others say, notwithstanding they call it English that they speak'. For long after this period, the same refrain would be heard. 'Bring together two clowns from Kent and Yorkshire, and I will wager a

[59]  Ibid. 23–6.
[60]  Defoe, *A Tour thro' the Whole Island of Great Britain*, ed. Cole, 219.

ducat that they will not be able to converse, for want of a dialect common to them both.'[61]

This communication problem goes some way towards explaining contemporary patterns of migration. Athough this was a society in which people were highly mobile, the great majority of movement and resettlement tended to be over relatively short distances. Youngsters who travelled in search of service or apprenticeship, for example, usually ventured no further than the nearest large town or the next parish, often a distance of less than a dozen miles. They rarely journeyed, in other words, outside their 'country', or speech community.[62] As for those individuals who were driven to seek subsistence or opportunity further afield, there is some evidence to suggest that they gravitated towards the neighbourhoods of towns or cities where other of their 'countrymen' and women or kinsfolk were already settled. This tendency may also have been influenced by speech recognition, among other factors of common culture. Most graphically of all, patterns of settlement in North America during the seventeenth century were highly determined by geographical origins, with the result that the dialects of particular English localities influenced regional speech patterns in the colony thereafter.[63]

It was not only long-distant migrants across Britain who might encounter dificulties in this respect, but also general travellers around the country on business or pleasure. At a time when the roads were poor and certain communities could be relatively isolated, strangers, or 'foreigners', were often rare and frequently regarded with suspicion. It must have

---

[61] Richard Foster Jones, *The Triumph of the English Language* (Stanford, Calif., 1953), 5 n.; Verstegan, *A Restitution of Decayed Intelligence*, 204–5; Samuel Pegge, *Anecdotes of the English Language: Chiefly Regarding the Local Dialect of London and its Environs* (2nd edn., London, 1814), 76.

[62] Peter Clark, 'The Migrant in Kentish Towns, 1580–1640', in Peter Clark and Paul Slack (eds.), *Crisis and Order in English Towns, 1500–1700* (London, 1972), 134–8; Keith Wrightson and David Levine, *Poverty and Piety in an English Village: Terling, 1525–1700* (2nd edn., Oxford, 1995), 74–82; Ann Kussmaul, *Servants in Husbandry in Early Modern England* (London, 1981), 56–60; John Patten, 'Patterns of Migration and Movement of Labour to Three Pre-Industrial East Anglian Towns', in Patten (ed.), *Pre-Industrial England: Geographical Essays* (Folkestone, 1979), 143–61; Phythian-Adams, *Re-thinking English Local History*, 27–34. Even in the late nineteenth century, Thomas Hardy could still depict Tess travelling across 'the barrier of the vale' of Blakemore and, although less than 20 miles from home, finding that 'even the character and accent of the two peoples had shades of difference': *Tess of the d'Urbervilles* (1891; New Wessex edn., London, 1974), 110.

[63] V. B. Elliott, 'Single Women in the London Marriage Market: Age, Status and Mobility, 1598–1619', in R. B. Outhwaite (ed.), *Marriage and Society: Studies in the Social History of Marriage* (London, 1981), 93–5; Peter Clark, 'Migrants in the City: The Process of Social Adaptation in English Towns, 1500–1800', in Peter Clark and David Souden (eds.), *Migration and Society in Early Modern England* (London, 1987), 273–6; David Hackett Fischer, *Albion's Seed: Four British Folkways in America* (Oxford, 1989), 57–62, 256–64, 470–5, 652–5.

been very easy for locals to make their own speech incomprehensible and to feign misunderstanding of an unwitting outsider. Thus, although by the Elizabethan period most Cornishmen spoke English, 'to a stranger they will not speake it', warned Richard Carew, and 'if meeting them by chance, you inquire the way or any such matter, your answere shalbe, "Meea nauidna cowz asawzneck", "I can speake no Saxonage"'. The same experience was suffered by one English visitor to Scotland in the 1670s. He found that in the border regions between Highlands and Lowlands the locals spoke both English and Gaelic, 'yet these people are so currish, that if a stranger enquire the way in English, they will certainly answer in Erst [Erse], and find no other language than what is inforc'd from them with a cudgel'.[64]

The reception given to travellers throughout England might be no different, as three soldiers from Norfolk discovered when they undertook a tour of the country in 1634. It was one thing to attend a service in Carlisle cathedral, to be struck by the 'Scottish tone' of the choir and find that 'the sermon in the like accent, was such, as wee would hardly bring away, though it was deliver'd by a neat young scholler . . . one of the bishop's chaplaines . . .'. But it was quite another to be out in the Westmorland countryside, riding between Penrith and Kendal, and to discover that in asking directions of 'the rude, rusticall, and ill-bred people, with their gainging and yating', they 'could not understand them, neither would they vnderstand vs'. A different triumvirate from Norfolk found the locals more willing but only slightly more comprehensible when they passed through Nottinghamshire in 1662. They were 'very ready to instruct us in our way. One told us our "wy lig'd" by "youn nooke" of "oakes" and another that wee "mun" goe "strit forth", which manner of speeches not only directed us, but much pleas'd us with the novelty of its dialect.'[65]

Meanwhile John Ray, an Essex man, was encountering so many dialect words as he toured around the country in the course of his scientific investigations that he found 'in many places, especially in the north, the language of the common people is to a stranger very difficult to be understood'. The geologist and physician, John Woodward, had similar difficulties when visiting Nettleton near Caistor, Lincolnshire, in the 1680s. 'I have allmost learnt to speake to them in their own language', he announced in due course. 'For instance, if any should ask me the way to

[64] Carew, *The Survey of Cornwall*, fo. 56ʳ; Thomas Kirke, *A Modern Account of Scotland by an English Gentleman* (1679), in *Early Travellers in Scotland*, ed. Hume Brown, 262.

[65] *A Relation of a Short Survey of 26 Counties*, ed. L. G. Wickham Legg (London, 1904), 37, 42; Edward Browne, 'Journal of a Tour in Derbyshire', in *Sir Thomas Browne's Works*, ed. Simon Wilkin (4 vols., London, 1835–6), i. 25–6.

Lincoln, I could say, "Yaw mun een goo thruft yon beck, then yaw'st com to a new yate, then turr off to th'raight, o'er a brig that lays o're a hoy doyke, and than yaw'st not hove ore a maile to th'next tawn".' When Thomas Kirke, an antiquary from Cookridge in the West Riding, was up at Berwick-upon-Tweed in May 1677, he was utterly bemused by the bellman proclaiming the death of a local man in the streets: 'he liggs aut thi sext dour wethin the hoord gawt closs on the hauthir haund, and I wod yaw gang to his [burial] before twa a clock'. Small wonder, then, that when the Lincolnshire man, William Stukeley, was in Newcastle in the mideighteenth century he found that 'as one walks the streets, one can scarce understand the common people, but are apt to fancy one's self in a foreign country'.[66]

Given such experiences, it becomes possible to understand why Daniel Defoe could form the opinion, on the basis of his extensive tours around Britain in the early eighteenth century, that the local dialects of England were as opaque to the outsider and as mutually exclusive to each other as the patois of provincial France. Through travel, he reported,

I became particularly acquainted with the common people, as well as with the country, in every place where I came; I observ'd their language, that is, the several dialects of it, for they strangely differ in their way of expressing themselves, tho' the same tongue; and there is as much difference between the English tongue, as spoken in the north of England, and the same tongue, as spoken in the west, as between the French spoken in Normandy and that of Gascogne, and Poictou...

The equally well-travelled William Marshall was later able to bear out this opinion. 'The languages of Europe are not more various, or scarcely more different from each other, than are the dialects of husbandmen in different districts of this island.'[67]

One peregrinatory group which regularly encountered such problems was the assize judges whose office required them to make biannual tours around one of the six jurisdictions in the course of presiding over the

    [66] Ray, *A Collection of English Words* (1st edn., 1674), sig. A3ᵛ; J. W. F. Hill, *Tudor and Stuart Lincoln* (Cambridge, 1956), 5; Thomas Kirke, 'Journeyings through Northumberland and Durham Anno Dom. 1677', in *Reprints of Rare Tracts and Imprints of Antient Manuscripts*, ed. Richardson, vii. 15–16; William Stukeley, *Itinerarium Curiosum* (2nd edn., 2 vols., London, 1776), ii. 65; cf. John Brand, *The History and Antiquities of the Town and County of the Town of Newcastle upon Tyne* (2 vols., London, 1789), i. 20n. For similar eighteenth-century comments, see T. S. Ashton, *An Eighteenth-Century Industrialist: Peter Stubs of Warrington, 1756–1806* (Manchester, 1939), 142; John Byng, *The Torrington Diaries*, ed. C. Bruyn Andrews (4 vols., London, 1970), ii. 174, 359.
    [67] Daniel Defoe, *The Great Law of Subordination Consider'd* (London, 1724), 48; William Marshall, *The Rural Economy of Norfolk* (2nd edn., 2 vols., London, 1795), ii. 373.

criminal courts. The different vocabulary and pronunciation of people in the various regions could make verbal testimonies very difficult for them as 'foreigners' to comprehend. Certainly Roger North, who rode the western circuit after the Restoration, noticed how much more difficult it became to understand the dialects the further he went from London and he recorded some of 'the gross difference . . . in the speech of several counties, by which they may be known'. Even to local officials, the testimony of country folk before the courts could be very difficult to understand. In a sermon before the Suffolk assizes in 1618 the Ipswich preacher Samuel Ward advised magistrates of the need to be

long-minded, to endure the rusticity and homelinesse of common people in giving evidence after their plaine fashion and faculty, in time, and multitude of words, happely with some absurdities of phrase and gestures, nor impatient towards their foolish affected eloquent tearmes, nor any thing else whereby the truth of their tale may be guessed at.[68]

It is for this reason, however, that transcriptions of depositions given before the courts can provide such a vivid insight into the spontaneous speech of ordinary men and women in this period. Unfortunately, the value of such records is seriously impaired by the way in which the clerk of the court often glossed what was said and sometimes even replaced dialect words and expressions with conventional ones. A graphic example of this is afforded in the evidence given by a Yorkshire tradesman during a case before the court of Chancery at Westminster in 1609. The clerk went back over what he had taken down and deleted the word 'vurse' before replacing it with the standard 'horse'. Three years earlier, in a Star Chamber case brought up to Westminster from the West Country, the clerk who heard the word 'strayeshorne' simply wrote it out in large clear letters, so that there could be no ambiguity. The vicar of Box in Wiltshire, John Coren, was suing some of his parishioners for defamation after they had alleged that he had been spending too much time with Phillipa Bewshin, wife of the vicar of Claverton, Somerset. The neighbours had begun to talk, saying that he 'should be strayeshorne' or that 'he must be shorne strayer'.[69]

[68] North, *The Lives of the Norths*, ed. Jessopp, iii. 130; Samuel Ward, *Jethros Iustice of Peace* (1618), in *A Collection of Such Sermons and Treatises as have been Written and Published by Samuel Ward* (London, 1636), 413–14.

[69] C. J. Sisson and R. E. Zachrisson, 'New Materials for the Study of Tudor and Stuart English', *Studia Neophilologica*, 3 (1930), 104; PRO, STAC8/98/20, m. 27. For other examples of deposition evidence, see Kenneth Hudson, 'Shakespeare's Use of Colloquial Language', in Kenneth Muir (ed.), *Shakespeare Survey*, 23 (Cambridge, 1970), 39–48; Jonathan Hope, 'The use of *Thou* and *You* in Early Modern Spoken English: Evidence from Depositions in the Durham

Despite this heavy level of mediation between the actual words of the deponent and the resulting transcript, it is still possible in some cases to detect the popular voice sounding through the text. In September 1591, for example, John Massee, a tailor from Minster in Kent, was overheard to exclaim 'That there woulde never be a myrrie worlde before there were a newe alteracon. "And for my pecke of maulte, sett the kell one fyer, and by God's wounds, the queene ys a whore!"' About the same time, William Clarke, a minstrel, and William Charles, both of Hornchurch in Essex, were being censured for having said to their neighbour Hugh Wylcockes that he was 'a basket butcher and he should flea a cow in the wood with Alison's wife, meaning that he should have his pleasure of her'. On the evening of Monday, 4 September 1648, goodwife Northcliffe of Sowerby in Yorkshire was cooking in her kitchen when Samuel Smith, Nathan Townsend, and Robert Cham heard her say, '"That is a sharpe thwitle. It cutts such thyn collops."'[70]

In cases of personal abuse popular speech would often be at its most expressive. Hence, when, a little before Christmas 1587, Isabell Swan and Lawrence Thompson were walking together past the shop of George Smith in the high street of Wearmouth, County Durham, they met Anne Walton who said to Lawrence, '"Will you presume to goe in a ladies companie?". Whereunto the said Isabell made aunswer, "I may as tite be a ladye as thou arte!"' At which point George Smith turned to Isabell and said, '"Thou art a tanterband and a tanterbande whore!"' Equally fierce words were being exchanged at an alehouse in Bury, Lancashire, one day in September 1604 when Martin Kaye, a husbandman of the town, shouted at the landlord, Lawrence Whiteheade, '"Thou arte a mutner, a sheepe stealer, and a pulterer!"' At Wakefield, in the West Riding, the inhabitants found their peace disturbed in December 1639 by Henry Dicconson, a yeoman from Bramley, bawling the insult, '"Thou shakeragg blewe beard!"', at Henry Sikes of Hunslet.[71]

---

Ecclesiastical Court Records', in Dieter Kastovsky (ed.), *Studies in Early Modern English* (Berlin, 1994), 141–51.

[70] *Calendar of Assize Records: Kent Indictments Elizabeth I*, ed. J. S. Cockburn (London, 1979), 336; F. G. Emmison, *Elizabethan Life: Morals and the Church Courts* (Chelmsford, 1973), 51; PRO, ASSI45/2/2/19. (A 'thwitle' is a knife; a 'collop' is a piece of bacon or ham.)

[71] *Depositions and other Ecclesiastical Proceedings from the Courts of Durham, extending from 1311 to the Reign of Elizabeth*, ed. James Raine (Surtees Society, 21, London, 1845), 322; *Lancashire Quarter Sessions Records, 1590–1606*, ed. James Tait (Chetham Society, new ser., 77, Manchester, 1917), 239–40; *West Riding Sessions Records*, ed. John Lister (2 vols., Yorkshire Archaeological Society, Leeds, 1888–1915), ii. 173. (A 'tanterband' is a scold; a 'mutner' is a 'mutton-monger', used either literally in the sense of sheep-stealer or euphemistically in the sense of haunter of prostitutes; 'pulterer' could similarly refer either to poultry or women.)

When such insults and allegations were written down on paper in the form of a defamatory letter or scurrilous rhyme it becomes possible to see both the vocabulary and the pronunciation of provincial people who wrote as they spoke. Thus in May 1612 a group of Devonshire villagers, including Richard Fowler and John Yeo, scrawled out a libellous verse suggesting that Richard Painter and Mary Wise of neighbouring Launcells in Cornwall were guilty of fornication. Together with various phonetic spellings and local words, it demonstrates the replacement of 'f' with 'v', characteristic of West Country speech, and suggests the pronunciation of 'Wise' to rhyme with 'feast' and 'November' with 'timber'. The composition, 'folded up in manner of a letter' and affixed to a horse which was tethered to a stile in the highway near its victims' home, began thus:

> I thought it fitt to write unto you all in a few talls,
> That all of you must remember the mowheis pals.
> How Richard Penter and Marie Wisc,
> When they were at Yeo to the feast.
> Begin yf you will know the 29 of November,
> He proved himself a veri come timber.
> But yf there be anie that are willing to know,
> Let them aske of Dick Voller or els of John Yeo.
> And the will tell you in plaine tals,
> That the found them two out by the mowheis pals.
> The pals are bad and verie ferking,
> But the ould abed but a litle gerking.[77]

In certain cases, especially those of slander perhaps, the validity of the whole cause might depend on the meaning of particular words which, because of their local or vulgar usage, were not generally known and understood by the court. One evening in 1629, for example, Elizabeth Poynton, Isabell Roberts, and Winifred Beardsley all dined together at the inn of Thomas Maylyn in the parish of St Mary's, Nottingham. After the meal, Roberts and Beardsley fell into an argument 'very lowde togeather' in which a number of those present overheard the one say to the other: '"Thou sitest like a saynt. Thou art a little dule, but thou art as cunning as the great dule. But take heed the old dule catch thee not, for thou goest

---

[72] PRO, STAC8/236/29, m. 2. By the eighteenth century, when ability to use a pen was more widespread, such texts begin to survive in their originals, rather than merely as transcriptions in legal records. In them 'the dialect or lilt of regional speech can be detected', for these were people 'who knew their letters, but whose writing was guided by their ear rather than by the standards of memory and eye': E. P. Thompson, 'The Crime of Anonymity', in Douglas Hay, et al., *Albion's Fatal Tree: Crime and Society in Eighteenth-Century England* (London, 1975), 298 and *passim*.

tetling and tatling from one house to another and thou art enough to sit a whole end of a towne togeather at debate or strife".' Clearly the bench did not know the meaning of the word 'dule', the import of which was crucial to Beardsley's claim to have been defamed. Thus, Elizabeth Poynton and two other witnesses, Sara Ludlam and Theodore Greanes, were brought forward to give their understanding of the term. Once enlightened, the counsel, or 'proctor', to the plaintiff, Mr Hatfield Reckles, could assert that 'when any body doth use in the[ir] speech the worde "dule", mencioned in the deposicions of the said three witnesses, the intention and meaninge of the party speakinge is of the devell, the common enemy of mankinde . . .'.[73]

Students of regional dialect have long realized the importance of legal records in general, and defamation cases in particular, as sources of evidence for popular speech in former centuries. In the 1850s the canon and chancellor of York, James Raine, whose father had been a founder member of the Surtees Society and the editor of many extracts from documents relating to the north-east of England, began work on a substantial 'Glossary of the Northumbrian Dialect' which remained uncompleted on his death in 1896. Among hundreds of examples gleaned from ecclesiastical proceedings in the diocese of Durham, he discovered, for example, 'fosson', meaning 'use' or 'advantage', when he came across a case from 1601 in which one woman called another 'an arrant theefe, for I bought a whie at Durham and thou haist had the fooson of her ever since'. A 'dub', he noted, meant a reach, or piece of still water, as revealed when Isabel Walker said to Ralph Blakeston in 1624 that 'the devill and he danced in a dubb together and there the devill traled him by his head hare'. Interesting social customs lay behind words such as 'stang', or the name given in the north to the wooden pole used for carrying scolds. In 1609 a woman from Heighington heard a report that another 'did so much abuse her husband, as in reproch thereof, [by] her next neighbors was caried upon a stang about the town'.[74]

Similarly, in 1912 an Essex clergyman, Andrew Clark, worked through some of the archdeaconry papers relating to his native county for the first half of the seventeenth century and brought to light many local words and expressions.[75] A more recent analysis of cases from the quarter sessions

---

[73] The depositions for this case are in Nottingham University Library, LB 225/3/32–35; the proctor's defence is in Nottinghamshire Record Office, M463, 457.

[74] BL, Egerton MS, 2868, fos. 90ʳ, 66ʳ, 244ᵉ. Raine, sen. had earlier appended a glossary of old local words to *The Charters of Endowment, Inventories, and Accounts of Rolls, of the Priory of Finchale, in the County of Durham*, ed. James Raine (Surtees Society, 6, London, 1837), 417–54.

[75] Bod. Lib., MS Eng. Lang. e. 6.

and assizes from the Elizabethan period in Essex also throws up a variety of dialect words clearly in use well before lexicographers began systematically to record the local vernacular in the nineteenth century. It reveals certain vocabulary drawn from agricultural life such as 'boar's frank' (a pig pen), 'cronge' (a handle), and 'scavell' (a small spade); and others related to hunting and warrening, such as 'jebots' (clamorous horn notes blown to frighten game), 'muses' (holes in a park fence for rabbits to pass through), and the verb 'to withstall' meaning to snare. It brings to light local terms related to weaving such as 'packlane' (pack for wool) and 'bay chain' (type of wool), and the names for weapons, including a 'dag' (handgun) and a 'loakstake' (pikestaff). Among other words it recovers are 'flue' (a mouth-pipe) and 'wholve' (a culvert), while 'to fetch a wanlace' meant to form an intercepting party, and a 'warp of ling' referred to four of these fish. Insight into pronunciation is also given in the rendering of expressions such as 'wossarwante' (whose servant), 'were fellen' (very villain), and 'worccelle' (wassail).[76] By the same token, a small sample of suits taken from the splendid run of quarter sessions rolls from seventeenth-century Wiltshire unearths a completely different set of local words. A few of those relating to the cloth trade, for example, would include: 'cipers' (fine gauze), 'fardle' (bundle), 'harnys' (coarse linen), 'kiddier' (huckster), 'thrumes' (end of a weaver's warp).[77]

Other forms of parochial record can be equally valuable as guides to both local vocabulary and pronunciation. The partially educated and semi-literate officials who often made entries in manorial rolls or local accounts, clearly wrote as they spoke in a broken and phonetic English which gives some insight into speech patterns. This is rarely more graphically illustrated than when the constable of Fixby, near Huddersfield, wrote 'omney beney' in his returns for April 1640. These documents of local administration can cast much light on traits of pronunciation. The churchwardens' accounts of sixteenth- and seventeenth-century London, for example, evidence the frequent and systematic use of certain spellings which distinguish them from written documents penned by the capital's learned elite at this time and appear to indicate some quite clear characteristics. Their orthography suggests, among other things, the pronunciation of a short 'o' as a short 'a', as in 'caffen' for coffin and 'band' for bond. Equally, a short 'a' seems often to have been sounded as a short 'e', as in 'Jenuarie' for January and 'perresh' for parish. Long 'a' and 'ai'

[76] F. G. Emmison, *Elizabethan Life: Disorder* (Chelmsford, 1970), 109, 301, 182, 243, 297–8, 163, 155, 4, 24, 244, 266, 34.

[77] *Records of the County of Wiltshire being extracted from the Quarter Sessions Great Rolls of the Seventeenth Century*, ed. B. H. Cunnington (Devizes, 1932), 21, 62 189.

were frequently replaced with 'i' or 'y': thus 'byes' for bays and 'rile' for
rail. And 'ou' or 'ow' were often represented by 'u': thus 'shutt' for shout
and 'fulle' for fowl. Meanwhile, a careful analysis of twenty-two sets of
churchwardens' accounts of the period from Cornwall, Devon, Somerset,
and Dorset, identifies nine clear characteristics of West Country pronunciation and grammatical form which consistently differentiate it from
that of London. One contemporary was in so little doubt that the broad
dialect of people from that part of the world was reflected in their writing
that he claimed 'we see their jouring speech even upon their monuments
and grave-stones'.[78]

At the same time, dialect words were not infrequently used in such
sources. Thus, from the corporation minutes of early Tudor York we hear
of 'kirk' for church, 'lig' for lie, and the expression 'ilkan' for 'every one'.
A set of archdeaconry records from Elizabethan Oxfordshire contains
'brat' for rubbish, 'earnes' for messages, and 'pack' for worthless person.
The manorial rolls of Wakefield for the 1660s return a variety of terms
from the West Riding countryside, such as 'shot' (corner of land), 'hebble'
(foot bridge), mistal (cow shed), 'nabbi' (hill), and 'slakki' (hollow). The
parish registers of Bakewell in Derbyshire, beginning in 1677, reveal as
many examples of another local vocabulary, including 'nugg' (pin), 'stale'
(handle), 'piggin' (small pail), 'wiskit' (basket), 'droughts' (teams), and
'urchants' (hedgehogs).[79]

In the same way, personal manuscript writings such as diaries, account
books, and letters can be suggestive of particular dialects and idiolects.
For example, the devotional treatises of Robert Parkyn, curate of
Adwick-le-Street near Doncaster until 1569, have been said to represent
'some of the most authentic specimens of dialect prose dating from the
mid-Tudor period', in which the author 'continues unaffectedly to use
many . . . dialect forms even when copying the works of recent southern
writers like More and Stapleton'. The diary of Henry Machyn provides

---

[78] *The Court Rolls of the Manor of Wakefield from October 1639 to September 1640*, ed. C. M. Fraser
and Kenneth Emsley (Yorkshire Archaeological Society, Leeds, 1977), 156; William Matthews,
*Cockney Past and Present* (London, 1938), 18–23; William Matthews, 'South Western Dialect in the
Early Modern Period', *Neophilologus*, 24 (1939), 193–209; Martyn F. Wakelin, 'Significant
Spellings in the St. Ives Borough Accounts', *Neophilologus*, 57 (1973), 284–6; Defoe, *A Tour thro'
the Whole Island of Great Britain*, ed. Cole, i. 221.

[79] D. M. Palliser, 'Civic Mentality and the Environment in Tudor York', *Northern History*, 18
(1982), 99; *The Archdeacon's Court: Liber Actorum, 1584*, ed. E. R. C. Brinkworth (2 vols.,
Oxfordshire Record Society, 23–4, Oxford, 1942–6), i. xxi–xxii; *The Court Rolls of the Manor of
Wakefield from October 1664 to September 1665*, ed. C. M. Fraser and Kenneth Emsley (Yorkshire
Archaeological Society, Leeds, 1986), xxi; Hilda M. Hulme, 'Derbyshire Dialect in the
Seventeenth Century', *Journal of the Derbyshire Archaeological Society*, new ser., 15 (1941), 99–103.

the very different example of a London merchant-taylor of the same period. If Machyn's spelling can be taken to reflect his pronunciation then he seems to have dropped his 'hs' in cases such as 'olles' for holes, but sounded them in others, as in 'hoythe' for oath. In some instances the 'th' sound might be pronounced as 'd', as in 'doys' for those, and in others as 'f', as in 'frust' for thrust. Sometimes a 't' sound might be pronounced 'th', as in 'a-boythe' for about, and a 'v' might be sounded as 'f', as in 'a-boyffh' for above. The account book of Richard Bax, a yeoman farmer who lived near Dorking, Surrey, in the mid-seventeenth century, suggests the articulation of the letter 'i' as an 'e' in words such as dinner ('denner'), timber ('tember') and mill ('mell'), as well as the sounding of a 'c' in words such as sawing ('scaeing'), supper ('scoper'), and sold ('scoulde').[80]

Dialects could vary, particularly in terms of their vocabulary, not only between regions and localities but also between particular trades and groups of workers. Occupational speech patterns were thus superimposed upon an already complex configuration of geographically determined ones and individuals might belong simultaneously to a number of separate linguistic communities. Most specialized trades and crafts had their own words for their particular tools and practices and in many cases different professions might use different terms to describe the same object. 'Each company would be thought a little nation | And coyn a dialect in their own fashion', commented one seventeenth-century poet. There were, noted William Congreve in 1695, 'country-clowns, sailers, tradesmen, jockeys, gamesters, and such like, who make use of cants or peculiar dialects in their several arts and vocations'. In 1688 the Cheshire gentleman, Randle Holme, included short glossaries of the terms peculiar to most of the major trades and callings in his monumental *Academy of Armoury*. But when Samuel Johnson came to compile his famous English dictionary two generations later, he was compelled to omit this bewildering terminology of 'art and manufacture' owing to its sheer size and the fact that so little of it was written down. 'I could not visit caverns to learn the miner's language, nor take a voyage to perfect my skill in the dialect of navigation, nor visit the warehouses of merchants, and shops of artificers,

[80] *Tudor Treatises*, ed. A. G. Dickens (Yorkshire Archaeological Society, 125, Wakefield, 1959), 27, 59–88; *The Diary of Henry Machyn, Citizen and Merchant-Taylor of London, from A.D. 1550 to A.D. 1563*, ed. John Gough Nichols (Camden Society, 1st ser., 42, 1848), 259, 268, 282, 284, 42, 79; 'Notes and Extracts from the Account-Book of Richard Bax, a Surrey Yeoman (kept between 1648–1662)', ed. Alfred Ridley Bax, in G. L. Apperson (ed.), *Gleanings after Time* (London, 1907), 207, 208, 209, 210, 213, 218, 219. Cf. 'Furse of Moreshead. A Family Record of the Sixteenth Century', ed. H. J. Carpenter, in *Report and Transactions of the Devonshire Association*, 26 (1894), 168–84.

to gain the names of wares, tools and operations, of which no mention is found in books.'[81]

In the countryside many farming practices and rural crafts had particular vocabularies and modes of expression associated with them. In the 1660s the agricultural writer John Worlidge described the bewildering variety of names for tools, livestock, and techniques existing between husbandmen in different parts of the country. There was amongst them

such a Babel of confusion as well in their terms and names of things, as there is in the practice of the art of agriculture itself, that remove a husbandman but sixty, or an hundred miles from the place where he hath constantly exercised his husbandry, to another, and he shall not onely admire their method and order in tilling the land, but also their strange and uncouth language and terms, by which they name their several utensils, instruments or materials they use.[82]

Thus the countrymen whom Sir Anthony Fitzherbert knew in Derbyshire in the early sixteenth century had various languages all of their own. Ploughmen would tell that the oxen's harness was made up of a number of constituent parts such as the 'stylkynges', the 'wrethynge-temes', and the 'bowes'. This was then attached to the 'togwith', or part of the draught apparatus of the harrow, which, in turn, was linked to the 'swingle tree' or 'sharbeare', a wooden frame to which the 'share' of the plough was fixed. Holding firmly to the 'plough-style' (right-hand handle) the husbandman could then take his 'landes' (part of the ploughing gear) and make his 'raines' (furrows) and 'rest balkes' (ridges) on his 'hades' (strips at end of arable land). Meanwhile, the farriers had an equally specialized vocabulary to describe the anatomy and equipment of horses. The horse's fundament, for example, was known as its 'tuell': the genitals were called 'scote' in the case of a colt and 'shap' in that of a mare. There were innumerable names for the various diseases afflicting horses, of which 'morfounde', 'farcyon', 'affreyd', 'rynbone', and 'myllettes' represent only a small sample. If a swelling was on the animal's back it was a 'nauylgall'; if above its fetlock, a 'wind-gall'; if under its ear, a 'vives'.[83]

---

[81] J.S., 'To my honoured friend T.B.', in Blount, *Glossographia*, sig. A8ʳ; William Congreve, *Concerning Humour in Comedy* (1695), in *Critical Essays of the Seventeenth Century*, ed. Spingarn, iii. 248; Randle Holme, *The Academy of Armoury* (London, 1688), iii. 73–129; Samuel Johnson, *A Dictionary of the English Language* (2 vols., London, 1755), i. sig. C1ʳ; some of these omissions were remedied by Jonathan Boucher, *A Supplement to Dr. Johnson's Dictionary of the English Language: Or, a Glossary of Obsolete and Provincial Words* (London, 1807).

[82] John Worlidge, *Systema Agriculturae, The Mystery of Husbandry Discovered* (London, 1669), 266. For a more recent glossary, see James Britten, *Old Country and Farming Words* (English Dialect Society, 30, London, 1880).

[83] Sir Anthony Fitzherbert, *The Book of Husbandry*, ed. W. W. Skeat (English Dialect Society, 37, London, 1882), 9, 11, 12, 14, 22, 25, 66–72.

Meanwhile the arable farmers of East Anglia would talk in terms of their 'brank' (buckwheat) and their 'bullimonge' (mixture of oats and barley), their 'hawme' (straw) and their 'edish' (stubble). They would speak of 'casting' (cleaning) their grain, of 'dew-retting' (steeping) their flax, and 'feying' (cleaning) their ditches. Around their farms one would meet a 'tilman' (ploughman) and a 'neathered' (cowherd), together with a 'patch' (labourer) and a 'droie' (servant). Among their instruments, or 'pelfe', could be found a 'crotch' (weeding tool), a 'didall' (triangular ditching spade) and a 'doong crone' (crook); in their fields might be seen some 'dallops' (tufts of corn) and some 'compas' (manure), while the 'swatches' (rows) of 'drink corn' (barley) were waiting to be bundled up in 'coemes' (four bushels).[84]

A different set of vocabulary, again, was known to the shepherds up in the pastoral country of the East Riding. They had different words to describe sheep according to sex, age, and condition. Thus a 'gimmer' was a young female only once shorn; a 'hogge' was a youngster for weaning before first shearing; a 'waster' was a sheep that would not fatten; and a 'moone rider' was a barren ewe. Rams could be 'hunge tuppes', 'close tuppes', 'riggon tuppes', or 'dodded tuppes': once castrated, or 'libbed', they were called 'weathers'. At the same time, various names described parts of the sheep's anatomy: its 'claggs', 'hough', 'kell', and 'liske'. Shepherds designated ownership of a sheep by making a 'botte' (mark) on the fleece or else by 'stowinge' it (cutting off the tip of its ear). They would count them by into the 'creave' (small pen) by making 'fagget-markes' (a sign for five) on a 'nickstick'. A lamb's testicles, or 'stones', could be fried with parsley as a delicacy called 'anchitricoes', while the sheepskins, or 'pelts', could be made into 'pellitt moyles' (sheepskin slippers).[85]

The differences between other occupational dialects are vividly illustrated by a legal dispute at Middlewich, Cheshire, in May 1599 which revolved around the meaning of the word 'stole', or 'scole'. Charles and James Mainwaring had agreed to supply timber to Philip Oldfield and others from trees chopped at Compton Lea in Middlewich, with the condition that the order include no wood from smaller saplings or 'stoles'. When their customers claimed that the Mainwarings had failed to meet this condition, the definition of what exactly constituted a stole became important. On the one hand, Charles Mainwaring, who 'cannot wryte or

[84] Thomas Tusser, *Five Hundred Points of Good Husbandry*, ed. Geoffrey Grigson (Oxford, 1984), 321–36.
[85] *The Farming and Memorandum Books of Henry Best of Elmswell, 1642*, ed. Donald Woodward (British Academy, Records of Social and Economic History, new ser., 8, London, 1984), 285–323.

reade wrytten hannd', stated that 'hee thinketh in his consciens, that all trees aboue the length of three yeards are reputed and taken to bee trees, and all of three yeards or under to be called stoles and are not trees'. On the other hand, the plaintiffs understood a stole rather differently than this. When they sent for John Ameson to draw up their indictment, he 'asked them what a stole was' to which 'they answered that a stole was such a one as a man standinge at the roote of ytt might reach the toppe of the bodie with his hannd'. The court then took evidence from two carpenters, William Prestbury and Richard Hulme, but found that to them it meant the stump of a fallen oak tree. The former 'saith that is commonly called a stowle or stoole of an oak tree whiche remaynethe after that the oke ys fallen or cutt downe, and so he hath knowen and reputed the same to be by the space of thirty yeres or more thereabouts, by reason so longe tyme he hath used the craft or occupation of a carpenter'. Moreover, among them, 'those of trees which be in length one, two or three yards or thereabouts and beane cropps are comonly called stubbs and stubb trees, and not stoles'.[86]

Another cluster of occupational groups renowned for their peculiar language were miners. The lead miners of Derbyshire and the Mendips, the tinners of Cornwall, the silver miners of Cardiganshire, and the iron ore and coal miners of Staffordshire, are all recorded as having their own unique and bewildering terminology known only to themselves and completely opaque to outsiders.[87] These dialects contributed significantly to the widespread contemporary perception of all subterranean workers as some kind of heathen race apart. In the mid-eighteenth century the colliers of Kingswood Forest, near Bristol, were said to be 'so barbarous and savage' that 'it was dangerous to go among them, and their dialect was the roughest and rudest in the nation'. In fact, these distinctive linguistic systems were no more than signifiers of particular work communities, each with their own practices, customs, and norms.[88]

---

[86] PRO, CHES 15/21 (I am grateful to Steve Hindle for this reference). The diversity of tools formerly used in carpentry is revealed in R. A. Salaman, *Dictionary of Tools Used in the Woodworking and Allied Trades, c.1700–1970* (London, 1975).

[87] BL, Lansdowne MS, 1033; R. Offer, 'Two Mining Account Books from Farnley Colliery, 1690–1720', *Transactions of the Yorkshire Dialect Society*, 5/34 (1933), 9–28; J. W. Gough, *The Mines of Mendip* (London, 1967), 71, 78–9, 89, 97, 113, 117, 138, 139, 140, 141–2, 147–9, 167, 186, 233. Nineteenth-century glossaries include James Mander, *The Derbyshire Miners' Glossary* (Bakewell, 1824); H. English, *A Glossary of Mining Terms of . . . Cornwall and Derbyshire* (London, 1830); W. E. Nicholson, *A Glossary of Terms used in the Coal Trade of Northumberland and Durham* (Newcastle, 1888).

[88] R. W. Malcolmson, '"A Set of Ungovernable People": The Kingswood Colliers in the Eighteenth Century', in John Brewer and John Styles (eds.), *An Ungovernable People* (London, 1980), 126. For similar perceptions of other groups of miners, see David Levine and Keith

In the mid-seventeenth century Edward Manlove, a former steward of
the barmote court for the lead mines in the wapentake of Wirksworth,
Derbyshire, collected some of the 'strange and uncouth' terms used by
the local miners in the form of a verse.

> Bunnings, polings, stemples, forks, and slyder,
> Stoprice, yokings, soletrees, roach, and ryder,
> Water holes, wind holes, veyns, coe-shafts and woughs,
> Main rakes, cross rakes, brown-henns, budles and soughs,
> Break-offs, and buckers, randam of the rake,
> Freeing, and chasing of the stole to th' stake,
> Starting of oar, smilting, and driving drifts,
> Primgaps, roof works, flat-works, pipe-works, shifts,
> Cauke, sparr, lid-stones, twitches, daulings, and pees,
> Fell, bous, and knock-barke, forstid-oar, and tees,
> Bing-place, barmoot court, barghmaster, and stowes,
> Crosses, holes, hange benches, turntree, and coes,
> Founder-meers, taker-meers, lot, cope, and sumps,
> Stickings, and stringes of oar, wash-oar and pumps,
> Corfes, clivies, deads, meers, groves, rake-soil, the gange,
> Binge-oar, a spindle, a lampturn, a fange,
> Fleaks, knockings, coestid, trunks and sparks of oar,
> Sole of the rake, smytham, and many more.[89]

As one commentator put it, the miners' vocabulary could 'not bee
understood without interpretor of theire owne expression'. It was for this
reason that Thomas Houghton needed to include a glossary of forty-
three 'terms of art' used by the Derbyshire lead miners in the edition of
their laws and customs which he printed in 1681. Defoe actually required
a translator when he came across one of their number in the early eighteenth century. This 'most uncouth spectacle' had 'some tools in a little
basket which he drew up with him, not one of the names of which we
could understand but by the help of an interpreter. Nor indeed could we
understand any of the man's discourse so as to make out a whole sentence;
and yet the man was pretty free of his tongue too . . . We asked him, how
deep the mine lay which he came out of: he answered us in terms we did

Wrightson, *The Making of an Industrial Society: Whickham, 1560–1765* (Oxford, 1991), 274–7; Andy
Wood, 'Custom, Identity and Resistance: English Free Miners and their Law, c.1550–1800',
in Paul Griffiths, Adam Fox, and Steve Hindle (eds.), *The Experience of Authority in Early Modern
England* (Basingstoke, 1996), 254–5.

[89] Edward Manlove, *The Liberties and Cvstomes of the Lead-Mines within the Wapentake of
Wirksworth in the County of Derby* (London, 1653), 8. This rhyme is reproduced in *Reprinted
Glossaries*, ed. Skeat, ii. 7–20, and discussed in Wakelin, *English Dialects*, 145–6.

not understand; but our interpreter, as above, told us, it signified that he was at work 60 fathoms deep . . .'.[90]

Seamen were another group renowned for having their own particular dialect. Elizabethan sailors clearly had a variety of words to decribe the many different types of seafaring vessel and to denote their constituent parts. They also had a huge range of terms to denote the equipment on board and a special array of verbs to describe its use. In 1635 Sir William Brereton noted down twenty-four of the peculiar 'names and terms which mariners use' as he had heard them on the voyage home from Holland. Sir Henry Manwayring thought it damaging to the national interest that gentlemen such as Brereton were completely baffled by the language of the sea. In 1644 he published *The Sea-mans Dictionary* in an effort to explain some of it, since 'the vulgar sort of sea-men hate land-men so much' they are 'unwilling to instruct them in that art'. Soon afterwards John Smith contributed *The Sea-Mans Grammar*, a nautical manual which included 'plain exposition of all such terms as are used in the navie and fight at sea'. Such tracts proved invaluable to an Admiralty official such as Samuel Pepys who had to deal with sailors and shipwrights all the time. He read one of them in March 1661 and later had them both bound up together.[91]

Many people, however, seem to have reciprocated the seamen's distrust of 'land-men' and regarded them, like miners, as a distinct and dangerous fraternity with 'a dialect and manner peculiar to themselves'. At the end of the seventeenth century Ned Ward looked with disgust on the sailors come ashore in London, such 'uncouth animals' in their habits, so 'rude in their behaviour'. He came across a group of carousers in a 'tavern kitchen' by the Exchange and 'soon found by their dialect they were masters of ships'.

'Cheer up, my lads, pull away, save tide; come, boys'. Then handling the quart, being empty, 'What, is she light? You, sir, that's next, haul the bar-line, and call the cooper's mate'. The drawer being come, 'Here, you fly-blown swab, take away this damned tankard, and ballast her well. Pox take her, there's no stowage in her hold. Have you ne'er a larger vessel?'

[90] Bod. Lib., MS Ashmole 816, fo. 43ʳ; Thomas Houghton, *Rara Avis in Terris: Or the Compleat Miner* (London, 1681), sigs. F1ʳ–F5ʳ; Defoe, *A Tour thro' the Whole Island of Great Britain*, ed. Cole, 571–2. Cf. Charles Leigh, *The Natural History of Lancashire, Cheshire, and the Peak, in Derbyshire* (Oxford, 1700), 117.

[91] Richard Hakluyt, *The Principal Navigations, Voyages, Traffiques and Discoveries of the English Nation*, ed. Jack Beeching (Harmondsworth, 1972), 430–3; Sir William Brereton, *Travels in Holland, the United Provinces, England, Scotland and Ireland, 1634–5*, ed. Edward Hawkins (Chetham Society, 1, London, 1844), 169; Sir Henry Manwayring, *The Sea-mans Dictionary* (London, 1644), sig. A2ʳ; John Smith, *The Sea-Mans Grammar* (London, 1653); *The Diary of Samuel Pepys*, ed. Robert Latham and William Matthews (11 vols., London, 1970–83), ii. 53.

It is not surprising, perhaps, that sailors tended to keep to themselves, living with their families in discrete districts within port towns, usually by the docks, which formed highly localized speech communities. Any visitor to the London seafaring neighbourhoods of Rotherhithe and Wapping, it was said in the mid-eighteenth century, 'would be apt to suspect himself in another country'. Even at Poole in Dorset it was later reported that a small part of the town 'appears to be inhabited by a peculiar race of people, who are, and probably long have been, the fishing population of their neighbourhood. Their manner of speaking is totally different from that of the neighbouring rustics.'[92]

In the case of all these vocabularies of work and craft, however, what was impenetrable and sometimes threatening to outsiders, was an important facet of occupational solidarity and craft identity to their users. Part of learning any trade was to be initiated into its unique linguistic system, to be apprenticed in its terms of art and specialized nomenclature no less than in its skills and techniques. A powerful sense of belonging could accrue from the language of work no less than from the language of place and as with all professional jargon there could be a vested interest in excluding the unschooled. This is no more explicitly illustrated than in the most famous of all the argots of this period and beyond, that of the 'criminal underworld'. A swathe of pamphlets appeared from the mid-sixteenth century detailing the 'canting tongue' of the 'fraternity of vagabonds', pick-pockets and prostitutes who were said to inhabit London streets and tramp the country. By the early seventeenth century this speech was beginning to be represented on the stage and it was dignified with the first of its 'dictionaries' in 1673 when Richard Head published *The Canting Academy*.[93]

The cant of the 'criminal underworld' demonstrates the way in which language can both express and create group identities and even subcultures. The jargon of con-artists and cutpurses enshrined their methods and described their familiar objects no less than many other occupational

[92] Marcus Rediker, *Between the Devil and the Deep Blue Sea: Merchant Seamen, Pirates, and the Anglo-American Maritime World, 1700–1750* (Cambridge, 1987), 162; Ned Ward, *The London Spy: The Vanities and Vices of the Town Exposed to View*, ed. A. L. Hayward (London, 1927), 241, 268; Peter Linebaugh, *The London Hanged: Crime and Civil Society in Eighteenth-Century England* (London, 1991), 134–5; J. O. Halliwell, *An Historical Sketch of the Provincial Dialects of England* (London, 1847), 7. Cf. Pablo E. Perez-Mallaina, *Spain's Men of the Sea: Daily Life on the Indies Fleets in the Sixteenth Century* (Baltimore, 1998), 225.

[93] *The Elizabethan Underworld*, ed. A. V. Judges (London, 1930); *Cony-Catchers and Bawdy Baskets*, ed. Gamini Salgado (Harmondsworth, 1972); Richard Head, *The Canting Academy* (London, 1673); *A New Canting Dictionary* (London, 1725); Francis Grose, *A Classical Dictionary of the Vulgar Tongue* (London, 1785). For discussion, see Blank, *Broken English*, 52–67.

dialects and perhaps more than most it provided a defence and protective from outside encroachment. It was invented, as one observer appreciated, 'to th' intent that (albeit any spies should secretly steale into their companies to discouer them) they might freely vtter their mindes one to another, yet auoide the danger'. Thomas Harman, author of one of the earliest pamphlets on the subject, offered this example of their conversation.

What stowe you bene cose and cut benat whydds and byng we to rome vyle to nyp a bong so shall we haue lowre for the bousing ken and when we byng back to the deuseauyel we wyll fylche some duddes of the ruffemans or myll the ken for a lagge of dudes.

The translation of which was:

What holde your peace good fellowe and speake better wordes, and go we to London, to cut a purse, then shal we haue money for the ale house, and when wee come backe agayne into the countrey, wee wyll steale some lynnen clothes of one hedges, or robbe some house for a bucke of clothes.[94]

Harman was a Kentish magistrate who claimed to have gathered material for his pamphlet in the course of interviews, at his house in Crayford near Dartford, with vagabonds who had been arrested travelling through the county. And lest this language be thought to be a mere literary fabrication or stylized representation, a remarkable document drawn up half a century later, from similar sources, confirms its genuine use. In 1615–16, John Newbolt, governor of the Bridewell at Winchester in Hampshire, interrogated various of the counterfeiters, pickpockets, fencers, and 'gamesters alias cheaters that live in London and come into the cuntry at fayres to deceave people of ther mony with false dice and cardes'. On the basis of their depositions he drew up a glossary of 107 'canting wordes' which they 'use amongst themselves as their language'. These itinerant fraudsters and thieves hailed not just from London but from all over the south of England: Thomas Baker 'a Devonshire man', John Dolby, 'a Cambridgeshire man', John Clapham 'pentioner at Bury in Suffolk', Hugh Masterson 'borne at Andover in Hampshire'. Yet they were united in a common 'canting tounge' which Newbolt seems to have recorded as an aid to other officials. To take the single example of money, these 'counterfett egiptians' called a penny a 'hyrow', a halfpenny a 'pushera', a groat a 'gorisha', five pence 'shogh hayra', five shillings 'pang shellony' and twenty shillings 'tromen'.[95]

    [94] Thomas Dekker, *Villanies Discouered by Lanthorne and Candle-light* (London, 1616), sig. M1ᵛ;
Thomas Harman, *A Caueat for Commen Cvrsetors Vvlgarely Called Vagabones* (London, 1567), sig. G4ᵛ.
    [95] Hampshire Record Office, 44M69/G3/159.

All of these many and varied vocabularies of region and community, of occupation and manufacture, point to the highly variegated nature of popular culture in this period. Each of these linguistic systems was the signifier of mentalities and world views which were often quite specific to particular places or groups of people. That communication could be difficult between localities and trades reflects the fact that early modern England was less a unified nation and more a constellation of communities which, while they may have shared some common cultural features, stubbornly clung to chauvinistic and exclusive ways of acting, perceiving, and speaking. There is no more graphic reflection of this than the lack of a national market economy at this time, due, among other reasons, to the fact that many agricultural 'countries' or specialist crafts had their own weights and measures and used different words to describe them. Much quantifying was done simply by rule-of-thumb. There were various dialect terms which recall the typically impressionistic definition of a 'stole' in Cheshire as a tree with a trunk which a man might reach the top of with his hand. In Essex John Ray noted that his neighbours spoke of a 'yaspen' or 'yeepsen', which meant as much of something 'as can be taken up in both hands joyn'd together'. With them, a 'seame' of corn signified a 'horse load', or eight bushels. In the north of England, meanwhile, an equivalent word was a 'tother', although in some places it meant two 'horse loads' and in others just one.[96]

Bushels, strikes, and pecks all varied, not only from town to town and manor to manor but also according to the commodity in question. Wheat and corn, peas and potatoes, apples and pears, all had their own standards and all were contingent on place: a strike could be anything from half a bushel to four bushels.[97] Equally, in the case of land, measures depended on the region, as well as both the type of soil and the nature of the crops grown in it. As Robert Thoroton explained in the 1670s, these gauges had 'been taken from the plow as long as memories of things are extant', and therefore were bound to vary 'according to the lightness or stiffness of the soyl, whereof one plow might dispatch more or less accordingly'. Thus a 'curucat', or 'plowland', 'defined to be as much land as one ox might till through the year . . . could not be equal in all places, but in some places was

---

[96] Ray, *A Collection of English Words Not Generally Used* (2nd edn., 1691), 121, 111; *The Farming and Memorandum Books of Henry Best of Elmswell*, ed. Woodward, 296; Joseph Wright (ed.), *The English Dialect Dictionary* (6 vols., London, 1898–1905), ii. 435. Cf. Thomas Hardy's Henchard: 'He used to reckon his sacks by chalk strokes all in a row like garden-palings, measure his ricks by stretching with his arms, weigh his trusses by a lift, judge his hay by a chaw, and settle the price with a curse': *The Mayor of Casterbridge* (1886; New Wessex edn., London, 1974), 130.

[97] Wright (ed.), *English Dialect Dictionary*, i. 475–8, iv. 449–50, v. 816. See, E. M. Wright, *Rustic Speech and Folk-Lore* (Oxford, 1913), 328–31.

twelve, in some sixteen, in some eighteen or more acres'. So the meaning of oxgangs, virgates, and roods also varied in their turn, while there was not even a standard acre since the number of feet to a perch and perch to an acre were highly localized. Even 'the foot itself was also customary', recognized Thoroton, 'in some place twelve inches, in some eighteen or less'.[98]

This lack of standardization is also evident in the many dialect words used to denote animals and plants. There were, for example, over 120 different names nationwide to describe the smallest of a litter of pigs. The hickwall (*Gecinus viridis*) went by over twenty titles around the country, while other common birds such as the sparrow, or fish such as the stickle-back, were also prolifically described. Meanwhile there were as many as fifty seperate names for the marsh marigold (*Caltha palustris*). *Tragopogon pratensis* was variously called goat's beard, Joseph's flour, star of Jerusalem, noon tide, and go-to-bed-at-noon; *Arum maculatum* might be cuckoo pint, cuckoo pintle, or cuckoo point, wake-robin, priest's pintle or calve's-foot, aron, barba-aron, janus, ramp or starchwort; *Capsella bursa-pastoris* was known in the south of England as shepherd's purse, shepherd's pouch or poor man's parmacetie, but in the north as toy wort, pick-purse or case-weed.[99]

Such names given to animals and plants often betray the popular beliefs held about them or the uses to which they were put, and the same applies to much of the prolific dialect vocabulary. In this now obsolete local terminology can be found evidence of everyday practices and habits, of social customs and modes of thought, which might otherwise have remained obscure or forgotten were it not for the words which denoted them. Thus Ray exposed some interesting household practices when he recorded the verb 'to leint' applied in parts of the north to ale and meaning 'to put urine into it to make it strong'. Other brewing techniques are revealed in his noting of the term 'slape-ale' used in Lincolnshire for 'plain ale as opposed to ale medicated with wormwood or scurvey-grass'. Long before Ray, John Gerard had pointed out that women in north Wales and Cheshire would put 'ale-hoofe' into their brews, but then, depending on the part of the country, this plant might also be called 'ground ivy', 'gill go by ground', 'turne-hoofe' or 'cats-foot'.[100]

[98]  Robert Thoroton, *The Antiquities of Nottinghamshire* (London, 1677), sig. A3. See also Carew, *The Survey of Cornwall*, fo. 54. Cf. Wright (ed.), *English Dialect Dictionary*, i. 13, iv. 397, 472, v. 147.

[99]  Wright, *Rustic Speech and Folk-Lore*, 7; Keith Thomas, *Man and the Natural World: Changing Attitudes in England, 1500–1800* (London, 1983), 81–3; John Gerard, *The Herball or General Historie of Plantes*, ed. Thomas Johnson (London, 1633), 736, 834, 276.

[100]  Ray, *A Collection of English Words* (2nd edn., 1691), 42, 64; Gerard, *The Herball or General Historie of Plantes*, ed. Johnson, 856.

If these usages of women in the domestic sphere were unlikely to be recorded otherwise, so too were the practices of children. White Kennett made reference to several of the local words by which children's games or toys were known thus providing earlier evidence of their use than might be suspected. So the phrase 'to play at knur' alluded to 'a game among the boys in Yorksh[ire] with a little round cheas-ball (which they call a knur) struck from one to another with little landy sticks . . .'. Another game in the same county using stick, or bat, and ball was 'bad', played with a 'cat stick', 'bad-stick', or hippal-stick'. Interestingly Kennett thought that a variant form of this game, known as cricket, was still sufficiently localized, 'a game most usual in Kent', to consider it a dialect word. In Norfolk and Suffolk the word for ball was 'campers' and 'to camp' was to play at football. Elsewhere, 'aws-bones' referred to 'bones of the legs of cows or oxen with which boys play at aws or yawse'.[101]

Finally, something may be inferred about popular religion, or at least popular attitudes towards the established Church, by the dialect names given to its major feasts and festivals. For example, Maundy Thursday was termed 'skirisfurisday' in Scotland, Northumberland, and Durham until the late seventeenth century, a survival of pagan ceremony and Old Norse; the Invention of the Holy Cross was known as 'crouchmas' in many areas until the nineteenth century, a hangover from medieval Catholicism and late Old English. The feast of Epiphany was called 'wassailing' day in Sussex, Somerset, and Devon, or 'howling' or 'hollering' in other regions, after the name given to the gathering and selling of apples. The day before Shrove Tuesday was known as 'collop Monday' in many northern places, after the word for the bacon customarily eaten on that day, and 'carling Sunday' took its name from the brown peas then consumed. Good Friday was 'cave Friday' in Cheshire and 'long Friday' in Lancashire, while 'cattern' was the name given to St Catherine's Day in Buckinghamshire, Shropshire, Sussex, Wiltshire, and Worcestershire, following the practice of children begging apples and beer from door to door, which gave rise to the noun 'catterning' or 'cattering'.[102]

---

[101] BL, Lansdowne MS, 1033, fos. 213ᵛ, 28ᵛ, 72ʳ, 54ʳ, 25ᵛ. For 'nur and spel', 'bad', and the similar 'cat', see J. O. Halliwell, *Dictionary of Archaic Words* (London, 1850), 583, 131, 235; cf. A. B. Gomme, *The Traditional Games of England, Scotland, and Ireland* (2 vols., London, 1894–8; rep. 1984), i. 11, 421–3. On the early development of cricket, see David Underdown, 'Regional Cultures? Local Variations in Popular Culture during the Early Modern Period', in Tim Harris (ed.), *Popular Culture in England, c.1500–1850* (Basingstoke, 1995), 42–6.

[102] Wright (ed.), *English Dialect Dictionary*; Forby, *The Vocabulary of East Anglia*, ii. 387; Wright, *Rustic Speech and Folk-Lore*, 283–306; Wakelin, *English Dialects*, 78–9.

### THE LANGUAGE OF DEGREE

One of the most significant developments in the perception of language at this time was a more self-conscious identification of speech patterns with social status. No doubt the idea that accents and dialects might be a reflection of social rank was already an old-established one by the Tudor period, and may well have crystallized as early as the late fourteenth century with the emergence of a standard form of English. It was only in the mid-sixteenth century, however, that commentators on both the language and the social order began to articulate this notion explicitly and to insist, moreover, that people should speak in ways befitting their status and position. Perhaps the new technology of print, which facilitated the circulation of debate on the subject among contemporaries and has preserved evidence of it for posterity, creates the illusion of new urgency and new attitudes in this respect. But the reign of Elizabeth may have marked new departures in the social stratification of English.[103]

In the first place, this was a period of immense linguistic change. More loan words enriched English vocabulary in the years 1570–1630 than at any time before or since. At the same time, there were extensive debates over correctness and propriety in terms of orthography and pronunciation, grammatical rules and stylistic conventions, and these had considerable influence on both the written and spoken word. In the second place, this was an era of enormous social and economic upheaval. A doubling of the population in the century after 1540, a much brisker land market in the wake of monastic dissolution, and huge price inflation as a consequence of these and other factors, all precipitated tremendous instability in almost every area of economy and society. It was for this reason that the governors of Tudor and early Stuart England were so concerned with the problem of 'order', both in their rhetoric and their social policy. Their concern manifested itself in a number of ways, including in a much greater insistence on the regulations and conventions which had long upheld hierarchy and degree. Proper codes of dress, forms of address, and rules of behaviour were all urged upon people with renewed vigour at a time when daily experience demonstrated their increasing fragility in practice. Just as William Harrison's highly traditional description of the Elizabethan social order was ceasing to bear any relationship to recognizable reality at the very moment at which it was written, so sumptuary laws and behavioural regulations were being proclaimed loudest at precisely the point when they were no longer reflecting actual circumstances.[104]

---

[103] Williams, "'O! When Degree is Shak'd'", 77.

[104] Ibid. 77–83. For a summary of these social and economic changes, see Keith Wrightson,

Manner of speech was another of the symbols of order and degree to come under scrutiny in this period of significant and rapid social development. In the sixteenth century orthoepists and educationalists began to stress that 'the King's English' was not merely more 'correct' in the grammatical and philological sense, but actually 'better', in a qualitative and emotive one. It was not only more 'lawful' but also more 'civil'. Writing in about 1570, George Puttenham made the point most clearly when he pointed out that the best usage was determined not so much by regional origins as by social status. The 'better brought vp sort . . . men ciuill and graciously behauoured and bred', spoke and wrote correctly wherever they lived just as the lower orders spoke badly irrespective of their habitat: 'a craftes man or carter, or other of the inferiour sort, though he be inhabitant or bred in the best towne or citie in this realme . . . doe abuse good speaches by strange accents or ill shapen soundes, and false ortographie'. Thus 'in euery shyre of England there be gentlemen and others that speake but specially write as good southerne as we of Middlesex or Surrey do, but not the common people of euery shire, to whom the gentlemen, and also their learned clarkes do for the most part condescend . . .'. This was a picture confirmed soon afterwards by Robert Reyce on the basis of the evidence in Suffolk. Among a certain rank of person, he observed,

I find no dialect or idiom in the same different from others of the best speach and pronunciation . . . so having no naturall defect proper to this soile, doe wee disgrace that with any broad or rude accent which wee receive at the hands of gentility and learned schollers, whereof wee haue many trained up in the best and purest language. Howbeit I must confesse our honest country toyling villager to express his meaning to his like neighbour, will many times lett slip some strang different sounding tearmes, no wayes intelligible to any of civill education, vntill by the rude comment of some skillfull in that forme, which by dayly vse amongst them is familier, they bee after their manner explaned.[105]

---

*English Society, 1580–1680* (London, 1982), chs. 1–2. On this greater regulation, see J. R. Kent, 'Attitudes of Members of the House of Commons to the Regulation of "Personal Conduct" in Late Elizabethan and Early Stuart England', *Bulletin of the Institute of Historical Research*, 46 (1973), 41–71; N. B. Harte, 'State Control of Dress and Social Change in Pre-Industrial England', in D. C. Coleman and A. H. John (eds.), *Trade, Government and Economy in Pre-Industrial England* (London, 1976), 132–65; Paul Slack, 'Books of Orders: The Making of English Social Policy, 1577–1631', *Transactions of the Royal Historical Society*, 5th ser., 30 (1980), 1–22.

[105] Puttenham, *The Arte of English Poesie*, 120, 121; *Suffolk in the XVIIth Century: The Breviary of Suffolk by Robert Reyce, 1618*, ed. Lord Francis Hervey (London, 1902), 54–5. On the author's own usual spelling of his name, 'Ryece', and the dating of his survey to the end of Elizabeth's reign, see Diarmaid MacCulloch, *Suffolk and the Tudors: Politics and Religion in an English County, 1500–1600* (Oxford, 1986), xix, 13.

As these comments suggest, problems of communication existed not only between people from the various regions of England, but between those of different social classes living in close proximity. Thus by the Elizabethan period in Cornwall most of the common people spoke English, but to a gentleman such as Richard Carew they seemed to 'disgrace it, in part, with a broad and rude accent' and they used, moreover, 'certayne peculiar phrases, which require a speciall dictionarie for their interpret-ation'. In mid-seventeenth-century Derbyshire, Philip Kinder seems to have been at a complete loss to characterize the impenetrable dialect of his neighbours. 'They have no thunder in theire speech in coughing in the teeth like the lower Britans in France. They have noe querulous tone like the Irish, noe wharleing like them of Carleton in Leic[ster]shire: but sumething a broad language much like the Dorsett dialect in Greeke.' A few generations later it was confirmed in Derbyshire that these 'particularities are not the language of the better sort, but of the vulgar; for they, except by chance, speak as elegantly and correctly as in any part of England'.[106]

Given the contemporary anxiety about status and the concern to main-tain demarcations of rank and degree amid alarming fluidity in the social structure, conservative commentators upbraided the nobility and gentry who failed to speak in the pure and proper way befitting their place and position. Equally they spurned the vulgar sort who dared to ape the lan-guage of those above them in a manner which was at best insubordinate and at worst a dangerous progenitor of upward mobility. On the one hand, it was 'a pitty when a noble man is better distinguished from a clowne by his golden laces, then by his good language' chided a Jacobean observer. On the other hand, remarked another, citizens were 'never so out of countenance, as in the imitation of gentlemen', be it in 'habite, manner of life, conversation, and even the phrase of speech'. It was com-mon for critics of the English stage, from the Elizabethan period onwards, to blame the breakdown of order and morality on the way in which dramatists blurred social distinctions by making gentle folk speak like clowns and country bumpkins sound like lords. 'Nothing put into the mouths of persons' which does not agree with their 'age, sex, and condi-tion', Jeremy Collier advised playwrights in the 1690s. 'An old man must

---

[106] Carew, *The Survey of Cornwall*, fo. 56; Philip Kinder, 'Historie of Darby-Shire', ed. W. G. D. Fletcher, *Reliquary*, 22 (1881–2), 198; Samuel Pegge, *Two Collections of Derbicisms*, ed. W. W. Skeat and Thomas Hallam (English Dialect Society, 78, London, 1896), xix. For other eighteenth-century comment on such social cleavages, see Thomas Sheridan, *A Course of Lectures on Elocution* (London, 1762), 30.

not appear with the profuseness and levity of youth; a gentleman must not talk like a clown, nor a country girl like a town jilt.'[107]

One of the notable social consequences of economic change during the sixteenth century was the increase in wealth, education, and political responsibilty enjoyed by those in the lower middle ranks of both rural and urban society. Many of the freeholders and secure tenant farmers who were able to benefit from market conditions in the countryside and the skilled craftsmen and modest tradesmen of the larger towns who contributed to an expanding service sector, enjoyed significant improvements in their material circumstances. At the same time, the increases in educational provision and the expansion of central government in the localities which were such features of the century after 1540, reached down to include and co-opt these social groups to an ever greater degree.[108] Significantly, the phrase 'middle sort of people' emerged in the mid-sixteenth century, and was being used quite regularly by the 1620s, to describe those groups whose modest economic competence or petty political authority gave them a degree of substance and status within local society. It is precisely these groups which, so modern research into speech patterns reveals, are most concerned to imitate the language of their 'betters', to ratify their social and economic gains with this and other cultural symbols of 'civility'.[109]

A varied body of evidence exists from the late sixteenth century to suggest that the lower 'middling sorts' were already displaying this tendency towards linguistic emulation. In the 1590s Thomas Nashe thought that exposure to greater amounts of literature had 'made the vulgar sort, here in London . . . aspire to a richer puritie of speach, than is communicated with the comminalitie of any nation vnder heauen'. At the same time, Robert Reyce noticed in Suffolk that while 'the ruder sort' spoke an unintelligible dialect, 'the artificer of the good townes scorneth to follow them, when he naturally prideth in the counterfitt imitation of the best sort of language'. In the countryside, meanwhile, the yeomanry were also

---

[107] Williams, '"O! When Degree is Shak'd"', 75; Jeremy Collier, *A Short View of the Immorality and Profaneness of the English Stage* (1698), in *Critical Essays of the Seventeenth Century*, ed. Spingarn, iii. 269, 282. Cf. George Whetstone, 'The Dedication to Promos and Cassandra', in *Elizabethan Critical Essays*, ed. G. Gregory Smith (2 vols., Oxford, 1904), i. 59–60; Dryden 'Preface to Troilus and Cressida', in *Essays of John Dryden*, ed. Ker, i. 214.

[108] Mildred Campbell, *The English Yeoman under Elizabeth and the Early Stuarts* (London, 1960); Christopher Hill, *Society and Puritanism in Pre-Revolutionary England* (London, 1964), ch. 4; Wrightson, *English Society*, 140, 169–72, 194, 196–9; Jonathan Barry and Christopher Brooks (eds.), *The Middling Sort of People: Culture, Society and Politics in England, 1550–1800* (Basingstoke, 1994).

[109] Keith Wrightson, '"Sorts of People" in Tudor and Stuart England', in Barry and Brooks (eds.), *The Middling Sort of People*, 41–5; Williams, '"O! When Degree is Shak'd"', 96–7.

following the example of the best English. In 1600 Samuel Rowlands referred to the way in which 'barbarisme' was being banished by 'the goodman . . . at his plow' who had become so marked by his 'new printed speech, that cloth will now compare with veluet breech'. A tract of 1598 apparently identified a social trend when it offered advice to the yeoman's son aspiring to be the servant of a gentleman. As well as altering his appearance and manners, 'he must as well as he can, make satisfaction for the queenes currant English before by him clipped: he must now make it full wayght, good and currant lawfull English.'[110]

That the attempts of the aspiring 'middling sorts' to imitate 'the best sort of language' was a common phenomenon, is suggested by the fact that it was already becoming a source of amusement among the social elite in the sixteenth century. As early as the 1530s, when Thomas Wilson was a student at Cambridge, he had witnessed a townsman offering a gift to the new Provost of King's College, 'that lately came from the court'. The 'simple man beyng desirous to amende his mother tongue' among scholars said: '"Cha good even my good lorde, and well might your lordship vare: Understandyng that your lordship was come, and knowyong that you are a worshipfull Pilate, and keeps a bominable house: I thought it my duetie to come incantivantee, and bryng you a pottell a wine, the whiche I beseeche your lordeship take in good worthe".' So it was that the servant in elevated company, the upwardly mobile tradesman or the socially ambitious aritsan's wife, who tried to affect the best English but slipped unwittingly into solecism and mispronunciation, would become comic stereotypes long before Fielding's Mrs Slipslop and Sheridan's Mrs Malaprop perfected the form in the eighteenth century. A number of Shakespeare's humble characters, such as Juliet's nurse, the cockney Mistress Quickly, the plodding constable Dogberry, and Bottom the weaver, are rendered ridiculous by their malapropisms and linguistic infelicities. Such caricatures remained a source of humour on the London stage throughout the seventeenth century and beyond.[111]

---

[110] Thomas Nashe, *Pierce Pennilesse* (1592), in *The Works of Thomas Nashe*, ed. McKerrow and Wilson, i. 193; Reyce, *Suffolk in the XVIIth Century*, ed. Hervey, 55; Samuel Rowlands, *The Letting of Hvmovrs Blood in the Head-Vaine* (London, 1600), sig. D8ʳ; I.M., *A Health to the Gentlemanly Profession of Seruingmen: Or, the Seruingman's Comfort* (1598), in *Inedited Tracts: Illustrating the Manners, Opinions, and Occupations of Englishmen during the Sixteenth and Seventeenth Centuries*, ed. W. C. Hazlitt (Roxburghe Library, London, 1868), 137–8.

[111] Blank, *Broken English*, 42–3, 81; Helge Kökeritz, 'Shakespeare's Use of Dialect', *Transactions of the Yorkshire Dialect Society*, 60 (1951), 10–25; C. V. Wedgwood, 'Social Comedy in the Reign of Charles I', in her *Truth and Opinion: Historical Essays* (London, 1960), 203–4; J. L. Styan, *Restoration Comedy in Performance* (Cambridge, 1986), 175, 182; John Loftis, *Comedy and Society from Congreve to Fielding* (Stanford, Calif., 1959), 105.

Another butt of stage humour was the broad dialect of country folk. To urban dwellers, of course, rustics had always provided stock figures of fun. But the new heights to which comic acting rose in the first age of London's established theatres gave this age-old trope an added dimension by exploiting the increasingly conspicuous differences between the speech of court and country. It is surely significant that Elizabethan comedians typically wore the garb of a countryman. The greatest of them, Richard Tarlton, was renowned for it. 'You should ha' seene him ha' come in', says the stage-keeper at the beginning of Jonson's *Bartholomew Fair*, 'and ha' beene coozened i' the cloath-quarter, so finely!' The russet coat was one of old Dick's trade marks, and his habit of 'mistaking words, as the fashion is, in the stage-practice', was another. At this time, the common English name for a countryman was 'clown', derived from the Latin *colonus*. Tarlton may well have been responsible for the fact that the first recorded usage of the word in its modern sense, of stage buffoon, is around 1600 (see Plate 2).[112]

In the seventeenth century, Tarlton was succeeded as the greatest comedian of his day by John Lacy. Lacy was a brilliant impressionist whose imitations of country bumpkins and foreigners made him a favourite of Charles II. Aubrey recorded that Ben Jonson 'tooke a catalogue . . . of the Yorkshire dialect' from Lacy, who hailed from near Doncaster, as 'his hint for clownery' in *A Tale of a Tub*. On four occasions in the 1660s Samuel Pepys saw him in one of his most celebrated roles, the 'country fellow' or 'clowne', Johnny Thump, in Shirley's *Changes, or Love in a Maze*. In 1667 he also attended Edward Howard's *Change of Crowns* in which 'Lacy did act the country gentleman come up to court'. In addition, Pepys made reference to his having appeared in Richard Brome's *Jovial Crew*, one of the best comedies to be based around thieves' cant. Lacy may actually have been too skilful for his own good: his accent as Sauny the Scot in his own version of Shakespeare's *The Taming of the Shrew* was so strong that Pepys could not understand him. But his Irishman seems to have been more accessible to London audiences. John Evelyn saw him play the part of Teague in Sir Robert Howard's popular comedy, *The Committee*, in November 1662 and thought 'that mimic Lacy acted the Irish-footeman to admiration'. The following summer Pepys considered his interpretation of the character, 'beyond imagination' (see Plate 3).[113]

[112] Baskervill, *The Elizabethan Jig*, 90–9; Ben Jonson, *Bartholomew Fayre* (1631), 'Indvction', in *The Works of Ben Jonson*, ed. C. H. Herford and Percy Simpson (11 vols., Oxford, 1925–52), vi. 14; *OED*, s.v. 'clown'.

[113] Aubrey, *Brief Lives*, ed. Clark, ii. 14, 28; *The Diary of Samuel Pepys*, ed. Latham and Matthews, iii. 88, iv. 179, 181, viii. 158, 167–8, 195–6, 384, ix. 177–8, 411–12; *The Diary of John*

Thus characteristic features of the 'country clown' were well established in the minds of Londoners by the time Henry Peacham summed
him up in 1638.

> His ordinary discourse is of last year's hay, which he hopes will give six pounds
> the load at Smithfield, and of the rate of swine in Rumford market. All his jests
> consist in rude actions with the hand or foot. His speech is Lincolnshire about
> Wrangle and Frieston; if he be westward, about Taunton and ten miles beyond.

Restoration drama continued to be cluttered with provincial simpletons
and rustic boors who came up to town and betrayed their clownish manners and course dialects. John Dryden could not understand why gentlemen found the conversation of 'Cobb and Tib' a jest in 'the theatre, when
they would avoid it in the street', but the appetite for such material
remained undiminished.[114]

In the 1660s and 1670s Londoners were delighted by the jigs which
Thomas Jordan composed for civic pageants, such as 'A dialgoue betwixt
Tom and Dick, the former a country-man, the other a citizen'; 'The
Cheater's Cheated', which had as the butt of its joke the speech of Wat,
the Somerset clown; 'A countryman, a citizen, and sedition' which featured
Tom Hoyden of Taunton Dean; and the 'Musical Interlude' starring
'Crab, a west-countryman'. By the later seventeenth century, the dialect
speech of country lovers in wooing ballads was being accompanied by the
ridiculous love letters written between them in chapbook tales. Typically,
the Somerset man, Dick Downright, was made to pen one such epistle in
*True Lover's New Academy* which Pepys bought and added to his collection
of 'Penny Merriments'. In *Bog Witticisms* another choice example was
written by a country scrivener on behalf of a servant to his sweetheart, a
Welsh kitchen maid. These rustic characters were ridiculed not simply
because they were provincial but because they were ill-educated,
uncouth, and lowly. Significantly in George Stuart's dialogues of 1686
between two provincials of different rank, 'a Northumberland gentleman
and his tenant, a Scotchman', only the latter spoke in broad dialect.[115]

Crude as these comic stereotypes of popular drama and cheap print
were, they may well have been symptomatic of very marked differences in

*Evelyn*,ed. E. S. de Beer (6 vols., Oxford, 1955), iii. 345; Edwin Nungezer, *A Dictionary of Actors*
(Ithaca, NY, 1929), 230–3.

[114] Henry Peacham, *The Truth of Our Times* (1638), ed. Virgil B. Heltzel (Ithaca, NY, 1962),
216–17; Dryden, 'Defence of the Epilogue', in *Essays of John Dryden*, ed. Ker, i. 177.

[115] Baskervill, *The Elizabethan Jig*, 178–9, 316–18, 428–31, 473–90; Margaret Spufford, *Small
Books and Pleasant Histories: Popular Fiction and its Readership in Seventeenth-Century England* (London,
1981), 51–2, 55–6; Görlach, *Introduction to Early Modern English*, 399–401; George Stuart, *A
Joco-Serious Discourse: In Two Dialogues between a Northumberland-Gentleman and his Tenant a Scotchman*,

the texture of urban and rural life. Many of the important cultural developments of the period such as the growth of educational institutions, the ownership of books, and the consequent increases in literacy levels were much more evident in towns and cities than in the countryside.[116] This served to accentuate, or add another dimension to, the distinctions which had always existed between the social and intellectual environment of London and that of the provincial capitals, as between them and the smaller market centres, and then, in turn, between these and their surrounding hinterlands. The hierarchy of urbanization, which was mirrored by the hierarchy of educational provision and literacy levels, seems also to have been reflected in the hierarchy of 'purity' and 'civility' in speech. There was a big difference, thought Puttenham, between the English 'spoken in the the kings court, or in the good townes and cities' and that 'in the marches and frontiers, or in port townes', and the latter was different again from that to be heard 'in any vplandish village or corner of a realme, where is no resort but of poore rusticall or vnciuill people'.[117] The gulf between urban and rural English was a constant refrain of commentators on the language. 'Olde and obsolete wordes are most vsed of country folke', commented one Elizabethan. 'And what I say here of dialects is pertinent only to country people,' remarked Alexander Gil in 1619.[118] Other opinions from around the nation confirmed this distinction. Thus, Sir Thomas Smith made it clear in the 1540s that the peculiarities of pronunciation in his native Essex were confined only to the 'rustici'. In Suffolk, Reyce was later struck by the difference between the speech of the 'artificer of the good townes' and that of the 'honest country toyling villager'. 'And most of all if you listen to country people', it was said of Jacobean Somerset, 'it is easily possible to doubt whether they are speaking English, or some foreign language'. At the end of the seventeenth century, Hugh Todd boasted that 'in the citty and greater towns' of the diocese of Carlisle, 'they speak English with more propriety and a better accent than is done in most counties in England', although he was notably

---

both *Old Cavaliers* (London, 1686). Cf. Keith Thomas, 'The Place of Laughter in Tudor and Stuart England', *Times Literary Supplement* (21 Jan. 1977), 77.

[116] Peter Clark and Paul Slack, *English Towns in Transition, 1500–1700* (Oxford, 1976), 14, 23, 73, 153–4; Peter Clark, 'The Ownership of Books in England, 1560–1640: The Example of some Kentish Townsfolk', in Lawrence Stone (ed.), *Schooling and Society: Studies in the History of Education* (Baltimore, 1976), 108–9; David Cressy, *Literacy and the Social Order: Reading and Writing in Tudor and Stuart England* (Cambridge, 1980), 132–5.

[117] Puttenham, *The Arte of English Poesie*, 120.

[118] E.K., 'Epistle' to Edmund Spenser, *The Shepheardes Calender* (1579), in *Spenser: Poetical Works*, ed. J. C. Smith and E. De Selincourt (Oxford, 1912), 417; Gil, *Logonomia Anglica*, 18 (my trans.)

silent about the country districts. This same distinction clearly applied on
the 'Celtic fringes' no less. 'They have many words in the country that
citizens understand not', commented Sir William Brereton as he passed
through Lowland Scotland in 1635. A satirical attack on the Welsh in 1682
recognized similarly that 'their native gibberish is usually prattled through
the whole of Taphydom except in their market towns, whose inhabitants
being a little raised up do begin to despise it'.[119]

Significantly, it was in the last quarter of the sixteenth century that the
word 'rustical' came to be used not only to denote a rural dweller but also
to imply someone with the manners and speech to be found in the countryside. The cultural and behavioural connotations of the word are clear
when the city gentleman says to the country gentleman in a dialogue of
1579, that if youngsters are 'brought vp in the countrey till they bee six-
teene or eyghteene yeares olde, before which time they are so deeply
rooted in rusticitie', they will be beyond all civility. For, 'through rusticall
company in childehoode, [they] doo get them selues as it were an habite
in loughty lokes, clownish speech, an other ungentlemanly iestures, as it is
a good while (yea many times neuer) that these rusticities bee leaste'. By the
seventeenth century the standard dictionary definition of 'rusticity', and
even of 'rural', was 'clownish, vplandish, or churlish and vnmannerly', or
'rudeness: clownish behauiour'. It was then coming to be employed in the
language of differentiation within local society, as when the respectable
inhabitants of Manningtree petitioned the Essex county quarter sessions
in 1627 because the behaviour of local alehouse-keepers had grown 'so
rusticall that for the better sort it is almost no living with them'. By the
later seventeenth century, the adjective 'rustic' had more to do with
uncouth, and 'slovenly speech', than it had to do with things rural.[120]

In parallel with this, the term 'urbanity' was also coming to be used in
the sense of the best manners and speech, those to be found in the city. In
1586 Angel Daye defined it as meaning 'ciuile, courteous, gentle, modest

[119] Dobson, 'Early Modern Standard English', 27; Reyce, *Suffolk in the XVIIth Century*, ed.
Hervey, 55; Gil, *Logonomia Anglica*, 17 (my trans.); Hugh Todd, *Account of the City and Diocese of
Carlisle*, ed. R. S. Ferguson (Cumberland and Westmorland Antiquarian and Archaeological
Society, 5, Kendal, 1890), 33; Brereton, *Travels in Holland, the United Provinces, England, Scotland and
Ireland*, ed. Hawkins, 188–9; W. J. Hughes, *Wales and the Welsh in English Literature* (London, 1924),
45. For eighteenth-century comments to the same effect, see Sybil Rosenfeld, *Strolling Players and
Drama in the Provinces, 1660–1765* (Cambridge, 1939), 27; William Chapple, *A Review of Part of
Risdon's Survey of Devon* (Exeter, 1785), 55 n.
[120] *Cyuile and Vncyuile Life* (1579), in *Inedited Tracts*, ed. Hazlitt, 69; Cawdrey, *A Table
Alphabeticall*, sig. H4ᵛ; Bullokar, *An English Expositor*, sig. N4ᵛ; Cockeram, *The English Dictionarie*,
pt. i, sig. K1ᵛ; Blount, *Glossographia*, sig. Ll6ᵛ; Wrightson, *English Society, 1580–1680*, 170; Thomas
Fuller, *The History of the Worthies of England* (London, 1662), ii. 18; Holme, *The Academy of Armoury*,
iii. 72.

or well ruled, as men commonly are in cities and places of good gouern-
ment', but thought that, as yet, 'the word is not comon amongst vs'.
Within a generation, however, it had found its way into the new English
dictionaries where its linguistic connotations were clear: 'courtesie in
speech or behauiour', 'gentle in speech and gesture, pleasant in behaviour
and talk, comely, seemly'.[121] At the same time, in an age becoming increasingly preoccupied with manners and decorum, 'urbanity' was frequently
contrasted with 'rusticity' in discussions of propriety in wit and humour.[122]

These attitudes clearly had a significant influence on the emulative tendencies of the middling sort and others. As long as the 'rustic' dialects of
the countryside were considered comical and the 'smooth' speech of the
city was thought to be superior, there would be a natural tendency to be
embarrassed by the former and aspire to the latter. The 'mere gull citizen'
was no better than the typical country clown in John Earle's estimation,
only he was somewhat more 'polite' and 'the quality of the city hath
afforded hime some better dresse of clothes and language', which made
him 'sillily admir'd' by his rural neighbour. In Elizabethan Suffolk it was
already clear what an advantage in business it could be to speak in the best
London fashion. The tradesman 'of the good towne', whose imitative
tendencies struck Robert Reyce, found that his 'smooth speech, and civil
conversation increase the number of his customers'. He could also appeal
to a better class of clientele, and on purveying the goods, acquired
through his contact with London, 'to his best customers of the next neighbour villages, hee in short time climeth to much credit and wealth'.[123]

Such exposure to London fashion was highly significant, and the influence of the capital on the standards and tastes of the rest of the nation was
clearly enormous in this respect as in others. Young people, in particular,
poured into the metropolitan melting pot where they were exposed to the
latest modes and trends at an impressionable age. In the early seventeenth
century, 85 per cent of London's apprentices were from outside the city.
One of them was the 14-year-old John Lilburne, product of a minor gentry family from County Durham, who was immediately conspicuous by
his north-country speech, 'rough-hewen' manners, and ignorance of the

---

[121] Angel Daye, *The English Secretorie* (London, 1586), 39; Cawdrey, *A Table Alphabeticall*,
sig. I5ᵛ; Bullokar, *An English Expositor*, sig. P3ʳ; Cockeram, *The English Dictionarie*, pt. i, sig. L4ʳ;
Blount, *Glossographia*, sig. Tt8ʳ.

[122] Lodowick Bryskett, *A Discovrse of Civill Life* (London, 1606), 245–6; Edward Reyner, *Rules
for the Government of the Tongue* (London, 1656), 223–7; Dryden, 'A Discourse Concerning the
Original and Progress of Satire', in *Essays of John Dryden*, ed. Ker, ii. 75; Anthony Ashley Cooper,
*Sensus Communis: An Essay on the Freedom of Wit and Humour* (London, 1709), 19.

[123] John Earle, *Micro-cosmographie: Or, a Peece of the World Discovered; in Essayes and Characters*
(London, 1629), sig. G9; Reyce, *Suffolk in the XVIIth Century*, ed. Hervey, 59.

best etiquette, all of which deficiencies he set out to amend. When such people later returned to the provinces, as often happened, they became transmitters of the new refinements from centre to locality. In the century after 1650, one in every six adults is estimated to have lived in the capital city at some point during his or her life. That this had a strong influence on the emulation of its speech in the provinces is suggested by the proverb common in Cheshire, that 'She has been at London to call a "strea" a "straw" and a "waw" a "wall"', which was said in 1670 to be one 'the common people use in scorn of those who having been at London are ashamed to speak their own country dialect'. At the same time, Cornish people were said to speak better English than their West Country neighbours by virtue of copying 'the gentry and merchants' who had brought the language from London and 'imitated the dialect of the court, which is the most nice and accurate . . .'.[124]

So it was that linguistic development in the early modern period may be said to have accentuated and exacerbated some of the fundamental distinctions within English society. There had always been disparities of wealth and status which were underscored by variations in manners and tastes. The cultural differences between urban and rural environments, or between the ambience of larger cities and that of smaller towns, were scarcely new in the sixteenth and seventeenth centuries. But linguistic change added new dimensions to these existing cleavages. Patterns of speech both reflected the important social changes of this period and in many ways contributed to them. At the same time, however, these developments had assimilating tendencies which were felt quite far down in society. Artisan's wives and tradesmen, servants and apprentices, all adapted to the circumstances in which they found themselves; they too had to come to terms with a social system in which speech both expressed and determined place.

Patterns of speech in sixteenth- and seventeenth-century England confirm the picture of a society in which for the majority of people local affinities and identities still subsumed national ones, in which 'country' meant neighbourhood, and mental horizons were fundamentally

---

[124] Elliott, 'Single Women in the London Marriage Market', 84; Pauline Gregg, *Free-Born John: A Biography of John Lilburne* (London, 1961), 37; E. A. Wrigley, 'A Simple Model of London's Importance in Changing English Society and Economy, 1650–1750', *Past and Present*, 37 (1967), 49–51; John Ray, *A Collection of English Proverbs* (Cambridge, 1670), 218; William Camden, *Britannia*, ed. Edmund Gibson (London, 1695), 146. For this kind of emulation with regard to dress, see *The Life of Adam Martindale Written by Himself*, ed. Richard Parkinson (Chetham Society, 4, Manchester, 1845), 18.

parochial. Local dialects remained intact in their myriad diversity and mutual opacity as a demonstration of the limits of national incorporation and cultural standardization. Despite this, however, they were not immune from the significant changes in the spoken language at this time as people of all ranks were encouraged to participate in the process of linguistic reform by a social system in which speech was an important determinant of position. The standard was set by the upper ranks in and around London, and the extraordinary growth of the metropolis during these centuries had a huge influence on the wider nation, as an agent of cultural integration no less than a motor of economic growth.

# 2
## Proverbial Wisdom

Among other thyngs profityng in our tong
Those whiche much may profit both old and yong
Suche as on their fruite will feede or take holde
Are our comon playne pithy prouerbes olde.
Some sence of some of whiche beyng bare and rude
Yet to fyne and fruitefull effect they allude.
And theyr sentences include so large a reache
That almost in all thinges good lessons they teache.

John Heywood, *A Dialogue Conteinyng the Nomber*
*in Effect of all the Prouerbes in the Englishe Tongue*
(London, 1546), sig. A1ᵛ.

That which is in euerye mans mouthe, is not spoken without
cause . . . The Englyshe prouerbe sayeth thus: It is lyke to be true
that euery man sayeth.

Richard Taverner, *Proverbes or Adagies, Gathered oute of the Chiliades*
*of Erasmus* (London, 1552), fo. 57ᵛ.

OF central importance to the modes of thought and expression which
epitomize England in the sixteenth and seventeenth centuries was the
proverb. This period, it may justly be said, witnessed the golden age of
proverbial expression in European intellectual life. English society, in
common with other contemporary cultures, was one which relied heavily
on oral traditions and supported a wide variety of unstandardized vernacular forms. At the same time, however, in an age of expanding formal
education and the rapidly emerging technology of print, sententious wisdom assumed the status of a didactic tool and a literary genre to a degree
which it has enjoyed neither before nor since.

Contemporaries repeatedly laced their conversation with old adages,
filled their writings with trusted maxims, and delighted in making collections of choice dicta. Not surprisingly, many attempts were made to
define this most popular of verbal and literary forms. To the Elizabethan
antiquary, Richard Carew, proverbs were 'concise in words but plentifull
in number, briefely pointing at many great matters, and vnder the circuite

of a few syllables prescribing sundry auaileable caueats'. The churchman
Thomas Fuller later agreed that 'a proverb is much matter decocted into
few words'. The six properties which he believed essential to it, 'namely
that it be, 1. Short 2. Playn 3. Common 4. Figurative 5. Antient 6. True',
were transcribed approvingly into the diary of the Reverend John Ward
who took the living at Stratford-upon-Avon in 1662. Proverbs, according
to one early eighteenth-century student, were 'short, dogmatical concise
sentences, accommodated to the principal concerns of life; commonly
used, and commonly known: and, for the most part, conceived in figurative expressions . . .'.[1]

In sixteenth- and seventeenth-century England there were some
12,000 proverbs and proverbial phrases in regular use, many times more
than the number currently circulating.[2] It is the sheer ubiquity of gnomic
sayings at this time, and the frequency with which they were recorded in
all manner of writings, which both demands their analysis and makes it
readily possible. To students of popular mentalities, moreover, proverbs
represent a source of particular value. They express the 'common sense'
by which a people is defined; they preserve the knowledge which they
find most useful; they enshrine the values which they hold most dear. To
those interested in the evolving relationship between oral and literate
modes of cognition and communication, proverbs provide a vivid insight
into the structure of mental categories and the ways in which verbal
forms can migrate between the spoken and textual realms.

## SAYINGS OF THE PHILOSOPHERS

By the early modern period, proverbs had been the object of reflection
and veneration for many centuries. A variety of fragmentary evidence
confirms their collection in Anglo-Saxon England and during the renaissance of the twelfth century a greatly enhanced repertoire of adages and
wise sentences entered common circulation via schoolmen and scholas-
tics. Even in the early Middle Ages the study of proverbs had been integral to a training in rhetoric: the brief, pithy, memorable, and authoritative

---

[1] Richard Carew, 'The Excellencie of the English Tongue', in William Camden, *Remaines,
Concerning Britaine* (2nd edn., London, 1614), 39, and cf. 301; Thomas Fuller, *The History of the
Worthies of England* (London, 1662), i. 5; *The Diary of the Rev. John Ward, A.M., Vicar of Stratford-
upon-Avon, Extending from 1648 to 1679*, ed. Charles Severn (London, 1839), 110; James Kelly, *A
Complete Collection of Scottish Proverbs, Explained and Made Intelligible to the English Reader* (London,
1721), sig. A3.

[2] M. P. Tilley, *A Dictionary of the Proverbs in England in the Sixteenth and Seventeenth Centuries* (Ann
Arbor, Mich., 1950); F. P. Wilson, *The Oxford Dictionary of English Proverbs* (3rd edn., Oxford, 1970);
John Simpson and Jennifer Speake, *The Concise Oxford Dictionary of Proverbs* (3rd edn., Oxford, 1998).

quality of these phrases recommended them in oratory and preaching, no less than in the writing of letters and treatises. By the later medieval period they were being employed and disseminated widely in imaginative literature, featuring prominently in the works of Gower, Lydgate, and especially Chaucer. Thus the standard dictionary of proverbs and proverbial phrases compiled from sources mostly before 1500, lists a total of 9,233 items. Many express a body of morality, wisdom, and advice which was common across medieval Europe, the accumulated intellectual capital of Western civilization and the Judaeo-Christian tradition.[3]

From the beginning, the Church had been an essential vehicle for the dissemination of this heritage and many proverbs were clearly fed into popular circulation via the pulpit. Preachers had long disseminated sententious wisdom in their sermons, drawn both from the Bible and from the collections of 'Proverbys of Phylosopherys' which circulated in manuscript as source-books for pulpit orators. Latin sermons of the later Middle Ages were full of sayings which would become well known in the vernacular: 'Many hands make light work'; 'Enough is as good as a feast'; or that favourite adage attributed to St Bernard, 'He who loves me, loves my dog'. In the fifteenth century, for example, the Latin 'proverbs of certain philosophers' compiled by John Hall, Fellow of King's College, Cambridge, and later rector of Garboldisham in Norfolk, included some future household favourites well before their appearance in vernacular sources: 'Cut your coat according to your cloth'; 'Remember the past; set the present in order; provide for the future'; and 'Virtues, not parents, constitute nobility'.[4]

The English sermons of the fourteenth and fifteenth centuries, meanwhile, abounded with the homely saws through which preachers sought to appeal to the sensibilities of unlearned audiences. They were replete with the idiom of everyday life, the language of ordinary men and women in market-place, tavern, and field: 'as it is seid in comen proverbe—"Pride goth bifore, and schame cometh after"'; 'It is an olde sawe—"Swych lord, swyche meyne"'; 'for it is seyd—"He that fool sendyth, fool abydeth"'. Thanks to this pulpit literature we know that then, as now, people would say of children, 'He is his father's son', or 'As the mother, so is the

---

[3] W. W. Skeat, *Early English Proverbs Chiefly of the Thirteenth and Fourteenth Centuries* (Oxford, 1910); Janet E. Heseltine, 'Introduction', in W. G. Smith, *The Oxford Dictionary of English Proverbs* (Oxford, 1935), viii–x; B. J. Whiting, *Chaucer's Use of Proverbs* (Cambridge, Mass., 1934); B. J. Whiting, *Proverbs, Sentences, and Proverbial Phrases from English Writings mainly before 1500* (Cambridge, Mass., and London, 1968).

[4] G. R. Owst, *Literature and Pulpit in Medieval England* (2nd edn., Oxford, 1961), 42–3, 183; *The Dicts and Sayings of the Philosophers*, ed. Curt F. Buhler (Early English Text Society, orig. ser., 211, London, 1941); William Worcestre, *Itineraries*, ed. John H. Harvey (Oxford, 1969), 364–6.

daughter'; and that it was 'a comone proverbe bothe of clerkes and of lay men—"yonge seynt, old dewell"'. In these habitual sooths we hear some immemorial themes. Thus the dull tones of patriarchy resonate in the 'old Englysch sawe' which decreed that 'a mayde schulde be seen but not herd', or the proverbial phrase that women are 'ever jangelynge as a pye, other a jay'. We detect also in these sermons the grudging attitude of the commonality towards their clergy grumbling through the text. 'It is a comon seynge of the pepull' complained one preacher '"ye latt God and me alone!"'; 'But there is many that carythe not for the preste, ne for the chyrche', lamented another, 'For thei wil sey—"it is no wilde catt, ne it wyll not flee"'. And the quiet resignation of the poor, downtrodden multitude echoes across the centuries: 'As it is seide in olde proverbe— "Pore be hangid bi the necke; a riche man bi the purs"'; 'Yf hope were not, herte shulde breke'; 'And therefore hit is seide in proverbe that he, that best is, most loweth him'.[5]

Together with the Church, the schools also played an important part in the dissemination of wise and edifying sayings. By the fifteenth century it had long been a didactic technique of schoolmasters to quote Latin proverbs at their charges for identification and explanation: 'Quis? Quid? Quomodo? Cur? Quibus auxiliis?' were the accompanying questions. In addition, it was common practice to provide collections of familiar English phrases, with Latin translations underneath, as a means both of teaching language and imparting morality. Through the rendering of these sentences and aphorisms, or 'vulgars', much proverbial wisdom was formally inculcated at an impressionable age.[6] Thus, one notebook, probably written by a Lincolnshire schoolmaster around 1425–50, contains early recordings of some well-known vernacular saws. Among them were, 'Better a friend at court than a penny in purse'; 'The burnt hand dreads the fire'; 'Pepper is black but has a good smack'; 'Be the summer day never so long, at last comes evensong'.[7] Two of these proverbs were also among those which boys attending Magdalen College school, Oxford, under John Stanbridge's tutelage between 1488 and 1494 were required to render into 'latins'. Others included: 'Thou hyttes the nayle on the heed'; 'A gyuen hors may not [be] loked in the teethe'; 'He is an euyll

[5] Owst, *Literature and Pulpit in Medieval England*, 41–6, 463 n. Cf. Chaucer's Pardoner with his Latin tags 'To saffron with my predicacioun, And for to stire hem to devocioun': *The Riverside Chaucer*, ed. Larry D. Benson (3rd edn., Boston, Mass., 1987), 194.

[6] Archer Taylor, 'The Study of Proverbs', in his *Selected Writings on Proverbs* ed. Wolfgang Mieder (Helsinki, 1975), 74; Nicholas Orme, *English Schools in the Middle Ages* (London, 1973), 99; id., *Education and Society in Medieval and Renaissance England* (London, 1989), 78–80.

[7] Orme, *Education and Society in Medieval and Renaissance England*, 82–5.

coke that can not lycke his owne lyppes'; 'Wysshers and wolders be small hous holders'. Robert Whittinton was one of Stanbridge's pupils to propagate these methods in his own pedagogy. Whittinton's *Vulgaria* offered many wise observations to his schoolboys, which 'it is comenly sayd'. 'Therefore is wysdome to be ware of had I wyste', they advised: do not 'offereth a candell to the deuyll', they warned. Remember 'many a ragged colt proued to [be] a good horse'; 'it is better a chylde vnborne than vntaught'; 'for maners (as they say) maketh man'; and 'one scabbed shepe (as they saye) marreth a hole flocke'.[8]

In the early sixteenth century, however, there were two important developments which greatly increased the influence of both church and school as vehicles for the purveying of proverbial wisdom. The first was the Reformation with its renewed emphasis on preaching and its insistence that people should experience the word of God for themselves. This, allied to the revolution in production and distribution of the written word occasioned by printing, transformed the extent to which the Bible and its immense stock of phrases and formulae entered the fabric of the language. By the 1630s the clergy had become an entirely graduate profession, while at least 500,000 copies of the Bible had been printed in England by the end of the seventeenth century. The influence of these developments is suggested by the fact that 179 of the 11,776 proverbs listed in Tilley's modern dictionary are of biblical origin.[9]

The Book of Proverbs, in particular, provided a fund of moralistic wisdom which fed into the commonplaces of the nation. 'The dog returns to his vomit'; 'Answer a fool according to his folly'; 'Hope delayed afflicts the heart'; 'A contented mind is a continual feast'; 'A good name is better than riches'; 'The tongue breaks bone though itself has none'.[10] At the same time, the Gospel of St Matthew, in particular, provided a large quantity of aphoristic wisdom which seeped into subliminal values and

---

[8] *The Vulgaria of John Stanbridge and the Vulgaria of Robert Whittinton*, ed. Beatrice White (Early English Text Society, orig. ser., 187, London, 1932): for these and other proverbs, see 15, 18, 23, 26, 27, 30, 71, 72, 84, 89, 93, 94, 98, 107, 108, 109, 115, 116. For other examples, cf. *A Fifteenth-Century School Book*, ed. William Nelson (Oxford, 1956); William Horman, *Vulgaria* (London, 1519).

[9] Rosemary O'Day, 'The Anatomy of a Profession: The Clergy and the Church of England', in Wilfrid Prest (ed.), *The Professions in Early Modern England* (London, 1987), 47; T. W. Laqueur, 'The Cultural Origins of Popular Literacy in England, 1500–1850', *Oxford Review of Education*, 2 (1976), 262; Tilley, *Dictionary of the Proverbs in England*.

[10] For these and others, see Proverbs 25: 11 (Tilley, A297); 20: 14 (B445); 26: 11 (D455); 26: 5 (F442); 27: 22 (F447); 14: 15 (F456); 17: 28 (F531); 20: 3 (F546); 13: 12 (H600); 15: 15 (M969); 22: 1 (N22); 19: 17 (P471); 15: 30 (R85); 19: 4 (R103); 28: 20 (R106); 23: 5 (R111); 13: 24 (R155); 30: 18 (S349); 6: 9 (S547); 11: 15 (S1009); 25: 15 (T403); 1: 17 (V3); 10: 26 (V64); 9: 17 (W131); 28: 1 (W333); 16: 16 (W526); 15: 1 (W822).

everyday speech. From it people learned to 'do as you would be done to' and to beware 'a wolf in sheep's clothing'. They were told not 'to strain at a gnat and swallow a camel', not to let 'thy left hand know what thy right hand doeth', not 'to hide your light under a bushel', not to 'cast pearls before swine' and not 'to build on sand'. They were reminded that they 'cannot serve God and mammon', that 'no man can serve two masters' and that 'no man is prophet in his own country'. They became accustomed to asking, 'Is it not lawful for me to do what I will with mine own?', and to saying, 'With what measure you mete, it shall be measured unto you'. They could take comfort from the fact that 'he that seeks finds' and 'blessed are the peacemakers', but they knew that while 'the spirit is willing, the flesh is weak' and though 'many are called, few are chosen'.[11]

Together with the Reformation, the other important development of the early Tudor period was the spread of Renaissance humanism. The fresh impetus given to classical learning entailed by its intellectual developments had a huge influence on European education and by the second decade of the sixteenth century the curricula of the English grammar schools were beginning to reflect the influence of the New Learning. The renewed emphasis on ancient authors further enhanced the use of gnomic sentences as a didactic technique. Works which illustrated or collected proverbial wisdom, such as the *Fables* of Aesop and the *Distichs* of Cato, became standard textbooks and writings which were replete with wise sayings, such as the comedies of Terence or the orations of Cicero, were adopted as required reading.[12]

Most significant of all in this respect was the work of Erasmus. In ten editions of *Adages* printed between 1500 and 1536 he was responsible for collecting and publishing a total of 4,251 quotations, tags, and proverbs gathered from ancient Greek and Latin authors. This 'Herculean labour' of editorial scholarship was responsible for popularizing a huge corpus of phrase and formula in sixteenth-century Europe. It was largely thanks to Erasmus' intellectual mediation between ancients and moderns that people in Tudor England first learned, for example, 'to squeeze water out

---

[11] See Matthew, 12: 34 (Tilley, A13); 22: 21 (C9); 24: 28 (C73); 4: 6 (D230); 7: 12 (D395); 18: 9 (E226); 26: 41 (F363); 23: 24 (G150); 6: 24 (G253); 6: 3 (H79); 5: 15 (L275); 6: 24 (M322); 13: 57 (M329); 7: 2 (M801); 5: 7 (M895); 7: 3 (M1191); 20: 15 (O99); 5: 9 (P155); 7: 6 (P165); 7: 26 (S88); 7: 8 (S213); 23: 27 (S225); 26: 41 (S760); 5: 45 (S985); 6: 21 (T485); 12: 33 (T497); 7: 15 (W614).

[12] Orme, *English Schools in the Middle Ages*, 111; Foster Watson, *The English Grammar Schools to 1660: Their Curriculum and Practice* (Cambridge, 1908), 121–2, 315, 357–8, 370–1; T. W. Baldwin, *William Shakspere's Small Latine and Lesse Greeke* (2 vols., Urbana, Ill., 1944), i. 181, 581–606; 'Introduction', in *John Heywood's 'A Dialogue of Proverbs'*, ed. Rudolph E. Habenicht (Berkeley and Los Angeles, 1963), 3–12; Kenneth Charlton, *Education in Renaissance England* (London, 1965), 110, 243; David Cressy, *Education in Tudor and Stuart England* (London, 1975), 81–4.

of a stone', 'to leave no stone unturned', and not to put 'the cart before the horse'. It was from this influence that they came to think that 'the grass is greener in the next field' and that 'there's many a slip twixt cup and lip'; that 'one swallow does not make a summer', and that 'God helps those who help themselves'. They came to appreciate the virtue of having 'an iron in the fire', of calling 'a spade and spade', and enduring 'a necessary evil'; they came to realize when someone was 'blowing their own trumpet', was 'like a dog in a manger', or was 'in the same boat' as themselves. Now they might 'sleep on it'; then they could be 'up to their ears'; and when they were not 'ready to die laughing', their 'hearts were in their boots'.[13]

The principal purpose of the *Adages* was educative, and in England a number of schoolmasters published their own compilations of sentences and proverbs taken from Erasmus' works. A huge new corpus of Latin tags and phrases entered the grammar schools which pupils were required to identify and translate, repeat, and write upon. The first known epitome of Erasmian adages was the *Dicta Sapientum* published by Thomas Berthelet in the 1520s, 'very necessary and profitable for children to lerne and good for all folkes to rede or to here redde'. In 1539 Richard Taverner, clerk of the privy seal under Thomas Cromwell, issued a collection of 178 'proverbes or adagies' from the same source, with English translations and glosses, as part of his literary efforts in the Protestant cause. In the 1540s the Eton schoolmaster, Nicholas Udall, rendered a further 140 examples in the tradition of the 'sayings of the philosophers', preferring these themes to write upon over 'suche as been commenly vsed' which contained 'for the moste parte . . . nothyng but litle trifleyng senses voide of all pith or fruite'.[14]

In addition, most of the English-Latin dictionaries aimed at schools during the sixteenth century contained proverbial phrases in their illustrations. 'Nor I haue omitted prouerbes, called adagia, or other quicke sentences, whiche I thought necessarie to be had in remembraunce', advised Sir Thomas Elyot in 1538, prefacing the first work of its kind in England to be inspired by the Renaissance rediscovery of classical Latin. Subsequent editions of his dictionary were produced by Thomas Cooper

---

[13] Margaret Mann Phillips, *The 'Adages' of Erasmus: A Study with Translations* (Cambridge, 1964), 3, 7.

[14] Desiderius Erasmus, *Dicta Sapientu[m]: The Sayenges of the Wyse Me[n] of Grece in Latin with the Englysshe Folowyng* (London, 1527?); Richard Taverner, *Proverbes or Adagies with Newe Addicions Gathered out of the Chiliades of Erasmus* (London, 1539); Desiderius Erasmus, *Apophthegmes*, trans. Nicholas Udall (London, 1542), ***i. See *John Heywood's 'A Dialogue of Proverbs'*, ed. Habenicht, 21–6.

in 1548, 1552, and 1559. Cooper's own monumental *Thesavrvs Lingvae Romanae et Britannicae* was reported to be still 'chained to the desk' in schools in the mid-seventeenth century, and it remained 'a most useful worke' long after that.[15] These lexicons were joined by those of Richard Huloet, John Baret, and John Withals, which went through various editions between 1553 and 1634, in purveying gnomic wisdom to young scholars.[16]

Following in the Erasmian tradition, many of the standard textbooks of the Tudor grammar school consisted of ancient *dicta*. William Baldwyn's, *A Treatise of Morall Phylosophie, Contaynyng the Sayinges of the Wyse* was first published in 1547 and had gone through twenty-three different editions by 1651. This, together with Nicholas Ling's *Politeuphuia* (1597), was among the works of reference still being recommended by Charles Hoole in 1660 as sources from which schoolboys should gather 'witty sentences'.[17] In 1621 Bartholomew Robertson provided accompanying translations to 500 proverbs from Erasmus, published in a slim octavo volume for the benefit of those 'who aspire to further perfection in the Latine tongue', while in the 1630s, John Clarke, the master of Lincoln grammar school, issued *Paroemiologia Anglo-Latina*, a similar collection of Erasmian adages with English parallels. 'These proverbs though excellent in all mens discourse, use-full upon all occasion to every man', he advised, 'be chiefly intended for the use of grammar-schooles; and therefore the industrious schoolemaster may please, every day to cause his scholars to repeat a head or two after their parts, and interpret them . . .'. One of Clarke's pupils at Lincoln was William Walker who went on to be master himself at Grantham grammar school. In 1672 he published his own version of *Paroemiologia*, 'for the use of schools'.[18]

[15] Sir Thomas Elyot, *The Dictionary* (London, 1538), sig. A3ᵛ; Thomas Cooper, *Thesavrvs Lingvae Romanae et Britannicae* (London, 1565); Thomas Fuller, *The Holy State* (Cambridge, 1642), 109; John Aubrey, *Brief Lives*, ed. Andrew Clark (2 vols., Oxford, 1898), i. 183.

[16] Richard Huloet, *Abcedarivm Anglico-Latinvm* (London, 1552); John Baret, *An Alvearie or Triple Dictionarie, in Englishe, Latin, and French* (London, 1573); John Withals, *A Dictionary in English and Latine; Devised for the Capacitie of Children, and Young Beginners* (London, 1634), 539–84.

[17] William Baldwyn, *A Treatise of Morall Phylosophie, Contaynyng the Sayinges of the Wyse* (London, 1547), esp. bks. 3–4; Nicholas Ling, *Politeuphuia: Wits Common Wealth* (London, 1597), esp. fos. 166ᵛ–172ᵛ; Charles Hoole, *A New Discovery of the Old Art of Teaching Schoole* (London, 1660), 182. See, Louis B. Wright, *Middle-Class Culture in Elizabethan England* (Chapel Hill, NC, 1935), 146–53; Baldwin, *William Shakspere's Small Latine and Lesse Greeke*, i. 24–5, 704, ii. 291; Charlton, *Education in Renaissance England*, 243–4.

[18] Desiderius Erasmus, *Adagia in Latine and English*, trans. Bartholomew Robertson (London, 1621); John Clarke, *Paroemiologia Anglo-Latina in Usum Scholarum Concinnata* (London, 1639), sig. A6; William Walker, *Idiomatologia Anglo-Latina* (3rd edn., London, 1680), sig. A2ʳ; id., *Paroemiologia Anglo-Latina* (London, 1672).

This same method of instruction by translating familiar sayings was adopted not only in learning Latin but also modern European languages. Thus in 1573 James Sanforde included 'certayne Italian prouerbes and sentences, done into Englishe' in his celebration of that nation's worthy deeds and learned insights. At the same time, the great mediator between the Italian and English tongues, John Florio, published 'diuers prouerbes, sentences, and golden sayinges' in his two books of *Fruits*. 'Touching prouerbs' he opined, who 'inuents them, no man finer; and aplyes them, no man fitter . . .'. And in 1642 Giovanni Torriano produced the first volume entirely dedicated to Italian proverbs.[19] Meanwhile, collections of Spanish maxims were included in the textbook of William Stepney, annexed to the grammar and incorporated into the dialogues of John Minsheu, and interspersed in the dictionary of John Sanford.[20] Equally, choice Gallic examples were cited throughout the French–English lexicons of Claudius Hollyband, Randle Cotgrave, and Guy Miege, while both G. Delamothe and John Wodroephe printed scores of French proverbs and sayings with English equivalents in their guides to that language.[21]

It was also commonly believed that much could be learned about foreign countries and gleaned about national characteristics through the study of indigenous proverbs. 'The genius, wit, and spirit of a nation, are discovered by their proverbs,' Francis Bacon is said to have opined. It was for this reason that Fynes Moryson, in his extensive travels through Europe between 1591 and 1617, collected the proverbs, 'by reading and discourse', which epitomized the character of 'divers nations and provinces'. Meanwhile, 'the proverbs of sev[er]all nations were much studied' by the Jacobean bishop, Lancelot Andrewes, 'and the reason hee gave was, because by them he knew the minds of sev[er]all nations, which is a brave thing: as wee count him a wise man that knowes the mindes and insides of men, which is done by knowing what is habituall to them'.[22]

---

[19] James Sanforde, *The Garden of Pleasure* (London, 1573), fos. 101ᵛ–110ᵛ; John Florio, *Florio His Firste Fruites* (London, 1578), epist. ded., 31–4, and *passim*; John Florio, *Florios Second Frutes* (London, 1591), sig. A4ʳ; Giovanni Torriano, *Select Italian Proverbs* (Cambridge, 1642).

[20] William Stepney, *The Spanish Schoole-master* (London, 1591); John Minsheu, *A Spanish Grammar* (London, 1599), 75–84; John Minsheu, *Pleasant and Delightfull Dialogves in Spanish and English* (London, 1599), esp. 10–11, 21, 60; John Sanford, *An Entrance to the Spanish Tongve* (London, 1611).

[21] Claudius Hollyband, *The Frenche Littleton* (London, 1576), sigs. D6ᵛ–E2ʳ; Randle Cotgrave, *A Dictionarie of the French and English Tongves* (London, 1611); Guy Miege, *A New Dictionary French and English with another English and French* (London, 1677); G. Delamothe, *The Treasvre of the French Tovng* (London, 1592); John Wodroephe, *The Spared Hovres of a Sovldier in his Travels: Or the True Marrowe of the French Tongue* (London, 1623), 474–523; and see also Edward Leigh, *Analecta de XII. Primus Caesaribus* (2nd edn., London, 1647), sigs. P5–Q7.

[22] Bacon quoted on title-page of Kelly, *A Complete Collection of Scottish Proverbs*; Fynes

The same spirit informed the desire to publish collections of sayings drawn from the stock of various European countries. In the 1630s the poet George Herbert, rector of Fugglestone-with-Bemerton, Wiltshire, assembled a list of 910 'Outlandish Proverbs', and he was to have many followers over the succeeding century.[23]

The literary fashion for collecting English sayings began in 1546 when the poet and dramatist John Heywood published his *Dialogue of Proverbs*, a conversation in rhyme containing some 1,267 proverbs, proverbial phrases, and epithets. All subsequent compilers of English proverbs took their starting point from Heywood. His work was the origin of the proverbs which William Camden included in the second edition of his *Remaines, Concerning Britaine* in 1614, as it was of those which the future Historiographer Royal, James Howell, published together with examples from foreign nations in 1659. Soon afterwards Thomas Fuller built his *Worthies of England* around the canon of saws which could be said to be county specific, on the basis that 'you may behold how each county is innated with a particular genius, inclining the natives to be dextrous, some in one profession, some in another'. Finally, in 1670 the naturalist John Ray culled material from all of the major printed collections since Heywood for his *Collection of English Proverbs*, a volume which he enlarged with contributions from friends and correspondents eight years later.[24]

Beyond mere dictionaries, many other works of the period were based around familiar gnomic sayings and by the Elizabethan period 'proverb literature' had become a popular genre. Thus the poet, John Davies of Hereford, wrote *Upon English Proverbs*, an epigram in the manner of John Heywood which comprised rhymes on 418 favourite old saws. In 1590 Robert Greene produced *The Royal Exchange*, a work 'contayning sundry

Moryson, *An Itinerary Containing His Ten Yeeres Travell* (4 vols., Glasgow, 1907–8), iii. 426–63; *Table Talk of John Selden*, ed. Sir Frederick Pollock (London, 1927), 115.

[23] George Herbert, 'Outlandish Proverbs', and 'Jacula Prudentum', in *The Works of George Herbert*, ed. F. E. Hutchinson (Oxford, 1941), 321–62; James Howell, *Proverbs, or, Old Sayed Sawes and Adages, in English (or the Saxon Tongue), Italian, French and Spanish* (London, 1659); N.R., *Proverbs English, French, Dutch, Italian, and Spanish: All Englished and Alphabetically Digested* (London, 1659); Robert Codrington, *A Collection of Many Select, and Excellent Proverbs out of Several Languages* (London, 1672); Thomas Fuller, *Gnomologia: Adagies and Proverbs, Wise Sentences and Witty Sayings, Ancient and Modern, Foreign and British* (London, 1732).

[24] John Heywood, *A Dialogue Conteinyng the Nomber in Effect of all the Prouerbes in the Englishe Tongue* (London, 1546); Camden, *Remaines, Concerning Britaine*, 301–15; Howell, *Proverbs, or, Old Sayed Saws and Adages*; Fuller, *The History of the Worthies of England*, i. 53; John Ray, *A Collection of English Proverbs* (Cambridge, 1670; 2nd edn., 1678). The county proverbs arranged by Fuller were reproduced by Ray and copied again by antiquaries such as Browne Willis, Samuel Pegge, and Francis Grose during the eighteenth century: see Bod. Lib., MS Willis 2, fo. 84; Bod. Lib., MS Eng. Lang. e. 4, 151–216; Francis Grose, *A Provincial Glossary with a Collection of Local Proverbs and Popular Superstitions* (London, 1787), sigs. K5–S6.

aphorisms of phylosophie, and golden principles of morall and naturall quadruplicities'. Typical of these were, 'to shutte the stable doore when the steede is stolne, is to wishe for a showre of rayne when haruest is past'; and '*Ex abundantia cordis os loquitur*: alluding to our olde English prouerbe, what the hart thinketh, the tongue clacketh'. The vogue both for proverbs and for 'quadruplicities' was also exploited by Nicholas Breton in *The Figure of Foure* (1597) and *Crossing of Proverbs* (1616).[25]

Throughout the seventeenth century popular literature continued to reflect the appeal of witty, improving, and useful sentences to an ever expanding reading public. A collection of the sayings attributed to James I was published posthumously in a handy octavo: among its general observations were aphorisms such as 'false miracles and lying news, are the food of superstition', and 'a good pastor is the phisitian of the soule'. There followed works such as *The Country-mans New Common-Wealth* (1647), a tract containing 'witty sentences, pithy sayings, quaint observations, both divine and moral', or John Spencer's *Things New and Old* (1658), a 'storehouse of similies, sentences, allegories, apophthegms, adagies, apologues, divine, morall, politicall'. Similar flowers of rhetoric were included in the fashionable genre of conversation manuals which included Thomas Blount's *Academie of Eloquence* (1654), with its collection of 'common places', together with Edward Phillips' *Mysteries of Love and Eloquence* (1658) and William Winstanley's *New Help to Discourse* (1669), both of which contained short lists of proverbs.[26]

Formal education and the printed word clearly bore much responsibility for the dissemination and inculcation of proverbial wisdom, therefore. It was through the didactic process and their own reading that many people learned the goodly morals and ancient maxims which guided and sustained them throughout their lives. However casually some sayings may have been absorbed in conversation, a large number were clearly instilled in a quite deliberate fashion. 'At grammer-scole I lerned a verse', recalled the early Tudor agricultural writer Sir Anthony Fitzherbert, 'that is this,

[25] John Davies, *Vpon English Prouerbes*, in *The Complete Works of John Davies of Hereford*, ed. A. B. Grosart (2 vols., Edinburgh, 1878), ii. 41–50; Robert Greene, *The Royal Exchange* (1590), in *The Life and Complete Works in Prose and Verse of Robert Greene*, ed. A. B. Grosart (15 vols., London, 1881–6), vii. 245, 255; Nicholas Breton, *Crossing of Proverbs* (1616), and *The Figure of Foure* (1636), in *The Works in Verse and Prose of Nicholas Breton*, ed. A. B. Grosart (2 vols., Edinburgh, 1879), ii. e, f, and see appendix, 57–9.

[26] James I, *Flores Regij: Or, Proverbes and Aphorismes, Divine and Morall . . . Collected by J.L.S.* (London, 1627), 163, 165; *The Country-mans New Common-Wealth* (London, 1647); John Spencer, *Kaina Kai Palaia: Things New and Old* (London, 1658); Thomas Blount, *The Academie of Eloquence* (London, 1654), 49–118; Edward Phillips, *The Mysteries of Love and Eloquence* (London, 1658), 158–64; W[illiam] W[instanley], *The New Help to Discourse* (London, 1669), 310.

*Sanat, sanctificat, et ditat surgere mane.* That is to say, Erly rysyng maketh a man hole in body, holer in soule, and rycher in goodes.' His successor Thomas Tusser later recalled his days at Eton, where 'the latin phraies' were drummed in by the translator of Erasmus, Nicholas Udall. '*Sed non nascitur ridiculus mus*, as the proverbe of Erasmus is', recorded the Gloucestershire estate steward, John Smyth, a product of Derby Free School in the 1570s.[27]

References in the works of a number of dramatists and popular authors suggest that they also learned their proverbs in this way. Among the strings of adages lacing the works of Robert Greene, for example, is 'wysshers and wolders be small hous holders', which is first known from Stanbridge's *Vulgaria* and may well have been learned during his time at Norwich grammar school in the 1570s. He says of Francesco in *Never Too Late* that 'hee being a scholler' and 'thinking this olde sentence to be true, *that wishers and woulders were neuer good householders*, therefore he applied himself to teaching of a schoole . . .'. Meanwhile, the Farmer in George Peele's play *Edward I* is made to confuse the standard grammar school textbooks, the *Sententiae Pueriles* and the *Distichs of Cato*, and then to attribute to them a sentence actually found in William Lily's *A Shorte Introduction of Grammar*: ''Tis an olde saide saying, I remember I redde it in Catoes *Pueriles*, that *Cantabit vacuus coram latrone viator.*' No doubt Peele was drawing on his own experience as a 'free scholar' at Christ's Hospital, London, in the later 1560s and the contents of these texts must have been sufficiently well known that he could rely upon his audiences getting the joke. Given William Camden's love of proverbs it is certain that Ben Jonson would have imbibed them under his tutelage at Westminster school. '*Omnia secunda*; you could not haue pray'd, to haue had it so wel: *saltat senex*, as it is i' the prouerbe . . .', says Cutberd in *The Silent Woman*, quoting the Erasmian adage, 'all is well, the old man dances'.[28]

The principal means by which youngsters were instructed to lodge in their minds the wise sentences and witty proverbs garnered from reading was the commonplace book. In this personal aid to memory and reflection,

[27] Sir Anthony Fitzherbert, *The Book of Husbandry*, ed. W. W. Skeat (English Dialect Society, 37, London, 1882), 101, and cf. 91, 99; Thomas Tusser, *Five Hundred Points of Good Husbandry*, ed. Geoffrey Grigson (Oxford, 1984), 203; John Smyth, *The Berkeley Manuscripts*, ed. Sir John Maclean (3 vols., Gloucester, 1883–5), iii. 307.

[28] Robert Greene, *Greenes Neuer Too Late* (1590), in *The Life and Complete Works*, ed. Grosart, viii. 64–5; George Peele, *The Famous Chronicle of King Edward the First, Sirnamed Edward Longshankes* (London, 1593), xii. 1922–4 (sig. G4ᵛ); Ben Jonson, *Epicoene, or The Silent Woman* (1616), II. vi. 11–13, in *The Works of Ben Jonson*, ed. C. H. Herford and Percy Simpson (11 vols., Oxford, 1925–52), v. 196–7.

they were encouraged, in a manner which many of them never lost, to make their own collections of sayings and observations. 'Writing is the tongue of the hand, and the herrald of memory,' advised the Elizabethan Nicholas Ling, whose *Politeuphuia* was, in effect, a printed commonplace book for schoolboys containing aphoristic sentences and observations listed under different heads. Such phrases would then act as a prompt in public speaking and private conversation, an outlet for moral contemplation, and a practical guide to steer them through the challenges of life.[29] One proposal for educational reform in the 1680s continued to stand by the practice of centuries in recommending that boys study and copy proverbs.

Proverbs would be useful for them to learn and read and also set down in the Real Character which will fix it better in their minds. The Italian proverbs are the better done into English, and I think the Spanish, which are the best . . . The wisdom of a nation is much discerned by their proverbs and there is no nation so dull but have some sayings worth remembrance. There is a French grammar called the *French Alphabet* to which is annexed a *Treasury of the French Tongue*, wherein are all the French proverbs. Mr Camden in his *Remains* has a collection of English proverbs, but Mr John Ray has made a greater. Let these be sometimes read a quarter of an hour and repeated: it will mightily open understanding and their judgements. These hints will be as *granum sinapis*—nest eggs. Their excerpts of observations in their note books will be repositories or stories from observations and experience, away beyond the common way of precepts as the knowledge of a traveller exceeds that which is gotten by a map.[30]

An abundance of commonplace books survive from the period as testimony to the popularity of gathering these verbal nest eggs as a source of guidance in life's journey. Thus the London grocer, Richard Hill, recorded over 100 'diwes good prowerbis' in Latin and English in his commonplace book compiled in the third and fourth decades of the sixteenth century.[31] Around 1586, John Maxwell the younger, of South Barr, Renfrewshire, similarly noted down 232 'reasownes and prowerbes', mostly copied from the printed works of George Pettie and John Lyly.[32]

---

[29] Ling, *Politeuphuia*, fo. 44ᵛ. On this practice, see W. F. Mitchell, *English Pulpit Oratory from Andrewes to Tillotson* (London, 1932), 82–5; Baldwin, *William Shakspere's Small Latine and Lesse Greeke*, ii. 290–4; Joan Marie Lechner, *Renaissance Concepts of the Commonplaces* (New York, 1962), 153–99; Quentin Skinner, *Reason and Rhetoric in the Philosophy of Hobbes* (Cambridge, 1996), 111–19.

[30] *Aubrey on Education*, ed. J. E. Stephens (London, 1972), 56–7.

[31] *Songs, Carols, and other Miscellaneous Poems, from the Balliol MS. 354, Richard Hill's Commonplace-Book*, ed. Roman Dyboski (Early English Text Society, orig. ser., 101, London, 1907), 128–41.

[32] Edinburgh University Library, MS La. III. 467; M. P. Tilley, *Elizabethan Proverb Lore in Lyly's 'Euphues' and in Pettie's 'Petite Pallace' with Parallels from Shakespeare* (New York, 1926), 4–6.

Another typical collection of commonplaces of the same date contains an agglomeration of apophthegms, anecdotes, and quotations garnered from both biblical and classical sources.[33] A Baconian-like example of the 1590s included among its 'elegancies' and 'formularies promus', various adages in English and Latin together with 'some choice French proverbs'. Among the English examples, 'He is the best prophite that telleth the last fortune' and 'You must sowe with the hand not with the basket', provide sayings apparently unknown in any other sources.[34] A further Elizabethan commonplacer combined the standard lists of Latin proverbs and English equivalents, with sayings from the Bible, and memorable extracts from a speech by the character of 'Time' in a play.[35]

One early seventeenth-century commonplace book included in its six-teeen 'observations' in English, 'If a man get but peace with his conscience he cannot do amisse, ther is no ioy lyke this'.[36] The preferred method of another compiler was to balance Latin sentences on the recto leaves of his book with English proverbs on the verso. The latter included many well-known favourites, and also a number of otherwise unknown gems, such as 'An unbydden ghost knowes not where to sytt' and 'A legge of a lack is better then the whole body of a kyte'.[37] Another Jacobean example, comprised of phrases and proverbial expressions apparently taken from some printed book, was chiefly concerned with political subjects.[38]

After the Restoration, the Kentish gentleman Henry Oxinden jotted down proverbs on a pocket-sized roll of paper. Many were taken from the Bible, while others followed his own advice to 'run ouer the prouerbs of euery country and cull out the choicest of them, for manie of them carry much weight, wit and caution'. He was also fond of copying out aphoristic wisdom from Ecclesiasticus: 'All flesh consorteth according to kind, and a man will cleave to his like'; 'A wise man will hold his tongue till hee see opportunity: but a babler and fool will observe no time'; 'Better is the life of a poore man in a mean cottage, then delicate fare in another mans house'.[39] Naturally enough, the Bible also provided the source for the 'sayings' noted down by the Essex clergyman, Ralph Josselin, at about the same time.[40] A commonplace book of Archbishop William Sancroft, meanwhile, included nuggets from Erasmus, as well as other modern authors such as Francis Bacon, James Howell, Izaak Walton, and John

---

[33] BL, Additional MS, 29971.     [34] BL, Harleian MS, 7017, fos. 83–132.

[35] PRO, SP12/288/71–3.     [36] BL, Sloane MS, 2628, fos. 60–3.

[37] BL, Lansdowne MS, 701, fos. 47ᵛ–70ʳ.     [38] PRO, SP14/189/7.

[39] BL, Additional MS, 28013, quoting Ecclesi. 13: 16; 20: 7; 29: 22.

[40] *The Diary of Ralph Josselin, 1616–1683*, ed. Alan Macfarlane (British Academy, Records of Social and Economic History, new ser., 3, London, 1976), 657–8.

Spottiswood. The proverbs which he saw fit to record ranged from favourites such as 'He who hath glass-windows of his own, sh'd take heed how he throws stones at those of his neighbour', and 'Goods lost, nothing lost; credit lost much lost; soul lost all lost', to the less than charitable, 'A Scottish man is like a fart, never at ease till he be out of his own countrie'.[41] Another commonplacer of the period chose to record Latin proverbs beginning with the letters L, M, Q, and R, followed by their English equivalents: thus, '*Qui prior est tempore, potior est jure*. First come, first served'.[42] Print also came to the aid of this habit of commonplacing. John Clarke's *Paroemiologia*, for schoolmasters and their pupils, left 'vacant spaces . . . under every head, that alterations might be made, additions inserted', while John Ray's pocketable *English Proverbs* was published in interleaved editions for owners to supplement with observations and quotations of their own.[43]

With minds and commonplace books thus filled with formulaic wisdom, the learned elite habitually used proverbs to garnish their discourse and dignify their speech. In an age which prized so highly the venerable authority of ancient adages, an appropriate saying carefully chosen and aptly applied would lend gravity to any assertion, amplify any argument, clinch any debate. As Nicholas Ling put it in his printed commonplace book:

seeing euery continued speech is of more force and efficacie to perswade or disswade, being adorned and strengthened with graue sentences, then rude heapes of idle wordes, and that wee ought to haue an especiall regard, not howe much we speake but howe well, I haue thus boldly aduentured, to make thee pertaker of my trauailes, which I haue imployed in gathering of certaine heades or places, that with more ease thou maist discourse of any subiect tending to vertue or vice.

'Certainly they are of excellent use', agreed Bacon of the apophthegms which he amused himself in recording during the ill-health of old age. 'They serve to be interlaced in continued speech. They serve to be recited upon occasion of themselves. They serve, if you take out the kernel of them, and make them your own.'[44]

[41] Bod. Lib., MS Sancroft 130, fos. 23, 53. Cf. the political aphorisms interspersed throughout William Sancroft, *Modern Policies, Taken from Machiavel, Borgia, and Other Choice Authors* (4th edn., London, 1653).

[42] PRO, SP29/444/90.

[43] Clarke, *Paroemiologia*, sig. A8ʳ; see the MS notes in the interleaved copy of Ray's *English Proverbs* in the Wren Library, Trinity College, Cambridge (shelf mark: Adv. d. 1. 7). Ray's *Collection of English Words* was similarly annotated: see the copies in the British Library (shelf mark: 626a.6) and at Magdalen College, Oxford (shelf mark: I. 7. 21).

[44] Ling, *Politeuphuia*, sig. A3ʳ; Francis Bacon, *Apophthegms New and Old* (1625), in *The Works of*

Moreover, grammar school education, which was as much as anything a training in the skills of classical rhetoric based upon the models of Cicero and Quintilian, urged the utility of choice quotations in public speaking. All of the great sixteenth-century manuals on rhetoric, such as those by Richard Sherry, Thomas Wilson, Richard Rainolde, Henry Peacham, and George Puttenham, recommended the use of wise sentences or pithy gnomes as the foundation of successful oratory. Proverbs could be invaluable in this context: they were authoritative, memorable, and concise, 'leaping ouer the heads of a great many words', as Puttenham put it.[45] So it was that politicians, lawyers, and preachers regularly employed proverbial phrases in their speeches, pleadings, and sermons. The Elizabethan member of parliament for Hereford, Thomas Jones, even interjected in a debate of 1601, on a bill to avoid the double payment of debts, with a contribution made up entirely of old saws.

It is now my chance to speake something, and that without humming or hawing. I think this law is a good law; even reckoning makes long friends, as far goes the penny, as the penny's master. *Vigilantibus non dormientibus jura subveniunt.* Pay the reckoning over night, and you shall not be troubled in the morning. If ready money be *mensura publica*, let every man cut his coat according to his cloth. When his old suit is in the wain, let him stay till that his money bring a new suit in the increase. Therefore, I think the law to be good, and I wish it a good passage.[46]

The rhetorical training of lawyers was bound up with the maxims and precepts in which so many principles of law were enshrined.[47] Classical dicta such as 'ignorance of the law excuses no one', or 'silence gives consent', remained important foundations of jurisprudence. English custom and practice also evolved its own series of guiding aphorisms. 'In our common law', wrote James Howell, 'there are some proverbs that carry a kind of authority with them . . .'. He cited as examples the adage in paternity suits, 'which began in Henry the Fourth's time, He that bulls the cow must keep the calf', or the phrase which epitomized the ancient

*Francis Bacon*, ed. James Spedding, Robert Leslie Ellis, and Douglas Denon Heath (7 vols., London, 1857–9), vii. 123.

[45] Richard Sherry, *A Treatise of the Figures of Grammer and Rhetorike* (London, 1555), fos. 54ᵛ, 57ʳ; Thomas Wilson, *The Arte of Rhetorique*, ed. G. H. Mair (Oxford, 1909), 119; Richard Rainolde, *A Booke Called the Foundacion of Rhetorike* (London, 1563), fo. 20ʳ; Henry Peacham, *The Garden of Eloquence* (London, 1577), sig. U3; George Puttenham, *The Arte of English Poesie* (London, 1589), 10, 152, 157.

[46] Quoted in Heseltine, 'Introduction', in Smith, *Oxford Dictionary of English Proverbs*, xiv–xv.

[47] W. R. Prest, *The Inns of Court under Elizabeth I and the Early Stuarts, 1590–1640* (London, 1972), 116; Richard Ross, 'The Memorial Culture of Early Modern English Lawyers: Memory as Keyword, Shelter, and Identity, 1560–1640', *Yale Journal of Law and the Humanities*, 10 (1998), 277–95.

Kentish inheritance custom of gavelkind, 'The father to the bough the son to the plow'.[48] The interest of lawyers in proverbs as an augment to rhetoric is reflected in the commonplace book of the barrister John Manningham, who, at the beginning of the seventeenth century, collected many sayings from reading, listening to sermons, or from everyday conversation around the Middle Temple.[49]

It was already common in the early modern period, therefore, to say that 'there is a salve for every sore' and that 'no one is above the law'. In criminal trials one would often hear that 'all men are presumed innocent until proven guilty' and that 'murder will out'. In property cases it was accepted that 'omittance is no quittance' and that 'possession is eleven points of the law'. Judges and juries knew that 'seeing is believing' and that 'one eye witness is better than ten ear witnesses'. Criminals realized that they were 'as well hanged for a sheep as for a lamb' and that 'the receiver is as bad as the thief'. Everyone was aware 'that which is mine is my own' and that 'necessity knows no law'. Many such sayings passed into common parlance, of course, and enjoyed a currency beyond mere legal contexts. So too, those sayings which we owe to the practices of medieval torture: 'To go through fire and water'; 'To put the screws on'; 'To be put on the rack'; 'To be hauled over the coals'. And it is the church courts which we have to thank for 'playing the devil's advocate', for 'being on the side of angels', and for 'cursing with bell, book and candle'. Even the very courtroom oath, to tell 'the truth, the whole truth, and nothing but the truth' entered the language as everyday usage.[50]

Clergymen also relied heavily on proverbial wisdom, biblical or otherwise, in order to illustrate their morals and provide pithy lessons which might be borne away by their hearers. The famous sermons of the Edwardian bishop of Worcester, Hugh Latimer, son of a Leicestershire yeoman, were full of tags and sayings, proverbial allusions, and similes. Thus, 'as they commonly say', or 'according to the proverb', '"He that walketh plainly, walketh safely"'; 'as the old saying is, "Happy is the child whose father goeth to the devil"'; 'it is a true saying, *Radix omnium malorum avaritia*, "Covetousness is the root of all wickedness'; 'we have the old proverb, *Omnia venalia Romae*, "All things are sold for money at Rome"'.

---

[48] Archer Taylor, *The Proverb* (Cambridge, Mass., 1931), 86–97; Howell, *Proverbs, or, Old Sayed Sawes and Adages*, 5–6.

[49] *The Diary of John Manningham of the Middle Temple, 1602–1603*, ed. Robert Parker Sorlien (Hanover, NH, 1976), 38 and *passim*.

[50] Donald F. Bond, 'English Legal Proverbs', *Publications of the Modern Language Association*, 51 (1936), 921–35. Cf. Natalie Zemon Davis, 'Proverbial Wisdom and Popular Errors', in her *Society and Culture in Early Modern France* (Stanford, Calif., 1975), 244.

John Bridges was one of those who carried this homely style through Elizabeth's reign and beyond. He liked to string familiar sayings together, as in a sermon of 1571 which included: 'nay it is now the old prouerbe vp and downe, trim tram, such maister, suche man, suche cuppe, suche couer, neyther barrell better herring, both maister and man may go in a line together, for a great many of men and maisters now a dayes'. In 1616 Thomas Draxe, the minister of Harwich and Dovercourt, Essex, published a collection of proverbs in English and Latin arranged under alphabetical heads apparently as an aid to good sermonizing.[51]

The tendency to amplify sermons with abundant proverbs and elaborate similes as part of a self-conscious rhetorical style reached its height with the metaphysical preachers of the first half of the seventeenth century. Many of the great pulpit orators of this generation, including Thomas Adams, Lancelot Andrewes, Joseph Hall, Thomas Fuller, George Morley, and John Donne all made extensive use of proverbial phrases and epithets in their public performances. They repeatedly drew not only on classical *sententiae* but also on popular sayings, which were much valued, as Thomas Adams put it, for their 'antiquitie, brevity, significance, experience and truth'.[52] Here, for example, is Adams on the question of where we shall find truth.

You would wonder to find her in a courtier, in a politician; whose element and position is, *Qui nescit dissimulare, nescit vivere*: he that knowes not how to dissemble, knowes not how to live. Or in a country mans budget, shut up with snaphance: no, you shall have as much deceit under russet, as under velvet, though a little more bungerly . . . You would smile to find her *in pueris et fatuis*; in children and fooles: yet they say, children and fooles tell truth. But if it be child-hood or follie to tell truth, I am sure we have but a few children, a few fooles. Or in a drunkard; yet they say, *in vino veritas*, drinke utters the truth. But take the ale-bench without a malicious lie, or at least an officious lie; a very lie, or a merry lie, and make a pew of it. Where then shall we find truth? I hope in the church, in the pulpits: oh God forbid else! Yet often truth keepes only in the pulpit, and does not goe downe staires with the man . . . *Omnis homo mendax*, God is true, every man a lyar. There is no certaine place to find truth, but in the word of God; there let us seeke her, there we shall find her.[53]

---

[51] *Sermons by Hugh Latimer*, ed. G. E. Corrie (Parker Society, Cambridge, 1844), 89, 114, 146, 184–5, 185; John Bridges, 'The Effects of Example', in *In God's Name: Examples of Preaching in England from the Act of Supremacy to the Act of Uniformity, 1534–1662*, ed. John Chandos (London, 1971), 85, and cf. 84; Thomas Draxe, *Bibliotheca Scholastica Instrvctissima* (London, 1616).

[52] Mitchell, *English Pulpit Oratory from Andrewes to Tillotson*, pt. II, esp. 237–8; Horton Davies, *Like Angels from a Cloud: The English Metaphysical Preachers, 1588–1645* (San Marino, Calif., 1986), 289–92.

[53] Thomas Adams, *A Commentary or, Exposition upon the Divine Second Epistle Generall, Written by*

Those clergyman who addressed audiences in country parishes were especially aware of the value of homely morals and familiar sayings in their sermonizing. The Norfolk doctor Sir Thomas Browne was surely correct to observe that it was more in 'parables than propositions, and proverbs more powerful than demonstrations', that many ministers might best appeal to the sensibilities and affections of their listeners. William Glibery, the Elizabethan vicar of Halstead, north Essex, certainly knew this to be true. 'It is no matter', he jested from the pulpit one Sunday in the 1580s when the puritan Richard Rogers came to preach in his parish. 'Every man as he loves quoth the good wife when she kissed you wot what.' The firebrand, Stephen Marshall, son of a glover from neighbouring Finchingfield, was said to be such a popular preacher in the 1640s because he was 'acquainted with all the vulgar proverbs and odd country phrases and by-words, which he would sprinkle up and down in his sermon, which captivated people at a strange rate'.[54]

Adam Martindale realized that the 'vulgar hearers' to whom he ministered in parishes around Lancashire and Cheshire in the middle years of the seventeenth century needed their doctrine in this 'briefer way'. He punctuated his autobiographical writings with collections of 'pithie matter' such as, 'Unequally delt (as the proverbe is) is soone chosen'; 'The old proverbe is very true, as many find by woefull experience:—"He that will not when he may, when he would he shall have nay"'; 'Much would have more, as the proverbe is'; 'Home is home (as the proverbe sayes) though never so homely'. Equally, the poor cottager's son, John Bunyan, would appreciate the value of being able to speak to his Bedfordshire brethren in their 'own native language'. The narrative in his *Pilgrim's Progress* is full of proverbial phrases, and his characters often mouth them. 'That proverb, "A bird in the hand is worth two in the bush", is of more authority with them, then are all the divine testimonies of the good of the world to come'; 'according to the true proverb, "The dog is turned to his vomit again, and the sow that was washed, to her wallowing in the mire".' Talkative tells us: 'Thus say the common people that knew him, "A saint abroad, and a devil at home".' Faithful warns: 'The proverb is true of you, which is said of a whore; to wit, that she is a shame to all women; so you are a shame to all professors.'[55]

the *Blessed Apostle St. Peter* (London, 1633), 70–1. For other examples, see *The Workes of Tho: Adams* (London, 1629).

[54] Sir Thomas Browne, *Pseudodoxia Epidemica* (1646), in *The Works of Sir Thomas Browne*, ed. Geoffrey Keynes (4 vols., London, 1964), ii. 26; Patrick Collinson, *The Elizabethan Puritan Movement* (London, 1967), 373; William Hunt, *The Puritan Moment: The Coming of Revolution in an English County* (Cambridge, Mass., 1983), 280–1.

[55] Adam Martindale, *The Life of Adam Martindale Written by Himself*, ed. Richard Parkinson

Meanwhile, the transferral of rhetoric on to the written page in the form of letters or persuasive position papers demonstrates this similar reliance on adages and maxims as a means to move the reader or hearer. 'It is to be noted', approved William Fulwood in 1568, 'that diuers epistles may begin with a perfect sentence, authoritie, or common prouerbe: prouided that it be altogether agreeable to the purpose that we entend to perswade or disswade'.[56] Many letters of the sixteenth and seventeenth centuries demonstrate this advice in action. In June 1599, for example, after eighteen years under royal banishment, poor Charles Paget could write to Thomas Barnes from Paris citing the 'olde prouerbe' about taking heed of trusting a friend. When in January 1614 John Chamberlain related to Dudley Carleton the hope that James I would soon create some new officers of state, he quoted the saying familiar to schoolboys since the Middle Ages: 'be the day never so long, at last comes even song'. Responding in like kind to the Scottish colonel, Robert Monro, from an embattled Berwick in October 1640, Sir John Conyers was able to 'answeare your Scottish prouerb with our English one, which sayes, that threatned men liue long'. In a letter concerning Admiralty business in November 1666 the naval commander at Portsmouth, Thomas Middleton, reminded Samuel Pepys of another school favourite, 'the burnt child dreads the fyer'. 'You know the proverb', wrote Secretary of State, Henry Coventry, to the Attorney-General, Sir William Jones, in September 1678, '"A fool may ask more queotiono than a wise man can answer" . . .'.[57]

Indeed, in an age in which texts of all kinds were often written to be read aloud it was appropriate that they should be infused with the formualic and familiar sayings which facilitated *viva voce* delivery. In general, the prose style of the sixteenth and first half of the seventeenth century is said to have contained a heavy 'oral residue', a rhapsodic structure and a high degree of colloquiality which reflects the close association between

(Chetham Society, 4, London, 1845), 174, 24, 182, 237, 238; and for other examples, see 8–10, 22–3, 42–4, 101–3, 120–22, 126, 182–5, 200–1, 217–18, 237–9; John Bunyan, *The Pilgrim's Progress*, ed. J. B. Wharey and R. Sharrock (Oxford, 1960), 168, 31, 68, 78, 84; and for other examples, see 39, 57, 99, 102, 105, 130, 145, 169, 203, 216, 291.

[56] William Fulwood, *The Enimie of Idlenesse* (London, 1568) fo. 15ʳ. Cf. Angel Daye, *The English Secretorie* (London, 1586), 69, 231. On letter writing as a form of rhetoric, see Jean Robertson, *The Art of Letter Writing: An Essay on the Handbooks Published in England during the Sixteenth and Seventeenth Centuries* (London, 1942), 23–4.

[57] PRO, SP12/271/10; PRO, SP14/76/6; PRO, SP16/470/71; PRO, SP29/179/28; *CSPD, 1678 and Add. 1674–79*, 394. For other examples, see PRO, SP12/199/13; SP12/239/158i; PRO, SP14/72/31; PRO, SP16/148/54i; PRO, SP29/126/100; SP29/215/78; SP29/429/51; SP29/434/64.

the spoken and written realms at this time.[58] Proverbs and mnemonic verbal patterns were an instrumental part of this. Given the contemporary vogue for aphoristic wisdom as a pedagogic tool, a rhetorical device, and a literary ornament, moreover, it is hardly surprising that much of the poetry, prose, and drama of the period should be, unconsciously or otherwise, laden with proverbial allusions and phrases. Some printers even highlighted sententious remarks and popular sayings for a reader's attention by typographical devices such as quotation marks, italics, or pointers in the margin.[59]

Many professional writers kept a commonplace book of brief and clever quotations, memorable phrases, and familiar proverbs as an essential tool of the trade. The large number of such expressions contained in the works of the Elizabethan authors George Chapman and Thomas Nashe, for example, were clearly supplied in part by the saws and adages, many of them deriving from Erasmus, which they collected through commonplacing. For dramatists this practice was invaluable. John Webster jotted down proverbs, rhymes, and sentences culled from modern authors such as Sidney, Montaigne, and Bacon which he interspersed throughout his own work. Ben Jonson kept extensive notebooks, compiled from wide reading, and his plays, particularly the speeches of his common characters, are said to be 'as full of proverbs as an egg of meat'. It is not known whether Shakespeare kept a similar aid to memory but it is at least a possibility since his works have been calculated to contain 4,684 proverbs and proverbial allusions. Plays must then have had a considerable influence in popularizing proverbial sayings among their audiences and in disseminating the fruits of commonplacing into everyday circulation and common discourse. 'Besides', commented the Devonshire minister Thomas Trescot, 'the very language it selfe, what is it oft times, but a few shreds and scraps dropt from some stage-poet, at the Globe or Cock-pit, which they have carefully bookt up, to serve them for such an occasion.'[60]

[58] Walter J. Ong, 'Oral Residue in Tudor Prose Style', _Publications of the Modern Language Association_, 80 (1965), 145–54; D. F. McKenzie, 'Speech-Manuscript-Print', in Dave Oliphant and Robin Bradford (eds.), _New Directions in Textual Studies_ (Austin, Tex., 1990), 89–93.

[59] Louis B. Wright, 'William Painter and the Vogue of Chaucer as a Moral Teacher', _Modern Philology_, 31 (1933–4), 165–74; G. K. Hunter, 'The Marking of _Sententiae_ in Elizabethan Printed Plays, Poems and Romances', _Library_, 5th ser., 6 (1951), 171–88; A. C. Partridge, _Orthography in Shakespeare and Elizabethan Drama_ (London, 1964), 191.

[60] Franck L. Schoell, 'G. Chapman's Commonplace Book', _Modern Philology_, 17 (1919–20), 199–218; _The Works of Thomas Nashe_, ed. R. B. McKerrow, rev. F. P. Wilson (5 vols., Oxford, 1958), v. 111–15; Charles Crawford, _Collectanea: First Series_ (Stratford-on-Avon, 1906), 20–46, esp. 33, and id., _Collectanea: Second Series_ (Stratford-on-Avon, 1907), 1–63, esp. 44–5; _The Works of Ben Jonson_, ed. Herford and Simpson, ii. 439–40; F. P. Wilson, 'Shakespeare and the Diction of

It was natural, of course, that characters on stage should habitually mouth proverbs in the interests of recreating spontaneous speech. The 'proverb play', in which the dramatic action exemplified the proverbial title, even became a popular genre in its own right during the sixteenth century. Equally, the literary dialogue, so favoured a vehicle of didactic and polemical writers of the Renaissance, was likely to be full of 'old said saws' traded by the characters in its stylized representation of conversation.[61] In works of prose fiction, meanwhile, the vogue for sententious wisdom was no less evident. George Pettie's *Petite Pallace* (1576) has been shown to contain a total of 261 proverbs, for example, while the two parts of John Lyly's *Euphues* (1578–80) quote some 643. The two great novels of early modern Europe, Rabelais's *Gargantua and Pantagruel* and Cervantes's *Don Quixote*, which reached English audiences through the translations of Sir Thomas Urquhart in 1653 and Thomas Shelton in 1612, respectively, are both infused with proverbial imagery, reference, and personification.[62]

In the sixteenth and seventeenth centuries, then, proverbs supplied much of the mortar which held the edifice of prose together. They were also the subject of a literary genre, and their stylized use became an art form in itself. At the same time, ancient adages and moral maxims provided the building blocks for rhetoric and preaching, for academic debate and learned conversation. Many derived from biblical and classical sources and owed their dissemination to learned texts and the formal processes of edification and education. The intellectual prestige and acknowledged utility of the proverb was never greater (see Plate 4).

## VULGAR WISDOMS

The large part played by wise sentences and ancient adages in formal education and their use in intellectual and professional life notwithstanding, it was also true that proverbial wisdom was everybody's wisdom.

Common Life', in his *Shakespearian and other Studies*, ed. Helen Gardner (Oxford, 1969), 115; R. W. Dent, *Shakespeare's Proverbial Language: An Index* (Berkeley and Los Angeles, 1981), 3–4; Thomas Trescot, *The Zealous Magistrate* (London, 1642), 14.

[61] Paula Neuss, 'The Sixteenth-Century English "Proverb" Play', *Comparative Drama*, 18 (1984), 1–18; *John Heywood's 'A Dialogue of Proverbs'*, ed. Habenicht, 50–62. For examples of proverbs in dialogues, see *Inedited Tracts: Illustrating the Opinions and Occupations of Englishmen during the Sixteenth and Seventeenth Centuries*, ed. W. C. Hazlitt (Roxburghe Library, London, 1868), 9, 77, 112, 117, 133, 166, 173, 178, 184, 188, 192, 193, 199.

[62] Charles G. Smith, *Spenser's Proverb Lore* (Cambridge, Mass., 1970); Tilley, *Elizabethan Proverb Lore*, 2; Mikhail Bakhtin, *Rabelais and his World*, trans. Helene Iswolsky (Cambridge, Mass., 1965), ch. 2; U. R. Burke, *Spanish Salt: A Collection of all the Proverbs which are to be found in Don Quixote* (London, 1877) (lists 352 examples).

Proverbs were truly 'popular', both in the sense of being frequently invoked and enjoyed, as in that of being known as much to the illiterate masses as to the classically trained elite. The 'best of them', said Francis Bacon of his little collection, 'are of course in everybody's mouth'. For, no matter how much old saws depended upon text for their preservation and propagation, they were, first and foremost, 'sayings', spoken formulae which might be given literary form but were, in essence, oral. The moralist Samuel Palmer may well have been correct to say of proverbs that their 'original method of instruction was by oral tradition from father to son'. They were, as they remain, an important part of those verbal patterns of which speech is made up and as such they scarcely needed to be learned in any deliberate sense, being known simply by virtue of knowing the language. Thus, even the bluntest of English people did not disdain to preface their discourse with 'an old prouerbe', thought the churchman John Earle in 1628. The Scots, meanwhile, were said by one of their countrymen to 'abound with proverbs' and, by another, to be 'wonderfully given to this way of speaking . . . especially among the better sort of the commonalty, none of whom will discourse you any considerable time, but he will confirm every assertion and observation with a Scottish proverb'.[63]

The majority of the population imbibed their customary sayings not from books or deliberate instruction but from experience and unconscious emulation: they were implicit and subliminal, or that 'which we suck in with our mother's milk', as contemporaries often put it. Proverbs were handed down the generations, absorbed by word of mouth from parents and nurses, or 'habituall to a nation, being transmitted from father to sonne', as the great John Selden was heard to say. James Howell agreed that these 'traditionall sayings, precepts and memorandums' were 'handed over as it were from father to son, from mother to daughter, from nurses to children time out of mind, and will be so as long as sermocination lasts among men'.[64]

It was from this venerability, from their transmission by the old and the wise over many generations, that proverbs derived their moral authority. Their invocation was often prefixed by the adjectives 'old' or 'rusty',

---

[63] Francis Bacon, 'Promus of Formularies and Elegancies', in *The Works of Francis Bacon*, ed. Spedding, Ellis, and Heath, vii. 202; Samuel Palmer, *Moral Essays on Some of the Most Curious and Significant English, Scotch and Foreign Proverbs* (London, 1710), iii; John Earle, *Micro-cosmographie. Or, a Peece of the World Discovered; in Essayes and Characters* (London, 1628), sig. G5ᵛ; *A Collection of Highland Rites and Customes*, ed. J. L. Campbell (Folklore Society, Cambridge, 1975), 21; Kelly, *A Complete Collection of Scottish Proverbs*, sig. A3.

[64] Oswald Dykes, *English Proverbs with Moral Reflexions* (2nd edn., London, 1709), xxxv; *Table Talk of John Selden*, ed. Pollock, 115; Howell, *Proverbs, or, Old Sayed Sawes and Adages*, 7.

'stale' or 'musty'. They were wise because they were ancient. Like good books, thought Sir William Temple in 1690, proverbs 'receive their chief value from the stamp and esteem of ages through which they have passed'. A century before, Thomas Nashe had referred to 'a hackny prouerb in mens mouths euer since K. Lud was a little boy', and one of John Lyly's characters had captured the sense in which longevity of tradition added weight: 'I haue heard my great grandfather tell how his great grandfather shoulde saie, that it was an olde prouerbe, when his greate grandfather was a childe, that it was a good winde that blew a man to the wine'.[65]

Being 'habitual' from an early age, a great store of sayings and saws was carried around by people in memory. Catchy and rhythmical, often alliterative and sometimes rhymed, they had a mnemonic quality which made them stay in the mind and slide trippingly off the tongue. Significantly, many of those who wrote collections of proverbs seem to have relied purely on memory, in the first instance at least. Thus, Francis Bacon's substantial compilation of 'apophthegms new and old' was said to have been 'made out of his memory, without turning any book'. At the beginning of the eighteenth century Oswald Dykes assembled sayings and saws 'having consulted few books, and had few books to consult'. Meanwhile, the collector of Scottish proverbs, James Kelly, could spontaneously 'and in a very short time' note down 'above one thousand two hundred, as they offered in discourse, or occurred to my memory'.[66]

Thus, there was something inherently popular, and even populist, about proverbs. They were 'the voice of the people' and, as such, embodied the wisdom of Everyman, the collective psyche of the nation. 'Proverbs may not improperly be called the philosophy of the common people . . .', considered James Howell, being 'the truest franklins or freeholders of a countrey; they have no other parent but the people . . .'. John Ray believed them to be, above all, 'generally used and well known to the vulgar'. The antiquary, John Aubrey, agreed that they 'are drawn from the experience and observation of many ages; and are the ancient and natural

[65] Sir William Temple, 'An Essay upon the Ancient and Modern Learning' (1690), in *Critical Essays of the Seventeenth Century*, ed. J. E. Spingarn (3 vols., Oxford, 1908), iii. 34; Thomas Nashe, *Haue with you to Saffron Walden* (1596), in *The Works of Thomas Nashe*, ed. McKerrow and Wilson, iii. 129; John Lyly, *Mother Bombie* (1594), ii. v. 4–7, in *The Complete Works of John Lyly*, ed. R. W. Bond (3 vols., Oxford, 1902), iii. 193, quoted in Wilson, *Oxford Dictionary of English Proverbs*, vii. Cf. Robert Blau, *Libamina Junioribus Philologis Degustanda, or the Locutions of the Latine Tongue* (Edinburgh, 1702), 2.

[66] Bacon, *Apophthegms New and Old* in *The Works of Francis Bacon*, ed. Spedding, Ellis, and Heath, vii. 123n. Dykes, *English Proverbs with Moral Reflexions*, v; Kelly, *A Complete Collection of Scottish Proverbs*, sig. A3.

philosophy of the vulgar, preserved in old English; in bad rhythms handed downe to us . . .'.[67]

That proverbs were ubiquitously traded and invoked by ordinary people in their everyday conversations is not in doubt. If we use the depositions given before the courts in order to eavesdrop on the domestic chatter, market-place gossip, and alehouse discussion of men and women as they went about their daily business, the formulaic nature of popular speech is evident. In 1570, for example, Robert Fawcus, a 78-year-old glazier from the city of Durham, called at the house of a neighbour where he met Robert Smith and his wife, together with Bertram Robson, 'sittinge by the fyer, and the said Robson playin of one pair of clavicords, and William Smith, their son, of another pair'. This jolly scene he greeted with an appropriate proverb and 'said to them "Litle mirth is worth moch sorro"'. As Jonas Cooke, a yeoman of Brandeston, east Suffolk, stood passing the time of day with his vicar, John Lowes, some time in 1615, he chanced to remark that the cleric had 'had good lucke to horsfleshe sethance that he did marrye his wife, she being the weddowe of a grave parson, ther withall not thinkeing any hurt did repeat an ould merie proverbe that he that would haue good lucke to horsefleshe must lye wth a parsons wife'. Unfortunately Lowes took offence at the adage and promised to make Cooke repent his insolence. On Trinity Sunday in June 1641 the proverbial taunt, 'win it and wear it', spiced the summer-game rivalry between two neighbouring communities when around eighty revellers from Malmesbury descended upon the churchyard of Long Newnton and, according to the old custom, attempted to carry off the village's festive garland of flowers. Amongst the raiding party was 'John Browne, sometymes a chymney sweeper, with a hobby horse and bells on his legs, and David Tanner, a fencer, and when they saw John Comyn and his companions going with the garland they had them to stand, saying "Wynn it and weare it. Come three score of you, you are but boies to wee!" And thereupon there was a great fight and many of the Newnton men were sorely beaten.'[68]

Other examples of the sayings and saws with which people peppered their conversations and their disputes could be multiplied. In January 1605

---

[67] Howell, *Proverbs, or, Old Sayed Sawes and Adages*, 7; Ray, *A Collection of English Proverbs* (1st edn., 1670), sig. A3ᵛ; Bod. Lib., MS Aubrey 1, fos. 7ᵛ–8ʳ.

[68] *Depositions and other Ecclesiastical Proceedings from the Courts of Durham, extending from 1311 to the Reign of Elizabeth*, ed. James Raine (Surtees Society, 21, London, 1845), 207 (Tilley, O86; Wilson, 601); C. L'Estrange Ewen, *Witchcraft in the Star Chamber* (n. pl., 1938), 47–8 (Tilley, L575; Wilson, 496: this case predates the reference there cited); *Records of the County of Wiltshire being extracts from the Quarter Sessions Great Rolls of the Seventeenth Century*, ed. B. H. Cunnington (Devizes, 1932), 141 (Tilley, W408; Wilson, 892).

when the vicar of Elm in Cambridgeshire, Mr Gyles, accused one of his parishioners, William Mosgrave, of unseemly 'brawlinge and chiding', he received a sharp proverb in reply as 'Mosgrave said before the neighbors in reproche of the said Mr Gyles, "Like shepheard like flocke!"' During Allhallowtide 1609 a group of neighbours was gathered at the house of Thomas Willett in Chipping Norton, Oxfordshire, when Anne Trevis claimed in heated discussion that a neighbour's son was the bastard child of William Carricke for 'he was as like him as yf he had beene spatt out of his mouth'. An Essex man was equally expressive in June 1637 when he told the bishop of London's commissary court that 'he would not come to Rome but he would see the Pope'. A parishioner of St Peter's Westcheap, London, claimed in 1649 that 'William Bird in a publick place told me I was like a dog in a manger and he said that I would neither do good nor suffer others.'[69]

By the same token, people often incorporated proverbs into the mocking rhymes which they invented to ridicule the foibles and slander the good names of others. One bawdy ballad which began life as a ditty sung around the alehouses of Worcestershire and Staffordshire in the spring of 1607 included a dialogue in which a miller quotes the proverb, 'If you be angry you may turn the buckle of your girdle behind you'. In May 1616 William Pennell of Barnslands in Shropshire was accused of 'making and singinge a rime' in derogation of his neighbours, one line of which claimed that 'the Goodwief Camebridg will not parte from the dropping of her nose &c' This proverb said of misers, that 'they would not give away the droppings of their nose on a frosty morning', was still circulating in the west of England in the nineteenth century when it was recorded from oral tradition. In September 1621, two Devonshire men set out to blacken the name of Roger Neck, a yeoman from Kings Nympton, by alleging that he was a cuckold and composing a song against him which included, 'tys well knowne a ticklishe beast hath tricks, and the oulde proverbe saieth "a gald Jade kickes"'.[70]

When people were talking politics the flow of proverbial imagery was

[69] CUL, EDR/B/2/20, fo. 122ᵛ (Tilley, P583 and S328; Wilson, 647 and 732); ORO, ODR c. 25, fo. 8 (Tilley, M1246; Wilson, 464); Bod. Lib., MS Eng Lang. e. 6, fo. 2ᵛ (otherwise unrecorded); William Matthews, *Cockney Past and Present* (London, 1938), 17 (Tilley, D513, Wilson, 195).

[70] PRO, STAC8/220/31, mm. 15–16 (see below p. 324; Tilley, B698; Wilson, 14); *Records of Early English Drama: Shropshire*, ed. J. A. B. Somerset (2 vols., Toronto, 1994), i. 51 (Tilley, D619; Wilson, 485); G. F. Northall, *Folk-phrases of Four Counties (Glouc. Staff. Warw. Worc.) gathered from Unpublished MSS. and Oral Tradition* (English Dialect Society, 73, London, 1894), 15; PRO, STAC8/221/9, m. 2. The proverb, 'touch a galled horse and he will kicke' was also invoked by William Pinge during a quarrel with Roda Greenrise at Colchester, Essex, in 1610: Laura Gowing, *Domestic Dangers: Women, Words and Sex in Early Modern London* (Oxford, 1996), 77–8, cf. 172–3.

no less profuse. Following the death of Elizabeth I, for example, Thomas Browne, a grocer from Buntingford in Hertfordshire, was heard express-ing his radical opinions at Royston in March 1603 when he urged his com-rades to solidarity: '"We whoe looked for the queenes death theis twentye yeares will not be made fooles now, for byrdes of a fether would hold together!"' In July 1638 a Reading man, Henry Spicer, was at an inn down in Chichester when, during a discussion about the threatened uprising in Scotland, he said 'that the winde did sometymes blow in the east and sometymes in the west and that wee should have the cart sett on his right wheeles'. When in July 1662 John Elliot, who had recently returned from a trip into Devonshire, was at a house in Taunton, Somerset, he was asked 'what news there was abroad in the country'. He replied that he had heard some dangerous news against the government which he dared not repeat, at which one of the company, John Hooper, approved of his caution with the old proverb, 'If you tell tayles out of schoole you must be whipt'.[71]

A notebook kept by the Norfolk squire Sir Nicholas L'Estrange up until his death in 1655 is revealing in this respect since it records material gathered not from reading but from conversations with local people. L'Estrange noted jests, anecdotes, and aphorisms which were told to him by the people with whom he met regularly and chatted: his mother and father, his wife and brother, the future licenser of the press, the local parson, and various other friends. He wrote down at least twenty jokes which embodied or elaborated famous old saws in the tradition of proverbial tales. But as many of the sayings which he committed to paper were apparently known only parochially or were of his own invention. For example, the parson, Mr Derham, told him, 'This proverbiall saying passeth upon marriages: that a young man and woman is a match of Gods making . . . but a young man and an old woman, of the divells making.' From his friend, Mr Spring, he heard, 'I have turned up as much in a hollow tooth, as will last me this fortnight', referring to a sufficiency of drink. His father informed him that, 'I come to thee to mend braines'; Mr Russell relayed that he had heard a 'serving-wench' say 'my master hath sent you some open-arses, and sayes if you keepe them not till they be rotten as a turd, they will not be worth a fart'. At the same time, a neighbour, Ned Gourny, furnished him with an anecdote from which to 'see the old saying is true, that ther's no creature upon earth, but the rater ha's the same'. And his wife advised him, 'There is a pretty fallacie in the

[71] *Calendar of Assize Records: Hertfordshire Indictments James I*, ed. J. S. Cockburn (London, 1975), 4–5 (Tilley, B393; Wilson, 60); PRO, SP16/397/40 (Tilley, W442; Wilson, 893); PRO, SP29/58/16i (Tilley, T54; Wilson, 803). See also below p. 339 (Tilley, M1029; Wilson, 536).

old proverbiall saying; that whatsoever hath not a palme in their hand on Palme-Sunday, must have their hand cutt of'.[72]

Such sources reveal only a few of the thousands of proverbs in regular circulation and constant conversational use in early modern England. Old and wise sayings existed to meet every conceivable situation. They provided consolation and comfort in the face of adversity; they admonished vice and commended virtue. To meet a problem with a trusted maxim was to acknowledge implicitly that similar difficulties had arisen before and could be coped with. 'Patch grief with proverbs; make misfortune drunk', was advice well heeded.[73] Consider, for example, the scenario depicted in a chapbook of the 1680s in which poor Susan, a seamstress, seeks advice at the hands of old Mother Bunch, 'weeping and wringing her hands' and crying '"Frank the Fidler has left me and swears he won't have me"'. She receives comfort from the sagely matron.

'Prithee child, be of good cheer, she that's afraid of every grass must not think to piss in a meadow. One swallow makes no summer, nor one frosty day a winter. Set your stool in the sun, and if one knave goes, an honest man may come. Therefore never grieve, but mind these old proverbs, for if he's worth any thing, he'll come again, if not 'tis well you are rid of him: I hope he has not plaid at wag-tail with thee?'[74]

There was reassurance to be found in those familiar prefaces to a saying which appealed to its age and its universality: 'As I have heard say', 'As the oulde proverbe sayth', 'It's an awd sayin', an' it's a true un . . .'. The repeated use of old saws could thus serve to reaffirm the ethical standards of a community, latently underscoring its mental solidarity and spiritual identity. It could provide a code of conduct, a series of counsels to 'come patly into that man's head which is furnished with such materials, as to prevent him doing some ill or folly which he would afterward repent of; or to put him upon what he might not otherwise have thought to do at that time, or in that matter'.[75]

[72] 'Merry Passages and Jeasts': A Manuscript Jestbook of Sir Nicholas Le Strange (1603–1655), ed. H. F. Lippincott (Salzburg, 1974). For allusions to well-known proverbs see, 17, 18, 22, 24, 30, 43, 64, 70, 77, 106, 128, 150, 160, 161, 163 (Tilley, W462; N216; W746; M1093; E232; F452; C267; S513; B95; T460; S885; H495; D3; W247; P365; S300; C309; S260; T537). For these personal and parochial sayings see, 89, 70, 78, 57, 105, 107; and for others, 161–6.

[73] Shakespeare, *Much Ado about Nothing*, v. i. 17.

[74] *Mother Bunch's Closet Newly Broke Open* (London?, 1685; 1715 edn.), 9–10.

[75] John Mapletoft, *Select Proverbs* (London, 1707), sig. A5. On these values and functions of proverbs, see E. O. Arena and Alan Dundes, 'Proverbs and the Ethnography of Speaking Folklore', *American Anthropologist*, 66/6 (1964), 70–85; Roger D. Abrahams, 'Introductory Remarks to a Rhetorical Theory of Folklore', *Journal of American Folklore*, 81 (1968), 143–58; id., 'Proverbs and Proverbial Expressions', in Richard M. Dorson (ed.), *Folklore and Folklife: An*

Occasionally it is possible to catch sight of the way in which proverbial wisdom could correct conduct, dictate action, or provide advice for ordinary people in just such a way. In 1650, for example, a Warminster man was before the Wiltshire grand jury for slandering a neighbour and pleaded for mercy with the proverbs, 'the tongue is an unruly evil full of deadly poison, and that no man is wise at all seasons'. Four years later two youngsters from Chitterne similarly accused before the same authority promised in future 'to observe the saying of the wise man, "He that keepeth his mouth and his tongue keepeth his soul from trouble" which they pray God will imprint in their memories'. In January 1678 a Kentish seaman, Edward Barlow, married a servant girl from London at the parish church in Deal, and afterwards at the King's Head. He reassured himself of the wisdom of his choice by contemplating the proverb that a man always marries a good woman the first time around. He also remembered that 'it is an old saying "A good Jack makes a good Jill" and "The proof of the pudding must be in the eating"'.[76]

Another famous saying applied to affairs of the heart during an alehouse discussion at Ashton-in-Makerfield, Lancashire, in 1663, was the Aesopian 'catch not the shadow and lose the substance'. One Thursday in October of that year, Roger Naylor and Thomas Insworth called to see their friend, the apprentice mercer Roger Lowe, and offered to buy him a drink. Over their ale they set to 'discourseing of Esop's fable' and Lowe began 'spakeing of the fable of dogge and peece of flesh, who, swiminge over river, caught shadow and lost substance'. The proverbial tale struck Naylor as being applicable to its teller, who was then attempting to court more than one woman at a time. 'Says Roger, "Take [care] of you doeing so", which speach', recalled Lowe, 'did much amaze me, for I was troubled at it very sore.'[77]

Anyone thus contemplating marriage would have had around sixty proverbs readily to hand offering the benefit of experience on the subject.

Tis true, that marriages are made in heaven, it is also true that marriage and hanging goeth by destiny; but if you are disposed to marry, marry a shrew rather than

*Introduction* (Chicago, 1972), 117–27; Barbara Kirshenblatt-Gimblett, 'Toward a Theory of Proverb Meaning', *Proverbium*, 22 (1973), 821–7; Alan Dundes, 'On the Structure of the Proverb', *Proverbium*, 25 (1975), 961–73; James Obelkevich, 'Proverbs and Social History', in Peter Burke and Roy Porter (eds.), *The Social History of Language* (Cambridge, 1987), 43–55.

[76] *Records of the County of Wiltshire*, ed. Cunnington, 219; HMC, *Various Collections*, vol. i (London, 1901), 129 (Tilley, T407; Wilson, 830; and Tilley, M335; Wilson, 571); Ralph Houlbrooke (ed.), *English Family Life, 1576–1716: An Anthology from Diaries* (Oxford, 1988), 34 (Tilley, J6; Wilson, 408; Tilley, P608; Wilson, 650).

[77] *The Diary of Roger Lowe of Ashton-in-Makerfield, Lancashire, 1663–74*, ed. William L. Sachse (London, 1938), 42 (Tilley, S951; Wilson, 110).

a sheep, for a fool is fulsome, yet ye run a risk also in the other, for a shrew may so tye your nose to the grindstone, that the gray mare will prove the better horse; besides, there is another old sayed saw, that every one knowes how to tame a shrew but he who hath her; if it be your fortune to meet with such a one, she may chance put you to the charge of buying a long spoon, for he must have a long spoon who will eat with the devill.[78]

In this case, as in others, there was little consistency about proverbial wisdom, indeed many sayings could be flatly contradictory and derived their meaning only from the specific circumstances in which they were used. Where they can be set in context, however, the 12,000 or so proverbs known to be circulating regularly in early modern England provide a remarkable repository of attitudes, opinions, and beliefs among contemporaries and an analysis of their contents reveals much about the salient values and common preoccupations of this society. Certain themes recurred in them with regularity. There were, for example, 172 saws which revolved around the Devil or devils, a number balanced almost exactly by the 178 which mention God; 102 sayings concerned women, while 56 mentioned death. Significant numbers dealt with issues such as the family, neighbours and kin, or poverty and riches, law and order, the spread of news, and opinions about foreigners.[79]

A glance at the proverbs popular in the sixteenth and seventeenth centuries would provide grist to the mill of anyone seeking to identify enduring continuity in English attitudes, aspirations, and sensibilities over the long period. Many of the cliches of today which might be considered rather modish, turn out to have a long and venerable ancestry. When, for example, the professional footballer tells us in defeat that he is 'as sick as a parrot' he invokes a phrase already familiar when Aphra Behn referred to it in the late seventeenth century; when the language of modern competitiveness reminds us, 'no pain, no gain', it draws on a phrase which was well known even to the ancients; and when the inconsistent or unreliable 'play fast and loose' with us, it is as well to remember that they have been doing so since Tudor times, at least.[80] It comes as no surprise, therefore, to find that by the early modern period people were already long used to 'minding their Ps and Qs' or to 'being all in a quandary'. The price inflation of the last three centuries has conspicuously failed to undermine the value of being 'in for a penny and in for a pound'. It was as axiomatic to contemporaries as it is to us that 'one man's meat is another man's poison'

---

[78] Howell, *Proverbs, or, Old Sayed Sawes and Adages*, 8.

[79] These figures are based on an analysis of Tilley, *A Dictionary of the Proverbs in England*. For proverbs about women, see below, p. 177.

[80] Tilley, P59; Tilley, N305, P413, P420, and Wilson, 581, 633; Tilley, P401.

and that we must 'make hay while the sun shines'. They, too, could be as 'cool as a cucumber' as 'fit as a fiddle' or as 'stiff as a board'; they were every bit as likely to have 'two bites of the cherry', 'beat about the bush' or 'kill two birds with one stone'. The enduring familiarity of these and many other sayings tends to demonstrate the wisdom of Ecclesiastes, that 'there's nothing new under the sun'.[81]

Many sayings display an earthy and irreverent quality, a crude and sometimes scatological flavour which owes less to the distillations of classical and patristic wisdom and more to the brisk physicality of popular culture. A seventeenth-century Scottish collector quite cheerfully recorded 'Ane drunken cunt had never ane good dore bar [has no porter]', 'Ye eat all and dryts [shit] all and harles [drag] the barrow at your ars', and 'Ye ar all cunts bennisone [quarrelsom]', among the familiar expressions of his countrymen.[82] Reference to bodily functions was, it seems, never far from people's lips. 'Piss and fart, a sound heart'; 'He that is afraid of every fart must go far to piss'; 'You may lend your ass and shit through your ribs'. At the same time it was well known that 'shitten luck is good luck', but that 'the more you stir a turd the more it stinks'.[83] There was a blunt realism about much proverbial wisdom which reflects an unsentimental, matter-of-fact approach to life: 'There came never a large fart out of a wren's ass'; 'Tell a tale to a mare and she will let a fart'; 'You cannot make honey of a dog's turd'; 'Who lives by hope dies breaking of wind backwards'; 'Look high and fall into a cow turd'.[84]

Many proverbial sayings echo the experiences and sensibilities of their humble speakers. We hear in them a stoical resignation, a sober acceptance of the world around, a world of economic hardship and social inferiority. It was, after all, 'better a bare foot than no foot at all'; 'better half a loaf than no bread'; 'better half an egg than an empty shell'. It was foolish to 'look for a golden life in an iron age'; it was well to remember that 'the weakest goes to the wall'; in the end, it was 'better to die a beggar then live a beggar'. Inequalities were fundamental and life could be brutal: 'the pleasures of the mighty are the tears of the poor'; 'the difference twixt the poor man and the rich is that the one walketh to gett meet for his stomach, the other to get a stomach for his meat'; the poor 'pay for all' and 'suffer all the wrong'.[85] Hungry people would remind the authorities that

---

[81] Tilley, P1; Q1; P196; M483; H235; C895; F202; B485; B423; B742; B400; T147.

[82] *Fergusson's Scottish Proverbs from the Original Print of 1641 Together with a Larger Manuscript Collection*, ed. Erskine Beveridge (Scottish Text Society, new ser., 15, Edinburgh and London, 1924), 16, 115, 116 (Tilley, A215; C901; A216).

[83] Tilley, H322; F67; A385; L581; T603.    [84] Tilley, F70; T47; H562; H609; C781.

[85] Tilley, F561; H36; H37; L267; W185; B231; P422; M366; M357; P469.

'the belly hath no ears' because 'words will not fill it', as did the destitute weavers at Maldon in Essex during the riots of 1629.[86] Or they might threaten, 'a hungry man, an angry man', that 'hunger breaks down stone walls', and that one day 'the ram may kill the butcher', as Shakespeare well knew. The risings of 1607 around his native Warwickshire having just abated, he gave Coriolanus occasion to despise the 'vulgar wisdoms' of the people.

> They said they were an-hungry; sigh'd forth proverbs—
> That hunger broke stone walls, that dogs must eat,
> That meat was made for mouths, that the gods sent not
> Corn for rich men only. With these shreds
> They vented their complainings.[87]

A popular suspicion of the law and distrust of lawyers also resounds in these shreds of complaint. For there was 'one law for the rich and another for the poor' and 'laws catch flies and let hornets go free': no wonder it was so often said that 'the law is an ass'. As for the practitioners of law, a good lawyer proverbially made an evil neighbour and had to be a great liar. His opinions were worth nothing unless paid for; his gown was lined with the wilfulness of his clients; and his house was built on the heads of fools. What chance, then, for the poor 'countryman' who between two lawyers was 'like a fish between two cats', or 'a goose 'twixt two foxes'?[88] There was some satisfaction, perhaps, in the knowledge that few lawyers died well and few physicians lived well; for physicians were another group perceived as prospering undeservedly on the backs of the helpless. 'The physician owes all to the patient, but the patient owes nothing to him but a little money'; 'Where there are three physicians there are two atheists'; 'Physicians kill more than they cure'.[89] And finally, proverbs reveal a similarly jaundiced attitude towards the clergy. 'If you would live well for a week, kill a hog; if you would live well for a month, marry; if you would live well all your life, turn priest'; 'The parson always christens his own child first'; 'Take heed of an ox before, an ass behind, and a parson on all sides'; 'Three things are insatiable: priests, women and the sea', or, otherwise, 'women, priests and poultry have never enough'.[90]

---

[86] Tilley, B286; John Walter, 'Grain Riots and Popular Attitudes to the Law: Maldon and the Crisis of 1629', in John Brewer and John Styles (eds.), *An Ungovernable People: The English and their Law in the Seventeenth and Eighteenth Centuries* (London, 1980), 70.

[87] M187; H811; R26; Shakespeare, *Coriolanus*, i. i. 152–6.

[88] Wilson, 445–7; Tilley, L116; L124; L125; L130; C713; C411.

[89] Wilson, 245, 622–3; Tilley, L129; P268.

[90] Wilson, 474–5, 610, 604, 817, 911; Tilley, M1107; C318; H376; W717.

Amid the grumblings, there was also a certain resigned consolation in many popular platitudes. Comfort might be taken from the fact that 'riches and sin are often married together', that 'riches bring care and fears' and that 'the rich know not who their friends are'. It was axiomatic that rich men were miserable, and often said that a rich man was either wicked himself or the heir of a wicked man. In any case, it was suspected that 'content lodges oftener in cottages than palaces', undeniable that 'love lives in cottages as well as in courts', and plainly true that 'the sun shines on all alike'. At least 'he that lies upon the ground can fall no lower', and remember that 'necessity is the mother of invention'. In the end, life was merely a question of expectations: after all, 'a humble bee in a cow-turd thinks himself a king'.[91]

This air of cheerful stoicism hangs over many other vulgar wisdoms, betraying a degree of whimsy in the face of life's struggles. When all was said and done, it was 'better a snotty child than his nose wiped off' and 'better to marry than to burn'. It was wise not to 'piss against the wind' and not to 'scold thy lips on another man's pottage'. The proverbs of courtship and marriage, in particular, exude a certain wry humour. 'He that woos a maid must feign, lie and flatter; but he that woos a widow must down his breeches and at her'; 'When a couple are newly married, the first month is honeymoon or smick smack, the second is hither thither, the third is thwick thwack, the fourth, the devil take them that brought you and I together'. Everyone should accept that 'a husband must be deaf and his wife blind to have quietness', and it was well to remember that there was much 'more to marriage than four bare legs in a bed'. People expressed themselves in a stream of vivid similes which gave their speech an exuberant and evocative quality. Thus, great eaters were said to 'dig their graves with their teeth'; the person 'who tells a lie to save his credit wipes his nose on his sleeve to save his napkin'; to state the obvious was to 'teach your grandame to grope her ducks'; to be precipitate was to 'kiss my ass before my breeches are down'; to be 'a man of words and not of deeds' was to be 'like a garden full of weeds', for 'fair words butter no parsnips'. Anyone with great hopes for some improbable undertaking would be met with the deriding, 'Fire, quoth the fox when he pissed on the ice'.[92]

Given that proverbs were such an integral part of the spoken language, therefore, they hardly needed to be learned in any formal sense but were

---

[91] Tilley, R106; R109; R104; M363; M364; C626; L519; S985; G464; N61; H806.

[92] Tilley, C296; M692; W427; L328; M18; C714; H834; M1146; E53; L240; G407; A386; M296; W791; F263. Cf. Eugen Weber, *Peasants into Frenchmen: The Modernization of Rural France, 1870–1914* (Stanford, Calif., 1976), 419–28.

merely absorbed by people, without thinking, in the process of daily inter-
course. It was scarcely necessary to attend a school or a church in order to
be saturated with a wealth of proverbial imagery and aphoristic wisdom at
an early age and to have it always on the tip of the tongue, ready to meet
any situation. Occasionally it is possible, nevertheless, to see the ways in
which the lessons which proverbs contained might be inculcated more
self-consciously from parents or elders to their children in the domestic
sphere. In the 1660s, for example, the Yorkshire gentlewoman, Alice
Thornton, was carrying out the educative function of many mothers in
teaching her son 'to read, and heare him his catechisme, prayers, and
psalmes, gitting proverbs by heart, and many such like dutys'. Her father
before her had kept a 'Booke of Advice to his Son George' which was
clearly full of wise words and goodly lessons, the benefit of which Alice
sought to pass on to her own progeny.

> I charge you, therefore, all my deare children and grandchildren, to keepe fast
> those good instructions, advice, and councells, which are writt in my said hon-
> ored father's booke, and to make it your indeavours to walke answerable to those
> precepts in the frameing your lives and conversations uprightly and just, in your
> thoughts, words, and actions.[93]

Further down the social order such moral teachings and proverbial
wisdoms were probably less likely to be committed to paper. In the book
kept by Robert Furse of Dean Prior in Devon, however, we have a
remarkable record of this didactic process at work in the household of an
Elizabethan yeoman farmer. In 1593 Furse decided to set down the
lessons for his son which he himself had learned both from oral tradition
and from his personal practice, or 'evydenses, som by reporte off old
awncyente men and som of my on knowlege and experyens'. He commended the wisdom of his ancestors 'allthoffe some of them wer but
sympell ande unlernede and men off smalle possessyenes substance
habillyte or reputasion'. Thus, for a great many of the important realms
and crucial decisions of life Furse had an old saying to impart. He invoked
a pair of medieval saws in order to warn against the regrets which result
from not being certain of a thing before acting upon it: 'beware of "hadde
I wyste" but as the olde saynge ys "knowe or you knytte so maye you well
slacke but knytte not before you knowe for then hyt may be to late"'. He
advised his successors not to concern themselves with the affairs of
others but to 'lett everye man shutt his own bowe'; he pointed to the sense
of not spending the inheritance before his death, 'here remember the

---

[93] *The Autobiography of Mrs Alice Thornton, of East Newton, Co. York*, ed. Charles Jackson
(Surtees Society, 72, Durham, 1875), 261, 191–2.

comon saynge that "the catte dothe not growne before he hathe the mowse so surelye"'. Concerning education his counsel was similarly supported:

> Geve yourselves to the redynge and herynge of the holy scryptures and suche like good docteren to be lerned in the laws of the realme and have to rede the old cronnenekeles and shuch like awnshyente hystoryes rememburynge yt ys a commone saynge 'yt is a shame for a man to be ignorante of that whyche he ofte to knowe'.

Finally, in encouraging his male heirs to find good wives, he proffered more gnomic suggestions:

> But whate so ever she be inquyre dylygentelye of what nature quallytes or condysyones her mother ys of for comenly the dofter do lerne the quallytes and maners of ther mother and marke also howe and yn what companye she hathe bynne brofte uppe from her yuthe for the proverbe ys 'loke what ys fyrste brofte or putte ynto an newe vessell the vessell shall ever savor thereof'.[94]

There were other means, too, by which ordinary men and women might absorb or learn proverbial wisdom more deliberately than simply by osmosis in conversation. For one thing, it was common at this time to write up proverbs and moral sentences on walls. All manner of public buildings, as well as great houses and humble cottages, could be decorated with well-chosen counsels upon which to reflect. It was almost as if walls everywhere could speak, commented the Elizabethan composer, Thomas Whythorne, when he read a mural proverb in an Italian house. Churches had long been adorned with biblical sentences and pious aphorisms painted aloft to edify their viewers. An ecclesiastical canon of 1604 prescribed that such 'sentences' should be drawn in churches and chapels to be read aloud by those who were able. Typically, it was reported from one Cambridgeshire parish in 1662 that 'the Ten Commandments are sett up in our parishe church where the people may read them, and other chosen sentences are written upon the walls . . . in places convenient'.[95]

In secular buildings, meanwhile, the walls might confront the reader with a variety of wise sayings. Thus, the outer chambers at Wressell Castle in the East Riding, owned by the earls of Northumberland and demolished in 1650, were covered with moral maxims.

---

[94] 'Furse of Moreshead: A Family Record of the Sixteenth Century', ed. H. J. Carpenter, in *Report and Transactions of the Devonshire Association*, 26 (1894), 170, 172, 179.

[95] *The Autobiography of Thomas Whythorne*, ed. James M. Osborn (Oxford, 1961), 63; Tessa Watt, *Cheap Print and Popular Piety, 1550–1640* (Cambridge, 1991), 193, 217–20; *Episcopal Visitation Returns for Cambridgeshire: Matthew Wren, Bishop of Ely, 1638–1665*, ed. W. M. Palmer (Cambridge, 1930), 80.

Pronounce thes proverbis indefferently,
Withe remors of reason and not sensually,
For as soundithe the instrument,
So shalbe judged the entent.
Parabillis symylitudis and reasons morall,
Be comprysede and left for a memoriall,
Of vertues information and goodly doctryne,
They whiche be goode of reason will inclyne.

'The olde saw sayethe that measure is a treasure, For in short tyme thy goode may well waste away', shouted out one sentence from the side of an inner chamber.[96]

Similarly, at the Percys' manor house at Leconfield, near Beverley, many of the walls and ceilings had proclaimed sententious morality since the reign of Henry VII. Proverbs were exchanged by characters in illustrated dialogues in order to create the impression of wisdom spoken. Among the cries from the roof of the highest chamber in the garden lodge were, 'Esperaunce in fortune when she smylithe, Nay beware for she begilithe'; 'Esperaunce in glory and magnificens hye, Nay beware thou may fall sodcynly'; 'Esperaunce en dieu in hym is all, Be thou contente and thou art above fortunes fall'. The roof of his Lordship's closet advised, 'He that in his memory goode lernyne will bere away, Nedithe not to be a disciple and study all day'; 'An olde proverbe it is meane is a treasure, Why shoulde not youthe at tymes enjoye his pleasure'. The ceiling in the library warned, among its rhymed verooo, 'Drede God and fle from syn, Of hym all goodnes dothe begyn'; 'In many wordis is syn comonly, Speke litill and trewly'; 'This proverbe lerne of me, Avaunt nevyr of thy degree'.[97]

Further down in society, inns and alehouses were often decorated with painted cloths or 'steyned hangings' upon which were frequently bespatttered wise words and old proverbs. 'Who fears a sentence or an old man's saw, shall by a painted cloth be kept in awe', as Shakespeare had it. In 1564, William Bullein could conjure up the image of an inn at Barnet, north of London, in which the 'comlie parlour' was 'trimlie apparelled' with 'faire clothes with manie wise saiynges painted vpon them' in 'golden letters'. One suggested the moral of Aesop's fable of the hare and the tortoise. *'Melius est claudus in via quam cursor praeter viam.* That is, better is an halting

---

[96] *The Antiquarian Repertory*, ed. Francis Grose (4 vols., London, 1775–84), iv. 182–7, 256–60.

[97] Ibid., iii. 265–71; iv. 9–15, 77–81, 112–15. For other examples, see F. W. Reader, 'Tudor Domestic Wall-Paintings', *Archaeological Journal*, 92 (1935), 277 and plate XVI; id., 'Wall-Paintings of the Sixteenth and Early Seventeenth Centuries Recently Discovered in Bosworth House, Wendover, Bucks', *Archaeological Journal*, 87 (1930), 85.

man whiche kepeth the right waie, then the swift ronner besides, that wandereth a straie.' That such sights were becoming rarer by the late seventeenth century is suggested by the nostalgia of John Aubrey's reflection upon them.

In former times, as in some old houses is yet to be seen, which argues the goodness of that age, on the painted hangings were writ good, moral sentences. Sir Ralph Hopton, afterwards Lord, was wont to say that he learned more philosophy once from a painted cloth in an alehouse than in all the books he had read; sc: 'Never lament or make any moan | For either there's remedy, or there is none'.

Aubrey continued to believe that an excellent way to teach children was to 'have several emblems well-painted to delight their ingenious young spirits with their mottoes selected proper for their fancy: they will both delight and instruct'.[98]

This practice of proverbing the walls is no less evident in ordinary dwellings. In the first floor room of a very modest sixteenth-century cottage by the London road in Chalfont St Peter, Buckinghamshire, for example, was inscribed: 'When any thinge thou takest in hand to do or enterpryse, fyrst markewell the fynall end there of that maye aryse. Feare God.' Around 1597 a yeoman of Cowden in Kent adorned his farmhouse with, 'For hee that will not heare ye crye | of them that stande in neede | Shall crye him selfe and not be hard | when he doth hope to spede'. The same maxim was one of those which filled the house of the estate steward, John Smyth, at North Nibley in Gloucestershire. During the first decade of the seventeenth century he jotted down a list of 'moral notes and sayings' to be painted up in his hall, chamber, and parlour 'above the waynscott'. Together with the biblical quotations which he reserved for the private rooms, he chose certain aphorisms for public display, including 'They that perceive not deceipt are often deceived themselves'; 'Crowes will not peck a man til he be dead, but flatterers will devour a man being alyve'; and the marital adage, 'Happy is hee that wooeth vertue, but more happy is hee that is contracted to her'.[99]

---

[98] Shakespeare, *The Rape of Lucrece* (1594), lines 244–5; William Bullein, *A Dialogue bothe Pleasaunt and Pietifull wherein is a Godlie Regiment against the Fever Pestilence* (London, 1564), fo. 60; *Aubrey on Education*, ed. Stephens, 63, 62. Cf. Henry Porter, *The Pleasant History of the Two Angry Women of Abington* (London, 1599), sig. D1ᵛ. In the 1720s Nathaniel Salmon also thought that these 'hangings' full of 'useful lessons' belonged to 'our grandfathers' day': *The History of Hertfordshire* (London, 1728), 303.

[99] F. W. Reader, 'Tudor Mural Paintings in the Lesser Houses in Bucks', *Archaeological Journal*, 89 (1932), 171 and plate XXIV; Philip Mainwaring Johnston, 'Mural Paintings in Houses', *Journal of the British Archaeological Association*, new ser., 37 (1932), 84; David Rollison, 'The Bourgeois Soul of John Smyth of Nibley', *Social History*, 12 (1987), 326–8.

It is likely that, as in the case of biblical sayings, printed texts often provided the inspiration for this mural sentencing. Thomas Tusser recommended a number of versified adages, or 'posies', with which the husbandman and his wife might aptly furnish their rooms, for example. Those suitable for the hall included, 'The wise will spend or give or lend, yet keepe to have in store, If fooles may have from hand to mouth, they passe upon no more'; among the suggested parlour wisdom was, 'Oft times a friend is got with easie cost, Which used evill is oft as quickly lost'; the guest-room might warn, 'The sloven and the carles man, the roinish nothing nice, To lodge in chamber comely deckt, are seldome suffred twice'; and the main bed chamber may well enquire, 'What better bed than conscience good, to passe the night with sleepe? What better worke than daily care fro sinne thy selfe to keepe?'[100]

Moreover, with the spread of printed broadsides from the second half of the sixteenth century, many of which were pasted on walls for purposes of edification and entertainment, the popular press also came to the aid of mural proverbing. Various examples of cheap print were specifically devoted to the inculcation of aphoristic wisdom, among them Jacobean titles such as, *Table observations, Solomon's sentences, The Christian's ABC,* and *Keep within compasse.*[101] Much later, *Old Mr Dod's Sayings* (1667), posthumously attributed to the puritan divine, John Dod, seem to have been displayed in this way: in the mid-eighteenth century it was reported that 'many of them on two sheets of paper, are still to be seen pasted on the walls of cottages'.[102] At the same time, the ubiquity of *King Charles's Twelve Good Rules* was also indicative of the popularity of sententious advice on the printed sheet. These dicta were thought to have been left in the study of Charles I: 'Prophane no Divine Ordinances; Touch no State Matters; Urge no Healths; Pick no Quarrels; Maintain no Ill Opinions; Encourage no Vice; Repeat no Grievances; Reveal no Secrets; Make no Comparisons; Keep no Bad Company; Make no Long Meals; Lay no Wagers.' For many generations they were posted up in schools, alehouses, and cottages throughout England.[103]

---

[100] Tusser, *Five Hundred Points of Good Husbandry*, ed. Grigson, 186–8.

[101] Watt, *Cheap Print and Popular Piety*, 234–5, 301–3.

[102] *Old Mr Dod's Sayings* (London, 1667); J. O. Halliwell, *Descriptive Notices of Popular English Histories* (Percy Society, 23, London, 1848), 94; William Haller, *The Rise of Puritanism* (New York, 1938), 59–60; Isaac D'Israeli, 'The Philosophy of Proverbs', in his *A Second Series of Curiosities of Literature* (3 vols., London, 1823), i. 426. In the mid-eighteenth century an old woman from Shiplake, Oxfordshire, told James Granger, 'that she should have gone distracted for the loss of her husband, if she had been without Mr. Dod's *Sayings* in the house': James Granger, *A Biographical History of England from Egbert the Great to the Revolution* (2 vols., London, 1769), i. 255–6.

[103] Morris Martin, 'The Case of the Missing Woodcuts', *Print Quarterly*, 4 (1987), 343–61;

A wide variety of other cheap printed material clearly served to disseminate proverbial wisdom at the lower and semi-literate levels of society. Ballads, for example, could offer advice on good conduct in a more
whimsical way. *GoodAdmonition, Or to al sorts of people this counsell I sing, That
in each ones affaire, To take heed's a faire thing* (1633) was a typical collection of
didactic proverbs in verse. Many ballads had proverbial titles, such as
Martin Parker's *A Prouerbe old, yet nere forgot, Tis good to strike while the Irons
hott. Or, Councell to all Young men that are poore, To Marry with Widowes now while
there is store.* Carolled in alehouses and bawled in market-places, anyone
might hear *Anything for a Quiet Life, A Fooles Bolt is Soone Shot, I Smell a Rat,
Jone is as Good as My Lady*, or *The Proverbe is True that Weddinge is Destyne.* Frequently these songs pointed up their old saws for listeners to take note:
'this prouerbe old, hath oft bene told, Tis good to strike while the iron's
hott'; 'The common proverb, as it is read, That a man must hit the nayle
on the head'; 'It is an old saying, that few words are best'; 'And, as the
prouerbe doth show very playne, A hood for this foole, to kepe him from
the rayne'. More casually, they were crammed full of familiar sayings and
aphoristic phrases, as was natural in a form intended to be sung aloud and
easily retained. It has been calculated, for example, that of the 305 titles in
Child's collection of *English and Scottish Popular Ballads*, 211 contain proverbial material in one or more of their versions. Stock formulae and
repeated refrains such as these had been an aid to memory in the oral performance of both professional ballad singers and their audiences for millennia, of course.[104]

Another influential publication in this respect was the astrological
handbook *Erra Pater* which, together 'with sundry like ancient surebies,
and old sokers', commented John Harvey in the 1580s, 'haue set down'
many 'wholsome rules, and goodly maximes', 'forlorne said saws, and tri-
fling gewgawes' for the benefit of the 'meaner and baser sort' of people.
These, and the growing number of almanacs, were full of 'pretended

Thomas Holcroft, *Memoirs of the late Thomas Holcroft, Written by Himself* (3 vols., London, 1816),
i. 135–6; Thomas Bewick, *A Memoir of Thomas Bewick Written by Himself*, ed. Iain Bain (Oxford,
1975), 193; George Deacon, *John Clare and the Folk Tradition* (London, 1983), 50.

[104] Wright, *Middle-Class Culture in Elizabethan England*, 225 n., 429; Natascha Wurzbach, *The
Rise of the English Street Ballad, 1550–1650* (Cambridge, 1990), 72–3, 75–6, 77–8, 93, 204–5, 219, 324,
331; Hyder E. Rollins, 'Concerning Bodleian MS. Ashmole 48', *Modern Language Notes*, 34 (1919),
343; C. R. Baskervill, *The Elizabethan Jig and Related Song Drama* (Chicago, 1929), 488; B. J.
Whiting, 'Proverbial Material in the Popular Ballad', *Journal of American Folklore*, 47 (1934), 22–44;
James H. Jones, 'Commonplace and Memorization in the Oral Tradition of English and Scottish
Popular Ballads', *Journal of American Folklore*, 74 (1961), 97–112. For other examples of proverbial
phrases in ballads, see Wurzbach, *The Rise of the English Street Ballad*, 45, 63, 71, 84, 86, 94, 104, 109,
111, 113, 168, 175, 201, 206.

prophesies, old said saws, antique prognosticates and shepheardly sooth-sayings' aimed at ordinary rustics. The almanacs of Thomas Bretnor pub-lished between 1609 and 1618, for example, contained lists of good and evil days with accompanying proverbs. Given that, as Henry Peacham said dismissively of the country clown, '*Erra Pater* and this year's almanac, if he can read, are the only books he spends his time in', the impact of such works in popularizing proverbial sayings should not be underestimated.[105]

## USEFUL KNOWLEDGE

So it was that proverbial wisdom could express the accumulated ethical values of ordinary people in early modern England. At the least literate levels of society this source of guidance and authority was indispensable to the many people for whom written instruction was inaccessible and on the many issues on which it was simply unavailable. Prescriptive adages constituted a kind of oral textbook or mental reference in which to seek help and find advice. This might extend, moreover, beyond moral and emotional issues to the practical tasks of daily life. For it was in this form that people carried much of their knowledge of meteorology, medicine, and the law; in this way that they transmitted and retained the tried and trusted methods of agriculture and husbandry, the intimate techniques of art and craft, the useful tips of manufacture and trade. This was a period in which, as Isaac D'Israeli later put it, 'the workman condensed some traditional secret of his craft into a proverbial expression' and those 'who gave counsel gave wealth'.[106]

In what was a predominantly rural and agricultural society it was nat-ural that an immense stock of proverbial wisdom should have existed to guide and dictate the ways of life on the land. The countryman, as John Earle observed, always had 'some thrifty hobnaile prouerbes to clout his discourse'. Thus, to stop and pass the time of day with a husbandman in early Tudor Derbyshire would have been to hear a flow of old saws, ready to meet any circumstance. 'It is an olde saying, "The oxe is neuer wo, tyll he to the harowe goo"'; another 'olde sayinge: he that hath bothe shepe, swyne, and bees, slepe he, wake he, he maye thryue'; and 'there is a olde common sayenge, that seldom doth the housbande thryue, withoute the

---

[105] John Harvey, *A Discoursive Probleme Concerning Prophesies* (London, 1588), 98–9, 128–9; John Crow, 'Some Jacobean Catch-Phrases and Some Light on Thomas Bretnor', in Herbert Davis and Helen Gardner (eds.), *Elizabethan and Jacobean Studies Presented to Frank Percy Wilson* (Oxford, 1959), 250–78; Bernard Capp, *Astrology and the Popular Press: English Almanacs, 1500–1800* (London, 1979), 204, 229–30; Henry Peacham, *The Truth of our Times* (1638), ed. Virgil B. Heltzel (Ithaca, NY, 1962), 215.

[106] D'Israeli, 'The Philosophy of Proverbs', in his *A Second Series of Curiosities of Literature*, i. 418.

leue of his wyfe'. One might have met 'thopinion of olde husbandes' that peas should 'be sowen in the olde of the mone . . . that they shoulde the better codde, and the sooner be rype'; and would likely 'haue harde olde houswyues saye, that better is Marche hurdes than Apryll flaxe'. At Walden in Essex, meanwhile, one 'saying of old husbend men' in the 1550s reminded:

> That the hoyty as tymly sewyng
> Som tyme yt faylyth
> Butt to late sewyng
> Seldom as men wyll provyth.[107]

Thus, it was hardly surprising that when, between 1557 and 1580, Thomas Tusser came to set down the wisdom learned from his farming experience in East Anglia, much of it was expressed in the form of proverbs and sayings, rhymed and alliterative the better to be kept 'in memorie fast'. In Tusser's couplets we hear the language of the country-side, abounding with old saws which were probably ancient when he chanced to weave them into the fabric of his text, so providing some of their earliest recordings. 'Who soweth in raine, he shall reape it with teares, who soweth in harmes, he is ever in feares' was among the advice to the husbandman and his wife in October. In December, 'Give cattle their fodder in plot drie and warm, and count them for miring or other like harme'; and then, 'Calves likely that come between Christmas and Lent, take huswife to reare, or else after repent.' A reminder for February was, 'Go plow in the stubble, for now is the season, for sowing of fitchis, of beanes, and of peason'. Thereafter, 'Sowe barlie in March, in April and Maie, the latter in sand, and the sooner in claie'; 'Good flax and good hemp for to have of hir owne, in Maie a good huswife will see it be sowne'; and 'In June and August, as well doth appeere, is best to mowe brakes, of all times in the yeere'. A number of sayings dealt specifically with the tasks of housewifery. When brewing, for example, it was well to remember, 'Brew somewhat for thine, Else bring up no swine'; 'Well brewed, worth cost, Ill used, halfe lost'; 'Remember good Gill, Take paine with thy swill'. Advice for baking ran, 'New bread is a drivell. Much crust is as evill'; in the dairy, guidance included, 'Good droie woorth much. Marke sluts and such'; and in the malthouse it was true that 'Ill malting is theft, wood dride hath a weft'.[108]

---

[107] Earle, *Micro-cosmographie*, sig. F6ʳ; Fitzherbert, *The Book of Husbandry*, ed. Skeat, 24, 74, 93, 22, 96; BL, Lansdowne MS, 210, fo. 80ᵛ.
[108] Tusser, *Five Hundred Points of Good Husbandry*, ed. Grigson, 41, 55, 76, 83, 93, 106, 121, 167–70.

Every region clearly had a similar body of lore relevant to its own farm-ing conditions. The yeoman Richard Shanne, who farmed at Methley, south of Leeds in the West Riding of Yorkshire, during the Elizabethan and Jacobean period, transcribed a series of Tusser-like mnemonics into his commonplace book. For each month he had a series of rhymed proverbials which could be remembered easily and applied year upon year. Thus in February:

> Sowe beanes pease and oates, in ground hote and drie,
>> When as the newe moone, appeared to thine eye,
> Superfluous brannches, from trees prune awaie,
>> And suffer not mosse upon them to staie,
> Plash and twist hedges, risse up youre ley lande,
>> Lay quiellsetts, plant roses, the springe is at hande.

And later in the year another verse reminded:

> September is come, and therefore applie,
> In lande that is stronge, to sowe wheat and rie,
>> Nowe reape up youre barlie, least that it be loste,
> Youre beanes and youre peasome, to quite care and coste,
>> Remembringe allwaies, the age of the moone,
> So shall youe do nothinge, to laite or to soone.[109]

An interesting example of the relationship between the oral and written traditions in this context is provided by the farming and memo-randum books of Henry Best who owned the manor of Elmswell, over in the East Riding, between 1618 and 1645. Best clearly used and applied Tusser's saws in his own husbandry. Thus, on sheep shearing: 'Lette lambs goe unclipped till June bee halfe worne, The better the fleeces will growe to bee shorne'; and 'Tusser's advice: you are to provide:—"A sheep-marke, a tarre-kettle little or much, Two pottles of tarre to a pottle of pitch".' But in the particular pastoral conditions of his region he generally found the oral tradition of the local shepherds, their 'usuall sayinges', 'country proverbes', and other 'shorte remembrances', a far more reliable guide to practice than the formulations of a book based upon experience elsewhere.

Husbandmen usually begin to folde their sheepe about May-day and continue folding them till the begininge of September according to Tussers direcktions:— 'Sette then noe barre, Whilst moneth hayth an R'. But the truth is, men cannot leave theire sheepe unfolded soe longe as there is any corne in the field.

---

[109] BL, Additional MS, 38599, fos. 59ʳ–64ᵛ.

At every phase of the sheep-rearing calendar a local proverb came to mind. When breeding, 'The usuall sayinge is, "at St Luke lett Ewe goe to tupe", which is aboute the 18th of October'; during this period, 'The most judicious sheep-men endeavour by all means possible to provide good tuppes for ewes, for they say "a bad ewe may bringe a bad lambe, yett shee spoyles but one; but an ill tuppe is likely to spoyle many".' Local experience recommended putting a ewe into a good pasture three weeks before giving birth and for three weeks afterwards, both to strengthen the mother and to encourage the lamb to feed: 'hence ariseth the shepheards phrase that "Whiles the grasse groweth, Ewe dryeth, lambe dyeth".' At shearing time, 'the country proverbe is:—"The man that is aboute to clippe his sheepe, Must pray for two faire dayes and one faire week"', a maxim which concisely captured the shepherd's need for 'a faire day the day before hee clippe, that the wooll may bee dry, a faire day when hee clippes, a week of faire whether after hee hath clipped, that the sheepe may be hardened and theire woll somethinge growne before a storme come'.[110]

The weather was, of course, vital to the fortunes of all farmers and this is reflected in the large number of sayings and saws, many of them quite local, which were relied upon to predict changes in climate and season. It was often observed that country people were skilled in observing 'prognostics' of the weather and the 'fore-knowledges' which interpreted 'the signes and token of every particular season'.[111] Much of this experience was captured in proverbial rhymes which were easily remembered and much trusted. Thus many of the 'western vulgar proverbs' which John Aubrey 'rakt-up' in the course of conversation with his neighbours during the second half of the seventeenth century naturally concerned changes in the weather. A typically earthy prognostic ran,

> The moon does always pisse, when she is pale,
> When red, she farts, when white, she wipes her tayle.

Or, as Aubrey explained, 'contry-men observe as a certain rule, that a dripping moon (i.e.) perpendicular, presages wett, especially the moon being of a clowdy and blackish colour . . . and that the weather will last so a good while: e.g. if it last to the full, it will be wet after the full; if till the new, it will be so after'. In the same vein was the 'Wiltshire proverb',

---

[110] *The Farming and Memorandum Books of Henry Best of Elmswell, 1642*, ed. Donald Woodward (British Academy, Records of Social and Economic History, new ser., 8, London, 1984), 6, 7, 10, 16, 22, 23, 25, 29, 36–7.

[111] See, for example, Francis Bacon, *Sylva Sylvarum: Or A Natural History* (1627), in *The Works of Francis Bacon*, ed. Spedding, Ellis, and Heath, ii. 603–9; Gervase Markham, *The English Husbandman* (London, 1635), 9, 11–12, 20; John Worlidge, *Systema Agriculturae: The Mystery of Husbandry Discovered* (London, 1669), 219–64.

When the wind is north-west,
the weather is at the best:
If the raine comes out of the east,
'twill raine twice twenty-four howres at the least.

Among other 'old Wiltshire country prognosticks of the weather' was,

When the hen doth moult before the cock,
the winter will be as hard as a rock;
But if the cock moults before the hen,
the winter will not wett your shoes seame.

Armed with such sayings the husbandman could determine his practice accordingly. Thus 'a proverbial rithme observed as infallible by the inhabitants on the Severne-side' ran,

If it raineth when it doth flow,
then yoke your oxe, and goe to plough;
But if it raineth when it doth ebb,
then unyoak your oxe, and goe to bed.

Equally, a proverbial prediction 'generally agreed on to be matter of fact' in south Wiltshire was 'the constant observation . . . that if droppes doe hang on the hedges on Candlemas-day    it will be a good pease year'.[112]

At the same time Aubrey observed that 'there are certain popular prognosticks drawn from the festivals in the kalendar and conceived opinions of certain daies in the months'. At the beginning of the year he found that the local 'vulgar' preserved 'a proverb in Welsh of great antiquity, sc. "Haf hyd gatan, Gaiaf hyd Fay", that is, if it be somerly weather till the kalends of January; it will be winterly weather to the kalends of May. They looke upon this as an oracle.' For the next month, he recorded that 'the shepherds, and vulgar people in south Wilts call Februarie "Sowlegrove": and have this proverbe of it, viz. "Sowlegrowe sil lew". That is, February is seldome warme.' Another 'proverbial distich' which followed thereafter was, 'April borroweth three daies of March, and they are ill'. In general, it was 'usual among us to qualifie, or conditionate the twelve months of the yeare, answerably unto the temper of the twelve daies in Christmas'. All such things, he noted, 'men believe upon some borrowed experience of their owne, and received traditions of their forefathers'.[113]

---

[112] Bod. Lib., MS Aubrey 1, fo. 7ᵛ; John Aubrey, 'Observations', in *John Aubrey: Three Prose Works*, ed. John Buchanan-Brown (Fontwell, 1972), 337; Aubrey, *The Natural History of Wiltshire*, ed. Britton, 16.

[113] Aubrey, 'The Remaines of Gentilisme and Judaisme', in *Three Prose Works*, ed. Buchanan-Brown, 222, 223.

A general preoccupation with the weather is reflected in the fact that something like fifty proverbs relating to the subject were in common circulation during the period. Typically, it was said that 'a burr around the moon bodes wind and rain', and 'so many days old the moon is on Michaelmas day, so many floods'. Old saws foretold that 'A fair day in winter is mother of a storm', that 'the gull comes against a tempest', and 'hail brings frost in the tail'. Daily experience demonstrated that 'an evening red and a morning gray is the sign of a fair day', 'a red morning fortells a stormy day', and 'a red sky in the evening is the sign of a fair day'. Otherwise, 'a mackerel sky' always meant rain. Clearly few people then, as now, heeded the saying that 'change of weather is the discourse of fools'.[114]

In hilly regions there was a host of variations on a theme which predicted rain if the local peak 'wore a cap' of cloud. Thus, one visitor to Cleveland early in the seventeenth century noted that 'towards the weste there stands a highe hill called Roseberry Toppinge, which is a marke to the seamen, an almanacke to the vale, for they have this ould ryme common, "When Roseberrye Toppinge weares a cappe, Let Cleveland then beware a clappe". For indeede yt seldom hath a cloude on yt that some yll weather shortly follows yt not...'. At the same time it was observed in the communities beneath the Cumberland peaks that 'the inhabitants judge of the weather, and have this rhyme common amongst them: "If Skiddaw hath a cap | Scrufell wots full well of that"'. Equally, in north-east Lancashire the locals under Pendle Hill knew that 'when the topp weares a black capp, tis a signe he is rheamatike and rayne', while another old saying around Bolton warned: 'If Riving[ton] Pike do wear a hood | Be sure that day will ne'er be good'.[115]

A popular mind which still marked the passage of time in terms of saints' days and conceived the calendar in terms of their feasts, gave rise

---

[114] Tilley, B733; D120; D72; G478; H12; E191; M1175; S515; M2; C231. For some later compilations on this subject, see M. A. Denham, *A Collection of Proverbs and Popular Sayings, Relating to the Seasons, the Weather, and Agricultural Pursuits; Gathered Chiefly from Oral Tradition* (Percy Society, 20, London, 1846); Charles Swainson, *A Handbook of Weather Folk-Lore* (Edinburgh, 1873); Richard Inwards, *Weather Lore: A Collection of Proverbs, Sayings, and Rules Concerning the Weather* (London, 1893).

[115] *The Topographer and Genealogist*, ed. John Gough Nichols (3 vols., London, 1846–58), ii. 409; William Camden, *Britannia*, ed. Edmund Gibson (London, 1695), 822; BL, Sloane MS, 241, fos. 35ʳ, 73ᵛ; Grose, *A Provincial Glossary with a Collection of Local Proverbs and Popular Superstitions*, sig. O3ʳ. For later recordings of similar rhymes, see John Brand, *Observations on the Popular Antiquities of Great Britain*, ed. Henry Ellis (3 vols., London, 1849), i. 51, 340–2, 351; ii. 43; William Hone, *The Every-Day Book* (2 vols., London, 1825–7), i. 669–70; Robert Forby, *The Vocabulary of East Anglia* (2 vols., London, 1830), ii. 416–17; G. F. Northall, *English Folk-Rhymes* (London, 1892), 73, 88.

to a wide variety of sayings which predicted the weather on this basis. Thus it was said that St Bartholomew's day would bring cold dew, and that St Luke's and St Martin's would be warm. If St Vincent's day was sunny there would be fair weather all year, but 'if St Vitus's day be rainy weather, it will rain for thirty days together'. Most oracular of all was, 'St Swithin's day, if thou dost rain, for forty days it will remain; St Swithin's day, if thou be fair, for forty days t'will rain na mair'. The importance of saints' days was equally evident in the lore of husbandry. So, ran the advice, 'St Benedick, sow thy pease, or keep then in thy rick'; 'Before St Chad every goose lays, both good and bad'; 'St David's day, put oats and barley in the clay'; 'Till St James's day be come and gone, you may have hops or you may have none'; 'St Luke's day the oxen have leave to play'; 'St Matthias take thy hopper and sow'; 'If you bleed your nag on St Stephen's day, he'll work your work for ever and aye'; 'St Thomas divine, brewing, baking, and killing of fat swine'; 'On St Valentine's day cast beans in clay, but on St Chad's sow good or bad'.[116]

More generally, a survival from the Catholic past was the great variety of taboos and observances associated with saints' days and religious feasts which were encapsulated in proverbial sayings. Thus, according to old saws it was bad luck to marry in Lent, in May and 'between sickle and scyth', or to do anything on St Distaff's day; but good luck to borrow on St George's or St John's day. It was an 'old verse so much observed by countrey-people', that 'If Paul's day be faire and cleare | It will betyde a happy yeare'.[117] At the same time, much of the widespread belief in lucky and unlucky days was enshrined in proverb lore. Thus, Friday, as the Elizabethan clergyman William Harrison noted, was 'commonly called among the vulgar sort either king or worling, because it is either the fairest or foulest of the seven'. Sunday was a good day to begin a journey, but to go a-wooing led to ruin. Henry Best observed of farm servants in the East Riding that 'theire desire (hereaboutes) is to goe to theire newe masters eyther on a Tewsday or on a Thursday, for on a Sunday they will seldome remoove, and as for Munday, they account it ominous for they say, "Munday flitte, neaver sitte"'.[118]

[116] Tilley, S37; S62; S38; S39; S40; S45; S52; N2; S67; Wilson, 693–6.

[117] Tilley, S422; S41; Wilson, 515–16, 693–4; Whiting, *Proverbs, Sentences, and Proverbial Phrases*, 500; Aubrey, 'Remaines of Gentilisme and Judaisme', in *Three Prose Works*, ed. Buchanan-Brown, 223.

[118] William Harrison, *The Description of England*, ed. Georges Edelen (Ithaca, NY, 1968), 382–3; Wilson, 42, 788; *The Farming and Memorandum Books of Henry Best*, ed. Woodward, 141. On lucky and unlucky days, see Brand, *Observations on the Popular Antiquities*, ed. Ellis, ii. 44–51; Keith Thomas, *Religion and the Decline of Magic* (London, 1971), 239, 615–23.

The beliefs in the particular properties of days and seasons were also manifest in the popular sayings relating to health, diet, and medicine, and these constituted another important part of useful knowledge which people carried in gnomic form. At a time when professional medicine was either unavailable or inadequate in treating most illness and disease, families passed on traditional domestic remedies from generation to generation, for as the proverb had it, 'kitchen physic is the best physic'. Much counsel of this sort concerned diet. 'The vulgar in the west of England doe call the month of March, Lide', observed Aubrey, and they had 'a proverbiall rhythm. "Eate leekes in Lide, and ramsins in May | And all the yeare after physitians may play".' Equally common advice included, 'eat an apple before going to bed, make the physisian beg his bread'; 'after dinner sit awhile, after supper walk a mile'; 'much meat, much malady'; 'one dish shall serve the turn'; and 'feed by measure and defy the physician'. 'The proverb saith, that many dishes make diseases,' noted Thomas Muffett.[119]

Experience predicted that herbs good for the liver may be bad for the spleen; potions good for the back were bad for the head; and, 'according to the olde prouerbe, That which is good for the head, is euill for the necke and the shoulders'. Other common sayings offered reassurance or warning: 'an ague in the spring is physic for a king'; but 'autumnal agues are long and mortal'; 'quartan agues kill old men and cure young'; and 'agues come on horseback but goe away on foot'. Many proverbs encapsulated tried and trusted remedies for familiar maladies: it was always best to 'stuff a cold and starve a fever'. The phrases, 'hair of the dog' and 'like cures like' captured the popular belief that in the cause of the complaint lay the cure: thus one could tend a bite from a dog with its fur, salve a bee sting with its honey, ease a snake bite with a balsam made of its skin, and soothe a nettle rash with its near neighbour the dock leaf. It was already the case, too, that 'our ale-knights often vse this phrase, and say, "giue vs a haire of the dog that last bit vs"'.[120]

Not surprisingly, professional physicians were rather less enthusiastic

---

[119] Andrew Borde, *Hereafter Foloweth a Compendyous Regyment or a Dyetary of Helth, made in Mou[n]tpyllier* (London, 1542), sig. J5ᵛ; Aubrey, 'Remaines of Gentilisme and Judaisme', in *Three Prose Works*, ed. Buchanan-Brown, 273; Thomas Muffett, *Healths Improvement*, ed. Christopher Bennet (London, 1655), 272; Tilley, P260; L178; D340; M829; D371; M802; D378; Wilson, 17.

[120] James I, *A Covnter-Blaste to Tobacco* (London, 1604), sig. C2ᵛ; Ray, *A Collection of English Proverbs* (2nd edn., 1678), 32–42; Cotgrave, *A Dictionarie of the French and English Tongves*, sig. K2ᵛ; Tilley, H267; A79; A84; A82; A83; F195; D421; H23; Wilson, 319, 464. See also, W. G. Black, *Folk Medicine: A Chapter in the History of Culture* (Folklore Society, London, 1883), 50–2; Roy Porter, 'The People's Health in Georgian England', in Tim Harris (ed.), *Popular Culture in England, c.1500–1850* (Basingstoke, 1995), 124, 130.

about 'kitchen physic'. 'The common people most commonly are disposed to thwart and contradict physicians', lamented James Primrose in the mid-seventeenth century, dismissing their proverbial remedies as 'vulgar errors'. The widespread notion that milk was bad for the liver urged him to stress 'that the common proverbe is false, "milk must be washed from the liver". Because this so familiar and ordinary proverbe is not of any great moment, we will speake but little of it.' He rejected the idea that women in labour, according to the proverb, should only be given hot drinks such as mulled wine, after having 'heard women in child-bed complaine of a grievous thirst and heat, because it is a maxime received by evil observation, that they should take no cooling thing . . .'. 'It is the custom of many', he observed suspiciously, to take exercise if they begin to feel ill, 'following herein the old saying' that '"unto diseases give no way | be hold and let them beare no sway"'. He was prepared to countenance some of the general aphorisms which applied to health. Thus, 'they think it better to bee cured slowly, for that they bee safely and surely cured: "soon enough (saith the proverbe) is well enough"'. In diagnosis it was also 'an axiome of physicians; "one thing is indicated or betokened by one"'. It was unhealthy to smoke too much for, 'the proverb is true, "too much of one thing is good for nothing"'.[121]

Husbandmen and healers were not the only groups to have their particular proverbial lore, of course. Blacksmiths, for example, have contributed to the common stock phrases such as 'to strike while the iron is hot', 'to come to buckle and bear thong'; 'to pull out of the fire', 'to get you off the hook', 'to hit the nail on the head', 'to hammer it out', 'as dead as a door nail', and 'as plain as a pikestaff'. Cheesemakers in Somerset would say: 'If you will have good cheese, and have'n old | You must turn'n seven times before he is cold.' Anglers knew that, 'when the wind is south, | It blows your bait into a fish's mouth'. Sailors were renound for their proverbial lore. They would 'bid the wind blow-devil', for '(a rude sailor's proverb) the more the wind the better the boat'. The seamen off the Suffolk coast had 'a rude verse of their own using' which ran: 'Swoul and Dunwich, and Walderswick, | All go in at one lousie creek.' At Milford Haven it was 'an olde adagie or p[ro]verbe amonge the maryners and sea fareing men . . . sayeing that "Dangers in Milford there is none, | Save the Crow the Carre and the Cattelstone"', alluding to the three great rocks guarding the harbour.[122]

[121] James Primrose, *Popular Errours: Or the Errours of the People in Physick*, trans. Robert Wittie (London, 1651), 290, 166–7, 177, 194, 220, 237, 350, 327.

[122] Wurzbach, *The Rise of the English Street Ballad*, 93–4; Ray, *A Collection of English Proverbs* (2nd edn., 1678), 352, and Aubrey, *The Natural History of Wiltshire*, ed. Britton, 105; Izaak Walton,

Particular regions also had their own distinctive maxims and sayings. Many counties or parishes characterized themselves in terms of 'the north for greatness, the east for health; the south for neatness, the west for wealth', or divided their constituent parts into a schema of 'health and wealth; health without wealth; neither health nor wealth'.[123] Every locality had proverbial rhymes relating to its topographical features and notable landmarks. Thus the 'common saying' recorded in north Lincolnshire that 'between Trent-fall and Whitten-ness, many are made widdows and fatherless', alluded to the tendency for the river Humber to flood its banks. Similarly, further south 'old sawes' predicted that, as the river Welland went, it 'shall drowne all Holland with his excrement'; in Derbyshire, by contrast, 'the people have this saying: "In April, Dove's flood, is worth a king's good"'. Meanwhile, Wiltshire folk would claim that Salisbury Plain was 'never without a thief or twain'; and oft boasted in Herefordshire was 'blessed is the eye, that is betwixt Severn and Wye'.[124] People frequently characterized their county by rhymes based on the proverbial qualities of certain communities. So in Essex it was 'Braintree for the pure, and Bocking for the poor, Coggeshall for the jeering town, and Kelvedon for the whore'; in Suffolk, 'Beccles for a puritan, Bungay for the poor, Halesworth for a drunkard, and Bilborough for a whore'; and in Surrey, 'Sutton for mutton, Cashalton for beeves, Epsom for whores, and Ewel for thieves'.[125]

Clearly such sayings could contribute strongly to a sense of identity and parochial consciousness amongst their users. To know the maxims and

*The Complete Angler* (Everyman edn., London, 1906), 95; Daniel Defoe, *A Tour thro' the Whole Island of Great Britain*, ed. G. D. H. Cole (London, 1927), 101, 55; BL, Additional MS, 22623, fo. 22ʳ; Huntington Library, Ellesmere MS, 1145, 41.

[123] See, for example, William Lambarde, *A Perambulation of Kent: Conteining the Description, Hystorie, and Customes of that Shyre* (London, 1576), 200; Fuller, *The History of the Worthies of England*, i. 278; Aubrey, 'Observations', in *Three Prose Works*, ed. Buchanan-Brown, 316; James Brome, *Travels over England, Scotland and Wales* (London, 1700), 262.

[124] *The Diary of Abraham de la Pryme, the Yorkshire Antiquary*, ed. Charles Jackson (Surtees Society, 54, Durham, 1869–70), 139; Edmund Spenser, *The Faerie Qveene* (1596), IV. xi. 35, in *Spenser: Poetical Works*, ed. J. C. Smith and E. De Selincourt (Oxford, 1912), 270; Charles Leigh, *The Natural History of Lancashire, Cheshire, and the Peak, in Derbyshire* (Oxford, 1700), 23; Aubrey, *The Natural History of Wiltshire*, ed. Britton, 69; Fuller, *The History of the Worthies of England*, ii. 35. For similar examples, see *The Itinerary of John Leland in or about the Years 1535–43*, ed. Lucy Toulmin Smith (5 vols., London, 1906–10), v. 85; Thomas Westcote, *A View of Devonshire in 1630*, ed. George Oliver and Pitman Jones (Exeter, 1845), 111, 425; John Lewis, *The History and Antiquities Ecclesiastical and Civil of the Isle of Tenet in Kent* (London, 1723), 7.

[125] Ray, *A Collection of English Proverbs* (1st edn., 1670), 228, 253; Grose, *A Provincial Glossary*, sig. R4ᵛ. Cf. Sidney O. Addy, *Household Tales with Other Traditional Remains Collected in the Counties of York, Lincoln, Derby, and Nottingham* (London, 1895), 143, 144; E. M. Wright, *Rustic Speech and Folk-Lore* (Oxford, 1913), 178–82.

saws which governed a particular trade or craft was part of what it meant to belong to that occupational group; to understand proverbial allusions to local landmarks and the reputations of particular communities was integral to notions of belonging and the sense of place. The extent to which this was so is no more vividly captured than in the description of the hundred of Berkeley in Gloucestershire, written by John Smyth of Nibley during the late 1630s. For when Smyth came to define the people of the hundred, his neighbours, he chose to do so in terms of nothing else than their language and proverbs. It clearly seemed to him that what captured the very essence of the hundreders, what gave them a sense of themselves, were the habitual sayings of the locality. To be privy to these commonplaces, which epitomized their ethical values and encapsulated their practical wisdom, was to be 'a native'. In the hundred, Smyth commented, were 'frequently used certaine words, proverbs and phrases of speech' which the inhabitants held to be their own. Accordingly, he transcribed 100 of them which, he believed, were the 'peculiar' linguistic heritage of this particular 'country', the birthright of its denizens.[126]

Smyth's jottings reveal a great deal about the function and application of proverbs in one particular local setting and shed much light on the world view of their users. The parochiality of life in early modern England is evident in the various sayings of Smyth's neighbours which are unknown elsewhere. One such was 'Lide pilles the hide', a dialect phrase which meant that the month of March is likely to steal the poor man's beast. Equally unique were, 'he never had a bad lease that had a good landlord', and 'as nimble as a blinde cat in a barne'. At the same time, the hundreders had their own particular versions of sayings which were generally well known in other forms. Thus, instead of looking for a needle in a haystack they would seek 'for stuble in a fallowe feild'; and instead of saying, 'no penny, no pater noster', they would say, 'no pipe, noe puddinge'. The adage of the fool and his money was expressed as 'money is noe foole, if a wise man have it in keepinge'; the reproach about selling a pound and buying a penny took the form of 'hee hath sold Bristoll and bought Bedminster'. In the case of the proverb, 'hee'l proove, I thinke, a man of Durseley', referring to 'a man that will promise much but performe nothinge', they claimed responsibility for a phrase which had gained national currency, 'now dispersed over England'.

The proverbs recorded by Smyth confirm much of the evidence from

---

[126] Smyth, *The Berkeley Manuscripts*, ed. Maclean, iii. 26–33. For a discussion of Smyth's proverbs, see David Rollison, *The Local Origins of Modern Society: Gloucestershire, 1500–1800* (London, 1992), ch. 3.

other sources as to the nature of 'vulgar wisdoms'. Many sayings had a typically earthy flavour: 'Hee that feares every grasse must never pisse in a meadowe'; 'Things ne'ere goe ill where Jacke and Gill pisse in one quill', 'If thou lov'st mee at the hart, thou'lt not loose me for a fart'; and the favourite of schoolboys still, 'Hee first smels the fart that let it'. The 'durty proverb' warning that 'a great housekeeper is sure of nothinge for his good cheare, save a great turd at his gate', Smyth held to blame, in a familiar lament of the time, for 'havinge from thence banished the greater halfe of our ancient hospitality'. The hundreders had a stream of figurative and expressive sayings which also convey something of the quality of contemporary popular speech, rich in metaphor and simile. Thus, 'Hee mends like sowre ale in somer' referred to going from bad to worse; 'Soone crookes the tree, that a good cambrell will bee' conveyed the sense of the wayward youth who matures well; 'He drew it as blith as a robin reddocke' conjured up an image of adeptness. 'The crowe bids you good morrow' was an allusion to knavery; 'Il'e make abb or warp of it' suggested that something was neither one thing nor the other; and 'As proud as an Ape of whip' described a lack of pride.

There is a sturdy, yeomanly common sense about a number of these saws, counselling industry and thrift, vigilance and moderation. Thus, hard work reaps rewards: 'Hee that will thrive must rise at five: but hee that hath thriven may lye till seaven.' Save for the future: 'store is noe sore; plenty never rings its master by the eare'. Face up to challenges and do not neglect details: 'bones bringe meat to towne: meaning, difficult and hard things are not altogether to bee reiected, or things of small consequence.' Remember where your true interests lie: 'Be the counsell better, be it worse, follow him, that beares the purse.' Mind your own business: 'In little medlinge is much ease, of much medlinge, comes no sound sleepinge.' Be on your guard: 'Beware the fox in a fearne bush. i.e. . . . hypocrisy often clokes a knave.' Never forget the harsh realities of life: 'He that worst may, must hold the candle. Or, the weakest goes to the wall.'

A variety of proverbs offered practical advice. On the subject of marital relations, for example, they insisted that men should wear the trousers: 'the gray mare is the better horse—meaninge, that the most master goeth breechlesse.' A little chastisement never did a wife any harm, remembering that 'a woman, a spaniell, and a walnut tree, the more they are beaten, the better they bee'. At the same time, a little praise might go a long way: 'my catt is a good moushunt' was 'an vsuall speach when wee husbands comend the diligence of our wives. Wee hundreders maintaininge as an orthodox position, that hee that sometimes flattereth not his wife canot alwaies please her.' And there was a recognition that wives will have their way: 'As the good man saies, so it should be, but as the good wife saies, soe it must bee'. That women were by no means powerless in sexual politics was suggested by the 'widowe's wanton proverbe' announcing, 'hee that's cooled with an apple, and heated with an egge, over mee shall never spread his legg'; and, in the same spirit, 'an head that's white to mayds brings noe delight: or an head that's gray serves not for maydens play'.

Naturally enough, the hundreders had a rich proverbial lore of agriculture and the seasons, born of the soil and hewn from the landscape. Once again, they had parochial variations on many familiar refrains. 'When Westbridge wood is motley, then its time to sow barley' was the Berkeley rendition of a versatile saying. Similarly, 'on St Valentine's day cast beanes in clay, but on St Chad sowe good and badd'. The maxim, 'when the daies begin to lengthen the cold begins to strengthen' alluded to 'the rule of husbandry: that at Candlemas a provident husbandman should have halfe his fodder, and all his corne remaininge'. Equally infallible were the old saws, 'my milke is in the cowes horne, now the zunne is 'ryv'd at Capricorne'; 'when the crow begins to build then sheepe begin to yeald'; and 'Michaelmas rott comes short of the pott', all of which Smyth explained in detail. In typical fashion, the weather-lore in the hundred adapted well known prognostics to particular local landmarks. 'When Wotton Hill doth weare a cap, let Horton towne beware of that.' At the same time, 'Neighbor, w'are sure of faire weather, each ha beheld this morne, Abergainy hill', was a 'frequent speach with vs of the hilly part of the hundred; and indeed', admitted Smyth, 'that little picked hill in Wales over that towne is a good alminake maker; wherof my selfe have often made vse in my husbandry'. In the same vein, 'A misty morne in th'old o'th moone doth alwaies bringe a faire post-noone' was 'an hilly proverb about Simondshall'.

The more fragmentary evidence from other parts of England suggests that the hundred of Berkeley was by no means unique in having its own distinctive proverbial lore. Every region, and perhaps every community, had certain sayings which encapsulated some nugget of local tradition or alluded to some parochial reference point which made sense only within a confined area. Even old saws which were well known throughout the country could effectively be 'naturalized' to a place by their specific application, or merely by being rendered in the particular dialect. In the 1670s Andrew Paschall of Chedzoy near Bridgwater sent a collection of Somerset proverbs to John Ray. Many were consistent with sayings familiar elsewhere, but a significant number had a distinctive character by their reference to county landmarks, their use of peculiar words and phrases or their relevance to farming conditions which would have been meaningless in other places.[127]

Arguably, it is possible to detect something of the spirit and character of different regions in the flavour of their habitual sayings. The sober realism and plain speaking attributed to Yorkshire folk can be heard perhaps in some of the 113 old saws which George Meriton, a lawyer and antiquary from Northallerton, North Riding, noted down in the late seventeenth century. 'Hee'll never dow [be good], egg nor bird'; 'Weel and woemen cannot pan [close together] but way and woemen can'; 'A vaunter [boaster] and a lyar is baith yay thing [both one thing]'; 'A new bissome [broom] sweeps clean'; 'Better sit idle then work teaum [for nothing]'; 'Draff [grains] is good eneugh for swine'; 'He that gives all his geir [property] to his bairns [children] may tack a mell [mallet] and knock out his harnes [brains]'.[128]

By contrast there might be said to be a greater whimsy and humour about the proverbs common in Cheshire at the same time. 'Ossing [intention] comes to bossing'; 'No more sib'd [a-kin] than sieve and riddle, that grew both in a wood together'; 'I'll tent [look to] thee, quoth Wood; if I cannot rule my daughter I'll rule my good'; 'Maxfield measure, heap and thrutch [thrust]'; and 'We will not kill but whoave [cover]' which was 'spoken of a pig or fowl that they have overwhelmed with some vessel in readiness to kill'.[129] The folklorists of later centuries, invested with a good measure of regional pride, were able to supply ample such evidence in support of the particular characteristics and 'genius' of their people.[130] They found that in many rural areas proverbial wisdom continued, as it had done for countless generations, to play an important part in

---

[127]  Ray, *A Collection of English Proverbs* (2nd edn., 1678), 342–55.

[128]  George Meriton, *The Praise of Yorkshire Ale* (3rd edn., York, 1697), 83–7, and reprinted in *Nine Specimens of English Dialects*, ed. W. W. Skeat (English Dialect Society, 76, London, 1896), 177–81. See also the proverbs communicated to Ray by Francis Brokesby of Rowley, East Riding: Ray, *A Collection of English Proverbs* (2nd edn., 1678), 355.

[129]  John Ray, *A Collection of English Words*, ed. W. W. Skeat (English Dialect Society, 3, London, 1874), 58, 63, 69, 70, 74.

[130]  See, for example, Samuel Pegge, 'An Alphabet of Kenticisms', in *Original Glossaries*, ed. W. W. Skeat (English Dialect Society, 12, London, 1876), 58–78; Charlotte S. Burne and Georgina F. Jackson, *Shropshire Folk-Lore: A Sheaf of Gleanings* (London, 1883) 577–99; Arthur Benoni Evans and Sebastian Evans, *Leicestershire Words, Phrases, and Proverbs* (English Dialect Society, 31, London, 1881), 299–303; *The Denham Tracts*, ed. James Hardy (2 vols., Folklore Society, London, 1892–95), ii. 65; C. A. Markham, *The Proverbs of Northamptonshire* (Northampton, 1897); E. Gutch, *Examples of Printed Folk-Lore Concerning the North Riding of Yorkshire, York and the Ainsty* (Folklore Society, London, 1901), 429–34; E. Gutch and Mabel Peacock, *Examples of Printed Folk-Lore Concerning Lincolnshire* (Folklore Society, London, 1908), 404–16; E. Gutch, *Examples of Printed Folk-Lore Concerning the East Riding of Yorkshire* (Folklore Society, London, 1912), 222–5.

describing and defining the world for the majority. It provided them with both local knowledge and practical guidance; a sense of belonging and a moral code.

## CARICATURES AND CRITICISMS

In the sixteenth and seventeenth centuries, then, proverbial wisdom was a ubiquitous ornament to the English language both spoken and written. In oratory and academic discourse no less than in rustic soothsaying and common conversation, in official documents and learned treatises no less than in personal memoranda and popular literature, proverbial wisdom infused the phrase and fable of communication. This universal reliance on the proverb was not without discrimination, however. On the one hand, as we have seen, the gnomic wisdom of all contemporaries drew on a common classical and biblical heritage and enshrined values, morals, and opinions which were normative throughout society. On the other hand, there could be a great difference between the *adagia* and *sententia* carefully selected by the educated classes for their commonplace books and their professional rhetoric, and the homely saws and hobbling rhymes employed by husbandmen and housewives in their daily toil.

To some extent, therefore, differing social circumstances dictated the kinds of proverbial wisdom employed by different individuals and groups and influenced the contexts in which it was applied. In addition, the educated elite often looked down upon those whose lack of learning and discrimination led them to overuse or misuse well known adages. Quoted with discretion, sayings could provide valuable amplification of an argument and lend authority to a moral; applied without reason or judgement they could seem banal and trite. Employed sparingly and propitiously they might be an elegant ornament to style; mouthed randomly and to excess they would appear ridiculous and nonsensical. The veracity of many proverbs is contingent rather than universal; their wisdom is founded upon the contexts in which they are used, and only judgement can furnish the speaker with the saying appropriate to the circumstance. For 'although proverbs be popular principles', observed Sir Thomas Browne, 'yet is not all true that is proverbial'.[131]

In the late sixteenth and early seventeenth century satirists were already mocking 'the proverb-monger', a caricature of an ill-bred, ill-educated person who spouts old sooths in uncritical profusion. Sir William

---

[131] Browne, *Pseudodoxia Epidemica*, in *The Works of Sir Thomas Browne*, ed. Keynes, ii. 147.

Cornwallis blamed uncouth influences at an impressionable age for the excesses of

prouerb-mongers, whose throates are worne like roade-wayes with, 'Little saide is soone amended'; 'It is no halting before a cripple', and such like. When I heare one of these, I looke for his drie nurse; for from her armes he plucked his language.[132]

Henry Porter's comedy, *The Pleasant History of the Two Angry Women of Abington* (1599) contains the character of a serving-man, Nicholas Proverbs, who has a 'mouth thats made of olde sed-saws'.

> This formall foole your man speakes nought but prouerbes,
> And speake men what they can to him, hee'l answere
> With some rime, rotten sentence, or olde saying,
> Such spokes as the ancient of the parish vse,
> With neighbour tis an olde prourbe and a true,
> Goose giblets are good meate, old sacke better then new.[133]

As in this case it is servile characters, in particular, who are thus exposed to ridicule. In Ben Jonson's *Every Man in His Humour*, critics point out that it is Downright who uses proverbs, rather than Wellbred. 'By his discourse, he should eate nothing but hay. He was borne for the manger, pannier, or pack-saddle! He ha's not so much as a good phrase in his belly, but all old iron, and rustie prouerbes! a good commoditie for some smith, to make hob-nailes of.' In the proverbially entitled *A Tale of a Tub*, one purpose was to prove that 'ancient proverbs may illustrate a cooper's or a constable's wit', but were scarcely fit for the educated and the civilized:

> Of antick proverbs, drawne from Whitson-lords,
> And their authorities, at wakes and ales,
> With countrey precedents, and old wives tales;
> Wee bring you now, to shew what different things
> The cotes of clownes, are from the courts of kings.[134]

Restoration drama is full of country bumpkins, fools, and coxcombs who lace their speech with hackneyed proverbs, mouthed without rhyme or reason. In the early eighteenth century, Samuel Palmer could reflect

---

[132] Sir William Cornwallis, *Essayes*, ed. D. C. Allen (Baltimore, 1946), 176.

[133] Porter, *Two Angry Women of Abington*, sig. D1ʳ.

[134] Tilley, *Elizabethan Proverb Lore*, 3–4; Ben Jonson, *Euery Man in His Hvmovr* (1616), I. v. 93–8, and 'Prologue' to *A Tale of a Tub* (1640), both in *The Works of Ben Jonson*, ed. Herford and Simpson, iii. 320, 10. Apparently Jonson took notes on Yorkshire proverbs from the comic actor John Lacy for *A Tale of a Tub*: Aubrey, *Brief Lives*, ed. Clark, ii. 28.

with regret on the way in which old sayings were becoming the object of ridicule and the adage had gained currency that 'wise men make proverbs, but fools repeat 'em'. It was a trend which he blamed in large part on these literary caricatures.

To this abuse some of our authors of the first rank have very much contributed; for the modern poets and novelists have put 'em in the mouths of their lowest characters. They make fools and clowns, little and mean people, speak sentences in abundance, string 'em like necklaces and make sport with 'em, and ridicule the remains of our ancestors. By this means 'tis esteem'd pedantry, if we find one in the mouth of a gentleman; and an author of honour and very fine parts, has made the reciting an adage or two the sign of a coxcomb. Thus they are condemn'd to the use of the mob, thrown out of the minds of our people of birth, and the influence of 'em lost in the manage of education.[135]

No doubt such influences contributed something to the denigration of the proverb among the socially self-conscious and professionally ambitious. The indiscriminate and infelicitous use of old sayings had long been regarded as at best comical and at worst uncouth among those whose upbringings had taught them to know better. But the ridicule of 'proverbs mongers' on stage and in popular fiction probably confirmed the stereotype. Amid what appears to be an ever more pointed concern to cultivate 'civility' during the seventeenth century, in terms of manners and style, forms of behaviour and codes of decorum, proverbs associated with the 'vulgar' were to be desparaged and eschewed.[136]

New sensibilities with regard to etiquette and social propriety dealt blows to the respectability of proverbs on a number of fronts. In the first place, many old sayings came to be regarded as just too scatological. Thus John Ray was obliged to omit all sayings 'as are openly obscene' from his *Collection of English Proverbs* in 1670. But even then some of the specimens which he included gave 'offence to sober and pious persons, as savouring too much of obscenity, being apt to suggest impure fancies to corrupt minds' and he dropped them from the second edition of 1678. As he conceded, a large number of them referred to bodily excrements and denoted 'those actions and parts of the body by which they are expelled, and therefore the mention of them is uncivil and contrary to good manners'.[137]

In the second place, a large number of old saws savoured of the days of popery or tended towards superstition in their concern with saints' feasts,

[135] Palmer, *Moral Essays on . . . English, Scotch and Foreign Proverbs*, viii–ix.

[136] Anna Bryson, *From Courtesy to Civility: Changing Codes of Conduct in Early Modern England* (Oxford, 1998); Peter Borsay, *The English Urban Renaissance: Culture and Society in the Provincial Town, 1660–1770* (Oxford, 1989), chs. 10–11.

[137] Ray, *A Collection of English Proverbs* (1st edn., 1670), sig. A3ᵛ (2nd edn., 1678), sig. A3ᵛ.

their use in soothsaying and their reference to lucky and unlucky days. Again, Ray was sensitive to this. 'All superstitious and groundless observations of augury, days, hours, and the like, I have purposely omitted', he claimed of the first edition of his proverb collection, 'because I wish that they were quite erased out of peoples memories, and should be loath to be any way instrumental in transmitting them to posterity'. In the same vein, the churchman Thomas Fuller had been concerned to exclude any items that were 'frivolous, scurrilous, scandalous' from the local sayings included in his *Worthies of England*.[138]

Finally, the world view epitomized by many traditional adages became increasingly out of step with the new spirit of the age by the later seventeenth century. Among a generation attempting to define itself as progressive and 'modern', they seemed intolerably conservative and referential; in an era of increasing individualism they represented the ethics of community; in a climate of optimism and opportunity they were resignedly stoic and hopelessly parochial. As they ceased to speak to the values, experiences, and expectations of certain sections of society they were more likely to be associated with the lower orders, with country folk and the uneducated. As such they became tainted with the stigma of uncouth: they were 'vulgar' not only for what they said and the way in which they said it, but also because they were the idiom of the multitude. Whereas, at the beginning of the seventeenth century, Francis Bacon had unrepentantly collected sayings, 'not omitting any, because they are vulgar; (for many vulgar ones are excellent good) nor for the meannesse of the person', by the end of it John Aubrey would feel bound to apologize for having included the saws of Wiltshire rustics in his antiquarian writings: 'it may seem nauseous to some that I have rak't up so many western vulgar proverbs'.[139]

Attitudes towards the proverb which were thus beginning to crystallize in certain quarters after the Restoration were to develop into the normal opinion of polite society during the eighteenth century. By 1738 Jonathan Swift expressed the feeling of the 'best companies of England' when he drew a sharp distinction between the uttering of 'proverbs and those polite speeches which beautify conversation: for as to the former, I utterly reject them out of all ingenious discourse'. 'Do not dispise me for my proverbs' is the famous apology made by Lovelace's old-fashioned uncle, Lord M., in Richardson's *Clarissa* (1748). 'It is other men's wisdom, and

---

[138] Ray, *A Collection of English Proverbs* (1st edn., 1670), sig. A3ʳ; Fuller, *History of the Worthies of England*, i. 5.

[139] Bacon, *Apophthegms New and Old*, in *The Works of Francis Bacon*, ed. Spedding, Ellis, and Heath, vii. 123; Aubrey, *Natural History of Wiltshire*, ed. Britton, 6.

not my own, that I am so fond of', he confesses to his nephew in a letter containing a dozen old saws. The earl of Chesterfield would later sum up the sensibilities which demanded such contrition when he warned his son against the use of 'false English, bad pronunciation, old sayings, and common proverbs; which are so many proofs of having kept bad and low company'. For 'a man of fashion never has recourse to proverbs, and vulgar aphorisms'.[140]

In addition to social decorum, there were also certain intellectual trends during the seventeenth century which already conspired to anticipate this change in attitude. As early as Bacon's day, the term 'commonplace' had connotations of the mundane and platitudinous.[141] By the second half of the seventeenth century the first manifestations of those changing educational fashions which would contribute to the long-term decline of the classical curriculum were already emerging. The study of ancient wisdom, so characteristic of intellectual life during the Renaissance, was no longer uncritically accepted as the purpose of learning, and rendering the adages in which it was couched, no longer unquestionably approved as a didactic technique. In 1670 the outspoken divine, John Eachard, warned that abstracting choice sayings from classical authors actually discouraged the reading of their works and denied youngsters their benefit. The 'main business' of school boys, he complained 'is to search out cunningly the antecedent and the relative, to lie at catch for a spruce phrase, a proverb, or a quaint and pithy sentence' and 'having gargl'd only those elegant books at school, this serves them instead of reading them afterward, and does in a manner prevent their being further lookt into'.[142]

This was still far from being accepted wisdom, however, and the most advanced writers on education in the late seventeenth century continued to extol the virtue of studying proverbs.[143] Nevertheless, after the Restoration the grammar schools began to find themselves in competition with a range of new unendowed schools and dissenting academies offering more vernacular, vocational, and technically based forms of

---

[140] Jonathan Swift, *A Complete Collection of Genteel and Ingenious Conversation* (London, 1738), xii; Samuel Richardson, *Clarissa* (4 vols., Everyman edn., London, 1932), ii. 408–13; Lord Chesterfield, *The Letters of the Earl of Chesterfield to his Son* (2 vols., London, 1774), i. 147, 464.

[141] Skinner, *Reason and Rhetoric in the Philosophy of Hobbes*, 119.

[142] John Eachard, *The Grounds and Occasions of the Contempt of the Clergy and Religion Enquired into* (London, 1670), 10.

[143] Obadiah Walker, *Of Education, Especially of Young Gentlemen* (London, 1673), 130; Christopher Wase, *Considerations Concerning Free-Schools, as Settled in England* (Oxford, 1678), 102; John Locke, *Some Thoughts Concerning Education*, ed. J. W. and J. S. Yolton (Oxford, 1989), 233; *Aubrey on Education*, ed. Stephens, 56–7, 63, 69.

instruction. The study of ancient texts and training in rhetoric declined as the standard basis of education at this level in Georgian England.[144] In the early nineteenth century William Motherwell stated what by then had long been the case, that 'our present system of education, and what, for want of a more precise term, we might call the spirit of the age, are hostile to the oral enunciation of these ancient sentences of wisdom and worldly prudence'.[145]

Changes in educational methods also had implications for changes in the language, both spoken and written. During the seventeenth century, the 'oral residue' which had typically infused Tudor prose style began to be undermined. The written word gradually shed the colloquial devices and formulaic refrains through which it had once sought to evoke the cadences of live voice; its loosely serial structure was slowly supplanted by a tighter, more sequential form in which there was less room for illustrative devices. The growth of silent reading no doubt had an important influence on the evolution of the literary language, as texts were less often constructed with verbal delivery in mind. The very typography and punctuation of printed works came to reflect this development in the structure of prose.[146]

During the second half of the seventeenth century there was a more self-conscious attempt to effect a reform in prose style. The principles of classical rhetoric as advocated by Renaissance humanism were rejected in favour of the virtues of 'plain style'. This owed something to the new science of the period which demanded a language, both spoken and written, which was capable of expressing ideas simply and directly. The oratorical and literary tropes so much valued in the past were now seen as impediments to clarity and precision. The pulpit also played its part in this transformation. By the 1660s many churchmen were turning their backs on the baroque style which had characterized the great metaphysical preachers of the recent past. The wealth of metaphors and similitudes, allegories and anecdotes, the habitual citation both of Latin and Greek phrases and more homely proverbs, were all rejected in favour of an unadorned and less discursive mode. Ungarnished brevity was seen as the best vehicle for

---

[144] Obelkevich, 'Proverbs and Social History', 59; Rosemary O'Day, *Education and Society, 1500–1800* (London, 1982), ch. 11; Nicholas Hans, *New Trends in Education in the Eighteenth Century* (London, 1951).

[145] William Motherwell, 'Preface', to Andrew Henderson, *Scottish Proverbs* (Edinburgh, 1832), ix.

[146] L. C. Knights, *Drama and Society in the Age of Jonson* (London, 1937), 250–60; Walter J. Ong, *Orality and Literacy: The Technologizing of the Word* (London, 1982), 128–35, 147–51; Partridge, *Orthography in Shakespeare and Elizabethan Drama*, 182, 186–7, 192–4.

the communication of both scientific and religious truth, whereas the art of rhetoric tended to be equated with the art of deception.[147]

'Who can behold, without indignation, how many mists and uncertainties, these specious tropes and figures have brought on our knowledg?', asked Thomas Sprat in 1667. 'How many rewards, which are due to more profitable, and difficult arts, have been still snatch'd away by the easie vanity of fine speaking?' Clergymen, agreed the chaplain to Charles II, Joseph Glanvill, should spurn 'phantastical phrases' in favour of 'plainness', and he denounced 'in some men's preaching a certain sordidness, which though ignorant people may like as plain and familiar preaching; yet 'tis such a familiarity as begets contempt. Such is the use of vulgar proverbs, and homely similitudes, and rude and clownish phrases.' In 1694 William Wotton summed up the change in fashion which had taken place and its implications for public speaking, whether in law court, parliament or pulpit.

Besides all this, the humour of the age which we live in is exceedingly altered. Men apprehend or suspect a trick in every thing that is said to move the passions of the auditory in courts of judicature or in the parliament-house. They think themselves affronted when such methods are used in speaking, as if the orator could suppose within himself that they were to be catched by such baits. And therefore, when men have spoken to the point, in as few words as the matter will bear, it is expected they should hold their tongues. Even in the pulpit, the pomp of rhetorick is not always commended; and very few meet with applause who do not confine themselves to speak with the severity of a philosopher as well as the splendour of an orator,—two things not always consistent.[148]

Thus the decline in the intellectual, literary, and social status of the proverb which took place during the eighteenth century had its antecedents in changing fashions, tastes, and sensibilities, which were already evident by the later Stuart period. There was not yet, however, the widespread denigration of proverbial wisdom in learned and polite society which subsequent generations affected to cultivate. And as for those less concerned with the priorities of academe and the dictates of

[147] 'Introduction', in *Critical Essays of the Seventeeth Century*, ed. Spingarn, i. xxxvi–xlviii; Richard Foster Jones, 'Science and English Prose Style in the Third Quarter of the Seventeenth Century', *Publications of the Modern Language Association*, 45 (1930), 977–1009, and id., 'The Attack on Pulpit Eloquence in the Restoration', *Journal of English and Germanic Philology*, 30 (1931), 188–217, both reprinted in his *The Seventeenth Century* (Stanford, Calif., 1951), 75–110, 111–42; Mitchell, *English Pulpit Oratory from Andrewes to Tillotson*, ch. 10; Joan Bennett, 'An Aspect of the Evolution of Seventeenth-Century Prose', *Review of English Studies*, 17 (1941), 281–97.

[148] Thomas Sprat, *The History of the Royal-Society of London* (London, 1667), 112; Joseph Glanvill, *An Essay Concerning Preaching* (London, 1678), 77; William Wotton, *Reflections upon Ancient and Modern Learning* (1694), in *Critical Essays of the Seventeenth Century*, ed. Spingarn, iii. 212.

decorum, they continued to speak, to enjoy and to rely upon old said saws for many generations to come.

Proverbs provide a good illustration of the relationship between oral and literate culture in sixteenth- and seventeenth-century England. Although they were fundamentally a spoken form, they had been an integral part of written culture and formal education for many hundreds of years before this period. By 1500 this form of gnomic wisdom had long been at the heart of the classical curriculum and a staple of rhetorical training; for generations it had provided a standard trope in letters and official documents no less than in imaginative literature. During the Renaissance, however, this tradition was enormously enriched and through the figure of Erasmus in particular, and the New Learning in general, a large corpus of formulae entered the English language and took root. So many of what became the naturalized platitudes of the vernacular derived from these learned pan-European origins.

Thus, proverbs no less than many other elements of verbal expression owed their dissemination, and often their origin, to textual sources. They reveal not only the inextricable reciprocity between the spoken and written realms at this time, but also a degree of universality in the attitudes and values which they enshrine. The crude dichotomies of 'oral' and 'literate' communication, and of 'elite' and 'popular' culture, fail to acknowledge the webs of interpenetration and mutual infusion which so often provide societies with shared forms of expression and common modes of thought.

At the same time, however, there remained distinctive strains and variegated elements within this cultural repertoire. There were sayings which spoke particularly to the realities of life at the bottom of society, a life normally tainted with hardship, sometimes threatened by oppression and often lacking in opportunity. There were old saws which applied particularly to life on the land or in certain trades and they too might have little relevance to the experience of the social and professional elite. Many of these 'vulgar wisdoms' were thoroughly homely; they found their way into writings only by chance, they owed little to classical or biblical inspiration and they employed a language abhorred by 'civility'. In few sources do we detect so well the sensibilities of those who have bequeathed little written record to posterity; in few instances do we hear so clearly the voice of the people.

# 3
## Old Wives' Tales and Nursery Lore

Old customes, and old wives fables are grosse things: but yet ought
not to be quite rejected: there may some truth and usefulnese be
elicited out of them: besides 'tis a pleasure to consider the errours
that enveloped former ages: as also the present.

> John Aubrey, 'Remaines of Gentilisme and Judaisme',
> BL, Lansdowne MS, 231, fo. 103ʳ.

> O spirit of the days gone bye
> Sweet childhoods teartul extacy
> The witching spells of winter nights
> Where are they fled wi their delights
> When listning on the corner seat
> The winter evenings length to cheat
> I heard my mothers memory tell
> Tales superstition loves so well
> Things said or sung a thousand times
> In simple prose or simpler ryhmes.

> John Clare, *The Shepherd's Calendar*,
> ed. Eric Robinson and Geoffrey
> Summerfield (Oxford, 1964), 18.

MOST of the oral culture which can be recovered from sixteenth- and
seventeenth-century England is adult male culture. The public sphere
which has generated so many of our texts was the man's sphere, and it is
his voice which we most often hear across the centuries. Just as our
written, and certainly our printed sources, fail, in their standard English,
to register the dialect languages in which the great majority of people
spoke, so they mostly fail to convey the assumptions and priorities of the
female and juvenile part of the population who far less frequently entered
the written realm on their own terms. Even legal records, in which it is
often possible to hear the words of the people most graphically, were
largely created by and for men.

In order to have anything like a fully rounded sense of the forms and
content of oral expression in this period, therefore, attention must be
paid to the majority of those who by virtue of their sex and age rarely

expressed themselves in writing and only infrequently intrude into textual sources. The world of the household in which gender roles often conditioned women to operate and in which children were nurtured had a rich and distinctive oral tradition of its own. This environment, no less than others, was not one immune from the influence of the printed word. Mothers were frequently to be found reading to and educating their children within the home. By the sixteenth century, the printed ballad had entered the nursery and the winter hearth as a stimulus to the edification and entertainment of youngsters. Even the fable and folklore, the medical remedies and kitchen recipes, in which women were wont to specialize, were the product of centuries of transmission in written as well as oral sources.

Despite this, however, the domestic sphere was one characterized by a high degree of oral transmission. There were recipe books, but children were still shown how to cook by their elders. There were herbals and treatises on health, but 'kitchen physic' was passed from mother to daughter as it had always been. There were broadsides and chapbooks, but the vast majority of the nursery rhymes and fairy-tales which once circulated have left no text behind them. Indeed few forms better illustrate the resilience and the importance of oral transmission than this nursery lore which has endured over centuries largely independent of the written realm. The faith and fable of mothers and nursemaids was passed down the generations and imbibed by infants before they were old enough even to be aware of absorbing it, and then, as now, it was retained into adult life in memory not in writing. Such things were rarely deemed worthy of transcribing, still less of dignifying in print. As the province of 'women, children and fools', they were simply too commonplace to require recording, too trivial to be worthy of reflection.[1]

## FOR WOMEN THEY ARE WORDS

By the early modern period England was the inheritor of a long tradition of prejudice against the products of female culture as at best trivial and erroneous and at worst dangerous and corrupting. From the fourteenth

---

[1] For a range of variations on this refrain, see Reginald Scot, *The Discouerie of Witchcraft* (London, 1584), 152; Michel de Montaigne, *The Essayes or Morall, Politike and Millitarie Discourses*, trans. John Florio (London, 1603), 87; Francis Bacon, *Sylva Sylvarum: Or A Natural History* (1627), in *The Works of Francis Bacon*, ed. James Spedding, Robert Leslie Ellis, and Douglas Denon Heath (7 vols., London, 1857–9), ii. 641; Thomas Ady, *A Perfect Discovery of Witches* (London, 1661), 84; Keith Thomas, 'The Place of Laughter in Tudor and Stuart England', *Times Literary Supplement* (21 Jan. 1977), 80.

century, at least, 'old wives' were synonymous with tale-telling.[2] By the Tudor period, the phrase 'old wives' tale' had been in use for generations as a euphemism for any story, tradition, or belief which was thought to be inconsequential or false. At the beginning of the sixteenth century, Alexander Barclay could claim that anyone was 'a fole' whose 'moste fely-cyte is to byleue the tales of an olde wyfe'. George Turberville would later treat as synonymous 'a thing not only friuolous to talke of, and a verie olde womans fable, or Cantorburie tale', while in the 1590s John Florio was able to dismiss, as of a piece, 'flim flam tales, old wiues fables, a ribble rabble discourse, idle words, speeches of no worth'.[3]

It was the rhetoric of the Reformation which did much to help secure for this phrase, and the assumptions which it betrayed, a place in the fabric of the language and the commonplaces of the learned elite. Early Protestant reformers lambasted the medieval Church and their Catholic opponents for allowing centuries of fabulous clerical invention to corrupt the pure word of God. 'They bryng forth old wyues fables for sounde and true thynges,' was how William Turner put it in 1537. Such 'unwritten tradicions' were no more than 'hethenyssh, old wiuyssh and capcyos fables' with no basis in Scripture, concurred the Scottish reformer Alexander Alane soon afterwards. At the same time the Eton schoolmaster Nicholas Udall ridiculed the 'olde wiuco foolyshe tales of Robyn Hoode and suche others, whiche many preachers haue in tymes past customably vsed to bryng in, taken out euen of the veraye botome and grossest parte of the dreggues of the commen peoples foolyshe talkyng'.[4]

Before long, such refrains were a standard feature of the triumphalist Protestant orthodoxy. 'You see gentleman', wrote John Lyly in 1580, 'into what blynde and grosse errours in olde time we were ledde, thinking euery olde wiues tale to be a truth, and euery merry word, a very witchcraft . . . They inuented as many enchauntments for loue, as they did for the tooth-ach . . .'. Francis Bacon joined the chorus when he ridiculed the old stories of miracles and relics as being 'old wives' fables, impostures of the clergy, illusions of spirits, and badges of antichrist, to the great scandal

[2] *OED*, s.v. 'old wives' tales'; F. P. Wilson, *The Oxford Dictionary of English Proverbs* (3rd edn., Oxford, 1970), 593.

[3] Alexander Barclay, *The Ship of Fools*, ed. T. H. Jamieson (2 vols., Edinburgh, 1874), i. 72; George Turberville, *The Booke of Faulconrie or Hauking* (London, 1575), 260; John Florio, *A Worlde of Wordes, Or Most Copious, and Exact Dictionarie in Italian and English* (London, 1598), 125.

[4] Urbanus Regius, *A Co[m]parison betwene the Olde Learnynge and the Newe*, trans. William Turner (Southwark, 1537), sig. C6ʳ; Alexander Alane, *Of the Auctorite of the Word of God against the Bishop of London* (Strasbourg, 1544?), sig. C2ᵛ, and cf. F1ʳ, F1ᵛ; Desiderius Erasmus, *Apophthegmes*, trans. Nicholas Udall (London, 1542), *** i.

and detriment of religion'. Not surprisingly the seventeenth-century Protestant preachers who, in order to illustrate the workings of divine providence, so often published collections of anecdotes showing wicked sinners inexplicably stuck down, were quick to say that these examples were not the 'fained miracles, nor fabulous stories, nor old wives tales' of the past, but verifiable recent incidents for which there were 'both eare and eye witnesses'.[5]

In almost every area of cultural and intellectual life the phrase 'old wives' tale' came to denote all the erroneous and superstitious rubbish which needed to be stripped away from the essence of truth. It was the idiom adopted by many of the academic disciplines whose new standards of empirical enquiry instilled an ever greater desire to differentiate findings based upon demonstrable evidence from beliefs grounded in hearsay and tradition. Thus, the historian of Worcestershire, Thomas Habington, could dismiss the notion that the salt pits of Droitwich had once been obtained from God by the prayers of a local saint as no more than 'the traditions of old wyfes . . . synce we have ould recordes to testify the contrary . . .'. Similarly, Anthony Wood ridiculed stories that there had been a mint in Oxford at the time of the ancient Britons as nothing but 'old wives' tales', on the grounds that they 'can noe way agree to the place designed'. The Derbyshire historian Philip Kinder was prepared at least to evaluate such tenuous evidence: 'and for fables, ould wife's-tales and legends, I shal sett downe including my conjectures of the truth or falsities'.[6]

In natural history, no less than antiquarian research, the same desire to sift the wheat of verifiable knowledge from the chaff of erroneous tradition was evident. Bacon was one among many who argued for the rigid separation of 'superstitious stories' from empirical data, 'for I would not have the infancy of philosophy, to which natural history is a nursing-mother, accustomed to old wives' fables'. Similarly, in 1600 William Gilbert could dismiss many of the old beliefs about the natural world as no more than 'the maunderings of a babbling hag'. The herbalists, meanwhile, were equally insistent on distinguishing their truths, derived from

---

[5] John Lyly, *Euphues and His England* (1580), in *The Complete Works of John Lyly*, ed. R. W. Bond (3 vols., Oxford, 1902), ii. 116; Francis Bacon, *The Advancement of Learning* (1605), in *The Works of Francis Bacon*, ed. Spedding, Ellis, and Heath, iii. 288; Henry Burton, *A Divine Tragedy* (London, 1641), 2.

[6] Thomas Habington, *A Survey of Worcestershire*, ed. John Amphlett (2 vols., Worcestershire Historical Society, Oxford, 1895–9), i. 468; '*Survey of the Antiquities of the City of Oxford*', *Composed in 1661–6, by Anthony Wood*, ed. Andrew Clark (3 vols., Oxford Historical Society, 15, 17, 37, Oxford, 1889–99), i. 472; Philip Kinder, 'Historie of Darby-Shire', ed. W. G. D. Fletcher, *Reliquary*, 23 (1882–3), 10.

classical authors such as Dioscorides or founded on sound experimenta-
tion, from the 'doltish dreams' and 'many fables' embodied in the herbal
lore of ordinary women. Such things, thought John Gerard, were just 'too
full of scurrilitie to set forth in print'. 'All which dreames and old wives
tales you shall from henceforth cast out of your books and memory,' he
instructed his readers.[7]

This language, and the attitudes which lay behind it, were no more than
one manifestation of a prevailing, male-dominated, culture which typically characterized women as creatures of the spoken word. In an intellectual universe accustomed to thinking in binary opposites, women were
private while men were public; women were fickle when men were constant; and women were passion as men were reason. The essence of a
woman was her loquaciousness: she was defined by her tongue; the
spoken word personified. 'For words they are women, and deeds they are
men', ran one familiar saying; 'a woman's tongue is the last thing about her
that dies', ran another. Indeed the unconscious cliches of everyday conversation bore witness to the myriad ways in which this ancient commonplace was articulated: 'a woman's tongue wags like a lamb's tail'; 'where
there are women and geese there wants no noise'; 'many women many
words'; 'women are great talkers'; 'women will have the last word';
'women will say anything'.[8]

Verbal aggression, or scolding, whether as a disruption to domestic
harmony or an infringement of neighbourhood peace, was by definition
a female misdemeanour. Gossiping, no less, was something which
women were thought to do, and to be 'a gossip', with all its associations of
trivial tittle-tattle, of useless, senseless verbal effusion, was regarded as
being inextricably bound up with the female personality (see Plate 6).[9]

[7] Steven Shapin, *A Social History of Truth: Civility and Science in Seventeenth-Century England*
(Chicago, 1994), 90, 201; John Gerard, *The Herball or General Historie of Plantes*, ed. Thomas
Johnson (London, 1633), 351, and cf. 718.

[8] Wilson, *The Oxford Dictionary of English Proverbs*, 909–12; M. P. Tilley, *A Dictionary of the
Proverbs in England in the Sixteenth and Seventeenth Centuries* (Ann Arbor, Mich., 1950), 741–9.

[9] David Underdown, 'The Taming of the Scold: The Enforcement of Patriarchal Authority
in Early Modern England', in Anthony Fletcher and John Stevenson (eds.), *Order and Disorder in
Early Modern England* (Cambridge, 1985), 116–36; Martin Ingram, '"Scolding Women Cucked or
Washed": A Crisis in Gender Relations in Early Modern England?', in Jenny Kermode and
Garthine Walker (eds.), *Women, Crime and the Courts in Early Modern England* (London, 1994),
48–80; Laura Gowing, *Domestic Dangers: Women, Words, and Sex in Early Modern London* (Oxford,
1996), chs. 3–4; Steve Hindle, 'The Shaming of Margaret Knowsley: Gender, Gossip and the
Experience of Authority in Early Modern England', *Continuity and Change*, 9 (1994), 391–419;
Bernard Capp, 'Separate Domains? Women and Authority in Early Modern England', in Paul
Griffiths, Adam Fox, and Steve Hindle (eds.), *The Experience of Authority in Early Modern England*
(Basingstoke, 1996), 117–45.

Thus, one of the worst jibes that could be levelled at a man was that 'he has a woman's tongue in his head', and older women, in particular, were the victims of implicit male assumptions in this respect. The normal identification of an 'old woman' with 'a prating gossip' is documented as early as the twelfth century and by the early modern period the two concepts had long been synonymous. Indeed the term 'old woman' or 'old wife' was adopted in a range of pejorative contexts. It was already a term of abuse levelled at men thought to be weak or inadequate.[10]

It was perhaps inevitable that the marvellously expressive terminology used to denote species in the natural world should pick up this sobriquet. In many parts of England the popular local name for the long-tailed duck (*Harelda glacialis*) was an 'oldwife', the reason being, as one commentator explained in 1634, 'the oldwives, be a fowle that never leave tatling day or night'. We can only speculate on the assumptions which lay behind the name 'old wife' being commonly given to one variety of apple: no doubt it was quickly wizened or especially sour. Meanwhile, at least four different families of fish went under the vernacular name 'old wife' in different places around the country, 'because of their mumping and soure countenance', Thomas Muffett tells us.[11] Indeed, the adjective 'mumping' was often applied to old wives and women in general. It conjured up images of some grimacing old crone, mumbling ancient sooths and croaking idle tattle from her gnarled and toothless mouth.[12]

## THE OLD BELDAM'S CATECHISM

In the sixteenth and seventeenth centuries, therefore, it was taken for granted by men that women were the more superstitious sex and were likely to be a corrupting influence on those around them. 'Often have you heard how much a superstitious wife, by her certaine lectures, hath wrought upon her Christian husband,' lamented Thomas Adams: 'when did you heare a beleeving husband prevaile with his misbeleeving wife?' ''Tis strange what women and children will conceive unto themselves, if

[10] Wilson, *The Oxford Dictionary of English Proverbs*, 593, 909; Keith Thomas, 'Age and Authority in Early Modern England', *Proceedings of the British Academy*, 62 (1976), 245.

[11] William Wood, *New Englands Prospect* (London, 1634), 31; Keith Thomas, *Man and the Natural World: Changing Attitudes in England, 1500–1800* (London, 1983), 83; Thomas Muffett, *Healths Improvement*, ed. Christopher Bennet (London, 1655), 184.

[12] See, for example, Sir Philip Sidney, *The Countess of Pembroke's Arcadia*, ed. Jean Roberston (Oxford, 1973), 270; Thomas Nashe, *Nashes Lenten Stuffe* (1599), in *The Works of Thomas Nashe*, ed. R. B. McKerrow, rev. F. P. Wilson (5 vols., Oxford, 1958), iii. 200; Natascha Wurzbach, *The Rise of the English Street Ballad, 1550–1650* (Cambridge, 1990), 207; *Cavalier and Puritan*, ed. Hyder E. Rollins (New York, 1923), 298–303.

they go over a churchyard in the night', observed Robert Burton, and when they 'lie or be alone in a dark room, how they sweat and tremble on a sudden'. The poets of old, thought Sir William Davenant, would conjure up the 'resemblance of hell out of the dreams of frightened women'.[13]

One of the very few educated male contemporaries who was able to see beyond this prejudice and appreciate the importance of women as the harbingers of folklore and the purveyors of oral tradition was John Aubrey (see Plate 5). Almost alone in his day, Aubrey possessed both the flexibility of mind and the imaginative sympathy to be fascinated by those varieties of knowledge and belief system which appeared to be the special inheritance of women. And he recognized, as few others did, the enormous cultural significance of the transmission of this faith and folklore to children at their most impressionable ages. Repeatedly, he harked back to his own childhood in the rural Wiltshire of the 1630s and early 1640s, a world which he felt to be very much in retreat by the end of the seventeenth century. It was an environment in which women had played an enormous, perhaps even a dominant, role in constructing the terms and categories through which a young mind perceived the world. In their customs and 'superstitions', stories and songs, mothers and nurse maids nurtured particular ways of seeing and believing and bequeathed them anew to the next generation. Even in later life Aubrey did not disdain to learn all he could 'from ignorant old women'.[14]

He could not help but remark, for example, on the many rhymes and rituals which they would rehearse in order to foretell the future. Love charms to identify a prospective husband were especially popular, and thus 'the women have several magical secrets handed down to them by tradition for this purpose'. One such, for performance on St Agnes' eve, the most potent time for such soothsaying, ran: 'Take a row of pins, and pull out every one, one after another, saying a Pater Noster, or Our Father, sticking a pin in your sleve, and you will dream of him or her you shall marry.' Alternatively a young girl might sleep in another county and tie her left garter around the stocking of her right leg while repeating

[13] Thomas Adams, *A Commentary or, Exposition upon the Divine Second Epistle Generall, Written by the Blessed Apostle St. Peter* (London, 1633), 555; Robert Burton, *The Anatomy of Melancholy*, ed. Holbrook Jackson (3 vols., Everyman edn., London, 1932), i. 262, and cf. iii. 338–9; Sir William Davenant, 'Preface' to *Gondibert, An Heroick Poem* (1650), in *Critical Essays of the Seventeenth Century*, ed. J. E. Spingarn (3 vols., Oxford, 1908), ii. 5. Cf. Alexander Roberts, *A Treatise of Witchcraft* (London, 1616), 42–3.

[14] See, in particular, John Aubrey, 'Remaines of Gentilisme and Judaisme', BL, Lansdowne MS, 231; printed in *John Aubrey: Three Prose Works*, ed. John Buchanan-Brown (Fontwell, 1972), 127–304; Michael Hunter, *John Aubrey and the Realm of Learning* (London, 1975), 195–6.

certain verses with each knot. Equally, a hard boiled egg with the yolk extracted and replaced by salt and eaten before bed without any supper was another 'magicall receipt to know'. By the same token, if women put a newly laid egg in a beer glass and exposed it to the hot sun they would 'perceive their husband's profession'. Another practice among 'the mayds (especially the cooke-mayds and dayry-mayds)', was to use slips of orpins, or blades of grass, as divining rods to predict mutual attraction between couples. They would try to influence the process by using the 'merry-thought', or 'wish-bone', in a particular way, 'as I have it from the woemen'.[15]

To this catalogue, Aubrey might have added the practice among young girls of crushing up certain leaves or seeds and throwing them onto the fire 'thinking to know their loves'. This, too, was a distinctive legacy of female oral tradition. 'We have also sometimes among our silly wenches', it was said in 1640, 'some that out of a foolish curiosity they have, must needs be putting in practice some of these feats that they have receaved by tradition from their mother, perhaps, or nurse . . .'. Or there was the practice of pealing a 'St Thomas' onion', putting it under the pillow at night, spreading out the arms and repeating:

> Good St Thomas do me right,
> And bring my love to me this night
> That I may look him in the face,
> And in my arms may him embrace.

In the summer girls would stick three pins in an apple, put it in a left hand glove under their pillow on Saturday night, clap their hands and say, 'If thou be he, ye must have me to be thy wedded Bride | Make no delay, but come away this night to my bed side.' On St Luke's day they would make an ointment to spread on breasts, stomach and lips, lie on their beds and chant, 'St Luke, St Luke, be kind to me | And let me now my true love see.'[16]

There was a host of such charms and among them, perhaps, some element of regional variation. In north Wiltshire, Aubrey remembered from boyhood, 'the mayd servants were wont at night (after supper) to make smoothe the ashes on the hearth, and then to make streakes on it with a stick', with which they could perform a kind of 'divination to know

---

[15] Aubrey, 'Miscellanies' and 'Remaines of Gentilisme and Judaisme', in *Three Prose Works*, ed. Buchanan-Brown, 83–4, 207–8, 214.

[16] Jacques Ferrand, *Epotomania, or A Treatise Discoursing of the Essence, Causes, . . . and Cure of Love, or Erotique Melancholy* (Oxford, 1640), 176; *Mother Bunch's Closet Newly Broke Open* (London?, 1685; 1715 edn.), 5, 5–6, 11.

whom they should marry'. Meanwhile, a parallel practice observed by Bishop White Kennett among 'the maids in Oxfordshire' was 'a way of foreseeing their sweet hearts by making a dumb cake' and eating one part of it before laying the other part on their pillows at night, all of which was to be done without uttering a word. Women were said to believe that the new moon had particular properties in these and other respects. Up in Yorkshire and other northern parts, 'some country woemen doe worship the new moon, on their bare knees, kneeling upon an earthfast steane' and repeating these words:

> All haile to the Moon all haile to thee!
> I prithee good moon declare to me,
> This night, who my husband must be.

The salting of meat on a new moon was also a practice 'religiously observed by some of our housewives', and there was no better cure for warts than wringing one's hands before it. Meanwhile in Northumberland, another love charm later told to John Brand 'in my childhood by my nurse', ran:

> An oven-ash, or a four-leaved clover
> You'll see your true love before the day's over.

She 'never, I think, forgot it when we passed by an ash tree or through a clover field', he remembered.[17]

The divining power of the ashes in the hearth at the end of an evening served not just for love divination. Aubrey recalled that 'the maydes were very fond of this kind of magick' and also used the smouldering embers to predict death. On New Year's eve they would smooth them before bedtime and if in the morning they found 'the likenesse of a coffin, one will dye; if of a ring one will be married'. On Midsummer eve there was the different custom of 'sitting-up ... in the church-porch, to see the apparitions of those that should dye, or be buried there, that year', something 'mostly used by women; I have heard 'em tell strange stories of it'. Of like sort was the way 'the woemen have ... of divining, whether the husband or wife shall die first by the number of letters in Latin, or the husbands, and wives christian-names'.[18]

---

[17] Aubrey, 'Remaines of Gentilisme and Judaisme', in *Three Prose Works*, ed. Buchanan-Brown, 84, 207–8, 212, 241, 242; John Brand, *Observations on the Popular Antiquities of Great Britain*, ed. Sir Henry Ellis (3 vols., London, 1849), iii. 290. Cf. *Mother Bunch's Closet Newly Broke Open*, 8, 15. There were innumerable observances based upon the cycles of the moon: see Iona Opie and Moira Tatem, *A Dictionary of Superstitions* (Oxford, 1989), 260–6, 279–83.

[18] Aubrey, 'Remaines of Gentilisme and Judaisme', in *Three Prose Works*, ed. Buchanan-Brown, 143, 207, 212, 242; BL, Lansdowne MS, 1039, fo. 12ᵛ.

Thus, the desire 'to know future things' was believed to be, as John Melton put it, 'especially heredetary to women'. And a myriad other such 'superstitions' they were thought to cherish and make it their business to impress upon children. There were the unflinching beliefs in the special properties of each day of the week and cycle of the moon, the religious observances relating to all manner of domestic practices and common customs, the traditional lore reverentially applied to the world all around. The Elizabethan writer Thomas Nashe remembered how, as a boy growing up at Lowestoft, Suffolk, in the 1570s, he had been spellbound by the faiths and fables which the old women had solemnly handed down around the home fire.

I haue heard aged mumping beldams as they sat warming their knees ouer a coale scratch ouer the argument verie curiously, and they would bid yong folks beware on what day they par'd their nayles, tell what luck euerie one should haue by the day of the weeke he was borne on; show how many yeares a man should liue by the number of wrinkles on his forhead, and stand descanting not a litle of the difference in fortune when they are turnd vpward, and when they are bent downward; him that had a wart on his chin, they would confidently assertaine he should haue no need of anie of his kin: marry, they would likewise distinguish betweene the standing of the wart on the right side and on the left. When I was a little childe, I was a great auditor of theirs, and had all their witchcrafts at my fingers endes, as perfit as good morrow and good euen.[19]

So it was, according to the old wives' catechism, that Friday was the unluckiest day. 'Now Friday came, your old wives say, of all the week's the unluckiest day.' Despite this, however, every milkmaid knew that a dream on Friday night was sure to come true. 'Of the signification of dreames, whole catalogues could I recyte of theirs,' recalled Nashe of his 'aged mumping beldams.'[20] On the one hand, ill omens might manifest themselves at any moment. Thus, spilling a drink would always presage misfortune and there were 'manie women, and effeminat men . . . that make great diuinations vpon the shedding of salt, wine, &c.' At the same time, others would affirm that a nose bleed was a sure prognostication of death, and housewives would tell that the crowing of a cock 'boded ill luck' for any venture.[21] On the other hand, such dangers could be resisted with

---

[19] John Melton, *Astrologaster, or, The Figure-Caster* (London, 1620), 53, and see 45–7, 67, 69, 71; Thomas Nashe, *The Terrors of the Night* (1594), in *The Works of Thomas Nashe*, ed. McKerrow and Wilson, i. 369.

[20] Richard Flecknoe, *The Diarium, or Journall: Divided into 12. Jornadas* (London, 1656), 38; Sir Thomas Overbury, *New and Choise Characters* (London, 1615), sig. K5ᵛ; Nashe, *The Terrors of the Night*, in *The Works of Thomas Nashe*, ed. McKerrow and Wilson, i. 369.

[21] Scot, *The Discouerie of Witchcraft*, 203; George Gifford, *A Discourse of the Subtill Practices of*

judicious preventatives. Thus, 'three knots in a thred, or an odde grandams blessing in the corner of a napkin, will carrie you all the world ouer'. A sprig of rowan knitted to the hair or tail of a person or animal was one of the many 'such kinde of charmes as commonlie dafte wiues vses' to protect against the evil eye. And every midwife would affirm that the possession of a baby's caul, 'called by our women, the sillie how', brought with it good luck for life.[22]

The natural world was full of prognostics and prophetical charms which women seem to have specialized in perpetuating down the generations. For example, robbing a swallow's nest, was 'from some old belldames catechismes, held a more fearefull sacrilege, than to steale a chalice out of a church'. And, as the Jacobean minister, Thomas Jackson, put it, 'besides tradition they haue no reason so to thinke'. Equally, ravens were said to be 'birds of omen', teaching 'both conj'rers and old women to tell us what is to befall'. Magpies often boded ill and in Lancashire it was unlucky to see two of them together. 'far I heard my gronny sey', remembered one of John Collier's characters of an early eighteenth-century childhood, 'hoode os leef o seen two owd harries [devils] os two pynots [magpies].' In Northumberland, meanwhile, it was an 'observation, frequent in the mouths of old women, that when the pye chatters we shall have strangers'.[23]

The environment all around was also the source of an immense amount of medical lore with which it was expected that every housewife would be conversant and pass on to her daughters. Women, the herbalist John Gerard noted, had their own peculiar names for certain plants. Cottonweed or cudweed was known particularly to women as 'live-long, or live-for-ever'; marigolds were 'called of the vulgar sort of women, jack-an-apes on horse back', a name which they also gave to oxlips; milkewort was 'vulgarly known in Cheapside to the herbe women by the name of hedge-hyssop'; the flowers of the antirrhinum were thought to be shaped liked a dragon's mouth, 'from whence the women have taken the name

*Deuilles by Witches and Sorcerers* (London, 1587), sig. C2ʳ; Aubrey, 'Remaines of Gentilisme and Judaisme', in *Three Prose Works*, ed. Buchanan-Brown, 220.

[22] Nashe, *The Terrors of the Night*, in *The Works of Thomas Nashe*, ed. McKerrow and Wilson, i. 359; James VI, *Daemonologie: In Forme of a Dialogue* (Edinburgh, 1597), 11–12; Roberts, *A Treatise of Witchcraft*, 65–6.

[23] Thomas Jackson, *A Treatise Containing the Originall of Vnbeliefe* (London, 1625), 177; William Cowper, 'A Fable', in *The Poems of William Cowper*, ed. John D. Baird and Charles Ryskamp (2 vols., Oxford, 1980), i. 401; John Collier, *The Miscellaneous Works of Tim Bobbin, Esq. Containing his View of the Lancashire Dialect* (London, 1775), 35; Brand, *Observations on the Popular Antiquities of Great Britain*, ed. Ellis, iii. 215. See Thomas, *Man and the Natural World*, 75–6; Opie and Tatem, *A Dictionary of Superstitions*, 387, 324, 235–6.

snapdragon'; the white satin flower had various different names around the country, but 'among our women is called honestie'; ground ivy was known to women in the north of England as 'ale-hoofe' as they used it in their brewing. John Parkinson could confirm that, among many other examples, women called the double wild campion, 'batchellors buttons', the garden poppy, 'Jone silver pinne', the red adonis flower, 'rosarubie', and the speckled variety of sweet william, 'London pride'.[24]

Gerard also commented upon some of the superstitious beliefs concerning plants and herbs cherished by 'those good house-wives that delight not to have any thing but from hand to mouth'. He, and other scornful contemporaries, often referred to such oral traditions as 'mother Bombie's rules'. Among them were several 'old wives tales' concerning the Mandrake, occasioned by the fact that it seemed always to be found growing under the gallows. Equally, of vervain 'many odde old wives fables' were told 'tending to witchcraft and sorcerie'. Such things tended to be branded as witchcraft by the medical and religious establishments alike and, as with all the magical arts of old women, they were said to 'go by tradition'. For 'witches are wont to communicate their skill to others by tradition, to teach and instruct their children and posteritie', observed the puritan divine William Perkins. The Northampton physician John Cotta, condemned such 'inchanted spels' as no more than the 'superstitous babling, by tradition of idle words and sentences, which all that have sense, know to be voide of sense'. Their substance was often difficult to discover precisely because, as John Webster explained in 1677, they were learned 'secretly and by tradition'.

And so these secrets of mischief are for the most part kept in obscurity, amongst old women, superstitious, ignorant, and melancholy persons, and by them delivered over from hand to hand, and commonly one learns it of another according to the proverb, popery and witchcraft go by tradition.

Thus it was only after the utmost 'importunacie' that the Lancashire shopkeeper Roger Lowe prevailed upon one of his customers in the 1660s to reveal to him the rhymed charm 'usd in staunching bloud, which is privatly usd amongst countrie persons, and not publickly knowen'.[25]

---

[24] Gerard, *The Herball or General Historie of Plantes*, ed. Johnson, 642, 740, 780, 564, 548, 464–5, 856; John Parkinson, *Paradisi in Sole Paradisus Terrestris* (London, 1629), 254, 286, 293, 320. Cf. John Evelyn, *Acetaria: A Discourse of Sallets* (London, 1699), 12. On the subject of popular biological vocabulary, see Thomas, *Man and the Natural World*, 81–7.

[25] Gerard, *The Herball or General Historie of Plantes*, ed. Johnson, 74, 351–2, 718–19; William Perkins, *A Discourse of the Damned Art of Witchcraft* (Cambridge, 1608), 193; John Cotta, *A Short Discoverie of the Unobserved Dangers of Severall Sorts of Ignorant and Unconsiderate Practisers of Physicke in England* (London, 1612), 50; John Webster, *The Displaying of Supposed Witchcraft* (London, 1677),

Most observers believed, often quite rightly, that such rhymes were medieval in origin, and regarded them as hangovers from the days of popery. They were increasingly perceived as accompanying the groundless traditions which the progress of religion and learning was beginning to explode but which lingered on in the conservative ways of ignorant and illiterate women. Thus 'it appeareth still among silly country people', Thomas Ady could lament in 1656, 'how they had learned charmes by tradition from popish times, for curing cattel, men, women and children; for churning of butter, for baking their bread, and many other occasions'. He traced their origin to the insidious seeds which the Catholic clergy had first sown in the minds of women. As a youngster growing up in Essex he had known an old woman who as a young girl 'in Queen Maries time', the 1550s, had learned 'many popish charms' in this way. 'Every night when she lay down to sleep she charmed her bed saying: "Mathew, Mark, Luke and John | The bed be blest that I lye on". And this would she repeat three times, reposing great confidence therein . . .'. He knew of another old woman who helped a maid in her butter churning with a charm which had been common when she was a girl 'and also in her mother's young time', which ran:

> Come butter come,
> Come butter come,
> Peter stands at the gate
> Waiting for a buttered cake
> Come butter come.[26]

Similarly, in the 1580s Reginald Scot recalled a number of the charmes and chants which he had first heard from his 'grandames maids' in Kent just after the Reformation. Like those known to Ady, the rhymes of these Kentish serving maids were clearly the product of a female oral tradition set on foot by the old Catholic Church. The verses for reciting in order to cure a 'heavie humor' were addressed to 'S. George, S. George, our ladies knight'. Those for ensuring peaceful rest, ran:

> In nomine Patris, vp and downe,
> Et Filii et Spiritus Sancti vpon my crowne,
> Crux Christi vpon my breast;
> Sweet Ladie, send me eternall rest.[27]

243; Roger Lowe, *The Diary of Roger Lowe of Ashton-in-Makerfield, Lancashire, 1663–74*, ed. William L. Sachse (London, 1938), 76–7.

[26] Ady, *A Perfect Discovery of Witches*, 58–9. On these rhymed charms, see Keith Thomas, *Religion and the Decline of Magic: Studies in Popular Beliefs in Sixteenth- and Seventeenth-Century England* (London, 1971), 180–1.

[27] Scot, *The Discouerie of Witchcraft*, 87, 246, 260, 273. For a similiar series of charms, see

Little verses such as these were easily transmitted and easily remembered by the illiterate. As Henry Howard appreciated when he heard a charm on the lips of Mother Joane of Stowe, said to 'cure eyther beastes, or men and women from diseases', she was not 'able to defend it by authority', it was 'altogether chyldishe and ridiculous, and so much the worse to bee lyked, as it runnes in ryme', and, sure enough, 'the woman is so fonde and simple as shee speaketh, onely lyke a parrette, and is not able to delyuer any reason of her dealing'. This was the oral tradition of the ignorant, drawn from the 'registers of olde wyues tales'.[28]

Such traditions were still very much alive among women in particular when John Aubrey was a boy in the 1630s. At the age of about 6 he lived for a short while in Bristol where, he recalled, it was 'a common fashion for the woemen, to get a tooth out of a sckull in the church-yard: which they wore as a preservative against the toothach'. In the case of gout, some would make a plaster 'with the earth or mucilage newly scraped from the shin-bones' acquired from the same source. When children lost their teeth 'the women use to wrap, or put salt about the tooth and so throw it into a good fire'. White Kennett could confirm on the basis of his Kentish childhood in the 1660s that this had been 'a constant custom of nurses and old women' there. As a medical practitioner in Norfolk at this time, Sir Thomas Browne clearly encountered many such 'common female doctrines', of the sort

that the first rib of roast beef powderd is a peculiar remedy against fluxes; that to urine upon earth newly cast up by a moll, bringeth down the menses in women; that if a child dieth, and the neck becommeth not stiff, but for many howers remaineth lythe and flaccid, some other in the same house will dye not long after; that if a woman with child looketh upon a dead body, her child will be of a pale complexion...

'I pray you', James I had asked, 'what foolish boy, what sillie wench, what olde doting wife, or ignorant countrey clowne, is not a phisician for the toothach, for the cholicke, and diuers such common diseases?'[29]

There was also a variety of such beliefs and observances which women entertained regarding pregnancy and childbirth. Sitting cross-legged was

*The Diary of Samuel Pepys*, ed. Robert Latham and William Matthews (11 vols., London, 1970–83), v. 361–2.

[28] Henry Howard, *A Defensatiue against the Poyson of Supposed Prophesies* (London, 1583), sigs. Ooiv, Ppi.

[29] Aubrey, 'Remaines of Gentilisme and Judaisme', in *Three Prose Works*, ed. Buchanan-Brown, 229, 265, 266; BL, Lansdowne MS, 1039, fo. 12ᵛ; Sir Thomas Browne, *Pseudodoxia Epidemica* (1646), in *The Works of Sir Thomas Browne*, ed. Geoffrey Keynes (4 vols., London, 1964), ii. 397; James I, *A Covnter-Blaste to Tobacco* (London, 1604), sig. C1ᵛ.

said to hinder the onset of labour: 'woemen are superstitious as to this at
woemens labours still', observed Aubrey. After the delivery, the 'mid-
wives [woemen] have some custome, of saving the after birth; or burning
of it: in relation to the long or short life of the new-borne babe'. And once
the baby was safely lodged in its cradle it was the 'ordinary superstition of
old women', White Kennett recorded, 'that they dare not intrust a child
alone in a cradle without a candle' fearing that without one it would come
to harm.[30]

Another fundamental belief among 'maids' and 'housewives' which
long survived the Reformation was in the the power of the fairies.[31]
'Robin Goodfellow', it was said in 1590, was 'famosed in every old wives
chronicle for his mad merry pranks'. At that time, 'women and maid servants lookd upon the fairies as a sort of household-gods', recalled
Kennett. Such beliefs were already ancient by the sixteenth century and
had a long lineage in written as well as oral tradition. They were not merely
confined to women, of course, but they seem to have had a particular
place in female belief and the main characteristics of fairy behaviour by
this period were centred on the household and on childrearing. Thus the
fairies were said both to punish the dirty or 'sluttish' housewife and
reward the clean and tidy one, while they also had the capacity to steal
away babies and replace them with 'changelings'. Aubrey remembered
how, in his childhood, the 'countrey-people' would religiously maintain
hearth and home in order to 'please the fairies', and 'that the fairies would
steale away young children and putt others in their places: verily believed
by old woemen in those dayes: and by some yet living'.[32]

These beliefs gave rise to a whole host of tales in 'the old wive's chronicle' of exploits performed by the little people, and many communities
had sites, landmarks, or artefacts with which they were associated. In the
1670s, Aubrey discovered the magical cauldron in the church at Frensham
in Surrey, 'brought hither by the fairies, time out of mind, from Borough
Hill about a mile from hence'. Many fabulous stories were told of its

---

[30] Aubrey, 'Remaines of Gentilisme and Judaisme', in *Three Prose Works*, ed. Buchanan-
Brown, 252, 206; Browne, *Pseudodoxia Epidemica*, in *The Works of Sir Thomas Browne*, ed. Keynes, ii.
386–7; BL, Lansdowne MS, 1039, fo. 8[r].

[31] These beliefs have been amply discussed in Brand, *Observations on the Popular Antiquities of
Great Britain*, ed. Ellis, ii. 476–516; *Illustrations of the Fairy Mythology of 'A Midsummer Night's Dream'*,
ed. J. O. Halliwell (London, 1845); M. W. Latham, *The Elizabethan Fairies* (New York, 1930);
K. M. Briggs, *The Anatomy of Puck: An Examination of Fairy Beliefs among Shakespeare's Contemporaries
and Successors* (London, 1959); Thomas, *Religion and the Decline of Magic*, 606–14.

[32] *Illustrations of the Fairy Mythology*, ed. Halliwell, vii, 122; BL, Lansdowne MS, 1039, fo. 13[v];
Aubrey, 'Remaines of Gentilisme and Judaisme', in *Three Prose Works*, ed. Buchanan-Brown,
203–4; Bod. Lib., MS Aubrey 3, fo. 185[v].

powers, and these 'verily believ'd by most of the old women of this parish, and by many of their daughters, who can hardly be of any other opinion, so powerful a thing is custom joyn'd with ignorance'. Similarly, the 'old landlady' at Brough in Nottinghamshire could tell William Stukeley some time later that her alehouse was built on 'fairy ground and very lucky to live on'. Visitors to Ward's Hole in Derbyshire, meanwhile, might learn of its enchantment and find that 'the old women told . . . strange storyes of pharyes, often seen in this place'.[33]

### AROUND THE WINTER FIRESIDE

Many of these old wives' stories about the fairies were spun, as were so many tales, around that hub of domestic life and focus of narrative tradition, the winter fireside. As the flames cast shadows in the night and played tricks on the imagination, mothers and nurses conjured up images of the sprites and spirits who inhabited the darkness, and 'old wiues trattles about the fire' told of witches magically transporting themselves from place to place. 'When I was a child (and so before the civill warres)', recalled John Aubrey, 'the fashion was for old women and mayds to tell fabulous stories nightimes and of sprights, and walking of ghosts &c'. This was the oral tradition of old, 'derived downe from mother to daughter'. And what Aubrey remembered of Wiltshire, Thomas Ady knew in Essex where 'old wives' would 'sit talking, and chatting of many false old stories of witches, and fairies, and Robin good-fellow, and walking spirits and the dead walking again . . .'. Equally, from the north-east of England it was later reported that 'nothing is commoner in country places than for a whole family in a winter's evening to sit round the fire and tell stories of apparitions and ghosts'. On this subject, realized Daniel Defoe, there was an 'abundance of merry tales scatter'd abroad in the oral tradition of antient times, and among those antient things called old women . . .'.[34]

---

[33] John Aubrey, *The Natural History and Antiquities of the County of Surrey: Begun in the Year 1673* (5 vols., London, 1718–19), iii. 366–7; William Stukeley, *Itinerarium Curiosum* (London, 1724), 98; Joseph Taylor, *A Journey to Edenborough in Scotland*, ed. William Cowan (Edinburgh, 1903), 19. For a variety of other places or natural phenomena with fairy associations, see *The Itinerary of John Leland in or about the Years 1535–1543*, ed. Lucy Toulmin Smith (5 vols., London, 1906–10), iii. 103; *Illustrations of the Fairy Mythology*, ed. Halliwell, 235–6; Robert Plot, *The Natural History of Stafford-Shire* (Oxford, 1686), 9, 14; John Morton, *The Natural History of Northamptonshire* (London, 1712), 397–9; Ralph Thoresby, *Ducatus Leodiensis: Or, the Topography of the Ancient and Populous Town and Parish of Leedes* (London, 1715), 493; *The Travels through England of Dr Richard Pococke*, ed. J. J. Cartwright (2 vols., Camden Society, new ser., 42, 44, London, 1888–9), i. 46, 97, ii. 217.

[34] James VI, *Daemonologie*, 40; Bod Lib., MS Aubrey 3, fo. 30; Ady, *A Candle in the Dark*, 169; Henry Bourne, *Antiquitates Vulgares; Or, the Antiquities of the Common People* (Newcastle, 1725), 76;

Tales of the supernatural were just some among the repertoire of yarns woven by wives and mothers as they sat and worked or sewed around the evening hearth. The Elizabethan, John Florio, was dismissive of the kind of 'flim-flam tale, as women tell when they shale peason', or 'ould wiues tales as they tell when they spinne', which had 'neither head nor foote, nor rime nor reason', but they seem to have delighted most youngsters. 'Come neere, take a stoole, and sit downe', says the old crone, Sybilla, in one of John Lyly's plays. 'Now, for that these winter nights are long, and that children delight in nothing more then to heare old wiues tales, we will beguile the time with some storie.' A vivid picture of just such a 'flim-flam' story and the pleasure which it gave to the young is provided in George Peele's comedy, *The Old Wives' Tale*, written about 1589. The action takes place around a winter's evening fireside where a smith's wife, Madge, is implored by three lads, Anticke, Frolicke and Fantasticke, to tell them 'a merry winter's tale'. 'Looke you, gammer', says Frolicke, 'of the gyant and the king's daughter, and I know not what; I haue seene the day, when I was a litle one, you might haue drawne mee a mile after you with such a discourse.' Madge consents 'to driue away the time with an old wiues' winter's tale'.

Once vppon a time there was a king or a lord, or a duke that had a faire daughter, the fairest that euer was; as white as snowe, and as redd as bloud: and once vppon a time his daughter was stollen away, and hee sent all his men to seeke out his daughter, and hee sent so long, that he sent all his men out of his land . . . O Lord, I quite forgot, there was a coniurer, and this coniurer could doo any thing, and hee turned himselfe into a great dragon, and carried the kinges daughter away in his mouth to a castle that hee made of stone, and there he kept hir I know not how long, till at last all the kinges men went out so long, that hir two brothers went to seeke hir. O I forget: she (he I would say) turned a proper yong man to a beare in the night, and a man in the day, and keeps by a crosse that parts three seuerall waies, and he made his lady run mad . . . [35]

Telling stories was thus an important part of the role of women as entertainers within the home. It was also central to their role as the instructors of children. 'The most innocent, grateful and universal discourse, is telling stories', considered the educationalist Obadiah Walker, 'and modern rather than ancient. Some are so well stocked with this trade as to be able to answer any question, or parallel any case by a story; which

Daniel Defoe, *A System of Magick; Or, a History of the Black Art* (London, 1727), 225. On the importance of the winter fireside, see pp. 30–1 above.

[35] Florio, *A Worlde of Wordes*, 124, 131; John Lyly, *Sapho and Phao* (1584), II. i. 21–4, in *The Complete Works of John Lyly*, ed. Bond, ii. 380–1; George Peele, *The Old Wiues Tale* (London, 1595), lines 103–58 (sig. B1).

is (if well done) a very great perfection of eloquence and judgement'. There must have been many devout women like Lady Anne North who could 'show how vertue may be mixt with delight' in the didactic stories which she told to her son Roger and his brothers in the 1650s. 'She used to tell us tales, allways concluding in morality, to which, as children use, wee were most attentive', and on Sundays she 'would tell some scripturall history, which was more pleasing to us becaus more admirable and extraordinary then others'.[36]

Women's stories also reflected the fact that they were frequently the custodians of family history and were responsible for its transmission to the young. Thus the servant, Roger, in a dialogue written by William Bullein in the 1560s, tells how his grandfather had taken part in 'Palme Sondaie battaile' at Barnet during the reign of Edward IV and only survived by hiding up a tree: 'I harde my grandame tell how he escaped', he remembers. Much later, the young Anthony Wood would be well aware that his great aunt, Alice Beare, who died 'a verie old woman' in 1634, had told his father 'many stories of the family', just as in the next generation Alice's daughter Elizabeth, who died at the age of 80 in 1668, passed on similar traditions to Wood himself.[37]

Historical tales and romances of wider import also entered this narrative repertoire where they were thought to provide uplifting examples or moral lessons for children. During John Aubrey's Wiltshire childhood the fashion had been for 'maydes to sitt-up late by the fire [and] tell old romantique stories of the old time, handed downe to them with a great deal of alteration'. In those days, 'the old ignorant times, before woomen were readers, the history was handed downe from mother to daughter'. Little had changed a generation later when Joseph Addison was growing up, not far from Aubrey, in the village of Milston near Amesbury during the 1670s. He later recalled the 'legends and fables, antiquated romances, and the traditions of nurses and old women . . . which we have imbibed in our infancy' (see Plate 9).[38]

Every town, village, and parish probably had its historical anecdotes and local traditions of which women were the special purveyors around winter hearth and nursery fire. Heroes of the community, in particular,

---

[36] Obadiah Walker, *Of Education, Especially of Young Gentlemen* (London, 1673), 248; Roger North, *The Lives of the Norths*, ed. Augustus Jessopp (3 vols., London, 1890), iii. 5.

[37] William Bullein, *A Dialogue bothe Pleasaunt and Pietifull wherein is a Godlie Regiment against the Fever Pestilence* (London, 1564), fos. 43ᵛ–44ᶜ; *The Life and Times of Anthony Wood, Antiquary, of Oxford, 1632–1695, Described by Himself*, ed. Andrew Clark (5 vols., Oxford Historical Society, 19, 21, 26, 30, 40, Oxford, 1891–1900), i. 4–5 n., v. 3.

[38] Aubrey, 'Remaines of Gentilisme and Judiasme', in *Three Prose Works*, ed. Buchanan-Brown, 445, 289; *The Spectator*, ed. Donald F. Bond (5 vols., Oxford, 1965), iii. 570.

provided an inspiration and an example to the young. From Elizabethan Pembrokeshire, for example, George Owen could report that 'our women' would explain the mysterious absence of nightingales in the county with a 'fable', like so many others, 'fathered upon St David'. At Weston in Hertfordshire romantic yarns were 'told by nursery fires' about the legendary deeds of one 'Strongbow', otherwise Richard de Clare, earl of Pembroke and sometime lord of the manor. At Sherston in Wiltshire the exploits of the village hero, 'Rattlebone', who 'did much service against the Danes', were celebrated in a rhyme which 'the old women and children have . . . by tradition'. In the parish of Upton in Warwickshire, meanwhile, one might hear the 'old wives story' of 'one Alcock, a great robber' who had once lived in a cave at the foot of the big hill in the wood. He had his ill-gotten gains hidden

in an iron-bound chest, whereunto were three keys; which chest, they say, is still there, but guarded by a cock that continually sits upon it: And that on a time, an Oxford-schollar came thither, with a key that opened two of the locks; but as he was attempting to open the third, the cock seized him. To all which they adde, that if one bone of the partie, who set the cock there, could be brought, he would yield up the chest.[39]

When Daniel Defoe travelled through Britain in the early eighteenth century he encountered many such local traditions, entrusted to the narrative skills of old women. Near the Scottish border, for instance, he was naturally curious about a famous battle. 'We had the Cheviot hills so plain in view, that we could not but enquire of the good old women every where, whether they had heard of the fight at Chevy Chace: they not only told us they had heard of it, but had all the account of it at their fingers end'. It was from the same source that he heard the rich historical legends passed down in the mountains of Radnorshire, for 'the stories of Vortigern, and Roger of Mortimer, are in every old woman's mouth here'. At St Bees in Cumberland he was told the fabulous tales of St Bee 'procuring, by her prayers, a deep snow on Midsummer day, her taming a wild bull that did great damage in the country', but resolved to leave 'these, and the like tales . . . where I found them, (viz.) among the rubbish of the old women and the Romish priests'.[40]

Defoe's dismissal of such 'rubbish' as the superstitions of old wives

---

[39] George Owen, *The Description of Pembrokeshire*, ed. Dillwyn Miles (Llandysul, 1994), 150; N[athaniel] Salmon, *The History of Hertfordshire* (London, 1728), 184; Bod. Lib., MS Aubrey 3, fo. 104ᵛ; Sir William Dugdale, *The Antiquities of Warwickshire* (London, 1656), 619.

[40] Daniel Defoe, *A Tour thro' the Whole island of Great Britain*, ed. G. D. H. Cole (London, 1927), 662, 453, 682.

and the dregs of popery was quite typical of educated male opinion in his day. It was symptomatic of the gulf which could exist between the beliefs and traditions of the upper ranks of society and those enduring among the lower orders. But these cultural worlds were by no means hermetically sealed or completely isolated from one another, for they met face to face in the world of childhood. It is an important, although often overlooked, fact that it was at the juvenile level where the repertoire of unlearned village women coincided for a brief but significant period with that of the educated male elite. Children of all classes were bewitched by fireside stories and songs and in so far as the wealthier in society employed humble women as servants and nurses, they exposed their infants to the influence of popular lore.[41]

In adult life many contemporaries would reflect upon the popular traditions and vulgar fancies peddled around the nursery fire by the old beldams who had their charge. Thus, George Puttenham recalled the saucy riddles heard from his nurse as a boy in the 1530s.

My mother had an old woma[n] in her nurserie, who in the winter nights would put vs forth many prety ridles, whereof this is one:

> I haue a thing and rough it is
> And in the midst a hole I wis:
> There came a yong man with his ginne,
> And he put it a handfull in.

The good old gentlewoman would tell vs that were children how it was meant by a furd glooue. Some other naughtie body would peraduenture haue construed it not halfe so mannerly.

Typically John Aubrey's nurse was a local woman, Katherine Bushell, from the village of Ford in south Wiltshire. She would tell romantic yarns about the old days, being 'excellent at these old stories', and she 'had the history from the Conquest down to Carl. I. in ballad'. A character in an early eighteenth-century ballad-opera sings the popular ditty 'A lass there lives upon the green', which she remembers as 'an old song of my nurse's, every word of which she believ'd as much as her Psalter, that used to make me long, when I was a girl, to be abroad in a moonlight night'. Then, of course, there were the superstitious tales of magic and enchantment. Lady Mary Wortley Montagu was not uncommon in recalling a nurse who 'took so much pains from my infancy', during the 1690s, 'to fill my head with superstitious tales and false notions, it was none of her fault I am not

---

[41] Cf. Richard M. Dorson, *The British Folklorists: A History* (London, 1968), 323: 'A whole monograph could be written on the relationship between the Victorian gentry and their house servants in terms of culture contact.'

at this day afraid of witches and hobgoblins . . .'. That some children were capable of giving back as good as they got is suggested by the little daughter of an old friend whom Richard Steele encountered in 1709. Her mother told him that she 'deals chiefly in fairies and sprights; and sometimes in a winter night, will terrify the maids with her accounts, till they are afraid to go up to bed'.[42]

The perils of exposing their children to the uncouth influences of village women did not go unremarked by well-to-do parents. Indeed, since it was believed in contemporary medical theory that an infant could absorb the character traits of a wet-nursing woman through the breast milk, they often worried about the corrupting influence of ill-educated and ill-bred matrons nurturing their young.[43] Although Sir William Cornwallis was prepared to concede that it was not innate inferiority, but rather lack of education, which kept women 'ignorant and so fearefull', it made him no less anxious about the damaging effect of a plebeian nurse suckling her employer's children. 'For from her teat they sucke somewhat of her constitution. In which I doubt whether there be not some fault, for we take the wives of our groomes and tenants to feede these little ones, and mingle grosse and heavy blood with their gentle and spirited natures.'[44] It is no wonder that observers who commented on the peculiar vernacular traditions of the common people which, though expunged from civilized society, continued somehow to perpetuate themselves stubbornly down the generations, often attributed their resilience to having been 'sucked in with nurses' milk'.[45]

Even more dangerous than the corrupting influences of inferior nature, however, were the damaging consequences of poor nurture: the

---

[42] George Puttenham, *The Arte of English Poesie* (London, 1589), 157; Aubrey, 'Remaines of Gentilisme and Judaisme', in *Three Prose Works*, ed. Buchanan-Brown, 287, 290, 445; W. Chappell, *Popular Music of the Olden Time* (London, 1859), 685; J. A. Sharpe, *Early Modern England: A Social History, 1550–1760* (2nd edn., London, 1997), 293; *The Tatler*, ed. Donald F. Bond (3 vols., Oxford, 1987), ii. 93.

[43] This classical belief is most clearly restated in Burton, *Anatomy of Melancholy*, ed. Jackson, i. 330–3. Cf. the medical opinion cited in Valerie Fildes, *Wet Nursing: A History from Antiquity to the Present* (Oxford, 1988), 73–4; Mary Abbott, *Life Cycles in England, 1560–1720: Cradle to Grave* (London, 1996), 54; David Cressy, *Birth, Marriage and Death: Ritual Religion and the Life-Cycle in Tudor and Stuart England* (Oxford, 1997), 90. It was probably for this reason that Jewish mothers would not let their children be suckled by Christian wet-nurses: BL, Lansdowne MS, 1039, fo. 8ᵛ.

[44] Sir William Cornwallis, *Essayes*, ed. D. C. Allen (Baltimore, 1946), 109.

[45] For a variety of comments to this effect, see E.K., 'Epistle' to Edmund Spenser, *The Shepheardes Calender* (1579), in *Spenser: Poetical Works*, ed. J. C. Smith and E. De Selincourt (Oxford, 1912), 417; John Smyth, *The Berkeley Manuscripts*, ed. Sir John Maclean (3 vols., Gloucester, 1883–5), iii. 23; Webster, *The Displaying of Supposed Witchcraft*, 32; *Life and Letters of Edward Lhwyd*, vol. xiv of *Early Science in Oxford*, ed. R. T. Gunther (Oxford, 1945), 331; Oswald Dykes, *English Proverbs with Moral Reflections* (2nd edn., London, 1709), xxxv.

risks of allowing vulgar women the responsibility of rearing one's children at precisely their most impressionable age. In the 1530s, Sir Thomas Elyot was already warning of the potentially contaminating effect of nurse-maids on their gentle and aristocratic charges. Seclude your children from 'barbarous nursses, clownish playing mates, and all rusticall persons', advised the Elizabethan schoolmaster William Kempe. 'For a child, like an emptie new vessell being voide of all learning, is most apt to receiue that which is first taught, and that which is first taught, sticketh deepest in memorie, whether it be good or bad.' These cautionary words appealed no less during the seventeenth century, as Obadiah Walker's concerns for the very young made clear. 'For very frequently the bland-ishments of nurses, and the foolish, vaine, or evil conversation of those about them, leave such impressions even upon their infancy, as are diffi-cultly defaced, even when the child arrives to discretion, and maturity. Besides, the nurses forme the speech, the garbe, and much of the senti-ments of the child.' The clergyman Ralph Josselin would thank the Lord for sparing him the 'poysonous infections from servants' to which his childhood in Bishop's Stortford during the reign of James I had exposed him.[46]

Not everyone was so fortunate, however. The stories told by nurses and maids and the beliefs which they instilled clearly remained with some youngsters all their lives, sticking deep in the memory as Kempe had pre-dicted, and sometimes returning to haunt them. Reginald Scot was born at Scots Hall in the village of Smeeth, near Ashford, in Kent, about 1538. Growing up in the 1540s he had been reared on a diet of 'old wives' tales' from his 'grandam's maides' and they left an indelible mark. The purpose of such stories was deliberately to frighten: to provide children with chas-tening examples of what might happen to them if they did not do as they were told. Discipline through fear was the aim. The devil and a host of other evil spirits lay in wait for the naughty child who disobeyed a parent or nurse. 'In our childhood', lamented Scot, 'our mother's maides have so terrified us with an ougliue divell' together with a myriad other wierd and wonderful creatures, 'that we are afraid of our owne shadowes'. Half a century later he could still evoke memories of 'fairies . . . coniurors, nymphes, changlings, incubus, Robin goodfellowe' and even then con-jure up the spectre of 'bull beggers, spirits, witches . . . kit with the can-

---

[46] Sir Thomas Elyot, *The Boke Named the Gouenour* (London, 1531), fo. 19ᵛ; William Kempe, *The Education of Children in Learning* (London, 1588), sig. E3ᵛ–E4ʳ; Walker, *Of Education*, 18; *The Diary of Ralph Josselin, 1616–1683*, ed. Alan Macfarlane (British Academy, Records of Social and Economic History, new ser., 3, London, 1976), 1.

sticke . . . the spoorne, the mare, the man in the oke, the hell waine, the firedrake, the puckle . . . hob gobblin . . . boneles, and such other bugs'.[47]

So commonplace were these frightening tales that the saying 'bugbears to scare babes' was a part of the everyday language. It was clearly normal, as Arthur Dent remarked, that 'a mother when her childe is waywarde' will 'scarreth it with some pokar, or bull-beggar, to make it cling more unto her, and be quiet'. Some parents, agreed Robert Burton, 'fright their children with beggars, bugbears, and hobgoblins, if they cry, or be otherwise unruly'. Not surprisingly, many boys and girls thus affrighted grew into adult life still shuddering at the thought of these early horrors. Significantly, when at the end of Elizabeth's reign, Sir William Cornwallis came to write an essay 'on fear', what came to mind was the way in which 'we heare from our nurses and olde women, tales of hobgoblins and deluding spirits that abuse travellers and carry them out of their way'. Stories of this whole 'visionary tribe', Sir William Temple later agreed, 'serve not only to fright children into whatever their nurses please, but sometimes, by lasting impressions, to disquiet the sleeps and the very lives of men and women, till they grow to years of discretion'.[48]

Such nightmares were clearly commonplace. 'The mare', mentioned by Scot, which gives its name to the term, was a goblin who was supposed to descend on children in the middle of the night and sit on their chests. An 'incubus' was a similar demon who might plague the sleep of young or old, and especially women. 'Boneless' and his companion 'bloodless' were clearly ghosts and they too had been haunting children since the Middle Ages.[49] John Bunyan's Bedfordshire childhood in the 1630s was not unusual in its being plagued by 'fearful dreams' and 'dreadful visions'.

---

[47] Scot, *The Discouerie of Witchcraft*, 85, 152–3, 256, 470, 471. An almost identical list is obviously borrowed from Scot in Thomas Middleton, *The Witch*, I. ii. 297–300, ed. W. W. Greg and F. P. Wilson (Malone Society Reprints, Oxford, 1950), 13.

[48] Tilley, *Dictionary of the Proverbs in England in the Sixteenth and Seventeenth Centuries*, 70; Arthur Dent, *The Plaine Mans Path-way to Heauen* (London, 1601), 123; Burton, *Anatomy of Melancholy*, ed. Jackson, i. 333; Cornwallis, *Essayes*, ed. Allen, 108; Sir William Temple, 'Of Poetry' (1690), in *Critical Essays of the Seventeenth Century*, ed. Spingarn, iii. 96. Cf. Montaigne, *The Essayes or Morall, Politike and Millitarie Discourses*, trans. Florio, 27; Flecknoe, *The Diarium, or Journall*, 40; Keith Thomas, 'Children in Early Modern England', in Gillian Avery and Julia Briggs (eds.), *Children and their Books* (Oxford, 1989), 67–8.

[49] On 'the mare', see Sir Thomas Elyot, *The Dictionary* (London, 1538), s.v. 'Incubus', sig. K5ᵛ; James VI, *Daemonologie*, 69; Michael Drayton, *Nimphidia: The Court of Fayrie*, in *The Works of Michael Drayton*, ed. J. William Hebel (5 vols., Oxford, 1931–41), iii. 126; Temple, 'Of Poetry', in *Critical Essays of the Seventeenth Century*, ed. Spingarn, iii. 97. That 'bloodless' was a ghost is suggested by the reference in *2 Henry VI*, III. ii. 161–2. An early fifteenth-century Bristol boy wrote in his school-book: 'Blodles and boneles stondyth by-hynd the dore': Nicholas Orme, *Education and Society in Medieval and Renaissance England* (London, 1989), 100.

In his sleep he would see 'the apprehensions of devils, and wicked spirits, who still, as I then thought, laboured to draw me away with them'. And it was, of course, in a dream that he later beheld the journey of Christian who encountered the 'hobgoblins, satyrs and dragons of the pit', and fought with fiend Apollyon: 'the monster was hidious to behold, he was cloathed with scales like a fish . . . he had wings like a dragon, feet like a bear, and out of his belly came fire and smoak, and his mouth was the mouth of a lion'. It also seems significant that the monster of the woods who terrorized the town of Vanity, with its dragon's body, seven heads, and ten horns, 'made great havock of children'.[50]

Another spectre which had been a particular terror of children since at least Reginald Scot's childhood in the 1540s, was 'Raw-head and bloody-bone.' One Elizabethan later referred to the 'hobgoblins or elfes, or such misshapen images or imagined spirits that nurces fraie their babes withall to make them leaue crying, as we say bug-beare, or els rawe head and bloodie bone'. Certainly John Aubrey never forgot 'Raw-head and bloody-bone feard by children.' His contemporary, John Locke, also noticed the 'indiscretion of servants, whose usual method is to awe children, and keep them in subjection, by telling them of Raw-head and bloody-bones'. In the early eighteenth century, the author of *Round about our Coal Fire, or Christmas Entertainments* recalled the similar tales of 'hobgoblins, Raw-heads and bloody-bones, buggybows, Tom-pokers, bull-beggars and such like horrible bodies' told to him by women in his infancy.

There was nothing kept me in greater awe when I was a child, than the frequent relations I had from my grandmother and nurse of hobgoblins and bull-beggars; they would tell me such stories of them daily, as would frighten me into a woful case, and sad disgrace . . .[51]

In some cases, Raw-head and bloody-bone could be a demon who lived in ponds ready to snatch naughty children who got too close to the water's edge, while Tom-poker was usually a bogey who lurked in dark cupboards and empty lofts. Many such traditions of the nursery grew out

---

[50] John Bunyan, *Grace Abounding to the Chief of Sinners*, ed. Roger Sharrock (Oxford, 1962), 6; John Bunyan, *The Pilgrim's Progress*, ed. J. B. Wharey and Roger Sharrock (Oxford, 1960), 56, 62, 64, 277–8.

[51] [Robert Devereux], *The Wyll of the Deuyll, and Last Testament* (London, 1548?), sig. C4ᵛ; Florio, *A Worlde of Wordes*, 215; Aubrey, 'Remaines of Gentilisme and Judiasme', in *Three Prose Works*, ed. Buchanan-Brown, 290; John Locke, *Some Thoughts Concerning Education*, ed. J. W. and J. S. Yolton (Oxford, 1989), 196; *Round about our Coal Fire, or Christmas Entertainments* (1734; London, 1740 edn.), i, ii, 9–10, 11. Cf. Ned Ward, *The London Spy: The Vanities and Vices of the Town Exposed to View*, ed. Arthur L. Hayward (London, 1927), 73.

of this attempt to frighten children away from the places in which they were not supposed to be or might come to harm. Youngsters were warned from playing by dangerous rivers and ponds with such tales of water demons; their natural curiosity for salt pits and caves was chastened by chilling narratives of underground spirits; and their tendency to gravitate towards steep cliffs and gorges was tempered by the legends of the devils who had made them. Boys were dissuaded from scrumping apples from orchards in the middle of night by the fairies said then to guard them. And adaptable to any situation was the fearful giant who would gobble up children for breakfast and grind their bones to make his bread: for even in the 1590s Thomas Nashe was speculating on 'the first inuention of *Fy, fa, fum,* I smell the bloud of an English-man'. The consequence, then, of this example of necessity being the mother of invention, was a rich vein of folklore inspired by deterrence and motived by the desire to keep youngsters 'in subjection'.[52]

By the latter part of the seventeenth century the efficacy of this traditional method of inspiring awe and subjection in children was being widely criticized, especially in advanced thinking on education. Such views were in part, no doubt, bound up with the increasing incredulity and distaste shown by the educated elite in general for the evil spirits in which earlier generations had believed, or at least been content to utilize. Anyone seeking the decline of 'superstitious' beliefs in early modern England would do well to identify when the tales and traditions grounded upon them ceased to be passed on in the nurseries of the gentry. 'Forbear also (chiefly if the child be naturally timorous) all discourse of witches, spirits, fayries, and the like', Obadiah Walker advised those with responsibility for the young, for such things 'intimidate the spirit, and fill the head with vain and frightful imaginations'. John Locke agreed that the kind of idle nonsense peddled by servants was likely to make a child afraid of being alone, 'especially in the dark', and lead to the kind of nightmares suffered by the young Bunyan. 'How many souls are ruin'd by mothers and nurses scaring their children with horrid and frightful names . . .?' wondered a rueful Thomas Tryon in 1695.[53]

---

[52] E. M. Wright, *Rustic Speech and Folk-Lore* (Oxford, 1913), 197–9; Temple, 'Of Poetry', in *Critical Essays of the Seventeenth Century*, ed. Spingarn, iii. 97; Sir William Brereton, *Travels in Holland, the United Provinces, England, Scotland and Ireland, 1634–1635*, ed. Edward Hawkins (Chetham Society, 1, London, 1844), 170; Thomas Nashe, *Haue with you to Saffron Walden* (1596), in *The Works of Thomas Nashe*, ed. McKerrow and Wilson, iii. 37, quoted in Iona and Peter Opie, *The Classic Fairy Tales* (London, 1974), 48; Shakespeare, *King Lear*, iii. iv. 170–2.

[53] Walker, *Of Education*, 42; Locke, *Some Thoughts Concerning Education*, ed. Yolton, 196; Thomas Tryon, *A New Method of Educating Children* (London, 1695), 13.

TEXT AND SUBTEXT

The rejection of these tales for children by the upper social ranks reflected the way in which their tastes and sensibilities were changing by the later seventeenth century. But the legitimacy of such beliefs and the efficacy of such methods had a long and respectable tradition, in learned culture as well as popular, in recorded tradition no less than oral. What were coming to be regarded by the end of this period as little more than the fables and superstitions of old wives had once been disseminated from the pulpits of educated preachers and perpetuated in the chronicles of monkish writers. Legends of mythical creatures, stories about malevolent fiends and evil spirits, and solemn accounts of miracles and prodigies had all comprised part of the orthodox teachings of church and schoolroom well back into the Middle Ages and before. As with other aspects of oral culture by the early modern period, nursery lore was the product of a long series of interactions between written and spoken transmission.

Some features of the 'old beldam's catechism' are well attested in writing from an early date. In the case of legends about fairies and their magical feats, for example, many of the classic tales owe their first recording to the great monastic chroniclers of the twelfth and thirteenth centuries. Remarkably, they appear to have been handed down thereafter with very little alteration over 700 years. Thus, 'The Fairy Midwife', a story about changelings recorded by Gervase of Tilbury around 1211, was still circulating early in the twentieth century when Ruth Tongue heard it from 'Annie's granny' at Taunton in Somerset. 'The Missing Sow', a tale describing the magical underworld also told by Gervase, was discovered by Walter Scott to be current among northern border folk at the end of the eighteenth century. William of Newburgh copied from Ralph of Coggeshall the still familiar story of 'The Green Children' who were said to have emerged from an underground cavern to live among mortals in Suffolk. Among the tales first committed to paper by Walter Map, writing in the reign of Henry II, was the legend of 'Wild Edric', a Shropshire nobleman of the eleventh century who had an elf-maiden for a wife. His deeds were still being recounted by the Shropshire folk known to Charlotte Burne in the Victorian period.[54]

In the case of other elements in the old wives' repertoire far fewer recordings were made or have survived. Fairy-tales were clearly widespread in the Middle Ages but very few received full literary treatment. Chaucer's 'broad-speaking, gap-toothed' Wife of Bath provides not only

---

[54] Katherine M. Briggs, *A Dictionary of British Folk-Tales in the English Language* (4 vols., London, 1970), iii. 235–6, 327, 262–3, 405–7; see also i. 363–5, iii. 304–5.

the literary archetype of the mumping beldam but also a comparatively rare example of a fully developed fairy tale from the medieval period. 'In th'olde dayes of the Kyng Arthour | Of which that Britons speken greet honour | Al was this land fulfild of fayerye.' That the classic motif which she elaborates, involving a hideous creature turned back into a beautiful damsel by the kiss of handsome prince, was already popular is attested by its inclusion in a variety of other fourteenth-century literature. Meanwhile, another contemporary of Chaucer, the Benedictine sub-prior of Durham, Robert Rypon, preached a sermon in which he alluded to the story of 'Cinderella'. Such tantalizing references hint at a manuscript tradition which has not come down to us and suggest a seam of oral transmission running beneath the firm ground of text.[55]

In the sixteenth and seventeenth centuries there was scarely any development in the literary evolution of the fairy-tale. There was no British equivalent of Charles Perrault's *Histoires ou contes du temps passé* (1697), which recorded stories from the mouths of the French peasantry in the seventeenth century. Instead, we are left with partial and fragmentary references in the drama and other writings of the period from which to speculate on the features of the English tradition. Peele's *The Old Wives' Tale* contains the first telling of the tale later known as 'The Three Heads in the Well'. This version is probably similar to 'The Wal at the Warld's End' which the shepherds in *The Complaynt of Scotlande*, an anonymous tract of 1549, considered a 'gude tayl or fabil, to pas the tyme quhil euyn', but it was not given full literary form until *The History of Four Kings*, a chapbook offered for sale in 1764. The shepherds also knew 'The taiyl of the reyde eyttyn vitht the thre heydis' and 'The tayle of the giantis that eit quyk men', but no such narratives appear to have been set down until the early eighteenth-century chapbook *The History of Jack and the Giants* published what may have been something similar. Equally, 'Jack and the Beanstalk' first found its way into print in a chapbook of 1734 which includes 'Enchantment demonstrated, in the Story of Jack Spriggins and the Enchanted Bean', although in this case it is impossible to tell whether it was known earlier.[56]

---

[55] John Dryden, 'Preface to the Fables', in *Essays of John Dryden*, ed. W. P. Ker (2 vols., Oxford, 1900), ii. 262; *The Riverside Chaucer*, ed. Larry D. Benson (3rd edn., Boston, Mass., 1987), 116; Opie, *The Classic Fairy Tales*, 15 n., 183–4; G. R. Owst, *Literature and Pulpit in Medieval England* (2nd edn., Oxford, 1961), 42, 209.

[56] Opie, *The Classic Fairy Tales*, 21–4, 156–61, 47–65, 162–74; Briggs, *Dictionary of British Folk-Tales*, i. 517–20, 551–3; Peele, *The Old Wiues Tale*, lines 253–96 (sig. B3ᵛ–B4ᶜ), 744–856 (sig. D4ᶜ–E2ᶜ), 960–93 (sig. E3ᵛ–E4ᵛ); *The Complaynt of Scotlande*, ed. J. A. H. Murray (Early English Text Society, extra ser., 17, London, 1872), 63; *Round about our Coal Fire*, 32–45. On the ancient motif of heads in wells, see Anne Ross, 'Severed Heads in Wells: An Aspect of the Well Cult', *Scottish Studies*, 6 (1962), 31–48.

Shakespeare's plays contain a number of allusions to fairy-tales which clearly needed no explanation to contemporary audiences but are only known today through later recordings. Elizabethan familiarity with 'The Owl was a Baker's Daughter' is betrayed by Ophelia: 'They say the owl was a baker's daughter', she lets slip in her distracted ramblings of grief. But its details are not known until a version was contributed to the *Gentleman's Magazine* in 1804, said to have been heard from an 'old lady' and to be 'an old fairy tale, well known to nurses in Herefordshire'.[57] References to 'The Man in the Moon' also appear twice in Shakespearean drama. The story, which was probably traditional long before mention was first made of it in the fourteenth century, involves a man who is punished for stealing some thorn bushes by being banished to the moon, so near and yet so far from heaven. Perhaps it was in the sabbatarian atmosphere of the early modern period that this theme was grafted onto an Old Testament moral and became the tale collected by the Victorians of a poor man condemned to lunar purgatory for gathering sticks on a Sunday.[58] 'Like the old tale, my lord—it is not so, nor 'twas not so, but indeed, God forbid it should be so', says Benedick in *Much Ado about Nothing*, quoting the crucial repeated refrain from the story of 'Mr Fox'. An 'old tale' it may have been in the 1590s, but it was not transcribed from oral tradition until 1821.[59]

One of the stories which Reginald Scot 'heard among my grandam's maides' in Kent during the 1540s was 'A Maid who Fetched Water in a Sieve'. This classic type, which is only partially rendered by Scot, told of some wicked sisters who sent their sibling to fetch water, giving her only a sieve in which to carry it. When she tried to fill the sieve, the water ran out as fast as it went in. But, as luck would have it, a crow noticed the poor maid and promised her that if she plugged her sieve with 'clam claie' she should have 'a cake of so great quantitie, as might be kneded of so much floure as she could wet with the water that she brought in a siue'. The maid did as she was told and 'clamd it with claie, and brought in so much water, as whereby she had a great cake, and so beguiled hir sisters'. The tale then completely disappears from the written word for three and a half

[57] *Hamlet*, IV. v. 41–2; *Gentleman's Magazine*, 74 (Nov., 1804), 1003–4; J. O. Halliwell, *Popular Rhymes and Nursery Tales* (London, 1849), 167.

[58] *A Midsummer-Night's Dream*, v. i. 253–4; *The Tempest*, II. ii. 137–40; Numbers 15: 32–6; Briggs, *Dictionary of British Folk-Tales*, i. 123–4; Opie and Tatem, *A Dictionary of Superstitions*, 264.

[59] *Much Ado about Nothing*, I. i. 203–4 (written 1598–9, printed 1600); Halliwell, *Popular Rhymes and Nursery Tales*, 47–8. Another tale, 'The Miser and his Wife', or 'Good Fortune', was alluded to by Ben Jonson: see Halliwell, *Popular Rhymes and Nursery Tales*, 31–2; Briggs, *Dictionary of British Folk-Tales*, ii. 104–5.

centuries before it was recorded, in slightly variant form, at a household in Calver, Derbyshire.[60]

Scot also heard from his grandam's maids all about 'Tom Thombe' and 'Tom Tumbler', together with 'imps' and 'elves', 'dwarfs' and 'giants'. Clearly stories of Tom Thumb were circulating orally at this time, and they may already have been in print too. On his death in 1640, Robert Burton bequeathed a copy of *The History of Tom Thumb* to the Bodleian Library in Oxford, one of the many 'little historical diverting pamphletts' with which he used to entertain himself, 'as he did with other little merry books'. A century later it was read by the antiquary Thomas Hearne in whose learned judgement it dated from the reign of Henry VIII. Hearne thought that the author might have been Andrew Borde, the well-known medic and popular author. This pamphlet apparently described Tom as 'King Edgar's dwarf' whereas the earliest extant copy of the tale, probably written by Richard Johnson and printed for Thomas Langley in 1621, has him as 'King Arthur's dwarfe'(see Plate 7). Tales of Tom were probably old by Scot's day and may well have been known to manuscript long before they reached print. At the same time, Johnson's claims for his long popularity in oral tradition were clearly justified.

The ancient tales of Tom Thumbe in the olde time, haue been the onely reuiuers of drouzy age at midnight; old and young haue with his tales chim'd mattens till the cocks crow in the morning; batchelors and maides with his tales haue compassed the Christmas fire-blocke, till the curfew bell rings candle out; the old shepheard and the young plow boy after their dayes labour, haue carold out a tale of Tom Thumbe to make them merry with: and who but little Tom, hath made long nights seeme short, and heauy toyles easie?[61]

The fact, therefore, that so few of what we now describe as fairy-tales were written down in full before the modern period is testimony to their circulation, and survival over many centuries, by word of mouth. Sufficient allusions to such tales in the sixteenth and seventeenth centuries make it clear that they were then well known to contemporaries, but apparently almost no one thought them worth writing down or printing.

[60] Scot, *The Discouerie of Witchcraft*, 256; Sidney O. Addy, *Household Tales with Other Traditional Remains Collected in the Counties of York, Lincoln, Derby, and Nottingham* (London, 1895), 40; Briggs, *Dictionary of British Folk-Tales*, i. 267–8. Folklorists were later to collect a number of versions of tales which involved carrying water in a sieve: see 'The Well of the World's End', 'The Frog Prince', 'The Frog', and 'The Paddo', in Briggs, *A Dictionary of British Folk-Tales*, i. 561–2, 563–4, 259–60, 258–9, 443–5. They also discovered many examples of tales featuring wicked sisters and step-sisters: see 'Ashpitel', 'Rashin Coatie' and 'The Red Calf', ibid., i. 138–40, 456–8, 460–2.
[61] Scot, *The Discouerie of Witchcraft*, 153; *The Remains of Thomas Hearne*, ed. John Buchanan-Brown (London, 1966), 410, 424–5; Opie, *The Classic Fairy Tales*, 30–46.

They were told one to another down the generations running as a stream beneath the surface of literary discourse, scarcely recorded at the time, scarcely recoverable by posterity. A fundamental reason for this, no doubt, was their particular possession by women and children, their particular inhabitance of the domestic and private sphere.

Much the same could be said of the songs and lullabies with which mothers and nurses soothed their children around the evening hearth. Typically, we rely on casual references in contemporary literature or occasional vignettes from the popular stage to capture fleeting glimpses of this otherwise unremarked and unremarkable world. Thus in William Wager's *The Longer Thou Livest, the More Foole Thou Art*, a 'very mery and pythie commedie' written about 1559, the character of Moros the clown sings a medley of snatches from apparently well-known and long-standing songs. When asked whether he is not troubled 'thus vainly the time to spend', he replies: 'My mother, as I war wont in her lappe to sit, she taught me these'. Among these nursery rhymes, which are thus dated at least to the early sixteenth century and may well be much older, are some still known among children today. Similarly, in Thomas D'Urfey's play *The Campaigners* (1698) the character of Fardell, an 'affected tattling nurse', sings as she suckles her charge: 'Ah doddy blesse dat pitty face of myn sylds, and his pitty, pitty hands, and his pitty, pitty foots, and all his pitty things, and pat a cake, pat a cake bakers man, so I will master as I can, and prick it, and prick it, and prick it, and prick it, and prickt it, and throw't into the oven'. Were it not for this scene we might think of the still ubiquitous 'Pat-a-cake, pat-a-cake, baker's man' as an invention of *Mother Goose's Melody*, the book of nursery rhymes in which it was first printed in full around 1765.[62]

Many such examples could be cited which reveal how much older nursery rhymes are than their first existence in print. Thus the famous, 'To market, to market | To buy a plum bun | Home again, home again, | Market is done', was not written down in full until 1805. Only the fortuitous aside of an author in 1611, which suggests that he knew the jingle from childhood, reveals that it must have been popular since at least the mid-sixteenth century. An equally enduring classic, 'Cock a doodle doo! | My dame has lost her shoe', was another of those to make its first full appearance in *Mother Goose's Melody*: but a throw away reference to it in the most unlikely of places, a murder pamphlet of 1606, reveals that its face was already familiar in Shakespeare's day. The ABC rhyme beginning 'A was

---

[62] Iona and Peter Opie, *The Oxford Dictionary of Nursery Rhymes* (Oxford, 1951), 246–7, 1, 341–2.

an apple-pie' became a favourite for teaching the alphabet in the nine-teenth century. It might have been assumed to take its origin from a chil-dren's book of 1743 were it not for the fact that the Restoration divine, John Eachard, just happened to quote the first part of it in a pamphlet of 1671 defending the clergy.[63]

John Aubrey was almost unique among contemporaries in the anthro-pological interest which he took in the rhymes and songs chanted by women to children and perpetuated by the youngsters themselves. He transcribed a few of those which he heard, or remembered from his own childhood, and in so doing captured some gems of juvenile culture which might otherwise be dated no earlier than the Victorian period. 'Little chil-dren have a custome when it raines to sing, or charme away the raine; thus they all joine in a chorus and sing thus, viz. "Raine, raine, goe away | Come again a Saterday". I have a conceit that this childish custome is of great antiquity, and that it is derived from the gentiles.' In this context, as elsewhere, he preserved elements of a particularly female tradition, noting several rhymes which mothers taught to their daughters. Thus, 'Hempe-seed I sow | And hempe-seed I mowe | And he that is my sweetheart | Could follow me, I trowe'. He also knew this 'old filthy rhythme' sung by young girls:

> When I was a young maid,
> and wash't my mothers dishes,
> I putt my finger in my cunt,
> and pluck't-out little fishes.

He noticed, too, that 'young wenches' used the word 'cockle' inter-changeably with the word 'arse' and had 'a wanton sport which they call moulding of cocklebread'. In this saucy game, 'they gett upon a table-board, and then gather-up their knees and their coates with their hands as high as they can, and then they wabble to and fro with their buttocks as if the[y] were kneading of dowgh with their arses, and say these words, viz.— "My dame is sick and gonne to bed | And I'le go mowld my cockle— bread"'. White Kennett, who borrowed and annotated Aubrey's notes, gave a fuller version of the rhyme, which he had heard in Oxfordshire. There the girls, 'when they have put themselves into the fit posture, say thus:

> My granny is sick and now is dead,
> And wee'l goe mould some cockle-bread.
> Up with my heels, and down with my head,
> And this is the way to mould cockle bread.

[63] Halliwell, *Popular Rhymes and Nursery Tales*, 12, 138; Opie, *Oxford Dictionary of Nursery Rhymes*, 30–1, 47–8, 128–9, 299.

Kennett also observed girls 'dancing the candle rush' and in so doing recorded 'The Tailor of Bicester' a century and a half before it would be written down again. 'The young girls in and about Oxford have a sport called Leap-candle', he reported, 'for which they set a candle in the middle of the room in a candlestick, and then draw up their coats in the form of breeches, and dance over the candle back and forth, with these words':

> The taylor of Bisiter,
> He has but one eye;
> He cannot cut a pair of green galagaskins,
> If he were to die.

Another children's game of which Kennett contributed a description was 'pace-egging', or the practice of begging eggs or other treats just before Easter. 'It is the custom for boys and girls in country schools in several parts of Oxfordshire (as Bletchingdon, Weston, Charlton &c.) at their breaking up in the week before Easter to goe in a gang from house to house with little clacks of wood...'. On arrival at someone's door, 'they fall a beating their clacks' and 'all strike up very loud' with the following song:

> Harings, harings white and red,
> Ten a penny Lent's dead.
> Rise dame and give a negg,
> Or else a piece of bacon.
> One for Peter, two for Paul,
> Three for Jack a Lents all.
> Away Lent away.

For this they 'expect from every house some eggs or a piece of bacon, which they carry baskets to receive, and feast upon them at the week's end'. If they receive these treats from the housewife 'they begin the chorus':

> Here sits a good wife,
> Pray God save her life.
> Set her upon a hod,
> And drive her to God.

If, on the other hand, they are turned away empty-handed, then, 'with a full cry', they sing:

> Here sits a bad wife,
> The devil take her life.
> Set her upon a swivell,
> And send her to the devill.

'And in farther indignation, they commonly cut the latch of the door, or stop the keyhole with dirt, or leave some more nasty token of displeasure.'[64]

Aubrey appreciated how marvellously scrupulous and tenacious children are in preserving and perpetuating these ancient practices and oral traditions. He noticed the way in which, a full century and a half after the Reformation, 'the plough-boies, and also the schooleboies will keep-up and retaine their old ceremonies and customs and priviledges', despite the fact that these survivals of the Middle Ages had been lost to adult society. Certainly, many of the children's games and rhymes still current in Aubrey's day were of ancient origin. The chant 'Give a thing | And take a thing | To weare the divell's gold-ring', for example, referred to the juvenile principle that 'things that are truly given must not be taken away again' which, as Thomas Fuller pointed out, Plato had said 'that in his time it was a proverb amongst children'. The distich accompanying the guessing game, 'Handy-dandy, prickly prandy | Which hand will you have', was probably venerable when it was alluded to in the mid-fourteenth century. Several other rhymes were first recorded in the Elizabethan period in explantion of games which were thought to have been familiar in antiquity. Thus boys engaging in 'a kind of sport or play with an oister shell or a stone throwne into the water, and making circles yer it sinke', could be heard reciting 'A ducke and a drake | And a halfe penie cake'.[65]

In the twentieth century the researches of the Opies have confirmed the remarkable capacity of children to preserve oral tradition. 'An oft-doubted fact attested by the study of nursery rhymes', they suggest, 'is the vitality of oral tradition. This vitality is particularly noticeable where children are concerned . . .'. This is so not only because they are 'conservative and exact' in repetition, but also because they 'tend to be in touch with the non-working (oldest) members of the family, who themselves delight in recounting their earliest memories'. At the same time, however, even the inheritance of the nursery was not immune from the influence of the written word in the early modern period. Two-thirds of the 550 items in the Opies' dictionary of English nursery rhymes are believed to date from

[64] Aubrey, 'Remaines of Gentilisme and Judaisme', in *Three Prose Works*, ed. Buchanan-Brown, 256, 255, 254, 140. It is hardly surprising the preachers so often lamented the obscenity of children's songs: see, for example, Thomas Gouge, *The Young Man's Guide* (London, 1670), 144; Richard Baxter, *Gildas Salvianus: The Reformed Pastor* (London, 1656), 333. Cf. *King Lear*, III. iv. 72; William Coe, 'The Diary of William Coe of Mildenhall, Suffolk. A.D. 1680–1729', *East Anglian*, new ser., 11–12 (1906–8), 11: 290, 339, 341; 12: 112.

[65] Aubrey, 'Remaines of Gentilisme and Judaisme', in *Three Prose Works*, ed. Buchanan-Brown, 137; Halliwell, *Popular Rhymes and Nursery Tales*, 15, 116–18, 182; Thomas Fuller, *The Holy State* (Cambridge, 1642), 231.

before 1750. About one-quarter of them can be shown to have been already in likely circulation before the end of the sixteenth century. That a further quarter were apparently coined during the seventeenth century can be attributed to the proliferation of books and broadsides at this time.[66]

Children, no less than adults, lived in a world increasingly saturated by the products of both manuscript and print culture and they appear to have been highly receptive to its influences. Rhymes and songs fed from written sources into oral circulation and came down from parents and nurses to their young ones. So, for example, the popular song-books produced by Thomas Ravenscroft for genteel audiences in the reign of James I were responsible for introducing to print six rhymes which became children's classics. His *Deuteromelia* (1609) launched 'Three blind mice' and 'Nose, nose, jolly red nose', while to his *Melismata* (1611) we owe the earliest printed version of 'A frog he would a-wooing go'. The spate of song books appearing after the Restoration included such titles as *Westminster Drollery* (1671), which contained the first printing of 'I saw a peacock with a fiery tale', and Henry Playford's *Wit and Mirth* (1684) which provided the debut for 'When I was young, I then had no wit.'[67]

The vast production and extensive circulation of cheap broadside ballads at the same time clearly had a significant influence on the culture of youngsters as it did on that of adults. In the 1620s Robert Burton commented on the way in which 'carmen, boys, and prentices, when a new song is published with us, go singing that new tune still in the streets'. The sort of thing which he might have had in mind included *A New Yeares Guift for Shrews*, a print of about 1620 typical of the contemporary satires on scolding women, which carried the verse 'Who marieth a wife vppon Moneday'. Another appropriation by children was 'There were three men of Gotam', already an old song when it was printed as a broadside in 1632, and still going strong today in its 'three Welshmen' variant. The opening stanza of ballads was frequently adopted by children, retained, and added to their repertoire. 'There was an old woman sold puddings and pies' derives from the first verse of a broadside of 1675; another ballad of similar date begins with 'Lavenders green, diddle diddle | Lavenders blue'; while the initial lines of *The Wiltshire Wedding*, printed about 1680, would become the favourite nursery rhyme 'One misty, moisty, morning'.[68]

[66] Opie, *Oxford Dictionary of Nursery Rhymes*, 7, 8, 15; and see Iona and Peter Opie, *The Lore and Language of Schoolchildren* (Oxford, 1959).

[67] Opie, *Oxford Dictionary of Nursery Rhymes*, 21–2, 306, 330, 177–81, 342–3, 95–6.

[68] Burton, *Anatomy of Melancholy*, ed. Jackson, iii. 109; J. O. Halliwell, *The Nursery Rhymes of*

The way in which political songs and satires were adopted by children and made their own provides a particularly striking example of the influence of scribal and print culture upon them. This sensitivity to topical events is a notable feature of juvenile culture and must be set alongside the conservative capacity of children to maintain long-standing traditions. Many rhymes which became favourites in the nursery began as partisan songs or comments on current affairs but were clearly picked up by youngsters and remembered by them long after they ceased to have relevance to adults. Thus, 'The King of France' was probably coined following Henry IV's last and fatal campaign against the Spanish in 1610 but, despite frequent allusion to it subsequently, it was not written down in full until the mid-nineteenth century.

> The King of France went up the hill
> With forty thousand men;
> The King of France came down the hill,
> And ne'er went up again.

'There was a monkey climbed a tree | When he fell down, then down fell he', had its origins in a topical political satire on the duke of Buckingham's failed expedition to Cadiz in 1625. Meanwhile, internal evidence in a favourite riddling rhyme involving Oliver Cromwell appears to date it from around 1648, although it would be another two centuries before it was written down from oral tradition.

> Purple, yellow, red and green,
> The king cannot reach it, nor yet the queen;
> Nor can Old Noll, whose power's so great:
> Tell me this riddle while I count eight.[69]

This same tendency is apparent in children's chants and verbal games. The game of 'Similes', said to be 'mightily play'd at' during the reign of James I, was, according to one contemporary, 'invented to ridicule the forced innuendoes and arbitrary judgments of the Star-Chamber'. 'Cross Purposes', included by Robert Burton in his catalogue of 'ordinary recreations which we have in winter', was said to be especially popular with children before the Civil War. Another favourite, which apparently came into vogue during Cromwell's Protectorate, was 'The Parson has lost his fiddling cap', a name which suggests its accompaniment by the 'Cock a

*England, Collected Principally from Oral Tradition* (Percy Society, 4, London, 1842), 29, 43; Opie, *Oxford Dictionary of Nursery Rhymes*, 19–21, 410, 422, 433, 265–7, 314.

[69] Halliwell, *The Nursery Rhymes of England*, 12, 93, and (5th edn., London, 1853), 11–12, 129; Opie, *Oxford Dictionary of Nursery Rhymes*, 176, 310–11, 355–6.

doodle doo' rhyme. At the same time, 'Questions and Commands', also listed by Burton, was being adapted by every youngster in the land to the ridicule of the monarchy. One child would play the part of the king and another his servant: 'as, for instance, "King I am", says one boy; another answers, "I am your man"; then his majesty demands, what service he will do him; to which the obsequious courtier replies, "The best and worst, and all I can".' After the Restoration, when scatological prints and bawdy songs flooded London in ridicule of the Rump Parliament, Samuel Pepys noticed how in the streets 'boys do now cry "kiss my parliament" instead of "kiss my arse"'.[70]

Another type of word game which benefited from the influence of written and printed sources was riddles. These had long been well known to both adults and children by the early modern period and a number of collections survive in medieval compilations and school-books.[71] In the sixteenth century they quickly found their way into print in the form of *The Demaundes Joyous*, published by Wynkyn de Worde in 1511, and later in *The Book of Riddles*. The fact that in the 1570s both of these works were said to be included in the remarkable library of the mason of Coventry, Captain Cox, and were mentioned by the 'country gentleman' in a dialogue as among the 'pleasant bookes' employed to pass time, suggests that such reading was certainly familiar to urban and rural elite alike in the mid-Elizabethan period.[72] That they were also integral to the 'ordinary recreations' of youngsters is suggested in the popular novella, *The Pinder of Wakefield*, in which George a Green and his friends sit around in the evening posing riddles to each other. Seven of the seventy-seven items in *The Booke of Meery Riddles*, extant in an edition of 1600, are still recited by children today.[73]

[70] Burton, *Anatomy of Melancholy*, ed. Jackson, ii. 81; *Gentleman's Magazine*, 8 (Feb. 1738), 80–1; Brand, *Observations on the Popular Antiquities of Great Britain*, ed. Ellis, ii. 427; Halliwell, *Popular Rhymes and Nursery Tales*, 19; *The Diary of Samuel Pepys*, ed. Latham and Matthews, i. 45. 'Similes' appears to have been being played by adults at an alehouse in Woodstock, Oxfordshire, in March 1540: *Letters and Papers, Foreign and Domestic, of the Reign of Henry VIII*, ed. J. S. Brewer and James Gairdner (21 vols., London, 1862–1910), xv. 136. Pepys joined in a game of 'Questions and Commands' at the Dolphin tavern in February 1661: *The Diary of Samuel Pepys*, ed. Latham and Matthews, ii. 30.

[71] See, for example, *The Riddles of the Exeter Book*, ed. Frederick Tupper (Boston, Mass., 1910); W. A. Pantin, 'A Medieval Collection of Latin and English Proverbs and Riddles, from the Rylands Latin MS. 394', *Bulletin of the John Rylands Library*, 14 (1930), 109–14; Nicholas Orme, 'The Culture of Children in Medieval England', *Past and Present*, 148 (1995), 77–9.

[72] *The Demau[n]des Joyous* (London, 1511); cf. *The Booke of Merrie Riddles* (London, 1617); Robert Laneham, *A Letter* (London, 1575), 35; *Cyuile and Vncyuile Life* (1579), in *Inedited Tracts: Illustrating the Manners, Opinions, and Occupations of Englishmen during the Sixteenth and Seventeenth Centuries*, ed. W. C. Hazlitt (Roxburghe Library, London, 1868), 57; and cf. *The Merry Wives of Windsor*, i. i. 184–8 (for use at Allhallowmas).

[73] *The Pinder of Wakefield*, ed. E. A. Horsman (Liverpool, 1956), 77, 85–6; Halliwell, *Popular*

A signal example of the relationship between oral, scribal, and printed media in the transmission of children's riddles is afforded by the unique nursery jotter in which, during the 1640s, the Holme children of Bridge Street in Chester wrote down their favourite examples. Randle Holme was still a teenager at the time and he seems to have been helped by his younger brothers and possibly his sisters in compiling a collection of 144 questions and answers, many of them in rhyme. Some may have been copied from familiar publications: thus, one-third of the items in the Holmes' notebook were known to *A Booke of Merrie Riddles* (1631), for example. But the majority of their gleanings do not appear in other written sources, and even those which do are often so poorly worded and incomplete in these juvenile scribblings as to suggest noting from memory rather than copying from text. In short, this book provides remarkable evidence of oral circulation at work.[74]

Among the tricky posers which delighted the Holmes are fourteen rhymes still known to children today. We have these Cheshire youngsters to thank for the introduction to literature, and the first recording before the nineteenth century, of what have become nursery classics. They wrote out an incomplete version of 'Little Nancy Etticoat'; they set down an early variant of 'Gray Grizzle'; and they copied this, in more or less the form still recited:

> Q:  There was a king met a king
> In a narrow lane,
> Said the king to the king,
> Wher hast thou bin?
> I have bin in the wood
> Hunting a doe.
> I pray thee lend me the dog
> I may do soe:
> Call him to thee
> And tell me his name.
> I count him a wise man
> That tells me the same.
> A:  The mens names were King
> and the dogs name was Bin.[75]

---

*Rhymes and Nursery Tales*, 141–54; Opie, *Oxford Dictionary of Nursery Rhymes*, 15–17. For a full collection of contemporary riddles, see Archer Taylor, *English Riddles from Oral Tradition* (Berkeley, Calif., 1951).

[74] 'The Holme Riddles (MS. Harl. 1960)', ed. Frederick Tupper, *Publications of the Modern Language Association*, 18 (1903), 216–18; *A Booke of Merrie Riddles* (London, 1631).

[75] 'The Holme Riddles (MS. Harl. 1960)', ed. Tupper, 223, 235, 237; Opie, *Oxford Dictionary of Nursery Rhymes*, 16, 326, 194, 253–4.

The overwhelming impression given by this commonplace book is just how much of such material must have been circulating in the oral tradition of the sixteenth and seventeenth centuries; just how venerable much of it must already have been by that time; and just how much has been lost over the succeeding centuries. When we read the rhyme beginning, 'As I was walking late at night | I through a window chanced to spy | A gallant with his hearts delight | He knew not that I was so nigh', we behold the first part of riddle which is not dissimilar to one that was inscribed on an Anglo-Saxon beaker: it has no other known recording and is apparently now extinct. We realize just how much of what we would now like to know about the cultural life of the past never found its way into writing when we see, for the first and only time before the modern period, nuggets such as 'As I went over Hottery Tottery, I looked into Harbora Lilly | I spied a cutterell playing with her cambril.' The spirit of this was often recorded in contemporary sources, but nowhere else does it appear as:

> Q:     There is a bird of great renown,
>        Usefull in citty and in town,
>        None work like unto him can doe:
>        Hes yellow, black and green
>        A very pretty bird I mean,
>        Yet he is both firce and fell,
>        I count him wise that can this tell.
> A:     The painfull bee.[76]

As the Holme children swapped their riddles, therefore, they epitomized the way in which nursery lore was transmitted in early modern England. Like much in the popular repertoire, juvenile culture was infused by elements drawn from a long tradition of manuscript circulation and it was greatly enriched by the dissemination of new and varied materials in print. At the same time, however, much of what youngsters told and sang was apparently unknown in written sources and relatively untouched by their influence. Most of it is completely lost and but for stray references in print and chance survivals in manuscript little of it would even be suspected. It endured and replenished itself as a domestic conversation beneath the public discourse of society.

---

[76] 'The Holme Riddles (MS. Harl. 1960)', ed. Tupper, 236, 237, 238, 269, 271; Opie, *Oxford Dictionary of Nursery Rhymes*, 82–3. Halliwell was the first to print some of the Holme riddles, in *Popular Rhymes and Nursery Tales*, 149–50.

In large part, therefore, the oral traditions of many women and most children remained relatively untouched by the influence of the written word. Their superstitions and fairy-tales, nursery rhymes and riddles, very rarely found a way into print and they perpetuated themselves down the generations outside and beyond the influence of literary culture. Much of what has come down to us owed its survival to transmission by word of mouth up until the modern period and it clearly represents only a small part of the repertoire once in circulation.

At the same time, however, the enormous increase in the quantity of popular print during the sixteenth and seventeenth centuries had an impact in this sphere as in most others. In some ways it may have served to dissipate the superstitions of old women and undermine the independence of the traditions around the winter fireside. Aubrey was certainly elegiac to this effect.

Before printing, old-wives tales were ingenious: and since printing came in fashion, till a little before the civil-warres, the ordinary sort of people were not taught to reade: now-a-dayes bookes are common, and most of the poor people understand letters: and the many good bookes, and variety of turnes of affaires, have put all the old fables out of dores: and the divine art of printing and gunpowder have frighted away Robin-good-fellow and the fayries.

How terrified he had once been by the prospect of 'Raw-head and bloody-bone' and the visionary tribe of walking spirits. 'Now', he observed in the later seventeenth century, 'children feare no such things, having heard not of them, and are not checked with such feares.'[77]

These reflections were, of course, nostalgic and overdrawn but they rightly identified the significant influence which the growth in reading ability and the expansion in cheap literature was having on popular culture. Nor were the consequences of print as destructive as Aubrey made out. Here, as in other contexts, pamphlets and printed sheets tended to reinforce and reinvent oral tradition rather than simply to destroy or replace it. People now learned broadside ballads and read chapbook tales of *Robin Goodfellow; his Mad Prankes and Merry Jests*, as they did on a whole host of such subjects (see Plate 8). In 1718 Francis Hutchinson listed twenty-two books published since the Restoration on the theme of witchcraft and popular superstition. 'These books and narratives', he observed, 'are in tradesmen's shops and farmer's houses, and are read with great eagerness, and are constantly levening the minds of youth, who

---

[77] Aubrey, 'Remaines of Gentilisme and Judaisme', in *Three Prose Works*, ed. Buchanan-Brown, 290, and cf. 207; Bod. Lib., MS Aubrey 3, fo. 30.

delight in such subjects'.[78] In other words, print was feeding back into popular belief and juvenile culture, informing, fashioning, and sustaining them rather than undermining their vitality. By an irony, one of the items on Hutchinson's list was a book entitled *Miscellanies*, which, he thought, 'teaches people charms and sorcery'. It was the only one of John Aubrey's works to appear in print during his lifetime.

[78] *Illustrations of the Fairy Mythology*, ed. Halliwell, 120–70; *The Pepys Ballads*, ed. W. G. Day (5 vols., Cambridge, 1987), i. 80–1; Francis Hutchinson, *An Historical Essay Concerning Witchcraft* (London, 1718), xiv.

# 4
## *The Historical Imagination*

Why doe the rude vulgar so hastily post in a madnesse
To gaze at trifles, and toyes not worthy the viewing?
And thinke them happy, when may be shew'd for a penny
The Fleet-streete Mandrakes, that heauenly Motion of Eltham,
Westminster monuments, and Guild hall huge Corinaeus,
That horne of Windsor (of an Unicorne very likely)
The caue of Merlin, the skirts of old Tom a Lincolne.
King Iohn's sword at Linne, with the cup the Fraternity drinke in,
The Tombe of Beauchampe, and sword of Sir Guy a Warwicke:
The great long Dutchman, and roaring Marget a Barwicke,
The Mummied Princes, and Caesars wine yet i' Douer,
Saint Iames his Ginney Hens, the Cassawarway moreouer,
The Beauer i' the Parke (strange beast as er'e any man saw)
Downe-shearing willowes with teeth as sharpe as a hand-saw.
The Lance of Iohn a Gaunt, and Brandons still i' the Tower:
The fall of Niniue, with Norwich built in an hower.
King Henries slip-shoes, the sword of valiant Edward.
The Couentry Boares-shield, the fire-workes seen but to bedward.
Drakes ship at Detford, King Richards bed-sted i' Leyster,
The White Hall whale-bones, the siluer Bason i' Chester;
The liue-caught Dog-fish, the Wolfe and Harry the Lyon,
Hunks of the Beare-garden to be feared, if he be nigh on.

> Henry Peacham, 'To the famous Traueller', preface to Thomas
> Coryate, *Coryats Crudities* (London, 1611), sig. K4ᵛ.

I leave the ruins of Tintagel to those that search into antiquity; little
or nothing, that I could hear, is to be seen at it; and as for the story of
King Arthur being both born and killed there, 'tis a piece of tradition,
only on oral history, and not any authority to be produced for it.

> Daniel Defoe, *A Tour thro' the Whole Island of Great Britain*,
> ed. G. D. H. Cole (London, 1927), 257.

ONE of the most important features of the oral culture of sixteenth- and
seventeenth-century England was the repertoire of stories and songs
which concerned the past. An awareness of history and tradition was
something which was well developed at all levels of society and many

people held a strong sense of certain events and individuals of former times. The way in which history was perceived by different social groups and communities could vary greatly, of course, and in the early modern period, no less than today, people drew upon competing and often contradictory versions of the past to inform their actions and justify their opinions in the present.

The media through which historical information, reminiscences, and traditions were transmitted could also vary. As with the dissemination of so much cultural product in these centuries, both oral and written forms coexisted and overlapped to an inextricable extent. On the one hand, written versions of the past, in the form of chronicles, hagiographies, sermons, and romances, had long been widely dispersed. They provided the origin of so much historical knowledge and understanding that any attempt to differentiate between the oral and scribal realms in this respect can be difficult and misleading. On the other hand, even those versions of the past which owed their provenance to some written authority could develop and be elaborated in wholly new ways as they circulated by word of mouth, while many other historical traditions and anecdotes probably never found their way into writing at all. At the lower and least literate levels of society, in particular, information could be passed from father to son and mother to daughter down the generations with little existence outside memory and the spoken word. This was so at the end of the early modern period no less than at the beginning.

During the course of the sixteenth and seventeenth centuries, however, new versions of, and views about, English history did emerge which were to transform the ways in which scholars and common people alike understood their heritage. The tremendous flowering of antiquarian research and writing, which was such a feature of the intellectual life of this period, revolutionized historical thinking and ultimately brought about a change in perceptions at all social levels. At the same time, some of the dramatic events and upheavals which marked these centuries were conspiring to create, in due course, a new stock of reference points in the mental map of the past.

### OLD MEN SPEAK FABLES

The principal means by which the majority of people received their knowledge about the past in early modern England was by word of mouth. Historical traditions formed a crucial part of that culture of fireside storytelling which was so much a part of social life in this period. Thus, in Elizabethan Wales, it was said, folk would climb their mountain tops to tell tales of battles against the English and listen to the exploits of Taliesin, Merlin, 'and such others, the intended prophets and saints of this country'. In the Scottish borders they told stories of the great struggles with the English and swashbuckling tales of reivers and robbers. Throughout England they sat up 'late by the fire [to] tell old romantique stories of the old time' (see Plate 9).[1]

Many of these fireside stories remained unwritten because they were too narrow in interest, or too local in scope, to make the recording of them either necessary or desirable. They had meaning for particular communities and it was this parochial relevance which both kept them alive and ensured their confinement. It was events which were significant to the neighbourhood that were remembered, while even historical incidents or individuals of national renown tended to be conceived of within a familiar setting. Many traditions served an aetiological function, purporting to explain the origin of local place names or account for the evolution of the topographical landmarks which provided people with their mental reference points. Indeed, the landscape all around was a vast repository of memory.[2] Memories of the past comprised part of that local knowledge from which people derived a sense of identity and pride based upon place. They provided an imagined heritage which helped to underscore the emotional solidarity of the community and they were expressed in the 'common voice', 'common fame', or 'common report' of the inhabitants which antiquaries and travellers frequently encountered as they toured the country.[3]

The fanciful fables which some small towns or villages liked to cherish about their former greatness, for example, were often sustained by local memory and by the physical evidence all around rather than by any written documents. In the 1530s the 'commune voyce' at Billericay in Essex informed the passing John Leland that the town had once been much greater, and the locals could show a fine ceremonial horn and mace to prove it. The Elizabethan inhabitants of Overburrow in Lancashire were

---

[1] R. R. Davies, *The Revolt of Owain Glyn Dŵr* (Oxford, 1995), 336; *A Memoir of Thomas Bewick Written by Himself*, ed. Iain Bain (Oxford, 1975), 8; John Aubrey, 'Remaines of Gentilisme and Judaisme', in *John Aubrey: Three Prose Works*, ed. John Buchanan-Brown (Fontwell, 1972), 289–90.

[2] On the general importance of landscape as a mnemonic of historical traditions, see Jan Vansina, *Oral Tradition as History* (London, 1985), 45–6; James Fentress and Chris Wickham, *Social Memory* (Oxford, 1992), 87, 93, 113, 121, 166. On England, see Walter Johnson, *Folk Memory: Or the Continuity of British Archaeology* (Oxford, 1908); Jennifer Westwood, *Albion: A Guide to Legendary Britain* (London, 1985); Keith Thomas, *The Perception of the Past in Early Modern England* (Creighton Trust Lecture, London, 1984), 4–5; D. R. Woolf, 'The "Common Voice": History, Folklore and Oral Tradition in Early Modern England', *Past and Present*, 120 (1988), 31; Jacqueline Simpson, 'The Local Legend: A Product of Popular Culture', *Rural History*, 2 (1991), 25–35; David Rollison, *The Local Origins of Modern Society: Gloucestershire, 1500–1800* (London, 1992), 70–1.

[3] Woolf, 'The "Common Voice"'.

equally keen to tell visitors that their 'small country village' had been 'formerly a great city', as they knew 'by a tradition handed down from their ancestors' and a variety of Roman remains confirmed. By the same token, large foundations uncovered in the village of Cogges, Oxfordshire, made the 'vulgar people that live here think that in old time here was a castle', but there was seemingly no documentary evidence to support this idea. *'Immensa cani spirant mendatia folles'*, was John Norden's reaction to similar traditions recounted by the ancients at the ruin in one Middlessex village during the 1590s: 'olde men speake fables'.[4]

Indeed, one of the most striking features of local historical tradition in early modern England is the extent to which it was inspired, nurtured, and perpetuated by the visual evidence of the immediate environment. Very often the source of a legend or old tale would be some landmark such as a hill or barrow, an extraordinary chasm or unusual outcrop. The great megolithic rock formations which littered the countryside, for example, prompted a host of aetiological legends seeking to explain their origin. Thus at 'The Hurlers' by Liskeard in Cornwall, it was 'the country peoples report, that once they were men, and for their hurling vpo[n] the Sabboth, so metamorphosed'. At the Rollright Stones, near Chipping Norton in Oxfordshire, the locals would tell the tale of 'a king, his nobles and commons turn'd into stones', while the stone circles at Stanton Drew, near Bristol, were said to be a wedding party frozen in rock: 'one of the stones they call the Bride, another is called the Parsons stone, and another the Cookes stone'.[5] By the same token, popular tradition could inform the curious enquirer that the gnarled rocks around Whitby on the north Yorkshire coast were actually

[4] *The Itinerary of John Leland in or about the Years 1535–1543*, ed. Lucy Toulmin Smith (5 vols., London, 1906–10), iv. 67; William Camden, *Britannia*, ed. Edmund Gibson (London, 1695), 794; BL, Sloane MS, 241, fo. 35ᵛ; *Parochial Collections (First Part) Made by Anthony à Wood, M.A. and Richard Rawlinson, D.C.L., F.R.S.*, ed. F. N. Davis (Oxfordshire Record Society, 2, Oxford, 1920), 100; *The Life and Times of Anthony Wood, Antiquary, of Oxford, 1632–1695, Described by Himself*, ed. Andrew Clark (5 vols., Oxford Historical Society, 19, 21, 26, 30, 40, Oxford, 1891–1900), i. 253; BL, Additional MS, 31853, fo. 5ʳ. For other such examples, see BL, Cottonian MS, Julius F. VI, fo. 341ʳ; [John] Coker, *A Survey of Dorsetshire* (London, 1732), 55; Treadway Nash, *Collections for the History of Worcestershire* (2 vols., London, 1781–2), i. 521.

[5] Richard Carew, *The Survey of Cornwall* (London, 1602), fo. 129ᵛ; Camden, *Britannia*, ed. Gibson, 254; Robert Plot, *The Natural History of Oxford-shire* (Oxford, 1677), 337; John Aubrey, *Monumenta Britannica*, ed. John Fowles and Rodney Legg (Sherborne, 1980–2), 46, 71–2; William Stukeley, *Abury: A Temple of the British Druids* (London, 1743), 13, 83. On Rollright, see also A. J. Evans, 'The Rollright Stones and their Folk-Lore', *Folk-Lore*, 6 (1895), 6–51; and for a full version of the Stanton Drew wedding tale, recorded much later, see Katherine M. Briggs, *A Dictionary of British Folk-Tales in the English Language* (4 vols., London, 1970), iii. 95–6. For the rich traditions of this sort in Scotland, see 'Professor James Garden's Letters to John Aubrey, 1692–1695', ed. Cosmo A. Gordon, in *The Miscellany of the Third Spalding Club*, iii (Aberdeen, 1960), 12–14, 24, 34; Martin Martin, *A Description of the Western Islands of Scotland circa 1695* (Glasgow, 1884), 9, 151–3, 220, 364, 387–8.

serpents frozen in stone by St Hilda; that the salt pits at Droitwich were procured by the prayers of St Richard of Wick; and that the indentations to be seen outside Melrose were prints of the devil's cloven hoof on the spot where he had been cudgelled by St Cuthbert.[6]

At the same time, it would have been possible to visit the hill above Uffington in Berkshire, with its mysterious white horse cut in the turf, where local tradition claimed that St George had slain the dragon; to pass by the great stagnant pool on Threlkeld fells in Cumberland where 'the cuntry [people] do fable' that King Arthur threw his sword; or to trace the Hull river back to its source at Driffield in the East Riding where, it was said, King Alfred lay buried.[7] Whenever there was a natural phenomenon not easily accounted for, legend stepped in to provide an answer. So those living in the vicinity of the huge Brecknock mere in south Wales, said to be 2 miles long, a mile wide, and 6 miles around, faithfully explained its ori gins as a once great city which an earthquake had caused to be subsumed by water.[8] Equally, it was an oral tradition, there being 'no such thing in our stories upon record', which solved the mystery of the walnut tree at the end of Page Green in Tottenham Highcross which never grew any bigger: 'the people do commonly tell the reason to bee, for that there was one burnt upon that place, for the profession of the gospell'. Meanwhile, the large hole in the ground outside the village of Slingsby in the North Riding, and the otherwise unaccountable fact that the Hovingham to Malton road detoured a whole mile south to avoid it, were conveniently reconciled by the story that a terrible dragon had once made its lair there.[9]

Just as important as geological and topographical features in promoting historical tales in a community, were the man-made constructions which every day summoned up the past for all to behold. In most cases, the chief example of these was the parish church with its medieval monuments and

---

[6] *The Topographer and Genealogist*, ed. John Gough Nichols (3 vols., London, 1846–58), ii. 419; Thomas Habington, *A Survey of Worcestershire*, ed. John Amphlett (2 vols., Worcestershire Historical Society, Oxford, 1895–9), i. 468; BL, Sloane MS, 1322, fo. 5ᵛ. For other similar examples, see BL, Sloane MS, 241, fo. 51ᵛ; Sir Robert Atkyns, *The Ancient and Present State of Gloucestershire* (2nd edn., London, 1768), 188.

[7] *The Travels through England of Dr Richard Pococke*, ed. J. J. Cartwright (2 vols., Camden Society, new ser., 42–4, London, 1888–9), ii. 249; Sampson Erdeswicke, 'Certaine Verie Rare Observations of Cumberland, Northumberland, etc.', in *Reprints of Rare Tracts and Imprints of Antient Manuscripts*, ed. M. A. Richardson (7 vols., Newcastle, 1843–9), vii. 9; BL, Sloane MS, 241, 71ᵛ.

[8] Camden, *Britannia*, ed. Gibson, 592; BL, Sloane MS, 241, 62ʳ; BL, Harleian MS, 7017, fos. 249ʳ, 256ʳ, 258ʳ; Daniel Defoe, *A Tour thro' the Whole Island of Great Britain*, ed. G. D. H. Cole (London, 1927), 452.

[9] Wilhelm Bedwell, *A Brief Description of the Towne of Tottenham Highcrosse in Middlesex* (London, 1631), 28; Roger Dodsworth, *Yorkshire Church Notes, 1619–1631*, ed. J. W. Clay (Yorkshire Archaeological Society, Record Series, 34, 1904), 174.

statues, carving and iconography. The legend of the Slingsby dragon, for example, was happily confirmed in the popular mind by the thirteenth-century statue of a knight in armour, standing in the south chapel of the church, who was said to have perished in slaying the fiery serpent. Scores of similar legends were planted on the effigies and images which adorned ecclesiastical architecture. Thus the huge monument in Penrith church-yard was said to commemorate Sir Owen Caesarius 'an heroick champion of monstrous strength and stature' and gave rise to many fabulous tales of his life as a knight errant, killing monster, man and beast. Aldworth church in Berkshire contained a fine collection of knightly statues around which a body of legend accrued. One of the figures was known locally as John Stronge, while to another, called by the 'common people' John Ever Afraid, attached the familiar folktale 'that he gave his shirt to the divel if ever he was buried either in church or churchyard'.[10]

Typically enough, the twelfth-century tympanum of St George slaying the dragon above the church porch at Brinsop in Herefordshire gave rise to the tradition that it was actually here that the famous event had occurred. Since the devil was so often represented as a dragon in ecclesiastical iconography, this provided another stimulus to the many legends about fire-breathing serpents through which parochial notoriety could be claimed and fireside stories embellished. The thirteenth-century wall painting of a dragon above the north or devil's door in the church at Wissington, for example, may well have been responsible for the tales of dragon-fighting told along that part of the Suffolk and Essex border.[11] Pictures in the stained glass very often claimed to capture some nugget of parish tradition, or more often perhaps, were responsible for instigating it. Such was the tableau, reputedly depicting a local miller and his wife with bow and arrows, to be seen in the middle of the south window at

[10] Sir Daniel Fleming, *Description of the County of Cumberland*, ed. R. S. Ferguson (Cumberland and Westmorland Antiquarian and Archaeological Society, 3, Kendal, 1889), 18; Defoe, *A Tour thro' the Whole Island of Great Britain*, ed. Cole, 686; BL, Harleian MS, 965, fos. 57ᵛ, 59ʳ. For other examples, see Richard Butcher, *The Survey and Antiquitie of the Towne of Stamford, in the County of Lincolne* (London, 1646), 27; Richard Izacke, *Antiquities of the City of Exeter* (London, 1677), 66–7 (second pagination).

[11] Westwood, *Albion: A Guide to Legendary Britain*, 382, 153. Durham Cathedral, for example, contained a number of dragon carvings together with pictures in the stained glass of St George and St Michael killing dragons: *Rites of Durham*, ed. J. T. Fowler (Surtees Society, 107, Durham, 1903), 5, 10, 110, 115, 116. An observation of John Aubrey's points to what was probably a common source of confusion and of bogus legend: 'Methinks the picture of St George fighting with the dragon hath some resemblance of St Michael fighting with the devil, who is pourtrated like a dragon': Aubrey, 'Remaines of Gentilisme and Judaisme', in *Three Prose Works*, ed. Buchanan-Brown, 156. Cf. Sir Thomas Browne, *Pseudodoxia Epidemica* (1646), in *The Works of Sir Thomas Browne*, ed. Geoffrey Keynes (4 vols., London, 1964), ii. 373.

Whitchurch in Oxfordshire; 'he being a famous archer', it was said. In Lincolnshire one could speculate on the meaning of the emblem of a man with a kite's head found in one of the windows of Barnetby church, or at Tathwell admire the fenestral picture of Guthlac, 'the saint of the fens', of whom many fabulous tales were told.[12]

The survival of visual evidence, then, was often crucial to the preservation of local tradition. By the same token, it was equally the case that historical memory was likely to die out if the landmarks or monuments which kept it in mind were once destroyed or allowed to crumble. 'Notwithstanding the eagerness of the vulgar in harkening to stories relating to the parochial churches to which themselves particularly belong', observed the Oxford antiquary Thomas Hearne, 'when such churches fall or are destroyed, they soon forget what they had been, or even what benefactions had been made to them.' This was certainly the experience of Hearne's contemporary Browne Willis. When he went to Winchcombe in Gloucestershire early in the eighteenth century to try to learn more about the famous abbey which had been demolished after the Reformation, he found that the inhabitants had very little recollection of it. He managed to 'learn from tradition' that the buildings had once stood on the east side of the present parish church, but otherwise the locals 'could not give me the least description of any part of it'.[13]

A good example of the way in which the destruction of a monument could lead within a couple of generations to its lapse from popular memory is provided by the case of the statue of Our Lady of Gillingham and the Rood of Chatham which once stood in the churchyard of this Kentish village. They were described in the 1570s by the local antiquary, William Lambarde, who also recorded the legendary miracle associated with them 'as I have often heard (and that constantly) reported', and he thought it 'not amisse, to commit faithfully to writing, what I have received credibly by hearing'. But he found the images 'now many yeres sithence defaced' and thus the legend, although 'receaved by tradition from the elders', and 'long since both commonly reported and faithfully credited of the vulgar sort', was now not to be 'learne[d] at euery mans mouth'. Yet, he conceded, 'many of the aged number remember it well'.[14]

[12] BL, Harleian MS, 965, fo. 22ᵛ; BL, Harleian MS, 6829, 148, 187.

[13] *The History and Antiquities of Glastonbury*, ed. Thomas Hearne (Oxford, 1722), xiv; Browne Willis, *An History of the Mitred Parliamentary Abbies and Conventual Cathedral Churches* (2 vols., London, 1718–19), i. 210.

[14] William Lambarde, *A Perambulation of Kent: Conteining the Description, Hystorie, and Customes of that Shyre* (London, 1576), 286–7; John Weever, *Ancient Funerall Monuments* (London, 1631), 343–4.

As this comment suggests, the memories of aged inhabitants could be of great importance in the retention of local knowledge about the past. The evidence here confirms the picture given of other societies with strong oral traditions that older people were vital in the preservation and transmission of customary practice and intellectual capital.[15] As such, they were revered as the repositories of ancient wisdom and the custodians of communal memory. Their recollections were often sought on events and practices in the relatively recent past which were unlikely to be recorded in writing and for which they represented the best or only source of information. When, for example, Sir Thomas More led a commission into Kent in order to enquire 'what was the cause of Goodwin sands, and the shelf that stopped up Sandwich haven', he summoned all the 'men of experience' and questioned, in particular, 'an old man, with a white head, and one that was thought to be little less than an hundred years old'. Naturally enough, when the vicar of Radwinter in Essex, William Harrison, later wanted to learn of the changes in domestic comfort which had taken place during the sixteenth century, it was the 'old men yet dwelling in the village' to whom he turned. By 1590 much of Dunwich on the Suffolk coast had already fallen victim to the sea, but it was then still possible to learn about many of its swallowed-up churches which yet remained 'within the memorie of man'. Considering agricultural practice in Devon during the reign of Charles I, Thomas Westcote could report innovations 'begun within the memory of old men'.[16]

As a young boy growing up in Wiltshire before the Civil War, John Aubrey 'did ever love to converse with old men, as living histories'. Principal among these was his own maternal grandfather, Isaac Lyte, from whom he gathered a myriad historical anecdotes, local customs, and family traditions. Lyte himself had drawn on the reminiscences of old men, such as his own father and old father Davis, to provide vivid images of what life had been like before the Reformation. The young Aubrey listened agog to the tales of long ago related by old Mr Jacob of Wootton Bassett who was 80 years of age in 1648. He lapped up the stories of other ancients, like his 'old cosen' Ambrose Brown of Winterbourne Bassett 'who lived to 103', or 'old Jaquez' of Kington St Michael, and old

[15] Jack Goody, *The Interface between the Written and the Oral* (Cambridge, 1987), 150, 164; M. T. Clanchy, *From Memory to Written Record: England, 1066–1307* (2nd edn., Oxford, 1993), 295–6; Keith Thomas, 'Age and Authority in Early Modern England', *Proceedings of the British Academy*, 62 (1976), 233–4; and see Chapter 5 below.

[16] *Sermons by Hugh Latimer*, ed. G. E. Corrie (Parker Society, Cambridge, 1844), 251; William Harrison, *The Description of England*, ed. Georges Edelen (Ithaca, NY, 1968), 200; BL, Additional MS, 23963, fo. 2ᵛ; Thomas Westcote, *A View of Devonshire in 1630*, ed. George Oliver and Pitman Jones (Exeter, 1845), 56.

Bartholomew of Malmesbury. Old women, no less, inspired his tender imagination. He realized in the Broad Chalke of his childhood what might be learned at the hands of wise matrons such as old goodwife Holly or old goodwife Dew, who also died aged 103 in 1649, just as he would later consult the memory of old goodwife Faldo of Mortlake.[17]

The length of such memory might stretch back with a good deal of reliability for at least the period of a long life, therefore. In the mid-seventeenth century the Lancashire clergyman Henry Newcome heard all about the last great famine to afflict the county from old aunt Key of Bury who told him that it 'was then sixty years past'. A curious visitor to Skinningrove on the Cleveland coast some time before had heard 'ould men, that would be loath to have their credytes crackt by a tale of a stale date, reporte confidentlye' an incident said to have taken place 'sixty years since, or perhaps eighty or more'. Goodwife Dew could remember the visit of Edward VI to Wiltshire almost a century before. And when more than one generation was involved, inherited memory could reach back with some reliability for far longer. John Smyth of Nibley, estate steward to the earls of Berkeley in Gloucestershire, lived between 1567 and 1640 and during this period he 'often heard many old men and weomen' of the neighbourhood, born in the reign of Henry VII, 'relate the report of their parents, kinsfolks and neighbours' who as children themselves had witnessed the great local battle of 1469 between William, marquis of Berkeley, and Thomas Talbot, Viscount Lisle, over land rights. Smyth heard in vivid detail how Lisle had been slain by the arrow of one 'Black Will' and carried from the field, together with 'many other perticularyties . . . not possible almost by such plaine country people to be fained'. Old Mr Charles Hiet was able to tell the same story in 1603, as 'delivered from the relation of his father and grandfather as if the same had been but yesterday'. The inherited memory here, then, spanned at least a century and a half.[18]

In many of the reminiscences of eldest inhabitants is a nostalgia for the old days which can be characteristic of any age. It had been, after all, a

[17] John Aubrey, *Brief Lives*, ed. Andrew Clark (2 vols., Oxford, 1898), i. 43; John Aubrey, *The Natural History of Wiltshire*, ed. John Britton (London, 1847), 69, 76; Aubrey, *Three Prose Works*, ed. Buchanan-Brown, 162, 226, 353; Anthony Powell, *John Aubrey and his Friends* (London, 1948), 34–7; Michael Hunter, *John Aubrey and the Realm of Learning* (London, 1975), 168–9; Bod. Lib., MS Aubrey 3, fos. 3, 25ᵛ, 57ᵛ, 59, 76ᵛ, 80ᵛ, 92, 97, 98, 185ᵛ; Bod. Lib., MS Ashmole 1788, fos. 147–8. He also knew another 'goodwife' of Deverill in south Wiltshire who was said to be 111 years old in 1686: Bod. Lib., MS Aubrey 1, fo. 152.

[18] *The Autobiography of Henry Newcome, M.A.*, ed. Richard Parkinson (2 vols., Chetham Society, 26–7, Manchester, 1852), i. 82; *The Topographer and Genealogist*, ed. Nichols, ii. 416; Aubrey, *The Natural History of Wiltshire*, ed. Britton, 69; John Smyth, *The Berkeley Manuscripts*, ed. Sir John Maclean (3 vols., Gloucester, 1883–5), ii. 114–15; Woolf, 'The "Common Voice"', 36.

much 'merrier world' in the past: hospitality was greater and life was sim-
pler, there were fewer lawyers and all things were cheap.[19] To this extent,
there could be something inherently subversive about popular perceptions of the past. What ordinary men and women remembered was not
usually the stuff of learned or officially approved versions of the past but
instead interpretations of events which attempted to make sense of and
justify the world as they saw it. As such their memories could be irreverent and even seditious in the details which they chose to retain, or forget,
and the way in which they chose to construe them. At the time of the Civil
War, for example, the inhabitants of Evesham in Worcestershire were
eager to relate the exploits of Simon de Montfort, earl of Leicester, who
had fallen there while leading the baronial revolt against Henry III, for
such tales sat well with their view of the present monarchy. 'It is reported
the dead body of the earl of Leicester being fouly and barbarously
deformed with wounds was there discovered, whom neverthelesse the
vulgar sort reverence as a martir, because as they said he suffered all this
for the commonwealth, but not for the king, who forbad this the
people's cannonizacion . . .'.[20]

Thus, popular traditions might bear little relationship to the significant
historical events as recorded by antiquarian scholarship in this period.
Take, for example, the disafforestation, drainage, and enclosure of
Hatfield Chase on the Yorkshire–Lincolnshire border in the reign of
Charles I. This was apparently consented to by the 'better sort' of the
inhabitants of the area at the time and, after initial protests by some of the
dispossessed, occasioned no further contention. Sir William Dugdale was
to write up this history of 'improvement' in 1662 and no other verdict on
the issue would be recorded were it not for the enquiries of Abraham de
la Pryme who became vicar of Hatfield in November 1696. De la Pryme
was a great collector of local traditions and here, as elsewhere, he was
always 'examining and talking with . . . my eldest parishioners . . . about
what was memorable relating thereto'. He found that the 'old men' of
Hatfield would often talk nostalgically of the days before the destruction
of the chase when 'the poor people got a good liveing out of the same and
venison was no greater a rarity then in a poor man's kitchen than mutton
is now'. They also related in loving detail the intricacies of their poaching
technique, seeming to delight in its skill and craft as well as in its defiance
of authority. Moreover, they had a popular hero in Sir Robert Swift, the
last Bowbearer to the king in the chase, whose responsibility it was to

---

[19] Thomas, *The Perception of the Past in Early Modern England*, 11–22.
[20] Habington, *A Survey of Worcestershire*, ed. Amphlett, ii. 82.

protect the game but whose lovable incompetence seems to have endeared him to all and occasioned 'many traditional stories'.[21]

Exactly the same kind of discrepancy in interpretations of the past may be detected in the rather different versions of an eventually famous tale collected at Tilney Smeath in Norfolk. In the churchyard there stood a monument commemorating the deeds of one Hikifricke. In 1631 John Weever recorded the tale, 'as it hath gone by tradition from father to the sonne', of how 'upon a time (no man knowes how long since)', Hikifricke had saved the rights of the seven villages in the parish over the large common which they surrounded from the encroachments of the local landlord.[22] When, however, the heralds Elias Ashmole and William Dugdale were touring the fenlands in the early summer of 1657, they both seem to have derived different versions of events from the locals at Tilney. Ashmole understood their hero to have 'killed a gyant and recovered marshland from him', while Dugdale believed that Hikifricke himself had been the lord of Tilney and had fought not for but against the inhabitants over the bounds of the common (see Plate 10).[23] Such variance provides signal evidence of the way in which interpretations of a tale might depend upon the disposition of both tellers and recipients. In the minds of some Hikifricke was a champion of the common cause of the people, while in the view of others he was invoked as a defender of the rights of property and lordly authority.

Many communities seem to have cherished hero figures such as Hikifricke who had at some time defended the rights of the common people or flouted authority. Outlaws, in particular, were the epitome of those who spurned the conventions of society and appeared to live a life of freedom outside the bounds and burdens which usually kept people in their place. Theirs were deeds of daring and adventure, romantic and exceptional. To hear of them was to be transported momentarily to a time and a place in which the powerful might be defied and even conquered.

[21] Sir William Dugdale, *The History of Imbanking and Drayning* (1662), 145–9; Keith Lindley, *Fenland Riots and the English Revolution* (London, 1982), 13–4, 23–4, 64, 71–2; *The Diary of Abraham de la Pryme, the Yorkshire Antiquary*, ed. Charles Jackson (Surtees Society, 54, Durham, 1869–70), 71; BL, Lansdowne MS, 897, fos. 50–1, 55ᵛ.

[22] Weever, *Ancient Funerall Monuments*, 866; and cf. Sir Henry Spelman, 'Incenia: Sive Norfolciae Descriptio Topographica', in *Reliquiae Spelmannianae* (Oxford, 1698), 138; Francis Blomefield and Charles Parkin, *An Essay towards a Topographical History of the County of Norfolk* (5 vols., Fersfield, 1739–75), iv. 691–2. Equally, local tenants might seek to deface or destroy such monuments when there were traditions associated with them which were prejudicial to their land rights and usages: see Sampson Erdeswicke, *A Survey of Staffordshire* (London, 1723), 192.

[23] *Elias Ashmole (1617–1692): His Autobiographical and Historical Notes, his Correspondence, and other Contemporary Sources Relating to his Life and Work*, ed. C. H. Josten (Oxford, 1966), 708–9; Bod. Lib., MS Ashmole 784, fo. 23ᵛ; Dugdale, *History of Imbanking and Drayning*, 244.

Such had been the appeal of Hereward the Wake in the centuries after the Norman Conquest and then of Robin Hood who by the thirteenth century seems to have taken his place in the popular imagination.[24]

Ubiquitous as Robin was in popular legend, he had plenty of local equivalents who may have been unknown other than in the parochial context and were probably remembered only in oral tradition. Thus, the people living around the Forest of Exmoor in Devon would tell of one Symon, 'another Robin Hood', who 'standing in outlary, kept this forest'. Among the trees was 'a large deep pool which they name Symon's Bath . . . and in the moors of Somerset there is a burrow or fort called, by the inhabitants, Symon's Burrow, which he made his winter strength to retire unto'. Such tales suggest all the swashbuckling elements of the conventional Robin Hood narratives and many seem to have adopted the motif of a man of high birth forced to live on the margins of society. At Myddle in Shropshire, for example, they had a local hero in 'wild Humphry' Kinaston, a knight-errant turned fugitive of whom 'the people tell almost as many romantick storyes, as of the great outlawe Robin Whood'. Among these was the tale of how 'wild Humphry' had escaped from the ambush of the sheriff and 'a considerable company of men' by leaping over the river Severn. He sought shelter in a cave near Nesscliffe 'which, to this day, is called Kinaston's Cave'. Such also was the history of Poole's Hole, an underground cave by Buxton in Derbyshire, the refuge of 'one Pool, of Pool's Hall in Staffordshire, a man of great valour who, being outlawed, resided here for his own security', and yet to be seen were his stone table, bed, and shelf. Likewise, at Bristol in the years before the Civil War one could still hear tell 'as fresh as but of yesterday' of the exploits of 'black Will' Herbert, future earl of Pembroke, 'a mad fighting young fellow' who in the reign of Henry VIII had killed one of the sheriffs and escaped through the city gates to France.[25]

---

[24]  Maurice Keen, *The Outlaws of Medieval Legend* (rev. edn., London, 1977). For Hereward see also Michael Swanton trans., 'The Deeds of Hereward', in Thomas H. Ohlgren (ed.), *Medieval Outlaws: Ten Tales in Modern English* (Stroud, 1998), 12–60; Westwood, *Albion: A Guide to Legendary England*, 149–50; on the subversive aspect of Robin Hood's appeal, see Christopher Hill, 'Robin Hood', in his *Liberty against the Law: Some Seventeenth-Century Controversies* (London, 1996), 71–82.

[25]  Westcote, *A View of Devonshire in 1630*, ed. Oliver and Jones, 95; Richard Gough, *The History of Myddle*, ed. David Hey (Harmondsworth, 1981), 56–7; *The Diary of Ralph Thoresby, F.R.S.*, ed. Joseph Hunter (2 vols., London, 1830), i. 91–2; Edward Browne, 'Journal of a Tour in Derbyshire', in *Sir Thomas Browne's Works*, ed. Simon Wilkin (4 vols., London, 1835–6), i. 35; Aubrey, *Brief Lives*, ed. Clark, i. 314–15; Powell, *John Aubrey and his Friends*, 31–2. The celebrated escape of the border reiver Kinmont Willie from Carlisle Castle in April 1596 continued to be remembered in Cumberland: Edmund Sandford, *A Cursory Relation of all the Antiquities and Familyes in Cumberland*, ed. R. S. Ferguson (Cumberland and Westmorland Ant. and Arch. Soc., 4, Kendal, 1890), 49. Sir Walter Scott was later to transcribe from oral tradition and immortalize

If it was true that the memories of ancient inhabitants might provide a strong and relatively reliable link with the recent past, it was certainly the case that the further back in time historical tradition sought to reach the more prone to distortion it was likely to become. There was a large gap in terms of factual accuracy between what was inherited directly at first or second hand from elders and ancestors and what was believed to have taken place in the very distant past.[26] There was a tendency to 'telescope', to shorten or omit entire portions of the past, which is familiar in many societies with strong oral traditions.[27] For most people their understanding of times long ago was vague and episodic: theirs was a history with little sense of chronology, in which names and places, dates and events could be hopelessly conflated and confused. Seminal episodes, such as Noah's Flood, the Roman and Danish invasions, or later the Reformation and civil wars of the seventeenth century, acted as 'dating tools' against which everything was measured and in terms of which everything was explained. The influence of certain great historical figures, such as Julius Caesar, King Arthur or Robin Hood, loomed so large as to account for almost any landmark or occurrence of note.[28] When the short limits of memory were exhausted, myth began.

This vague sense of date was clearly evident among 'the country people' of Lincolnshire who were reported to labour under the 'notion that the Foss road is the oldest in England, and that it was made by William the Conqueror'. Meanwhile, Ethelbert's Tower in Canterbury was not in fact built by Ethelbert himself, 'as vulgar tradition will fabulously tell you it was', but merely in his honour in about 1047. Castles seemed particularly prone to this kind of fanciful dating. Some were post-dated, like Reigate in Surrey, thought to be built by the Saxons, 'tho a vulgar error has generally given the credit of it to one of the Warrens, earls of Surrey'. Most, however, were dignified with a more or less bogus antiquity, like Devizes Castle,

in print the ballad of this triumphant episode: *Minstrelsy of the Scottish Border*, ed. Thomas Henderson (London, 1931), 179–90.

[26] See, for example, Johnson, *Folk Memory: Or the Continuity of British Archaeology*, 13; M. T. Clanchy, 'Remembering the Past and the Good Old Law', *History*, 55 (1970), 167; Thomas, *The Perception of the Past*, 8–9; Rosalind Thomas, *Oral Tradition and Written Record in Classical Athens* (Cambridge, 1989), 283.

[27] Jan Vansina, *Oral Tradition: A Study in Historical Methodology*, trans. H. M. Wright (London, 1965), 101–2; David Henige, *Oral Historiography* (London, 1982), 100–1.

[28] Fentress and Wickham, *Social Memory*, 99, 110–12. For examples of dating events from 'the Flood', see Carew, *The Survey of Cornwall*, fo. 7ᵛ; George Owen, *The Description of Pembrokeshire*, ed. Dillwyn Miles (Llandysul, 1994), 191–2; *The Topographer and Genealogist*, ed. Nichols, ii. 420–5; Joshua Childrey, *Britannia Baconica: Or, the Natural Rarities of England, Scotland, and Wales* (London, 1660), 129, 163; John Byng, *The Torrington Diaries*, ed. C. Bruyn Andrews (4 vols., London, 1970), ii. 174; for the other events and individuals, see below.

actually built by Roger, bishop of Salisbury, in the twelfth century, but said, 'upon the authority of tradition', to have been the work of Alfred the Great. The Norman Winchester Castle was claimed to have been the work of King Arthur; tradition attributed Tedworth Castle in Wiltshire to King Lud, who apparently lived there for its 'good air as he was infirm'; while Bamburgh Castle on the Northumbrian coast, was built, so local people affirmed, 'before our Saviour's time'.[29]

In the popular construction of the past, a few particular heroes were promiscuously accredited with almost any monument of antiquity, any landmark of exception. Most prolific of all in this respect was King Arthur. Scores of sites around the country bore witness to the impact which his legend had made on historical consciousness. It was possible to cross his bridge and pass through his gate; to climb his hill and inspect his round table; to visit his castle and kneel by his gravestone. There were his 'seats' and his 'chairs' aplenty, his 'ovens' and his 'stones' in abundance; there were his hunting wells and resting places, his causeways and battle grounds. Here he held court, there he won victory, here he fell in combat. In several spots, they claimed, he lay sleeping, ready to awaken one day and rescue his people in their hour of need.[30]

Only Julius Caesar could rival Arthur for ubiquity. He seems to have impressed himself on the popular imagination, in particular, as the natural builder of fortifications, of whatever age they may actually have been. 'Vulgar chronology will have Norwich Castle as old as Julius Caesar', it was said, while the castles at Chepstow, Exeter, Canterbury, and Dover, where visitors could inspect his 'old brass trumpet', were among those similarly attributed.[31] Patrons in an alehouse at Woodstock, Oxfordshire,

[29] William Stukeley, *Itinerarium Curiosum* (London, 1724), 99; William Somner, *The Antiquities of Canterbury* (London, 1640), 40; John Aubrey, *The Natural History and Antiquities of the County of Surrey* (5 vols., London, 1718–19), iv. 189; Camden, *Britannia*, ed. Gibson, 103; *Travels through England of Dr Richard Pococke*, ed. Cartwright, ii. 122, 246; Thomas Kirke, 'Journeyings through Northumberland and Durham Anno Dom. 1677', in *Reprints of Rare Tracts and Imprints of Antient Manuscripts*, ed. Richardson, vii. 11.

[30] For a selection of examples, see Kendrick, *British Antiquity*, 95; Westwood, *Albion: A Guide to Legendary Britain*, 5–8; William Worcestre, *Itineraries*, ed. John H. Harvey (Oxford, 1969), 6, 94; *Itinerary of John Leland*, ed. Smith, i. 151, iii. 106, 119, v. 48; Carew, *The Survey of Cornwall*, fo. 122ᵛ; Camden, *Britannia*, ed. Gibson, 11, 545, 620, 628–9; Fynes Moryson, *An Itinerary Containing his Ten Yeeres Travell* (4 vols., Glasgow, 1907–8), ii. 118; BL, Harleian MS, 6726, fo. 244ᵛ; Sir Daniel Fleming, *Description of the County of Westmorland*, ed. G. F. Duckett (Cumberland and Westmorland Ant. and Arch. Soc., 1, Kendal, 1882), 30; Aubrey, *Monumenta Britannica*, ed. Fowles and Legg, 113–14, 955; James Brome, *Travels over England, Scotland and Wales* (London, 1700), 22; Stukeley, *Itinerarium Curiosum*, 142; Robert Hunt, *Popular Romances of the West of England* (2 vols., London, 1865), ii. 59–71; *The Denham Tracts*, ed. James Hardy (2 vols., Folklore Society, London, 1892–5), ii. 125–31.

[31] Sir Thomas Browne, *Hydriotaphia Urne-Burial* (1658), in *The Works of Sir Thomas Browne*, ed. Keynes, i. 142; *The Life of Marmaduke Rawdon of York*, ed. Robert Davies (Camden Society,

boasted to one Elizabethan tourist that the Roman conqueror had been responsible for a 'palace' there; nor were such notions mere village fancy, for even in the capital city 'common opinion' erroneously ascribed the Tower of London to his offices.[32] Small wonder then that 'the vulgar' were thought to be 'generally uncapable of judging of antiquities'.[33]

## THE MONKISH BALANCE

This confused sense of chronology was not merely the product of popular ignorance or the distortion caused by oral transmission, however, but was in essence the fruit of learned fiction and often derived from written sources. At a time when studious historical scholarship was only just beginning to develop standards of documentary reference and corroboration and to question many of the long-established legends, inherited from the medieval chronicles, which continued to dominate the learned view of the past, ignorance was by no means confined to 'the vulgar'. Moreover, new and spurious versions of the past were being written in the early modern period which did as much to generate error. It was the arriviste gentry of Tudor England, with the aid of the heralds, who were as responsible as anyone for the creation of bogus versions of history in the fantastic genealogies which they fabricated in an attempt to dignify family lines with spurious longevity.[34]

A sense of learned fiction feeding into popular lore is evident in much that can be recovered of generally held views about the past. In practice few historical narratives which circulated orally were completely 'pure', in the sense of owing nothing to the written word. A number of recent studies drawing upon evidence gathered from societies around the world and over time have demonstrated the interaction and reciprocal infusion of

1st ser., 85, London, 1863), 187; Brome, *Travels over England, Scotland and Wales*, 21; John Hooker, *The Description of the Citie of Excester*, ed. W. J. Harte, J. W. Schopp, and H. Tapley-Soper (Devon and Cornwall Record Society, Exeter, 1919), 31; Camden, *Britannia*, ed. Gibson, 205; 'A Relation of a Short Survey of the Western Counties', ed. L. G. Wickham Legg, in *Camden Miscellany*, xvi (Camden Society, 3rd ser., 52, London, 1936), 19, 24; BL, Additional MS, 19990, fo. 6ʳ; BL, Sloane MS, 1911–13, fo. 195ʳ.

[32] *Thomas Platter's Travels in England, 1599*, ed. Clare Williams (London, 1937), 223; John Stow, *A Survey of London*, ed. C. L. Kingsford (2 vols., Oxford, 1908), i. 44, 136.

[33] *The History and Antiquities of Glastonbury*, ed. Hearne, vii, and quoted in Woolf, 'The "Common Voice"', 46.

[34] On these bogus genealogies, see Michael Maclagan, 'Genealogy and Heraldry in the Sixteenth and Seventeenth Centuries', in Levi Fox (ed.), *English Historical Scholarship in the Sixteenth and Seventeenth Centuries* (London, 1956), 41–2; Lawrence Stone, *The Crisis of the Aristocracy, 1558–1641* (Oxford, 1965), 23–5; A. R. Wagner, *English Genealogy* (2nd edn., Oxford, 1972), 358–66; Felicity Heal and Clive Holmes, *The Gentry in England and Wales, 1500–1700* (Basingstoke, 1994), 34–7.

written and unwritten sources in the communication of information about the past, whether in story or song.[35] So too in Tudor and Stuart England, much of the historical tradition which circulated among ordinary people had some basis in literary and learned culture even if the embellishment and corruption effected by generations of oral transmission had taken it far from its origins. By the early modern period, centuries of chronicle and hagiographic writing, of chivalric romance, sermon exempla, poetry, and drama, had been providing a variety of written sources of knowledge about the past and they provide the key to understanding the genesis of a large part of popular tradition.[36] Time and again, the kind of local anecdote which was increasingly coming to be dismissed as erroneous by antiquarian scholarship in the seventeenth century can be found to derive from some written source, perhaps long forgotten.

In addition to initiating much of what subsequently passed into oral circulation, the written word was also responsible for augmenting and enhancing it; for reviving an oral narrative which might otherwise have died out were it not for its preservation, elaboration and dissemination in text. Again, written culture was probably more culpable than oral in the fabrication and perpetuation of distorted, exaggerated, and spurious versions of the past. Thomas Westcote commented perceptively in the 1630s that 'some things seem more fabulous, interposed perchance by some augmenting transcribers' than many others 'left unto us as a tradition . . . from mouth to mouth'. By the same token, it was said of the 'miraculous storys' told of St William of Lindholme by 'the country people' in south Yorkshire, that they remained purely local and rather muted as a consequence of never having been writtten down: 'the pitty is that this worthy saint has not had any one to set forth his strang works or else perhaps they might have been as great, wonderfull and fabulous as K[ing] Arthur's are'.[37]

---

[35] See the evidence reviewed in Ruth Finnegan, *Oral Poetry: Its Nature, Significance and Social Context* (Cambridge, 1977), ch. 5; Ruth Finnegan, *Literacy and Orality: Studies in the Technology of Communication* (Oxford, 1988), ch. 6. The point is made with regard to early modern England in Thomas, *The Perception of the Past*, 7–8.

[36] See, for example, G. R. Owst, *Literature and Pulpit in Medieval England* (2nd edn., Oxford, 1961), esp. 126–34, 158–61; P. R. Coss, 'Aspects of Cultural Diffusion in Medieval England: The Early Romances, Local Society and Robin Hood', *Past and Present*, 108 (1985), 35–79; C. L. Kingsford, *English Historical Literature in the Fifteenth Century* (Oxford, 1913); E. K. Chambers, *English Literature at the Close of the Middle Ages* (Oxford, 1945). One thinks of the preaching technique of Chaucer's Pardoner: 'Thanne telle I hem ensamples many oon | Of olde stories longe tyme agoon. | For lewed peple loven tales olde; | Swiche thynges kan they wel reporte and holde': *The Riverside Chaucer*, ed. Larry D. Benson (3rd edn., Boston, Mass., 1987), 195.

[37] Westcote, *A View of Devonshire*, ed. Oliver and Jones, 30; BL, Lansdowne MS, 897, fo. 73ʳ. Local tradition later held that William of Lindholme was either a giant or a magician: E. Gutch and M. Peacock, *Examples of Printed Folk-Lore Concerning Lincolnshire* (Folklore Society, London,

Even contemporaries who believed that they were witnessing pure oral tradition passing down the generations unadulterated by the infiltration of writing were usually mistaken in this. Elias Ashmole seems to have thought that the legend of St Joseph of Arimathea and the Holy Thorn of Glastonbury Abbey provided an example of one such tradition, for until the work of a few recent writers he could 'not remember to have read any author who hath taken notice of this thorne in print'. Otherwise, 'all the remembrance we have of it, hath past along among us by tradition only, which I have often heard spoken of . . .'. In reality, however, the monks at Glastonbury had been fabricating miraculous stories of St Joseph since the thirteenth century and they had enjoyed wide manuscript circulation long before the Tudor herbalists popularized the legend of the Thorn.[38]

Many such legends which had come to enjoy widespread currency by the early modern period probably had their origins in the attempts of religious houses to assert or invent certain claims. Equally, from an early date it had been common for noble or gentle families to try to explain their origins, justify their ownership of a piece of land, or account for the heraldic dragon on their coat of arms, by claiming for an ancient forebear some feat of heroism or conquest. Such 'charter myths' might then pass into popular belief and they provide the source for much dragon lore of the period.[39] The lordship of Moston in Cheshire, for example, had been in the possession of the Venables family for many generations when it was recorded in 1560 that their ancestor, Thomas, had earned the inheritance by slaying 'a terrible dragon' which had once terrorized the neighbourhood, piercing it with an arrow while in the very act of devouring a child. The dragon on the Berkeley family crest derived, so an early seventeenth-century document explains, from the dragon-slaying exploits of Sir John Berkeley at Bisterne in Hampshire, where a Dragon Field can be seen to this day. At Sockburn, in County Durham, a monument in the church commemorated the valiant deeds of Sir John Conyers, who 'before the Conquest', tradition told, had fought and slain the

1908), 322. On the way in which writing can infuse and augment oral traditions, see Henige, *Oral Historiography*, 81–7 ; for another good example, see Woolf, 'The "Common Voice"', 34.

[38] *Elias Ashmole (1617–1692)*, ed. Josten, 1286–7; and cf. *The History and Antiquities of Glastonbury*, ed. Hearne, 302; Antonia Gransden, 'The Growth of the Glastonbury Traditions and Legends in the Twelfth Century', *Journal of Ecclesiastical History*, 27 (1976), 358; C. E. Raven, *English Naturalists from Neckam to Ray* (Cambridge, 1947), 21.

[39] Tales of dragons had been fed into popular circulation for centuries via sermons, romances, and imagery: Owst, *Literature and Pulpit in Medieval England*, 15 n. 108 n. 111, 145, 161 n.; Ohlgren (ed.), *Medieval Outlaws*, 152–4; Clanchy, *From Memory to Written Record*, 174–5, 190, 290. Belief in dragons was still common in the sixteenth century: see, for example, John Maplet, *A Greene Forest, or a Naturall Historie* (London, 1567), fo. 81.

dragon, a 'monstrous venom'd and poison'd wiverne, ask or worme, which overthrew and devour'd many people in fight, for the scent of the poyson was so strong that noe person was able to abide it'. In the reign of Charles I people were still showing the spot known as Graystone where the dragon had fallen, and the deeds of Sir John were commemorated in local ceremonial into the nineteenth century.[40]

Another set of charter myths which provided a written source for what would enter into popular oral tradition were those which certain towns fabricated in support of their antiquity and venerability. In the late fifteenth century the Warwickshire antiquary John Rous had attributed the foundation of Cambridge, both town and university, to one Cantaber, a Spaniard who came to Britain in the time of King Gurguntius, about 375 BC. This was the view endorsed by John Caius in the 1570s, among others, so that the duke of Württemberg, visiting the town in 1592, was rightly told that this was the orthodoxy 'as affirmed by the principal historians'.[41] At Oxford, meanwhile, it was possible for the curious enquirer to choose from a number of contending hypotheses about its origins, all of them derived from learned written authorities. Some attributed its provenance to one Mempric, 'who was king of the Britannes in the year of the world 2954 and before Christ 1009'; others gave the plaudits to his son Ebranc; while still others preferred the claims of Olenus Calenus 'a Roman, about 70 years before Christ'. But it was equally possible to find support for the view that it had been the creation of 'certain philosophers out of Graece', a theory which the existence of 'Aristotle's well' near Walton did much to confirm; 'that Cassisbulan, king of the Britaines about 58 years before Christ, built it; as he did Exeter, Colchester and Norwich'; that it was 'originally founded by a British king called Arvizagus about 70 years after our Saviour's nativity'; that it had been 'built or at least restored' by King Vortigern in 474; or, finally, that it was the work of King Alfred, '(as some, and these not mean historians, assert) in the year 872'.[42]

[40] BL, Harleian MS, 2119, fo. 40; Westwood, *Albion: A Guide to Legendary Britain*, 45, and cf. 250–1, 341–2; BL, Harleian MS, 2118, fo. 39ᵛ; W. C. Hazlitt, *Tenures of Land and Customs of Manors* (London, 1874), 285 n.

[41] John Rous, *Historia Regum Angliae*, ed. Thomas Hearne (2nd edn., Oxford, 1745), 25–6; John Caius, *De Antiquitate Cantebrigiensis Academiae* (1574), in *The Works of John Caius, M.D.*, ed. E. S. Roberts (Cambridge, 1912), 11–14; *England as seen by Foreigners in the Days of Elizabeth and James the First*, ed. William Brenchley Rye (London, 1865), 33. Cf. Kendrick, *British Antiquity*, 25–6; BL, Harleian MS, 6768, 48; 'Diary of the Journey of Philip Julius, Duke of Stettin-Pomerania, through England in the Year 1602', ed. Gottfried von Bülow', *Transactions of the Royal Historical Society*, new ser., 6 (1892), 33; 'Thomas Baskerville's Journeys in England, Temp. Car. II', in Historical Manuscripts Commission (HMC), *Thirteenth Report, Appendix, Part II* (London, 1893), 284.

[42] Rous, *Historia Regum Angliae*, ed. Hearne, 21–2; '*Survey of the Antiquities of the City of Oxford*',

Such myths were hardly mere 'vulgar errors', therefore, but learned fictions endorsed in the universities and supported by the most respected antiquarian opinion. Many of them derived from Geoffrey of Monmouth's *Historia Regum Britanniae* or else from the elaborations and imaginings of subsequent monastic writers. The abundance of such literature was evident to William Worcestre when he toured the south of England in 1478–80. He found chronicles in a number of abbeys and libraries which variously told that Salisbury was the first city in Britain, that Bristol had been founded by one Brennus, brother of King Berlin of Britain; that the building of Cambridge and Grantham was the work of King Grandebodran, and that Pickering owed its origins to Peredur, another king, 'elected by the commons of Britain, who reigned after Artogall'.[43] Scholarly opinion in the sixteenth and early seventeenth century did little to dispel, and often did much to encourage, such legend. The Elizabethan antiquary Joseph Holland, for example, maintained that Totnes was the oldest town in Britain and claimed to be able to show the stone on which the founding Brutus had rested. In the 1620s, William Slatyer, the Kentish clergyman, was happy to substantiate the traditional view that Chester had been built by the giant Leon-Gavere.[44] For some time to come, it remained perfectly legitimate to believe that Grimsby was named after a poor fisherman called Grim, and that the present site of Bristol was due to the good offices of St Werburg, just as it remained quite orthodox to attribute the foundation of Devizes to King Divitiacus and to believe that Colchester was the work of old King Cole.[45]

Inevitably such learned fictions passed into the oral tradition of the majority. Thus, when the 'old attendant' at the Angel Inn in Leicester assured three soldiers resting there in 1634 that the town had been 'built by the British King Leir, neare 1000 yeeres before Christ', he was doing no more than repeating the testimony of Geoffrey of Monmouth. And Geoffrey's *Historia* was also the source of the tale which these same three travellers found in York, 'as tradition and story tells', that the town was founded by King Ebraucus 'in the reign of K[ing] David' of Judaea. It is no less to be wondered at that Hertfordshire people should believe Nesting to take its name from 'King Alfred's finding a child in an eagle's

Composed in 1661–6, by Anthony Wood, ed. Andrew Clark (3 vols., Oxford Historical Society, 15, 17, 37, Oxford, 1889–99), i. 41–3, 354–5; *England as seen by Foreigners*, ed. Rye, 21.

[43] Worcestre, *Itineraries*, ed. Harvey, 94, 96, 278.

[44] Kendrick, *British Antiquity*, 75, 101.

[45] BL, Harleian MS, 6829, 1–2; BL, Additional MS, 24891, fo. 2ᵛ; Stukeley, *Abury: A Temple of the British Druids*, 27; 'Thomas Baskerville's Journeys in England', in HMC, *Thirteenth Report, Appendix, Part II*, 282. For other foundations attributed to legendary British kings, see Coker, *A Survey of Dorsetshire*, 2; *M. Misson's Memoirs and Observations in his Travels over England: With some Account of Scotland and Ireland*, trans. John Ozell (London, 1719), 101.

nest' there, or that Elstree was derived for similar reasons from 'Eagle's tree', for 'a monkish tale' had first set these ideas on foot.[46]

The Elizabethan inhabitants of Halifax told Camden a story, clearly a legacy of the monastic past but still very much current, that the town had been merely a village known by the name of Horton until this miraculous incident, 'not many ages since'.

A certain clergyman of this town, being passionately in love with a young woman, and by no means able to move her to comply with his lust, grew stark mad, and in that condition villanously cut off her head. Her head was afterward hung upon a ew-tree, where it was reputed holy by the vulgar, till quite rotten; and was often visited in pilgrimage by them; every one plucking off a branch of the tree (as a holy relique). By this means the tree became at last a meer trunk, but retain'd its reputation of sanctity among the people, who even perswaded themselves that those little veins, which are spread out like hair in the rind between the bark and the body of the tree, were indeed the very hair of the virgin. This occasion'd such resort of pilgrims to it, that Horton, from a little village grew up soon to a large town, assuming the new name of Halig-fax or Halifax, which signifies holy hair. For fax is used by the English on the other side [of the] Trent, to signifie hair.[47]

The heritage of medieval historiography was no less evident in the saints' legends which continued to provide popular explanations for place names. In Restoration Oxford it was still believed that the city took its name, according to 'an old tradition that goeth from father to son of our inhabitants', from the eighth-century St Frideswyde who returned to it in triumph after trials and tribulations 'mounted on a milk white ox betokening innocency; and as she rode along the streets, she would forsooth be still speaking to her ox, "ox forth", "ox forth" . . . and hence they undiscreetly say that our city was from thence called Oxforth or Oxford'.[48]

Many such legends of saints and their miracles which still enjoyed widespread currency in the early modern period had their origins in this kind of monastic fabrication. Accounts of their lives had been written by chroniclers since the early Middle Ages and by the twelfth and thirteenth centuries had assumed a standard format. In this guise they became a staple of manuscript culture and sermon exempla and represented some of the most widely known of all traditionary tales in late medieval England. Given that they were, in G. R. Owst's words, 'definitely presented as true

---

[46] *A Relation of a Short Survey of 26 Counties*, ed. L. G. Wickham Legg (London, 1904), 14, 64, deriving directly from Geoffrey of Monmouth, *Historia Regum Britanniae*, II, xi, II, vii; N[athaniel] Salmon, *The History of Hertfordshire* (London, 1728), 59. On Leicester, cf. BL, Additional MS, 15917, fo. 5; and on York, cf. BL, Egerton MS, 2578, fo. 6ʳ.

[47] Camden, *Britannia*, ed. Gibson, 708.

[48] Wood, '*Survey of the Antiquities of the City of Oxford*', ed. Clark, ii. 132.

history, not to be confused in the popular mind with lighter forms of pulpit illustration', it is hardly suprising that they were widely and faithfully believed by the majority. Many of them were included in compilations such as the *South English Legendary*, or the famous *Golden Legend*, a thirteenth-century continental collection which was to be translated and printed by Caxton in 1483 and reissued seven times by 1527. There were scores of individual lives too, especially of English martyrs like St Thomas of Canterbury, St Oswald, and St Edmund.[49]

Thus the origin of a tradition in Canterbury that the devil had once tried to prevent St Augustine preaching at the chapel of St Pancrace, was, according to William Somner, the work of some monastic chronicler which he had seen. But it had passed subsequently into popular tradition and 'of latter time ... became vulgarly received'. Similarly, the tales which travellers often encountered from the mouths of local people at Crowland Abbey in Lincolnshire, of the torments once inflicted by fright-ful devils upon St Guthlac and the monks, could be traced back, so it was said, to 'the chronicler Felix'. The life of St Aldhelm had been written by William of Malmesbury in the twelfth century: 500 years later John Aubrey listened to the 'old men of Malmesbury' tell stories of the many miracles performed by the celebrated Saxon abbot.[50]

Given that the legends of Thomas Becket were some of the most prolif-ically written up of all in literature of the later Middle Ages it is hardly surprising to find them passing similarly into local oral tradition. At Bramfield in Hertfordshire could be found 'Becket's pond' from which he 'brewed good ale'; at Otford in Kent, site of the archiepiscopal palace, was St Thomas's well which he had made by striking his staff on the dry ground; and typically at Todenham in Gloucestershire, where there was one of the numerous parish churches dedicated to Becket, 'many miracles were reported of him'. It was even possible to see, on display at Isel in Cumberland, the sword which had struck him down on that fateful day in 1170.[51]

[49] *The South English Legendary*, ed. Charlotte D'Evelyn and Anna J. Mill (2 vols., Early English Text Society, 235–6, London, 1956); *The Golden Legend*, trans. William Grainger Ryan (2 vols., Princeton, 1993); Owst, *Literature and Pulpit in Medieval England*, 125–6; Keith Thomas, *Religion and the Decline of Magic* (London, 1971), 26; G. H. Gerould, *Saints' Legends* (Boston, Mass., 1916).

[50] Somner, *The Antiquities of Canterbury*, 61–2; Camden, *Britannia*, ed. Gibson, 460–1; Bod. Lib., MS Aubrey 3, fos. 107, 185ᵛ.

[51] Salmon, *The History of Hertfordshire*, 48; Weever, *Ancient Funerall Monuments*, 344–5; Atkyns, *The Ancient and Present State of Gloucestershire*, 409; John Denton, *An Accomt of the Most Considerable Estates and Families in the County of Cumberland*, ed. R. S. Ferguson (Cumberland and Westmorland Antiquarian and Archaeological Society, 2, Kendal, 1887), 68. On the medieval literary tradition of Becket legends, see Owst, *Literature and Pulpit in Medieval England*, 126–34.

Thus while the hagiographic tradition was thoroughly the product of learned written and clerical culture it was quickly assimilated and perpetuated by popular oral tradition. Indeed, the vibrant survival of saints' legends for several centuries after the Reformation, when they had ceased to be officially propagated, is testimony to the strength of this transmission by word of mouth. While it is not unexpected, for example, that in the reign of Henry VIII John Leland should find at Alcester many tales of St Chad, the seventh-century bishop of Lichfield, 'and of the injuries there done to him', it is more remarkable that two centuries later Daniel Defoe was still told 'a long story' of his life by local people. The dedication of parish churches was certainly one factor which helped to keep the legendary deeds of patron saints in mind long after they had ceased to be actively recounted in pulpit and chronicle. At a church in Cardiganshire dedicated to St David, Camden was told that it was here that the famed bishop had 'confuted the palagian heresie ... by miracle: for 'tis reported, that the ground on which he stood preaching, mounted up to a hillock under his feet'. And when Edmund Gibson visited the same church a century later the sexton could still show him a large horn 'which he told me had been preserv'd there ever since the time of St David, adding the fabulous tradition of the oxen call'd Ychen bannog'. In Cornwall it is unsurprising to find the miracles of patron saints still celebrated in Elizabethan parishes, but as late as 1750 the people near Penzance were telling Dr Pococke 'a great many additional stories of the saints of these places to whom their churches are dedicated, as well as to many Irish saints'.[52]

If the dedications of parish churches helped to keep such stories alive, so too did the occasional surviving shrine. Such was St Winifred's well at Holywell in Flintshire which remained a popular tourist attraction long after this period. Typically, when the lawyer Justinian Paget visited in 1630 he found that the locals 'told us many ridiculous fables' of the saint, including the miracle that 'her head was cutt off and sett on again and she lived 15 yeares after'. At the end of the seventeenth century James Brome found the story no less current among a local population still 'much addicted to popish superstition'.[53] So too did Celia Fiennes, and she also

[52] *Itinerary of John Leland*, ed. Smith, ii. 51, 99, cited in Thomas, *The Perception of the Past*, 5; Defoe, *A Tour thro' the Whole Island of Great Britain*, ed. Cole, 480; Camden, *Britannia*, ed. Gibson, 641, 643–4; Carew, *The Survey of Cornwall*, fo. 69ᵛ; *Travels through England of Dr Richard Pococke*, ed. Cartwright, i. 136; and for their continuation into the nineteenth century, see Hunt, *Popular Romances of the West of England*, ii. 3–33.

[53] BL, Harleian MS, 1026, fo. 31ᵛ; Brome, *Travels over England, Scotland and Wales*, 223–4. Cf. BL, Sloane MS, 241, fo. 39ᵛ; *Life and Letters of Edward Lhwyd*, vol. xiv of *Early Science in Oxford*, ed. R. T. Gunther (Oxford, 1945), 156; Francis Jones, *The Holy Wells of Wales* (Cardiff, 1954), 65, 70. The belief in severed heads in wells has been widespread in Celtic tradition over many

came across St Mungo's well at Copgrove near Harrogate where the associated fable was still going strong. Another of these 'old fabulous legends' accompanied St German's well on the Cornish coast at Rame, which even in the 1770s was 'yet in report'. In Northumberland, meanwhile, the legends of St Cuthbert prospered for just as long, prompted by such survivals as his coffin, which remained on display near the chapel dedicated to him at Hetton.[54]

Another legacy of the learned and literate tradition of the medieval Church which was to have a significant and enduring impact on popular tradition was the large and well-developed repertoire of moralizing tales featuring the devil. By the early modern period, many centuries of preaching and didactic writing had firmly established the notion of a malevolent fiend active in the temporal world who endeavoured to tempt mankind from virtue and wreak havoc wherever he could. These accounts of diabolical evil, which were such a standard feature of sermon exempla, both drew from and fed into what was one of the largest corpus of folktales to come down from the Middle Ages. Once again, in their telling and retelling such stories tended to be conceived of in local terms and to be prompted and sustained by features in the immediate landscape. Unusual topographical landmarks often had an explanation associated with them which involved the work of Satan: rocky outcrops, stone circles, caves, ditches, and gorges were all likely to be attributed to the malignant efforts of 'Old Nick'. 'It is a strange taste which our ancestors had', William Cobbett could later muse, 'to ascribe no inconsiderable part of these wonders of nature to the devil.'[55]

One of the most famous such landmarks at this time was the four large boulders standing upright by the side of the road near Boroughbridge in Yorkshire, variously called the devil's bolts, arrows, or darts, which the evil one was supposed to have hurled at neighbouring Aldborough. Richard Shanne, yeoman of nearby Methley in the earlier seventeenth century, knew the stories associated with them better than most.

My owne selfe have hard this taile verie often tould concerning these boults. That a spiritt was sekinge an auncient citie harde by called Aldborrowe, who metinge with some by the way did aske howe farr it was to such a citie, and they

centuries: see, Anne Ross, 'Severed Heads in Wells: An Aspect of the Well Cult', *Scottish Studies*, 6 (1962), 31–48.

[54] *The Journeys of Celia Fiennes*, ed. Christopher Morris (London, 1947), 81–2, 180–1; *The Antiquarian Repertory*, ed. Francis Grose (4 vols., London, 1775–84), ii. 76–7; William Hutchinson, *A View of Northumberland* (2 vols., Newcastle, 1778), ii. 23; *The Denham Tracts*, ed. Hardy, i. 8–9. Cf. Hunt, *Popular Romances of the West of England*, ii. 35–59.

[55] William Cobbett, *Rural Rides* (2 vols., Everyman edn., n.d.), i. 205.

tould him they knewe it not. And the spirit said, 'I have beene sekinge of the same so manie years and yet could never fynd it', and in a rage shott those boults away and so fledd and was never hard of anie more.[56]

Of a like formation of stones in Merionethshire 'the people make no difficulty in saying the devil set them there', and other monuments to dia-bolical ammunition included the devil's quoits by Stanton Harcourt in Oxfordshire or those at Avebury in Wiltshire. At neighbouring Stonehenge, meanwhile, many such fabulous stories were told.

One of the great stones that lies downe on the west side hath a cavity something resembling the print of a man's foot: concerning which the shepherds and coun-trey people have a tradition (which many of them doe stedfastly believe) that when Merlin conveyed the stones from Ireland by art magick, the devill hit him in the heale with that stone, and so left the print there.[57]

By the same token, travellers could wonder at the large chasm in the rock near Castleton in the Derbyshire peak district, 'vulgarly called the devil's arse . . . of which many fables are told' or encounter the equally famous Stiperstones in south-west Shropshire, 'great heapes of stones, which the vulgar sort dreame to have been the divel's bridge'.[58] In the same vein were the devil's brook near Sturminster in Dorset, the devil's punchbowl between Lambourn and Wantage in Berkshire, the devil's jumps by Chertsey in Surrey, the devil's kettles in Cleveland, the devil's drop outside Dover, or the devil's chair above Glastonbury.[59] Ravines and crevices invariably had some legend associated with them involving huge leaps made by the devil in the course of making his

---

[56] BL, Additional MS, 38599, fo. 98ᵛ. Among many other references to these rocks, see *The Topographer and Genealogist*, ed. Nichols, ii. 425; Camden, *Britannia*, ed. Gibson, 716; Aubrey, *Monumenta Britannica*, ed. Fowles and Legg, 109–12; Robert Plot, *Natural History of Stafford-shire* (Oxford, 1686), 398; Defoe, *Tour thro' the Whole Island of Great Britain*, ed. Cole, 627–8; *Travels through England of Dr Richard Pococke*, ed. Cartwright, i. 59; Thomas Parkinson, *Yorkshire Legends and Traditions* (2 vols., London, 1888–9), i. 115–19.

[57] Defoe, *A Tour thro' the Whole Island of Great Britain*, 461–2; Aubrey, *Monumenta Britannica*, ed. Fowles and Legg, 95, 107, 823; Plot, *The Natural History of Oxford-shire*, 343; *Travels through England of Dr Richard Pococke*, ed. Cartwright, ii. 52.

[58] Moryson, *An Itinerary Containing his Ten Yeeres Travell*, iv. 152, 154. For other references to the 'devil's arse', see Camden, *Britannia*, ed. Gibson, 495; Edward Browne, 'Journal of a Tour in Derbyshire', in *Sir Thomas Browne's Works*, ed. Wilkin, i. 32–3; Charles Leigh, *The Natural History of Lancashire, Cheshire, and the Peak, in Derbyshire* (Oxford, 1700), 43; HMC, *13th Report, Appendix, Part IV* (London, 1892), 475.

[59] *Itinerary of John Leland*, ed. Smith, v. 108; Aubrey, *Monumenta Britannica*, ed. Fowles and Legg, 904; Aubrey, *Natural History and Antiquities of the County of Surrey*, iii. 185; Cobbett, *Rural Rides*, i. 204, 205; *Topographer and Genealogist*, ed. Nichols, ii. 409; *Travels through England of Dr Richard Pococke*, ed. Cartwright, ii. 92–3.

mischief: vivid examples were recorded of Birtley Holywell in north Tyneside, Cheddar gorge in Somerset, and Bayard's Leap in Lincolnshire.[60]

At the same time, ditches, dykes, causeways, and the Roman roads always had such tales associated with them: 'for the vulgar', observed William Stukeley, 'generally think these extraordinary works made by help of the devil'. Aubrey commented upon the devil's causeways at Boxgrove near Chichester, at Wood Ditton near Newmarket, and Ockley near Dorking, and there were very many others. Passing the 'devil's bank', a large trench located betweeen Sheffield and Rotherham, Defoe reflected that such things were often attributed to Satan 'as if he had more leisure, or that it was less trouble to him than a whole army of men', and it was frequently believed that he made these structures in an instant, perhaps in a fit of rage or in order to win an evil bet. At the great ditch, 'called by the neighbouring inhabitants Wansdike', Camden had heard the 'groundless tradition that it was made by the devil upon a Wednesday'. Equally, both Hadrian's Wall and the Roman road Watling Street were said by locals in the north-east to have been built overnight night by Satan and his friend, the fabled wizard Michael Scot.[61]

Frequently the devil was tricked into building these structures by his own stupidity or else by the ingenuity of the local people. The 'fabula anilis' which Aubrey recorded about Stane Street, the Roman road between London and Chichester, was typical. In Surrey 'it is made of flints and pebbles; but there are no other flints nearer than seven miles, and the pebbles are such as are at the beaches in Sussex, from whence the common people say they were brought, and that it was made by the devil'. At Dorking, where the road passed through the churchyard they told the story of how Old Nick had fallen in love with 'a faire lady, a great man's daughter'. He struck a bargain with her father that he might have her if he could build a great causeway in a single night and complete it 'before sun riseing'. Working furiously to win his prize, he may have succeeded had not the local people played the trick of building 'a great fire to make the devil believe the sun was up'. So startled was he to see the dawn breaking that he 'let fall a lap full of stones' and tumbling from the sky they 'made

[60] *The Denham Tracts*, ed. Hardy, ii. 216–7; R. L. Tongue and K. M. Briggs, *Somerset Folklore* (Folklore Society, London, 1965), 123–4; Sidney O. Addy, *Household Tales with Other Traditional Remains Collected in the Counties of York, Lincoln, Derby, and Nottingham* (London, 1895), 25–6. For early references to Bayard's Leap, see N. J. O'Conor, *Godes Peace and the Queenes: Vicissitudes of a House, 1539–1615* (London, 1934), 120; Stukeley, *Itinerarium Curiosum*, 81.

[61] Stukeley, *Itinerarium Curiosum*, 171; Aubrey, *Monumenta Britannica*, ed. Fowles and Legg, 381, 881, 891, 923; Defoe, *Tour thro' the Whole Island of Great Britain*, ed. Cole, 592; Camden, *Britannia*, ed. Gibson, 85; Hutchinson, *A View of Northumberland*, i. 80; David Ure, *The History of Rutherglen and East-Kilbride* (Glasgow, 1793), 133; *The Denham Tracts*, ed. Hardy, i. 348, ii. 116–19.

a hill at one of the causewayes'.[62] There is always a sense of justice which surrounds these stories, for the devil, though evil, is ultimately rather stupid and capable of being outwitted by mere mortals. It is a message which owes its origin to the sermon exempla and was to remain a fundamental part of English folklore throughout the nineteenth century.[63]

Finally, together with the legends of saints and the fabulous exploits of devils and dragons, another staple of popular tradition in early modern England which had thoroughly literary origins was the repertoire of tales about giants. The idea that giants had once inhabited the earth had Old Testament authority, of course, and it was Geoffrey of Monmouth's *Historia* which popularized notions, probably much older, that the island of Albion had been populated by gargantuan figures before the conquest of the Trojan Brutus.[64] Once again, then, it is hardly surprising to find this weight of written orthodoxy feeding into general historical consciousness. Camden believed, for example, that the many tales told by Cornish folk of the giants who occupied St Michael's Mount, still much talked of in the nineteenth century, owed their creation to verses penned in the reign of Henry III.[65] And, as with much other medieval fable, these ideas were taken up and popularized anew by scholars in the sixteenth and early seventeenth centuries. Thus in 1610 the astrologer Simon Forman wrote a genealogy of all the giants from the days of Noah, while at the same time the antiquary William Burton could invoke a variety of scriptural and other authorities to prove their former existence.[66] Meanwhile, this legendary history of Britain found its way into the great poetry and prose of the period.[67]

In this case, too, visual evidence was vital in the stimulation and perpetuation of such tradition at the popular level. Reminders of the legendary past were everywhere to be seen in those many towns which, in an effort to assert their origins in the earliest days of Albion, claimed to have been founded by giants. The images which decorated their midsummer

---

[62] Aubrey, *Natural History and Antiquities of the County of Surrey*, iv. 187; Aubrey, *Monumenta Britannica*, ed. Fowles and Legg, 273, 925.

[63] Briggs, *A Dictionary of British Folk-Tales*, iii. 43–4, 82–3, 95–6.

[64] Genesis, 6: 4; Kendrick, *British Antiquity*, ch. 1; D. R. Woolf, 'Of Danes and Giants: Popular Beliefs about the Past in Early Modern England', *Dalhousie Review*, 71 (1991), 183–7.

[65] Camden, *Britannia*, ed. Gibson, 4. For legends of Cornish giants, as they were recorded in the mid-nineteenth century, see Hunt, *Popular Romances of the West of England*, i. 3–61.

[66] Bod. Lib., MS Ashmole 244, fos. 192–9; William Burton, *The Description of Leceister Shire* (London, 1622), 277.

[67] Among the most famous examples are Edmund Spenser, *The Faerie Queene* (1596), in *Spenser: Poetical Works*, ed. J. C. Smith and E. De Selincourt (Oxford, 1912); Michael Drayton, *Poly-Olbion* (1613), in *The Works of Michael Drayton*, ed. J. William Hebel (5 vols., Oxford, 1931–41), iv. 26. For discussion, see C. B. Millican, *Spenser and the Round Table* (Cambridge, Mass., 1932); Ernest Jones, *Geoffrey of Monmouth, 1640–1800* (Berkeley and Los Angeles, 1944), 406–17.

pageants and civic processions did much to make immediate for the citizenry this venerable past.[68] On Christmas Eve in Chester, for example, the Recorder would make 'a speech of the antiquity of her, founded by gyants', while at midsummer 'the giants, and some wild beasts (that are constantlie kept for that purpose) are carry'd about the towne . . .'.[69] Corporations such as Nottingham, Bristol, and Southampton had figures of giants set upon the gates of the castle or city wall, leaving visitors in no doubt as to the antiquity of the place which they were entering.[70] At the same time, gigantic figures adorned the frescos and murals in palaces, cathedrals, and great houses, and provided a subject for the wall paintings in taverns and inns.[71]

Against this background, therefore, the popular traditions which celebrated the feats of some gigantic hero in the community are neither exceptional nor surprising. As with the devil, the remarkable exploits of a giant readily accounted for huge features in the landscape, either natural or man-made. Hills and rock formations, ruins and causeways, were all explained in terms of the debris left by the gargantuan figures who had once occupied the land. Like the devil of local folktale, whose stupidity allowed him to be tripped up by wily mortals, these giants of historical belief were not the threatening man-eaters of nursery lore. Their role was not so much to frighten as to be a friend and even a patron to the neighbourhood. There was a benign, sometimes almost comical, quality about them, and in their very names an air of familiarity. Thus the inhabitants of Silchester in Hampshire claimed for their own the giant Onion, a sometime resident whose coins, 'Onion-pennies', were not infrequently dug up by the plough. The village of Weston in Hertfordshire could point to the stones

[68] For a variety of the many examples of pageant giants, see *The Diary of Henry Machyn, Citizen and Merchant-Taylor of London, from A.D. 1550 to A.D. 1563*, ed. John Gough Nichols (Camden Society, 1st ser., 42, London, 1848), 33, 45, 89, 186, 201; Plot, *The Natural History of Oxford-shire*, 349; Robert Withington, *English Pageantry* (2 vols., Cambridge, Mass., 1918–26), i. 50–64; C. J. Sisson, *Lost Plays of Shakespeare's Age* (Cambridge, 1936), 168; *Records of Early English Drama: Newcastle*, ed. J. J. Anderson (Toronto, 1982), xv; *Records of Early English Drama: Norwich, 1540–1642*, ed. David Galloway (Toronto, 1984), 9.

[69] *A Relation of a Short Survey of 26 Counties*, ed. Wickham Legg, 51–2; and cf. *Records of Early English Drama: Chester*, ed. Lawrence M. Clopper (Toronto, 1979), 415. The origin of this belief was at least Ralph Higden's *Polychronicon* of the mid-fourteenth century; it was endorsed by Daniel King, *The Vale-Royall of England. Or, the County Palatine of Chester Illustrated* (London, 1656), 7–8, 12.

[70] *Itinerary of John Leland*, ed. Smith, i. 95; *Life of Marmaduke Rawdon of York*, ed. Davies, 174–5; 'Thomas Baskerville's Journeys in England', 286; Defoe, *A Tour thro' the Whole Island of Great Britain*, ed. Cole, 141.

[71] See for example, *Thomas Platter's Travels in England*, ed. Williams, 165–6; Aubrey, *Monumenta Britannica*, ed. Fowles and Legg, 477; *Diary of Henry Machyn*, ed. Nichols, 186.

in the churchyard which marked the grave of the local giant, a hero of
Robin Hood-like reputation called Jack of Legs who, 'as fame goes, lived in
a wood here'. At nearby Brent Pelham, meanwhile, there was a monument
in the church to its particular giant, Shonk. An 'old farmer . . . who valued
himself for being born in the air that Shonk breathed', explained to
Nathaniel Salmon in the 1720s how 'Shonk was a giant that dwelt in this
parish, who fought with a giant of Barkway, named Cadmus, and worsted
him; upon which Barkway hath paid a quit rent to Pelham ever since'.[72]

Ruined buildings always attracted romantic tales and the remains of
large structures were often thought, plausibly enough, once to have been
home to some evocatively named giant. Roman buildings had been 'so
very stately', observed Camden, that 'the common people will have
these . . . to be the work of gyants'. The once 'stupendious' Roman
defences which lay beyond the south gate of Leicester, for example, were
celebrated by 'the vulgar . . . as the works of giants'.[73] And medieval
castles were equally likely to be so regarded. Thus local people at
Corbridge in Northumberland told John Leland that the nearby ruin had
been the sometime residence of 'one Yoton, whom they fable to have
beene a gygant', while at Mulgrave Castle in the North Riding he was
shown the former dwelling of the legendary Wade, 'whom the people
there say to have been a gigant'. At Defford in Worcestershire the old ruin
was known locally as Coppin's Court and it was 'receaved from the forefathers of the auncient inhabitants heereabouts that one Coppin, a man
once of extraordinary estimation, was master heereof'. At Knock Castle
near Manchester locals would give 'a fabulous report of Turquin a giant
living there, kill'd by Sir Lancelot de Lake, a knight of King Arthur's',
while at Brougham Castle in Westmorland 'the country people have a
story' that Sir Lancelot had killed a 'giant of the name of Braidforth'. In
Staffordshire the remains of Healy Castle by the village of Betley were
said to have been the home of Baldwin the Giant who 'lived in it three or
four generations, as the country people express it'. Of the ruins above
Aldridge, the locals had 'a tradicion that there lived a gyant . . . and another
att a castle in Wall[sall] and that when either went from home he used to
throwe the key to the other'. Once upon a time, the story went, a throw
fell short and the key plummeted into a pit of water below where it was
found by a poor man who used it as 'a share and coulter for a plow'.[74]

[72] Camden, *Britannia*, ed. Gibson, 126; Salmon, *History of Hertfordshire*, 184, 289–90.
[73] Camden, *Britannia*, ed. Gibson, lxv; BL, Additional MS, 15917, fo. 7ʳ.
[74] *Itinerary of John Leland*, ed. Smith, i. 59, v. 57; Habington, *Survey of Worcestershire*, ed.
Amphlett, i. 187; Stukeley, *Itinerarium Curiosum*, 55; *Travels through England of Dr Richard Pococke*, ed.
Cartwright, i. 6, 31; Aubrey, *Monumenta Britannica*, ed. Fowles and Legg, 387–9. The legend at

Caverns, too, provided a natural habitat for these monstrous men. There was the giant's hole at Clifton outside Bristol, a giant's cave in the Avon gorge nearby, and another at Luckington near Malmesbury in Wiltshire. The visitor to Somerset would find the giant's lair at Poole's Hole, while Wookey Hole in Mendip was known locally as 'the gyant's table'. In the Peak District of Derbyshire, just outside Brassington, was the cave called 'Ward's hole . . . where the Giant Ward liv'd' and not far away his chair, pulpit and gravestone.[75] Given the extent of such beliefs it is hardly surprising that any large bones turned up by the plough, perhaps those of elephants brought over by the Romans or else of dinosaurs, were invariably thought to belong to the giants of old.[76] Nor is it to be wondered at that any hill or barrow was liable to be explained as the burial place of some giant, likely slain in titanic battle.[77]

Equally predictable, was the fact that causeways and large ditches were given similar associations. Oxfordshire had a number of Grim's ditches, for example, and 'the country people will tell you that this Grymes was a gyant', while the Roman road on Wheeldale Moor in the North Riding was known as Wade's Causeway after the giant and his wife who were said to have built it in an instant.[78] Similarly, the propensity of giants to hurl objects between hill tops accounted for the constitution of unusual rock formations and stone circles. Stonehenge had been known as 'the Giant's Dance' since Saxon times. Meanwhile, 'the common people tell this incredible story' that the lone boulder next to the stone circle at Stanton

Knock Castle clearly involved a confusion with that of Sir Tarquine, enemy of King Arthur, who was fabled to have lived in Manchester Castle: Richard Hollingworth, *Mancuniensis; Or, an History of the Towne of Manchester* (Manchester, 1839), 21–2. The castle of Abergavenny in Monmouthshire was built after the Norman Conquest, 'as auncient monuments and writtings make mencion', on the same spot 'where before time, a gyant called Ayres had builded a stronge forte or holde': PRO, SP12/219/17.

[75] Aubrey, *Monumenta Britannica*, ed. Fowles and Legg, 811, 1025, 1037, 1043; Childrey, *Britannia Baconica*, 45; *Life of Marmaduke Rawdon of York*, ed. Davies, 178; *The Denham Tracts*, ed. Hardy, ii. 217; Joseph Taylor, *A Journey to Edenborough in Scotland*, ed. William Cowan (Edinburgh, 1903), 19–20. Cf. *The Journeys of Celia Fiennes*, ed. Morris, 201.

[76] See, for example, Woolf, 'Of Danes and Giants', 186; Stow, *Survey of London*, ed. Kingsford, i. 292, ii. 337; Smyth, *The Berkeley Manuscripts*, ed. Maclean, iii. 193; *The Life and Times of Anthony Wood*, ed. Clark, ii. 141; Aubrey, *Monumenta Britannica*, ed. Fowles and Legg, 116, 391; Bod. Lib., MS Aubrey 1, fo. 154; *The Diary of Abraham de la Pryme*, ed. Jackson, 105, 141–2; BL, Lansdowne MS, 897, fos. 188ᵛ–189ᵛ; Leigh, *The Natural History of Lancashire, Cheshire, and the Peak*, 41; Byng, *The Torrington Diaries*, ed. Bruyn Andrews, i. 24.

[77] *Itinerary of John Leland*, ed. Smith, iii. 119; Camden, *Britannia*, ed. Gibson, 197; Enid Porter, *Cambridgeshire Customs and Folklore* (London, 1969), 186–8.

[78] *The Remains of Thomas Hearne*, ed. John Buchanan-Brown (London, 1966), 199, 205; Westwood, *Albion: A Guide to Legendary Britain*, 343–6. Cf. Addy, *Household Tales with other Traditional Remains*, 27 n.

Drew in Somerset was the quoit of the giant Hakewell; and the same 'vulgar fancy' explained the great stone in the road by Armley near Leeds, hurled by the occupant of giant's hill across the river, 'upon which stone the credulous can see the impressions of his fingers'. Typically, the large rock standing between the two Comptons in Staffordshire was said to have been thrown there by a giant from Aston, while the series of stones at Barrasford, north Tyneside, were supposed to be the legacy of a dual between 'two ancient giants'.[79]

### THE IMPACT OF PRINT

To the manuscript culture of the Middle Ages, then, can be traced the foundation of much of what passed into oral tradition, where it was to take on a life of its own. Moreover, by the early modern period these written sources were being enhanced by printed ones which would, in turn, enormously stimulate the creation and augmentation of the legendary repertoire. In particular the tremendous growth of antiquarian writings in the form of chronicles, county histories, and itineraries from the sixteenth century was responsible not only for recording much popular belief but also for helping to create and sustain it. Once again, this cautions against the notion that writing necessarily destroys memory and undermines oral tradition. Rather, it is more instructive to view it in many cases as an agent of invigoration and recreation.

A number of examples of printed history infusing oral culture are discernible. Thus local tradition in London knew the great building in Basing Lane as 'Gerrards Hall' after its supposed one-time inhabitant Gerard the Giant. When the curious John Stow went to investigate in the 1590s he was assured by the master of the house that the story was true and was advised to 'reade the great chronicles, for there he heard it'. This was a reference to the mention of Gerard in Harrison's *Historicall Description of the Iland of Britaine* which in 1577 had been included in the first part of Holinshed's *Chronicles*.[80] In the late seventeenth century, the clergyman White Kennett discovered the view among the inhabitants around Otmoor in Oxfordshire that the Roman road, Akeman Street, had run

---

[79] L. V. Grinsell, 'The Legendary History and Folklore of Stonehenge', *Folklore*, 87 (1976), 5–20; Aubrey, *Monumenta Britannica*, ed. Fowles and Legg, 46, 68; Ralph Thoresby, *Ducatus Leodiensis: Or, the Topography of the Ancient and Populous Town and Parish of Leedes* (London, 1715), 194; Plot, *The Natural History of Stafford-shire*, 397–8; *The Denham Tracts*, ed. Hardy, ii. 217. Cf. *Life and Letters of Edward Lhwyd*, 201.

[80] Stow, *A Survey of London*, ed. Kingsford, i. 348–9, ii. 353; Raphael Holinshed, *Holinshed's Chronicles of England, Scotland and Ireland* (6 vols., London, 1807–8), i. 21.

# The Unhappy Memorable Song of
## The HUNTING of
# CHEVY-CHASE

Plate 1  *The Unhappy Memorable Song of the Hunting of Chevy-Chase*. The ballad of *Chevy-Chase* was one of the most popular songs in sixteenth- and seventeenth-century England. Its several versions enjoyed widespread circulation in oral, manuscript, and printed form, demonstrating the reciprocal exchange between these three media. (National Library of Scotland, Crawford EB. 430.)

Plate 2 A drawing of the famous Elizabethan comedian, Richard Tarlton, d. 1588 (British Library, Harleian MS, 3885, fo. 19ʳ). Tarlton was famed for his rustic garb and 'mistaking words' in ridicule of country folk. 'You should ha' seene him', reminisces the stage-keeper in the Induction to Jonson's *Bartholomew Fair*.

Plate 3 Portrait of John Lacy (d. 1681) by John Michael Wright. (The Royal Collection). Lacy was the greatest mimic and character-actor of the seventeenth century. He did a brilliant imitation of a country bumpkin as well as celebrated impressions of Scotsmen and Irishmen. According to Aubrey, Lacy provided Ben Jonson with a catalogue of 'words and proverbes' from his native Yorkshire as a 'hint for clownery' in *A Tale of a Tub*. Wright depicts him here in three of his most famous stage roles: Sauny the Scot in *The Taming of the Shrew*, either Galliard or Lord Vaux in *The French Dancing Master*, and Parson Scruple in *The Cheats*.

**Plate 4** *Netherlandish Proverbs*, 1559, by Pieter Bruegel depicts around 120 popular sayings, many of which were well known throughout northern Europe during the Renaissance. In the building lower left, for example, a man can be seen 'falling between two stools'. To his right in the foreground is another 'banging his head against a brick wall' while above him a man 'armed to the teeth' is trying 'to bell the cat'. At the front centre is someone 'casting roses among swine' and to his right is a woman 'crying over spilt milk'. Towards the back right is a figure 'swimming against the tide'; in the middle at the back a man 'turns his coat according to the wind'; and in the far distance can be seen 'the blind leading the blind'. (Staatliche Museen Zu Berlin.)

**Plate 5** Portrait of John Aubrey by William Faithorne, 1666. Aubrey was much ahead of his time in the systematic interest which he took in oral traditions and popular beliefs. (Ashmolean Museum, University of Oxford.)

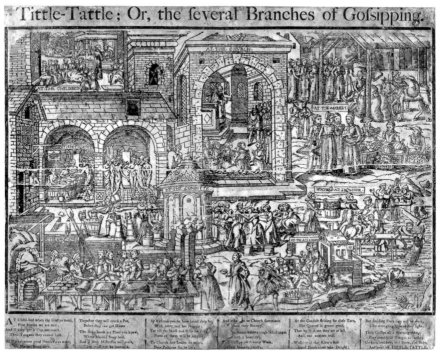

**Plate 6** *Tittle-Tattle; Or, the Several Branches of Gossipping, c.*1600. This remarkable print depicts some of the sites where women met and were said to swap gossip and news. (British Museum, Department of Prints and Drawings, BMSat 61.)

# The History of *Tom Thumbe*, the

*Little*, for his small stature surnamed,
*King* ARTHVRS *Dwarfe:*

Whose Life and aduentures containe many
strange and wonderfull accidents, published for
*the delight of merry Time-spenders.*

Imprinted at London for *Tho: Langley*. 1621.

# The mad-merry prankes of Robbin Good-fellow.

### To the tune of *Dulcina*.

Obrion in Fairy Land
King of Ghosts and shadowes there,
ᵒᶦⁿ I at his command,
t to view the night-spozts here.
at revell rout
ept about
cozner where I goe,
vill oze see,
o merry be,

Sometimes I meet them like a man,
sometimes an oze, sometimes a houn
And to a hozse I turne me can,
to trip and trot about them round.
But if to ride
We backe they stride,
Moze swift then winde away I goe,
Oze hedge and lands,
Through pooles and ponds,

---

**Plate 8** *The Mad-Merry Prankes of Robbin Good-fellow.* In the sixteenth and seventeenth centuries tales about fairies, together with much other traditional lore, were being disseminated via popular print and feeding back into oral circulation. (Pepys Library, Magdalene College, Cambridge.)

**Plate 9** *The Legend* by George Paul Chalmers, *c.*1864. Women played a very important role in imparting oral traditions to children within the home. (National Gallery of Scotland.)

**Plate 10** A sketch by Elias Ashmole of the churchyard monument at Tilney in Norfolk, 1657. It was believed by local people to be the burial place of their hero, the giant Hikifricke. (The Bodleian Library, University of Oxford, MS Ashmole 784, fo. 23ʳ.)

**Plate 11** *Rent Day* by Pieter Breughel the Younger, *c.*1618. This scene gives an impression of the ubiquity of documentation in local society by the early seventeenth century. (Burghley House, Stamford, Lincolnshire.)

**Plate 12** Detail from the 'Agas' Map of London, dated between 1561 and 1570, showing Westminster Hall and the Star Chamber. (Guildhall Library, London.)

CAP. CXXXVIII.
De iniurijs per scripta.
¶ Summę rerum tractatarum in Commenta.    CAP. 138
1 Scri

**Plate 13** Joos de Damhouder, *Praxis Rerum Criminalium* (Antwerp, 1562), 398. A rare contemporary depiction of the practice of posting up and distributing 'libels'.

# The Post of Ware:
## With a Packet full of strange Newes out of diuers Countries.
### To a pleafant new Tune.

Plate 15 *The Post of Ware: With a Packet Full of Strange Newes out of Diuers Countries.* The seventeenth century witnessed seminal developments in the public postal service. (Pepys Library, Magdalene College, Cambridge.)

Plate 16 Wenceslaus Hollar, *The World is Ruled and Governed by Opinion* (1642). Hollar's famous etching depicts the rash of polemical pamphlets printed in 1641. The verses below are signed by his associate Henry Peacham. (British Museum, Department of Prints and Drawings, BMSat 272.)

north–south across the county between Wallingford and Banbury, when it actually ran east–west through Thame and on to Bath. The origin of this error he attributed to William Camden, who had indeed published it in the sixth edition of his *Britannia* in 1607, and now the misapprehension had 'resolv'd into the oral tradition of the common people'.[81]

A good example of this process of 'feedback' is also evident in the tradition of the 'Danish yoke'.[82] One of the most potent themes in the popular memories of the past in early modern England was a strong sense of the ravages and atrocities committed by the Danish armies during their occupation from the ninth century. Hundreds of communities up and down the country harboured traditions about battles once fought between local people and the brutal armies who oppressed them. Place names and buildings, barrows and natural features of all sorts were explained in these terms. But it is doubtful that there was much continuous folk memory of such events passing in oral tradition from the time of their occurrence down to the seventeenth century when they are most plentifully recorded. Instead, the demonization of the Danes seems to be a product quite specifically of the late fifteenth century. The historian John Rous may have been responsible for initiating it in his influential *Historia Regum Angliae* which recounts the Danish conquest of Mercia. In the fields of his native Warwickshire he pointed to the red flowering dwarf elder (*Sambucus ebulus*), or walwort as it was popularly known, which marked the spots where blood had been shed. By the time that William Turner published his list of plant names in 1538, walwort was called for the first time 'danewort'. By 1590 Camden was using the name 'danesbloud' when he discovered it growing on the Bartlow Hills in Essex and found that the 'country people' knew it 'by no other name'. It has been suggested that the etymological derivation of walwort from the Old English *wealh* could imply the shedding of foreign, or specifically Welsh, blood. Could it be that Rous, whose *Historia* was fulsomely dedicated to Henry VII, replaced the association of battle grounds long regarded as the scenes of victory over the old Welsh enemy with that of a new foe in order to flatter, or not to offend, his new Tudor master? If so, he may have instigated a rich theme in English folklore which was to last for a least two centuries.[83] Credence to this theory is given by the fact that the famous

---

[81] White Kennett, *Parochial Antiquities attempted in the History of Ambrosden, Burcester, and other Adjacent Parts in the Counties of Oxford and Bucks* (Oxford, 1695), 16; William Camden, *Britannia* (6th edn., London, 1607), 267.

[82] On the concept of 'the Danish yoke', see Thomas, *The Perception of the Past*, 26; Woolf, 'Of Danes and Giants', 193–7.

[83] Westwood, *Albion: A Guide to Legendary Britain*, 103–4, drawing on Rous, *Historia Regum*

Hocktide plays performed on the second Monday and Tuesday after Easter seem also to have become widely popular from the late fifteenth century. This drama, together with the processions led through towns and symbolic fights enacted between men and women which commemorated the defeat of the Danes, must have done much to create and keep alive these traditions.[84]

Rous's writing may also have given a boost to the Danish dimension in the story of Guy of Warwick. During the fifteeenth century, the family tradition of the Beauchamps, earls of Warwick, was busy reinventing the hermitage of Kibbecliva or Gibbeclyve as 'Guy's Cliff', the place where their famous ancestor was supposed to have retreated to live a hermit's life after returning from the Holy Land. A chantry was founded there in 1422 to which Rous was appointed a chaplain in 1445. 'Guy's chapel' was added in the 1450s and in it was carved a huge statue of the great knight. Rous's *Historia*, and his now lost *Antiquity of Guy's Cliff*, contributed to a legend which had already long circulated in manuscript.[85] It was to find its way into print in the early days of the new technology: Wynkyn de Worde was publishing versions of it after 1500 and the verse romance *The Booke of the Most Victoryous Prince Guy of Warwicke* is extant in an edition of 1560. Soon after this, broadside ballads of *The Famous History* were being produced in abundance along with plays, and later chapbooks, which continued to be popular throughout the eighteenth century.[86]

*Angliae*, ed. Hearne, 1–2, 101–6; Wood, '*Survey of the Antiquities of the City of Oxford*', ed. Clark, i. 326; William Turner, *Libellus De Re Herbaria Nouus: In Quo Herbarum Aliquot Nomina Greca, Latina, & Anglica Habes* (London, 1538), sig. A4ʳ; William Camden, *Britannia* (3rd edn., London, 1590), 352.

[84] Hockday is mentioned by Rous as commemorating the 'liberation of England from Danish servitude': Rous, *Historia Regum Angliae*, ed. Hearne, 106. On these Hocktide ceremonies and plays, see John Brand, *Observations on the Popular Antiquities of Great Britain*, ed. Sir Henry Ellis (3 vols., London, 1849), i. 186–91; E. K. Chambers, *The Mediaeval Stage* (2 vols., Oxford, 1903), i. 154–6, 187, ii. 264–6; Ronald Hutton, *The Stations of the Sun: A History of the Ritual Year in Britain* (Oxford, 1996), 207–13. They were staged in Coventry as early as 1416 but do not seem to have become widely popular until later in the century: Charles Phythian-Adams, 'Ceremony and the Citizen: The Communal Year at Coventry, 1450–1550', in Peter Clark and Paul Slack (eds.), *Crisis and Order in English Towns, 1500–1700* (London, 1972), 69; Woolf, 'Of Danes and Giants', 194. For a useful discussion of the mnemonic value of ceremony and ritual, see Paul Connerton, *How Societies Remember* (Cambridge, 1989), 41–71.

[85] Rous, *Historia Regum Angliae*, ed. Hearne, xxiii–xxxvi, 97–8, 208; Kendrick, *British Antiquity*, 19, 23; Westwood, *Albion: A Guide to Legendary Britain*, 220–3; *Fragments of an Early Fourteenth-Century Guy of Warwick*, ed. Maldwyn Mills and Daniel Huws (Medium Aevum Monographs, new ser., 4, Oxford, 1974); V. B. Richmond, *The Legend of Guy of Warwick* (New York, 1996), 127–34.

[86] Ronald S. Crane, 'The Vogue of Guy of Warwick from the Close of the Middle Ages to the Romantic Revival', *Publications of the Modern Language Association*, 30 (1915), 125–94; *Bishop Percy's Folio Manuscript*, ed. J. W. Hales and F. J. Furnivall (3 vols., London, 1867–8), ii. 509–58; Margaret Spufford, *Small Books and Pleasant Histories: Popular Fiction and its Readership in Seventeenth-Century England* (London, 1981), 225–7; John Ashton, *Chapbooks of the Eighteenth Century* (London, 1882), 138–55.

So it was that during this period travellers would be shown the statue and other artefacts, both in the chapel of Guy's Cliff and at Warwick Castle, said to be associated with the hero. In the locality, meanwhile, 'the vulgar' were found to believe that Guy, like his famous Danish opponent Colebrand, had been a giant-like figure.[87] In the ballad and chapbook accounts of Guy, his exploits were said to have taken place in the reign of Athelstan and this notion may have been responsible for the reinvention of the Saxon king as a popular hero. In certain parts of the country numerous communities could be found by the seventeenth century laying claim to some glorious association with Athelstan. In towns and villages around Oxfordshire, for example, local people identified as their own the spot where he had defeated King Rollo in a famous victory. In the area around Malmesbury in Wiltshire, where tradition sited his palace, his exploits were legion. At Brokenborough was 'the seate of King Athelstan, which the inhabitants still show'; on Dane's Hill was the spot where he was supposed to have vanquished this enemy in battle; at Bishopstone was the 'hocker bench' where 'Aldermen of the hocker bench' presided every year over the Hocktide revels which celebrated the death of Harthacnut. Every Trinity Sunday the people of Long Newnton recalled in another ceremony and tradition how Althelstan had granted them their common land as a reward for service against the Danes.[88]

The Danes also stepped in to help satisfy the need for local heroes. Evidence from many communities demonstrates how tales of daring and bravery, which drew from the motifs of chivalric romance, were grafted onto this powerful theme and invested with meaning by their parochial setting. Thus in the village of Colerne, near Chippenham, they related with pride the achievement of the farmer's son of Hall Farm who, according to the 'tradition from the old people', was said to have 'shott his arrow through a hole in Colerne Park wall, and killed one of the chieftans, or generalls of the Danes'. Once again, where some kind of monument existed on which to pin a tale and renew it in the popular mind, such invented traditions were likely to endure. At Sherston near Malmesbury a famous battle between Edmund 'Ironside' and King Cnut had taken place in 1016. Onto this fact was grafted the story of one Rattlebone 'who, the tradition is, did much service against the Danes'. A little statue carved above the church porch,

---

[87] See, for example, G. R. Elton, *Policy and Police: The Enforcement of the Reformation in the Age of Thomas Cromwell* (Cambridge, 1972), 52; *Itinerary of John Leland*, ed. Smith, ii. 45–6; Camden, *Britannia*, ed. Gibson, 121–2, 512; Sir William Dugdale, *The Antiquities of Warwickshire* (London, 1656), 183, 185, 299–301, 343; *The Journeys of Celia Fiennes*, ed. Morris, 116–17; *Travels through England of Dr Richard Pococke*, ed. Cartwright, ii. 283.

[88] Camden, *Britannia*, ed Gibson, 253, 269; Bod. Lib., MS Aubrey 3, fos. 23–4, 25ᵛ, 35ʳ, 151ʳ.

actually of the fifteenth century and clearly depicting some saint or churchman, was now claimed for an effigy of their hero. By the same token, a stone
statue in the churchyard at Algarkirk in Lincolnshire was hailed by the locals,
no doubt with equally little justification, to be 'the famous count Algar,
commander of the Holland men in the many battles against the Danes'.
Meanwhile, village tradition at Overton Longueville, Huntingdonshire,
claimed that the ancient monument of an armoured knight in the church
was a Lord Longueville, 'who in fighting with the Danes near this place
received a wound in his belly, so that his entrails fell out; but wrapping them
round the wrist of his left arm, he continued the combat with his right hand
till he had killed the Danish king, and soon after fell himself'.[89]

Many towns and villages across the south of England were able to
point to a spot on which local people had once turned out to give the
marauding Danes their just deserts. Local tradition in the parish of
Charlwood, Surrey, had it that Kilman bridge derived its name 'from a
great slaughter committed on the Danish plunderers by the inhabitants of
the county of Sussex, who fell on the rear of their forces and g[a]ve them
an entire defeat'. The field behind Barton church in Bedfordshire was
called Dunstall or Danestall field, 'where, they say, the Danes had an over-
throwe in battell'. In this field, it was reported, 'doth yet grow Dane-weed,
or Danes bloud, soe called they beleve bicause the Danes bloud there spilt
did bring up this weed which here (as in some other places) will not be
destroyed'. Equally, 'dane's blood' could be shown by the locals at Gatton
in Surrey and at Yatton, near Bristol, where the plant, 'as it were, spotted
with blood', grew in abundance.[90]

Although the name 'danewort' was not recorded before the reign of
Henry VIII and 'dane's blood' was not known before 1590, they very
quickly appear to have fed into popular historical consciousness and were
soon being used to account not only for former Danish battle grounds but

---

[89] Aubrey, *Monumenta Britannica*, ed. Fowles and Legg, 807, 817; Bod. Lib., MS Aubrey 3,
fo. 104ᵛ; Stukeley, *Itinerarium Curiosum*, 22; William Pinnock, *The History and Topography of
Huntingdonshire* (London, 1822), 29 n.; Westwood, *Albion: A Guide to Legendary Britain*, 61–2. The
hero of Sherston was still faithfully remembered in the early nineteenth century: J. O. Halliwell,
*Popular Rhymes and Nursery Tales* (London, 1849), 198–9. The Rattlebone Arms in the village continues to commemorate his name.

[90] Aubrey, *History and Antiquities of the County of Surrey*, iv. 261, 217; BL, Additional MS, 6223,
fos. 11ʳ–13ᵛ; '*Survey of the Antiquities of the City of Oxford*', ed. Clark, i. 326; Camden, *Britannia*,
ed. Gibson, 352; Childrey, *Britannia Baconica*, 100. The red cliff at West Teignmouth in Devon,
where the Danes landed in 970, was said 'to memorize the bloodshed and calamaties of their
times, according to these verses: "In memory whereof, the clift exceeding red, | Doth seem
thereat again full fresh to bleed"': Tristram Risdon, *The Chorographical Description or Survey of the
County of Devon* (London, 1811), 143.

also for associated place names. Thus, the 'dane's blood' growing by Slaughterford in Wiltshire simply emphasized, if emphasis were needed, whence that village drew its name. The fields around Seckworth in Oxfordshire, also spattered with danewort, provided conspicuous corroboration, 'according to the vulgar', of the traditions surrounding the adjacent village of Danecourt. That the town of Daventry in Northamptonshire, or 'Daintrey' as the locals called it, similarly owed its name to the Danes was confirmed by 'the road hereabouts ... being over-grown with daneweed: they fancy it sprang from the blood of the Danes slain in battle, and that if upon a certain day in the year you cut it, it bleeds'.[91]

Indeed, Northamptonshire was not unusual in harbouring a fund of popular traditions about the Danes, as the county's historian John Morton was to find in the early eighteenth century. He noted the abundance of danewort growing in certain parts of the county and rejected the tradition concerning the naming of Daventry, 'there being no foundation for it in history'. He was equally dismissive of the local story that the barrow by the village of Lilbourne marked a Danish battle ground, considering 'that 'tis the way of the vulgar with us to attribute all such actions to the Danes, and that there are many such erroneous traditions'. The moorland known as Danesmoor, 'or Dunsmore (as the country people now frequently call it)', was believed to mark a similar spot as 'a constant tradition of the neigh-bour' delivered. 'The people there have a notable rhime', he reported, 'which they make the Danes say upon the point of battel.' It ran:

> If we can Pad-well overgoe, and Horestone we can see:
> Then Lords of England we shall be.

In Northampton itself, meanwhile, local tradition had it that the wide ditch surrounding the northern part of the town was first built as a defence against the Scandinavian enemy while it was they who were responsible, so 'the antientest inhabitants' told, for the entrenchment at nearby Hunsbury Hill. At the same time, the towns and villages around Rainsborough all perpetuated the communal memory that they had once been destroyed by the Danes, this 'firmly believ'd by all the neighbour-hood, upon a tradition successively handed down to them'.[92]

---

[91] Aubrey, *Monumenta Britannica*, ed. Fowles and Legg, 807; Wood, '*Survey of the Antiquities of the City of Oxford*', ed. Clark, i. 326; Stukeley, *Itinerarium Curiosum*, 107.

[92] John Morton, *The Natural History of Northamptonshire* (London, 1712), 378, 530–48. For a selection of other explanations for place names and landmarks in these terms, see *The Topographer and Genealogist*, ed. Nichols, ii. 411; Plot, *Natural History of Stafford-Shire*, 432; Aubrey, *Monumenta Britannica*, ed. Fowles and Legg, 807; BL, Sloane MS, 1899, fos. 6ʳ, 7ʳ; Defoe, *A Tour thro' the Whole Island of Great Britain*, ed. Cole, 15; John Lewis, *The History and Antiquities Ecclesiastical and Civil of*

So it was, then, that one of the most powerful historical myths in early modern England owed much of its currency to the printed stories and songs, and to the plays and annual Hocktide rituals, which were so popular between the late fifteenth and early eighteenth centuries. Another equally ubiquitous series of traditions which the Tudor dynasty and the new technology of print did much to reinvent and nourish were those of King Arthur. The fabulous Arthurian legends, made famous by Geoffrey of Monmouth and endlessly rehearsed by other monastic writers, had been popularized anew by the renaissance in chronicle and romance writing during the fifteenth century. Thomas Malory's *Morte d'Arthur*, completed in 1469, was first printed by Caxton in 1485 and would be reprinted in a furthur six editions by the mid-seventeenth century.[93] It was under the Tudors, for whom Geoffrey's Welsh Arthur had particular appeal, that his myth reached the status of a cult with the help of an outpouring of poetry, prose, and drama.[94] The dissemination of such literature was clearly widespread. The Elizabethan mason from Coventry, Captain Cox, was said to have a copy of 'king Arthurz book' in his remarkable little library of vernacular literature, while the 'book of king Arthures knights' was one that the 'poore husband-man' proposed to buy for his son in a tract of 1586. 'Shewe mee King *Arthur*, *Beuis*, or Syr *Guy*, | Those are the bookes he onely loues to buye', was Henry Parrot's view of the 'countrey-farmer'. Thus, whatever evidential basis there may have been for a historical Arthur figure, 'the many incredible stories that have been reported of this prince', lamented one contemporary, had long 'made his history little better than a romance'.[95]

In this context, too, the development of the broadside ballad must have been greatly influential in bringing historical legend to the widest possible audiences. *A Pleasaunte History of an Adventurus Knyghte of Kynges Arthurs Couurte* was printed by Richard Jones in 1566. The great balladwriter Thomas Deloney was responsible for *The Noble Actes Nowe Newly Found of Arthure of the Round Table* which was entered in the Stationers'

*the Isle of Tenet in Kent* (London, 1723), 120; Stukeley, *Itinerarium Curiosum*, 10; Salmon, *History of Hertfordshire*, 220.

   [93] Kendrick, *British Antiquity*, chs. 1–2; Kingsford, *English Historical Literature in the Fifteenth Century*; Sir Thomas Malory, *Le Morte D'Arthur* (2 vols., Everyman edn., 1906), i. viii.

   [94] Kendrick, *British Antiquity*, ch. 3; Irving Ribner, *The English History Play in the Age of Shakespeare* (2nd edn., London, 1965), ch. 8; Sydney Anglo, 'The *British History* in Early Tudor Propaganda', *Bulletin of the John Rylands Library*, 44 (1961–2), 17–48; E. K. Chambers, *Arthur of Britain* (London, 1927); R. F. Brinkley, *Arthurian Legend in the Seventeenth Century* (Balitmore, 1932).

   [95] Robert Laneham, *A Letter* (London, 1575), 34; John Ferne, *The Blazon of Gentrie* (London, 1586), ii. 23; Henry Parrot, *The Mastive, or Young-Whelpe of the Olde-Dogge* (London, 1615), sig. I1r; *Antiquities of Glastonbury*, ed. Hearne, 145.

register in June 1603. In 1598, Fynes Moryson was already describing the many monuments attributed to Arthur's name as 'famous among all ballad-makers'. ''Tis great pity', John Aubrey was later to lament, 'that so famous and great a worthie should have ever been abused, either by monkish verses, or vile painting in an alehouse'.[96]

Despite this view, however, Aubrey, who still believed that 'antiquaries, when they cannot meet with better authority, will not disdaign to give an old ballad in evidence', borrowed Elias Ashmole's copy of Robert Laneham's *A Letter* (1575), which contained a song said to be taken from 'king Arthurz book', and transcribed it into his 'Monumenta Britannica'. Meredith Lloyd had told him that at Cynllwyd near Bala in Merioneth 'the common people to this day' would show the 'heap of stones of the length of four pershes' at the foot of a great hill which they said was 'Bedd Rita Gawr' or 'the grave of Rita the Giant', slain upon that spot by King Arthur. The tale comes straight from Geoffrey of Monmouth's account of the giant Ritho of Mount Aravius, or Snowdon, who has a cloak made of the beards of the kings he has killed and taunts Arthur to shave off his. Here, it seems, is a good example of the intersection of medieval chronicle, popular print, and oral tradition. It is likely that the legend of Ritho and Arthur had been handed down by word of mouth in North Wales well before Geoffrey wrote it down in the early twelfth century. There is evidence here of unbroken oral transmission over at least seven centuries, therefore, although it is likely that the widespread influence of the printed ballad had done much to elaborate, invigorate, and keep this story fresh in the minds of people by John Aubrey's day.[97] It is interesting to consider that two of the major episodes in the *Historia* which J. S. P. Tatlock considers obviously to be drawing upon twelfth-century oral tradition, this story of Arthur and that of King Lear's foundation of Leicester, should also be among the few legends in Geoffrey that were found still to be alive in the popular memory of the early modern period.[98]

As the examples of Guy of Warwick and King Arthur demonstrate, the influence of cheap print in the form of the broadside ballads, chapbooks, and plays which poured from the presses in this period was clearly of great importance in inventing and sustaining popular versions of the past. The

---

[96] Hyder E. Rollins, 'An Analytical Index to the Ballad-Entries (1557–1709) in the Registers of the Company of Stationers of London', *Studies in Philology*, 21 (1924), 169, 183; Moryson, *An Itinerary Containing his Ten Yeeres Travell*, ii. 118; Aubrey, *Monumenta Britannica*, ed. Fowles and Legg, 543. Cf. BL, Harleian MS, 6726, fo. 244ᵛ.

[97] Bod. Lib., MS Aubrey 2, fo. 145; Aubrey, *Monumenta Britannica*, ed. Fowles and Legg, 540–3, 809; Laneham, *A Letter*, 53–4; Geoffrey of Monmouth, *Historia Regum Britanniae*, X, iii.

[98] J. S. P. Tatlock, *The Legendary History of Britain: Geoffrey of Monmouth's Historia Regum Britanniae and its Early Vernacular Versions* (Berkeley and Los Angeles, 1950), 381–2, 388–9.

content of such material was, thought George Puttenham around 1570, 'for the most part stories of old time, as the tale of *Sir Topas*, the reportes of *Beuis of Southampton, Guy of Warwicke, Adam Bell*, and *Clymme of the Clough*, and such other old romances or historicall rimes'. The most famous of these, the rhymes of Robin Hood, were again not born so much of popular oral tradition as of the literary romances written for performance among the social elite. But it was probably the widespread dissemination of his story in the famous *Gest*, which was reprinted several times during the sixteenth century, together with broadsides such as *A ballett of Robyn Hod* (1562), and the play-books informing mummings and May games, which was responsible for fixing the legend in its present form.[99]

It also ensured the place of Robin in local folklore. For Robin Hood's Bay is not known to have been so named before 1544 and his many 'strides', hills and mills, or the examples of his 'butts' which are to be found in at least six counties of England, were probably attributed no earlier.[100] His famous well with accompanying chair at St Anne's, about a mile to the north of Nottingham, is of similar date, while there is no reference to that by the side of the Great North Road between Doncaster and Pontefract before the early years of the seventeenth century.[101] Robin Hood's grave at Kirklees in the West Riding was first noted by Richard Grafton in 1565. A generation later, the early fifteenth-century tomb of Elizabeth Fitz Walter in the church at Little Dunmow, Essex, was reinvented as the resting place of Matilda the Fair, or Maid Marian, thanks to two plays by Anthony Munday, *The Downfall of Robert, Earl of Huntingdon* (1601) and its sequel *The Death* (1601), which ensured the currency of the fable well into the nineteenth century. It may also have been around this time that the

[99] George Puttenham, *The Arte of English Poesie* (London, 1589), 69; Coss, 'Aspects of Cultural Diffusion in Medieval England', 38–40; *Rymes of Robyn Hood: An Introduction to the English Outlaw*, ed. R. B. Dobson and J. Taylor (2nd edn., Stroud, 1989); Rollins, 'An Analytical Index to the Ballad-Entries', 199–200; Stephen Knight, *Robin Hood: A Complete Study of the English Outlaw* (Oxford, 1994), chs. 3–4; David Wiles, *The Early Plays of Robin Hood* (Cambridge, 1981); Hutton, *Stations of the Sun*, 270–4.

[100] Westwood, *Albion: A Guide to Legendary Britain*, 206–8. For a variety of contemporary references to these topographical landmarks, see *Elias Ashmole (1617–1692)*, ed. Josten 625, 961; 'Thomas Baskerville's Journeys in England', in HMC, *Thirteenth Report, Appendix, Part II*, 303; Aubrey, *Monumenta Britannica*, ed. Fowles and Legg, 273; Aubrey, *Natural History and Antiquities of the County of Surrey*, iii. 320; Brome, *Travels over England, Scotland and Wales*, 160, 217; *Travels through England of Dr Richard Pococke*, ed. Cartwright, ii. 271; Byng, *The Torrington Diaries*, ed. Bruyn Andrews, ii. 192.

[101] Dodsworth, *Yorkshire Church Notes*, ed. Clay, 12; *A Relation of a Short Survey of 26 Counties*, ed. Wickham Legg, 13; Brome, *Travels over England, Scotland and Wales*, 85; Charles Deering, *Nottingham Vetus et Nova* (Nottingham, 1751), 73; Robert Thoroton, *The Antiquities of Nottinghamshire*, ed. John Throsby (3 vols., Nottingham, 1790–6), ii. 164–71; J. C. Holt, *Robin Hood* (2nd edn., London, 1989), 176–9.

huge grave in Hathersage churchyard, Derbyshire, 'with one stone set up at his head, and another at his feete, but a large distance between them', was first ascribed to Little John, whereafter local people would show part of his bow hanging up in the church.[102]

The same might also be said of the legend of Bevis of Southampton. Here too, local folklore was a literary invention. Bevis's story was first told in an Anglo-Norman romance of the thirteenth century, which itself probably derived from earlier models. *Sir Bevis of Hampton* was first printed around 1503 and *The History of the Life and Death of that Noble Knight* was later to become one of the most popular chapbook tales.[103] It was no doubt as a consequence of such accounts that during the sixteenth century Arundel Castle in West Sussex was reinvented as the foundation of Bevis who was said to have named it in honour of his trusty steed. At the end of the seventeenth century this was still 'a current opinion handed down by tradition' in the locality. At Southampton, meanwhile, Arundel Tower in the town wall, probably named after Sir John Arundel, governor of the castle in the 1370s, was now similarly attributed, while the large barrow on Portsdown near Havant became Bevis' Grave. In Elizabeth's reign, Downton, south of Salisbury in Wiltshire, was already 'famous for Bevis of Southampton's house'. It is not clear when it first became possible to inspect the huge staff in Bosham church, Sussex, which the hero was said to have used in wading across the sea, but by this time Bevis, too, had become firmly established in the popular mind as a giant. 'Whatever the fable of Bevis of Southampton, and the gyants in the woods thereabouts may be deriv'd from', commented Defoe in the early eighteenth century, 'I found the people mighty willing to have those things pass for true.'[104]

## CHANGING PERSPECTIVES

Despite the longevity of many of these traditions and their endurance throughout the early modern period and beyond, they were by no means unchanging over these centuries. Memory could be short and legends might fall out of use when they ceased to conform to the aspirations and

[102] Holt, *Robin Hood*, 41; Westwood, *Albion: A Guide to Legendary Britain*, 118–19; Dodsworth, *Yorkshire Church Notes*, ed. Clay, 52; *Elias Ashmole (1617–1692)*, ed. Josten, 625. Little John's bow was later removed to Cannon Hall near Barnsley where it may still be seen: *Folklore, Myths and Legends of Britain* (London, 1973), 294.

[103] Spufford, *Small Books and Pleasant Histories*, 7–8, 225; Ashton, *Chapbooks of the Eighteenth Century*, 156–62.

[104] Westwood, *Albion: A Guide to Legendary Britain*, 63, 82; Camden, *Britannia*, ed. Gibson, 181; BL, Sloane MS, 241, fo. 54ʳ; Defoe, *A Tour thro' the Whole Island of Great Britain*, ed. Cole, 141.

sensibilities of new generations. Many traditions survived only as long as
the physical evidence remained to keep them in mind. Moreover, there
were a variety of other significant factors which served to restructure the
popular perception of the past.

In the first place, local myths were by no means unaffected by the
changes in scholarly opinion and writing about the past during the
Renaissance and thereafter. Since the popular historical imagination was
so often structured by the orthodoxies within learned and written culture,
developments in the academic view of the past inevitably had an influence upon the folk repertoire. When assiduous enquiry began into the
Saxon period and the study of old English was undertaken in earnest it
became possible to explode many of the myths invented by the medieval
chroniclers about the early history of Britain.[105] The learning was then
available to explain the origin of place names through etymological
derivation rather than charter myths and to account for the origin of
towns or monuments without reference to the work of giants or fabulous
kings. The lack of evidence for the King Arthur legends and the inconsist-
encies and implausibilities in the stories attributed to him meant that by
the second half of the seventeenth century the majority of scholarly opinion could no longer sustain most of what was claimed in his name. These
conclusions were slow to attain the status of accepted wisdom even in
learned circles and it is hardly surprising that they long endured as artefacts in 'the archaeology of the rural mind'.[106] Nevertheless, as Brutus and
the giants and Arthur and his exploits were increasingly written out of the
official version of the British past, this sounded the death knell for the
hold of such legends upon folk tradition, even if their demise was to be
long and drawn out.

If changing antiquarian opinion played one important part in helping
eventually to revise the popular view of the past, then the long-term
impact of the Reformation played another. Not for Protestants the
medieval sermon with its illustrative exemplum, its legends of saints
delivered as truth, its mixing of historical anecdote with the stories from
Scripture. The pulpit, which had formerly been such an important instrument in inventing and disseminating fabulous tales of former ages, began
to turn its back on such things in the sixteenth century. They were

---

[105] On the development in academic history, see Kendrick, *British Antiquity*, chs. 7–8; F. Smith
Fussner, *The Historical Revolution: English Historical Writing and Thought, 1580–1640* (London, 1962);
May McKisack, *Medieval History in the Tudor Age* (Oxford, 1972); David C. Douglas, *English
Scholars, 1660–1730* (2nd edn., London, 1951).

[106] Phrase of John Fowles from introduction to Aubrey, *Monumenta Britannica*, ed. Fowles and
Legg, 609; reprinted as 'The Great Amateur of Archeology', *Natural History* (August, 1982),
18–24.

despised instead as the fabrications of Catholicism, a signal illustration of the way in which the old Church had corrupted and diluted the word of God. 'In our forefathers tyme', wrote Roger Ascham, 'whan papistrie, as a standyng poole, couered and ouerflowed all England, fewe bookes were read in our tong, sauyng certaine bookes of cheualrie . . . made in monasteries, by idle monkes, or wanton chanons: as one for example, *Morte Arthure.*' Even now, thought Reginald Scot in Elizabeth's reign, the papists were perpetuating such things, 'histories . . . so grosse and palpable, that I might be thought as wise in going about to confute them, as to answer the stories of Frier Rush, Adam Bell, or the Golden Legend'. At the end of the seventeenth century, Abraham de la Pryme repeated the, by then long familiar, denunciation of saints' legends as the 'idle storys and ridiculous inventions' of popery.

Tis a pretty romance to see what is recounted of St Frances's cord, the seapular of St Antony, St Bridgit, and other such favourites of heaven. He that has but read the atchivements of these may excuse the perusal of *Bevis of Southampton*, of *Guy earl of Warwick*, of *K. Arthur*, the *Seven Champions* or *Quevedo Visions*: for these are nothing to compare to the former either for the rair invention, wonderfull surprises or performance of impossibilitys . . .[107]

Together with the long-term consequences of the Renaissance and the Reformation there were other events in this period, no less dramatic and formative, which had a significant impact in reorientating the major reference points in the topography and chronology of the popular historical imagination. For these centuries took an enormous toll on precisely the kind of monuments and artefacts which were so crucial in inspiring and sustaining popular tradition. In particular, the break with Rome and the civil wars of the mid-seventeenth century were responsible between them for the destruction of an immense amount of ecclesiastical art and architecture. The iconoclasm and sheer vandalism which characterized these episodes denuded parish churches and other public buildings of so many of the wall paintings and windows, statues, and carvings in which people had beheld their past. It was not simply that preachers no longer recounted the lives of saints from the pulpit, but the shrines of these worthies were desecrated, their holy wells filled in, and their images erased from the fabric of religious life. In the way of such things, once the visual representations disappeared so the legends which they had evoked faded from memory.[108]

---

[107] Thomas, *The Perception of the Past*, 10; Roger Ascham, *The Scholemaster* (London, 1570), fo. 27ʳ; Reginald Scot, *The Discouerie of Witchcraft* (London, 1584), 498; BL, Lansdowne 897, fo. 128ʳ.
[108] Margaret Aston, *England's Iconoclasts* (Oxford, 1988); Paul Slack, 'Religious Protest and Urban Authority: The Case of Henry Sherfield, Iconoclast', in Derek Baker (ed.), *Schism, Heresy*

The zeal of the Cromwellian army was especially assiduous in finishing off much of what had managed to survive the iconophobia of the sixteenth century. Thus the Glastonbury thorn, for example, was destroyed by 'the malice and fury of the late wars'. Parish churches across the country were desecrated and looted, their monuments destroyed and their treasures dispersed. Many of the great cathedrals suffered a tragic loss of their beautiful imagery in which the past had been so vividly portrayed. At Canterbury the stained glass windows together with much of the internal fabric were completely smashed; at Chichester statues were broken and pictures defaced; at Lichfield tapestries were torn down; at Wells much of the frontage was badly damaged. Typically, it was reported from Lincoln early in the 1660s that over the west door 'were four or five pictures, but broken down in the late troubles', and 'the tombs in this church, as in most other, are very much defac'd'.[109]

This is what John Aubrey meant when he lamented that 'gunpowder' had destroyed so much of the popular culture and traditional belief with which he had grown up as a boy 'before the late wars'. Repeatedly he lamented the destruction wrought by the 'barbarous soldiers', the 'puritanicall zealotts', and by the 'fanatique rage of the late times'. He marked with sadness the old trees which had been cut down, the stained glass shattered, and the ancient buildings razed to the ground. Among the many old customs and beliefs which he remembered from childhood and which were now rapidly disappearing, was the rich folklore surrounding the saints. Even in the 1630s it had been the preserve of 'old men' who remembered the days before Protestant reforms had taken their toll on the hagiographic tradition and by the Restoration period a new generation was reaching maturity for whom such things were a distant shadow.[110]

Equally, many features in the natural landscape which had been so important as prompts to parochial legend were assaulted by a puritan zeal which saw them, not without some justification, as an inspiration to 'popish' tradition. Thus the locally famous rock-houses in the duke of

*and Religious Protest* (Studies in Church History, 9, Cambridge, 1972), 295–302; John Morrill, 'William Dowsing, the Bureacratic Puritan', in John Morill, Paul Slack, and Daniel Woolf (eds.), *Public Duty and Private Conscience in Seventeenth-Century England* (Oxford, 1993), esp. 188–203; David Underdown, *Revel, Riot and Rebellion: Popular Politics and Culture in England, 1603–1660* (Oxford, 1985), 139–40, 177–8.

[109] Childrey, *Britannia Baconica*, 36; Charles Carlton, *Going to the Wars: The Experience of the British Civil Wars, 1638–1651* (London, 1992), 276–8, 283–4; Edward Browne, 'Journal of a Tour in Derbyshire', in *Sir Thomas Browne's Works*, ed. Wilkin, i. 25.

[110] Hunter, *John Aubrey and the Realm of Learning*, 166; Aubrey, 'Remaines of Gentilisme and Judaisme', in *Three Prose Works*, ed. Buchanan-Brown, 162–3, 207.

Newcastle's park near Nottingham were ruined for this reason. In the mid-eighteenth century a man in his nineties told Charles Deering 'that he had heard his father say: "that in time of the Civil War, the Round-heads (for so he called the parliamentary party) had demolished a great part of the rock-houses in the park under pretence of their abhorence of popery"'. Throughout the country there were various huge boulders, commonly called 'rocking stones', which, although they could be made to sway with the force of just one finger, could not actually be moved off their spot by any number of men. They had been the source of much fable, like 'the stone of Ambrosius' in Cornwall, but this, together with its like near Balvaird in Fife, were among those destroyed by Cromwell's men with the 'notion of these works being superstitious matters'. In at least one case, however, such disruptions were less the reaper of tradition than the midwife. The two great stones in a meadow between Sutton and Hereford were mysteriously moved twelve paces 'in the late civil wars, about the year 1652'. When they were later replaced it took nine yoke of oxen to drag them, 'which gave occasion to a common opinion, that they were carry'd thither by the devil'.[111]

At the same time, events such as the Civil War were instrumental in creating a new series of battle grounds and symbolic sites which helped to supplant some of the old landmarks in the mental map of the past. These dramatic episodes threw up a fresh set of heroes and villains and provided the raw materials with which to construct entirely different myths about the past into the eighteenth century and beyond. The 1640s and 1650s may have been instrumental, for example, in helping to replace the Danes as the great evil responsible for the ruin of buildings with other bogey figures, such as Oliver Cromwell. A blackened image of Cromwell was deliberately fostered after the Restoration and only a small imaginative leap was required to lay responsibility for all the wartime destruction at his door. Throughout the Georgian and Victorian periods travellers and antiquaries were to find that the notion of Cromwell as the natural destroyer of all castles and old buildings had permeated deep into folk memory. By this time, one series of myths and dating tools had been subsumed in the popular mind by another.[112]

This was certainly the experience of John Byng in his travels around England and Wales in the 1780s and early 1790s. Byng shared, with the

---

[111] Deering, *Nottingham Vetus et Nova*, 189; William Stukeley, *Stonehenge: A Temple Restor'd to the Druids* (London, 1740), 49; Camden, *Britannia*, ed. Gibson, 581, and cf. Defoe, *A Tour thro' the Whole Island of Great Britain*, ed. Cole, 449.

[112] Alan Smith, 'The Image of Cromwell in Folklore and Tradition', *Folklore*, 79 (1968), 17–39; *The Denham Tracts*, ed. Hardy, i. 95; Briggs, *A Dictionary of British Folk-Tales*, iv. 25–7, 52–3.

benefit of a further century of hindsight, Aubrey's sense of the civil war years as amounting to a fundamental disruption and discontinuity in British social life, both in terms of the destruction of the built environment and the instigation of processes of national incorporation which were undermining distinctive regional and local cultures. 'Oh that a critical tourist had minutely described, before the civil wars, the state of the castles, and of the religious remains, and of the mode of living of the nobility, and gentry,' he lamented, 'er the former were dismantled, the monuments of religion demolish'd; and that the entrance of folly, by high roads, and a general society had introduced one universal set of manners, of luxury, and of expense'. In particular he was witness to the fact that the memory of a demonized Cromwell was now firmly fixed in the popular mind. 'Whenever I enquire about ruins I allways get the same answer', he noticed, 'that it was some papish place, and destroy'd by Oliver Cromwell, to whose share is laid even much more devastation than he really committed'. This was typically his finding at the ruined castle on Beacon Hill above Eynsham in Oxfordshire, as also at the remains of Pontefract Castle where the gardeners 'explained, or invented history very well'. At Barnard Castle in County Durham he was 'shown about by a fellow, who dealt out all the old stories of O. Cromwell', while at Shifnal in Shropshire, 'they spake here of Cromwell, of his cannen balls, and of his attacks upon the castle'. Ultimately he found it just too tedious, at every castle he came upon, 'to detail the demolitions, real or false, of O. Cromwell'.[113]

The common notion that any such ruin had formerly been 'some papish place' highlighted another interesting example of telescoping in the popular view of the past. For clearly the country folk whom Byng encountered were generally liable to confuse and conflate the legacy of destruction left by Oliver Cromwell, the destroyer of castles, with his namesake Thomas Cromwell who, at the Reformation, had implemented the dissolution of religious houses. Thus at an old deserted castle in the manor of Wingfield, Derbyshire, his guide 'spake of the siege it sustain'd in the civil wars; shew'd every rent in the walls as if made by cannon balls; and was puzzled, as all countrymen are, about the two Cromwells; the destroyer of monasteries, and the destroyer of castles'. Similarly, at Crowland Abbey in Lincolnshire, ruined at the Reformation, his guide showed him the destruction which, he said, 'was owing to O. Cromwell'. The ruin at Portland on the Dorset coast was presumably some kind of

---

[113] Byng, *The Torrington Diaries*, ed. Bruyn Andrews, i. 6, 284, ii. 29, 332, iii. 30, 68, 138, 272. Cf. Stukeley, *Itinerarium Curiosum*, 119; *Travels through England of Dr Richard Pococke*, ed. Cartwright, i. 56–7, 63, 88, ii. 216.

religious foundation for it was known locally as 'the vicar's house, of which no particular history is to be procur'd; but the old talk of Oliver Cromwell'. In general, traditions of Cromwell now seem to have loomed large in the memories of many communities. At the church in Faringdon, Oxfordshire, the 'voluble clerk' was eager to regale Byng with 'all the old stories of O. Cromwell, of loss of brasses, and demolition of tombs'. The innkeeper in Wansford, Northamptonshire, directed him to an old house a couple of miles distant where Cromwell was said to have resided; the bones in the chapel there were supposedly his, although Byng thought them 'none of Noll's I dare say'. At Little Bromwich in Warwickshire he was shown various relics and antiquities left from the days of the Lord Protector.[114]

Byng may also have stumbled somewhat unwittingly upon another change in the nature of the folklore of the sixteenth and seventeenth centuries in terms of the importance which such stories had in the lives and perceptions of their tellers. In 1789 he found himself at Mountsorrel in Leicestershire and heard the local tradition as to how it acquired its name. It told of a giant in some versions, or devil in others, by the name of Bell who mounted a sorrel horse at the place ever after called Mountsorrel. From there he had leapt a whole mile to the town now known as One-leap, or Wanlip; and from thence another mile to Birstall, so named because he burst himself and his horse; before finally jumping a third mile upon which he expired and was there buried at Bell's-grave, or Belgrave. Byng seems to have taken this anecdote seriously as an 'old popular tradition', and it is certainly the kind of tale which was once earnestly believed and told. But Byng's contemporary, the antiquary Francis Grose, was surely much more astute in recognizing this as something of a joke, perhaps one contrived in the recent past, 'calculated to ridicule those tellers of miraculous stories'. Such credulous tellers even had a name: 'shooters in the long bow'. Thus, by this time, even if 'country people' liked to tell such stories, it was as liable to be for reasons of amusement as much as sober attempts to explain local history. Even in the 1690s Edmund Gibson had been prepared to give popular beliefs about King Arthur the benefit of the doubt in this respect. The 'humour' of 'the vulgar', he said, 'to dedicate many unaccountable monuments to the memory of that hero' was 'not so much (as some have imagin'd) out of ignorance and credulity, as a kind of rustick diversion'.[115]

---

[114] Byng, *The Torrington Diaries*, ed. Bruyn Andrews, i. 99, 253, ii. 198–9, 220, 332, iii. 221.

[115] Ibid., ii. 83; Francis Grose, *A Provincial Glossary with a Collection of Local Proverbs and Popular Superstitions* (London, 1789), sig. O4ᵛ; Camden, *Britannia*, ed. Gibson, 628–9, quoted in Thomas, *The Perception of the Past*, 7.

The emergence of a mythologized Oliver Cromwell as one figure through whom all that was ancient and unusual in the landscape could be accounted for and explained, demonstrates the way in which historical memory was short. As in all circumstances where such memory is purveyed by word of mouth and accrues around visible remains, it is liable to be preserved only as long as the intellectual inheritance of eldest inhabitants endures and the physical survival of antique monuments permits.

Popular tales about the past are constantly being invented and reinvented, changing over time to meet new circumstances and to help make sense of a shifting environment. So much of that tradition recorded by folklorists in rural England during the nineteenth century which was believed to be the bequest of centuries or even millennia was actually of quite recent inception. And most of what was regarded as the pure fruit of oral transmission, unadulterated by the contaminating influence of the written word, was in fact the hybrid product of generations of cross-fertilization between oral, scribal, and printed sources. In this context, as in others, writing was not the threat to oral culture so often assumed by the post-Enlightenment mind. Rather, literary influences fed into the semi-lettered repertoire of the people, nourishing, sustaining, and making anew.

# 5
## Local Custom, Memory, and Record

We old men are old chronicles, and when our tounges go they are not clocks to tell only the time present, but large books unclasped; and our speeches, like leaves turned over and over, discover wonders that are long since past.

*The Great Frost* (1608), in *Social England Illustrated*, ed. Andrew Lang (London, 1903), 166.

Verbal reports we experimentally find so very inconstant and apt to err, and misrepresent things, done even in our own time and very neighbourhood, either by concealing the truth of narrations, or adding to them; and of this, indeed, common sense is a proper judge. Nay, why (if this be otherwise) do men take such wondrous care about their deeds and legal evidences, which concern their temporal estates only, if writing be not more certain and less apt to err than words?

John Evelyn, *The History of Religion*, ed. R. M. Evanson (2 vols., London, 1850), i. 425.

ANOTHER example of the relationship between oral and written culture in sixteenth- and seventeenth-century England is that of local custom. For the majority of people in this period one of the most important sets of traditions with which they grew up was the customary law of their community. This amounted to a body of knowledge, a set of rules and regulations, and a series of practices and rituals which defined and expressed the economic and social administration of their particular locality, trade, or institution. Unlike the imaginative traditions considered in the previous two chapters, the remembrance and preservation of custom was crucial to the livelihoods and material well-being of those whom it affected.

In manors, parishes, and boroughs throughout the country at this time, the legal, economic, and social relationships between landlords and tenants, masters and apprentices, clergymen and their flocks, or a corporation and its citizens were governed by customary rules and regulations which determined the rights and obligations of all parties. These customs might dictate the terms of tenancy and ownership, the occupational structure of a trade, the value of rents and tithes, or the amount and usage of common lands. They might act differently upon rich and poor, men and women, young and old. In both rural and urban areas, agricultural regions and industrialized communities they comprised a collection of rules and a body of lore which structured the practices and rhythms of daily life.[1]

Customs enjoyed full force at law so long as they could be shown to be 'reasonable', consonant with common right, binding upon those to whom they applied, certain and consistent over time, and anciently used.[2] Provided that it fulfilled these criteria, a local custom could not be broken, nor could it be overrridden by the national common law. Thus, in theory at least, for those such as the customary tenants of manors, the scale of their rents, the amount of the fines which they paid on the transfer of their leases, the extent to which their beasts could graze on the common land, and their rights of gleaning and extraction within the lordship were all matters determined not merely by vague convention or the will of the lord, but by the precise terms of their copyhold tenancies, or by prescriptive right established through long usage.

It followed from this that customary law and practice were highly local. 'It is an olde prouerbe, "Lawe and Countrie"', recorded John Marbeck, 'for euerie region hath certaine customes of their owne, which cannot easilie be chaunged.'[3] Each liberty and jurisdiction was likely to have a

---

[1] For some recent discussions of the many and varied contexts in which customary tenures and laws governed social and economic relationships, see C. E. Searle, 'Custom, Class Conflict and Agrarian Capitalism: The Cumbrian Customary Economy in the Eighteenth Century', *Past and Present*, 110 (1986), 106–33; R. W. Hoyle, 'An Ancient and Laudable Custom: The Definition and Development of Tenant Right in North-Western England in the Sixteenth Century', *Past and Present*, 116 (1987), 24–55; Louis A. Knafla, 'Common Law and Custom in Tudor England: Or, "The Best State of the Commonwealth"', in Gordon J. Schochet (ed.), *Law, Literature and the Settlement of Regimes* (Washington, 1990), 171–86; Donald R. Kelley, '"Second Nature": The Idea of Custom in European Law, Society and Culture', in Anthony Grafton and Ann Blair (eds.), *The Transmission of Culture in Early Modern Europe* (Philadelphia, 1990), 131–72; E. P. Thompson, 'Custom, Law and Common Right', in his *Customs in Common* (London, 1991), 97–184; Tim Stretton, 'Women, Custom and Equity in the Court of Requests', in Jenny Kermode and Garthine Walker (eds.), *Women, Crime and the Courts in Early Modern England* (London, 1994), 170–89; Andy Wood, 'Custom, Identity and Resistance: English Free Miners and their Law c.1550–1800', in Paul Griffiths, Adam Fox, and Steve Hindle (eds.), *The Experience of Authority in Early Modern England* (Basingstoke, 1996), 249–85.

[2] Charles Calthrope, *The Relation betweene the Lord of a Mannor and the Coppy-Holder his Tenant* (London, 1635), 21–3; Sir Edward Coke, *The Compleate Copy-Holder* (London, 1641), 68–75; Sir William Blackstone, *Commentaries on the Laws of England* (4 vols., London, 1765–9), i. 76–8; Charles Watkins, *Treatise on Copyholds* (London, 1797), 15. For a recent discussion, see J. W. Wellwood, 'Custom and Usage', in *Halsbury's Laws of England* (4th edn., London, 1975), xii. 1–60.

[3] John Marbeck, *A Booke of Notes and Common Places* (London, 1581), 270.

quite specific and unique set of customs grounded in the soil. They were as distinctive and defining as the physical landmarks and topographical features of the immediate environment, and as circumscribed as the legends and romantic tales which so often attached to them. This made for a bewildering diversity, a myriad of individual communities each with their own particular code and conduct, a plethora of the knowledge systems which governed life. Even within 'communities', geographically defined, there could be an immense variety of practice in this respect since the land of two or more manors could be intermixed, subjecting near neighbours to very different customary regulations. At the same time factors such as terms of tenancy, gender, or occupation variously determined the extent to which individuals were governed by local laws. 'Should I goe about to make a catalogue of severall customes', wrote the lawyer Sir Edward Coke in 1641, 'I should with Sisiphus *saxum volvere*, undertake an endless piece of worke . . .'[4]

Customs, then, served to prescribe the sense of place and define the limits of belonging. To owe duties and receive rights by virtue of the customary law of a locality was to be part of it; to know and practise its highly individual ways was integral to a psychological identification with the neighbourhood and to the definition of self. As with many other forms of local knowledge, custom was often intimated and transmitted most immediately by oral tradition and practical demonstration. It may also have had some existence in writing, but its principal means of communication was more likely to be recitation and emulation down the generations. Here, as in other contexts, the recall and the example of ancient inhabitants was of signal importance. The experience of elders provided a vital link between the past and the present: they were the repositories of local precedent and the custodians of communal memory.

This chapter seeks to explore the relationship between oral and written transmission in the communication of customary law. It examines custom as spoken word and lived experience and seeks to show how this form of tradition contributed to the fabric of life and the sense of belonging in many communities. It also seeks to gauge the role played by writing in the preservation and articulation of custom and to suggest that the written word assumed ever greater importance in this context during the course of the seventeenth century.

---

[4] Coke, *The Compleate Copy-Holder*, 69–70.

## CUSTOM AND TRADITION

'In Europe', it has been said, 'the distinction between law and custom is ultimately based on what was written and what was not.'[5] Custom was local, founded upon practice, whereas law was a codified system which was promulgated over a wider area. In sixteenth- and seventeenth-century England, contemporaries defined the particular customs of local jurisdictions, as they did the general customs of the realm which made up the common law, to be laws 'unwritten', by which they meant non-statutory or not matters of record. In the standard formulation, a custom was said to be 'a law, or right, not written, which being established by long use and the consent of our ancestors, hath been and is daily practised'.[6] Samuel Carter's late seventeenth-century discussion of parochial customs was taken directly from Sir John Davies's definition of the common law in 1612: 'A custom which hath obtained the force of a law, is always said to be *jus non scriptum*, for it cannot be made or created, either by charter or by parliament, which are acts reduced to writing, and are always matter of record: but being only matter of fact, and consisting in use and practice, it can be recorded and registered no where but in the memory of the people.'[7]

It was only the 'memory of the people', therefore, which could determine the validity of a custom. The condition for its legitimacy, that it be consistent, binding, and anciently used, was that it applied 'time out of mind to which the memory of no man is to the contrary': that is, that no one had known it to be any different within his or her lifetime or within the lifetime of any ancestor, as it had been reported. The actual longevity of the custom was immaterial in the view of the lawyer Charles Calthrope. What was cucial was 'that no man then in life, hath not heard any thing, nor know any proof to the contrary . . . for the number of yeares makes not the matter, but the memory of man'. If, on the other hand, 'any chance to be alive, that remembreth the contrary, then such prescription must give place to such proofe'. In 1607 the civilian John Cowell commented that if a custom was to be decided at common law 'by witnesses', it was sufficient 'if two or more can depose, that they heard their fathers

---

[5] Jack Goody, *The Logic of Writing and the Organization of Society* (Cambridge, 1986), 129.

[6] For examples of this definition, see John Cowell, *The Interpreter: Or Booke Containing the Signification of Words* (Cambridge, 1607), sig. V4ʳ; Coke, *The Compleate Copy-Holder*, 68; Richard Gough, *The History of Myddle*, ed. David Hey (Harmondsworth, 1981), 64; R. B. Fisher, *A Practical Treatise on Copyhold Tenure* (London, 1794), 34.

[7] Samuel Carter, *Lex Custumaria: Or, a Treatise of Copy-hold Estates* (2nd edn., London, 1701), 24–5; J. G. A. Pocock, *The Ancient Constitution and the Feudal Law* (Cambridge, 1957), 32–3.

say, that it was a custome all their time, and that their fathers heard their fathers also say, that it was likewise a custome in their time'.[8]

Thus, customs could not be established by written title but were born out of prescriptive rights and preserved in oral transmission and continual usage. Nor were they subsequently codified to provide a written guide to their use, there being neither the need nor the ability to do so. In London, for example, there were once said to be so many 'liberties, priviledges, and customes' that 'no man can remember them all to set them downe in writing being only recorded by mouth'.[9] In some cases, a charter or grant may have bestowed certain privileges on the inhabitants of a manor or borough which by continual exercise over time had become customary rights. But such documents were often unspecific as to whom precisely they entitled and what exactly they entailed. At best they established the basis of what became over time a much more complex fabric of densely woven rights and usages. These were fashioned and elaborated in the exercise of everyday social relations, in the reciprocities between landlord and tenant, citizen and corporation, which were constantly adapted and renegotiated over the centuries. Indeed, one of the virtues of custom being only partially written was that it allowed for such flexibility, for subtle changes over time to be accommodated without fear of contradiction from the records of past practice.[10]

Custom, then, was 'never fact. It was ambience.' It served to structure a lived environment of 'unwritten beliefs, sociological norms, and usages asserted in practice but never enrolled in any by-law'.[11] It was the foundation of a world which was informed by oral tradition and expressed in repeated exercise. Customs were the intellectual property of their users, and only those users really knew what they were. For many people, therefore, this gave the ordering of experience a fundamentally referential and

---

[8] Calthrope, *The Relation betweene the Lord of a Mannor and the Coppy-Holder his Tenant*, 18–19; Cowell, *The Interpreter*, sig. V4ʳ.

[9] 'The Ancient Customes and Approved Usages of the Honourable City of London', in *The City Law* (London, 1647), 20 (I am grateful to Craig Muldrew for this reference). In the bibliography of William Camden, *Britannia*, ed. Edmund Gibson (London, 1695), *The City Law* is said to have been 'translated out of an ancient MS'.

[10] On the failure of written evidence to record the more complex reality of customary practice, especially concerning customs of common right, see Jean Birrell, 'Common Rights in the Medieval Forest: Disputes and Conflicts in the Thirteenth Century', *Past and Present*, 117 (1987), 24–5; E. P. Thompson, 'The Grid of Inheritance: A Comment', in Jack Goody, Joan Thirsk, and E. P. Thompson (eds.), *Family and Inheritance: Rural Society in Western Europe, 1200–1800* (Cambridge, 1976), 337, 342–3, 352; J. M. Neeson, *Commoners: Common Right, Enclosure and Social Change in England, 1700–1820* (Cambridge, 1993), 77–80.

[11] Thompson, 'Custom, Law and Common Right', *Customs in Common*, 100, 102.

retrospective quality. Custom pervaded the routines of livelihood with the ambience of tradition. Practices were allowed because they had been anciently used; restrictions were imposed because time had honoured them; rituals were enacted because precedent dictated. In a fundamental sense, difficult to imagine today, the understanding of the past infused and informed the working of the present.

So, for example, the endurance of symbolic title deeds. Before the thirteenth century, it was common for the crown to confirm the granting of land to a subject by the giving of a sod of earth or other emblematic object as proof of title. A *factum*, or 'deed', was no more than a phyiscal act of conveyance which, together with the spoken words accompanying it, were sufficient evidence for its legitimacy both in law and in practice. But the reign of Edward I saw sustained demands for written proof of the rights over property. The famous, if apocryphal, story of Earl Warenne producing before the *quo warranto* judges a rusty old sword granted to his ancestors at the Norman Conquest and claiming 'This is my warrant!' was an elegiac evocation of a system of proof based upon word, action, and symbol at the very moment of its replacement by one based upon writing. Henceforth a 'deed' was a sealed document.[12]

Symbolic title 'deeds' endured, nevertheless, into the early modern period, at least in a vestigial form. The manor of Sockburn was held from the bishop of Durham by virtue of an ancient falchion. These terms of tenure were said to date from the reign of Richard I although the first certain reference to them is at the end of the fourteenth century. In a ceremony which lasted until 1826 successive lords of the manor would present this symbolic sword to every new bishop who crossed the river Tees on his first entry to the diocese. Together with swords, horns were the most common symbols of tenure. Thus, in the thirteenth century, Walter Agard had claimed to hold by inheritance the office of escheator and coroner through the whole honour of Tutbury and the bailiwick of Leek in Staffordshire, 'for which office he could produce no evidences, charter or other writing, but only a white hunter's horn' richly decorated and adorned. The depositions taken from some ancient inhabitants of Taxal, Derbyshire, in 1720 confirm that the manor continued to be held in the

---

[12] M. T. Clanchy, *From Memory to Written Record: England, 1066–1307* (2nd edn., Oxford, 1993), 35–6. For a good example, see Thomas Blount, *Fragmenta Antiquitatis: Antient Tenures of Land, and Jocular Customs of some Mannors* (London, 1679), 18–19: 'In King Henry the third's time, Walter de Plompton held certain lands in Plompton in the parish of Kingsbury and county of Warwick by a certain weapon, called a Danish axe, which being the very charter whereby the said land was given to one of his ancestors, hung up for a long time in the hall of the capital messuage, in testimony of the said tenure.'

seventeenth century by the blowing of such a horn on Midsummer's Day at the high rock called Windgather. And the manorial lord remained bound to perform the service of holding the royal stirrup and rousing the stag should a monarch ever come hunting in Macclesfield Forest. Such ceremonial services were common, and sometimes enduring, terms of tenure. The manor of Wimble in Cambridgeshire had been held since the thirteenth century on the terms that its lord would perform the duties of official cup-bearer at coronations. In 1660 the then incumbent, Lord Allington, was still waiting on Charles II in this capacity. Equally, symbolic rents such as garlands of flowers, roses, or peppercorns, from whence the current expression, remained common. In 1546 the manor of Elston in Nottinghamshire was said still to be held for an annual rent of a pound of cumin seed, two pairs of gloves, and three steel needles.[13]

By the same token, copyhold tenants in some manors only retained their lands by the performance of certain services which were hangovers from the days of serfdom. At Hecham in Norfolk, the twenty-four customary tenants had formerly been required to work for the manorial lord for one day per week for a period after Michaelmas in return for payment of one corredy at noon and one loaf of bread in the evening. Similar customs were once maintained in the manor of Fiskerton cum Morton, Nottinghamshire. Here 'natives and cottagers' had worked 'boon days' for the lord; customary tenants provided men to clean his dam at Fiskerton mill; fines were exacted for offences and misdemeanours of all kinds. At Ladbroke in Warwickshire each tenant had been required to pay annual 'swarf money' on pain of a significant forfeit: on the appointed day, 'before the rising of the sun, the party must go thrice about the cross and say "the swarf-money", and then take witness, and lay it in the hole'.[14]

Manorial courts could be instrumental in the perpetuation of such peculiar customary rituals in their insistence that archaic forms of suit be paid to them as conditions of tenancy. So the tenants of Rochford in Essex preserved their rights only by attendance at a peculiar tribunal, 'vulgarly called the lawless court', held once a year in the middle of the night. It was described by John Norden in 1595 as:

---

[13] William Camden, *Britannia*, ed. Richard Gough (3 vols., London, 1789), iii. 114; Jennifer Westwood, *Albion: A Guide to Legendary Britain* (London, 1985), 341–2; W. C. Hazlitt, *Tenures of Land and Customs of Manors* (London, 1874), 285, 309, 329–30; Blount, *Fragmenta Antiquitatis*, 25, 78, 87. Cf. John Smyth, *The Berkeley Manuscripts*, ed. Sir John Maclean (3 vols., Gloucester, 1883–5), i. 268, iii. 148, 302.

[14] Blount, *Fragmenta Antiquitatis*, 146, 153–4, 156. On such services, see G. C. Homans, *English Villagers of the Thirteenth Century* (Cambridge, Mass., 1941), ch. 18.

a courte of a straunge custome, for it is kepte the Wednesday after Michaels day, after midnighte, begun and ended before the sune riseth at a place in the feyldes called Kings Hill, a hill not exceding in a moll hill in quantetie. The stewarde writeth only by the lighte of a lanterne, not with an ordinarie pen but with a coale, the baylife calling the tenauntes with as softe and lowe voyce as posseblie can pronounce their names, and procedeth to the chardge in all polletique secrecie, to the ende the tenauntes may make defaulte, whoe for feare crie all at once, "Here, Here!", for that therby they may loose therr landes which they holde by their suyte at this courte. This straunge seruice is layde upon that lande which holdeth of this honour, in perpetuall memorie of the rebellion of their auncestors against the kinge as it seemeth.[15]

Throughout this period and beyond the manorial court leet of Combe Keynes in Dorset, and all the rights which it upheld, would have been abolished according to the customs of the manor, if a tithingman had not done suit at neighbouring Winfrith. He was obliged to repeat certain 'incoherent lines' there, before paying threepence and departing 'without saying another word'.

> With my white rod,
> And I am a fourth post,
> That three pence makes three,
> God bless the king and the lord of the franchise.
> Our weights and our measures are lawful and true,
> Good-morrow, Mr. steward; I have no more to say to you.[16]

In 1690 Sir William Temple commented that there were still such rhymes used in 'some deeds or conveyances of land' and 'have been so since the Conquest'.[17] On certain manors they accompanied the ceremonies which upheld a widow's customary right of 'free-bench', for example. At East and West Enborne in Berkshire, at Torr in Devon and a number of other West Country manors, a widow would forfeit her right to inherit her husband's copyhold tenancy, if she committed 'incontinency' with another man. The right could only be redeemed 'if she come into the next court held for the mannor, riding backward on a black ram, with his tail in her hand' and repeated these lines:

---

[15] BL, Additional MS, 31853, fo. 15. Cf. William Harrison, *The Description of England*, ed. Georges Edelen (Ithaca, NY, 1968), 93; Norden, *The Surveyors Dialogue*, 106; Blount, *Fragmenta Antiquitatis*, 147.

[16] John Hutchins, *The History and Antiquities of the County of Dorset* (2 vols., London, 1774), i. 127; Hazlitt, *Tenures of Land and Customs of Manors*, 80.

[17] Sir William Temple, 'Of Poetry' (1690), in *Critical Essays of the Seventeenth Century*, ed. J. E. Spingarn (3 vols., Oxford, 1908), iii. 98.

Here I am, riding upon a black ram,
Like a whore as I am;
And for my crincum crancum,
Have lost my bincum bancum;
And for my tailes game,
Am brought to this wordly shame.
Therefore good Mr. Steward
Let me have my lands againe.

At Kilmersdon in Somerset a variation on the the theme ran:

For mine arses fault take I this pain,
Therefore, my lord, give me my land again.[18]

Tradition remained the very essence of custom, therefore. Folkloric beliefs and symbolic rituals shaded into the local legal culture which determined and defined customary regulations; popular traditions and sociological norms could be as important as written titles and documentary precedents in the way in which they were perceived and enacted. It was consistent with this, for example, that many communities believed that they derived certain ancient rights, such as the licence to trade or access to common land, from a heroic act once performed on their behalf by some legendary figure. Most famous of all these 'charter mytho' was, of course, the ride of Lady Godiva naked through the streets of Coventry which was said to have persuaded her husband, Leofric, to grant the city its 'charter of freedom'. The south window of Trinity church helped to refresh the tradition in the popular memory with its depiction of the pair holding a charter on which was written 'I Luriche for the love of thee | Doe make Coventre tol-free'. Such foundation stories were common-place. The commons at St Briavels in Gloucestershire were believed to have been saved for the people by virtue of a similar naked ride on the part of the countess of Hereford. At Long Newnton tradition told that the commons had been awarded to the inhabitants by King Athelstan in return for their service against the Danes: he ordered the monks of Malmesbury to grant them as much land as a local woman could ride around 'upon a bare-ridged horse'.[19]

---

[18] Blount, *Fragmenta Antiquitatis*, 144, 149–50. The first of these rhymes was much noted in the seventeenth century: see, for, example, BL, Sloane MS, 3111, fo. 2ʳ; BL, Lansdowne MS, 1033, fo. 71ʳ. For the second of them, see also Norden, *The Surveyors Dialogue*, 103. The unusual inheritance customs at Taunton Dean were described by Thomas Gerard, *The Particular Description of the County of Somerset*, ed. E. H. Bates (Somerset Record Society, 15, London, 1900), 56.

[19] Sir William Dugdale, *The Antiquities of Warwickshire* (London, 1656), 86; Keith Thomas, *The Perception of the Past in Early Modern England* (Creighton Trust Lecture, London, 1984), 2;

Like the legends which accounted for the origins of these customary rights, the rituals which confirmed and maintained their existence were bound up with traditional understandings and practices. The periodic perambulations which beat the bounds of the parish, circumnavigated the manor, or confirmed the limits of the common land by the physical act of treading them and repairing boundary markers, were products of an age of ceremony, a world in which actions spoke louder than words. A local map was still a rare thing, and where one was to be found most folks probably thought of it as no more than 'a painted paper'. Boundary markers are not even recorded in village by-laws before the mid-sixteenth century, presumably because everyone would simply have known them by heart.[20] Especially in fielden areas, the steward, accompanied perhaps by the manorial lord, would guide tenants around the ancient watercourses and hedgerows, the venerable trees and merestones which delineated one customary universe from another. Sometimes horns were blown, songs were sung and rituals enacted, refreshments were taken at customary resting places, and solemn pause was given at crucial points along the way.

Equally, whole parishes would turn out to meet the minister at Rogationtide to walk the limits of their parochial existence. These occasions retained into the nineteenth century the name of 'gang days' by which they had been known since before the Normans. Sometimes the cross would be carried before, banners might be paraded, and bells were rung to ward off evil spirits. Prayers would be said for the protection of the crops, Psalms 103 and 104 were chanted in the fields, and the Gospels read at symbolic places. Deuteronomy 19: 14: 'Thou shalt not remove thy neighbour's landmark, which they of old time have set in thine inheritance'; and 27: 17: 'Cursed be he that removeth his neighbour's landmark'. Proverbs 22: 28: 'Remove not the ancient landmark, which thy fathers have set'.[21] Significantly the Elizabethan homily to be read in churches at this festival spoke of boundary markers as if they were texts, and so in a sense they were: the grid references of the illiterate in the mental map of

---

*Wiltshire: The Topographical Collections of John Aubrey, F.R.S., A.D. 1659–70*, ed. J. E. Jackson (Devizes, 1862), 272–3, and cf. Bod. Lib., MS Aubrey 3, fo. 23ᵛ.

[20] Norden, *The Surveyors Dialogue*, 15; W. O. Ault, *Open-Field Farming in Medieval England: A Study of Village By-Laws* (London, 1972), 53–4.

[21] A. R. Wright, *British Calendar Customs: England*, ed. T. E. Lones (3 vols., Folklore Society, London, 1936–40), i. 130–8; Homans, *English Villagers of the Thirteenth Century*, 368; Keith Thomas, *Religion and the Decline of Magic: Studies in Popular Beliefs in Sixteenth- and Seventeenth-Century England* (London, 1971), 62–5; George C. Peachey, 'Beating the Bounds of Brightwalton', *Berks, Bucks & Oxon Archaeological Journal*, 10/3 (1904), 75–81; Bob Bushaway, *By Rite: Custom, Ceremony and Community in England, 1700–1880* (London, 1982), 81–100.

the parish. If these 'auncient terries of the fieldes' were taken up, it warned, 'the lordes recordes (which be the tenauntes euidences) be peruerted and translated ...'.[22]

These perambulations were not merely picturesque old ceremonies but real ways of remembering and maintaining prescriptive rights to land which carried with them essential benefits and entitlements. On such occasions it was incumbent upon the ancient inhabitants to remember the boundaries and to ensure that the vital knowledge of them was preserved and maintained. This was just one of many contexts in which aged memories had long been valued as guides to past practice in an environment where so much went unrecorded in writing. Mr Kay, the parson of Huggate in the East Riding of Yorkshire had a perfectly reasonable excuse for not undertaking his perambulation in 1578 when he claimed that 'the auncyente men of the parishe dyd not offer them selfs', for it would have been impossible without them.[23] The duty of these elders, moreover, was to pass on what they knew to the younger generation. Small boys always accompanied the perambulations and the bounds of parish or manor were solemnly shown and ritualistically impressed upon their minds by the older men. Thus, on the boundary which divided the manor of Brigstock from Rockingham Forest in Northamptonshire, for example, lay 'King Stephen's Oak', an ancient marker from which 'according to tradition, King Stephen once shot at a deer'. So large was the trunk that during the Brigstock processions it was 'the constant custom' of the inhabitants 'to fill the hollow with a company of boys', of thirty or forty in number. None of these boys was likely to forget such an experience, or what it signified.[24]

There were many such devices employed as mnemonic aids for the young. Rewards were common, as in the parish of Purton, Wiltshire, where at Jaques Oak, Charnham Oak, and Gospel Oak, in turn, the boundaries were affirmed by a Bible reading, the marking of a cross, and the throwing of money 'amongst the boys'. The preferred method of the great Richard Hooker, as minister of Bourne in Kent at the end of Elizabeth's reign, was humour. Insistent on 'the customary time of procession' for the 'preservation of love, and their parish rights and liberties', he 'would then always drop some loving and facetious observations to be remembered against the next year especially by the boys and young people'.[25] But pain rather than pleasure was the more common stimulus

---

[22] *The Seconde Tome of Homelyes* (London, 1563), sig. Ssss ii[v].

[23] *Tudor Parish Documents of the Diocese of York*, ed. J. S. Purvis (Cambridge, 1948), 194.

[24] John Morton, *The Natural History of Northamptonshire* (London, 1712), 397.

[25] T. S. Maskelyne, 'Perambulation of Purton, 1733', *Wiltshire Archaeological and Natural History Magazine*, 40 (1918), 124; Izaak Walton, *The Lives of Doctor John Donne, Sir Henry Wotton,*

to memory. Since Norman times, at least, acts which could not afford to be forgotten, such as the conveying of land or granting of privileges, had been accompanied by the whipping of young boys, 'for the sake of memory', as if recollection of the pain would imprint the deed indelibly upon their minds.[26]

In early modern England it remained usual practice to throw boys into boundary streams, lay them across merestones and offer them blows or pinches, or bump them up against trees in order that they remember the vital spot. Samuel Pepys commented upon the beating of the parish bounds on Ascension Day in London. In 1661 he watched 'the little boys go up and down in procession with their broomestaffes in their hands as I have myself long ago gone', and in 1668 the tavern talk was of 'how heretofore, and yet in several places, they do whip a boy at every place they stop at in their procession'. Martin Martin's late seventeenth-century description of the practice among the Western Islanders was applicable throughout Britain.

They preserve their boundaries from being liable to any debates by their successors, thus: they lay a quantity of the ashes of burnt wood in the ground, and put big stones above the same; and for conveying the knowledge of this to posterity, they carry some boys from both villages next the boundary, and there whip them soundly, which they will be sure to remember, and tell their children.[27]

This, then, was the context in which custom had its existence. It reflected the world in which it had evolved, a world which was highly localized, in which formal and binding regulations could exist nowhere but in memory and practice and in which symbolic objects were the 'charters' of the people, ritual acts their 'title deeds'. To a great extent these circumstances were as relevant in early modern communities as they had

---

*Mr Richard Hooker, Mr George Herbert and Doctor Robert Sanderson*, ed. Vernon Blackburn (London, 1895), 155–6. For other treats given to boys, see Wright, *British Calendar Customs: England*, ed. Lones, i. 133, 136; M. K. McIntosh, *A Community Transformed: The Manor and Liberty of Havering, 1500–1620* (Cambridge, 1991), 202; Ronald Hutton, *The Rise and Fall of Merry England: The Ritual Year, 1400–1700* (Oxford, 1994), 182, 247.

[26] Emily Zack Tabuteau, *Transfers of Property in Eleventh-Century Norman Law* (Chapel Hill, NC, 1988), 149–50 (I am grateful to Leisbeth van Houts for this reference); Homans, *English Villagers of the Thirteenth Century*, 368.

[27] *The Diary of Samuel Pepys* ed. Robert Latham and William Matthews (11 vols., London, 1970–83), ii. 106, ix. 179; Martin Martin, *A Description of the Western Islands of Scotland circa 1695* (Glasgow, 1884), 114. The practice of impressing boundaries on the minds of boys by various means continued in some areas throughout the eighteenth and into the nineteenth century: W. E. Tate, *The Parish Chest: A Study of the Records of Parochial Administration in England* (3rd edn., Cambridge, 1969), 74; Bushaway, *By Rite*, 85, 87; Thompson, 'Custom, Law and Common Right', *Customs in Common*, 98 n.

been in the medieval past. But the sixteenth and seventeenth centuries were to see significant changes in the importance of customary culture in local society and in the nature of its recorded existence. For this period witnessed unprecedented struggles over the legitimacy and form of custom in a host of contexts, one consequence of which was the widespread attempt, often for the first time, to reify prescriptive rights into a codified system and transmute oral traditions into written records.

## THE MEMORY OF MAN

A variety of circumstances conspired to aggravate disputes over local custom and eventually to encourage the impulse to document. To begin with, there emerged during the sixteenth century a much more active land market than previously. The confiscation of monastic lands by the crown at the Reformation and their subsequent lease or sale on the open market helped to create a new breed of landlords who acquired their land not by inheritance but through investment. Such men had little knowledge of local customs, little empathy with the traditional mores of neighbourhood, and very often saw such things as inimical to their proprietorial freedoms and commercial interests. Moreover the heavy price inflation of the late sixteenth century, to which these circumstances contributed, increased the need for landlords to recoup ever greater returns on their investments. Where entry fines and rents on copyhold land were fixed by custom, however, their value in real terms fell sharply during Elizabeth's reign. Pressing from another direction was the rapid demographic growth, itself another stimulus to price inflation, which England experienced between the mid-sixteenth and the mid-seventeenth century. Increased population intensified the demands made on local resources. Commons became overstocked and attempts were made to assart the hitherto marginal land of forests, fens, marshes, and heaths: pressure was put upon customary allowances such as gleaning, turf cutting, fishing, and mining. In consequence, many landlords tried to restrict access to these rights by excluding those who could not justify them by satisfactory title. They also sought to compound with their tenants over the commons, encouraging them to surrender their use rights in return for a cash payment which would then allow their enclosure by the lord as private property.[28] The crown was one of the most active agents in this

---

[28] These developments are described in R. H. Tawney, *The Agrarian Problem in the Sixteenth Century* (London, 1912), pt. 2; Joan Thirsk (ed.), *The Agrarian History of England and Wales*, iv: *1500–1640* (Cambridge, 1967); Eric Kerridge, *Agrarian Problems in the Sixteenth Century and after* (London, 1969), 54–7; Andrew B. Appleby, 'Agrarian Capitalism or Seigneurial Reaction? The

respect, especially during the early seventeenth century when James I
sought to restore his ailing finances by raising the revenues from the royal
estates.[29]

The result was protracted and bitter disputes waged between landlords
and tenants up and down the country. Suddenly the definition and the
legitimacy of customs became a matter of urgency and importance as
never before. The lack of codification which in the past had been an asset
allowing for flexibility and adaptation now became a liability inspiring
contention and conflict. Landlords realized that the best way of forcing
up fixed rents and fines or restricting access to use rights was to prove that
these customs were illegitimate, that they failed to meet the defining criteria of being constant and unaltered within the memory of man. For this
they needed witnesses who were prepared to testify that they had known
practices to have been different in the past. Alternatively, they sought any
available documentary evidence which might support their case. Here the
court rolls of the manor could be of some use since, although they provided no formal record of customs, they might indicate whether or not
the levels of rents and fines had changed over time.

The manorial and other local courts were the tribunals before which
such disputes were heard in the first instance. Over the course of the sixteenth century, however, the nature of these complaints often made it
impossible for such institutions adequately to settle matters. At the same
time, the central courts became more active in recruiting cases of this sort
from inferior jurisdictions in the localities. The common law courts
began to attract copyhold litigation in the 1550s. When in the 1570s they
started to offer writs of trespass to protect this form of customary tenant,
and in the 1580s to make writs of ejectment available to landlords, the
demand for their services increased steadily from all sides. Meanwhile,
contested tithing customs, traditionally the preserve of ecclesiastical justice, entered the royal courts in 1588 from which date common law judges

Northwest of England, 1500–1700', *American Historical Review*, 80 (1975), 574–94; Roger B.
Manning, *Village Revolts: Social Protest and Popular Disturbances in England, 1509–1640* (Oxford, 1988),
ch. 6. Similar conditions were experienced in the late thirteenth and early fourteenth centuries:
Susan Reynolds, *Kingdoms and Communities in Western Europe, 900–1300* (Oxford, 1984), 137; Birrell,
'Common Rights in the Medieval Forest', 22–3.

    [29] Gordon Batho, 'Landlords in England, 1500–1640', in Thirsk (ed.), *The Agrarian History of
England and Wales*, iv. 268–73; R. W. Hoyle, '"Vain Projects": The Crown and its Copyholders in
the Reign of James I', in John Chartres and David Hey (eds.), *English Rural Society, 1500–1800*
(Cambridge, 1990), 73–104; eid., '"Shearing the Hog": Reforming the Estates, c.1598–1640', in
Hoyle (ed.), *The Estates of the English Crown, 1558–1640* (Cambridge, 1992), 204–62.

allowed clergymen to recover tithes using writs of debt, and they were soon issuing writs of prohibition to discourage them from taking cases to the church courts.[30]

At the same time, the equity tribunals at Westminster, such as Exchequer, Chancery, and Requests, became increasingly active in these contexts. The business of the equity side of the Exchequer, for example, rose steadily from the reign of Elizabeth I until the end of the seventeenth century. In the first instance, the court heard only suits in which the crown had some interest, but as it became increasingly popular it was able to assume a general jurisdiction in 1649 by means of the legal fiction that the plaintiff was a debtor to the crown. There was an annual average of 84 bills filed in the period 1558 to 1587, rising to 334 between 1587 and 1603, and growing again to 456 during the Interregnum, before finally reaching a peak of 739 at the time of William and Mary. A large proportion of these cases revolved around disputed customary rights of one kind or another.[31]

The role of evidence before such equity courts was problematic. For centuries before this they, in common with all other legal fora, had preferred written record as a form of proof. But in the cases where it was unavailable or unreliable they were compelled to rely on oral testimony as well. In suits involving custom, it seems, they sought corroboration in a combination of both verbal and textual witness. Masters in the Elizabethan court of Requests 'took heed of manorial records wherever they were available' in customary disputes, but 'they remained reluctant to pass judgement on the basis of documentary proof alone'. They sought the oral evidence of customary tenants because they remained the best guide to current and recent practice. Indeed, there appears to have been a sense, certainly on the part of the tenants, that as long as custom was consistent as far back as anyone could remember, it did not matter if an ancient document might suggest that practice had once been different: old deeds mattered nothing against what had held within lived experience. This appears to have been an opinion shared by Lord Keeper Thomas Egerton in the court of Chancery who, at the beginning of the seventeenth century, instructed a jury to decide some disputed manorial

---

[30] C. M. Gray, *Copyhold, Equity, and the Common Law* (Cambridge, Mass., 1963), chs. 2–3; W. J. Jones, 'A Note on the Demise of Manorial Jurisdiction: The Impact of Chancery', *American Journal of Legal History*, 10 (1966), 297–318; id., *The Elizabethan Court of Chancery* (Oxford, 1967), 264–304; Richard J. Ross, 'The Memorial Culture of Early Modern English Lawyers: Memory as Keyword, Shelter, and Identity, 1560–1640', *Yale Journal of Law and the Humanities*, 10 (1998), 262.

[31] W. H. Bryson, *The Equity Side of the Exchequer* (Cambridge, 1975), 16, 18–19, 33, 168–9.

customs by what 'had gone by usual reputation sixty years last, and not to
have it paired, and defalked by such ancient deeds'.[32]

There seems to have been no consistency, in practice at least, as to the
privilege given to spoken as against written testimony in these cases.
Certainly Egerton's attitude to recent oral memory in one case did not
stop him disregarding it when it threatened his own interests in another.
Four years later, as Lord Chancellor Ellesmere, he attended the chambers
in Gray's Inn of the solicitor-general, Sir Francis Bacon, to arbitrate with
his own tenants, from the manor of Great Gaddesden in Hertfordshire.
The copyholders, headed by one of their number, Thomas Wells, were
claiming 'a custome of certeyntye of fines upon dyscents and surrenders
after the rate of fower pence an acre and to paye but one harryott onlye
for severall copihoulde lands and tenements comeinge into one man's
possession'. Ellesmere and his 'learned councell', on the other hand, had
examined the manorial records and 'did finde by the ... court rolles that
the sayd fines ... were uncerten, sometymes more and sometymes lesse,
att the lord's will and pleasure, and that the most of the other pretended
customes weare not warranted by the sayde court rolles but meerelye con-
tradicted the same'. At the meeting these rolls were produced, extending
back from the reign of Elizabeth to that of Edward II, and they were read
aloud. Unfortunately for the tenants, 'by a continuall concurrence of them,
it appeared that the fines were uncertain'. They countered by claiming to
have an 'ancient customarie' which would bear them out, but they could
not produce it. They proffered instead 'a paper booke to prove the certainty of the said fines', but this indicated just as much variance. So it was
concluded that the customs were 'therefore held suspitious' and the tenants were forced to concede.[33]

Such inconsistency was no doubt a product, at least in part, of the fact
that neither written nor oral evidence could be trusted with any degree of
confidence. Records and documents, where they could be found, were
easily forged and corrupted. Indeed it was the increasing fluidity of land
transactions which was partly responsible for the statute 'agaynst the
forgyng of evydences and wrytinges' in 1563. It recognized that the falsi-
fication of written titles 'hathe of late tyme been verye muche more practised, used and put in use in all partes of this realme then in tymes passed'
and condemned anyone found fabricating a 'false dede, charter or writing

---

[32] Stretton, 'Women, Custom and Equity in the Court of Requests', 176; *The English Reports*
(176 vols., Edinburgh, 1900–30), xxi. 13, quoted in Jones, 'A Note on the Demise of Manorial
Jurisdiction', 306.

[33] Huntington Library, Ellesmere MS, 233.

sealed, court roll, or the will of any person or persons in writing' with the intent of defrauding another of hereditaments.[34] On the other hand the memories of ancient inhabitants, when they were not prone to amnesia, were often subject to partiality and selectivity in their own interests. Certainly 'overordennrie experience' taught the Elizabethan surveyor Sir Robert Johnson 'that the moste parte of tenannts in these daies, when inquisitions of surveigh or inquests of office are taken, do not so much studie to answere what is true as (by all possible meanes) devise to sett forth and aver such customes and usages as are eyther directly preiuditiall to the inheritance or at the least onelie good and profitable for theme selves, and I have scarcely found anie other course holden; spetiallie when they knowe not of court rolls or ancient surveighes to impunge theme'.[35]

The complex relationship between oral and written evidence in disputes over custom is explored in more detail in the following discussion based upon the depositions and decrees from a sample of such cases before the equity side of the court of Exchequer between 1560 and 1686.[36] The Exchequer, like other equity courts, placed considerable store in the oral testimony of witnesses, taken either centrally or by commission in the localities. Since the defining conditions of custom included current, consistent, and uninterrupted usage it followed that it could best be explained by those whose daily practice it was. From the depositions of ancient inhabitants called forth to recount the code by which they lived we gain some graphic insights into the workings of popular memory in early modern society which few other sources reveal with such clarity.

Many ordinary tenants seem to have displayed the long and accurate recall of those who had lived the customs they described for many decades. In a typical Exchequer dispute of 1630, ten witnesses were produced to testify that the tenants of the manor of Oaksey in Wiltshire had always enjoyed rights of common pasture in the Forest of Braydon: their average age was 78 years, the most senior being husbandman Thomas Wigmore, a centenarian who claimed to have known these rights for ninety years. In order to establish immemorial usage, however, it was necessary to reach back beyond direct experience into the realms of inherited tradition. In 1628, William Messenger, a yeoman of Chelworth in Wiltshire, testified that tenants from the manor of Leigh also enjoyed rights in Braydon Forest, something he knew to have existed not only

[34] 5 Eliz. c. 14, in *Statutes of the Realm* (11 vols., London, 1810–24), iv, pt. i, 443–5.

[35] PRO, SP12/283A/80.

[36] Depositions from 175 cases between PRO, E134/3 Eliz/Hil 2, and E134/2 Jac 2/East 31. Decrees from PRO, E126/1–8.

from personal experience 'dureinge all the time of his remembrance', which was fifty years, but also by report from 'before his tyme and tyme out of minde, as he has credibly heard by the relacion of [his] father who well knewe the same beinge aged one hundred yeares or thereabouts att the tyme of his death'.[37]

In this way, 'the memory of man' might extend back with some reliability for at least a century and could involve several generations, as many deponents were quick to establish. In 1565 Richard Hobbes, a 70-year-old husbandman, claimed to know the customs of the manor of Southam in Gloucestershire as one born and bred there, 'and also for that he hathe heard bothe his grandfather and his own father, sometyme beying tenants of Southam, so say and declare'. Richard Mogiar, a husbandman aged 56 in 1574, had been told the bounds of the manor of Gillingham in Dorset 'by ould auncient men, as by his grandfather and father'.[38]

As a result of such oral transmission there were many in Elizabethan and early Stuart England who had strong memories, at first or second hand, of the days before the dissolution of the monasteries, especially if they lived on lands formerly owned by religious houses. In 1603, for example, a 96-year-old butcher from Horsington in Lincolnshire could recapture the customs of the locality as he had 'hearde his father and other auncyent men of Horsington' speak of practice in the days of 'the Pryoresse of Stixwould'. A few years later, the husbandman Robert Tyllye, who had been born around 1540, still recalled the customs in the

---

[37] PRO, E134/6 Chas 1/Trin 9; PRO, E134/4 Chas 1/East 26. On the general importance of elders in societies with strong oral traditions, see Jack Goody, *The Interface between the Written and the Oral* (Cambridge, 1987), 150, 164; and in this context, see Keith Thomas, 'Age and Authority in Early Modern England', *Proceedings of the British Academy*, 62 (1976), 233–4. It is testimony, no doubt, not only to the tardiness of legal process but also to the seniority of most witnesses in disputes over custom that the Exchequer barons, in their not infrequent rulings to refer cases to the common law, would allow the depositions taken in their court to be used again at a future trial for the benefit of 'all such witnesses as shall be dead or not able to travel' by that time: see, for example, PRO, E126/5, fos. 48ᵛ, 54ʳ, 60ʳ, 162ʳ, 207ʳ, 262ʳ. Cf. *Quarter Sessions Records with other Records of the Justices of the Peace for the County Palatine of Chester, 1559–1760*, ed. J. H. E. Bennett and J. C. Dewhurst (Record Society of Lancashire and Cheshire, 94, 1940), 66, 83.

[38] PRO, E134/7 Eliz/East 1; PRO, E134/16 Eliz/East 6. In the later nineteenth century, Lord Hobhouse heard a dispute over common rights and concluded that 'the oral evidence', based upon 'what the old witnesses say of their own knowledge, and what they must in their boyhood have heard their grandfathers say, must go back for at least 100 years': G. J. Shaw-Lefevre, Lord Eversley, *Commons, Forests and Footpaths* (London, 1910), 107. Beyond first hand experience, oral transmission is notoriously unreliable: see Jan Vansina, *Oral Tradition: A Study in Historical Methodology*, trans. H. M. Wright (London, 1965), 101–2; M. T. Clanchy, 'Remembering the Past and the Good Old Law', *History*, 55 (1970), 166–7; David P. Henige, *The Chronology of Oral Tradition* (Oxford, 1974), ch. 1; Rosalind Thomas, *Oral Tradition and Written Record in Classical Athens* (Cambridge, 1989), 125, 180, 283.

days of the prior of Bath on the manor of Weston in Somerset, for 'he hath heard his father report' the same. William Bell, aged 74 in 1580, knew the limits of the manor of Benwell, Northumberland, since the days when he had 'sene the boundes thereof rydden and gone by one that was prior of Tynmouthe'.[39] Equally, in the later seventeenth century, there were many ancient inhabitants who had lived through the tumultuous events of the the 1640s and 1650s and could recall the different world in the 'days before the wars'. Typically, in 1675, ten deponents averaging over 72 years of age from parishes adjoining Kingswood Forest near Bristol recounted the features of their community, its wildlife, cottages, coalmining, commons, and enclosures, 'before the tyme of the late wars'.[40]

It was to these ancient men, therefore, that anyone wishing to learn manorial or parochial custom must turn. When a new landlord, ignorant of local ways, came into a manor for the first time, he often had no option but to summon the elders in order to have explained exactly those rights and duties which he was bound to allow and expect. Thus when John Warneforde purchased the manor of Cloteley, Wiltshire, in the mid-sixteenth century he immediately 'did call together the eldest inhabitants of the parish of Hankerton and mannor of Clotcley' so as to establish exactly what the boundary was between his land and the adjoining manor of Charlton. There was a real sense in which if these ancients died then the knowledge of which they were the sole possessors died with them. Hence deathbed scenes in which people huddled urgently around an old man as he passed on what he knew while he still had breath. In Elizabeth's reign, no one understood the boundary between the park belonging to the manor of Witham in Somerset and the limits of Brewham Forest, better than John Frye 'whoe was manie yeares servant to Sir Raffe Hopton', the then lord of Witham. As Frye 'laie on his death bed', Lady Rachel Hopton, Sir Raffe's widdow, implored him 'to deliver his knowledge concerning the said bounds', he 'being then of perfect memorie'.[41]

The ways in which these ancient inhabitants passed on their knowledge of local custom to the younger generation were usually rather more

---

[39] PRO, E134/1 Jas I/East 3, m. 10; PRO, E134/7 Jas I/Mich 12, m. 4; PRO, E134/22&23 Eliz/Mich 17, m. 3. On popular memories of the days before the Reformation, see Thomas, *The Perception of the Past*, 11–23.

[40] PRO, E134/27 Chas II/Mich 29; another case, eight years later, revealed more old men with these memories of Kingswood before 'the late troubles': PRO, E134/35 Chas II/Mich 48, m. 3. For similar examples from elsewhere, see PRO, E134/26 Chas II/Mich 32, m. 11; PRO, E134/28 Chas II/East 20.

[41] PRO, E134/37 Eliz/East 13, m. 3; PRO, E134/17 Jas I/Hil 9, m. 5.

deliberate, if no less solemn. Often they can be heard, summoning up the authority of the past, remembering how as young boys themselves they had been told of ancient usage or shown the bounds of manor or parish. The delivery of such knowledge seems almost to have been a ceremonial rite of passage, part of their induction into the adult community of which they were to become a part. The usual mnemonic devices were employed. In 1615 a Northumbrian yeoman remembered how, fifty years before, he had seen William Hall gravely showing his two sons, Nicholas and Edward, the line dividing the lands of Amble and Birling. Near Halsey dyke nook he had pointed to a stone 'and did knocke upon the said stone with his staffe and willed [them] to remember that yf the bounder betwixt the quene and the earle of Northumberland came in question that that stone was the bounderstone'. On another occasion, John Clarke was made to sit on this crucial marker with 'his bare buttocks' that he might 'remember the same soe long as he should live', while Edmund Finch was later taken up Beacon Hill to view the stone by an old man who willed him commit to memory 'that which his fore elders had tould him', which, he said, '"When I am dead and rotten you may saye of a truth . . ."'.[42]

Ongoing boundary disputes during the second half of the seventeenth century involving the demarcation between the Forest of Exmoor and the commons belonging to its adjoining manors and parishes in Somerset and Devon came to a head in a big battle in the court of Exchequer in 1678. In April of that year many old men attested to the bounds of the forest as they had been perambulated every seven years as far back as their memories went. They recalled the pain inflicted upon them by the then ancient inhabitants on the old markers so that they might remember that knowledge which was their birthright. William Gregory, a husbandman of Exford, recalled a graphic example of the mnemonic shock treatment administered to him as a boy of 7, seventy-two years before. On the perambulation led by the parson of Exford parish that day in 1606, one Richard Edbrooke had called him over to a merestone and told him

> to putt his finger upon the said stone, sayeing that it was soe hott that it would scald him, which, [he] beleiving, did putt his finger thereon and the said Richard Edbrooke imediately thereupon layd hold on [his] hand and did wring one of his fingers sorely that for the present it greived him very much, and said 'Remember that this is a bound stone and is a boundary to the parish of Exford'.

Humfry Stote, a 68-year-old yeoman from Romansleigh, remembered the perambulation of over fifty years before, at which time the techniques for aiding memory were only a little less painful. On that occasion he

⁴² PRO, E134/13 Jas I/Mich 4, m.3.

did accompany the minister who then served the cure of the parish church of
Exford and divers of the inhabitants in a perambulacon or prosession which was
then made aboute the bounds of that parish, and [he] doth well remember that in
such their perambulacon they did take in and perambulate all of the said comon
of Exford comeing up close home to the verge or bounds of the said forest
divided by the mearstones or boundaryes by [him] before described. And [he]
doth very well remember that at the time of the said perambulacion there was one
Silvester Gregory, being then an antient inhabitant of the said parish of Exford,
that did goe along . . . and if any of the said boundaryes or mearstones . . . were
found to be in decay or fallen downe, hee . . . would take one of the boyes who
went along with them following the said procession and lay him upon [it]
and then give him some gentle blowes and pinches willing and bidding him to
remember that that was an antient boundary or mearestone betweene the said
Forest of Exmore and Exford comon.[43]

Such vivid testimony as to the way in which customary knowledge was
remembered and transmitted down the generations in this period, as for
many centuries before, remained important evidence so far as equity
courts like the Exchequer were concerned. If old men reported that
they had known no different, that their fathers and grandfathers had
never told them anything to the contrary, then this was powerful evidence
towards establishing the legitimacy of a custom. In addition to this
the court sought wherever possible to corroborate such testimony with
the witness of written records. Such records were likely to be of limited
use, however, since legal theory stated that customs could not be created
by record. They were also unlikely to exist in the first place since in
former centuries there was no place and no need to commit customs to
paper.

Manorial courts were self-governing institutions presided over by a
homage or jury comprising the tenants themselves. They made rulings as
to manorial custom, which very often went unrecorded, in what they saw
as the interests of the community as a whole. Despite the legal theory that
a legitimate custom had to be constant and immutable since time
immemorial, the practice on the ground was very different: custom
changed constantly to meet developing socio-economic needs.[44] No one

---

[43] PRO, E134/30 Chas II/East 21, mm. 9, 10; and printed in Edward T. MacDermot, *The
History of the Forest of Exmoor* (1911; rev. edn., Newton Abbot, 1973), 353.

[44] For a good example of this, see Robert S. Dilley, 'The Cumberland Court Leet and Use of
the Common Lands', *Transactions of the Cumberland and Westmorland Antiquarian and Archaeological
Society*, new ser., 67 (1967), 150. Proverbial wisdom certainly endorsed this flexibility. 'A bad cus-
tom is like a good cake, better broken than kept'; 'Custom without reason is but an ancient error';
'A good custom must root out that which an ill has brought in': M. P. Tilley, *A Dictionary of the
Proverbs in England in the Sixteenth and Seventeenth Centuries* (Ann Arbor, Mich., 1950), 136.

required that customary practice be recorded and even in instances where there was some written indication of past practice it did not necessarily make any difference to subsequent generations. What had transpired at one time might well bear no relation to what happened at another: tenants were unlikely to be even aware of change if it had taken place beyond the relatively short period of their collective memory. The equity courts showed a willingness to accept this reality. In some cases they were prepared to acknowledge that if tenants had agreed to change or make a new custom then general consent was all that was required for it to be binding.[45]

Despite this, however, the involvement of the central equity jurisdictions in the business of the manor court tended to increase the premium put on evidence in writing. Certain documents, while they contained nothing approaching a formal statement of the complexity of customary rights, duties, and usages could offer some indication of their form. Court rolls might reveal in the process of recording land transactions the value of rents and fines or the rules of inheritance as they operated over time. Ancient grants or charters might bestow some privilege on 'inhabitants' or 'citizens'. In doing so they merely confirmed a right and said nothing about the way in which it would operate or exactly to whom it would apply, matters which remained the province of unwritten custom, but they did at least provide a documentary precedent which could be invoked by subsequent generations in the justification of claims. Occasionally a custumal might exist, drawn up perhaps as a consequence of some past dispute, which provided a snapshot of practices as they had once been.

Where such documents could be found, lawyers looked to them for vital corroborative evidence. The number of lawyers was expanding markedly in the late sixteenth and early seventeenth centuries, in tandem with the huge growth of business experienced by the central courts. Increasingly these men were educated first at the universities, whose curriculum centred around the study of classical texts, before graduating to the Inns of Court which, by the turn of the seventeenth century, were displaying an ever greater reliance on written precedents in their didactic method. The Elizabethan and Jacobean legal profession was the product of a legal culture which during the Tudor period had been becoming gradually more referential to written precedents as contained in the yearbooks and abridgements and the growing number of law reports and collections of judgments put into print. It was a profession often ignorant of the oral and malleable ways of customary law as it was administered in the manor

---

[45] Stretton, 'Women, Custom and Equity in the Court of Requests', 178–9.

courts and one more and more likely to be suspicious of its unwritten foundations. A consequence, then, of the arbitration of local custom by central equity courts was the invention a documentary basis for it. It encouraged not only the search for old records which could be invoked to corroborate the case of either party but also the writing down in a formal code of the precise form of customary practice.

## THE SEARCH FOR EVIDENCE

Aided by their legal counsel, both landlords and tenants, clergymen and parishioners, corporations and citizens, engaged in the battle for documentary proof. In the legal insistence that customs be unchanging, manorial lords saw a real opportunity to prove that they were 'uncertain' and therefore invalid. They began, with the help of lawyers and the ever growing numbers of estate stewards, to search back through court rolls, deeds, and any other records in the manorial chest to find evidence of the mutability of past practice. Such evidence was not difficult to find. Court rolls were likely to show the way in which, as economic circumstances changed over time, the value of rents rose and fell accordingly. Even though in theory tenants may have paid fixed fines on an inheritable estate, the rolls might show that in practice the levels had varied. Equally, there could be a marked difference between what the court rolls said went on and what actually went on in reality. On such grounds had Lord Ellesmere defeated his tenants of Great Gaddesden.

The Exchequer cases repeatedly demonstrate the strenuous efforts to which landlords went to use documents such as court rolls as a stick with which to beat their tenants in the light of legal theory. In February 1604, for example, the court ruled in favour of Edward, Lord Abergavenny, in a dispute with his tenants as to whether he as lord, or the copyholders sitting as the homage, had the right to assess the level of entry fines payable on the inheritance of land in his manor of Allesley, Warwickshire. The tenants lost, not only because in their oral evidence they 'utterlye disagreed' as to the number of copyholders whom custom dictated should assess the fines, together 'with diverse other disagreements', but because the court rolls, extending 'from the raigne of King Henry the fowerth to this tyme', contained no record of them ever making such an assessment. These sins of commission and omission in their evidence were no doubt consequences of the fact that practice had varied over time and that there had never been any need or desire to enroll their procedures for posterity. This kind of victory was one which landlords repeatedly won. Typically, in 1607 Henry Farre, lord of the manor of Ombersley,

Worcestershire, succeeded in defeating his copyhold tenants in a dispute over the level of rents and fines by producing the court rolls to show how variable they had been in the days before the dissolution of the monastery of Evesham, former lord of the soil. Alternatively, in May 1640, the dean and chapter of Hereford were able to substantiate their claim to heriots paid on the death of customary tenants in their manor of Preston-on-Wye when 'upon the reading of certaine leger bookes, court rolls and other records', the Exchequer barons ruled that it was 'a good custom'.[46]

In certain circumstances, however, the tenants might be able to turn such evidence to their own advantage. In the case of those belonging to the crown manor of Hemel Hempstead, Hertfordshire, a dispute in the reign of Henry VIII as to whether or not the fines and heriots were fixed or arbitrary and at the will of the king had resulted in a document being drawn up and ratified by royal commissioners which set out in twenty-five points 'the true and laudable services and customes that hath ben used of old tyme and of right ought to be used in the said mannor'. When the same issue became the subject of contention again in 1609 the court rolls could be produced to show that the level of fines and heriots as laid down in the Henrician award had been paid without alteration ever since. The Exchequer had no choice, therefore, but to rule that it was James I's 'disposion not to interrupt the antient and setled customes and privileges of any his tenants but to suffer them to enioy the same according to iustice and equitie'. In 1657, the copyholders of Barton under Needwood, Staffordshire, were finally able to defeat their landlords, Sir Edward and John Bromfield, after disputes lasting many years over the custom of entry fines. The tenants won an initial victory at the assizes, apparently being able to produce court rolls and other evidences to support their case. The Bromfields took the case up to the Exchequer only to have their appeal rejected, the equity court 'being satisfied that there is and, from all the time whereof the memory of man is not to the contrary, that there hath bine such a custome within the said mannor of Barton under Needwood'.[47]

Just as court rolls might be of some use in establishing the levels of rents and fines it was believed that ancient grants might provide legitimating evidence for or against such liberties as the right of a clergyman to tithes or of tenants to use common land. Documents of this sort

---

[46] PRO, E126/1, fos. 9ᵛ, 76ʳ–80ʳ, 82–6; PRO, E126/5, fo. 43ʳ. Often decrees were revoked when it was proved that since the time of their issue the level of fines had varied, making it arbitrary and at the will of the lord: PRO E126/1, fo. 283; PRO, E126/3, fos. 270ᵛ–272ʳ.

[47] PRO, E126/1, fos. 129ᵛ, 130ʳ, 133–6; PRO, E126/6, fos. 155ᵛ–156ʳ, 204ᵛ–209ʳ.

enshrined no custom as such, but they were clearly regarded by both lawyers and others as being capable of establishing precedents for usages which over time had become prescriptive rights. In the past, a monarch or lord may have granted certain privileges which were at his will but which 'the favour of tyme', as John Norden put it, had made into customs enforceable at law. When such rights were contested in the sixteenth and seventeenth centuries, therefore, interested parties repeatedly appealed to the witness of some ancient charter to bear out the justice of their claims. Thus in a dispute during the 1570s over rights of common on Alderholt Heath, part of the manor of Cranborne in Dorset, Henry Molineux deposed that almost sixty years before he had first been shown a copy of a court roll 'whereunto was a scedule annexed in parchement coteyninge an ancyent graunte, by one Kinge Edwarde at the instance of Edmonde his brother to one Dymes Dynell, then lady of the sayde migehame and to her heyers, of pasture for two hundred shepe in Alderholte Heath'.[48]

Such ancient records were invoked in a variety of circumstances to justify all manner of customary rights. In 1581 John Evelethe testified to the right of the customary tenants of Ottery St Mary, Devon, to do service of suit and grist at the mills within the manor based upon 'a customarye set downe uppon old recordes' which he had seen, 'made in the eleventh yere of Kinge Edward the third, between John Granston, the byshoppe of Exceter, being founder of the Colledge of Ottrey . . . and the tennantes of the sayd manner'. In 1624 it was said of the free minters of the Forest of Dean that 'by vertue (as they saye) of an ancient graunt made unto them by some kinge or kinges of England . . . they clayme a custome of free digginge in any namd freehold landes within the perambulacon of the saide forreste which they have used and doe use untill this daye'. Christopher Tucker, one of their number, confirmed that he 'hath seene an auncient deede dated in the raigne of Kinge Edward the second testifyinge the libertye and priviledge of the myners within the said forreste'.[49]

Meanwhile, the tenants of Rodley in Gloucestershire claimed their rights of common in the Forest of Dean by virtue of a charter dating from the reign of Henry II. In the early 1590s these rights came into question when villagers from neighbouring manors also tried to assert rights under the same warrant. The inhabitants of Minsterworth, Tibberton, Longhope, and Bulley all made their bid 'under collor of the saide charter

---

[48] Norden, *The Surveyors Dialogue*, 106; PRO, E134/15 Eliz/East 3, m. 6.

[49] PRO, E134/23 Eliz/East 16, m. 7; PRO, E134/22 Jas I/East 8, mm. 6–7, and cf. PRO, E134/13 Chas I/Mich 42, m. 3; Cyril E. Hart, *The Free Miners of the Royal Forest of Dean and the Hundred of St. Briavels* (Gloucester, 1953), 19.

of Rodleighe'. In December 1591, old Henry Yerworth deposed that about forty-six years previously the inhabitants of Tibberton and Bulley had had their cattle driven from the forest. A few days later they had gone to see Henry's brother, Christopher, then a bailiff at large, and 'broughte and shewed unto the said bayliff (beinge learned) their charter', but he had found that it 'contayned no sufficient matter for their freedom of comon in the same forrest'.[50] During an early seventeenth-century dispute over rights of common in the fens around Littleport, Isle of Ely, the tenants claimed their rights to cut turf and hedge on the authority of a licence granted to them in the thirteenth century by Bishop Hugh Northwold. They were able to produce the famous 'auncient coucher booke' of 1251, an 'ould booke written in parchment . . . late remaining in the custodye of the deane of Elye, which doth expresse or declare . . . the boundes of the fennes of Littleporte'.[51]

Such documents could assume iconic significance among commoners who looked upon them as symbols of their privileges and bulwarks against their attack. The reverenced piece of parchment in the big chest at the manor court or in the church became a hallowed artefact, no less so for the fact that most people could not read it themselves. Such was the status of the indenture granted to the inhabitants of the manor of Epworth in the Isle of Axholme, Lincolnshire, by their lord, Sir John Mowbray, during the reign of Edward III. It guaranteed no further improvements to the commons there and was invoked by the local people when repeated attempts were made to undermine their rights during the seventeenth century. In 1649 Thomas Taylor, yeoman, related the history of the precious deed, as 'hee hath heard it beene generally reported', and could remember that as a young boy, about fifty years before, he had once seen it, 'kept in a great chest with barrs of iron in the parish church of Haxey'.[52] When Sir Gervase Clifton was seeking to enclose part of the

---

[50] PRO, E134/34 Eliz/Hil 23, mm. 2–3; Cyril E. Hart, *The Commoners of Dean Forest* (Gloucester, 1951), 14.

[51] PRO, E134/4 Jas I/Hil 14, m. 6, and PRO, E126/1, fo. 46ʳ; and see Cambridgeshire Record Office [hereafter, CRO], P109/28/4.

[52] PRO, E134/1649/Mich 11. On the iconic status of the Mowbray charter, see Keith Lindley, *Fenland Riots and the English Revolution* (London, 1982), 26–7; Clive Holmes, 'Drainers and Fenmen: The Problem of Popular Political Consciousness in the Seventeenth Century', in Anthony Fletcher and John Stevenson (eds.), *Order and Disorder in Early Modern England* (Cambridge, 1985), 192. The veneration of ancient documents which were believed to enshrine popular rights was hardly new, of course. During the revolt of 1381, the crowd of St Albans demanded 'a certain charter of King Offa with letters of alternately blue and silver by which King Offa had granted their liberty to the people of St Albans—the common people, masons and workmen—as a reward for their help in building the town': Rosamond Faith, 'The Class Struggle

great wood within his large manor of Wakefield in the 1630s, the commoners tried to defend their rights by invoking an ancient charter granted to them by Earl Warren in the fourteenth century, which seems to have enjoyed similar status. Eighty-four-year-old Thomas Somester testified that many times 'he hath seene a deed or charter in wrytinge from Earle Warren with a great seale thereto affixed and bound about with silver haveing an impression of the [Ex]chequer of the one side and a man on horse backe of the other side, made to the burgesses of Wakefield, by which the earle did graunt comon unto them in his woods and wastes at Wakefield, excepting in his old parke and new parke and great meadowe', which charter was safe in the parish church, 'being the place where some evidences concerning the towne of Wakefield were usuallie kept'.[53]

It was not only tenants, of course, who looked to such documents for precedent. Just as often landlords can be found employing them to assert their own rights and defend their particular interests. When, for example, the inhabitants of Thetford tried to claim rights of common in the manor of Westwick, Suffolk, at the beginning of the seventeenth century, they were countered by the surveyor Robert Buxton who claimed to have seen, among various 'ancient evidences' in the church of All Saints, a 'wryting made in the time of Hamelyn, Earle Warren' and 'an old paper booke belonging to the monks of Thetford' dated 1337, from which he 'inferreth that this Westwick could be no common as is pretended'. Threatened with a claim in the early 1660s by inhabitants of a neighbouring manor to rights over a parcel of land which he believed to belong to his lordship of Cowling in the North Riding of Yorkshire, Thomas Jackson was able to produce, among other evidence 'an ancient deed . . . made in the three and twentieth yeare of the late King Henry the sixth between the late Abbott of Coverham and William Ascogh' in support of his case. In 1679, the lawyers of the earl of Devonshire, owner of the rectory of Tutbury, tried to settle some of the long-standing disputes involving bounds, commons, and tithes in and around Needwood Forest by producing a charter from the reign of King John given by Lord Ferrers, the earl of Derby, to the priory of Tutbury, 'whereby the sayd earle did grant tythes in the Forest of Needwood to the sayd pryor and pryorie of Tutbury in the county of Stafford'.[54]

in Fourteenth-Century England', in Raphael Samuel (ed.), *People's History and Socialist Theory* (London, 1981), 57.

[53] PRO, DL4/94/46. On the struggles over common rights in Wakefield, see Manning, *Village Revolts*, 147–51.

[54] PRO, E134/1 Jas I/Trin 7, mm. 5–6; PRO, E126/8, fo. 85ᵛ; PRO, E134/30&31 Chas II/Hil 5.

In the case of royal forests such as Needwood it was particularly likely that this kind of ancient documentary evidence would be available. The active assertion of rights over these jurisdictions by the crown, since Norman times at least, had created a relatively large amount of recorded precedent which could be consulted and utilized in subsequent centuries. Royal forests were governed by their own laws which were already being written down in the twelfth century: the 'Assize of Woodstock' drawn up in 1184 represents their earliest authentic statement. In the second decade of the thirteenth century a number of documents set down the administration of the Forest of Exmoor, for example. Henry III issued a 'Charter of the Forest' in 1217; soon after a series of articles known as 'The Customs and Assizes of the Forest' were set down; and in 1219 the first perambulation of its bounds was mapped and enrolled. The forest laws were administered by justices in eyre, the earliest surviving records of which in Exmoor date from 1257 and 1270. In addition, the valuable resources which forests contained gave rise to a number of early declarations of rights of common within them. In 1154 Henry II issued a charter to the monks of Flaxley Abbey granting them 'all easements within my Forest of Dean, to wit, common of pasture for their young cattle and hogs, and for all other beasts'. In 1288 an enquiry conducted into common rights in Needwood Forest brought forth a large number of free tenants who claimed these rights by virtue of charters granted to them or their ancestors by the earls of Ferrers, the earliest of which dated from around 1128. In the early fifteenth century, the Tutbury coucher attempted to list systematically the common rights in Needwood.[55]

It was precisely such records which lawyers sought to recover and press into the service of their clients' claims. No doubt they primed deponents to refer to such documents in court, whether they had any prior knowledge of them or not. In the case of the perambulation of royal forests, for example, many of them were made during the thirteenth century and the records deposited at Westminster. In the Forests of Exmoor and Mendip, for example, they were taken in 1219, 1279, 1298, and 1300.[56] Such documents could be of great value when, in the sixteenth and

---

[55] MacDermot, *The History of the Forest of Exmoor*, 47–8, 50–1, 55–8, 72, 77–93; Hart, *The Commoners of Dean Forest*, 3; Birrell, 'Common Rights in the Medieval Forest', 28, 25 n.

[56] MacDermot, *The History of the Forest of Exmoor*, 115–21, 129–31, 137–42, 142–7; *Mendip Mining Laws and Forest Bounds*, ed. J. W. Gough (Somerset Record Society, 45, Frome, 1931), 164–92. The perambulation of Waltham Forest in 1300 is printed in W. R. Fisher, *The Forest of Essex: Its History, Laws, Administration and Ancient Customs* (London, 1887), 393–9. For references to other thirteenth-century perambulations, see J. C. Cox, *The Royal Forests of England* (London, 1905), 99, 125, 148, 151, 204, 229, 234–5, 247, 276, 284, 290–1, 336, 341.

seventeenth centuries, rights of common within forests were fiercely disputed and the boundaries between them and their neighbouring manors became a matter of great importance. In such cases, the court of Exchequer sought, as was its practice, to gather both oral and written evidence. In addition to hearing the depositions of old men who remembered the processions around the merestones from their youth, they dispatched officers to the Tower of London in search of record.

Thus in 1610 a boundary dispute between the lordship of Geddington and the manor of Newton adjoining Rockingham Forest, Northamptonshire, was ruled upon on the basis of the perambulation of the forest made in the reign of Edward I. Similarly, when legitimate rights within the Forest of Frome Selwood, Somerset, were being decided in 1633, 'sundry ancient records now read' in court, including Edward I's perambulation, provided the crucial evidence. A few years before, various claimants to rights of common in Braydon Forest, Wiltshire, had been dismissed after it was shown that their lands lay outside the bounds of the forest by dint of 'a statute made concerning forrests in the xxxiiith yeare of Kinge Edward the first' and a perambulation taken in the twelfth year of Henry III. They, on the other hand, could not produce 'any aucthentick record or other allowance, or any clayme had therefore in any justice seate or otherwise for the maintenance of their pretended claymes, which is the proper and effectuall proofe of comon in a forrest'.[57]

During the big Exchequer hearing of 1678 concerning common rights in Exmoor Forest, deponents asserting their claim were shown a copy of the perambulation of 1300, 'now remayning in the Tower of London' together with 'a certain card or mapp' showing the boundaries between the forest and its adjoining lands. Various ancient inhabitants, such as Thomas Pearse, a 60-year-old yeoman of Withypool, gave a detailed account of the merestones and markers as he had trodden them every seven years and claimed that these agreed exactly with those described in the record of 29 Edward I. Peter Houndell, yeoman of Exford, aged 73, also bore witness to the fact that the evidence of this document was 'satisfied and confirmed as well by his owne knowledge and experience as by the sayeings of all antient people with who [he] hath discoursed concerning the same'. In many particulars this agreement was real, but in others deponents required strained efforts to make recent practice coincide with that of three and a half centuries before.[58]

Given that such written records seem often to have been regarded by

[57] PRO, E126/1, fo. 184ᶠ; PRO, E126/4, fo. 99ᵛ; PRO, E126/3, fos. 256, 269ᶠ.

[58] PRO, E134/30 Chas II/East 21, mm. 4–11; see also PRO, E134/30 Chas II/East 15; PRO, E134/30 Chas II/Mich 12; MacDermot, *The History of the Forest of Exmoor*, ch. 12.

the court as the clinching evidence, and sometimes even the 'proper and effectuall proofe' of the customs claimed before it, it is hardly surprising that all parties to a suit should place such store by their procurement and preservation. In addition, the Exchequer cases reveal just how often litigants tried to suppress or alter documentation which might be prejudicial to their cause. On the one hand, communities carefully guarded the valuable deeds, titles, and copies preserved in the padlocked chest at the church or manor court, while individuals kept their cherished 'evidences' in the family strong box at home. On the other, it is clear that in times of dispute considerable efforts might be made by both landlords and tenants to manipulate the written word: court rolls mysteriously disappeared, custumals were tampered with, and parish chests were robbed.

In 1606 it was claimed by inhabitants of former bishopric lands in the Isle of Ely that new owners of these manors had 'gotten and obteyned into their possession some auncient cowchers and legar bookes of the inheritance of the said bishoppricke' and by 'writinge some olde surveys or parts of surveyes in such bookes contrarie to the truth' they had sought 'to gett from them their lawfull and true right of comon and priviledge . . . which they and their predessessors have enioyed many hundred yeares'. At Wem in Shropshire, meanwhile, a long story of chicanery on both sides was already underway. An inquisition early in the seventeenth century found that someone had erased and altered a custumal in an attempt to validate the claimed entitlements of the copyholders there. Two generations later, however, it was the then landlord, Daniel Wytcherly, who was apparently appropriating all available documents and copies in his attempt to force up rents and fines. He was said to have removed 'a writing' from the penthouse adjoining the manorial court and to have stolen 'a roll, wherein the customes of the manor were expressed, kept in the parish church of Wem in a chest there', only to claim, when challenged, that they 'had beene lost and could not be gott or obtayned'. A similar theft appears to have occurred at Ottery St Mary, Devon, in the 1660s when, as 84-year-old Richard Channon later remembered, 'the court rolls, ledger bookes and other writinges' concerning the local customs suddenly vanished. Since the beginning of Elizabeth's reign they had been 'kept in a little roome within the church . . . under severall lockes and keys . . . for the safe keeping of the same and for the loan use of the lord and copyholders', who had always 'had free accesse to view the same as occasion required', being 'of great concernment to the copyholders and tenants . . . for defence of their titles to their . . . lands and the maintenance of their customes there'.[59]

[59]  PRO, E126/1, fo. 46ᵛ; Kerridge, *Agrarian Problems in the Sixteenth Century and after*, 56; PRO, E134/26 Chas II/Mich 48; PRO, E134/18&19 Chas II/Hil 13. Among many similar examples

Such actions give some idea of the importance attached to old records as legal evidence. In addition to stimulating the battle to recover and control written evidence from the past, however, resort to equity also encouraged the desire to create new transcripts of custom. Suits before courts such as the Exchequer were just one spur among a number, in the late sixteenth and early seventeenth centuries, to the first full recording of knowledge which had always been preserved in memory and exercised in practice. This was a period during which, in localities throughout England, flexible usages were being codified into fixed form and oral traditions transmuted into written records.

## THE DESIRE TO DOCUMENT

As we have seen, the increasingly active land market during the sixteenth century created a situation in many manors where a new landlord with little knowledge of local custom was required to learn its details as a matter of necessity and urgency. This was done by calling together the homage of the manor court and other elders in order to be told the intricacies of their laws and regulations. Since the complexity of such knowledge was too great for an outsider easily to remember, this process naturally encouraged the writing down of customs. In addition, where tenants were threatened by a new lord who sought to break local custom by forcing up rents or restricting common rights, they may have felt a greater need to have some formal record of their entitlements. 'Constant inquiry into the customs of manors and into the evidence of tenants' titles was', as one historian has put it, 'one of the outstanding features of Elizabethan and early Stuart times, as literally thousands of surviving documents testify'.[60]

In manor after manor, therefore, this period threw up written statements of local custom which apprised the lord of exactly what he had an

---

of the appropriation or corruption of records, see PRO, E126/2, fo. 9ʳ; PRO, E126/5, fo. 206ᵛ; PRO, E126/6, fos. 155ᵛ–156ʳ, 204ᵛ–209ʳ; Manning, *Village Revolts*, 137; MacDermot, *The History of the Forest of Exmoor*, 230, 374; Hart, *The Free Miners of the Forest of Dean and the Hundred of St. Briavels*, 137, 303–4; E. P. Thompson, *Whigs and Hunters: The Origin of the Black Act* (London, 1975), 179; Joanna Martin, 'Private Enterprise versus Manorial Rights: Mineral Property disputes in Eighteenth-Century Glamorgan', *Welsh History Review*, 9 (1978), 171. On the increasing number of parish chests from the sixteenth century, see Tate, *The Parish Chest*, 37, 44–51.

[60] Batho, 'Landlords in England, 1500–1640', 304; and see Mildred Campbell, *The English Yeoman under Elizabeth and the Early Stuarts* (London, 1960), 106–7; C. W. Brooks, *Pettyfoggers and Vipers of the Commonwealth: The 'Lower Branch' of the Legal Profession in Early Modern England* (Cambridge, 1986), 200.

obligation to allow and a right to expect and confirmed for the tenants their ancient rights and duties. Typically, an inquiry into local ways by the lord of Bushey, Hertfordshire, in 1563 provoked such a document, drawn up by twenty of the copyholders. It contained sixteen articles which were apparently cited from memory since they claimed to 'knowe not where the courte rolles, rentals, or customaryes of the manor are remayning or in whose custodye'. Very often such documents were the outcome of a process of arbitration, a great collective bargain between lord and tenants, in which the former would agree to recognize certain rights of the latter in return for the acceptance of liberties of his own.[61]

Various examples from Cambridgeshire are representative. In 1577 Richard Brackyn, lord of the manor of Chesterton, and fifty-seven of his customary tenants brokered a deed of composition confirming the mutually acceptable customs of the manor. 'Reciting that sundry quarrels had grown between the lords and copyholders and for finally ending the same it was agreed that the several tenants should enjoy their copyholds specified in the schedule according to the limitations after expressed and not otherwise.' Brackyn agreed to confirm fixed rents and fines in return for which the tenants released their rights of common over various lands. In 1580, Sir Francis Hinde entered an agreement with the 'greatest number of welthiest and substancyalist inhabitants and tenants of Cottenham' concerning rights over the sheep-walk and access to the common fields in the parish. This was to be the first in a long series of settlements and disputes between lords and tenants here over the next century. Not far away at Milton, the lord of the manor, Henry Cooke, compounded with his customary tenants to the same end in October 1591. The latter had their rents and fines set and secured certain timber rights in return for agreeing to the division of the marshes and fens, previously held in common and now to be held in severalty, apportioned among the parties according to the size and terms of their holdings.[62]

The late sixteenth and early seventeenth centuries, then, represented the great age of the document of local customs. Around 1565, for example, the copyholders of Bosham in Sussex were granted an 'indenture of confirmation of their customs' by their landlord, Henry, earl of Berkeley, and this 'they for the canonicalnes thereof called Bosham bible'. Shortly afterwards the various interested parties in the manor of Crondall, Hampshire, produced a similar customary 'to put an end to all

---

[61] Tawney, *The Agrarian Problem in the Sixteenth Century*, 126–8.

[62] CRO, 399/E6; 'Common Rights at Cottenham and Stretham in Cambridgeshire', ed. W. Cunningham, in *Camden Miscellany*, xii (Camden Society, third ser., 18, London, 1910), 177–81, 193–229, 230–45; CRO, L3/17/3.

uncertainties'. The inhabitants of Great Wishford in Wiltshire wrote down two such statements of custom, in 1597 and 1603. The latter, entitled 'The sum of the ancient customs belonging to Wishford and Barford out of the Forest of Grovely', set out their common rights of plowbote, hedgebote, housebote, and firebote in the forest while rejecting the claims of their neighbours, of whom 'very many doe often resort into Grovely woodes and fetche fearne and wood there without any auethoritie for the doeing thereof'. And 1647 saw the transcription of 'A customary conteyning the cheife points of the custome of the mannor of Taunton and Taunton Deane in the county of Somersett' which listed fifty items.[63]

In many instances, disputants looked to the manorial court or other local jurisdiction to confirm their explanations of customary practice in a written form. Typically, the inhabitants of the manor of Farlington, North Riding, went before the justice in eyre in the neighbouring Forest of Galtres in 1571 to recite their rights of common pasture and turbary therein. They were approved by the court and recorded by the steward who held them for safekeeping, being 'ingrossed in parchment conteyninge two or three skinnes, and sealed and subscribed'. In the same way, husbandman Henry Rutter remembered in 1629, the inhabitants of Purton Stoke knew their rights of common in Keynes Wood, Wiltshire, because they had 'made claym to such . . . at divers justice seats and swanimote courts held within the . . . Forest [of Braydon], which have been ratified there from time to time and allowed of'. The homages themselves often took the initiative in the business of documentation. When, in 1584 there was, at the court baron of the manor of Wigmore in Herefordshire, a jury of 'substanciall gents and yeomen . . . then impannelled', they made a presentment 'in writinge' directing 'that all and every of the auncyente tenants and inhabitants of Aston and Elton had and used to have their severall commons of pasture and estovers in Bringwood [Forest]'. A few years earlier, officials from the swanimote court at King's Cliffe were ordered to survey the royal forests in Northamptonshire, with the result that sets of written orders were drawn up which codified rights of pannage and common in the woods.[64]

[63] Smyth, *The Berkeley Manuscripts*, ed. Maclean, ii. 433; Campbell, *The English Yeoman*, 123 n.; R. W. Bushaway, '"Grovely, Grovely, Grovely and All Grovely": Custom, Crime and Conflict in the English Woodland', *History Today*, 38 (May, 1981), 39, 42, and id., *By Rite*, 209–11; BL, Egerton MS, 2223, fos. 1–12.

[64] PRO, E134/5 Jas I/East 12; PRO, E134/4 Chas I/East 26, m. 9; PRO E134/5 Jas I/East 7; P. A. J. Pettit, *The Royal Forests of Northamptonshire: A Study in their Economy, 1558–1714*

In the creation of such documents and the gathering of the information which underpinned them, the surveyor came into his own. It is no coincidence that the Elizabethan and early Stuart period saw a huge increase in the numbers of surveyors for whose services there was new and urgent demand.[65] They were employed to help settle the mass of uncertainty and controversy over exactly what were true and proper customs in numerous manors, parishes, and boroughs across the country. Such a task could only ever be accomplished by a combination of measurement and assessment on the ground, interviews with all of the parties concerned, and archival research among whatever documents were extant. As John Norden, the greatest practitioner of the day, put it, surveyors were bound, on the one hand, to hear the testimony of 'the most aunctient, and longest inhabitants within the mannor', and, on the other, to study all available 'deeds, evidences, court-rolls, rentals, sute-rolls, custom-rolles, bookes of survey, accounts, or any other escripts or monuments' before making any decisions. Despite this balance of oral and written evidence, however, he conveyed the clear impression that the latter was usually to be valued over the former. The 'two pillars upon which a surveyor must of force build his work', he recognized, were 'information and record', but 'record be alwaies preferred before verbal intelligence'. Only the 'ouer credulous' would take 'raw reports for matter of record'. Similarly, in pronouncing their judgments it was insufficient for surveyors merely to 'read and explain' the conclusions to the assembled manor, but necessary also to 'leaue them with you in writing for your better memorie: for I know, and haue often found, that a bare deliuerie of many words, and of diuers things . . . euen to eares well prepared, may be little effectuall'. The resultant documents, then, 'inrolled and ingrossed for peretuall memorie', preserved in fixed and ossified form a body of practices and usages which had hitherto ebbed and flowed down the generations.[66]

Among the many examples of such work was the survey drawn up by

(Northamptonshire Record Society, Gateshead, 1968), 153–4. For a later example, see Thompson, 'The Grid of Inheritance', 352 n., 354–5.

[65] Kerridge, *Agrarian Problems in the Sixteenth Century and after*, 26–31; F. M. L. Thompson, *Chartered Surveyors: The Growth of a Profession* (London, 1968), chs. 1–2; Victor Morgan, 'The Cartographic Image of "The Country" in Early Modern England', *Transactions of the Royal Historical Society*, 5th ser., 29 (1979), 134; Brooks, *Pettyfoggers and Vipers of the Commonwealth*, 198–203; Peter Clark, *English Provincial Society from the Reformation to the Revolution: Religion, Politics and Society in Kent, 1500–1640* (Hassocks, 1977), 121–2, 289–90.

[66] Norden, *The Surveyors Dialogue*, 22, 23, 94, 97, 109, 128. For examples of Norden's work, see BL, Additional MS, 6027, fos. 82–3; BL, Additional MS, 42508.

Francis Hinde, Robert Taylor, and William Humberston, by order of an Exchequer commission in 1575, for the queen's manor of Over in Cambridgeshire. Surveying in such fenland country was notoriously difficult, since by its very nature the land was constantly changing and boundaries were always uncertain. But the scale of this task was enormously increased by a manorial homage who, in typical fashion, habitually altered local custom to suit local needs. Use of the commons had become the cause of great 'contencons and quarrells' because 'the customs and uses thereof have and dayly to alter according to the disposition of the tenants and officers in the fens, [and the] wetness and dryness of season, as appeareth by the politique orders and by laws made in the courts to continue during the consent of the homage and officers for their better commodity and advantage. By reason whereof, we cannot set downe any custome certaine, but it may be broken by the discrecon of the inhabitants as the times and years shall serve . . . yet we thought good to declare how they be used at present.'[67]

Their resulting survey, therefore, like all such documents, presented only a snapshot of the customs as they operated at a particular moment It froze in time what had been a highly mutable set of usages adapting year by year in response to changing conditions; it fixed in text for posterity what memory had been able to forget and circumstance to forgo. Henceforth, such documents provided an unflinching reference point against which any future alterations in practice could be measured. They were preserved and drawn upon subsequently, as when the survey of Rutland, compiled in the first year of Edward VI's reign by Thomas Heyes, was produced in 1603 to help establish the true customs of copyholders at the manor of Wing.[68] But the consequences of this were a mixed blessing. On the one hand, written fixity may have helped to settle contention, or perhaps even to avoid it in the first place. On the other hand, all parties were now bound to a rigid system which denied the flexibility and sensitivity to change allowed in the past.

Despite the work of surveyors in determining custom and helping to fix it in written form, there were a variety of reasons why landlords and tenants still felt the need to resort to the equity courts for help. For one thing, the sheer difficulty of the surveyor's task in certain areas of the country left him unable to decide these complex and ever changing circumstances on his own. When John Rowe attempted to survey one

---

[67] CRO, 258/M22; PRO, E134/17&18 Eliz/Mich 6 (copy of the survey).
[68] PRO, E134/4 Jas I/Mich 1, m. 3.

manor in the barony of Lewes, Sussex, in 1622 he complained that 'its customs I find so variable as that I can not certainlye resolve myselfe thereof, much lesse satisfye others'. On another manor he found the tenants' 'estates to be intangled with the like difficultyes fitter for the reverend judges of this kingdome upon mature deliberacon then for mine insufficiency to determine'. Thus cases were referred up to courts such as the Exchequer where the barons were charged with the task of arbitrating in near impossible circumstances. In one such example involving the boundaries of various lands and parishes in the notorious fens of the Isle of Ely, Francis Underwood, gentleman of Thorney, deposed that over a twenty-year period from 1636 he had attempted to survey the locality and 'did oftentymes make it his business to enquire amongst the auntient people then liveing near unto the places and also to inspect all such writings and records' in any effort to determine metes and bounds, but could only conclude that he, 'without any equivocation or mental reservation, doth veryly in his heart beleeve that neither hee . . . nor any other man liveing can truely say' what they are.[69]

Another reason why surveyors felt compelled to recommend the resort to equity was the sheer lack of the kind of documentation by which the profession set so much store. In a report to Sir Robert Cecil in 1602, the surveyor Sir Robert Johnson lamented that, on the crown lands, 'of everie tenne mannors their is not one perfect surveigh, that not one court roll of a hundred that ought to be are to be seen or come by, and I think fewe or none (onelesse it be for Duchie lands in which I think some good course is holden) are to be found in anie of those storehowses in which they might and ought to have bene kept and preserved'. For this he blamed manorial stewards who do not trouble 'their heads with anie curious preservation of ancient customes, nor their pennes with ingrossing anie records at all, but kepe their momentarie remembrances . . . in rough paper bookes which are comonlie loste or embeseled with the death or change of the steward and almost suppressed altogether at the change of the quenes tenant'. This lack of written evidence made disputes intractable. 'To what height the controversies that have growen (through want of sucessyve preservation of records) have brought our comon lawiers, nedeth no argument,' as Johnson observed. The solution which he recommended was resort to the courts of equity. In disputes where '(for want of ancient records) little or nothing can be said or averred, yt were mete that pecemeale the points might be drawn into question before the

---

[69] Campbell, *The English Yeoman*, 123; PRO, E134/28 Chas II/Trin 7, mm. 4–5.

barons of her majesties Exchequer to be by theme allowed or reiected as to equitie appteieneth'.[70]

Finally, the central courts recruited cases from the manors even when contending interests had managed to reach an accommodation between themselves. In many cases landlords and tenants wanted the indenture of agreement which they drew up for the confirmation of their customs ratified by the authority of the Westminster tribunals. Sometimes they even concocted spurious disputes in order that the court of Chancery or Exchequer would issue a ruling in the form of a decree legally recognizing a settlement already reached between them. When, for example, Sir John Brown compounded with the tenants on his Worcestershire manor in 1572 for the fixing of rents and fines, the parties succeeded in having the agreement ratified by such a decree. On 5 October 1632 the freeholders and copyhold tenants from a group of neighbouring manors in Cambridgeshire drew up articles of agreement with their landlords 'touching the dividinge, apporconing and setting out in severaltye of the fenney marsh and common waste ground of and belonginge to the said severall mannors'. This was confirmed the following March by Chancery decree which was ordered 'to bee inviolubly kept and observed for ever by all and singular the said lordes and tenants of the said mannors, their heires and assignes'. Things were never that simple in the fens, of course, and it was not long before that majority of inhabitants and tenants excluded by the decree's provisions had filed an Exchequer bill claiming that it 'was unduely had and obteyned, and without their consent, being the greater number of the said tenants'.[71]

For all of these reasons, therefore, the rulings of equity courts were keenly sought in such matters. And the decisions which they made, issued in the form of decrees, were themselves a crucial part of the process of transmuting oral custom into written record.[72] The precious Exchequer or Chancery decree was to become a binding code, 'inviolably kept and observed for ever', setting out in precise and unequivocal terms the customs of the manor and the rights of all. They were carefully preserved in estate offices and parish chests and bound up by tenants in the form of

---

[70] PRO, SP12/283A/80. On the parlous state of records relating to the royal estates, see David Thomas, 'The Elizabethan Crown Lands: Their Purposes and Problems', in Hoyle (ed.), *The Estates of the English Crown, 1558–1640*, 64–5.

[71] Michael Zell, 'Fixing the Custom of the Manor: Slindon, West Sussex, 1568', *Sussex Archaeological Collections*, 122 (1984), 101–6; PRO, E126/1, fos. 82–6; CRO, 126/M88.

[72] For an excellent case study of this process, see Wood, 'Custom, Identity and Resistance', 266–72. On the 'growing authority accorded to decisions of the central courts' in such cases, see Jones, *The Elizabethan Court of Chancery*, 487–8, and id., 'A Note on the Demise of Manorial Jurisdiction', 315–18.

'a customary book' which was typically entrusted to one of the 'eldest and most sufficient' amongst them.[73] Thus in 1590 a decree was issued in the court of Exchequer settling tithing customs in the parish of St Mary's, Whittlesey, in Cambridgeshire. Thereafter a copy of it, 'commonly called the customarye booke', was kept by the inhabitants of the parish, 'as a rule and direction for payment of theire tithes'.[74]

Hence, if further dispute over customary rights arose subsequent to their issue, such decrees became vital evidence. Naturally, when deponents in Exchequer cases were defending their interests they set great store by earlier decrees issued by the court. In February 1628, for example, a decree from the court confirmed the rights of common in the Forest of Dean to existing commoners, either freeholders or tenants. Late in 1635 a further Exchequer suit over the same issue elicited several invocations of this document. John Bridgman of Littledean had 'seen a writing ingrossed in parchment purporting an exemplification of a decree under the seal of the Exchequer dated 4 February 3 Charles, concerning the claim of common and other privileges within the Forest of Dean by divers and several persons, townships, places and parishes'. Joseph White of Huntley, clothier, justified the grazing rights of the commoners of Westbury over Walmore Common with similar reference.[75] It was with far less fondness, on the other hand, that many people in the Isle of Axholme looked upon the Exchequer decree of 1636 which ratified the enclosure of Epworth Common. Fifty years later ancient men could still remember how they were persuaded to sign away their rights, regarding the decree as a symbol of their loss.[76]

The authority of these judgments as legal precedents is evident and knowledge of, or access to, them could be of great importance. This was known very well by Mr Hunt, the parson of Lidford in Devon, early in the

[73] For an example, see Peter Large, 'Rural Society and Agricultural Change: Ombersley, 1580–1700', in Chartres and Hey (eds.), *English Rural Society*, 123. Occasionally decrees and other such documents might even be printed: Wood, 'Custom, Identity and Resistance', 270; R. W. Bushaway, 'Rite, Legitimation and Community in Southern England, 1700–1850: The Ideology of Custom', in Barry Stapleton (ed.), *Conflict and Community in Southern England* (Stroud, 1992), 113; Thompson, 'Custom, Law and Common Right', *Customs in Common*, 99–100.

[74] PRO, E134/28 Chas II/Trin 7, m. 11. A further Exchequer decree of 1638 sanctioned drainage and enclosure at Whittlesey: see PRO, E134/27 Chas II/East 28; CRO, 126/M88–90. Cf. the extracts from the Exchequer decree for the manor of Stretham, 1607, printed in 'Common Rights at Cottenham and Stretham in Cambridgeshire', ed. Cunningham, 253–9.

[75] PRO, E134/11&12 Chas I/Hil 2, and Hart, *The Commoners of Dean Forest*, 36–8.

[76] PRO, E134/1&2 Jas II/Hil 25. On the enclosures at Epworth, see Lindley, *Fenland Riots and the English Revolution*, 27–33. The Exchequer barons could deal harshly with anyone who challenged the authority of their decrees, but they themselves were quite prepared to revoke decisions made by the court in former times: see, for example, PRO, E126/1, fos. 76ʳ–80ʳ, 109ᵛ, 283; PRO, E126/3, fos. 270ᵛ–272ʳ.

seventeenth century. One of his predecessors had lost a legal battle over tithes, 'the record whereof remained in the registers office of the bishop of Exeter'. Hunt was alleged somehow to have appropriated the ruling, for he could boast that he would have his due, 'by reason he had gotten the said recorde into his owne handes'. Indeed, the preservation, or at least the popular memory, of these decrees could endure, like the memory of medieval charters, for many centuries. As late as the 1880s, the tenants of Cadnam and Winsor, adjoining the New Forest, saved their rights over Wigley Common from extinction when it was remembered that one of their number had a strong box containing an 'old paper'. Inside was found to be a Chancery decree of 1591 ratifying their custom. 'But for the big box', it was said, 'which impressed itself on the traditions of the tenants, as connected with their rights, the deed might have been lost.'[77]

So it was that, in variously attempting to transmute oral or ill-defined customs into written and codified documents, people of all sorts tried to provide themselves with what they believed to be the best means of defending and advancing their rights and interests. The late sixteenth and early seventeenth century, in particular, witnessed an enormous amount of controversy and litigation over customary rights in a wide range of circumstances. One consequence of this was that much which had always been preserved in memory and practice was now entrusted to paper and parchment. The ensuing process of documentation may be seen in some cases as a conscious effort to protect and enhance by means of writing, and in others as a largely unintended result of the repeated resort to law.

The case of the writing down of local custom provides just one very graphic illustration of the evolving relationship between oral tradition and written record over these two centuries. In this context, as in others, the relative status of the two forms was complex and constantly changing. If the prestige and use of the word on paper was increasing at the expense of the word spoken then there was certainly no simple or linear substitution of the one by the other. But customary law does offer one instance in which a very largely oral system came to be very largely written down over a relatively short space of time. By the middle of the seventeenth century, it is said, there were 'few manors where ambiguous customs had not been spelt out one way or another'.[78] Disputes over such matters, in manors as

---

[77] PRO, E134/3&4 Chas I/Hil 11, m. 6; Shaw-Lefevre (Lord Eversley), *Commons, Forests and Footpaths*, 126–8; Thompson, 'Custom, Law and Common Right', *Customs in Common*, 159.

[78] Christopher Clay, 'Landlords and Estate Management in England, 1640–1750', in Clay (ed.), *Rural Society: Landowners, Peasants and Labourers, 1500–1750* (Cambridge, 1990), 325–6.

in other jurisdictions, did not end there, nor did the desire to document rights and usages, but the Elizabethan and early Stuart period seems to have represented a watershed in this respect. For the generations who lived through these years there must have been an ever clearer sense of the utility and authority of the written word, an ever greater appreciation of the fact that this was a world defined and governed by texts.

# 6
## Ballads and Libels

Bvt all the world could not keepe, nor any ciuill ordinance to the contrary so preuaile, but that men would and must needs vtter their
splenes in all ordinarie matters also: or else it seemed their bowels
would burst, therefore the poet deuised a prety fashioned poeme
short and sweete (as we are wont to say) and called it *Epigramma*
in which euery mery conceited man might without any long studie or
tedious ambage, make his frend sport, and anger his foe, and giue a
prettie nip, or shew a sharpe conceit in few verses: for this *Epigramme*
is but an inscription or writting made as it were vpon a table, or in a
windowe, or vpon the wall or mantell of a chimney in some place of
common resort, where it was allowed euery man might come, or be
sitting to chat and prate, as now in our tauernes and common tabling
houses, where many merry heades meete, and scrible with ynke with
chalke, or with a cole such matters as they would euery ma[n] should
know, and descant vpo[n]. Afterward the same came to be put in
paper and in bookes, and vsed as ordinarie missiues, some of
frendship, some of defiaunce, or as other messages of mirth.

George Puttenham, *The Arte of English Poesie*
(London, 1589), 43–4.

Though some may slight of libells, yet you may see by them how the
wind sitts; as, take a straw, and throw it upp into the aire, you shall
see by that which way the wind is, which you shall not doe by casting upp a stone—More solid things doe not shew the complexion
of the times so well as ballads and libells.

*Table Talk of John Selden*, ed. Sir Frederick Pollock
(London, 1927), 72.

IN seventeenth-century Warwickshire, they told many stories of old Will
Shakespeare. And none was more famous than that of how the local hero
came to flee his home town and seek fame and fortune in the capital city.
One day, tradition recounted, he had been caught poaching deer in
Charlecote Park, the ancestral home of Sir Thomas Lucy, about 4 miles
from Stratford. 'For this he was prosecuted by that gentleman, as he
thought, somewhat too severely; and in order to revenge that ill usage, he

made a ballad upon him. And tho' this, probably the first essay of his poetry, be lost, yet it is said to have been so very bitter, that it redoubled the prosecution against him to that degree, that he was oblig'd to leave his business and family in Warwickshire, for some time, and shelter himself in London."[1]

Nicholas Rowe may not have known the contents of Shakespeare's first poetic effort, but some people clearly did. For the ballad was apparently passed down in the area by word of mouth until, three or four generations later, 'several old people at Stratford' were discovered repeating it. One man who overheard it was Thomas Jones, of nearby Tardebigge in Worcestershire, and he was able to recall the first stanza well enough to write it down before he died, 'upwards of ninety', in 1703. It ran thus:

> A parliamente member, a justice of peace,
> At home a poore scarecrow, at London an asse.
> If lowsie is Lucy, as some volke miscalle it,
> Then Lucy is lowsie whatever befalle it:
> > He thinkes himselfe greate,
> > Yet an asse in his state,
> We allowe by his eares but with asses to mate.
> If Lucy is lowsie, as some volke miscalle it,
> Sing lowsie Lucy, whatever befalle it.

The ancients of Stratford also remembered that 'the ballad written against Sir Thomas by Shakespeare was stuck upon his park gate, which exasperated the knight to apply to a lawyer at Warwick to proceed against him'. This was no private joke, then, but a very public insult and a serious defamation of character. By beating a hasty retreat to London, the young poet had narrowly escaped a prosecution for libel.[2]

Whether there is any truth behind this story and whether Shakespeare was the author of the satirical song or not, its composition typifies a practice which was commonplace in sixteenth- and seventeenth-century England. One of the most effective ways of holding someone up for

---

[1] Nicholas Rowe, 'Some Account of the Life, &c. of Mr. William Shakespear', in *The Works of Mr. William Shakespear*, ed. Rowe (6 vols., London, 1709), i. v. For a full discussion of this legend and its sources, see S. Schoenbaum, *Shakespeare's Lives* (2nd edn., Oxford, 1991), 68–72.

[2] Edward Capell, *Notes and Various Readings to Shakespeare* (3 vols., London, 1775), ii. 75. Capell's grandfather transmitted it to his son 'by memory' and he also wrote it down. At the same time, the antiquary William Oldys (1696–1761) obtained an identical copy of this verse. His transcription was published in *The Plays of William Shakspeare*, ed. Samuel Johnson and George Steevens (2nd edn., 10 vols., London, 1778), i. 223 (second pagination). An entirely different version of the poaching ballad, which purported similarly to date from the end of the seventeenth century, was copied in the late 1720s and first printed in *The Plays and Poems of William Shakspeare*, ed. Edmond Malone (10 vols., London, 1790), i. I, 107n.

ridicule at this time was to compose a railing rhyme or bawdy ballad about them. If it could be written down, copied, and spread around the neighbours, or posted up in public for all to see, then so much the better. But its power was principally oral: it lived and breathed as a verse recited or a song sung, bawled out in the language of the locality, as in this case which depends on the fact that in Elizabethan Warwickshire 'Lucy' was pronounced 'lowsie'. How well, we may imagine, this must have delighted patrons in the alehouses around and about: how they must have laughed.

But as the humiliated Sir Thomas's response demonstrates, it was a risky business to libel another person in this way, especially one of such rank. It had long been an offence under canon law to defame someone in word or deed, thus to rob them of their good name and undermine their 'credit' in the world. Moreover, by Shakespeare's day the secular courts were increasingly providing redress for the offence. In this they followed the lead given by one of the royal prerogative courts at Westminster, the Star Chamber, which in the Elizabethan and Jacobean period became the forum of ultimate resort for the victims of slander or libel.

For years scholars have debated whether or not Shakespeare continued to take his revenge on 'lowsie Lucy' by finding in him the inspiration for Justice Shallow who appears in *The Merry Wives of Windsor*, as well as in *2 Henry IV*. The *Merry Wives*, written in about 1597, opens with Shallow, a gentleman 'in the county of Gloucester, Justice of Peace and Coram', complaining bitterly of the 'disparagements' which he has suffered at the hands of Falstaff. 'Sir Hugh, persuade me not. I will make a Star Chamber matter of it. If he were twenty Sir John Falstaffs, he shall not abuse Robert Shallow, Esquire.' The cause of his grief becomes clear: 'Knight, you have beaten my men, killed my deer, and broke open my lodge.' Had Sir Thomas Lucy, threatened Shakespeare with prosecution in the Star Chamber for poaching, and also for libel after consulting the lawyer of Warwick about the 'bitter ballad'? The punning on 'luces' and 'louses' which follow in this play's opening exchanges, in which Shallows' coat of arms evokes that of the Lucys, are suggestive of the connection.[3] Whether these allusions offer corroboration for the legend of Shakespeare the poacher, or merely provide the references upon which subsequently to construct it, remains a matter for speculation. What they do point to, however, is the value of Star Chamber records as a source through which to investigate the issue of defamation, and in particular the contemporary proclivity for inventing libellous verse.

For students of the interaction between oral and literate forms of

---

[3] *The Merry Wives of Windsor*, I. i; Schoenbaum, *Shakespeare's Lives*, 69.

expression in early modern England, libellous rhymes afford a fascinating and very revealing glimpse of the dynamic interplay between spoken and written word. When they occasioned lawsuits for defamation, the records produced in such cases shed valuable light on the process by which songs and verses were committed to paper and distributed among their audiences in this period. They also illustrate both the form and the content of this popular genre, since offending compositions were often cited in evidence during the legal process. Even the humblest and least literate sections of contemporary society could be involved in the invention and dissemination of such material and, as a result, prosecutions for libel are capable of illuminating the views and concerns of those people whose mental world and cultural milieu is always most difficult to penetrate.

As examples of popular literature, libellous ballads and verses are especially instructive. Whereas in the case of most printed broadsides, their authorship is very often unknown and relatively little direct evidence survives as to where and among whom they circulated, the legal records created by the prosecution of these defamatory compositions enable us to discover not only who wrote them but the ways in which they were transmitted and the audiences at which they were aimed. Unlike extant examples of cheap print, which by themselves can tell us nothing about how the texts were actually sung or read, the ways in which they were received, or the responses which they evoked, the documentation produced in libel cases affords insight into the practices of singing and reading among ordinary men and women of the period. The recovery of 'libels' enables us to move the history of popular literature beyond the study of form and content and towards the analysis of performance and reception.

## SLANDER IN SONG

Consider another incident which took place not 20 miles from Stratford, while Shakespeare was at the height of his powers on the London stage. It occurred in December 1605 at the inn of Edward Freme in Evesham, Worcestershire. In a room at the Swan, a group of the townspeople were hatching a plot to blacken the name of a certain George Hawkins, and so make him the laughing-stock of the neighbourhood. Hawkins, a local squire, an attorney of the borough court, and a steward of the hundred of Blakenhurst, was alleged to have fathered a bastard child. It was a transgression, real or imagined, for which the conspirators were to expose him to humiliation of just the kind which his distant neighbour, Sir Thomas

Lucy, had reputedly suffered twenty years before. For these people were composing a 'libel', and George Hawkins was to be 'balladed'.[4]

None of the libellers seem to have been able to write, since in order to commit their message to paper, and so give it maximum publicity, they sought the services of three travelling tradesmen from Coventry, Lancelot Ratsey, Alexander Staples, and William Hickman, who happened to be lodging at the Swan. They told them that Hawkins 'was a man of that lewdenes' which they claimed and persuaded them to serve their turn. Accordingly, Ratsey, 'dyd in paper drawe . . . three sevrall pictures or images, decyferinge and notefyinge one of them to be the pyctuer of [George Hawkins]; one other to be the picture of one who was supposed to be a whore and had had a bastarde; the thirde and other to be the picture of the bastard ytself'. Beneath these drawings, furthermore, he 'dyd wryte in the sayde paper . . . a moste false, filthye, slanderous and defamous lybell' to the following effect:

> I canne noe more,
> This is the whore,
> Of cowardye George Hawkins.
> He gott with childe,
> In a place moste wilde,
> Which for to name yt is a shame.
> Yet for your satysfactione,
> I will make relatione,
> It was in a privey,
> A place moste filthy.
> As gent you may judge,
> Yet nothinge to bade,
> For a knave and a drabbe,
> And soe they praye goe trudge.
>
> This is the bastarde,
> With his father the dastard,
> George Hawkins highte he soe.
> In all this shire,
> There is not a squire,
> More like a knave I trowe.
> O cursed seede,
> My harte dothe bleede,
> To thinke howe thowe woist born.
> To the whore thy mother,
> And the knave thy father,
> An everlastinge scorne.

[4] PRO, STAC8/178/20; PRO, STAC8/178/37.

This done, Ratsey made multiple copies of the ballad and 'did drawe the same uppon a walle'. He and the others then set out to, 'caste abrode, devulge, publishe, and singe the same in dyverse and sonderye open and publicke places, and dyd sett upp and fix the same uppon dyverse and sundry doors, walls and posts to the intente that the same might be made knowne unto all mannor of persones whatsoever, to the utter infame, scandale and disgrace of [Hawkins]'. At the Swan they performed the scurrilous ditty and 'dyd fix the same uppon walls and doors in the said house to the intent that all persones might take notice thereof'. They 'did laughe and jeste att the said pictures', encouraging strangers passing through to do the same. Finally, they gave copies to Freme's servant, George Hooke, to distribute in the other tippling-houses in and around Evesham throughout that and the following month. So it was, in the face of this highly public and carefully orchestrated defamation of character, that George Hawkins prosecuted his assailants in one of the highest courts with jurisdiction in such matters, that of Star Chamber at Westminster.

The case of George Hawkins vividly demonstrates the way in which people at this time composed and had written out extempore songs in order to publicize news or rumour, information or entertainment. In this semi-literate world, the value of couching a message in verse or song was clear: rhymes passed around quickly by word of mouth, tripping easily off the tongue and lodging firmly in the memory. At the same time, however, it was evidently appreciated that if a composition could also be set down on paper its impact might be much greater and its audience much wider. Even if ballad makers could not write themselves, it was always possible to find a 'pen-man' somewhere to oblige, and at a time when images could be more successful than words in communicating to the people, the drawing of pictures provided a powerful auxiliary. Once set down on paper, such material could be disseminated not only by singing it in public and teaching it others, but also by posting transcripts aloft and distributing them around the locality. Verses such as these, parochial in circulation and ephemeral in nature as they tended to be, would have left few traces behind them were it not for the fact that their victims sometimes sought redress in an action for libel.[5]

The many traces of these 'libels' in surviving court records from around the country throughout the early modern period give some

---

[5] See C. J. Sisson, *Lost Plays of Shakespeare's Age* (Cambridge, 1936); Martin Ingram, 'Ridings, Rough Music and Mocking Rhymes in Early Modern England', in Barry Reay (ed.), *Popular Culture in Seventeenth-Century England* (London, 1985), 166–97.

impression of the frequency with which people used this poetic medium in a variety of contexts. In 1574, for example, a group of people were said to be causing strife at Rye in Sussex by their 'accustome to affixe upon diverse men's dores certeine infamous libells and skrolls containing dishonest reproche . . .'. William and Elizabeth Trene of Rainham in Essex were accused a decade later of scandalously making 'a filthie ryme, of the most parte of the inhabitantes of this parishe'. Among numerous like rhymers was Joan Gomme of Thetford, Isle of Ely, presented in 1606 'for that she hath made and doth exercise the makeinge of libellous and lascivious ballads by divers of her neighbors'. In 1620, Robert Maundrell of Compton Bassett in Wiltshire was said to have 'framed, contrived and published a very infamous and scandalous wrightinge, in the nature of a libell, tending to the disgrace of his father-in-lawe Richard Miller and his wife and daughters and [John Burchall's] disgrace and his wife's, and have scattered copies thereof abroad, and singe it in the open hearing of divers persons'. John Vaux, the notorious conjurer-parson of St Helen's in Bishop Auckland, County Durham, was charged before the ecclesiastical authorities in 1633 that, among other misdemeanours, he 'did make and contrive scurrilous libells and epigrams' and that he had 'a written booke, in which there was verses made against Sir Charles Wrenn, knight, and divers other gentlemen of the countrie'. In like sort, Mary Shepperd of Furneux Pelham, Hertfordshire, was said in 1652 to have framed and contrived certain rhymes and songs against a neighbour, Robert Pompheritt; while late in 1684 a group of men from Long Lawford in Warwickshire was in trouble for similarly abusing a local widow and her daughter.[6]

Some people seem to have made it their continual and regular sport to engage in this kind of lyrical ridicule. 'Certeine lewde youthes' from Eccleshall in Staffordshire, for example, were said in 1605 to be such

---

[6] HMC, *Thirteenth Report, Appendix, Part IV* (London, 1892), 36; *A Series of Precedents and Proceedings in Criminal Causes, Extending from the Year 1475 to 1640; Extracted from Act-Books of Ecclesiastical Courts in the Diocese of London*, ed. W. H. Hale (London, 1847), 178; Cambridge University Library, EDR/B2/24, fo. 142ᵛ; *Records of the County of Wiltshire being Extracted from the Quarter Sessions Great Rolls of the Seventeenth Century*, ed. B. H. Cunnington (Devizes, 1932), 69; *The Acts of the High Commission Court within the Diocese of Durham*, ed. W. H. D. Longstaffe (Surtees Society, 34, Durham, 1858), 34–6; *Hertford County Records*, ed. W. J. Hardy (6 vols., Hertford, 1905–30), i. 96; *Warwick County Records*, ed. S. C. Ratcliffe and H. C. Johnson (9 vols., Warwick, 1935–64), viii. 182. For some printed cases quoting the actual verses, see *The Archdeacon's Court: Liber Actorum, 1584*, ed. E. R. C. Brinkworth (2 vols., Oxfordshire Record Society, 23–4, Oxford, 1942–6), i. 12; 'Extracts from the Records of the Wiltshire Quarter Sessions', ed. R. W. Merriman, *Wiltshire Archaeological and Natural History Magazine*, 22 (1885), 215–17; HMC, *Tenth Report, Appendix, Part IV* (London, 1885), 491; HMC, *Various Collections*, i. (London, 1901), 78, 90; F. G. Emmison, *Elizabethan Life: Disorder* (Chelmsford, 1970), 59–60, 68, 69, 72–3.

eavesdroppers that the good people of the town could 'speake nothinge in their beddes, the man with his wife, or one man with an other, but they heare what they talke, and make rythmes of yt when they have done, and scatter them abroade in the streetes to the breedinge of greate mischeefe, and malicious stomakinge of one man against an other'. A few years later, John Swifte, a cleric from Havant in Hampshire, was described as being 'a knowen and comon libeller and contriver of false and slaunderous libells and pamphlets' which he would 'by waye of jeste and merimente, sckoffinglye singe, divulge and publish . . . att diverse and sundrye tymes and in diverse places to diverse persons'. In 1648 the Quaker leader George Fox attended a court at Mansfield in Nottinghamshire and afterwards was 'moved to go and speak to one of the wickedest men in the country, one who was a common drunkard, a noted whore-master, and a rhyme-maker'.[7]

References in contemporary literature reinforce the impression that this phenomenon was a familiar part of the cultural landscape. The fifth book of Spenser's *Faerie Queene*, for example, makes mention both of the practice and its of punishment.

> There as they entred at the Scriene, they saw
> Some one, whose tongue was for his trespasse vyle
> Nayld to a post, adiudged so by law:
> For that therewith he falsely did reuyle,
> And foule blaspheme that Queene for forged guyle,
> Both with bold speaches, which he blazed had,
> And with lewd poems, which he did compyle;
> For the bold title of a Poet bad
> He on himselfe had ta'en, and rayling rymes had sprad.

Jacobean drama is full of allusions to the extempore ballads and libels exchanged in anger and mockery by all manner of people. 'I'll find a friend shall right me, and make a ballad of thee, and thy cattle all over', is the warning Joan Trash the gingerbread-woman offers to Leatherhead the hobby-horse seller at Ben Jonson's *Bartholomew Fair*. 'I am afraid of nothing but I shall be ballated,' frets the eponymous hero in George Chapman's *Monsieur d'Olive* (1606). Thomas Heywood's character, the Cripple of Fanchurch, claims to have stolen some 'songs and ditties' from a 'sharp-witted, bitter-tongu'd' versifier of his town, 'rolles, and scrolles, and bundles of cast wit, such as durst never visit Paul's Church-yard', and

---

[7] *The Staffordshire Quarter Sessions Rolls, 1581–1606*, ed. S. A. H. Burne (5 vols., William Salt Archaeological Society, Kendal, 1931–40), v. 238; PRO, STAC8/185/23, m. 2, and PRO, STAC8/263/15; *The Journal of George Fox*, ed. John L. Nickalls (Cambridge, 1952), 26–7.

from these he can, when 'in company at alehouse, taverne, or an ordinary, vpon a theame make an extemporall ditty'. In Philip Massinger's *The Parliament of Love* (1624), Charmont threatens to have Lamira

> Picterd as thou art now, and thie whole story
> Sunge to some villanous tune in a lewd ballet,
> And make thee notorious in the world,
> That boyes in the streetes shall hoot at the.[8]

Indeed, plays and interludes themselves were commonly composed to add a dramatic element to libellous verses. Some of the best writers of the day were apparently involved in what must have been, by its topicality, a popular satirical genre on the London stage. At a more amateur level in the localities, meanwhile, people regularly acted out the infamies of their neighbours in improvised jig and song-drama.[9]

### A STAR CHAMBER MATTER

Makers of ballads and libels were regularly being brought before the courts in early modern England. Libel and slander had traditionally been considered moral offences, dealt with by the ecclesiastical authorities, but during this period they also came to be defined as 'criminal'; seditious if directed against persons in authority and breaches of the peace if touching private individuals.[10] The court of Star Chamber was, until its abolition at the outbreak of the Civil War, principally responsible for this

---

[8] Edmund Spenser, *The Faerie Queene* (1596), v. ix. 25, in *Spenser: Poetical Works*, ed. J. C. Smith and E. De Selincourt (Oxford, 1912), 318; Ben Jonson, *Bartholmew Fayre* (1631), II. ii, in *The Works of Ben Jonson*, ed. C. H. Herford and Percy Simpson (11 vols., Oxford, 1925–52), vi. 41; George Chapman, *Monsieur d'Olive* (1606), III. i, in *The Works of George Chapman: Plays*, ed. R. H. Shepherd (London, 1874), 129; Thomas Heywood, *The Fayre Mayde of the Exchange* (1607), III. ii, in *The Dramatic Works of Thomas Heywood* (6 vols., London, 1874), ii. 46–7; Philip Massinger, *The Parliament of Love* (1624), IV. v, in *The Plays and Poems of Philip Massinger*, ed. Philip Edwards and Colin Gibson (5 vols., Oxford, 1976), ii. 158. For other examples, see W. Chappell, *Popular Music of the Olden Time* (London, 1859), 252–4, 422–3.

[9] C. R. Baskervill, *The Elizabethan Jig and Related Song Drama* (Chicago, 1929), ch. 2; N. J. O'Conor, *Godes Peace and the Queenes: Vicissitudes of a House, 1539–1615* (London, 1934), 108–26; Sisson, *Lost Plays of Shakespeare's Age*, chs. 2–4; C. L. Barber, *Shakespeare's Festive Comedy: A Study of Dramatic Form and its Relation to Social Custom* (Princeton, 1959); Mildred Campbell *The English Yeoman under Elizabeth and the Early Stuarts* (London, 1960), 152; *Records of Early English Drama: Cumberland, Westmorland, Gloucestershire*, ed. Audrey Douglas and Peter Greenfield (Toronto, 1986), 195–8, 235–8.

[10] J. F. Stephen, *A History of the Criminal Law of England* (3 vols., London, 1883), ii. 298–395; W. S. Holdsworth, *A History of English Law* (17 vols., London, 1903–72), v. 205–12, viii. 333–78; W. S. Holdsworth, 'Defamation in the Sixteenth and Seventeenth Centuries', *Law Quarterly Review*, 40 (1924), 302–15, 397–412, and 41 (1925), 13–31.

development. Through its judgments in a series of precedential cases in the late sixteenth and early seventeenth centuries, it was instrumental in the creation of new common law and the redefinition of much existing statute. The effect, which partly reflected Tudor and Stuart anxieties about 'disorder', was to upgrade the gravity of offences of cunning, such as defamation, as against those of force. Star Chamber, thereafter, became a natural forum for their redress (see Plate 12).[11] William Hudson's contemporary treatise on the court considered that after about 1600 the number of 'libels' prosecuted there had rapidly increased. Early in the reign of Charles I, Lord Keeper Coventry could reflect that:

> The Starrechamber of late hath had assumed to [it] the punishment of libells, for herby it is come to passe that people think that libells are punishable in noe other place but here and soe by reason of the great charge of suites here, many libells are unpunished, where in ancient times they were punished in court leetes, courts of credit formerly, though now debased in the esteeme of men.[12]

For this reason, the Star Chamber records yield important information about the way in which slander and libel were coming to be regarded in this period and about the forms which they most often assumed. The following analysis is based, therefore, upon the records of this particularly significant court during the Jacobean period. As the scattered evidence from other jurisdictions reveals, however, these Star Chamber findings may be taken to illustrate a practice which was widespread throughout the sixteenth and seventeenth centuries.

'Libels' before the court principally took the shape of derogatory songs or verses; derisive letters; pictures or objects with some scandalous imputation; or false allegations made before another authority against an individual or group. They were usually constituted, as William Hudson observed,

> either by scoffing at the person of another in rhyme or prose, or by the personating [of] him, thereby to make him ridiculous; or by setting up horns at his gate, or picturing him or describing him; or by writing of some base or defamatory letter, and publishing the same to others, or some scurvy love-letter to himself, whereby

---

[11] Holdsworth, *A History of English Law*, v. 208–12; T. G. Barnes, 'Due Process and Slow Process in the Late Elizabethan and Early-Stuart Star Chamber', *American Journal of Legal History*, 6 (1962), 221–49, 315–46; id., 'Star Chamber and the Sophistication of the Criminal Law', *Criminal Law Review* (1977), 316–26.

[12] William Hudson, 'A Treatise of the Court of Star Chamber', in *Collectanea Juridica: Consisting of Tracts Relative to the Law and Constitution*, ed. Francis Hargrave (2 vols., London, 1791–2), ii. 100; BL, Lansdowne MS, 620, fos. 50ᵛ–51ʳ. Cf. Richard Crompton, *Star Chamber Cases* (London, 1630), 10–11.

it is not likely but he should be provoked to break the peace; or to publish disgraceful or false speeches against any eminent man or public officer.[13]

All such things might detract from the name and reputation of a person and materially affect the 'credit' upon which so much of his or her ability to function within a community was based. Many libels alleged sexual misdemeanour or at least employed sexual imagery and innuendo, for regardless of circumstance this was the most ready and potent means to shame and to mock.[14]

Litigation at Westminster was an inconvenient and costly business, and this is reflected in the social status of those engaged in Star Chamber actions. Of the 8,228 cases of all types brought before the court during the reign of James I, 1603–25, 64 per cent involved plaintiffs stated to be from the wealthier ranks of society: nobles, gentlemen, professionals, and merchants. The remaining 36 per cent came from the middle and lower social orders: the yeomanry, in particular, together with husbandmen, artisans, and labourers. The rank of defendants, though less easy to determine, suggests equally that 'Star Chamber litigation was gentleman's business, first and foremost'.[15] The cases involving defamation reveal even more of a social bias among plaintiffs; of the 577 suits heard by Star Chamber in this period, only 115, or 20 per cent, were entered by litigants designated to be of 'yeoman' status or below. However, a total of 212 causes, or nearly 37 per cent, involved defendants from these middling and lower levels of society.[16] The latter statistic is, of course, the important one to bear in mind if one is discussing the composers of libels.

---

[13] Hudson, 'A Treatise of the Court of Star Chamber', in *Collectanea Juridica*, ed. Hargrave, ii. 100.

[14] The court deemed the composition of a 'libel' to be an offence, regardless of whether or not the allegations which it made were true. Early in the reign of Charles I, Richardson LCJ ruled in *Frere* v. *Bennett, Langdon and Aylett* that 'though the truth bee that the plaintiff is incontinent, yet it is a rule in lawe and in this court that a libell can noe way be justified': BL, Lansdowne MS, 620, fo. 35ᵛ; and see Houghton Library, Harvard University, fMS Eng. 1084, fo. 60ʳ.

[15] T. G. Barnes, 'Star Chamber Litigants and their Counsel, 1596–1641', in J. H. Baker (ed.), *Legal Records and the Historian* (London, 1978), 10. These figures include those of unspecified status who 'can be presumed to have been of the lower orders'.

[16] In the 577 cases involving defamation before the Jacobean Star Chamber the number of suits entered by principal plaintiffs, broken down according to social status, was as follows: King (6); Peer (15); Baronet (6); Knight (64); Esquire (98); Gentleman (153); Professional (76); Merchant (41); Yeoman (56); Husbandman (4); Artisan (18); Labourer (1); Corporate Body (3); Unspecified (36). The social status of principal defendants in these cases was: Peer (3); Baronet (4); Knight (48); Esquire (63); Gentleman (139); Professional (74); Merchant (34); Yeoman (41); Husbandman (14); Artisan (22); Labourer (1); Unspecified (134). In practice, many causes involved multiple plaintiffs, and the majority cited multiple defendants whose social status was usually the same or lower than the individual principally sued. These calculations are based on the data in T. G. Barnes et al. (eds.), *List and Index to the Proceedings in Star Chamber for the Reign of*

Clearly, the practice of inventing ballads and songs in order to ridicule and shame a rival or adversary was one well known at all social levels. Such rhyming could be employed by those of gentle and even of aristocratic stamp; it was most familiar, perhaps, to the various peoples of the 'middle sort' who comprised urban or parish elites. As a cultural form which was known to and shared in by all sections of the community, libelling defies the crude dichotomies implied by the labels 'elite' and 'popular'. Since the concern of this chapter, however, is to investigate the relationship between oral and written forms of expression at the least literate levels of society, it is on versifiers of relatively humble origin that it focuses.[17]

The extensive documentation produced by Star Chamber proceedings allows for the recovery of much of the background detail and attendant circumstances surrounding cases of defamation, as of other offences. Particular insight is afforded in libel suits, moreover, as the cause was considered invalid unless a copy of the text or a verbatim recitation of the offending words could be produced by the plaintiff.[18] In almost all cases, therefore, the entire song, rhyme, letter, or derogatory petition in question is contained within the indictment or annexed to it. For example, when John Peter, a fuller from Tiverton in Devon, was before the court in 1611 accused of inventing some scandalous verses against Robert Reede, a wealthy clothier and local worthy, Reede was obliged to admit that 'not having himself seene or heard them written or spoken as they were first devised, written, spoken, and published', he could not 'preciselie sett [them] downe for the better colouringe and strengtheninge' of his case. Peter was legitimately entitled to answer, as a result, that an accusation without the texts, 'without shewinge in what sort or what the same were, ys utterlye uncerteyne and insufficient in the lawe'.[19] Fortunately, the burden of proof ensures that, in the great majority of cases, both the circumstances and the precise contents of such compositions can be retrieved.

---

*James I, 1603–25, in the Public Record Office, London, Class STAC8* (3 vols., Chicago, 1975), iii. 351–61.

[17] For discussion of the libellous verses which could be produced and circulated at the highest social levels and which attacked great persons of state, see Richard Cust, 'News and Politics in Early Seventeenth-Century England', *Past and Present*, 112 (1986), 66–9; Pauline Croft, 'The Reputation of Robert Cecil: Libels, Political Opinion and Popular Awareness in the Early Seventeenth Century', *Transactions of the Royal Historical Society*, 6th ser., 1 (1991), 43–69; Alastair Bellany, '"Raylinge Rymes and Vaunting Verse": Libellous Politics in Early Stuart England, 1603–1628', in Kevin Sharpe and Peter Lake (eds.), *Politics and Culture in Early Stuart England* (Basingstoke, 1994), 285–310.

[18] BL, Lansdowne MS, 639, fos. 88, 105; Hudson, 'A Treatise of the Court of Star Chamber', in *Collectanea Juridica*, ed. Hargrave, ii. 154.

[19] PRO, STAC8/253/18, mm. 3–4.

## POPULAR LITERATURE

The difficulty in producing a copy of some libels was a consequence of the fact that many of them were intended to be chanted or sung; they were transmitted orally to the extent that some were never written down at all. This was so in the case of a ballad invented in the summer of 1611 by John Penne, a husbandman of Belbroughton in Worcestershire, against the local vicar, Thomas Tristram, and entitled 'The Parson and his Mare'. Tristram could not 'attaine to have anie copies therof in wryting in respect the said John Penne dooth only sing and utter the same by word of mouth'. He would perform it 'with a lowde and high voice . . . not only [at] great fayres and other great assemblies and concourses of people but also in publique tavernes and alehowses', claiming that all clerics simply 'conned a ballet without booke and thereof made a sermon'.[20] Penne was probably unable to write, and he was just one of many libellers who were illiterate in some sense. Of course, it must have been a good form of defence to claim as much in court when accused of having devised and copied a scurrilous text. But almost all bills of complaint were prepared to recognize that the defendants might not have drawn up the libel personally; that they 'did write and make, or cause to be written and made' was a standard formula.

But the inability to write by no means denied people access to the realm of script in this context, or in any other. All communities had at least one person, perhaps a cleric or a pedagogue, an apprentice or a schoolboy, who was able and willing to perform such functions. Indeed, some individuals seem to have been well known for their skill at this kind of versifying, and customers would approach them with a tale upon which to extemporize. Thus when Thomas Chitham, a schoolmaster from Boreham in Essex, called at the house of Hugh Barker, barber of Chelmsford, in October 1601, he was asked if he would make a ballad out of a piece of local gossip: '"It is nothing" (quoth Barker) "but to have you pen a few verses for me upon a pretty jest which I shall tell you".' Two months later, on the Wednesday before Christmas that year, George Warde was among a group travelling towards Allerton in Yorkshire when he told one of the party, Francis Mitchell, serving-man of Hilton in Cleveland, 'that he knewe a good jyste by a neighbour of his, Michaell Steele, and his supposed maid servante, and desired [Mitchell] to maik a songe thereof that they might bee merrie in Christmas withall', whereupon he 'did then declare to [him] the substance of the matter . . .'.[21]

---

[20] PRO, STAC8/281/13, m. 2.
[21] Emmison, *Elizabethan Life: Disorder*, 74; Sisson, *Lost Plays of Shakespeare's Age*, 132. For a

In other cases, the authors of scandal were perfectly capable of rhyming themselves and merely required scribal services in order to commit their work to paper. So, in January 1605, a servant girl, Elizabeth Maunder, went to see John Parker, an apprentice to a Mr Charles of Fleet Street, London, and instructed him 'to write certen libelling verses which [she] would tell [him] by word of mouth, which he did and for want of incke wrote them first with black leade and afterwards with incke'. When in June 1632 a number of men, including Benjamin Martin and Joseph Turpin, were drinking and making merry at a tavern in Rye, Sussex, they hit upon a scurrilous 'lybell in meeter or verses' against some of the godly inhabitants, or 'purer sort', of the town. Apparently none of them could write, for 'Turpin said there were verses of some of the purer sort and that he would give a pott of beear to see them.' Fortunately, they found a fellow-drinker called Spirling who agreed to set them down, in return for which Turpin paid him a quart of wine. Thus the revellers could 'afterwards maliciously scatter and publish the same verses, to the great scandall of the complainants and of religion'.[22]

Many other alleged libellers were unable to write, or so they said. Thus, two apprentice tanners from Northamptonshire tried to extricate themselves from suspicion of having had a hand in a pair of offensive ballads by claiming that they could 'neither write, nor read written hand'. Protesting an inability to read was also an effective means by which the accused might distance themselves from a scandalous text, of course, but it was probably not without foundation in some cases. Richard Jerard, a serving-man of Beckington in Somerset, charged with writing an obscene rhyme against a neighbour and his wife in September 1611, claimed that he had only chanced across a copy of it in the common field at Berkley, 'folded up and sealed with wax in the manner of a lettre. But being not able to reade it (for he cannot reade written hand)', he took it back to his master's house where someone who 'could reade written hand took the writing from [him] and opening the seale reade from parte of it in [his] hearing'. Such people may have been among many contemporaries whose reading ability extended to some form of the printed word, 'print hand', but who had difficulty deciphering handwriting, 'written hand'. Another such, perhaps, was Thomas Mumby, a yeoman of Marshchapel in Lincolnshire. He denied having any knowledge of two scurrilous songs he was charged with

---

cameo of a professional ballad writer who makes 'libels' into 'metre', see J.H., *Two Essays of Love and Marriage* (London, 1657), 91.

[22] Guildhall Library, London, Bridewell Court Books, vol. v, fo. 10ᵛ (I am grateful to Paul Griffiths for this reference); *Reports of Cases in the Courts of Star Chamber and High Commission*, ed. Samuel Rawson Gardiner (Camden Society, new ser., 39, London, 1886), 149–53.

writing against Thomas and Mary Dawson of the same village in July 1621, until his servant, Alice Hutchinson, had found copies in his yard and shown them to him; whereupon he 'opened the same and indeavoured to read [them] but could not, but here and there a part'. John King, a husbandman from Compton Abbas in Dorset, appears to have been completely illiterate: when he saw the libel he was accused of composing nailed upon the church door one Sunday in October 1603, he took it down in ignorance, so he said, for he 'could not himself read'.[23]

If a large number of those who invented songs and rhymes were themselves unable to read handwriting, this incapacity certainly applied to most of their potential audience. Nevertheless, they sought to have their compositions written down and transcripts made in order to facilitate their circulation and heighten their impact. Thus, when a group of villagers from Jacobstow in Cornwall wanted to publicize the misdemeanours of various of their neighbours in September 1616, they began to spread rumours and gossip about them. But in order that these 'matters of infamie and reproach might take the deeper roote and impression in the myndes of the comon and vulgar sorte of people within the said parish', they decided 'to reduce the same into rimes in the nature of a libell and then to publish and divulge the same'.[24] Rhymes were much more memorable than prose and 'papers' could easily be 'scattered abroad', distributed in the streets, left in 'places of common resort', or posted up in prominent positions. Indeed, there are many examples of libellous verses pinned to people's front gates, to church doors, or to alehouse walls, and there is evidence of them being left on the parish pump, the pillory, and the maypole; attached to a fence post, a stile, or a haystack; left on busy highways, posted on the market cross on market day, slipped inside the Prayer Book on Sunday, or pinned to the coffin at a funeral.[25] People would flock round them to discover the latest news or scandal, those who could understand a written hand reading them aloud to the others (see Plates 13 and 14).

[23] PRO, STAC8/288/12, fos. 3ʳ, 6ʳ, m. 46; PRO, STAC8/92/10, m. 3; PRO, STAC8/114/12, m. 1; PRO, STAC8/190/7, m. 14. On the extent and nature of contemporary literacy, see Keith Thomas, 'The Meaning of Literacy in Early Modern England', in Gerd Baumann (ed.), *The Written Word: Literacy in Transition* (Oxford, 1986), 97–131.

[24] PRO, STAC8/27/10, m. 2.

[25] For some representative examples of these various postings, see PRO, STAC8/16/10; PRO, STAC8/79/12; PRO, STAC8/85/15; PRO, STAC8/129/2; PRO, STAC8/186/12; PRO, STAC8/221/9; PRO, STAC8/236/29; PRO, STAC8/240/26; PRO, STAC8/246/14; *Staffordshire Quarter Sessions Rolls*, ed. Burne, v. 236–7; Alastair Bellany, 'A Poem on the Archbishop's Hearse: Puritanism, Libel, and Sedition after the Hampton Court Conference', *Journal of British Studies*, 34 (1995), 137–64.

Often the words were scrawled on anything available: a 'torne paper', 'an old fittered paper leafe'.[26] But, equally, the visual dimension could be exploited more fully, as in the case of one of a series of ballads, circulating in Gloucester against the aldermen of the corporation during the first decade of the seventeenth century, which was said to have been framed 'in Romaino lettres and written with a kinde of darke redd ynke'. Indeed, as in all societies in which literacy is limited, the influence of graphic representation, and of all imagery and symbolism, could have a powerful communicating effect. The drawing of insinuating pictures was, as the libellers of George Hawkins knew, a very effective means of amplifying a scurrilous song. When in August 1608 some villagers from Petworth in Sussex conspired to shame a local mercer, George Frye, with a libel scrawled on 'a longe rolle of paper', they elaborated their text, said to be 'evill written' and near illegible, by drawing 'on the backside thereof with a penn' a picture of a man's head with two great horns and next to it the letters G. F. 'in a large Romayne hand'. This image plastered on a post outside Frye's house and on the market cross in Petworth blazoned its message to all regardless of literacy, maligning its subject 'even amongst the baser sort of people who doe the better remember and take a greater apprehension of [his] shame and reproche . . . bye signes and pictures then by the bare report, seeing, reading or hearinge of the same libell'.[27]

Everyone could 'read' such a drawing, and the same applied to other symbols and effigies, 'signs of reproach' or 'tokens of shame'. For example, when, one night in November 1605, a serving-man scribbled a message on the four knaves from a pack of playing cards and fixed them to the front door of Richard Roupe, a gentleman of East Allington in Devon, the import was voluble to all.[28] No elaboration was needed for those pairs of cuckold's horns so often to be found fixed above a man's porch, thrown through his window, set upon his horse, or sent to him with the head and skin of an animal still attached.[29] The powerful symbolism of the

[26]  PRO, STAC8/53/7, m. 1; PRO, STAC8/94/17, m. 18.

[27]  PRO, STAC8/285/27; PRO, STAC8/146/27, m. 48. Among other later examples of such drawings, see *Warwick County Records*, ed. Ratcliffe and Johnson, ix. 72, 130; J. A. Sharpe, *Defamation and Sexual Slander in Early Modern England: The Church Courts at York* (Borthwick Papers, 58, York, 1980), 5; F. G. Emmison, *Archives and Local History* (London, 1966), 83; E. P. Thompson, *Customs in Common* (London, 1991), 481 and plate VI. In law a 'libel' was not necessarily a written defamation but could be *sine scriptis*, in pictures or signs: Sir Edward Coke, 'The Case De Libellis Famosis, or of Scandalous Libels', in *The English Reports* (176 vols., Edinburgh, 1900–30), lxxvii. 250–2.

[28]  PRO, STAC8/254/24.

[29]  See, for example, PRO, STAC8/152/7; PRO, STAC8/140/29; PRO, STAC8/92/10; PRO, STAC8/153/29; PRO, STAC8/237/26; and also, *Somerset Assize Orders, 1629–1640*, ed.

gallows cropped up not only in drawing but also in the mock scaffold that was sometimes built of sticks and set outside someone's door. Thus, in the second decade of the seventeenth century the tenants of the manor of Osmington in Dorset were battling against their landlord John Warham who was trying to enclose the commons. As well as breaking down his fences they erected various mock scaffolds near his house. One of them was built, in March 1620, from his own firewood, while the following September they did 'frame and make another gallowes and hange thereuppon certaine bundles of fetches which they had framed in resemblance of men', thereby hanging Warham in effigy.[30]

Libels, then, were the products of an environment in which literacy was not expected, but it was nevertheless relied upon in order to help get the message across. They were often intended to be sung and were couched in verse as a mnemonic aid, especially for a majority whose only access to them was through oral channels; yet there was a perceived utility in mak-ing written copies and considerable energies were expended in 'publish-ing' them. When, for example, the rancour of a group of tenants from Newton in Makerfield, Lancashire, was aroused by the local bailiff and rent-collector, John Wood, they resolved to 'devise, frame and put in writinge an infamous and scandalous lybell in rime' against him. On the night of 5 February 1619 this was secretly 'fasten[ed] and pinned[ed] ... to the comon whipstocke standing in the most publicke place of ... Newton, for the punishing of sturdy rogues and vagabonds, where it remayned a great part of the next day to be openly seene and redde of all that came nere ...'. They let it be known that 'there was a lettre of newes uppon the whipstocke ... and wished [others] to goe and see what it was. Whereby there was presently a great concourse of people gathered together ... insomuch that the whole towne was in uprore.' For the benefit of the illit-erate, the authors were ready, in addition, to 'reade and singe the said libell as a ballate with a lowde voyce so that all the rest of the companie might heare it' and, further, 'taught their children and boyes to singe the same in the streets in scoffinge manner in disgrace of [John Wood]'.[31]

T. G. Barnes (Somerset Record Society, 65, Frome, 1959), 42; *Staffordshire Quarter Sessions Rolls*, ed. Burne, v. 101, 210–11; G. R. Quaife, *Wanton Wenches and Wayward Wives: Peasants and Illicit Sex in Early Seventeenth-Century England* (London, 1979), 199–200; David Underdown, 'The Taming of the Scold: the Enforcement of Patriarchal Authority in Early Modern England', in Anthony Fletcher and John Stevenson (eds.), *Order and Disorder in Early Modern England* (Cambridge, 1985), 128; Ingram, 'Ridings, Rough Music and Mocking Rhymes', 170.

[30] PRO, STAC8/293/12. For other examples, see PRO, STAC8/77/4; PRO, STAC8/195/21.
[31] PRO, STAC8/307/9, m. 2.

The same combination of oral and literate dissemination was deployed in almost all instances of public ridicule by lyric and song; everywhere the two modes were side by side, interchangeable and mutually reinforcing. The striking feature that nearly all verses were also set down is indicative of the fact that England at this time was a society thoroughly permeated by the use of the written word, even down to the level of scurrillous entertainment in provincial alehouses. Libellers proclaimed almost unanimously that the world of purely oral tradition was long gone. The trouble to which they went in order to procure 'transcriptts and coppies' of their work reveals that the value of writing was appreciated quite clearly even at the lowest social levels. It also suggests, perhaps, a greater 'written hand' literacy among contemporaries than is usually assumed.[32]

The behaviour of Stephen Hewes and his two accomplices from northern Wiltshire conformed exactly to George Puttenham's depiction of tavern libellers around 1570. Conspiring to abuse a neighbouring gentleman, Virgil Pleydell, in June 1611, these men went to the market town of Highworth where, at an inn, they railed openly infront of the patrons. They then decided to 'wryte uppon the wall of the saide house with a peece of chalke playnlie and apparanntlie to be reade, that Virgill Pleydell . . . was a coward, base fellowe and an asse'. They 'much reioyced and tryumphed in their doeings' and when their scandalized hostess 'endeavoured to have wyped and rubbed the said letters from the wall', they prevented her. Finally, they composed a 'lybell, ryme and verse' which Hewes 'pasted and fixed' to the market cross. One of his partners in crime was not satisfied, however, 'sayeing yt was not sett up publiquely enough and enquirde of some there present uppon which poste of the crosse [the king's] proclamacons used to be sett and there caused the said Hewes to past[e] the said libell on that parte of the same crosse in open viewe of the towne'. Thereafter they stood in a shop doorway directing passers-by to their handiwork 'with great iollytie and laughter'.[33]

This interaction of spoken and written word was equally well illustrated by another Wiltshire libel, this time devised against one of the gamekeepers of the earl of Pembroke in the Forest of Grovely in June 1609. The perpetrators took both 'sundry copies of the said libell, and did make songes and rymes therupon'. A written version was 'set up on the top of a post of certain rails' adjoining the highway through High Wood 'to be seen and redd by all passengers that way'. But they also

---

[32] On manuscript circulation, see Harold Love, *Scribal Publication in Seventeenth-Century England* (Oxford, 1993).

[33] PRO, STAC8/240/26. Puttenham as above.

communicated the verse to the unlettered in neighbouring communities, 'as well by reading copies of [it] and by pronouncing the same by hart, as by teaching [it] to others'. Most reading in this period was done aloud in any case, and it was expected that the literate minority would speak up for the rest to hear. One song composed by about twenty labouring people from Southwark in 1613 was also 'written ... at large in a peece of paper', apparently by a young boy, Edward Cottell. It was prefaced by the enticing words: 'Within this doore | Dwelleth a verie notorious whore' and then fixed above its victim's porch in 'open and publique view of all the neighboures and passengers travayling to and fro ... who red the same as they passed by, at the first taking [it] to be a kinde of bill or declaracion that the house were to be let or solde, but yt beinge percyved to be a libell, great companie theruppon resorted thither to the hearinge and readinge thereof'.³⁴

There is much similar evidence of the vigorous efforts made by the authors of such material to read it aloud in the most populous places in order that their message might reach the widest audience. Many libels originated in market towns, or were at least disseminated in them, since their gatherings of people and public spaces facilitated the process of exposure. Thus, a verse composed at Droitwich in Worcestershire during the spring of 1615 was published by 'reading, singinge and repeating the same in alehowses, taverns and other places of resort and by coppying, lendyng and delivringe the same to others to read and coppie out'. In July 1622 William Wood, an ironmonger of Derby, could be found with his accomplices pronouncing some verses 'in the open marketts and els where', not only 'in words in the heareing of greate multitudes' but also 'in writing unto others, and [they] did give and offer to others monie to reade and publishe the same abroade in the open marketts'. Sometimes the records yield a sense of the performance involved in such public reading and singing, an impression of the way in which exponents rendered their compositions in order to draw an audience, to entertain, and to court complicity. Performance could be all: it was often fundamental in constructing the meaning and conditioning the response to a text, and yet it is something usually lost to the student of ballads. These libels, like printed broadsides, were not simply texts to be read but events to be experienced; not just dead letters to be passively received but live voices with which to engage and repeat anew. Consider the energetic delivery of William Burton, a yeoman of Ladbroke in Warwickshire. We find him in August 1607 reading out a libel 'with a highe and lowde voyce' at a

---

³⁴ PRO, STAC8/152/11; PRO, STAC8/151/7, m. 2 and STAC8/156/29, mm. 2–3.

meeting called at the local smithy 'in the presence and hearinge of above an hundred severall persons . . . usinge manie scornfull jestes and countenances and speeches . . .'.[35]

Even those written verses which were not necessarily intended to be chanted or sung were framed in an 'oral' style which indicated that they were clearly meant for vocal delivery. This libel, in the familiar guise of a news-sheet, was found fastened 'uppon a board under the pillory' in the market-place at Lyme Regis in March 1608 and was directed against one of the customs officials from the harbour.

> Give eare a while,
> And listen to this newes I shall you tell.
> Of a long meeching fellow,
> Which in the towne of Lyme doth dwell.
> His name in breef I will you tell,
> With two syllables you may it spell.
> A rope and a halter,
> Spells Robin Salter.[36]

Significantly, the fact that libels were at one and the same time both written and spoken, simultaneously oral and textual so that the distinction between the two had almost no meaning, was reflected in the contemporary law of defamation. 'For a libell may be in word as well as in writing', ruled Lord Chief Justice Richardson in a case of 'slander' before the Star Chamber in 1631.[37]

As written texts, then, libels were intended to be repeated aloud to those who could not read; as songs also, they were often set to popular tunes. 'Better to be sung than to be redd, to the tune of Bonny Nell', instructed one verse composed at Nottingham in 1617; an apothecary of the town, Thomas Aldred, certainly thought it was hilarious 'in regarde of the strangeness and conceyted tune sett to it'. The celebrated tunes 'Phillida Flouts Me' and 'Fortune my Foe' were among the musical backings to the libellous song drama performed by a group of travelling players at Osmotherley, North Yorkshire, in December 1601. A scatological ballad invented during the summer of 1608 by Thomas and William Tickell of Great Brickhill in Buckinghamshire to publicize the alleged for-

[35]  PRO, STAC8/160/15, m. 4; PRO, STAC8/221/21, m. 7; PRO, STAC8/159/6, m. 2. For another example of shouting a libel 'in a loud voice', see Essex Record Office (ERO), 'Calendar of Essex Session Rolls, 1536–1714' (26 vols. typescript), xx. 180.

[36]  PRO, STAC8/258/15.

[37]  *Reports of Cases in the Courts of Star Chamber and High Commission*, ed. Gardiner, 71; and see J. M. Kaye, 'Libel and Slander-Two Torts or One?', *Law Quarterly Review*, 91 (1975), 524–39.

nication of Dorothy Poole and William Abraham was set 'to a new tune called Pryde and Lecherie'.

> There dwelles a wenche in Much Brickhill,
> Singe dall didell dall, dall a-dall lee.
> Her maydenhead is not to sell,
> Dainty dall lee.

A few years later, Daniell Steward, a yeoman from Sutton in Surrey, framed a fifty-eight-line ballad of his invention with the familiar refrain of 'Hay downe a-downe, go downe a-downe'. An obscene ditty, 'To the tune of panders come away', concocted at Slapton, Northamptonshire, in 1619 'came afterwards to be a comon songe, and was sunge by boyes and others as they went upp and down the towne'. Joseph Turpin of Rye and his accomplices set their rhymes to 'Tom of Bedlam' and 'Watch Currants'. As well as making the song memorable, renowned tunes with distinctive associations such as some of these, conveyed their message regardless of words. The catch of 'Mad Tom', for instance, manifestly mocked the idiocy of a libel victim, while 'Fortune', known to everyone as 'the hanging tune' because of its performance at public executions, would have needed little explanation and was, no doubt, a common accompaniment to the many pictures or effigies of the gallows directed at those who were believed to have breached good charity.[38]

Sometimes composers even employed professional performers, town waits, minstrels, and ballad singers to set their tunes to music and render them at civic gatherings or disseminate them over several counties as they travelled the circuit of alehouses and fairs. The Nottingham version of 'Bonny Nell', for example, was hammered out in the streets to the rough music of candlesticks, tongs, and basins, but was also played in taverns by professional pipers, and 'prickt in 4 parts to the vyalls' in gentlemen's houses, demonstrating the way in which such material could simultaneously circulate in many forms and operate on many social levels. During the winter of 1613–14, Thomas Bevett, gentleman of South Kirkby in Yorkshire, and some accomplices, hired three separate groups of musicians, one each at Stainforth and Pontefract, and at Tuxford in Nottinghamshire, to play and sing their twelve-stanza ballad 'The Devil

---

[38] Sisson, *Lost Plays of Shakespeare's Age*, 135–40, 199, 201, 206–8; PRO, STAC8/27/7, mm. 29, 9; PRO, STAC8/36/6, m. 8; PRO, STAC8/90/24, m. 2; PRO, STAC8/288/12, fo. 2ᵛ; *Reports of Cases in the Courts of Star Chamber and High Commission*, ed. Gardiner, 152. For the tunes of 'Bonny Nell', 'Phillida Flouts Me', 'Fortune my Foe' and 'Tom of Bedlam', and the refrain 'Hey down a-down', see, respectively, Chappell, *Popular Music of the Olden Time*, 501–2, 182–5, 162–4, 332–6, 391–2; on the last, cf. *The Shirburn Ballads, 1585–1616*, ed. Andrew Clark (Oxford, 1907), 248.

of Doncaster' ridiculing Bryan Cooke of that town. Throughout 1621 George Thomson, vicar of Aberford in the West Riding, made use of various minstrels, 'profesing of pipeinge and fidling, running and ranginge upp and downe the countrie from place to place to gett their livings at fayres, marketts and idle meetings and merrements', to perform the many songs he had conceived in derogation of Thomas Shillito, the high constable of Barkston. At Aberford, Ferrybridge, Pontefract, and Knottingley, among other places, they entertained the locals, 'in diverse and sundrie alehouses and innes and in diverse and sundry companies drawne together of purpose to heare the same songs, rithmes and libells and to reioyce and laugh thereat in scornfull, derideinge and infamous manner'.[39]

The references to tunes suggest that some of those who made up extempore rhymes and songs may well have been drawing upon, or at least operating within, a milieu of established and familiar commercial print. In their named tunes or titles, their conventional division into two parts, and in other features of format, style, and length, a small number of libels echoed the world of the broadside ballad.[40] Some authors appear to have copied directly from favourite items of popular literature. A long ballad composed and circulated in the city of Gloucester on 20 February 1609 by James Cowarne and Morris Attwood, mercers, together with a group of other men, mostly servants, contained references to the renowned Reynard the Fox and to Pasquil, the great patron of anonymous lampoons. It also embodied a crude version of the famous song about the frog who woos a mouse, which predates the earliest previously known text of this enduring favourite.[41] One ditty, made in December 1612 by James Ball of Wellingborough, Northamptonshire, which he did

[39] Sisson, *Lost Plays of Shakespeare's Age*, 198; PRO, STAC8/113/3; PRO, STAC8/275/22, m. 2.

[40] For examples of printed broadsides, see *The Roxburghe Ballads*, ed. W. Chappell and J. W. Ebsworth (9 vols., Ballad Society, London, 1871–99); *The Pepys Ballads*, ed. W. G. Day (5 vols., Cambridge, 1987); for discussion, see Hyder E. Rollins, 'The Black-Letter Broadside Ballad', *Publications of the Modern Language Association*, 34 (1919), 258–339; Tessa Watt, *Cheap Print and Popular Piety, 1550–1640* (Cambridge, 1991).

[41] PRO, STAC8/285/27, m. 8. The first reference to such a song, 'The frog cam to the myl dur', dates from 1549; *A Moste Strange Weddinge of the Frogge and the Mowse* was licensed as a broadside ballad by the Stationer's Company in November 1580. The earliest version of a text known hitherto dates from 1611; in a very different form it has been a favourite of children since the nineteenth century as 'A frog he would a-wooing go': *The Complaynt of Scotlande*, ed. J. A. H. Murray (Early English Text Society, extra ser., 17, London, 1872), 64; Hyder E. Rollins, 'An Analytical Index to the Ballad-Entries (1557–1709) in the Registers of the Company of Stationers of London', *Studies in Philology*, 21 (1924), 158; Thomas Ravenscroft, *Melismata: Musicall Phansies, Fitting the Court, Citie, and Countrey Humours* (London, 1611), sig. F1ᵛ; Iona and Peter Opie, *The Oxford Dictionary of Nursery Rhymes* (Oxford, 1951), 177–81.

'openly and with a highe voice publishe and singe . . . in dyvers alehouses, tavernes and other open and publique places', was framed in the dialogic form so often employed by professional balladeers. It began:

> *A Discourse between a Traveller and a Shepherd Meeting upon Bareshanke Leyes*
> *Traveller*:  Well mett sheppard!
> From whence doth thou come and wither aweye?
> *Shepherd*:  From the good towne of Wellingborrowe,
> So bonnye and soe gay.
> *Traveller*:  From Wellingborrowe, sheppard;
> What newes at the Hinde?
> *Shepherd*:  Ill newes Sir. Good ale is deare,
> Though women are kinde.[42]

Libellers such as these were obviously adapting to their own purposes, perhaps by just inserting new names, ballads which they knew from printed broadsides. This may have been the case with George James, a serving-man from Lutterworth in Leicestershire. In February 1616 he was employed in the household of Warwickshire gentleman, Henry Bressye. He soon fell out with his mistress, however, who decided to lock away his livery coat, and in a fit of revenge and resentment, he contrived a 'libellous songe or dittye' against her. It began with a well-known rallying cry, 'Roysters give roome!', and James was able to claim, quite plausibly, that his supposed 'libel' was no more than a regular

songe or jygge and comedians which the servants to the late highe and mightie Prince Henrie, Prince of Wales, did often, in the presence of his highnes and manie nobles and peeres of this reallme, act, daunce and singe as a jygge in the end of their enterludes and plaies, being a generall song without particuler nomination or alusion to anie. Which said songe or jygge hath bene seene, approved and allowed by the right worshippfull the Maister of the Revells to his Majestie.[43]

Examples such as these provide valuable evidence of the penetration of cheap print at the lowest levels of provincial society before the Civil War. They indicate how broadsides might provide the basis for an extemporized song reworked and applied in a specific context.[44]

No ballads or rhymes composed by people of this social status mentioned by name any known title from commercial print, although this was sometimes the case among the more well-to-do and literate versifiers. During the famous feud between the Dymoke family of Lincolnshire

---

[42] PRO, STAC8/153/5, m. 14. On the dialogue form in printed broadsides, see Natascha Wurzbach, *The Rise of the English Street Ballad, 1550–1650* (Cambridge, 1990), 187–94.

[43] PRO, STAC8/59/4, m. 1.

[44] For another example, see Ingram, 'Ridings, Rough Music and Mocking Rhymes', 180.

and Henry, earl of Lincoln, a member of the former devised, as part of a dramatic slur on their adversary, a mock sermon involving 'a collaudation of the ... ancient story of *The Friar and the Boy*' performed as part of a May game at Horncastle in 1601.[45] Similarly, Edward Seede, whose father was lord of the manor of Claverton in Somerset, denied making and singing a 'bawdie lybell' or 'filthie songe' in August 1606 against John Bewshin the local vicar and his wife. He claimed that on the occasion in question he had simply been 'amongst diverse of his friends . . . whoe had bin anciently acquainted in their youth, and then occasion being given to remember, manie old songs and rymes', which they had performed, 'fyrst in dauncing the daunce called the *Jew of Malta* and thereunto singing one ditty or tune, secondly dauncing the *Irish Daunce*, singing to that another, with diverse such like . . .', but that he had not sung the libellous jig alleged.[46]

Thus, to a degree the culture of ridiculing rhymes could be informed and overlapped by the culture of print, the amateur performance inspired by the professional. Occasionally the relationship might be reciprocal, with some of the material for the London presses clearly provided, in turn, by libels supplied even by the humblest provincial authors. It represented, after all, the ultimate form of publicity, and caused the maximum potential shame to the victim, to have a derisive ballad actually printed. Of the Tickells from Great Brickhill, for example, it was said that they 'most wickedlie endeavoured, practised and laboured to putt the[ir] ... wicked and infamous libell in printe. And to that end and purpose sent [it] to a printer in London.' The libellers of George Frye from Petworth were also said to have conspired to this end. In 1631–2 Francis Stacey of Coleorton in Leicestershire came up with what was said to be no more than a 'rabblement of words without rime or reason' in derogation of his vicar, Thomas Pestell, but that he did then 'endeavour to have had the same put into verse, purposing to have had the same put into print'.[47]

On 1 March 1607 Richard Rotten, a weaver from Moseley in Warwickshire, together with his brother John, and William Pretty from Yardley, contrived three ballads accusing a local girl, Anne Bellamie, of an illicit affair with a married man, Richard Nightingale of Tipton in

[45] O'Conor, *Godes Peace and the Queenes*, 120. *The Frere and the Boye* was first printed in England by Wynkyn de Worde, 1510–13, and was registered as a ballad in 1586: Rollins, 'Analytical Index', 84.

[46] PRO, STAC8/98/20, m. 27. *The Murtherous Life and Terrible Death of the Riche Jew of Malta* was registered in 1594: Rollins, 'Analytical Index', 161–2.

[47] PRO, STAC8/36/6, m. 8; PRO, STAC8/146/27, m. 31; Huntington Library, California, Hastings MSS, Legal Box 5 (9), fo. 85ᵛ (I am grateful to Patrick Collinson for this reference); for other examples, see Huntington Library, Ellesmere MS, 2728; Sisson, *Lost Plays of Shakespeare's Age*, 96–7, 103–6.

Staffordshire. Several of those who happened to be in John Tomlinson's alehouse in Moseley four days later testified to hearing Richard Rotten singing them to a tune which they recognized as 'Jamey'. He was also said to have had copies made which he 'dispersed on the backside or neare . . . his dwelling howse', set up in his shop, 'spread and cast abroade . . . in divers places' and would 'laughe and reioyce at the verses and contents thereof'. In addition, the composition was sent to the capital to be set in type, for it was apparently 'Imprinted at London at the signe of the wood-cocke in Paules Churchyarde'. The polish and the standardized format of the printed forms suggest that a professional writer may have been employed at this stage to improve the quality of the work for the press. No copy of this broadside is extant, but the whole text survives in the Star Chamber file, transcribed by the clerk of the court. One ballad was entitled 'A Pleasant New History | Declaring of a Mysterie | Of Richard Nightingale by name | and Anne Bellamie of Dods Lane. You may sing it to a merry new tune'. Another was now set, rather loftily, 'To a pleasant new tune called Marcus Tullius Cicero'.[48] It ran:

> There is a maide of Moseley towne,
> Her leggs be short she will soon be downe.
> For she went on a time to Haselwall,
> But there she chauncte to catch a fall.
>
> Yf you will know who this same maide should be,
> Forsooth, it is Nan Ballamie.
> Her busines was to the mill as I did heare,
> With a batch for to make her woers good cheare.
>
> But marke you well what I shall say,
> Before this mayden came away.
> The miller gott her a topp of the baggs,
> But his breeches fell downe about his legges.
>
> Now how it fell out I cannot tell,
> But the miller sayd he used her well.
> But suer I thinke he dealt unkind,
> For she with him greate faulte did find.
>
> Her mother standing by and seeing of this,
> She was an angrye woman I wis.
> For no ill will she bore to the sporte,
> But bycause it was done in such sorte.

---

[48] PRO, STAC8/220/31, mm. 14–16 and fos. 1–9, and PRO, STAC8/222/31, between fos. 4 and 5.

Then she rapte out an othe and sweare by Gods bread,
She could find in her harte to breake his head.
Could he find no other place,
But putt her daughter to that disgrace?

There was a woer that came from Tolerin,
Which the milner cared not for of a pinne.
Did seeme to be greived in his mind,
And told the milner he dealt unkind.

'Oh I pray thee', said the milner, 'be content,
For no harme unto the was meant.
But if thou seemed to be greived in mind,
Thou maiest turne the buckell of thy girdell behind.

Oh in good faith I for my self,
Would scorne to be beaten at such an elf.
And I thinke the worst that was there in place,
Would not be ashamed to looke your worshipp in the face'.

Nightingale seeing the milner cared not for him,
Thought good to lett him alone and not beate him.
Saying, 'Milner to beate the I am very loathe,
Bycause thou tellest me the very trothe'.

Finis.

So it was that what started out as a short ditty extemporized by ama-
teurs in a locality could end up as a fully developed broadside, printed and
perhaps dispersed nationwide. The majority of verse libels, however, were
never intended to be thus set down nor owed much to the products of
print culture and professional entertainment. They targeted individuals
who were obscure other than in a local context; most of their references
were parochial and specific, directed at an audience 'in the know'. From a
literary point of view they were usually crude; corrupt in rhyme, irregular
in metre, and simple in content. Their rough-hewn nature, both in construction and idiom, reflected their generation in an environment accustomed to oral and aural transmission, one governed less by the rules of
written language than by the variable constructions and opaque phrases
of popular speech. Many of the versifiers who could record their work,
wrote as they spoke, rhyming in the cadences of regional pronunciation
and expressing themselves in the vocabulary of local dialect. The libels of
the unlettered were sometimes hardly songs or ballads in any formal
sense, but more like 'rabblements of words without rime or reason'.

## THE IDIOM OF ODIUM

In their deployment by people of humble origin, these railing rhymes and lampooning songs could be very much the products of the 'alternative' society of the alehouse. Almost all were said to have been composed over a pot of ale and handed out or repeated in taverns and inns. 'If anie man aske who made this rime | Yt was Steven Corkrum in a drinkinge time', concluded one squib composed at a tippling-house in Pyworthy, Devon, in May 1612 and sung on 'alebenches and other places in most scoffing, lewd and obscene manner'.[49] Denied the right openly to question those in authority, it was only away from their watchful eyes that people were able to vent grievances freely. The alehouse offered a sanctuary for relative freedom of speech, for cathartic release in story and song, jest and mockery; it provided the chance to ridicule in private those whom it was an offence to challenge in public. These ballads of popular invention were, like so much oral culture, inherently subversive and irreverent, implicitly running counter to the norms and values of society's elite and sometimes challenging them explicitly.[50]

Indeed, many of the libels brought before the Jacobean Star Chamber which were composed by those of lowly social status, and therefore tended to be directed at persons of higher rank, had subversive overtones of some kind. It was this perceived threat to the social order which caused the Star Chamber to take an ever more dim view of the crime. Counsel for the plaintiff in a case of 1608 made it clear that persons of 'good credit'

should not be defamed, scandalized or slaundered by men of base and lewde condicion which are evill affected, by publishinge of scornfull and reprochfull lybells and pamphletts. And wheras lybelles, lybellers and lybellinge and the publishinge, devulginge and castinge the same abrode are thinges very odyous and hatefull in anie well governed comonwelth, movinge muche contencion, malice and sedicion amongest the people and are often tymes the causes of breache of the peace of the lande and of insurrections and rebellyons, and are alsoe directly againste the lawes and government of this . . . realme of Englande . . . and hath ever byne accompted noe small offence.[51]

[49]  PRO, STAC8/236/29, m. 2.

[50]  Cf. the discussion in James C. Scott, *Domination and the Arts of Resistance: Hidden Transcripts* (New Haven, 1990). On the radical potential of popular mockery, see Keith Thomas, 'The Place of Laughter in Tudor and Stuart England', *Times Literary Supplement* (21 Jan. 1977), 78.

[51]  PRO, STAC8/159/6, m. 2. For the role of Star Chamber in tightening the laws of sedition, see Roger B. Manning, 'The Origin of the Doctrine of Sedition', *Albion*, 12 (1980), 99–121; Philip Hamburger, 'The Development of the Law of Seditious Libel and the Control of the Press', *Stanford Law Review*, 37 (1984–5), 691–7.

Such rhetoric was reinforced by sentences involving large fines, whipping and branding, and even the cutting-off of an offender's ears in cases with seditious implications.[52] But whatever the consequences, a great many people 'of base and lewde condicion' were clearly undeterred by them. John Pearse, a husbandman from Dorset, threatened with the Star Chamber for making a libellous song in 1618, boasted 'that hee did not care a straw for it, for he had aunsweared there far worse matters than these'. 'Wee care not for the Star Chamber!', shouted the ridiculers of the Lancashire bailiff, John Wood. 'Wee will have a trick that Wood . . . shall not be able to looke towards the Star Chamber'.[53]

Equal contempt for the law and its agents was evident among the group of artisans and tradespeople from Thaxted in Essex who, in March 1622, concocted a shaming ballad against a councillor and notable citizen of the town, Richard Turner, whom they accused of harshly beating his daughter, Anne. They laughed in the face of authority and when the mayor of Thaxted

> by way of reprofe, [told] them that makeinge of libells would indanger the losse of theire eares, [they] did make a scoffe of [him] and at his admonitions, and did thereupon publishe that a sow of one in the town had lost her eares for makinge libells and . . . [they] made a representation of the mayor and bayliffes of [Thaxted] in innes and alehouses as sitting in their sessions, to the great scandall of the government of the said corporacion.

Their composition, entitled 'Whip Her Arse Dick', had been 'reported and sunge, published and divulged . . . in divers innes, alehouses and other places in the said towne of Thaxted and county of Essex'. They had made copies and 'taught and instructed . . . young children to singe the same to wrong and provoke [Turner]'. It began:

[52] BL, Lansdowne MS, 639, fo. 103; BL, Lansdowne MS, 620, fo. 50ᵛ; Hudson, 'A Treatise of the Court of Star Chamber', in *Collectanea Juridica*, ed. Hargrave, ii. 224. On the background to this notorious corporal punishment, see J. A. Guy, *The Court of Star Chamber and its Records to the Reign of Elizabeth I* (PRO Handbooks, 21, London, 1985), 46. For some examples of Star Chamber sentences for libel, see John Hawarde, *Les Reportes del Cases in Camera Stellata, 1593* to *1609*, ed. W. P. Baildon (London, 1894), 152, 230, 341, 345–6, 373, 374. Spenser's depiction of a seditious rhymer with his tongue nailed to a post referred to usual practice. In 1554 the Mayor's Court of Norwich had a minstrel, Robert Gold, 'sett vppon the pillorye and his eare nayled to the same for devysing of vnfitting songes against the quenes maiestie': *Records of Early English Drama: Norwich 1540–1642*, ed. David Galloway (Toronto, 1984), 34. For lesser offences, local courts imposed more modest penalties. In 1607 the corporation of Bury St Edmunds ordered that anyone 'using unseemly songs, ballads, libels and rhymes' should be fined 12*d*.: HMC, *Fourteenth Report, Appendix, Part VIII* (London, 1895), 140.

[53] PRO, STAC8/77/4, m. 4; PRO, STAC8/307/9, m. 2.

Hye thee home Anne,
Hye thee home Anne,
Whippe Her Arse Dicke,
Will have thee anon.
All those that love puddinge,
Come unto Parke Street,
And learne the songe,
Of Whippe Her Arse Dicke.

Through this combination of oral and visual dissemination, the song, it was said, soon 'became publique, common and notorious in the eyes, eares and tongues' of all Richard Turner's neighbours.[54]

The effect of this kind of ridicule could be devastating on its victims. As local people, known by everyone, they were exposed to a public shaming from which there was no escape and little redress. To some, taking the matter up to Westminster may have represented the best form of satisfaction, but 'the blott of infamie' did not easily fade. Of course, the complaints of libel victims were likely to maximize or even exaggerate the extent to which they had been damaged by the offence, but it is likely that such claims were not without substance. Richard Turner was apparently ruined both privately and professionally by his detractors who succeeded in their plan to 'robb and take from [him] his good name, credit and reputation and to make and cause [him] to be contemptuous and ridiculous to the said town of Thaxted'. Thereafter he was 'often forced to neglect his busines abroad, [while] hopeing in time the said scandalous libell, rime or songe may cease and end'. The same fate awaited others similarly abused. That substantial inhabitant of Tiverton, Robert Reede, the victim of a rhyme and a pair of cuckold's horns fastened upon his door in February 1610, became a laughing-stock among his neighbours. Long after the incident, it was said that when people passed him in the street they 'still doe most disgracefullie poynt att [him], and with their hands and fingers make the signe or token of hornes and poynt att [him] therewith', with such resulting shame to him and his wife that it 'were likely not only to cause a seperacion between them but alsoe were lyke to have bereaved them both of their lyves through the grief, sorrowe and discontentment which they conceyved att the said scandalous imputations'. Such indeed came to pass in the case of Joan Cunde and her husband Henry, the vicar of Montford in Shropshire. Joan was the victim of an 'infamous lybell' in August 1604 which ruined their marriage and to which she 'tooke such an inward grief and sorrowe that she presentlye fell sicke and pyned, wasted and consumed away, and shortly afterward dyed'.[55]

Very similar circumstances surrounded the 'sundrie reproachefull, scandalous and infamous libells ... in words as in writings' directed against Henry Collins of Winscombe in Somerset. Collins was another wealthy clothier who employed 'many poore and distressed people', and was also a village constable who regularly presented miscreants to the authorities. In doing so he incurred the wrath of one John Hawker who, as a weaver and 'a common haunter of alehouses, a night walker, and a notorious offender in many other disorders and greevous misdemeanors', had both professional and personal reasons to resent Collins. On 16 May 1624, Hawker, together with fellow weavers William Staple and George Bullford, invented 'balletts, rymes, songs and other infamous speeches' claiming that Collins, a married man, had been seen in the trees of Maudlines Grove with Hawker's niece Ann. They alleged that he had also lived incontinently with many women, that he was a bad debtor, and thus a person of no credit. They deliberately sang these ballads in front of Collins's circle of friends, 'the better sorte' of the neighbours, and among his 'kinsfolkes'. The result, he claimed, was that he was shunned by all and became afraid even to leave his house. Professionally he was 'utterlie forbarred and frustrated from the following of his trade and thereby utterly undonne and overthrowne'. When the ill fame reached Collins's wife she believed the 'rumors and rimes to be true' and 'did theruppon become frantick'.[56]

The 'better sort', so often the victims of these scurrilous songs, could frequently be heard denouncing libellers and their alehouse culture. Such was the reaction to the ballad composed in 1612 by James Ball of Wellingborough, 'out of his evill and malitious mind', and directed against a local widow, Ellinor Grobye. One gentleman of the town, Hugh Chervock, deposed that while Ellinor was 'reported to be an honest and civil poore woman amongst her neighboures', Ball was 'held to be, amongst the more and better sorte of his neighboures, a man of a troublesome disposition'. Another of these respectable neighbours, John Hackney, claimed to be greatly shocked by the ballad which was 'such a thinge as he never heard of in his life and that he thought that yt was a libell' which Ball performed 'in a laughing and very scoffing manner and made a Maye game thereof'.[57]

As these examples suggest, it is sometimes possible to gauge the audience's response to such ballads and libels in a way that is rarely allowed by

---

[55] PRO, STAC8/253/18, m. 4; PRO, STAC8/100/18, m. 8.
[56] PRO, STAC8/88/7, m. 2.          [57] PRO, STAC8/153/5, mm. 4, 8.

cheap printed texts. Of course, reactions often depended upon the quality of the performance and the content of the material involved, and they might vary according to the attitudes of readers or hearers both to the authors and their subjects. Ridiculing material of this kind was very likely to evoke strong opinions on all sides. Hilarity was clearly the intended result and it usually seems to have been achieved. 'There was good laughing at the ... readinge' recalled Christopher Horder, a West Country husbandman, of a 'filthie libell' which he had heard in 1603. But other people, either from genuine indignation or a sense of feigned propriety, expressed distaste and disgust at the obscene or the irreverent. Christopher Auncell, an apprentice from Wimborne Minster in Dorset, who claimed to have found a copy of a very saucy rhyme on the ground in his master's back yard, protested that 'it was a fowle piece of worke and that he would not have been the contriver of it for forty pounds'. Most compositions were greeted with a mixture of reactions, no doubt. When in May 1609, for example, Simon Girdler of Tenterden in Kent flagrantly performed a drunken jig outside the house of John Tylden, a godly magistrate of the town, 'being a man of sober and very religious behaviour', it occasioned the hysterical merriment of some and the abhorrence of others: 'his said behaviour being so publique [it] was not only laughed at by divers then seeing him and by others who after heard thereof ... but also some others then seeing him so behave him selfe were much greeved and ashamed thereof and for shame went from him and left him alone in such manner'.[58]

Libels were obviously an effective way in which people might jeer at and wound, their betters. The effects might be just as damaging to victims as any physical assault, indeed perhaps much more so, for, whatever the widening horizons and affiliations of the 'better sort' in this period, the loss of reputation among their immediate neighbours still mattered greatly to most. Slanderous rhymes might be sung among the victim's friends and family and, if they could be written out, posted up in public or left on their doorsteps. Often they were inspired by malicious or spiteful motives and had no justification other than petty personal jealousies. But they might also be a powerful articulation of popular opinions and sensibilities, the communal expression of a sense of justice. Brought to bear upon those who offended against perceived norms, they could be an informal censor and regulator of the most potent kind. Thus, enclosing or battening landlords, forestalling or hoarding tradespeople, officials thought to be overbearing in the pursuit of their duties, all risked the ignominy of being 'balladed'.[59]

[58] PRO, STAC8/190/7, m. 13; PRO, STAC8/153/29, m. 1; PRO, STAC8/51/2, m. 2.
[59] For some later examples of such 'propaganda by poetry', see E. P. Thompson, 'The Crime

Such was the fate of Andrew Abington, lord of the manor of Over Compton on the Dorset–Somerset border. During a protracted dispute with his tenants over enclosure of the commons, he found himself the object of a number of libellous protests. Notwithstanding that they were said to be 'simple unlearned people', the local husbandmen and their families managed to find someone to draw up a bond, to which twenty-six of them subscribed, claiming release from their obligations to Abington. They sent him, in addition, a pseudonymous letter of derision which was also read out at public meetings; and finally, in August 1616, they fastened this 'infamous libell' to the church gate at Trent in Somerset, about a mile from the manor house.

> *Heere be Andrew Abington's Commandementes*
>
> Thou shalt do no right nor thou shalt take no wronge
> Thou shalt catche what thou canst
> Thou shalt paie no man
> Thou shalt comitt adulterye
> Thou shalt beare false wittnes against thy neyghbor
> Thou shalt covett thy neighbors wiefe
> Thou shalt sell a hundred of sheepe to Henrye Hopkines after
> Thou shalt drawe the best of them
> Thou shalt sell thy oxen twice
> Thou shalt denye thye owne hand

With this parody of the Ten Commandments, which emphasized their view of Abington's behaviour as a mockery of Christian charity, the tenants 'did not only singe, repeat, publishe and divulge the said slanderous and vicious libell in innes, taverns and other places in [the] countyes of Dorset and Somerset and elsewhere, [but also] sold abroad coppyes thereof'. Here, apparently, was another example of a particularly striking libel that had a commercial value in written form. All this was said to have had the desired effect of bringing the squire and 'his wiefe and children into publicke disgrace and infamye'.[60]

Millers were another group which might also feel the force of such communal censure. Their position of power within the local economy and community meant that they were traditionally figures of popular suspicion and even contempt, usually portrayed as lechers or misers. It was the former image upon which the Rotten brothers had drawn in their ballads of Anne Bellamie from Moseley. The latter image provided one

of Anonymity', in Douglas Hay et al., *Albion's Fatal Tree: Crime and Society in Eighteenth-Century England* (London, 1975), 264, 301, 303, 337–40.

[60] PRO, STAC8/42/14.

theme for 'A pleasante newe songe of a faithfull drunkard dwellinge in Essex who was a myller', which cropped up in the summer of 1608.[61] Similarly caricatured and riduculed was the Puritan, depicted as a zealous hypocrite no less often in these local libels than in the plays and pamphlets of professional humorists.[62]

The 'godly' were especially vulnerable to lampooning if, when they held positions of office, they were perceived as being too 'busy' or 'precise' in regulating the behaviour of their neighbours. For there were in general many examples of mocking verses composed against authority figures such as churchwardens and constables, bailiffs and justices, or the mayor and aldermen of corporations. Commonly would some allegation of corruption or abuse be so dispersed, as Isaac Cotton noted in 1622, 'cast forth [in] certain rhymes or libells conteyninge as it were a dialogue full of scurrility and rude terms, scoffing and inveighing against [the] authority of officers and civil government, with menances for subversion of the same and other base matter unfit to be spoken of'.[63]

Thus it was that the unpopular chief constable of a wapentake near Leeds, John Harrison, found himself the focus of a ridiculing jig sung at alehouses on May Day 1616 in flagrant celebration of neighbourliness and good fellowship.

> What nowe becomes of all idle talke,
> In alehouse and taverne and as you doe walke,
> Where some payed money and some did but chalke,
> What wise mirth is this good neighbours.
>
> You rage and malice him that did saye,
> The parish had right and would have a daie,
> Would not this yeild matter to make a stage playe,
> For a ripe witt good neighbours.

As we have seen, the libels composed against Thomas Shillito, the high constable of Barkston, West Riding, were widely popular partly because

[61] PRO, STAC8/185/23, m. 2. On the traditional perception of millers in popular culture and song, see Thompson, *Customs in Common*, 218–20.

[62] For examples, see PRO, STAC8/26/10; PRO, STAC8/27/7; PRO, STAC8/94/17; and see Patrick Collinson, 'Ecclesiastical Vitriol: Religious Satire in the 1590s and the Invention of Puritanism', in John Guy (ed.), *The Reign of Elizabeth I: Court and Culture in the Last Decade* (Cambridge, 1995), 150–70; Ann Hughes, 'Religion and Society in Stratford upon Avon, 1619–38', *Midland History*, 19 (1994), 58–84; David Underdown, *Fire from Heaven: Life in an English Town in the Seventeenth Century* (London, 1992), 27–32; ERO, Q/SR, 222/12 (I am grateful to Keith Wrightson for this reference) and cf. ERO, 'Calendar of Essex Session Rolls', xix[b], 322–3. On this genre in professional writing, see William P. Holden, *Anti-Puritan Satire, 1572–1642* (New Haven, 1954), esp. 52–86, 101–44.

[63] BL, Lansdowne MS, 639, fo. 88[r].

of their professional performances, but also because the tenor of their contents must have struck a chord with many.

> Would God I weare a head constable,
>   And had a Justice of my name,
> Then would I whipp and stock the poore,
>   And think it neither sinne nor shame.[64]

The 'Justice' referred to here was Shillito's brother, George, and men of this stamp were by no means immune from such treatment. 'You thinke to oppresse men with your riches and authorytie!', bawled a Nottinghamshire man at a squire and Justice of the Peace whom he was alleged to have libelled in 1608. 'Gaping and framinge a deformed mouthe in most scornefull manner', he 'putt out his tounge at [him]', uttering these 'and divers other such sawcye and malepart words to the great scorne and dyrision of justice'. At another level, the scandalous sexual behaviour of Thomas Smith, a Justice of the Peace for Berkshire, so offended a group of yeoman farmers from Buscot and Lechlade that they tried to shame him into repentance with various mocking nicknames like 'Justice balle, bald pated knave and whoremaster knave', and more forcibly with a ballad which they sang among the neighbours, including at a wedding.[65]

The wider threat to the social and political order which this kind of derogation of authority was seen to pose is well illustrated by some libels contrived in Northampton during the summer of 1607. A large and diverse group of the local inhabitants was responsible for what were clearly a very successful pair of ballads. One was 'made against the knightes and justices of the county', and was 'bought and sold for money' as far north as Leicester and as far south as Dunstable in Bedforshire, where an innkeeper, Thomas Holland, paid 12*d.* for a copy. The other was composed in scandal of the ecclesiastical officials within the diocese of Peterborough and published on 22 September, the day of Archbishop Bancroft's visit to the town. It was found in the church of Allhallows and at 'inns and alehouses, in sadlers and smiths, and other tradesmen's shops'; a gentleman, Thomas Burton, 'said he would give an angell for a coppie of it, and shewe it to his lord', while Edward Thorowgood, a

---

[64] PRO, STAC8/167/27, m. 2; PRO, STAC8/275/22, m. 2. For other libels against constables, see PRO, STAC8/161/1; PRO, STAC8/161/5; Underdown, *Fire from Heaven*, 148–9.

[65] PRO, STAC8/208/31, m. 3; PRO, STAC8/256/9; for other libels on justices of the peace, see PRO, STAC8/85/15; PRO, STAC8/205/20; PRO, STAC8/258/5; PRO, STAC8/271/14; HMC, *Tenth Report, Appendix, Part IV*, 441; and on libels against Leicestershire magistrates in 1607, see Richard Cust, 'Honour and Politics in Early Stuart England: The Case of Beaumont *v.* Hastings', *Past and Present*, 149 (1995), 82–3.

woolen-draper, promised to 'sende it into Cambridgeshire to his friendes'. This ballad, which took the form of a dialogue between a man and a woman, included a typical jibe at one dignatory:

> He turnes his hat up in the brim,
>     And lookes as though his eyes wold burne,
> He snappes poore people by the nose,
>     And scornfully from them doth turne.

The libellers were said to have claimed that it was legitimate to publish such material, provided that it did not touch the person of the king nor his privy councillors. In so doing, their indictment protested, they 'bredd a most dangerous opinion in the harts of the comon people as though it were lawfull to libel and traduce their governors both ecclesiasticall and temporall (so [long as] they be no Lords of the Counsaile)' and also helped to 'continue and maintaine the hatred and dispight bred in many of the baser sort of people against the gentlemen of the country' at the time of the uprisings in the Midlands.[66]

It may have been the case that in prosecuting their assailants at Westminster, some libel victims were seeking to exploit such official anxieties over subversion and disorder. In general, the very fact that those from the most humble levels of society were presented before the Star Chamber at all and, moreover, that they themselves might sometimes present others, is indicative of the fact that the law, even in the form of its most grandiose court, was coming to loom increasingly large in the lives of people all the way down the social order. This was an unprecedentedly litigious age and even Star Chamber business, dominated as it was by the gentry, involved people from the middling and lower ranks of provincial society as either plaintiff or defendant in almost half the defamation cases during James I's reign.[67] The paradox of the libels examined here is that they were usually a supremely parochial phenomenon but one disputed and settled at the most elevated of levels. As such they were the reflection of a society which was at once intensely disparate and localized, yet ever centralizing and moving in the directions of incorporation and nationality.

---

[66] PRO, STAC8/205/19; PRO, STAC8/205/20; Huntington Library, Ellesmere MS, 5956. In July 1607 a libel was thrown into the parish church at Caistor, Lincolnshire, entitled 'The Poor Man's Friend and the Gentlemen's Plague', and beginning, 'You gentlemen that rack your rents and throwe downe land for corne': HMC, *Twelfth Report, Appendix, Part IV* (London, 1888), 406.

[67] 265 out of the 577 defamation causes (46 per cent) involved men and women from these middling and lower levels of society as either plaintiff or defendant. On the massive increase in litigation during this period, see C. W. Brooks, *Pettyfoggers and Vipers of the Commonwealth: The 'Lower Branch' of the Legal Profession in Early Modern England* (Cambridge, 1986), chs. 4–5.

William Shakespeare was lucky. If Sir Thomas Lucy had prosecuted him
for libel in the Star Chamber he would probably have incurred a very large
fine at the least. Even his crude first effort at poetry, if such it was, rates
rather well when compared with the muse of many of his more humble
contemporaries. But whereas it is not surprising to find someone of
Shakespeare's stamp composing and disseminating 'bitter ballads', it is
altogether more remarkable to discover the practice among the obscure
tradesmen and artisans, yeomen, and husbandmen of England's small
towns and villages. To be able to observe the way in which such ordinary
provincial people concocted rhymes and songs, had them committed to
paper and then circulated, both by performance and public posting, provides us with one of the most graphic, immediate, and illuminating
insights into the relationship between oral and literate culture that we are
likely to find. In this context, as in other spheres of contemporary life,
writing provided not a substitute but a valuable supplement to dissemination by word of mouth; it added a visual and a physical dimension to the
ethereal quality of sound. Text was only ever an auxiliary and a stimulus to
the primary media of reciting and singing. And yet the fact that it was utilized at all for something as ephemeral as the doggerel verses of alehouse
scurrility, speaks volumes about the perceived value and the widespread
use of the written word in Shakespeare's England.

# 7
## *Rumour and News*

---

Libels and licentious discourses against the state, when they are
frequent and open; and in like sort, false news often running up and
down to the disadvantage of the state, and hastily embraced; are
amongst the signs of troubles.

> Francis Bacon, *The Essayes or Counsels, Civill and Morall*
> (1625), in *The Works of Francis Bacon*, ed. James Spedding,
> Robert Leslie Ellis, and Douglas Denon Heath
> (7 vols., London, 1857–9), vi. 407.

What's the best news abroad? So we must begin. 'Tis the garb (les
nouvelle) the grand salute and common preface to all our talk. And
the news goes not as things are in themselves, but as men's fancies
are fashioned, as some lust to report, and others to believe. To some
relation shall go for true or false, according to the key wherein
men's minds are turned; but chiefly as they stand diverse in religion,
so they feign and affect different news. By their news ye may know
their religion, and by their religion fore-know their news . . . Titius
came from London yesterday, and he says that the new chappel at
St James's is quite finished: Caius came thence but this morning,
and then there was no such thing on building. False news follows
true at the heels, and oftentimes outslips it.

> Thomas Lushington, 'Christ, Dead or Alive?', the
> 'Repetition' sermon preached April 1623, in *In God's Name:*
> *Examples of Preaching in England from the Act of Supremacy*
> *to the Act of Uniformity, 1534–1662*, ed. John Chandos
> (London, 1971), 256.

THE grapevine, or the spreading of news or information by word of
mouth, is a phenomenon which has not always received the historical
attention which it deserves. The reason for this is obvious enough: oral
communication leaves little visible trace behind it for subsequent analysis.
But this neglect is unfortunate, since the grapevine has, over the centuries, been of the utmost importance in the dissemination of intelligence
and report, rumour and gossip, throughout nations and across the world.
It has had a crucial impact on the greatest of events, helping to lose wars

by demoralizing entire armies, conspiring to ferment revolutions by panicking whole populations.

When, in sixteenth- and seventeenth-century England, contemporaries spoke, as they often did, of the 'noise', 'murmur', or 'mutter' in the country, they referred to the constant buzz of people talking to each other: asking for news, swapping stories, exchanging views. For the majority at this time, the communication of information on current affairs was primarily an oral business, therefore. Nevertheless, the early modern period was to witness a significant increase in the extent to which the written word, in both manuscript and printed form, influenced the transmission and the content of news. In this context, as in others, there was a complex relationship between the various media and a tremendous infusion of oral circulation by textual sources.

This chapter examines the means and the mechanisms by which news and rumour of a largely political nature circulated in Tudor and Stuart England. It tries to demonstrate precisely how information passed along the grapevine from person to person and community to community. Whereas it might be easy to observe that a news story has spread across a region or over the nation in this period, it is often much more difficult to see by what process this has actually happened. As with all grapevines, that which operated at this time produced some marvellous distortions and adaptations of the messages it conveyed. Wild rumours and fantastic reports sprang up and took on lives of their own as they passed from mouth to mouth, at a time when even the best informed members of society had few means of authenticating intelligence. Written sources were generally no more reliable than oral, and print could bear as much, if not more, responsibility for exaggeration and corruption as common talk.

At the same time, however, the proliferation of written media was conspiring in the creation of a new world of information. The gradual loosening of the grip of censorship, the ever growing commercialization of the market for print, and the insatiable appetite of an increasingly literate populace, all contributed to a culture of communication that was very different by the end of the seventeenth century. In 1700 England was a nation no less lubricated by the oral flow of news and speculation, no less subject to hyperbolic rumours, than it had been in the past, but it was by then a society which had created the spaces and established the constituent parts for the emergence of what would later come to be known as 'public opinion'.

THINK NO EVIL, SPEAK NO EVIL

One of the very few opportunities for historians to eavesdrop on the conversations of the past, to be able to listen to what ordinary men and
women actually said to each other on specific occasions, is when someone
at the time tried to silence them. Repression, at least in sixteenth- and
seventeenth-century England, a society bound by the rule of law and
highly bureaucratic, tended to produce records. These records very often
included transcriptions of the offensive speeches allegedly uttered
against the state or its prominent individuals. In particular, the depositions taken from witnesses in judicial procedures provide a level of
detailed reporting which was necessary as evidence for judges or juries at
the time and is invaluable as a window into the minds of the otherwise
silent majority for researchers now.

England in these centuries had strict laws of sedition and censorship
which made it a criminal offence to speak or write ill of the government,
its personnel, or anyone in authority. The regularity with which these laws
were strengthened and the severity with which they were applied varied
with different regimes and changing circumstances, and the limitations of
enforcement always circumscribed their effectiveness in practice. The
repressive machinery of the state was founded on laws of treason which
stretched back to 1352 and were progressively extended in scope during
the sixteenth century by acts of 1534, 1552, 1554, 1571, and 1585.[1] In addition, by virtue of statutes in 1275, 1378, and 1388, it had also been an
offence to utter words considered to be seditious, that is, speeches which
impugned the person of the monarch or spread false rumours which
might sow discord between government and people. The laws of sedition
were tightened in 1542 with a statute respecting political prophecies. New
legislation by Mary Tudor in 1555 imposed heavy punishments of pillory
and fine for speaking 'false, sedicious and sclaunderous news, rumours,
sayenges and tales, ageynst our most dreadd sovereigne lorde and king,
and ageynst our most naturall sovereygne ladye and quene . . . of whom
we ar forbidden to thincke evill and muche more to speake evell'. In 1581,
Elizabeth I made the authorship of any seditious writing, and a second
conviction for uttering seditious words, capital offences without benefit
of clergy. This legislation remained the basis for the restriction of speech
throughout the seventeenth century, although successive governments

---

[1] J. G. Bellamy, *The Law of Treason in England in the Later Middle Ages* (Cambridge, 1970); id.,
*The Tudor Law of Treason: An Introduction* (London, 1979), 14, 27, 45–6, 84, 184; G. R. Elton,
*Policy and Police: The Enforcement of the Reformation in the Age of Thomas Cromwell* (Cambridge, 1972),
ch. 6.

issued proclamations repeatedly urging its respect by the people and its implementation by the magistracy.[2]

The records produced in the pursuit of these policies provide the principal source for this chapter. They take the form of reports submitted to the Privy Council in London by officials in the provinces describing seditious words and often enclosing the testimonies of accusers and accused. Such witness statements may have been taken by summary procedures or else at the assize courts which biannually dealt with such matters in the regions. The records of the assizes themselves, where they survive, give some idea of the extent and frequency with which the offence was prosecuted. But perhaps the material passed to the Privy Council and preserved in the State Papers, because it has survived relatively consistently throughout this period, most readily demonstrates the changing intensity of vigilance by the authorities over time. Thus, it was richest first in the late 1530s when Thomas Cromwell's attempts to enforce adherence to the new religion were at their height. It was also plentiful in the latter years of the sixteenth century when economic crisis from within and the threat of invasion from without jeopardized the stability of the Elizabethan regime. And it survives in larger quantities from the period prior to the breakdown of political order in early the 1640s, and during particular moments of crisis in the reign of Charles II.[3]

The concern of the authorities over the raising of false reports about affairs of state, or the spreading of dangerous rumours which might engender panic and cause disquiet among the people, is of particular interest in any attempt to piece together the way in which information actually circulated. The process by which royal officials, justices, and magistrates hunted down the source of a seditious tale enables us to trace back with them along the thread of transmission, one person to another, which led to the point of origin. It also gives us particular insight into the

---

[2]  33 Henry VIII, c. 14; 1&2 Philip and Mary, c. 3; 23 Elizabeth, c. 2, in *Statutes of the Realm* (11 vols., London, 1810–24), iii. 850, iv. pt. i, 240–1, 659–61; *Stuart Royal Proclamations: Volume I*, ed. J. F. Larkin and P. L. Hughes (Oxford, 1973), 495–6, 519–21. For discussion, see Elton, *Policy and Police*, 80–2; Roger B. Manning, 'The Origin of the Doctrine of Sedition', *Albion*, 12 (1980), 99–121.

[3]  For attempts to use cases of seditious words in order to gauge popular opinion, see Elton, *Policy and Police*, ch. 2; Joel Samaha, 'Gleanings from Local Criminal-Court Records: Sedition amongst the "Inarticulate" in Elizabethan Essex', *Journal of Social History*, 8/4 (1975), 61–79; Buchanan Sharp, *In Contempt of all Authority: Rural Artisans and Riot in the West of England, 1586–1660* (Berkeley and Los Angeles, 1980), 36–42; id., 'Popular Political Opinion in England, 1660–1685', *History of European Ideas*, 10 (1989), 13–29; Dagmar Freist, *Governed by Opinion: Politics, Religion and the Dynamics of Communication in Stuart London, 1637–1645* (London, 1997), ch. 5; Tim Harris, *London Crowds in the Reign of Charles II* (Cambridge, 1987), 50–1, 158, 161–3, 165–6, 213, 220–1; Paul Kleber Monod, *Jacobitism and the English People, 1688–1788* (Cambridge, 1989), ch. 8.

communication networks of ordinary people as they went about their daily business, since underpinning these policies was a belief in the fundamental fickleness, irrationality, and instability of popular opinion.

The 'vulgar', it was always said, were credulous and gullible in all that they heard, ever liable to misunderstand the truth of things, prone to distort them still further, hasty to judge, and quick to criticize their betters. 'Howe redy vulgare peple ar to be abused by such and ar disposed to dispearse sedycyous rumors therby to procure trobles and mocons,' wrote the queen to the earl of Shrewsbury during the Scottish disturbances of 1565. 'This is the vulgar sorte', the Devonshire justice, Lionel Sharpe, told Sir Robert Cecil in April 1601, 'which ar carried more by rumors without an head, then by the truth of thinges.' When, in July 1628, Robert Melvill was imprisoned for repeating a seditious tale against the duke of Buckingham, he confessed to having been 'drawen by the reporte of the common people (which is *belluam multorum capitum*) into the vulgar error of the tyme'. The 'common people' it was lamented from Great Yarmouth in the 1660s, 'gennerally delight to inveigh against persons of honor, though for no other cause but that they are honorable'. In April 1681 the grand jury of the quarter sessions at Bristol could report that factious dissenters spent their time 'in debating of state matters and in reading and hearing news which, tho' oftentimes it proves false, yet is very glibly swallow'd by the credulous vulgar who commonly delight to be entertained with fables and falsehoods especially such as reflect on his majestic, his affayres or government'.[4]

Such prejudice about the lack of popular discretion is reflected in the social composition of those indicted for sedition before courts such as the quarter sessions or assizes. There were, for example, 154 people so charged from the five counties which comprised the Home circuit assizes in the period 1558–1625, and 228 people arraigned in a sample taken from the seventeen counties making up the Home, Northern, Norfolk, and Oxford circuits during the years 1660–85. In both cases, 86 per cent of the individuals were described as being of 'yeoman' status or below.[5]

---

[4] PRO, SP15/12/73; PRO, SP12/279/62; PRO, SP16/110/13; PRO, SP29/233/112; SP29/415/142. For other contemporary comments of this sort, see Christopher Hill, 'The Many-Headed Monster', in his *Change and Continuity in Seventeenth-Century England* (London, 1974), 181–204.

[5] The Home circuit indictments (Essex, Hertfordshire, Kent, Surrey, Sussex) for the Elizabethan and Jacobean periods are calendared in *Calendar of Assize Records*, ed. J. S. Cockburn (10 vols., London, 1978–82), from which this calculation is derived. The breakdown is: 8 gentlemen, 12 clerics, 1 merchant, 28 yeomen, 47 artisans, 10 husbandmen, 31 labourers, 11 women, 3 vagrants, and 3 others. The figure from the four circuits during the reign of Charles II has been calculated by Sharp, 'Popular Political Opinion in England 1660–1685', 14. It includes:

What emerges from such records is the frequent ability of people to talk about political events and issues and the apparent alacrity with which they were prepared to do so. Whenever two or more met together, it seems, the conversation was likely to turn to the state of the nation. To the authorities, of course, even the very consideration of such matters, hardly the business of the common people, was reprehensible. In 1599, Lord Keeper Egerton could lament the late increase of those who, 'at ordinaries and comon tables, wheare they have scarce mony to paye for their dynner, enter politique discourses of princes, kingdomes and estates and of counsells and counsellors, censuring everie one according to their owne discontented and malicious humors without regard of religion, conscience or honestie.' 'I cann[ot] come into meeting but I find the predominant humour to be talking of the warres of Christendome, the honnor of their country and such like treasons,' one pamphleteer feigned to protest in 1621, 'and would to God they would stop their mouthes and prophane noe more the thinges that are above them.'[6] This appetite for political discussion was clearly fuelled by a parallel hunger to discover the latest information about affairs within the realm and beyond. In lieu of access to other sources, this usually meant asking for news of anyone well met.

### SPINNING WEBS WITH WORDS

Spinning has long been a metaphor for gossiping. For centuries the carving or painting, engraving or woodcut, depicting a woman with distaff in hand has been a representation of gossip; for women, it was said, span webs with words like threads of yarn. This image of verbal strands linking up myriad individuals into a network of communication was not one lost on contemporary authorities. When in the late 1620s the corporation of Reading was worried about disorderly youngsters in the town it was because they were 'not onelye gadders and spinners of streete webbs in the daye time, but very unruly in the evenings, ordinary nightwalkers'. Such gadders and spinners of street webs abound in the records of the period as officials frowned on the disquiet and dissent which they tended to leave in their wake, whether domestic discord between private individuals or political dissonance between subjects and rulers. There were many like Elizabeth Hunt of Jacobean Essex, 'a common gadinge gossip from

---

17 gentry, 12 clerics, 1 merchant, 1 medic, 68 yeomen, 60 labourers, 35 artisans, 13 retailers, 3 husbandmen, and 3 single women, among others.

⁶ PRO, SP12/273/35; PRO, SP14/126/1.

house to house, leaving tales and newes'; or her contemporary, Nicholas Baily of Cambridgeshire, 'a sower of discord . . . in raising and speakinge of divers slandcrous crimes and speaches betwene neighbor and neigh-bor'. And those who travelled in the course of their business were likely to link different communities by the verbal thread, such as Alice Bennet, 'a very poore woman' from Oxfordshire, described in 1604 as one who 'goeth abroad to sell sope and candels from towne to towne to gett her lyving and she useth to carrie tales betwene neighboures'.[7]

Then, as now, people loved to gossip, to speculate, to express opinions. Their desire for news, their curiosity about the business of others, their need to be heard was as insatiable then as ever. Indeed, enquiry after the news was, thought John Florio in 1591, always 'the first question of an Englishman'. It was the customary greeting, the opening conversational gambit, for everyone. 'It is the language at first meetings used in all coun-tries; what news?' confirmed one seventeenth-century pamphlet. 'What newes? Every man askes what newes? Every man's religion is known by his newes . . .', it was said. It remained one of the few questions which was capable, so Robert Burton believed, of stirring the Jacobean gentry from their customary apathy. 'If they read a book at any time . . . 'tis an English chronicle, Sir Huon of Bordeaux, Amadis de Gaul, etc., a play-book, or some pamphlet of news, and that at such seasons only, when they cannot stir abroad, to drive away time, their sole discourse is dogs, hawks, horses, and what news?'[8]

What was true of gentlefolk applied to the common people no less. It was a frequent lament among preachers that while their flocks were ever ready to discuss current affairs, they fell strangely silent when it came to talk of spiritual matters. They 'reherse and tell nothing but gossips tales, and newes, that love to have their tongues to runne through the world, and to be medling in other mans matters', complained George Widley of his parishioners in Portsmouth, but 'if any question shall be put as con-cerning religion, they grow as mute as fishes'. Impart to them a piece of doctrine and they forget it as soon as they hear it, lamented William Harrison of his Lancashire congregation in 1614; but 'report to them an

[7] HMC, *11th Report, Appendix, Part VII* (London, 1888), 214; Bod. Lib., MS. Eng. Lang. e. 6., fo. 65ᵛ; Cambridge University Library, EDR/B2/21, fo. 50; Oxfordshire Record Office, ODR c. 24, fo. 219.

[8] John Florio, *Florios Second Frvtes* (London, 1591), sig. A2ʳ; Margaret Spufford, *Small Books and Pleasant Histories: Popular Fiction and its Readership in Seventeenth-Century England* (London, 1981), 65; *Diary of John Rous, Incumbent of Santon Downham, Suffolk, from 1625 to 1642*, ed. Mary Anne Everett Green (Camden Society, 1st ser., 66, London, 1856), 44, and cf. the epigraph to this chapter; Robert Burton, *The Anatomy of Melancholy*, ed. Holbrook Jackson (3 vols., Everyman edn., London, 1932), i. 320.

humane historie, tell them some strange newes, or a tale for their worldly profit, or corporall health, they will keepe it well enough, and at any time, and in any company will relate it very readily'. The generality would do anything on a Sunday rather than be at church, as it seemed to Thomas Shepard, preferring 'to tel tales, and break jests at home, or (at best) to talk of foren or domesticall news only to pass away the time, rather than to see God in his works and warm their hearts thereby'.[9]

Given the laws of sedition, however, the casual question 'what news?' was one which might plunge the unsuspecting enquirer into deep trouble. In the 1590s the London chronicler John Stow could still remember the tragic hanging, outside his very door in Aldgate, of a 'well-beloved' bailiff of Romford in Essex who had fallen foul of official overreaction. It had been during Kett's rebellion of 1549 in East Anglia when the authorities were highly sensitive to the dangers of loose talk. On a visit to the capital the poor bailiff had chanced to fall into conversation with the curate of Aldgate. 'He asked me, "what newes in the countrey?" I answered, "heauie newes". "Why?" quoth he. "It is sayde", quoth I, "that many men be vp in Essex, but thanks be to God al is good quiet about vs".' 'And this was all, as God be my judge', he protested on the scaffold before they executed him the following morning. As for the curate, on hearing this protestation of innocence and 'to auoyde reproach of the people', he 'left the cittie, and was never heard of sinc[e] . . .'.[10]

As the London magistrates well knew, it was in precisely this way, by casual contact and the questioning of travellers, that information and rumour most often spread around the country. In this sense the circulation of national and political news should be seen as no different from the spread of domestic and personal gossip which is known to have been so rife in communities. Analysis of the records of defamation has made familiar that environment of chatter and rumour-mongering generated by the intimacy of small town and village life where privacy was typically scarce and people were encouraged to know the business of others. Allegations about people's personal lives and sexual misdemeanours, accusations of behaviour which breached community norms, all thrived as news in such a setting. '"I will tell you some news . . ."', leered Edmund Serjeant as he left a wheelwright's shop at Stanton St Quintin, Wiltshire, in 1623. '"The Sparrow hath begotten Mag Bird with child . . . She sits now at Hullavington and will hatch very shortly".' Behind any such tale

    [9] George Widley, *The Doctrine of the Sabbath* (London, 1604), 114; William Harrison, *The Difference of Hearers* (London, 1614), 39; Thomas Shepard *Theses Sabbaticae* (London, 1655), 314.
    [10] John Stow, *A Survey of London*, ed. C. L. Kingsford (2 vols., Oxford, 1908), i. 144–5.

told to the authorities of Church or State was this undercurrent and atmosphere of public gossip. Very often, irregularities came to the ears of churchwardens and constables simply on the basis of communal suspicion, the notion of the 'common fame', or 'common voice', which could be sufficient basis for a presentment.[11]

For news of a larger significance and a wider import, these mechanisms of transmission worked no less. Professional carriers, chapmen, and travelling tradespeople were often discovered to be the factors and brokers of news, circulating information and spinning webs of communication in ways which few other sources could provide. 'I bring nothing, except those things which are tossed up and down in barbers shops, in carriers waggons, and in ships', says one dialogue character of the news. The records are full of individuals such as Edward Lymwoode, a petty chapman from Ongar in Essex, indicted in 1586 as 'a comon spredder of newes and such false rumours' concerning the fortunes of the queen's fleet; or the pedlar called Peale caught wandering around Lichfield in 1592 uttering 'certain lewde speeches tendinge to treason'. Later, in 1663, Zachary Crofton, a former preacher turned 'cheesefactor' was reported from Cheshire to be one who 'rides both up and downe this county, and sevearall others, where we are afraid he soweth sedition'. At the time of the Rye House Plot in 1683, justices in the south and eastern counties of England were worried about the increasing number of travellers from Scotland, 'pedlers and petty chapmen wandring abroad' suspected of being 'carryers of intelligence in relacion to the late conspiracy against his majestie'. On the other hand, back in the spring of 1640 one of the main sources of intelligence which the English government had of the preparations being made for a rebellion in Scotland was the Borderers who went north to market and the Scottish traders who would stop in Berwick on their way south to buy and sell in London.[12]

---

[11] Martin Ingram, *Church Courts, Sex and Marriage in England, 1570–1640* (Cambridge, 1987), 305. On this subject see also J. A. Sharpe, *Defamation and Sexual Slander in Early Modern England: The Church Courts at York* (Borthwick Papers, 58, York, 1980); Laura Gowing, *Domestic Dangers: Women, Words, and Sex in Early Modern London* (Oxford, 1996), chs. 3–4.

[12] Desiderius Erasmus, *The Colloquies or Familiar Discourses of Desiderius Erasmus of Roterdam*, trans. H.M. (London, 1671), 51; HMC, *10th Report, Appendix, Part IV* (London, 1885), 481; *Acts of the Privy Council of England, 1542–1631* (46 vols., London, 1890–1964) (hereafter, *APC*), *1591–92*, 410; PRO, SP29/82/51, 84/94; PRO, SP29/436/107, 436/148, 436/148i; PRO, SP16/451/71. For remarks on the relationship between carriers and news, see J. Crofts, *Packhorse, Waggon and Post: Land Carriage and Communications Under the Tudors and Stuarts* (London, 1967), 20–1; R. W. Scribner, 'Oral Culture and the Diffusion of Reformation Ideas', *History of European Ideas*, 5 (1984), 237–56; M. C. Frearson, 'The English Corantos of the 1620s' (unpublished Ph.D. dissertation, University of Cambridge, 1993), ch. 1.

Such itinerant traders were often deliberately employed by people who wanted to convey news or intelligence around the country. Messages of a sensitive nature, in particular, were simply too dangerous to commit to paper and were much safer entrusted to people, with legitimate reasons for being on the road, for delivery by word of mouth. The northern gentry responsible for galvanizing support for the Pilgrimage of Grace in the closing months of 1536 often communicated in this way. Rafe Sadler met a number of them on his way up to York in January 1537, 'divers posts coming Londonwards', who told him that most of the northern counties had risen up in a new insurrection. Not long afterwards, John Petenson of Felton in Northumberland was discovered to be one paid by people throughout the north of England and Lowlands of Scotland to convey messages over the border country: he was arrested as a vagabond and confessed only 'that he heard these communications at divers times of such vagabonds as himself'. In Elizabethan Oxford, John Bradburie was probably not unusual in that 'being a tayler and not free of the towne', and thus 'driven to bee moste abrode for [his] living', he was often employed as 'a man that vseth to goe of messages for gentlemen'. John Penrose, a Catholic from Mawgan in Cornwall and 'a man of meane estate and condicion', was in the service of John Arundell of Lawhitton when he was interrogated in February 1606 as 'an intelligencer to and from London to recusants'. Edward Miller was similarly engaged to communicate between the Jacobites after the expulsion of James II. On the road between Corbridge and Newcastle in February 1690 he was overtaken by a fellow traveller who, suspecting his business, asked him 'if he had any letters. He replyed that was a dangerous way of carrying intelligence, but that there was a communication betwixt the Papists of Scotland and England by word of mouth that the Protestants of England would never discover."[13]

The value of those who travelled around on business as purveyors of news and disseminators of information is well illustrated by the way in which intelligence was spread and support solicited for the planned uprising in Oxfordshire at the end of 1596. In November, Roger Ibill confessed to having 'harde latelie divers poore people saie (as he traveilled in this countie, beinge a loader to Hampton Gaie mill) that the prices

---

[13] Madeleine H. and Ruth Dodds, *The Pilgrimage of Grace, 1536–7, and the Exeter Conspiracy, 1538* (2 vols., Cambridge, 1915), i. 50; *Letters and Papers, Foreign and Domestic, of the Reign of Henry VIII*, ed. J. S. Brewer and James Gairdner (21 vols., London, 1862–1901) (hereafter, *L&P Hen. VIII*), xii, pt. I (1537), 84; *L&P Hen. VIII*, xii, pt. II (1537), 322–4; *The Archdeacon's Court: Liber Actorum, 1584*, ed. E. R. C. Brinkworth (2 vols., Oxfordshire Record Society, 23–4, Oxford, 1942–6), i. 131; PRO, SP14/18/73; PRO, ASSI45/15/4/74.

of corne weare so deere that there would be shortlie a risinge of the people . . .'; Roger Symonds, carpenter, claimed to have heard much the same, 'commonly as he went to marketts'. News of these murmurings passed quickly on the grapevine. Of Richard Bradshaw it was said that he, 'being a miller and traveling the countrie, took uppon him to persuade dyvers to ioyne with them'; his brother James, also a miller, had met Richard Heath in the street at Yarnton 'and being asked "What news?" ' replied that 'he knewe a hundred good fellowes that rather then they would be starved they would ryse'. Bartholomew Steer, another carpenter and an initiator of the plot, had 'saide that he would ride and goe and use all the meanes which he could' to apprise others of their cause.[14]

Indeed, a principal motive behind official concern over vagrants and wandering beggars throughout this period was the danger which they posed in the spreading of seditious rumours prejudicial to the stability of government and religion. Henry VIII issued a circular to justices of the peace in December 1538 directing them 'to punish spreaders of seditious rumours and expel and corect all vagabonds and valiant beggars'. In June 1554 the civic authorities in York were taking 'especiall regarde to vacabonds' as those likely to 'spriede any vagne prophesies, sediciouse, false and untrue rumours'. Orders issued to parish constables in Wiltshire in July 1571 instructed them to punish all beggars, 'for ther is no greater disorder nor no greater roote of theftes, murders, pickinge, stealinge, debate and sedicion then ys in those vagabonds and that riseth of them'. The Privy Council drew up one of a number of draft bills in 1593 amid fears over missionary priests and foreign spies, 'for restraining and punishing vagrant and seditious persons, who under pretence of conscience and religion corrupt and seduce the queen's subjects'.[15]

It was hardly surprising, therefore, that as political tension began to mount again in 1638, there should be particular concern about beggars and the unemployed who, it was believed, 'in tymes of suspition or trouble, may by tales and false rumors distracte the peoples mindes'. It was in response to the threat posed by a group of Ranters that the Wiltshire grand jury was worried in 1656 about the malicious people who 'do wander about spreading many evil and dangerous opinions to the dishonour

[14] PRO, SP12/261/10ii, 12/262/4, 12/261/15iv, and see John Walter, 'A "Rising of the People"? The Oxfordshire Rising of 1596', *Past and Present*, 107 (1985), 97.

[15] *L&P Hen. VIII*, xiii, pt. II (1538), 485; *York Civic Records*, ed. Angelo Raine (8 vols., Yorkshire Archaeological Society, Wakefield, 1939–53), v. 107; HMC, *4th Report* (London, 1874), 115; HMC, *15th Report, Appendix, Part X* (London, 1899), 50–1. For other fears of vagrants spreading sedition during this period, see *L&P Hen. VIII*, xii, pt. I (1537), 581; PRO, SP12/60/1; PRO, SP12/60/27; PRO, SP12/272/48; PRO, SP15/12/74; PRO, SP14/72/31.

of God and the blaspheming his name'. When, at the end of the seventeenth century, the godly Richard Baxter came to reflect upon those
people who experience predicted were most likely to 'raise any army to
extirpate knowledge and religion', it was to itinerants and illiterates that he
looked accusingly: 'the tinkers, sowgawters and cratecarryers and beggars
and bargemen and all the rabble that cannot reade'.[16]

In particular, traders and travellers were facilitators of information by
word of mouth in so far as they had regular contact with London, the
centre in which most news was generated and the origin of much political
speculation. Typically, when Denis Jones, a smith from London, was up in
Reading in May 1537 he happily passed on the news he had heard in the
capital to locals at the Bear hostelry. Ten months before a group of neighbours from Freshwater, Isle of Wight, had been 'drynking together in
their churche hows', when a pedlar came in and told them them 'that he
heard at London that Queen Anne was put to death and boiled in lead'. In
March 1629, Stephen ap Evan met William Jones on the highway outside
Reilth in Shropshire and asked him 'what was the newes at London', at
which Jones told him that Parliament had been dissolved. When a
Scottish minstrel, Daniel O'Farrell, called in at an alehouse in Brotherton,
West Riding, on his journey north in November 1678, and asked the
keeper, John Megan, '"What news?"' as he ordered his flagon of ale,
Megan quite naturally replied that 'he might know that of him because he
supposed he was lately come from London'.[17]

Around the Royal Exchange, along Cheapside to St Paul's churchyard
and walk, in the taverns and inns which lined Fleet Street and the Strand
on the way towards Westminster Hall, the latest news could be found on
everyone's lips. 'Men will tell you more than all the world, betwixt the
Exchange, Pauls and Westminster,' commented one visitor in 1631. The
Exchange was the great entrepôt where factors and merchants met from
around the country and over the seas. In addition to trade, it was said,
'they all desire newes'. Paul's walk was no less the locus of information
swapped, tales told, and rumour gestated. 'The noyse in it is like that of
bees', mused John Earle in 1628, 'a strange humming or buzze, mixt of
walking, tongues, and feet . . . It is the great exchange of all discourse, and
no busines whatsoever but is here stirring and a foot . . . It is the generall
mint of all famous lies', while many 'turne merchants here, and trafficke

---

[16] HMC, *Report on the Records of the City of Exeter*, ed. J. H. Wylie (London, 1916), 202; *Records of
the County of Wiltshire*, ed. B. H. Cunnington (Devizes, 1932), 231; 'The Reverend Richard
Baxter's Last Treatise', ed. Frederick J. Powicke, *Bulletin of the John Rylands Library*, 10 (1926), 182.

[17] *L&P Hen. VIII*, xii, pt. I (1537), 589; *L&P Hen. VIII*, xiii, pt. I (1538), 186; PRO,
SP16/147/27; PRO, ASSI45/12/2/69.

for newes'. This oral communication was the quickest and often the best or only available source of news; in lieu of other more reliable media, 'the means only lefte is to wayte at Powles or the Exchange for some communication of some ould acquayntance', as one Elizabethan put it.[18]

If the principal frequenters of the Exchange and the majority of 'Paul's walkers' were merchants and gentlemen, politicians and diplomats, these centres were not entirely socially exclusive. Young servants and apprentices, for example, seem often to have been sent to pick up news for their masters or to save them places at sermons and readings at Paul's cross. One such was Vernon Ferrar, a servant who was sitting at the cross on a Sunday morning in May 1629, 'keeping a place for his master as he usually doth', when he heard another 'young youth' read aloud from a libel against the king in front of the assembled crowd. From there, such youngsters could carry this information throughout the alleys and tenements, along the thoroughfares and into the shops where people gadded and gossiped. Young Stephen Plunket got into trouble in March 1624 for repeating one piece of news, 'and for his author can produce no other but comon rumor as he (being a boy) passed to and fro about the streets'. Equally, servants from outside the capital might have access to Paul's news through their masters or superiors and it could filter back to the localities via such channels. In March 1587, for example, another servant, Lawrence Perry, was heard repeating some false news at the house of a neighbour in Essex which clearly originated from 'Paules church, where his maister is accustometh dailye to walke'. In April 1600, George Clifford from Fotherby in north-east Lincolnshire, was questioned about the rumour-mongering activities of his uncle Richard Thimblebie, with whom he had come to lodge in Aldersgate Street, London, and he confessed to having noticed how he would 'goeth dailie forth unto ordynaries' and that 'he hath often seene him walking in Powles'.[19]

---

[18] John Smith, *Advertisements for the Unexperienced Planters of New England* (London, 1631), sig. A2, quoted in H. S. Bennett, *English Books and Readers, 1603 to 1640* (Cambridge, 1970), 179; Donald Lupton, *London and the Countrey Carbonadoed and Quartred into Severall Characters* (London, 1932), 24, 142; John Earle, *Micro-cosmographie: Or, a Peece of the World Discovered; in Essayes and Characters* (London, 1928), sigs. K1ʳ–K3ʳ; PRO, SP12/239/26. In 1632 the 'foryners and strangers' who frequented Paul's churchyard were described as being 'for the most part men of greater sort and qualitie'; the noise they made on a Sunday in 'walkinge and talkinge' was said to disturb divine service: PRO, SP16/214/94. For other contemporary comment on the newsmongering at Paul's and the Exchange, see Samuel Rowlands, *The Letting of Humours Blood in the Head-Vaine* (London, 1600), sig. C8ʳ; Richard Brathwait, *Whimzies: Or, A New Cast of Characters* (London, 1631), 17, 23; Harold Love, *Scribal Publication in Seventeenth-Century England* (Oxford, 1993), 193–4.

[19] PRO, SP16/142/102; PRO, SP14/185/95; PRO, SP12/199/14; SP12/274/113.

Another vehicle through which news and rumour could be transmitted out from these centres of information was provided by the watermen who ferried 'walkers' across the Thames from Paul's wharf to the Bankside in Southwark. They would often pick up titbits of gossip from their passengers and could usually be relied upon to satisfy enquiries after the latest reports. During the rising of the Northern Earls in December 1569, for example, Harry Shadwell heard, at the Bull's Head in Cheapside, various rumours concerning the duke of Alba and was subsequently told by his sculler from Paul's wharf that 10,000 Scots had joined the rebels, but that most were slain. On the same day, another waterman, Richard Whittarnes, also relayed this tale to two passengers whom he took across to Bear Garden 'beeinge demanded by one of them, "What newes out of the northe?"' In February 1606, Thomas East was interrogated about some speeches touching 'treason intended against his majestie or the state' which he heard from a passenger in his wherry coming back in the other direction, from Horsehead Down stairs to Tower Wharf stairs in London. On their journey over to Southwark one evening in May 1627, John Poole, a tanner, and John Cole, a silkweaver, fell to talking with various others about news of the duke of Buckingham's expedition to La Rochelle, before one of the company was heard to speak ill-advisedly of the king and his favourite.[20]

In general, London acted as a magnet, attracting in visitors and their news stories from around the country and then repelling them out once again. People flocked to Paul's or the Exchange in search of the latest information to take back home. Travelling back and forth on the road between London and Deal on the Kent coast during October 1639, the great adventurer Peter Mundy kept 'meeting many lords, knightts [and] gentry posting and riding to and fro, some aboutt businesse, butt most to see and hear newes. For this latter purpose went multitudes of the common sort.' At the same time, the inhabitants of the hundred of Berkeley in Gloucestershire could see the news arriving in the form of returning tradesmen appearing over Simondshall Hill on the Cotswold edge. John Smyth of Nibley mused that, 'The clothiers, horscarriers and wainmen of this hundred who weekly frequent London, knowinge by ancient custome, that the first question, (after welcome home from London) is "What newes at London?" doe vsually gull vs with feigned inventions, divised by them vpon those downes; which wee either then suspectinge vpon the

    [20] PRO, SP12/60/48, 12/60/49, 12/60/54; PRO, SP14/18/65; PRO, SP16/63/113. Cf. *The Diary of Samuel Pepys*, ed. Robert Latham and William Matthews (11 vols., London, 1970–83), vii. 221, viii. 82.

report, or after findinge false, wee cry out, "Simondshall newes!". A generall speach betweene each cobblers teeth.'[21]

Indeed, the roads and highways, inns and hostelries, up and down the country rang out with that question to travellers from the capital. In March 1535 Adam Fermour of Walden, Essex, was down in London where he learned of the enactment of the new Statute of Uses. On his return one of his neighbours naturally asked him what news he had heard in the capital. '"What news man?"', Fermour is said to have replied. '"By God's blood evil news! For the king will make such laws that if a man die his wife and children shall go a-begging".' Fermour probably heard the new statute being read aloud by the crier at one of the market crosses in London where government acts and proclamations were anounced to the semi-literate people. This was certainly so of Lewis Herbert from Abergavenny, Monmouthshire, who was in London in September 1538. On his way back he lodged 'at the sign of the Lambe' in Abingdon, Berkshire, and then, on the evening of Tuesday the 17th, he reached the George in Pucklechurch, Gloucestershire, about 5 miles from Bristol. At supper time some of the locals asked him '"What news at London?"', to which Herbert replied that 'there was a cry at the cross in Cheapside' the previous Friday 'that no unlawful games should be used, and that angel nobles should go for 8s. and cross groats for 5d. apiece'.[22]

When William Frauncis, a smith, got back to Hatfield Broad Oak in Essex, in February 1587, his neighbours enquired '"What newes at London?"' At this, he relayed the rumour which had come to his ears 'that there was one in the Tower which sayeth he is King Edward'. More of this kind of speculation was heard in London early in May 1630 by Joseph Hall, a tailor from Newhall in Cheshire. After the three days' ride home he was asked by various of the locals '"What newes at London?"', to which he replied that 'itt was spoaken in divers places' that the king 'was in the Tower and that there was an other to bee in his place'. During the mounting political tension in the spring of 1639, Edward Thursby from Pattiswick in Essex travelled down to the capital 'about some occasions

---

[21] Peter Mundy, *The Travels of Peter Mundy, in Europe and Asia, 1608–1667*, ed. Sir Richard Carnac Temple and Lavinia Mary Anstey (5 vols. in 6, Hakluyt Society, 2nd ser., Cambridge, 1907; London, 1914–36), iv. 41; John Smyth, *The Berkeley Manuscripts*, ed. Sir John Maclean (3 vols., Gloucester, 1883–5), iii. 30. Cf. John Walter, *Understanding Popular Violence in the English Revolution: The Colchester Plunderers* (Cambridge, 1999), 288–9. In London, the equivalent expression to 'Simondshall news' was 'Pye Corner news': Edinburgh University Library MS, La. III. 545, fo. 114ʳ.

[22] *L&P Hen. VIII*, xiii, pt. II (1538), 121 (Statute of Uses, 27 Henry VIII, c. 10), 158–9 (probably the proclamation of 1538 on unlawful games: *Tudor Royal Proclamations*, ed. P. L. Hughes and J. F. Larkin (3 vols., New Haven, 1964–9), i. 266–8).

of his owne and . . . there he heard some newes concerning the Scottish business'. It was generally 'spoken about the towne' and in particular, 'Rowland Keely, a taylor dwelling about Sheere Lane, told it him and reported it to him for truth', which, on his return, 'made [him] tell it with the more confidence'. When at the time of Monmouth's rebellion in June 1685, William Whittwell, a brasier from Kendal on his way to Lancaster, met a man at Slyne who said he had come from London he naturally enquired of him 'what newse of James Scott and his party'.[23]

London was also the principal centre of foreign news which was taken back to the provinces in the same way. This became particularly evident in the early 1620s as interest in events abroad rose at the time of the Thirty Years War, and during the negotiations for the Spanish match in particular. One Friday early in March 1620, for example, Issack Forrester was in Dolberry's Inn at Poole in Dorset when, as a carrier, he was naturally asked by his host 'what newes he heard from London'. He relayed a report, which he claimed to have had a fortnight before from the parson of Durweston 'who then was newly come from London', who had said 'that he heard att London that the match betweene the prince and the king of Spaines daughter was concluded on and that the Palsgrave had sent lettres to our king to know his pleasure whether he should undertake the crown of Bohemia and that the same lettres were intercepted and an aunsweare . . . was sent back . . . that he should use his discretion . . .'. On the evening of Saturday 17 December later that year, Alexander Whillegge, yeoman of North Petherton in Somerset, was having a drink at John Harris's alehouse in Bridgwater with Edward Cadwallider who, during their conversation, asked 'what news there was at London out of Bohemia or from the Palatine (the saide Whillegge cominge lately before from London)'. The reply came back that the general, Ambrogio Spinola, and the count of Bucquoy were both reported to be dead.[24]

But London was not, of course, the only concentration of people and gossip to act as a dynamic facilitator of information. Provincial towns could also serve as focal points, attracting London news to their

---

[23] PRO, ASSI35/29/1/33; PRO, SP16/163/61, 16/166/43; SP16/422/80; PRO, PL27/1 (*Whittwell* v. *Burrow*, 1685).

[24] PRO, SP14/121/90i–iv; SP14/118/37, 14/118/38. For a discussion of the newsbooks produced on these events and some of the reactions which they evoked, see M. A. Breslow, *A Mirror of England: English Puritan Views of Foreign Nations, 1618–1640* (Cambridge, Mass., 1970), 10–22, 63–71. The circulation of such news in the West Country is evident in the diary of the Devonshire gentleman, Walter Yonge: *Diary of Walter Yonge, Esq*, ed. George Roberts (Camden Society, 1st ser., 41, London, 1848), 33–7. News of the wars on the continent at this time could also be obtained, of course, by asking 'what news?' of any soldiers or travellers abroad on their return to the local alehouse: see BL, Additional MS, 38855, fo. 56; PRO, SP16/409/102i.

market-places and taverns and then spinning it out through the small towns and villages of the countryside. In the little Essex village of Aldham the locals looked to Colchester as their closest major entrepôt. Certainly, when Thomas Wendon, a servant, passed a group of his neighbours sitting on a bench outside Rafe North's door one Saturday in June 1596, he 'asked them if any manne there had bene at Colchester that day and what newes they heard there'. At the beginning of July 1635, John Berisford of Eagle Hall in Lincolnshire went down to Newark where troops had been mustering for the king; the following day in the kitchen of his neighbour, John Mounson, he was asked '"What newes at Newark?"' When William Penry, gentleman of Lancaster, returned from a visit to Preston in February 1685 following the public proclamation of James II as king, he met Thomas Cole and Thomas Simpson in the street who asked him '"What news at Preston?"' On his return to Croston a few years later one of the locals at the alehouse asked husbandman Thomas Wignall '"What newes from the assizes in Lancaster?"'[25]

The many people who travelled the trade routes and followed the marketing networks provided vital communication links from town to town and between commercial centres and their outlying areas. Fairs and markets were melting pots of rumour and gossip to which farmers and manufacturers, merchants and pedlars came from far and wide to listen for news and pass on reports as they did their business. In November 1625, for example, a Northumbrian labourer, Christopher Hogg, was returning home from Norfolk when he was overtaken on the road in Yorkshire by a clergyman, Martin Danby, who asked him 'what news there was in the south'. Hogg told him that the duke of Buckingham and the earl of Rutland had been imprisoned for attempting to poison the king, 'all which he saieth he heard privatelie rumord in Hempton in Norfolk wheare he had then bene driving beasts to the faire'. When in May 1640 Thomas Webb, a clothier from Devizes in Wiltshire, was at market in Maiden Bradley he met William Collyer of Bristol, a starchmaker, who wanted to buy his horse. Webb mentioned that he had brought the animal from the capital, at which Collyer asked 'what newes there were at London', before proceeding to tell of 'newes in Bristoll' about Archbishop Laud turning papist. Webb claimed also to have heard this story two months later when he was overtaken on the Kingston to Wantage road by William Horne, a husbandman from South Fawley in Berkshire, and they had each asked of the other 'what newes was in theire

[25] PRO, SP12/259/51; PRO, SP16/293/72; PRO, PL27/1 (*Cole* v. *Penry*, 1685); PL27/1 (*Boond* v. *Dandy*, 1688).

country'. The same curiosity greeted Thomas Robinson, a tailor from
Norfolk, when he returned home by sea via Wells from a cloth buying trip
in Yorkshire during the summer of 1661. At the alehouse in Holkham
John Tooley was naturally keen to know 'what newes was in those parts'.
Perhaps Robinson was at the same Yorkshire fairs as John Goad, a cattle
drover from Cartmel, who was over the Pennines three summers later
trading at Hornby and elsewhere when he heard news of trouble in the
south from 'the reports of chapmen mett in the markets and fairs'.[26]

Inns and alehouses were also crucial in this respect as the places where
travellers stopped and relayed what they heard as well as being the social
centres of most communities. The number of alehouses in the provinces
alone was estimated to be at least 25,000–26,000 in 1636. In such places
travellers with tales to tell rested overnight, people met together to
discuss current affairs, keepers and landlords often made it their business
to keep abreast of the latest reports. Agnes Filer, an alehouse keeper of
Ubley in Somerset, was doing no more than oiling the wheels of her trade
when, as Edward Loxton came in for a pot of ale one afternoon in March
1539, she asked him 'what newes he heard'. There must have been many
hostelries like the alehouse kept by John Welchman at Deddington in
Oxfordshire in the 1580s where the host would actively stimulate
business by gathering information as he travelled around the countryside,
before returning to relay it to eager paying customers 'being desyrous to
heare some newes'. In 1669, one Davill, the innkeeper of the Queen's
Head in Retford, Nottinghamshire, was actually employed by some
plotters against the government to gather intelligence: there can have
been few better conduits of local rumour. Everyone must have known a
local drinking establishment where it was possible to go and hear the
latest stories coming from London.[27]

An illustration of how a story from the capital would arrive at a provincial hostelry is provided by the case of Stephen Wootton and Thomas
Venterman. These two 'very poor fishermen' from Sandwich in Kent
decided to journey up to London about their business just after
Christmas 1675. During their visit they had some conversation in
Southwark with two women who told them news from court which, they
said, came on the authority of a kinsman of the king's secretary, no less.

---

[26] PRO, SP16/10/33, 16/10/55, 16/12/54, 16/21/61; SP16/456/36, 16/459/69i,
16/461/46i–ii; PRO, SP29/67/15; SP29/100/108i–ii. For another example, see PRO,
SP29/58/16i.

[27] PRO, SP16/321/19; *L&P Hen. VIII*, xiv, pt. I (1539), 215; *The Archdeacon's Court*, ed.
Brinkworth, i. 152; PRO, SP29/258/155i. For numbers of alehouses, see Peter Clark, *The English
Alehouse: A Social History, 1200–1830* (London, 1983), ch. 3.

On their return journey Wootton and Venterman lodged overnight at the Swan inn in Sittingbourne where they relayed the news to other patrons and to the landlord, James Gooden. These people passed it on in their turn, while the two fishermen continued with their tale as far as the Isle of Thanet.[28]

Inns and alehouses were thus revolving doors of news, rumour, and gossip, drawing in stories before radiating them out again via the many people who passed through. Consider the case of the spread of a typical anti-Catholic rumour in the spring of 1633. The false belief that, as a result of the king's forthcoming visit to Scotland, there would soon be a bloodthirsty rising of the papists, was being filtered through the Angel inn at Stilton in Huntingdonshire. At the beginning of April a travelling Scotsman had called there and told this tale. It was overheard by the ostler who confided it to other customers. One of them was Robert Johnson who passed the news on to his brother-in-law, Richard Sawyer of nearby Holme. Sawyer, in turn, told his son, Henry, who was soon after working for Lady Digby in Lathbury field outside Gayhurst in Buckinghamshire, when two Hanslope men passed by on their way from market in Newport Pagnell and enquired 'what newse hee did heare abrowde'. Young Sawyer let them know the shocking story, adding that the Digbys, known papists, had been stockpiling arms. '"I have hard birds singe so"', he said, but insisted that although his sources were reputable, 'non of the smaller but of the better sorte', he 'would not be called in question for these words willinglye'. When one of the men, husbandman Christopher Courssey, later met his neighbour, John Cooke, and was asked 'what was the news at Newport', he passed on the report once again. Cooke then went to the minister of Hanslope with this information and in due course a group of neighbours from the village was dispatched to search for young Sawyer. One of this number was subsequently dining with a friend over at Cosgrove in Northamptonshire when he told the assembled company of the report, and before long it was all over that county too. Henry Wilde, the rector of Alderton, heard it and informed the mayor of Northampton, advising that 'newes to that purpose, although with litle grounds, I finde in the mouths of so many'. So it was that a passing remark at an inn could spark a sequence of exchange which might send several neighbouring counties into panic.[29]

[28] PRO, SP29/376/76, 376/81, 378/31, 378/36.
[29] PRO, SP16/237/27–30, 16/237/42, 16/237/45, 16/237/60i–iv, 16/238/33i–ii, 16/239/61i–iv, 16/239/85. For discussion of the many rumours about papists rising, see Robin Clifton, 'The Popular Fear of Catholics during the English Revolution', *Past and Present*, 52 (1971), 23–55.

## THE NOISE IN THE COUNTRY

Along these channels of information and through this network of communication, news stories and rumours could spread with tremendous
speed. The towns and villages of England were linked with London, and
to some extent with each other, through a verbal web woven by travellers.
Very often the tales which passed along these grapevines were completely
false and sometimes extraordinary in their details. In a society which had
few means of confirming or denying news, in which political insecurity
was often of the highest order, and in which the authorities tried to
restrict and censor the circulation of intelligence, it is hardly surprising
that fervent speculation and wild rumour were rife.[30]

There are many examples of the rapidity with which stories could
spread by word of mouth in this period. They demonstrate that a message
did not need to be written down in order to travel quicky around a region
or over the whole nation and, indeed, they reveal that oral communication could be much the fastest form of transmission. The rebellions of the
sixteenth century provide graphic illustrations of this. For example, it
took less than a week in July 1549 for the rebels in East Anglia to establish
bases in the four corners of Norfolk and Suffolk: at Norwich, Downham
Market, Ipswich, and Bury St Edmunds. The rapidity of this communication and the organization behind it could scarcely be bettered today.[31]

Meanwhile across in the West Country a month before, the rumours
which kindled the rebellion against the changes in religion and the impos-
ition of an English Prayer Book flew with equal speed. John Hooker, later
long-serving chamberlain of the city of Exeter, was an eye-witness to
these events and provided a detailed account of them. The spark which
ignited the wildfire was the news that the parishioners of Sampford
Courtenay in Devon had rejected the new forms of worship on 11 June.

This newes as a clowde caried with a violente wynde and as a thunder clappe
soundinge thorowe the whole countrie is caried and noyse even in a momente
throughe oute the whole countrie: and the common people so well allowed and
lyked thereof that they clapped their hands for ioye: and agreed in one mynde to
have the same in everie of their seu[er]all p[ar]ishes.

---

[30] For analysis of the forms and functions of rumour, see in particular, Gordon W. Allport
and Leo J. Postman, *The Psychology of Rumour* (New York, 1947); Tamotsu Shibutani, *Improvised
News: A Sociological Study of Rumour* (New York, 1966); James C. Scott, *Domination and the Arts of
Resistance: Hidden Transcripts* (New Haven, 1990), esp. 144–5. A classic case study is Georges
Lefebvre, *The Great Fear of 1789: Rural Panic in Revolutionary France*, trans. Joan White (London,
1973); see also Hans-Joachim Neubauer, *The Rumour: A Cultural History*, trans. Christian Braun
(London, 1999).

[31] Diarmaid MacCulloch, 'Kett's Rebellion in Context', *Past and Present*, 84 (1979), 39–40.

When, ten days later, one of Sir Peter Carew's men torched the barns and farms which provided part of the rebel's defences,

The noyse of this fire and burnynge was in poste haste and as it were in a momente caried and blasted throughe oute the whole countrie and the common people vppon false reportes and of a gnott [gnat] making an elyphante noyse and spredd it abroad that the gentlemen were alltogether bente to overrunne, spoyle and destroye theyme.[32]

Hooker's image of news spreading 'as a cloud carried with a violent wind' strikingly conveys the sense of its almost instant and invisible blanketing of large areas. And the notion that the common people are as quiet as a gnat when acting as individuals, but capable of making the noise of an elephant when speaking as one, vividly illustrates the power and threat of the common voice.

In such an environment the scope for wild and unfounded stories was immense. The slightest of causes could throw whole regions into panic as some rumour passed along the grapevine, typically growing larger and more exaggerated as it travelled from mouth to mouth. 'Newes, like a snow-ball, is more by telling', went the popular saying. 'Wee see the common people for the most part when they give themselves to talking proceed from badd to worse and incounter every tyme more foolishly then other,' was how one Jacobean pamphleteer expressed it. A spark of falsehood, once kindled was quickly fanned by the breath of thousands. Thus the nonconformist meeting houses in Yarmouth were described by Richard Bower at the end of 1667 as 'no other but tinder boxes to strike fier upon all occassions to sett the nation on flame, blowne up by the tounges of the vulgar people which runnes every way amoungst the multitude like fier in a shed'. For, he lamented, 'one truth with the common people will gaine credditt for a hundred lyes'. The further a story travelled the more susceptible it may have been to hyperbole and distortion. By the time the rumour of a Jesuit plot in 1659 reached the ears of John Winthrop Jnr. out in Massachusetts, for example, it was telling of their successful deposing of Richard Cromwell and their attempt, while masquerading as Quakers, to establish a Jesuit college in Whitehall.[33]

The multitude of false rumours which seized people during these two centuries are too many and varied to consider in full. Some seem perfectly rational, given the context in which they arose and the limited sources of

---

[32] John Hooker, *The Description of the Citie of Excester*, ed. W. J. Harte, J. W. Schopp, and H. Tapley-Soper (Devon and Cornwall Record Society, Exeter, 1919), 57, 61.

[33] John Clarke, *Paroemiologia Anglo-Latina* (London, 1639), 228; PRO, SP14/126/1; PRO, SP29/224/77; Clifton, 'The Popular Fear of Catholics', 34.

information generally available to people. The frenzied stories flying around the country in 1538, for example, that the introduction of parochial registration of births, deaths, and marriages was a part of a scheme by Henry VIII to levy new taxes, seems reasonable enough given that such census-taking had always been associated with fiscal exaction.[34] On the other hand, the stories buzzing through Kent and Surrey at the same time that the king was going to levy 'horn money' on all horned beasts, or the bruits said to be universal in East Anglia and Lincolnshire at the same time that any unmarked cattle would be confiscated by the crown, seem to be founded more on irrational panic than any precedent or hard evidence.[35] Nor does the propensity of people to be caught up in such fevered scares seem to have diminished in any way over the course of this period. Whatever improvements in communications there may have been during the seventeenth century, people at the end of it were no less susceptible to wild rumour than their forebears early in the sixteenth century had been. Thus, an almost identical cattle-scare sprang up in October 1683 when it was reported that throughout Oxfordshire, Gloucestershire, and as far west as Wales, 'a panick fear has seized the whole country that the king's takers were coming to drive away their cattel, except that they were markt; whereupon they have bin up whole nights in driving their horses and kin[e]s and pigs together, and marking them: and there is scarce a village which has not taken this alarm'. In due course the panic subsided but only after the mutilation of many cattle which 'for hast were generally markt by cutting off pieces of their ears'.[36]

Another source of wild rumour which does not appear to have diminished in any way over the course of these two centuries was the perceived threat posed to the realm by scheming Catholics. This fear had been a constant feature of Elizabeth's reign and it endured thereafter. Speculation was rife in the late 1630s and early 1640s that Archbishop Laud had converted to popery, for example.[37] Many rumoured that the king had followed the same course.[38] And in the next generation gossip

---

[34] *L&P Hen. VIII*, xii, pt. I (1537), 30; *L&P Hen. VIII*, xiii, pt. II (1538), 158–9, 486; *L&P Hen. VIII*, xiv, pt. I (1539), 197, 214.

[35] *L&P Hen. VIII*, xiii, pt. I (1538), 148; *L&P Hen. VIII*, xiii, pt. II (1538), 18, 20, 215–6, 486. For other fears of new taxes see *L&P Hen. VIII*, xii, pt. II (1537), 142; *L&P Hen. VIII*, xiii, pt. I (1538), 37, 162, 173–4; *L&P Hen. VIII*, xv (1540), 265.

[36] PRO, SP29/434/18, 434/40.

[37] PRO, SP16/247/59; SP16/248/93; SP16/250/58–9; SP16/254/50; SP16/254/52; SP16/260/48; SP16/260/79; SP16/267/89i; SP16/327/140; SP16/361/117; SP16/417/97i–iii; SP16/421/21; SP16/422/113; SP16/423/83; SP16/429/30; SP16/453/96–7; SP16/456/36; SP16/458/110; SP16/461/46; SP16/469/95; SP16/487/48; SP16/506/34–5.

[38] PRO, SP16/171/37i; SP16/197/35; SP16/198/37; SP16/211/65; SP16/220/30;

continued to circulate that Charles II was a papist.[39] More dramatic still was the belief that hordes of Catholics were at large in the land, just waiting for the opportunity to rise up and murder Protestants in their beds. Again, such fears are partly understandable given their deliberate propagation by recusants, while the apparent inability of the Stuarts to appreciate the depth of popular anxiety over this issue did little to assuage it. Nevertheless, the resulting panics were totally disproportionate in their frenzied paranoia.

There were rumours of a Catholic uprising in Sussex in 1596, in Hampshire and Monmouthshire in 1605, throughout various Midland towns in 1613, and in the north-east two years later. 1625 saw another such rumour spread rapidly from the south-east coast up to the Midlands from where it span both west and northwards. Northamptonshire was similarly convulsed in 1630 as was Bristol in 1636. In the highly charged period between the calling of the Short Parliament early in 1640 and the outbreak of the Civil War late in 1642 there were panics of this sort recorded in all but three of the English counties. Soon after the Irish rebellion in the summer of 1641, for example, fear of a Catholic insurrection spread through eight towns and villages of the West Midlands causing the inhabitants to set up nightly vigils. The Great Fire of London in 1666 brought a fresh wave of rumours that papists had started the blaze and intended to torch other cities before overrunning the country. In this climate it is hardly surprising that the political turmoil caused by the Popish Plot of 1678 and the Exclusion Crisis of 1679–81 brought another wave of scares. Less predictable, perhaps, was the successfully orchestrated campaign of terror which swept the country surrounding the arrival of William of Orange in 1688, which induced the whole nation to believe that it was about to be massacred by marauding bands of Irish soldiers disbanded from the army of James II.[40]

An equally constant product of the ignorance, insecurity, and instability

---

SP16/222/48; SP16/231/56i; SP16/248/60; SP16/251/31; SP16/258/50i; SP16/262/16; SP16/272/18–19; SP16/290/18i; SP16/367/73; SP16/387/59; SP16/391/85; SP16/426/41; SP16/454/42; SP16/458/110; PRO, ASSI45/1/3/47; *Middlesex County Records*, ed. J. C. Jeaffreson (4 vols., Middlesex County Record Society, London, 1886–92), iii. 74, 81.

[39] PRO, ASSI45/5/7/81; ASSI45/6/3/138; ASSI45/7/2/40; ASSI45/14/1/6; PRO, SP29/64/18–19; SP29/214/80.

[40] Carol Z. Wiener, 'The Beleaguered Isle: A Study of Elizabethan and Early Jacobean Anti-Catholicism', *Past and Present*, 51 (1971), 27–62; Clifton, 'The Popular Fear of Catholics', 24–6, 30–1; W. G. Bell, *The Great Fire of London in 1666* (London, 1920), 196–209; J. P. Kenyon, *The Popish Plot* (London, 1972); Brian Magee, 'The Protestant Wind: Some Aspects of the Revolution of 1688', *Month*, 177/922 (1941), 334–43; William L. Sachse, 'The Mob and the Revolution of 1688', *Journal of British Studies*, 4 (1964), 23–40.

of these two centuries was fears about the health of the sovereign. At a time when plots against the monarchy, real or imagined, were a regular feature of political life and the means of verifying stories about the health of a king or queen were few, speculation and rumour thrived. Sometimes false reports about a royal death were deliberately planted by opponents of the regime to sow disquiet and panic among the people, and as long-lived rulers such as Henry VIII or Elizabeth I grew into old age the ground for such seeds must have been ever more fertile. Not surprisingly, when a monarch really did pass away it could take some time for people to credit the news. Two and a half weeks after the death of Edward VI on 6 July 1553, for example, the corporation of Shrewsbury was still dating orders in his name. The most spectacular example of such natural scepticism is provided by the Shetland islanders following the Glorious Revolution of November 1688. 'They had no account of the Prince of Orange's late landing in England, coronation, &c., until a fisherman happened to land in these isles in May following, and he was not believed, but indicted for high treason for spreading such news.'[41]

Prophecies of the death of Henry VIII were circulating at least as early as 1536, and rumours of his actual demise appeared at the same time, well over a decade before the event was to take place.[42] One wave of such rumours seems to have been triggered in October 1537 by the mere fact of 'the hasty riding of the duke of Norfolk in post through Newark', such was the sensitivity of popular alarm. By December and January the following year they were reported to be circulating down in the south-east around Kent and Sussex, up in Berkshire and Oxfordshire and the Midland counties of Leicestershire, Huntingdonshire and Northamptonshire, as well as over in Dorset and Gloucestershire in the south-west.[43] They were carried abroad, no doubt, by people like John Petyfer, a husbandman from Kingsthorpe, Northamptonshire. He had ridden into Leicestershire with a companion at the end of November to consult a 'wise man' about some stolen goods and on his return had paused at a wheelwright's in Lutterworth. There a local harper had enquired, '"What news hear you?"' before proceeding to tell him about the king. He heard the same news when he reached Theddingworth from a chaplain who said that 'his master had a letter from London to that

---

[41] HMC, *15th Report, Appendix, Part X* (London, 1899), 13; Martin Martin, *A Description of the Western Islands of Scotland circa 1695* (Glasgow, 1884), 372.

[42] For the prophecies, see *L&P Hen. VIII*, vi (1533), 685 (misdated); *L&P Hen. VIII*, xii, pt. I (1537), 133, 300; *L&P Hen. VIII*, xii, pt. II (1537), 283.

[43] *L&P Hen. VIII*, xii, pt. II (1537), 328, 418, 423, 423–4, 430, 439, 441, 448, 454; *L&P Hen. VIII*, xiii, pt. I (1538), 3, 19, 24–5.

effect', all of which encouraged Petyfer to spread the story around the neighbours when he returned home.[44] Three weeks later John Blake overtook Walter Byrdley on his way back from London into Gloucestershire and was told the news as it had been reported to him back in Dorchester. All those who were drinking at the Cheker in Canterbury on New Year's eve would have heard the same story and been able to disperse it around Kent. Perhaps one of them was the merchant whom fisherman Thomas Graunte met on Barham Downs on his way back from Dover three days later. Certainly he told him the sensational news which he, in turn, was able to relay to his customers on returning to Wingham with his catch.[45]

It is hardly surprising that both similar prophecies and rumours should loom up again in the 1590s when an ageing Elizabeth had been on the throne for forty years and economic crisis, coupled with the perceived threat of plotters from within the realm and invasion from without, created a climate ripe for such scaremongering.[46] In due course, tales were to circulate about the health of James I, stories would be spread that Charles I had murdered his father, and then that he himself had been done away with by the duke of Buckingham, or had otherwise disappeared.[47] The Commonwealth did not dampen the appetite for such speculation. In March 1651 the well-informed Essex clergyman Ralph Josselin heard a report of Cromwell's death which was not confirmed as being false until June. In 1655 there was a rash of such bruits.[48] With predictable regularity there followed rumours that Charles II had been done away with by his brother, and there was always talk in the air about the premature demise of one or both of the last two Stuart kings.[49]

An example of the slightest grounds upon which such rumours could be founded and, at the same time, the significant impact which they could

---

[44] *L&P Hen. VIII*, xii, pt. II (1537), 423–4.

[45] *L&P Hen. VIII*, xiii, pt. I (1538), 19, 24–5. For other rumours of the king's death, see *L&P Hen. VIII*, xi. (1536), 169; *L&P Hen. VIII*, xiii, pt. I (1538), 201, 470, 502–3; *L&P Hen. VIII*, xv (1540), 374. For discussion of such reports, see Elton, *Policy and Police*, 73–8.

[46] For the prophecies, see PRO, SP12/172/7; SP12/192/50; SP12/194/57i; SP12/200/28; SP12/251/69; SP12/252/94i; SP12/276/111; PRO, ASSI35/14/6/22; ASSI35/25/1/37; ASSI35/26/7/25; ASSI35/37/9/41; ASSI35/42/7/27; and for rumours of the queen's death, see PRO, SP12/272/49i; PRO, ASSI35/22/1/9; ASSI35/38/7/3; ASSI35/38/7/5.

[47] HMC, *13th Report, Appendix, Part IV* (London, 1892), 134; PRO, SP16/3/53; SP16/10/33, 16/10/55, 16/12/54, 16/21/61; SP16/491/78i; PRO, SP29/86/22i–ii; PRO, ASSI45/5/7/17.

[48] *The Diary of Ralph Josselin, 1616–1683*, ed. Alan Macfarlane (British Academy, Records of Social and Economic History, new ser., 3, London, 1976), 239, 247; PRO, SP18/100/125; SP18/100/129; SP18/100/155.

[49] PRO SP29/86/22i–iii; SP29/100/83; SP29/159/9–10; SP29/376/76, 376/81; SP29/406/247; SP29/434/18i; PRO, ASSI45/14/2/10–13; ASSI45/14/2/102.

have, is illustrated by one story of the death of Charles I which sprang up, apparently without written provenance, and seized hold of people in south Wales and the West Country during the summer of 1628.[50] The report seems to have arisen early in July from the Carmarthenshire countryside when an escaping robber succeeded in shaking off those in 'hott pursuite cominge after him' by crying that the king had met his end. Given perennial insecurities over such things, this tale was clearly believed and threw the authorities into panic. The news quickly spread to Llanelli and from there a remarkable chain of transmission was set in motion. About noon on Tuesday 8th, William ap Evan, keeper of the ferry over the river Loughor, was suddenly disturbed in his fishing by a great noise coming from the direction of Llanelli. He looked up to see 'a great number of people cominge towards him to the number . . . of one hundred persones at the least, crying most fearefully'. They poured into the town of Loughor protesting news of the king's death. Panic was now such that many had convinced themselves that the Spaniards had also landed on the coast. Gathering more raisers of the alarm they set off towards Swansea.

Before long they had reached the town, by which time a further embellishment to the story had developed to the effect that the king had been poisoned by the duke of Buckingham. Rumours that Buckingham was a poisoner had been in circulation since at least 1625 when speculation that he had disposed of James I in this way was the subject of common gossip.[51] In a panic situation, then, this well-established suspicion appears to have been given a fresh impetus. At Swansea, the portreeve Patrick Jones acted promptly upon the news, mustering the trained bands and sending word on to Neath where, by about three o'clock, it had been received by many of the county's chief inhabitants who were there gathered for the quarter sessions. Meanwhile, Jones and one of the aldermen, Henry Vaughan, publicly announced the report in the market square at Swansea which was met 'with a generall lamentacion of the whole people, who gave out that they feared that the papists would rise up in armes and kill them in theire sleep'. Among the crowd were two Cornish sailors, Nicholas Browne and Thomas Ematt, who also heard the subsequent gossip of the local tradeswomen which added authority to the news by saying that it had come by post from the Council of Wales. Browne and

---

[50] The events described in this and the following paragraph are based upon PRO, SP16/110/6i, 16/110/13, 16/110/41, 16/111/21i–ii, 16/114/23i.

[51] This speculation occasioned discussion both in Parliament and in print the following year: see George Eglisham, *The Forerunner of Revenge* (Franckfort, 1626). (I am grateful to Alastair Bellany for this reference.)

Ematt then put to sea, landing at Crantock in Cornwall on Thursday. The following day they had reached St Columb, where they were telling of the king's death at the hands of Buckingham who, they now claimed, had been imprisoned for the crime. By the time the two sailors were arrested, much of the south-west coast seems to have been on standby in readiness for a foreign invasion.

Perversely enough, in addition to all the rumours of the premature deaths of monarchs, were those which told that the genuinely dead were actually still alive. Throughout the first half of Elizabeth's reign such stories circulated about Edward VI, telling that he remained living and was imprisoned in the Tower of London. It was a false hope fuelled by the impostors who continued to turn up claiming to be the lost king. 'Amongst the vulgar sort . . . what histories, chronicles, or politique discourses are not copious, and plentifull in this kind?' asked John Harvey in 1588 with reference to these rumours.[52] Little had apparently changed well over a century later, following the death of the duke of Monmouth in 1685 Many people refused at the time to accept that he had been killed and continued for years, even generations, afterwards to speak of his return.[53]

In general, the fortunes and the conduct of royal persons and their ministers were fair game for gossip. Then, as now, there was endless verbal mileage in the half-truths which circulated about the apparent behaviour of the great and the good: 'as, you know, what great ones do the less will prattle of'.[54] Perhaps the best example of this is provided by the stories told and retold throughout Elizabethan England, which appear to have little or no written origin, claiming that the queen had borne various children by Robert Dudley, the earl of Leicester. Such speculation may

[52] John Harvey, *A Discoursive Probleme Concerning Prophesies* (London, 1588), 61–2; and for examples, see PRO, SP12/184/50, 12/184/70; PRO, ASSI35/20/5/36; ASSI35/21/7/19; ASSI35/28/2/37; ASSI35/29/1/33; ASSI35/36/2/39; *APC, 1552–54*, 363; *APC, 1554–56*, 122, 221; *APC, 1579–80*, 194, 214, 371; *APC, 1580–81*, 23–4, 29, 353–4; Keith Thomas, *Religion and the Decline of Magic: Studies in Popular Beliefs in Sixteenth- and Seventeenth-Century England* (London, 1971), 419–22.

[53] PRO, ASSI45/14/2/31; ASSI45/14/2/84; ASSI45/14/3/34; PRO, PL27/1 (*Wilkinson* v. *France*, 1685); PL27/1 (*Roader* v. *Cottam*, 1685); PL27/1 (*Cheernes* v. *Smith*, 1685); PL27/1 (*Harrison* v. *Carrison*, 1686); PL27/1 (*Tirkle* v. *Prescott*, 1686); PL27/1 (*Harrison* v. *Ashburnor*, 1686); PL27/1 (*Shuttleworth* v. *Denby*, 1686); PL27/1 (*Frith* v. *Sparm*, 1688); *CSPD, 1687–89*, 191; *Middlesex County Records*, ed. Jeaffreson, iv. 311, 312; *Depositions from the Castle of York*, ed. James Raine (Surtees Society, 40, Durham, 1861), 283–4; HMC, *13th Report, Appendix, Part IV*, 350; Thomas, *Religion and the Decline of Magic*, 419; Robin Clifton, *The Last Popular Rebellion: The Western Rising of 1685* (London, 1984), 228–9; Sharp, 'Popular Political Opinion in England, 1660–1685', 25–6; T. B. Macaulay, *The History of England*, ed. Hugh Trevor-Roper (Harmondsworth, 1979), 112–13.

[54] Shakespeare, *Twelfth-Night*, I. ii. 30–1.

have appealed both to opponents of the crown and its religion and to those supporters who hoped vainly for an heir to the throne. It was clearly widespread from the earliest years of the reign and, like so much rumour and news, it probably emanated from the capital originally. In December 1559, Thomas Holland, vicar of Little Burstead, took the story back into south Essex after 'beinge at London' where he had 'met with one in Chepeside that was sometyme vicar of Stortford in Hertfordshire ... who told hym that the quene's majestie was with childe'. Not far away, the following June, a group of women were gossiping about the queen and Dudley, much as people speculate today about royal romances. Soon afterwards, one of their number, Anne Dowe of Brentwood, met Mr Cooke on his horse. '"What newes mother Dowe?"' he asked, 'and she sayd that she knew no other newes but that she sayd a woman told her that Dudley had given the quene a new petycote that cost twentie nobles, and the sayd Cooke sayd to [her], "Thynks thou that it was a petiecote? No, no, he gave her a chyld, I warrant thee".'[55]

Over the succeeding years these rumours continued to spread, growing larger and more elaborate. By January 1580, for example, Thomas Playfere, a labourer from Maldon in Essex, could be heard saying among his neighbours that Elizabeth did have lawful successors since she 'had two children by my Lord Robert (meaning the earl of Leicester) and that he did see them whene they were shipped at Rye in two of the best shippes the quene hathe'. The tale had grown even taller by the time it was told in May 1585 by a Surrey woman, Alice Austen, who claimed that 'the queene is no mayd and she hath had thre sunnes by the earle of Leicester, and that they shold have bene made earles'. By 1590 there was still more to tell: the queen '"hath had alredye as manye childerne as I"', proclaimed Denise Deryck of Witham, Essex, in April. She was sure that 'too of them were yet alyve, the one beinge a man childe and the other a mayden childe and furder that the other[s] were burned. And beinge demanded by whome she had them, she said, "By my lord of Leycester who was father to them and wrapped them upp in the embers in the chymney which was in the chamber wher they were borne".' Two months later the yarn had moved on to Coopersale in Epping, 25 miles away, where Robert Gardner, a husbandman, had picked it up in a form yet further embellished: there had been four offspring 'wherof thre of them were dawghters and alyve and the fourthe a sonne that was burnte'. Robert Fowler, a blacksmith from Wisborough Green in Sussex, had got it into his head, and was heard to proclaim, early in 1600 'that the earle of Essex

---

[55] PRO, SP12/12/51; SP12/13/21i.

was the sonne of the queene of England and that the queenes majestie
... had an other sonne whom menn did suppose to be the brother of
Mr [John] Walwyn, late vicar of Wisborough Greene'.[56]


## WRITTEN ORIGINS

Clearly it did not take much to start a rumour in this period. An unusual
or suspicious action, a quiet word in the right ear, a deliberately mischiev-
ous public pronouncement, could each be enough to instigate a panic
and activate the grapevine. As such, the origins of many rumours owed
nothing to the written word, nor did they rely on it for their transmission.
The very essence of a rumour, what infuses it with life, is the breath of
people talking. And yet, although thoroughly dependent upon oral communication, rumours can be initiated and their circulation augmented by
other media. This was so even in the first half of the sixteenth century in
England, a society already long used to relaying information and news
among its people in written form. Indeed it is surprising just how often a
bruit or news story, however much it may have relied on dissemination by
word of mouth, can be traced back to some written provenance.

Thus the communication of news in early modern England was little
different from the other modes of transmission and expression studied in
this book. Its primary delivery from person to person may have been
based for the most part on the spoken word, but it was a spoken word
often influenced, shaped, and structured by written forms. Here, as in
other contexts, the oral and the textual fed in and out of one another in
reciprocal and mutually enriching ways. Some news stories began life on
paper and passed into common gossip; others began as mere talk and
found their way into script or print, before passing back into the national
conversation. In this respect, as in others, oral and literate cannot be
delineated with much ease or any profit because they were so often inter-
twined, so often indistinguishable voices in the same dialogue.

The sixteenth and seventeenth centuries witnessed a huge growth in
the production and accessibility of written news. The progressive
increase in literacy levels, the continued expansion of a thriving scribal
culture, and the steady growth of printed news in various forms all contributed to this process. The proliferation of private letters, manuscript
'separates' and uncensored libels, of propaganda pamphlets, broadside

---

[56] PRO, ASSI35/22/10/14; ASSI35/27/8/31; ASSI35/32/2/48; ASSI35/32/2/49;
ASSI35/42/9/15; and for other examples, see PRO, SP12/148/34; SP12/269/22; PRO,
SP14/4/2; PRO, SP16/118/35i; PRO, ASSI35/28/6/45.

ballads, and newsbooks could not fail to influence people's awareness of and opinions about current affairs. But it did so in a way which was complementary to, rather than undermining of, oral exchange. The laws of censorship and sedition always limited the scope of what might be put on paper and there was often little qualitative difference between the written and spoken news, mutually derivative as they were. Newsletters and printed works travelled the highways in the packs of traders and travellers alongside the tales which were carried in their heads; they were deposited for collection at inns and alehouses no less than were their whispered counterparts; they were pasted up on walls and market crosses just as they were read aloud in these public places.

A good example of the way in which rumour and speculation was being initiated by written sources even in the 1530s is provided by the political prophecies which circulated in such abundance at this time. In many ways the prophecy was a supremely oral vehicle for political comment and what passed for news, something told and retold in alehouses and around firesides, easily retained and accessible to all.[57] And yet it is clear that almost all of those which we hear of from the reign of Henry VIII and beyond were set on foot by learned authors who committed their inventions first to paper. It is not surprising that clerics, courtiers, or gentlemen wishing to ferment opposition to royal policies among the people should choose to invent or recycle semi-magical predictions about the downfall of the monarch, but it is noteworthy that they always saw the use of writing as crucial to the first phase of their purpose.

Consider the variety of seditious prophecies, quite typical of the period, which were circulating throughout Yorkshire in the later 1530s.[58] At the beginning of December 1537 a group of parishioners from Muston in the parish of Hunmanby, East Riding, went down to York to accuse their vicar, John Dobson, of spreading such prophecies around the village, repeating them 'both in the church porch and the alehouse'. But if these scandalous forebodings had become the stuff of common talk they had done so at the end of a long chain of scribal copying which clearly went hand-in-hand with their oral circulation. Over a year before

---

[57] For examples of prophecies heard and spoken, see L&P Hen. VIII, xii, pt. I (1537), 300; L&P Hen. VIII, xii, pt. II (1537), 283; L&P Hen. VIII, xiii, pt. I (1538), 171, 267–8; L&P Hen. VIII, xiii, pt. II (1538), 427–8; L&P Hen. VIII, xiv, pt. I (1539), 379; L&P Hen. VIII, xiv, pt. II (1539), 2–3, 21, 27. On the prophetic tradition, see Rupert Taylor, The Political Prophecy in England (New York, 1911); for prophecies in this period, see Thomas, Religion and the Decline of Magic, ch. 13; Elton, Policy and Police, ch. 2.

[58] The details in this and the next paragraph are based on L&P Hen. VIII, xii, pt. II (1537), 427–8, 432–3.

this accusation at York, Richard Stapleton, a priest of Sockburn, had met William Langley, the parish clerk of Croft, on the Hunmanby road where he was asked if he would like to see a prophecy, 'not past 12 lines, and went in metre' which Langley called 'crummers' and promised to send him. This verse was the reworking of a ballad framed in the reign of Henry VI and now adapted to predict the downfall of Cromwell. The first part apparently invoked the authorship of Merlin and Bede and 'A.B.C.', while the second part ran:

> When ill cometh of a small note,
> As Crumwell set in a man's throat,
> That shall put many other to pain, God note;
> But when Crumwell is brought a-low,
> And we rede out the Christ Cross rowe,
> To R. L. and M. then shall we know news.[59]

Such a short rhyme or song was clearly intended to be remembered easily and chanted or sung among the mass of the non-reading population. But if it was devised principally for ease of oral dissemination, it was clearly supplemented in certain circles by a vigorous scribal circulation. Thus Richard Stapleton carried his copy of the verse around with him and when he was later travelling on his master's business, he showed it to a kitchener in Gisburn, West Riding. When next visiting Thomas Bradley, a priest of Ayton, he read it out to him; Bradley took a copy for himself and in due course gave one to William Langdale, a gentleman over at Scarborough. So it was that when John Borobie, prior of the White Friars in Scarborough, was in Langdale's house sometime later he noticed the 'little roll of paper containing a prophecy in rhyme, otherwise called a "gargonne", which spoke of the learning of A, B, C, and K, L, M,' and asked if he could borrow it for a few days in order to make a transcript of his own. Borobie was obviously an active conduit for such material since a couple of years before one of his brothers had brought him a 'scroll of paper which spoke of the black fleet of Norway and a child with a chaplet', said to have come from a priest of Rudston in the East Riding, John Paikok. This was probably the 'long roll of prophecies' which he lent to Langdale on returning the 'crummers', perhaps as a sort of quid pro quo. And in the spring of 1537 Borobie was copying again. This time his source was a priest of Beverley whom he met at the Rogation celebrations and who showed him another set of prophecies, in two sheets of paper

---

[59] *L&P Hen. VIII*, xii, pt. I (1537), 146; and see *Political Poems and Songs Relating to English History, Composed during the Period from the Accession of Edward III to that of Richard III*, ed. Thomas Wright (2 vols., Rolls Series, 14, London, 1859–61), ii. 221.

and beginning 'Fra[nce] and Flanders, shall arise', which he wrote out and added to his collection.[60]

Enter now the vicar of Muston, John Dobson. On 20 October 1537 he was up at Scarborough when he met John Borobie and was invited by him back to his chambers in the White Friars. There Borobie produced the prophecies of his Beverley priest which he read aloud and said '"Vicar, ye shall have it home with you, and look upon it, and send it me again within fourteen days".' Dobson was later able to reciprocate, in what seems to have been a culture of 'swaps', by offering the prior another set of prophecies in return. But he obviously received the 'crummers', and the rest of the prior's collection, for it was the contents of all of these sources which he was to stand accused of feeding into the alehouse gossip of his parishioners. Clearly, then, such material travelled in both oral and written form with equal facility. The clergy and gentry who formed 'scribal communities' for the swapping and transcribing of texts passed this seditious material amongst themselves on paper.[61] They did so to augment and reinforce songs and sayings which would have passed even more quickly from mouth to mouth among the mass of the people.

The modes of circulation in this part of the East Riding and beyond were hardly unique, for the 'crummers' and other prophecies ran up and down the country in both written and spoken form. If the rest of the evidence from the single year of 1537 is considered, then the importance of copying and recopying texts of what were essentially sayings or songs is clear. In February, for example, the 'crummers' were said to be 'framed of late' in East Anglia where the duke of Norfolk hoped to identify the spreader from his handwriting. At the same time, some monks of Furness Abbey were disseminating a prophecy which foretold 'that a.b.c. and iij. ttt should set all in one seat and should work great marvels' and that 'the red rose should die in his mother's womb'. In May, Richard Bushop of Bungay, Suffolk, met Robert Seyman in Tyndale Wood, and after asking him '"What tidings hear you?"', proceeded to say in conversation that if he 'would come to Bungay he would show him a prophecy, which one man had watched in the night to copy'. The following month similar materials were being circulated by William Todd, the prior of Malton in Rydal, Westmorland; and in June a Hertfordshire saddler, Robert Dalyvell, was in Edinburgh when various locals 'read the prophecies of Marlyn in his hearing' to the prejudice of the English king. In August, Richard

---

[60] For the texts of this, or similar rhymed prophecies, see *Ballads from Manuscripts*, ed. F. J. Furnivall (2 vols., London, 1868–73), i. 316–17.

[61] For the notion of a 'scribal community', see Love, *Scribal Publication in Seventeenth-Century England*, 179–82.

coming, rather ominously, to assess the valuables in local churches. When asked later as to the source of his story he replied that 'one Thomas Lloid of Shrewsbury, then at London, sent a letter to the town reciting the said matters, but named not to whom the letter was sent'. The following December, a Horsham man was employed to deliver a letter from Lord Stafford in London to his wife in Sussex from which he was accused of learning a rumour that the king was dead. A year later, Thomas Lamkyn, a husbandman from Werrington in Northamptonshire, claimed to have found a letter in a purse in Peterborough market which he enjoined a clergyman, Giles Taylor, to read out in this public place. The letter spoke of 'the coming of the king of Scots' and was written by those who intended to take his part.[66]

It was about this time that the crown first began to try to regulate the postal service. Sir Brian Tuke was appointed as the first Master of the Post by Henry VIII in order to oversee the safe carrying of the king's dispatches. During Elizabeth's reign the Controller of the Queen's Posts would issue the earliest known instructions to postmasters at home and a royal monopoly controlling the flow of mail to and from foreign countries was proclaimed in 1591. By this time many of the larger urban centres had appointed postmasters whose responsibility it was to handle the royal correspondence to the provinces.[67] Exeter certainly had such an appointee by 1600; we first hear of Thomas Stapleford of Leicester in 1605. Places on the north road up to Berwick became important as post towns and needed the services of a master. Thus, the job of postmaster at little Scrooby in Nottinghamshire was filled in 1588 and again in 1590; Lincoln became a post town in the early seventeenth century and Newark followed in 1626.[68]

Since this service catered almost exclusively for official mail, however, private individuals still had to employ their own foot-posts or carriers. By the end of the sixteenth century the desire for news on the part of the provincial elite when they were away from London was growing ever

---

[66] *L&P Hen. VIII*, xii, pt. I (1537), 358; *L&P Hen. VIII*, xii, pt. II (1537), 448; *L&P Hen. VIII*, xiii, pt. II (1538), 138, 141.

[67] Howard Robinson, *The British Post Office: A History* (Princeton, 1948), 7–22; A. R. B. Haldane, *Three Centuries of Scottish Posts: An Historical Survey to 1836* (Edinburgh, 1971), 3–4; Brian Austen, *English Provincial Posts, 1633–1840: A Study Based on Kent Examples* (London, 1978), 1–2.

[68] Wallace T. MacCaffrey, *Exeter, 1540–1640: The Growth of an English County Town* (2nd edn., Cambridge, Mass., 1975), 241; Jack Simmons, *Leicester Past and Present*, i: *Ancient Borough to 1860* (London, 1974), 115; PRO, SP15/31/40; PRO, SP12/233/48; J. W. F. Hill, *Tudor and Stuart Lincoln* (Cambridge, 1956), 14–15. A proclamation of 1607 forbade any unauthorized person from carrying packets or letters: PRO, SP14/45/50. The postmaster of Ware, Hertfordshire, was reproved for failure to observe this in July 1617: PRO, SP14/92/100.

more avid and their demand for such services increased accordingly. The 1590s witnessed the emergence of 'intelligencers' in the capital, men such as Peter Proby, John Chamberlain, and Rowland Whyte who made it their business to provide intimates and employers in the country with the latest news stories from court or to keep them abreast of the rumours circulating at the Exchange or St Pauls. 'Powles newes', William Sterrell wrote to Thomas Phelippes in April 1593, was 'sufficient allwayes to furnishe a letter with.'[69]

By the 1620s, a new breed of professional newsletter writer was charging substantial fees to service clients with regular bulletins of events at court, copies of parliamentary speeches and news from abroad. This period saw the development of the 'separate', usually three manuscript pages containing a single text such as a speech or short topical discourse. These were copied in their hundreds and the large survival rate of such fragile objects testifies to the huge extent of their circulation.[70] After the Restoration, Under-Secretary of State, Joseph Williamson, following a pattern established by Cromwell's Secretary Thurloe, instituted a system of official newletters. These were informed by the regular reports which he received from provincial correspondents and envoys abroad together with his own knowledge of government business and parliamentary proceedings. Every week they were dispatched to select 'country friends' who received, for their annual subscription of £5, the best intelligence that money could buy. In the 1670s the Whigs began to circulate their own newsletters among the wealthy elite in the provinces and the professional classes in London. Meanwhile a growing army of full-time journalists continued to service the ever expanding appetite for news among the rest of the population, despite every effort on the part of the government to suppress them.[71]

The dissemination of official and other professionally written newsletters, as well as of other private correspondence, was facilitated by parallel developments in the postal system. The beginnings of a public postal service were signalled by the appointment of Thomas Witherings as first Postmaster-General in July 1635. Witherings's plan to create a

---

[69] Lawrence Stone, *The Crisis of the Aristocracy 1558–1641* (Oxford, 1965), 388; F. J. Levy, 'How Information Spread among the Gentry, 1550–1640', *Journal of British Studies*, 21/2 (1982), 20; PRO, SP12/244/123.

[70] Levy, 'How Information Spread among the Gentry', 21/2; Richard Cust, 'News and Politics in Early Seventeenth-Century England', *Past and Present*, 112 (1986), 62–4. For a good description of the 'separate', see Love, *Scribal Publication in Seventeenth-Century England*, 13.

[71] Peter Fraser, *The Intelligence of the Secretaries of State and their Monopoly of Licensed News 1660–1688* (Cambridge, 1956), 28–34, 114–15, 127–8, 130–1, 140–4; Love, *Scribal Publication in Seventeenth-Century England*, 9–22.

comprehensive network covering the whole country was frustrated by the outbreak of the Civil War, but about this time a system developed of 'farming out' the control of postal routes to tenants who paid fixed rents, something which the Cromwellian regime sought to regulate in 1657. The post was leaving London once a week in the late 1630s; by 1649 the service had increased to twice a week and in 1655 letters could be posted on Tuesday, Wednesday, and Saturday nights to all the important provincal centres. 1680 saw the introduction of a Penny Post, reflecting the huge increase in correspondence which had taken place since the Restoration, and three years later this was incorporated into the General Post Office (see Plate 15).[72]

In addition to this increasingly available and affordable system, the traditional means of conveyance long sufficed. Servants, professional carriers, or travelling traders who might be paid to take a letter in their packs, remained usual conduits for written messages no less than oral ones. And, as in the case of communication by word of mouth, such people provided a vehicle through which the contents of correspondence among the social and political elite might pass into more general circulation. The case of Francis Barrett may well have been typical. He was a sailor by trade, 'a poore stragling fellowe', who clearly supplemented his income as he moved around the country by carrying missives for people of substance. When arrested in Essex in December 1633 he was accused of having, over the previous sixteen years, 'carried divers letters for noblemen and gentlemen', although he claimed in his defence that only 'upon occasion, passeing from one place to another, he hath been intreated to convey sometimes a letter as a friend and not otherwise'. He also insisted that he never knew their contents, being unable to 'writte or reade anie other hande then printed hande'. His accusers, however, maintained that he had said that he 'never carried any letters but hee heard them read and knewe what they were before hee carried them'.[73]

Barrett had much in common with the 'footman in very poore clothes' who called in April 1671 at the mill of Thomas Ferris and his wife at Dean, Bedfordshire, to ask for lodging in their barn. He confessed that 'he had beene carrying letters about' on behalf of Catholics, 'till he [was] very weary and very drie'. Although the mysterious traveller would not reveal his name or place of origin, Ferris could tell that his 'speech differd from the speech of this country, and as neere as he could guesse by the manner of his language he was an Oxfordshire man or of some other Westerne

[72] Robinson, *The British Post Office*, 23–76; Haldane, *Three Centuries of Scottish Posts*, 4–5; Austen, *English Provincial Posts*, 2–13; Fraser, *The Intelligence of the Secretaries of State*, 20, 128–9.
[73] PRO, SP16/252/67i–ii.

county more remote than that'. Despite this, however, he had an excellent knowledge of all the towns in the area and their exact whereabouts, revealing 'that he had theyr names sett downe in writing in his note of directions for his iourny, and that he could read written hand, although he went so raggedly in his clothes'. He owned to having been as far east as Norfolk on this trip, 'to carry letters to a popish gentleman of 500l. a yeare who kept 30 houses furnished for warre in a vault underground', and 'also sayd that he was continually imployed in carrying about to papists all over England and very often to the citty of London'. Certainly the miller noticed what 'looked like a great bundle of letters' about his person.[74]

It seems likely that such privately hired itinerants often knew the contents of the letters which they transported, either by hearing or reading them, since they were probably employed for their sympathy with the cause of the correspondents. Evidently this was true of William Emerson, a shearman who also made his living by being 'sent from one nobleman to another about the papists buisenes to knowe their mynds'. He probably took messages by word of mouth but was also discovered in Buckinghamshire in September 1625 with letters about him. Quite without reservation, it seems, he was happy to divulge their contents to a local labourer whom he met on the Newport road, as perhaps to others whom he might have encountered on an itinerary which would have taken him as far west as Gloucestershire and as far east as Cambridgeshire and Suffolk. 'Before Christmas daye next', he confided, 'there would be old bustelinge and that a great nobleman of this kingdome . . . would ayed the Pope with 30,000 men.' Of such indiscretions were frenzied rumours made.[75]

In addition, there were various other means whereby the contents of both gentry correspondence and formal newletters could find their way into wider circulation. Sometimes such material might be actively disseminated by those with political motives: in 1634 it was said of the radical sectary, Thomas Cotton of West Bergholt in Essex, 'a greate depravour of government', that 'he maintaines some pevish intelligencer in London weekly to send him the newse of the time, which he usually reades in the streets every markett daye att Colchester, about whom the zealouts thronge as people use where balletts ar sunge'. Equally, letters could be dispersed openly, posted, and copied whenever large crowds were gathered. One example, written to a gentleman of Foulsham in Norfolk, was found in the streets of Norwich during the Lent assizes of 1627. It hinted that an army of papists was preparing to land at

74 PRO, SP29/289/22oii.        75 PRO, SP16/6/68i–ii.

Weybourne on the north Norfolk coast before May Day next. One copy
was picked up by the wife of Thomas Owldman of Cawston, tanner, and
she took it to 'ould Powell of Cawston to read for her' and, 'because hee
could not read it' either, she gave it to a schoolboy, Edward Lombe, who
passed it, in turn, to Henry Rychers, and he finally gave it to his father.
Meanwhile, another copy of the letter was found in a shop in the city by a
preacher of Wymondham who sent a transcript of it to a friend at
Westminster 'for great news'. It is tempting to wonder whether the
Suffolk clergyman John Rous came across it. Certainly Norwich was one
of the many market towns in the region which he visited at this time,
gathering as he went a regular flow of gossip, manuscript verses, newsletters, and printed pamphlets on current affairs, as well as reading the
government proclamations pinned on the corner post at the Bell inn in
Thetford or pasted up in the saddler's shop at Walton.[76]

By this time, the possibility of more humble people sending back
London news to friends and family in the provinces was an ever more
realistic prospect. Those who flocked to the capital in search of apprenticeship were especially likely to have the writing skills to keep in touch
with home in this way. One letter from a London apprentice back to his
parents in Wigan, Lancashire, worked in just this way. Mathew Mason was
bound to 'one that selleth bandes and cambricks' at the sign of the Falcon
in the Poultry, London, when he wrote home on 12 March 1619. Amid
personal wishes he decided to include details of one report circulating on
the streets of the capital.

This I thought it fitt to lett you here of our hearthes newes. I have but litle but that
there is like to be great changing in England. Many strange wonders about
London. There is a hand and a sword risen out of the ground at a towne called
Newmarkett, where the kinge is, and stands strikeinge at him. And the kinge went
to see it and ever since hee hath kepte his chamber and cannott tell what it
meanes; and other strange things which nowe I will not speake of.

Thus written, the young apprentice gave his letter to a porter for delivery
to William Hyton, 'a comon carryer betweene Lancashire and London'.
About twelve days later, Hyton handed it to Gilbert Mason of Wigan,
tanner, Mathew's father. He shewed it to the deputy mayor of the town, to
Mr Peter Marsh, and to others 'as a letter of newes'; his wife, Margaret,
'lent it out' among the neighbours and it quickly became public property.
Transcripts were soon made for distribution. Another of the Mason
children 'did take the said letter and plaistered it on a chiste' for all to see;

---

[76] PRO, SP16/276/42; SP16/60/25i–iii, 16/60/26; *Diary of John Rous*, ed. Everett Green.
Rous is discussed in Cust, 'News and Politics in Early Seventeenth-Century England', 65–6.

other copies were read aloud in the streets. Peter Green, yeoman, saw Roger Bulloughe, shoemaker, poring over a version and, asking to have a look at it himself, he read it aloud 'openly in the streets in Wigan'.[77]

If a letter was not delivered to hand it might be picked up direct from the carrier. Thus in September 1640 when Alexander Pricher, page to Sir William and Lady Thepton of Kirby Bedon, was in Norwich 'he went to the carriers to looke for letters that should come from London for his lady'. Much later, in February 1686, George Huntley a merchant of Newcastle, sent his servant Jonathan Carr to 'receive a letter from the post boy and open the same'. Such instructions were almost inviting the publication of its contents. Ann Baxter noticed Carr doing this 'and asking him "What news?", he replied, "Bad news. The king is ill of the same distemper his late majestie dyed of!"'[78]

Alternatively, it was common to leave letters at inns or other hostelries for collection. Since the beginning of the royal postal service innkeepers had been appointed as provincial postmasters. In 1636 the tenant at the Greyhound was suggested as the postmaster of Dover; the incumbent at the King's Arms in Norwich was appointed in 1668.[79] At the same time many inns, taverns, and alehouses seem to have acted as unofficial post offices. This had probably long been the case by the time that we find Edmund Manninge of Deddington in Oxfordshire popping into John Welchman's alehouse one Sunday morning in March 1584 to collect a letter left there for him, and drinking a halfpenny pot of ale in return for the service.[80] Everyone in the provinces must have had access to such an establishment, while every Londoner would have been able to find out the particular depository and collection point of carriers servicing all parts of the realm. In order to help them, John Taylor published a list in 1637 of all the 'inns, ordinaries, hostelries and other lodgings in and near London' frequented by the 'carriers, waggons, foot-posts and higglers' from each of the towns and shires, together with the days of the week on which to expect them, 'whereby all sorts of people may find direction how to receive or send goods or letters unto such places as their occasions may require'.[81]

[77] PRO, SP14/107/66i–v. For another example, involving a seditious letter sent from a son in London via the carrier to his father in Leicestershire during May 1637, see PRO, SP16/357/102i–iii.

[78] PRO, SP16/468/44Aiii; PRO, ASSI45/14/2/29.

[79] Crofts, *Packhorse, Waggon and Post*, 71; Haldane, *Three Centuries of Scottish Posts*, 3; Austen, *English Provincial Posts*, 7; 'Notes from two Court Books of the City of Norwich, from 1666–1688', ed. Walter Rye, *Norfolk and Norwich Archaeological Society*, 2 (1905), 123.

[80] *The Archdeacon's Court: Liber Actorum, 1584*, ed. Brinkworth, i. 230.

[81] John Taylor, *The Carriers Cosmography* (London, 1637).

Clearly such establishments provided another of the principal means whereby written news and rumour was disseminated to a wide audience, whether that audience could read for itself or not. After the Restoration, as one pamphlet claimed, newsletters were to be found in every village inn where, 'over a boull or nogg', the local squire could be heard expounding their contents 'like a little newsmonger'. In larger towns and cities there were probably several inns and taverns which acted as informal news centres. The Ship in Canterbury appears to have been one such. In December 1660 various people gathered there to meet the post from Deal and were soon discussing the news of 'the plott latelie discovered in London'. It was concern over just this kind of political speculation which moved the grand jury of Northamptonshire in February 1683 to demand the closer regulation of alehouse keepers and victuallers because of their 'great temptation in spreading seditious news'. Henry Hodgkinson's establishment in Preston was clearly acting as just such a conduit. On a typical evening in August 1689, many of the townspeople called in to peruse or hear the news as it arrived. John Matthew appeared 'when the post was newly come in'; John Brent turned up 'to read or hear the publique newes letter which usually came thither'; John Lance arrived with the mail, 'being desirous to heare that days news'; John Marsden, tailor, together with Joseph King and William Atkinson, 'went to the house . . . to read the publique newes that came thither that eveninge'.[82]

By this time, and probably well before, certain hostelries were acting as communications centres with particular religious or political affiliations and as such were often closely scrutinized by the authorities. In 1681, for example, the grand jury of Bristol reported the 'coffee house and tipling house' of John Kimbar which was 'commonly frequented . . . by many schismaticall and seditious sectaries and other disloyall persons where for their encouragement in tipling they are usually entertained with false news, lying and scandalous libells and pamphletts tending to the reproach and dishonour of the establisht religion and of his majestie and government and divers of his great officers and ministers of state'. It may also have kept a close eye on the Horse Shoe inn in the city: the political club meeting there, to which it gave its name, had 120 members in January 1682. In Northampton, meanwhile, the Swan inn was where, until 1690 or so, supporters of the local Whig party would meet to receive London newsletters, while the Tories appeared to have favoured the Goat inn in

---

[82] Crofts, *Packhorse, Waggon and Post*, 107; PRO, SP29/24/40–41; SP29/422/110; PRO PL27/1 (*Marsden* v. *Dale*, 1689). Preston also had a coffee house by this date, kept by a Mrs Jameson: PRO, PL27/1 (*Hodgkinson* v. *Walker*, 1689).

Gold Street for the same purpose. An alehouse in Hereford called the Catherine Wheel, kept by Bridget Andrewes, was suppressed in January 1695 after a riot occurred there and it emerged that 'divers persons disaffected to the present government do weekly and daily resort thither and read private, false and seditious newsletters to corrupt his majesty's subjects'.[83]

Coffee houses also provided, from their first appearance in the 1650s, another channel for the dissemination of letters of all types. Whatever the high price of official or other professionally written newsletters, they were brought to the shops of coffee sellers where they were left on the tables, pasted on the walls, and read aloud, giving access to them for all. By the late 1650s the London coffee houses were already being described as 'the markett place of news'. 'What news have you, master?' was the first question of the coffee man to his customer and on his tables lay pamphlets and lampoons, a 'store of mercuries' and the 'last coffee letter'.[84] Not surprisingly these new venues soon gained a reputation not only as principal sources of information but also as places where current affairs were openly discussed, political issues debated, and criticisms of Church and State articulated. Consequently they aroused the suspicion of the authorities from the first.[85]

In London, coffee houses were soon a familiar feature of the landscape: by 1663 the city was already home to eighty-three of them and there were many more in Westminster and the suburbs.[86] By this time they were also appearing in many provincial towns and cities. There were several at the university seats of Oxford, which had boasted the first, and Cambridge,

[83] PRO, SP29/415/142; SP29/429/61; Alan Everitt, 'The English Urban Inn, 1560–1760', in Everitt (ed.), *Perspectives in English Urban History* (London, 1973), 111; HMC, *13th Report, Appendix, Part IV*, 351. Taverns not infrequently became home to political clubs in this period. For examples in London with various affiliations, see PRO, SP29/420/6; HMC, *14th Report, Appendix, Part IV* (London, 1894), 297; Harris, *London Crowds in the Reign of Charles II*, 100, 132–3; *Poems on Affairs of State: Augustan Satirical Verse, 1660–1714*, v: *1688–1697*, ed. William J. Cameron (New Haven, 1971), 165–7.

[84] *The Diurnal of Thomas Rugg, 1659–1661*, ed. William L. Sachse (Camden Society, 3rd ser., 91, London, 1961), 2 and n.; Steve Pincus, '"Coffee Politicians Does Create": Coffeehouses and Restoration Political Culture', *Journal of Modern History*, 67 (1995), 819.

[85] Fraser, *The Intelligence of the Secretaries of State*, 115, 117–18, 119–21, 127, 128, 131–2; Bryant Lillywhite, *London Coffee Houses* (London, 1963), 17–20; Harris, *London Crowds in the Reign of Charles II*, 28–9, 99.

[86] *The Diary of Samuel Pepys*, ed. Latham and Matthews, x. 70. In the later 1690s the minister of Epworth, Lincolnshire, told his neighbour, Abraham de la Pryme, that when he had been in London he knew a parrot who was sent to a coffee house and within six months 'could say nothing but "Bring a dish of coffy"; "Where's the news?"', and such like': *The Diary of Abraham de la Pryme, the Yorkshire Antiquary*, ed. Charles Jackson (Surtees Society, 54, Durham, 1869–70), 176–7.

for example.[87] Tunbridge Wells acquired such an establishment after the Restoration, Bristol had one in 1666 and soon gained others, while there was one in York by 1669. The ports of Harwich and Yarmouth were among the other centres of trade supporting a coffee house at this date.[88] A similar institution clearly existed in Nottingham by July 1667 when it was reported to Secretary Williamson in London that 'a certain person, one Slater . . . pretends to have weekly newes from your office . . . Hee makes the worst use of what is communicated to him, for hee is zealous in publishing the ill newes and the meetings at his howse doe in a great measure resemble the coffee howses with you, for liberty of speech and descanting upon their intelligence.'[89] By the end of the century such thriving centres of information and news were widespread: Dorchester became home to two during the 1670s, Ipswich had the same number in 1696, at which time there were several in Exeter, and many others elsewhere.[90]

Like inns and taverns, they could act as provincial post offices where mail might be delivered and collected. So, for example, around Christmas 1680 a Northamptonshire gentleman, Henry Rushton, picked up 'a letter of news' from Frind's coffee house in Northampton which 'was sent downe by the post'. He took it to the house of John Whitfeld, vicar of Bugbrooke, and asked him 'to read [it] openly to his neighbours'. Whitfeld refused since it contained scandalous material about the government and the next day he went to Frind's 'and diligently searched the file of letters whence this was said by Rushton to be a copy but could not finde none there that had reference to any such thing'. Perhaps Joane Tackbread also had to search through a file of correspondence when, as servant to a nonconformist minister of Taunton, Somerset, she was sent in the summer of 1682 'to one Williams his coffee house, beinge the signe of the London, in Taunton . . . [to] enquire if there were any letter left there for her said master . . .'.[91]

---

[87] For comments on the news avidly exhanged in them, see Anthony Wood, *The Life and Times of Anthony Wood, Antiquary, of Oxford, 1632–1695, Described by Himself*, ed. Andrew Clark (5 vols., Oxford Historical Society, 19, 21, 26, 30, 40, Oxford, 1891–1900), i. 423, ii. 300, iii. 41, 45, 155; Roger North, *The Lives of the Norths*, ed. Augustus Jessopp (3 vols., London, 1890), i. 197–200.

[88] Aytoun Ellis, *The Penny Universities: A History of the Coffee-Houses* (London, 1956), 207, 213; Pincus, '"Coffee Politicians Does Create"', 813–14; Jonathan Barry, 'Popular Culture in Seventeenth-Century Bristol', in Barry Reay (ed.), *Popular Culture in Seventeenth-Century England* (London, 1985), 68–9.

[89] PRO, SP29/211/28.

[90] David Underdown, *Fire from Heaven: Life in an English Town in the Seventeenth Century* (London, 1992), 250; Peter Borsay, *The English Urban Renaissance: Culture and Society in the Provincial Town, 1660–1770* (Oxford, 1989), 145; W. G. Hoskins, *Industry, Trade and People in Exeter, 1688–1800* (Manchester, 1935), 24; Pincus, '"Coffee Politicians Does Create"', 814.

[91] PRO, SP29/417/59; SP29/428/26i.

At the same time, professional newsletter writers operated from London taverns and coffee houses where they could rely on picking up news before sending their missives on to similar establishments in the provinces. Typically, Rebecca Weedon's coffee house by the Exchange in London was reported in 1677 to be an establishment in which there 'constantly lay a paper of newes which she said could warrant and common to all persons'. A copy of the *Haarlem Courant* was seized there in January 1678 and among her customers was at least one person 'whose livelihood is nothing but newes, sending it to all parts of England'. In August 1682, Ralph Fisher, operating from the Green Dragon in Lombard Street, London, sent his newsletter to Joan Webb at her coffee house in Bristol. The last paragraph made reference to the strong report of another popish plot recently discovered at court and for this dangerous rumour it was confiscated and, within four days, sent back to the Secretary of State's office in Whitehall. Coffee-sellers themselves were often involved in the writing of newletters. In 1683, a Mr Combe was described as being one whose coffee business in the capital had almost dried up but whose newletters remained in great demand throughout England. Similarly a coffee man of Newgate Street called Monckreive was said at the same time to send many of his derivative epistles into the country.[92]

Wherever they were written, it was certainly to the coffee houses of both London and the main provincial centres nationwide that these newsletters were directed. In August 1681, for example, alarm was being expressed about the 'two very fanaticall letters full of sedition which come every week to Oxford and all over the kingdom'.

One of them is sent to Mrs Dayes coffee house in the High Street, written by one Gay a bookseller, who being lately broke hath set up again in a priviledged place called Whitefriars. The other is sent to Fagges his coffee house near the market place, written by one Smith a bookseller who is usually called Elephant Smith. These fellows do a great deal of mischeif by spreading lyes and false rumours about the nation to provoke people to sedition and rebellion.

Two years later, it was estimated in London that Giles Hancock, based at the Three Crowns near Bread Street, was earning up to £150 per annum by the newletters which he supplied to the city's coffee sellers and the thirty or more 'hee brought . . . oft times to the post'. At the same time a writer named Blackhall was said to specialize in servicing metropolitan establishments while another called Robinson served several more and a further twenty around the country. The team of Pike and Bill was also

---

[92]  PRO, SP29/396/116; SP29/401/60; SP29/420/1, 420/7; SP29/433/142.

reported to provide missives for 'an abundance of coffee houses' in the capital, among them Tome's in Birchin Lane. Other writers based at the General Post Office, including Sautell and Leeson, were reckoned to be even more prolific.[93]

In the early 1670s the government was expressing concern about the spreading of false news in coffee houses. Not until 29 December 1675, however, did it order their closure because 'diverse false malitious and scandalous reports are devised and spread abroad to the defamacon of his majestyes governement'. Another proclamation, on 10 January 1676, soon allowed their reopening again on condition that no such material circulated in them, but this was always an unrealistic hope. In September 1677, twenty coffee-house keepers had their licences revoked for allowing seditious newspapers onto their premises. The following year Chillingworth, master of a coffee house in Leadenhall Street, together with Kid, keeper of the Amsterdam in Bartholomew Lane, the principal gathering place for Whig sympathizers, and Rebecca Weedon, by the Exchange, were all censured for dispersing letters of false news.[94] By the early 1680s civic authorities all around the country were acting to this effect. In April 1680 the aldermen of Norwich were instructed to 'send to any publique house or coffee house or booksellers for such newletters as they have lately and do for the future receive from London'. The following year it was ordered in Bristol that 'no printed or written news or pamphletts be suffer'd to be read or published' in any 'coffee or tipling house but onely such as shall first be shewn to Mr mayor or the aldermen of the ward'. Similar action was being taken in Northampton soon after against the 'unlicensed coffee houses or places where false and seditious news is invented and spread' in the town.[95]

By this time, therefore, there was an even greater variety of channels through which written news, whether in the form of private epistle or professionally written newsletter, could easily become common knowledge.

---

[93] PRO, SP29/416/120; SP29/433/141, 433/142. On the remarkable career of Francis 'Elephant' Smith, seditious book printer of the Elephant and Castle, London, for over twenty-five years, see *Poems on Affairs of State: Augustan Satirical Verse, 1660–1714*, i: *1660–1678*, ed. George deF. Lord (New Haven, 1963), xxxiv–xxxvi; and regular references throughout the State Papers.

[94] PRO, SP29/294/64; SP29/311/112; SP29/376/80; SP29/378/40; David Ogg, *England in the Reign of Charles II* (2nd edn., 2 vols., Oxford, 1955), i. 101–2; *CSPD, 1677–78*, 338, 339. These edicts did not pass without comment. 'Then Charles, thy edicts against coffee recall | There's ten times more treason in brandy and ale', wrote the poet in 'A Dialogue between the Two Horses' (1676): *Poems on Affairs of State*, i, ed. deF. Lord, 283.

[95] 'Notes from two Court Books of the City of Norwich', ed. Rye, 157; PRO, SP29/415/142; SP29/422/110.

As a result, stories or rumours were much more likely to be initiated by some written source than simply by word of mouth. This was no less the case in the earlier sixteenth century, of course, but during the seventeenth century the range and quantity of such material grew much larger. After the Restoration it became increasingly common to find the false news spread by people in the provinces deriving from the bogus contents of some newsletter sent from London. In November 1679, for example, the rumour was buzzing around Halifax that the king was dead, the origin of the story being a servant who 'belonged to an eminent person as any was about Halifax and that this person of quality had it from London in a letter'. In just the same way some false news that James II had died later spread from mouth to mouth in North Shields as people asked each other, '"Neighbour did not you heare the post last night?"' During Monmouth's rebellion in the summer of 1685, a story circulated in Lancashire that 'a great army was landed beyond London' and it was said 'that this was the news by the poste'.[96]

As these examples make clear, however, the news on paper was certainly no more reliable than that spread orally. The two sources often depended upon one another and the authors of letters were often no better informed than the purveyors of gossip.[97] Indeed by increasing the circulation of false rumours, the greater availability of scripted news rendered a great service to the disinformation of the nation. Writing may have appeared to dignify the credibility of a story, especially if its source was considered to be reputable, with deleterious effects on popular beliefs and political stability. So it is that most of the wild rumours of the later seventeenth century, as many of those before, can be traced back in origin to some newsletter.

Perhaps the most spectacular example of this is provided by the huge Catholic fear which swept the land in the winter of 1688, either side of the arrival of William of Orange on 5 November. The rumours appear to have started at the beginning of October and lasted into the following January. In county after county, town after town, panic followed upon panic that at any moment a massive army of papists, aided by thousands of marauding Irish troops disbanded from the army of James II, would descend to massacre all Protestants who stood in their way, men, women,

---

[96] PRO, ASSI45/12/3/63; ASSI45/14/2/102; PRO, PL27/1 (*Lomax* v. *Brobin*, 1685). For another example, see PL27/1 (*Cowling* v. *Tootell*, 1680).

[97] It is striking just how often someone like Pepys, drawing on the best oral and written sources which London had to offer in the 1660s, received and believed news which turned out to be completely false: *The Diary of Samuel Pepys*, ed. Latham and Matthews, e.g. i. 260–1, ii. 38, 40, iii. 11, vii. 102.

and children. The highest point of the paranoia came between 14 and 18 December when many centres of population raised the alarm in readiness for imminent invasion. In the early hours of the 14th the news had reached Kent and before too long it was arriving in Surrey, Derbyshire, and Leicestershire. By that evening a post from Huntingdon brought the news to the people of Cambridge that 5,000–6,000 Irish had burned Bedford, cut throats there, and were heading towards them. The following day the mayor of Wigan wrote urgently to the mayor of Preston that 'at 5 this morning, an express came from Warrington with letters from Newcastle, Chester and four other towns, that 4,000 or more Irish and Scotch had committed a massacre in Birmingham, and were marching northwards'. The news reached Bristol where 'thousands of persons flew to arms to resist the barbarians'. On the 18th 'it was proclaimed in Settle market . . . that the Irish and Scotch had burned Halifax yesterday, and were expected at Skipton'. In total there is evidence that at least nineteen counties, in addition to London and Middlesex, were seized by this fear. At the time, no one quite knew why this particular wave of panic had been so comprehensive and so simultaneous across the country.[98]

The answer was that the rumour, deliberately engineered by opponents of the Protestant cause, was one systematically disseminated by letter. If we are to believe the retrospective account of the spy and seditionary Hugh Speke then this was a campaign which he orchestrated with precision by exploiting the workings of the postal system. Speke claimed that during the Popish Plot in 1678 he had had the opportunity to acquaint himself quite purposefully with prominent Whig sympathizers around the country. He had then set about a detailed study of the postal network so that he knew exactly when the mail arrived in every major town and how long it took to travel from place to place. By mid-December 1688 he was ready to send letters to selected gentlemen and merchants across England which were timed to arrive at exactly the same moment. 'All contained a surmise of the discovery of an universal conspiracy of the Irish and their Popish adherents to make some desperate attempt,' he remembered: 'these letters were severally contrived in such a manner that everyone believed the danger at his own door.' While it is questionable whether Speke's story can be entirely believed and it is unlikely that he was the sole instigator of this fright, it seems clear that this

---

[98] Magee, 'The Protestant Wind: Some Aspects of the Revolution of 1688', 341–2; and see also G. H. Jones, 'The Irish Fright of 1688: Real Violence and Imagined Massacre', *Bulletin of the Institute of Historical Research*, 55/132 (1982), 148–53; J. Anthony Williams, 'No-Popery Violence in 1688: Revolt in the Provinces', in G. A. M. Janssens and F. G. A. M. Aarts (eds.), *Studies in Seventeenth-Century English Literature, History and Bibliography* (Amsterdam, 1984), 245–60.

was very largely rumour by post, something which would have been much more difficult before the developments in mail carriage over the previous half-century.[99]

Of course once such letters were at large, those who revelled in the turmoil which they caused could rely on the grapevine to do its work. Another witness who was later to pen some reflections upon this panic was Abraham de la Pryme, who at the time had been a youngster in Lincolnshire. His recollection of that period was of oral reports travelling in advance of any written word. 'This newse or report ran . . . quite through the country, and for all it was some weeks a running northward, yet no one letter appear'd out of the south concerning any such thing there till it was always gone past those places where these letters were to go.' There were 'various reports . . . concerning the occation of this rumour', but he believed it to be 'nothing but a politick alarm raised and set on foot by the king and council to see how the nation stood affected to their new king'. It was 'wonderful how such rumours as then was could be invented', he mused.[100]

A further genre which might be considered in the context of oral circulation inspired by written origins, is that of political songs. For centuries before this, of course, songs, ballads, and rhymes had been used as a means of spreading news, propaganda, and polemic among an unlettered audience. Easily learned, easily retained and repeated, the most mnemonic and entertaining of all media, they were always one of the best means of communicating messages among the people. Many songs, and particularly shorter doggerel rhymes, may never have been written down at all, being learned in the first instance perhaps from professional minstrels or players and passed on one to another by word of mouth. Even if such material did have some existence in written form it would still have been through hearing that most people became familiar with it and, as remains the case with many songs today, paper copies would have played little part in their dissemination and memorization.

Here again, however, whatever the fundamentally oral nature of songs and ballads, it is clear that even in the earlier sixteenth century, their creation and circulation already owed much to written influences. Like prophecies, they were often invented and written down by a clerical or political elite with propagandist motives for fermenting discontent among the people. Once in textual form they could then be broadcast in public and repeated to others verbally. In some ways, it is surprising that

---

[99] Magee, 'The Protestant Wind: Some Aspects of the Revolution of 1688', 342.
[100] *The Diary of Abraham de la Pryme*, ed. Jackson, 15–16.

songs and rhymes of a seditious nature should have been committed to paper at all. Written transcripts surely provided much more tangible evidence against an accused than mere verbal recitation, while the identification of handwriting left an author or copier much more open to discovery than an anonymous lyric on the lips. They are testimony, therefore, to the extent to which England had become, even by the reign of Henry VIII, a society which drew heavily on written forms of communication.

The impact of the Reformation probably made a crucial difference in this respect. In his efforts to force through the revolution in Church and State demanded by his master, Thomas Cromwell exploited the propaganda potential of this genre as never before. Employing 'divers fresh and quick wits', as the martyrologist John Foxe would later put it, he was the sponsor of numerous 'excellent ballads and books . . . contrived and set abroad concerning the suppression of the Pope and all Popish idolatry'.[101] In this effort he utilized not only the traditional scope of scribal dissemination but also the new medium of print. Among his propagandists was William Gray, whose 'The Fantasie of Idolatory' denounced the false images, feigned miracles, and bogus shrines of the saints. It may have been this, or something like it, which William Hunte, a minstrel of Finchingfield in Essex, was disseminating in February 1538 when 'singing a song at a bridal, a song railing against saints, calling their images but idols'.[102]

A consequence of this strategy, however, may have been to encourage a response in like kind from the opponents of Henry's policies and Cromwell's enforcement. For these years throw up plentiful evidence of the use of seditious rhyme and song in denunciation of draconian royal coercion and defence of the old religion, all of which bears witness to the deployment of the written and even the printed word. A manuscript rhyme which came to light in June 1537 warned that 'he that ne rekketh where that he steppeth, he may lyghtly wade to depe'. In the winter of 1538–9, 'sundry books of balettes and defamatory railings' against the English king were written in Scotland and circulated throughout the Lowlands and Border counties. That oppositional material somehow found its way into print is suggested by the indictment of William Senes, master of the 'song scole' of the College of Jesus in Rotherham, West Riding, who was found in June 1537 with 'some printed ballads against

---

[101] John Foxe, *Acts and Monuments*, ed. S. R. Cattley (8 vols., London, 1837–41), v. 403, quoted in C. H. Firth, 'The Ballad History of the Reigns of Henry VII and Henry VIII', *Transactions of the Royal Historical Society*, 3rd ser., 2 (1908), 37. On Cromwell's propaganda techniques, see Elton, *Policy and Police*, ch. 4.

[102] *L&P Hen. VIII*, xiii, pt. I (1538), 227.

the prayers of the church used in the hallowing of water, the blessing of bread and of bells, and touching purgatory', which were apparently, 'not authorised by Parliament'. Senes is said to have denounced the new liturgy, claiming that 'such books as were sent down to the curates was made by heretics, and none of them true'.[103]

The use of writing, and particularly manuscript copies, for the conveyance of an essentially oral form, something which only came to life when chanted or sung, is striking. Having once been committed to paper, however, such material had then to be taught to other people, most of whom would not have been able to read handwriting. It was through public performance and popular emulation that such songs passed into the oral repertoire. In January 1539 a Gloucestershire man was arrested for singing a song against Henry and Cromwell of which there were copies. He claimed at first to have learned it from minstrels at Brailes before finally admitting that 'a cellarer of Wynscom taught him'. The previous May, Edward Eland, chaplain to the vicar of Wakefield was discovered 'teaching young folks seditious songs' against Cromwell. One of them, 'learned by heart by boys and others', derived from a text which was sent in evidence to its libelled victim in London, and it was probably in this form that Eland 'had it of one Byrkeheyd of Bole'.[104]

The Pilgrimage of Grace at the end of 1536 spawned many verses and ballads which were disseminated via script into oral circulation in this way. During the rebellion, John Lacy, bailiff of Halifax and his brother composed and wrote out another rhyme vilifying Cromwell, the archbishop of Canterbury, and the king, 'with words which any honest man would abhor', which first entered common currency by being read around the town. 'As for the king, an appyll and a fair wench to dally withall would please him very well,' it scoffed.[105] At the same time, a friar from the priory of Bridlington in Yorkshire, John Pickering, made a rhyme entitled 'An Exhortacyon to the Nobylles and Commons of the Northe'. It began 'O faithfull pepull of the boryalle region' and encouraged the rebels to resist the persecutions of 'naughty Cromwell'. Pickering confessed that he had written the rhyme at the suggestion of one Halom who had given him copies of other such verses made against Cromwell, the Lord Chancellor and various bishops of the new religion, 'which rhymes had been sung abroad by minstrels'. Various copies of his own work were later made in Bridlington and Scarborough but he acknowledged that he had

---

[103] *L&P Hen. VIII*, xii, pt. II (1537), 61; *L&P Hen. VIII*, xiii, pt. II (1538), 472, 476; *L&P Hen. VIII*, xiv, pt. I (1539), 54, 61, 62, 63, 92, 96, 107, 166, 371; *L&P Hen. VIII*, xii, pt. II (1537), 176.
[104] *L&P Hen., VIII*, xiv, pt. I (1539), 25; *L&P Hen., VIII*, xiii, pt. I (1538), 387–8.
[105] *L&P Hen., VIII*, xii, pt. I (1537), 340; *L&P Hen., VIII*, xii, pt. II (1537), 139.

expressed himself in verse specifically because it was an accessible and memorable oral medium, 'that the hearers might better bear it away'. The strategy clearly worked since before long the rhyme was said to be heard 'in every man's mouth' around Bridlington and Pontefract.[106]

Professional minstrels were one of the most effective brokers between the flysheets of author or scribe and the oral culture of the people. Much of their repertoire clearly drew upon written copies, like the ones which Halom gave to John Pickering, but it would have been received by the majority through listening to their performances at alehouses, fairs, and festivals. In the spring of 1537, an itinerant minstrel, John Hogan, found himself at Diss in Norfolk where at a butcher's and other houses he sang a compositon by Cromwell's ballad writer William Gray called 'The hunt is up' which had clearly been adapted in various ways and attacked the part played by the duke of Suffolk in the Pilgrimage.

> The hunte is vp, the hunte is vp, &c.
> The masteres of arte, and doctoures of dyvynyte
> haue brought this realme ought of goode vnyty
> The nobylle men haue take this to stey
> my lorde of Norffolk, lorde Surrey
> And my lorde of Shrewsbyry
> the duke of Suffolk myght a made Inglond mery.[107]

In June 1538, Alexander Stotson, a minstrel, or 'ryver abroad from place to place', was over in Windermere, Westmorland, not far from his native Cartmel, 'playing on a fedill and making merry' at an alehouse in Winster, when Isaac Dikson came in and demanded that he sing a 'song he had sung at one Fayrbank howsse in Crostwat . . . in the tyme of the rebellion, which song was called Crumnok', or 'Crumwell'. This could have been any one of the many songs so entitled which circulated in manuscript around the country over this period.[108]

The vigorous practice of using songs and ballads as an effective means of communicating political messages among a largely unlettered audience was one which would thrive and expand long after the first polemical battles over the Reformation had been fought. As the bishop of Winchester,

---

[106] *L&P Hen.*, *VIII*, xii, pt. I (1537), 460–4. The full text is printed in *Ballads from Manuscripts*, ed. Furnivall, i. 304–9. Cf. Firth, 'The Ballad History of the Reigns of Henry VII and Henry VIII', 38–9.

[107] *L&P Hen.*, *VIII*, xii, pt. I (1537), 206; *L&P Hen.*, *VIII*, xii, pt. II (1537), 119–20; *Ballads from Manuscripts*, ed. Furnivall, i. 310–12.

[108] *L&P Hen.*, *VIII*, xiii, pt. I (1538), 501, 508–9; and *Records of Early English Drama: Cumberland, Westmorland, Gloucestershire*, ed. Audrey Douglas and Peter Greenfield (Toronto, 1986), 214–15.

John Ponet, wrote to John Bale in exile during Mary's reign, 'Ballads, rhymes and short toys that be not dear, and will easily be born away, do much good at home among the rude people.'[109] Governments made ever greater use of the printed broadside as a vehicle for their self-presentation and the transmission of carefully selected news, while the laws of censorship, tightened by the monopoly of licensing granted to the Company of Stationers in 1557, ensured that oppositional verse was confined to a thriving and ubiquitous manuscript culture.

The evidence of this oppositional material which crops up in the records of the criminal prosecutions for sedition confirms the textually based nature even of dangerous songs. In 1553, Thomas Cundale was offering to show the locals at an alehouse in the remote Cambridge village of Orwell an anti-Catholic ballad called *Mistress Mass*, one of the many such titles printed in London in 1548 which had been widely dispersed at the time and must have continued to circulate underground after Mary's accession.[110] In 1554, John Cornet, 'prentice with a minstrel at Colchester' was at a wedding outside the town and being asked 'to sing some songs of the Scripture, chanced to sing a song called "News out of London", which tended against the mass and against the queen's mis-proceedings'. In Norfolk, meanwhile, another minstrel Robert Gold had been playing his harp 'at the signe of the Wassell' in Wymondham and singing a ballad 'against the mass and the godly proceedinges of the Catholike faythe of the churche'. James Wharton, a colleague from near King's Lynn who himself carried 'bookes of songes' containing scandalous material, borrowed this composition and on 10 May two of his apprentices were caught singing it in Norwich.[111]

This genre of seditious rhymes and songs, sometimes in print but most often in manuscript, already had a long and well-established history by the time that it re-emerged with a vengeance in the last third of Elizabeth's reign. What seems to have ignited it anew was the series of Martin Marprelate prose pamphlets against the bishops, circulating first in script and then in print, during 1588. The ecclesiastical authorities decided to

---

[109] Patrick Collinson, *The Birthpangs of Protestant England: Religious and Cultural Change in the Sixteenth and Seventeenth Centuries* (Basingstoke, 1988), 103.

[110] Margaret Spufford, *Contrasting Communities: English Villagers in the Sixteenth and Seventeenth Centuries* (Cambridge, 1974), 208, 245; Susan Brigden, *London and the Reformation* (Oxford, 1989), 436–8; J. N. King, *English Reformation Literature: The Tudor Origins of the Protestant Tradition* (Princeton, 1982), 248–9.

[111] Foxe, *Acts and Monuments*, ed. Cattley, viii. 578; 'Depositions taken before the Mayor and Aldermen of Norwich, 1549–1567', ed. Walter Rye, *Norfolk and Norwich Archaeological Society*, 2 (1905), 55; *Records of Early English Drama: Norwich, 1540–1642*, ed. David Galloway (Toronto, 1984), 34–5.

respond in like kind by sponsoring anti-Martinist invective from popular writers like Thomas Nashe and this appears to have set the tone for what followed. In the troubled 1590s a new wave of virulently satiric, audaciously critical, and often highly abusive writing began to circulate, much of it in verse.[112] For the next century, the pithy and salacious 'libel', whether poem, doggerel rhyme, or ballad, was to become one of the most popular, ubiquitous, and influential literary forms in England. The novelty of this genre should not be exaggerated: its antecedents were clearly well established in Thomas Cromwell's day. But it had taken on a new dimension in quantity and kind by the end of the sixteenth century.

A condemnation of 'seditious wrytings' in 1590 acknowledged that it had ever been 'a corrupt and perverse practise of evill subiectes to sow abroade libells and invectives of purpose to deface their gouvernors and by imbasing their estimation to supplante the allegeance and dutyes of the people and the quyet of their countryes'. And once again 'many are of late times dispersed and commen abroade within this realme . . . making evident digressions and excursions into matters of state, debating titles and jurisdictions, quarrellinge with lawes and acts of Parliamente, examining treatyes and negotiations and ever presuming to . . . undutyfull and dispitefull defamacon of their superiors, depravinge their accons publike and private'. In 1599 Archbishop Whitgift and Bishop Bancroft organized the public burning of some examples in London. Meanwhile, a speech by Lord Keeper Egerton in the Star Chamber condemned those 'monsters of men' who lately 'doe contrive and publish false and sedicious libells, scattering the same in many partes of the citie of London, yea and in her majestie's court itself', traducing not only councillors and ministers but also the queen herself. Nor was their distribution confined to political circles, for such libels were reported to be everywhere in the mouths of the common sort.[113]

At the same time Catholic conspirators from both within and without the realm sought to exploit this medium and there were constant fears of 'papistical libels' being spread abroad, some of which were discovered.[114] In 1594, Thomas Hale, recusant gentleman of Walthamstow, was indicted

---

[112] Patrick Collinson, 'Ecclesiastical Vitriol: Religious Satire in the 1590s and the Invention of Puritanism', in John Guy (ed.), *The Reign of Elizabeth I: Court and Culture in the Last Decade* (Cambridge, 1995), 150–70; Thomas Cogswell, 'Underground Verse and the Transformation of Early Stuart Political Culture', in Susan Amussen and Mark Kishlansky (eds.), *Political Culture and Cultural Politics in Early Modern England* (Manchester, 1995), 279–82.

[113] PRO, SP12/235/81; Cogswell, 'Underground Verse', 279; PRO SP12/273/35; SP12/273/37.

[114] PRO, SP12/158/51; SP12/275/141; SP12/279/12; SP12/284/67; PRO, SP15/27/93.

before the Essex assizes for having written eight years before a 'ballad or rhyme' lamenting the loss of the old religion and its replacement by 'a gosppell full of heresies'. In October 1600, 'a popishe ballett' was found in the streets in Hereford and the following year, Nicholas Foster, a Westminster schoolmaster, was discovered in possession of a 'scandalous ballett or libell in print betwixt a Papist and Protestant'. 'I am persuaded there are many such pamphlets', wrote John Rhodes at this time, 'together with other like Romish wares, that are sent abroad amongst the common people, both Protestants and Papists in London and in the country.'[115]

Under James I a variety of seditious manuscript libels circulated in court and country alike against prominent ministers such as Robert Cecil and Francis Bacon.[116] In the 1620s, royal favourite, the duke of Buckingham, became the most hated man in the kingdom thanks to the rash of poems, songs, and mocking ballads which passed around the country barely controlled by the authorities.[117] Evidence of the libels against Buckingham suggests that the circulation of this material was widespread around the country. The expedition to Spain by Buckingham and Prince Charles in September 1623 produced one wave of such critical compositions. The Dorchester gentleman, William Whiteway, was in London when 'there came newes of the prince his arrivall at Portesmouth, and ballads were made of it, but it prooved false; the ballad-singers were sent to prison'.[118]

Equally, the disastrous Île de Ré expedition occasioned many similar libels. It may have been such a ballad about the duke that a Kentish man 'lately come from London' was broadcasting around Sandwich in May 1626. The following month a scandalous libel in the form of a letter addressed to the duke was found in the buttery at the Middle Temple in

---

[115] PRO, ASSI35/36/2/34, and printed in F. G. Emmison, *Elizabethan Life: Disorder* (Chelmsford, 1970), 59–61; HMC, *13th Report, Appendix, Part IV*, 338; *Middlesex County Records*, ed. Jeaffreson, i. 272; Spufford, *Small Books and Pleasant Histories*, 11.

[116] Pauline Croft, 'The Reputation of Robert Cecil: Libels, Political Opinion and Popular Awareness in the Early Seventeenth Century', *Transactions of the Royal Historical Society*, 6th ser., 1 (1991), 43–69; C. H. Firth, 'The Ballad History of the Reign of James I', *Transactions of the Royal Historical Society*, 3rd ser., 5 (1911), 45; Lisa Jardine and Alan Stewart, *Hostage to Fortune: The Troubled Life of Francis Bacon* (London, 1998), 464–5.

[117] Cust, 'News and Politics in Early Seventeenth-Century England', 67–9; Alastair Bellany, '"Rayling Rymes and Vaunting Verse": Libellous Politics in Early Stuart England, 1603–1628', in Kevin Sharpe and Peter Lake (eds.), *Culture and Politics in Early Stuart England* (Basingstoke, 1994), 285–310. Some of these songs have been printed in *Poems and Songs Relating to George Villiers, Duke of Buckingham*, ed. F. W. Fairholt (Percy Society, 29, London, 1850).

[118] *William Whiteway of Dorchester: His Diary, 1618 to 1635* (Dorset Record Society, 12, Dorchester, 1991), 54; Firth, 'The Ballad History of the Reign of James I', 50–4.

London. In East Anglia, meanwhile, the clergyman John Rous came across much of this material in local towns. He transcribed one set of verses from June 1626 which 'came forthe, as I did heare, soone after the returne from Rees'. He suspected them to be based upon no more than 'vulgar rumor', but then, 'those which are in esteeme and greatest favour with princes are most subject to slander of tongues, the vulgar delighting herein, who judge all things by events, not by discretion'.[119]

During 1627 ballads mocking Buckingham were found in the mouths of minstrels at Ware in Hertfordshire, at Staines in Middlesex, and Windsor in Berkshire, and publicly posted at Dunmow in Essex and Bartholomew Fair in London. Three fiddlers from Middlesex named Moseley, Markehall, and Greene, 'being poore people', were convicted for singing several 'libellous songs against the duke of Buckingham and . . . the king and of the privy council, but principally they were intended against the duke'. One of them was the famous 'Clean Contrary Way' while another was entitled 'Take him Devil, Take him'. Small wonder that, in sentencing these ballad singers, Attorney-General Heath could describe libels as 'the epidemical disease of these days'. Buckingham may well have been implicated in the rumours of plots against the government which, during the spring of that year, were flying around Staffordshire, thanks to John Iremonger who was found dispersing two dangerous papers, claiming that 'he receved them as London newes most ordinary, the one as a songe usually sunge by fidlers, the other as newes of the tyme'.[120]

By 1628 such material was voluminous. In March, Rous noted: 'Newes was that the duke was in the Tower, and strange rimes and songs came abroade before the time.' Finally, Buckingham's assassination in August 1628 at the hands of the army officer, John Felton, occasioned another rash of manuscript verses celebrating the event. During the autumn Rous

---

[119] PRO, SP 16/27/80; BL, Additional MS, 38855, fo. 68; *Diary of John Rous*, ed. Everett Green, 19–22; C. H. Firth, 'The Ballad History of the Reign of Charles I', *Transactions of the Royal Historical Society*, 3rd ser., 6 (1912), 22. Such material was still circulating at the end of 1634 when William Eardly, an apprentice woollen-draper, was dining with a friend, Christopher Clough, in Fish Street, London, and 'among other discourse' Eardly 'repeated certain verses which were made some 7 years before of the late duke of Buckingham, which verses the said Clough desired to have and asked [him] whether they were new or noe, who answered he might have them and make them new if he pleased . . .': PRO, SP 16/278/12. For the full text of this Île de Ré ballad, see PRO, SP 16/85/84, and *Poems and Songs Relating to George Villiers, Duke of Buckingham*, ed. Fairholt, 19–24.

[120] PRO, SP 16/68/28, 16/70/10, 16/70/24, 16/70/45, and BL, Lansdowne 620, fos. 50–1; PRO, SP 16/64/11, and *APC, 1627*, 301. There must have been many with the modicum of invention displayed by Cornish gentleman Charles Tregion, a prisoner in the Fleet at this time, who 'used to sing a prophane songe, in the foote of which songe, in scandall and disgrace of the name of the duke of Buckingham, he would singe him by the name of the duke of Fuckingham': PRO, SP 16/89/69. For other verses deriding Buckingham, see PRO, SP 16/111/51.

received a verse epitaph on the duke, learned of another Île de Ré ballad posted at Bartholomew Fair, and heard it 'reported that the dole for the duke was farthings; and an ould rime was rehersed: "Brasse farthings in charity are given to the pore | When all the gold pieces are spent on a whore". Thus foully will the vulgar disgrace him whose greatness they hate."[121]

Rous's diary also bears witness to the huge number and variety of these manuscript libels which continued to circulate throughout the country during the 1630s and early 1640s. He received more verses in August 1629 and over the course of 1630. In April 1633 he collected 'To the Gentlewomen of the Newe Dresse' and 'The Ladies and Gentlewoman's Answer' both by Dean Corbet; 'Upon Sir Thomas Overbury', by 'Sir W.R.' and 'A Ladie with one Eye' by 'John Kn'. In 1635 he brought home a typical jibe at the 'new churchman of the times' and his perceived leanings back towards popery. 'He hopes to be saved by prevision | Of Good workes, but will doe none | He will be no Protestant, but a Christian | And comes out Catholicke the next edition', ran one of six stanzas. 'Many of these rimes came out in these late times, about 1634 and 1635', noted Rous, 'on both sides, some against the orthodoxe, others against these "newe churchmen", &c'. More verses attacking salvation by works and popish ceremonies circulated in the following years, including one in 1637 directed at James 'Ceremonius' Buck, the vicar of Stradbroke. Another flurry of 'railing rimes' on matters of doctrine and church government appeared in 1640 and 1641 when Rous collected 'A Dialogue between Two Zelots', 'A Dismall Summons to the Doctor's Commons', 'God Have Mercy, Good Scot', 'The Scholler's Complaint, to the Tune of Alloo, Alloo, Follow My Fancy', 'The Canterbury Bell', and 'The Masse-Priest's Lamentation | For the Strange Alteration | Begun in this Nation'. All of these and more he transcribed to 'keepe them for president of the times'.[122]

Many such manuscript verses, including some of those known to Rous, came to the attention of the authorities. Throughout the late 1630s and early 1640s there was a constant stream of poetic libels against Archbishop Laud detected circulating around London and elsewhere.[123]

---

[121] *Diary of John Rous*, ed. Everett Green, 14, 29–30, 31; PRO, SP16/117/10, 117/73; SP16/529/13; SP16/529/20i; *Poems and Songs Relating to George Villiers, Duke of Buckingham*, ed. Fairholt, 36–78. For a pair of anti-Felton verses, see J. A. Taylor, 'Two Unpublished Poems on the Duke of Buckingham', *Review of English Studies*, new ser., 40 (1989), 232–40.

[122] *Diary of John Rous*, ed. Everett Green, 42–3, 53, 54–5, 72–5, 77–9, 80, 83–4, 86–7, 101–3, 109–11, 115–19. Cf. Rous's commonplace book: BL, Additional MS, 28640. For another manuscript collection of poems and songs, compiled *c*.1630, see BL, Additional MS, 10309.

[123] Cogswell, 'Underground Verse', 277, 288, 289–90, 293; PRO, SP16/467/9 (printed); SP16/487/48; SP16/506/13; SP16/506/34; SP16/506/35.

Equally, manuscript verses were discovered denouncing ship money, attacking the bishops and episcopal government, lamenting the state of the nation, and libelling the king, particular ministers or other prominent individuals.[124]

During the Commonwealth, supporters of the crown maintained their morale with anti-Cromwellian songs, which naturally tended to circulate orally or in handwritten copies. As early as May 1649 a group of Royalist soldiers were proclaiming Charles II as their king in the market-place at Malton in the North Riding and went from the 'old cross, singing' to Williamson's tavern with 'divers children and apprentices flocking over them to see what the matter was'. In May 1653, Symon Warryner, a dyer from Knaresborough in the West Riding, was reported to have 'pend a song with his owne hand about halfe a yeare since' urging 'all gallant souldiers to display their banners and sett Kinge Charles in his right againe.' In London, Charles Staynings came to official notice in August 1654 for writing verses denouncing the regicide and the election of a Protector. Such may well have been the burden of the song of William Withers, sent to the House of Correction in Devizes, Wiltshire, the following year 'for singing of ballets contrary to the statute'. Just before Christmas 1656, William Higgory was discovered at the Black Boy in Ashcott, Somerset, rousing the patrons with the refrain, 'Let us drink, let us sing, here's a health to our king, and it will never be well, until we have one again!' When, on 24 April 1658, Samuel Buckberry, a barber from Tutbury in Staffordshire, was at the alehouse of Henry Heyes in the mining area around Newhall in Derbyshire, 'to trimme colliers', a number of his customers heard him 'sing a certain song in relation to the late king and his eldest sonn Charles Stuart'. By the end of 1659 and beginning of 1660, 'Rump songs' were already finding their way into print, and after the Restoration such material flooded out into the open to be sung and published with impunity.[125]

---

[124] PRO, SP16/438/93; SP16/455/42; SP16/468/141; SP16/472/65; SP16/473/48; SP16/473/113; SP16/487/46; SP16/487/47; SP16/490/51; SP16/493/63; SP16/503/103; SP16/538/140 (printed). For a manuscript collection of 'songs and sonnets' from this period containing social and political comment, see BL, Harleian MS, 2127.

[125] PRO, ASSI45/4/1/40, 4/1/132; ASSI45/4/3/98; PRO, SP18/74/4i; *Records of the County of Wiltshire*, ed. Cunnington, 230, and cf. HMC, *Various Collections*, i: (London, 1901), 131; *Quarter Sessions Records for the County of Somerset*, ed. F. H. Bates (4 vols., Somerset Record Society, 23, 24, 28, 34, 1907–19), iii. 347; *Three Centuries of Derbyshire Annals, as Illustrated by the Records of the Quarter Sessions of the County of Derby, from Queen Elizabeth to Queen Victoria*, ed. J. C. Cox (2 vols., London, 1890), ii. 66–7; *The Diurnal of Thomas Rugg*, ed. Sachse, 11, 13, 28–30, 48. Pepys sang a Rump song in April 1660, 'to the tune of "The Blacksmith"': *Diary of Samuel Pepys*, ed. Latham and Matthews, i. 114. Cf. *Catalogue of the Pamphlets, Books, Newspapers, and Manuscripts . . . collected by George Thomason*,

Following the Licensing Act of 1662, however, manuscript remained the principal supplement to word of mouth for the circulation of political songs and ballads. Thousands of libellous verses on affairs of state are known to have been written in the last four decades of the seventeenth century: about 500 have survived from the period between the Glorious Revolution of 1688 and the Treaty of Ryswick in 1697 alone. Almost all of them were disseminated through scribal publication, in the first instance at least, and the majority were never printed at all. Many were collected by interested parties and bound together in aggregations of flysheets, or else transcribed into manuscript anthologies.[126] Verses containing biting personal attacks on successive kings and scathing invectives against their ministers, among many other polemical and controversial matters, were constantly circulating throughout London in particular and were regularly brought to the attention of the authorities.[127]

Material of this sort could easily be picked up in the streets, as George Piggott discovered in December 1663 when he claimed that 'in the night goeing in the streets he accidentally found a copy' of a manuscript 'ballad or paper of verses' which he took away to have printed. Equally such things might be bought or copied from the taverns and coffee houses in which they were regularly distributed, as in the case of the verses of 1681 or 1682 which were actually addressed, in a fashion not uncommon, to 'Sam's coffee house, Ludgate Hill'. Otherwise they might simply be taken down from the prominent places, or the walls and doors around the city in which they were daily posted aloft for all to see. Even the titles of some of those verses or ballads which eventually made it into print reveal where they were first publicly displayed in their original state: *A Lampoon on Lord Scroggs Put on his Door* (1679); *A Bill on the House of Commons' Door* (1680); *A Stanza Put on Westminster Hall Gate* (1686); *A New Ballad, as it was Fixed on the Lord Dorset's Door at the Cockpit* (1689).[128]

---

*1640–1661* (2 vols., London, 1908), ii. 275–8, 288. See *Rump: Or an Exact Collection of the Choycest Poems and Songs Relating to the Late Times*, ed. H. B[rome] and H. M[arsh] (London, 1662).

[126] *Poems on Affairs of State*, i, ed. deF. Lord, xxxvii–xxxviii; *Poems on Affairs of State*, v, ed. Cameron, xxvii. A useful bibliography of the major manuscript collections is given in *Poems on Affairs of State: Augustan Satirical Verse, 1660–1714*, iv: *1685–1688*, ed. Galbraith M. Crump (New Haven, 1968), xv–xviii.

[127] For examples of such rhymes or songs, see PRO, SP29/61/161; SP29/143/147; SP29/173/136; SP29/197/21i–ii; SP29/211/132; SP29/381/78; SP29/417/132; SP29/421/221; SP29/442/80; SP29/443/47; *CSPD, June 1687–Feb. 1689*, 386–7.

[128] PRO, SP29/86/3, 96/55; SP29/421/221; *Poems on Affairs of State: Augustan Satirical Verse, 1660–1714*, ii: *1678–1681*, ed. Elias F. Mengel (New Haven, 1965), 288–9, 344–6; *Poems on Affairs of State*, iv, ed. Crump, 93; *Poems on Affairs of State*, v, ed. Cameron, 102–3. L'Estrange was well aware that 'Upon examining any man where he had this or that libell, his ready answer is, "I found it in

Scores of people were brought to book as Sir Roger L'Estrange and his officials hunted them around London. The 1680s, for example, saw some notable prosecutions in the capital. Famously, the great Whig polit-ician Algernon Sidney was actually executed for treason in 1683 merely for possessing a manuscript lampoon. The following year, the well-known scribal publisher, Robert Julian, who had already lost an ear for writing and distributing libels, was given a large fine and ordered to stand in the pillory at Westminster, Charing Cross, and Bow Street for composing seditious songs which circulated widely but were never printed. His prin-cipal offence was 'Song. Old Rowley the King. To the tune of "Old Simon the King"', the first verse of which is typical of the satirical attacks on Charles II:

> 'This making of bastards great,
> And duchessing every whore,
> The surplus and Treasury cheat,
> Have made me damnable poor,'
> Quoth old Rowley the King,
> Quoth old Rowley the King,
> At Council Board,
> Where every lord
> Is led like a dog in a string.

In November 1689, the crypto-Catholic Ralph Gray, sometime resident of the Latin coffee house near Gray's Inn, was pilloried as 'a composer of verses and lampoons against the government', one of which was 'The Coronation Ballad' written to denounce King William's investiture the previous April. It must still have been sung among Londoners four years later when Bridget Laytus, a mantua maker, suffered a similar punishment for making a pair of libellous songs on the royal couple which employed Gray's refrain 'A dainty fine king, A dainty fine queen, indeed, indeed'.[129]

## THE PRINTED WORD

When compared with manuscript texts, the role of printed works as vehicles for the dissemination of news was relatively limited for much of this period. The regimes of government censorship which operated with

my street"; "It was left at my house by I know not whom", or the like: and there's an end of the search': PRO, SP29/51/10i.

[129] *Poems on Affairs of State*, i, ed. deF. Lord, xxxvii–xxxviii; *Poems on Affairs of State: Augustan Satirical Verse, 1660–1714*, iii: *1682–1685*, ed. Howard H. Schless (New Haven, 1968), 478–83; *Poems on Affairs of State*, v, ed. Cameron, 39–45. On Julian, see Love, *Scribal Publication in Seventeenth-Century England*, 253–9.

more or less intensity throughout these two centuries strictly controlled the kind of topical reporting and political comment that found its way to the press. A proclamation of 1538 required the licensing of all printed books for 'expellinge and avoydinge the occasion of erroneous and seditious opinions' concerning matters of government and religion. In 1557 Mary Tudor granted a charter to the Stationers' Company, which was confirmed by a Star Chamber decree of 1586, giving it extensive powers of search and seizure and the authority to restrict the number of printers. With the abolition of the Star Chamber and High Commission at the Civil War, however, the major courts with jurisdiction in such matters were removed and thereafter newsbooks began to flood London. In September 1649 the Rump Parliament introduced stringent measures to try to control such publications which Cromwell enforced with particular rigour between August 1655 and his death in 1658. After the Restoration, the Licensing Act of 1662 provided an even tighter framework for control of the press until its lapse for the final time in 1695.[130]

Despite these restrictions, however, there were important precedents set during the seventeenth century in the printing of news and political opinion. Single-sheet corantos, dealing only with foreign affairs, were first published in London in 1621, to be followed by quarto newsbooks which ran from 1632 until their suppression six years later. The lapse of control over the press during the Civil War gave rise to an explosion of journalism. By 1644, a dozen newsbooks were appearing in the capital every week with some selling over 500 copies. In all there were no less than 350 separate news titles to appear between 1641 and 1659; the London stationer George Thomason had a collection of 7,216 news items compiled over this period in stock at his death in 1666. Both Royalists and Parliamentarians created their own propaganda mouthpieces and London's near monopoly on printing was broken by the multitude of small presses which began to spring up around the country. With

---

[130] For full details, see F. S. Siebert, *Freedom of the Press in England, 1476–1776* (Urbana, Ill., 1952), 165–263; G. A. Cranfield, *The Press and Society from Caxton to Northcliffe* (London, 1978), 1–2, 6, 9–10, 18–20; D. M. Loades, 'The Theory and Practice of Censorship in Sixteenth-Century England', *Transactions of the Royal Historical Society*, 5th ser., 24 (1974), 141–57; Christopher Hill, 'Censorship and English Literature', in *The Collected Essays of Christopher Hill* (3 vols., Brighton, 1985–6), i. 32–71; Sheila Lambert, 'The Printers and the Government, 1604–1637', in Robin Myers and Michael Harris (eds.), *Aspects of Printing from 1600* (Oxford, 1987), 1–29; A. B. Worden, 'Literature and Political Censorship in Early Modern England', in A. C. Duke and C. A. Tamse (eds.), *Too Mighty to be Free: Censorship and the Press in Britain and the Netherlands* (Zutphen, 1987), 45–62; J. Walker, 'The Censorship of the Press during the Reign of Charles II', *History*, new ser., 35 (1950), 219–38; Lois Schwoerer, 'Liberty of the Press and Public Opinion, 1660–1695', in J. R. Jones (ed.), *Liberty Secured: Britain before and after 1688* (Stanford, Calif., 1992), 199–230.

the return of licensing, the government-authorized *London Gazette*, which began in 1666 and was also confined largely to foreign reports, became the main official source of news. In practice, however, the tradition of open and partisan journalism which the mid-century upheavals had spawned could never be suppressed effectively and by the late 1670s factions of all political stripes were again publishing their own weekly and periodical bulletins under the nose of government regulation.[131]

In addition to these newsbook publications, a bewildering range of printed pamphlets and broadsides, almanacs and ballads, appeared from all sides of the political spectrum, especially during the extraordinary upheavals of the 1640s and 1650s, and in the mid-century period print may well have superseded manuscript as the principal medium through which written information and polemic were circulated (see Plate 16). The remarkable collection of publications compiled by Thomason at this time was said, after the Restoration, to contain every pamphlet issued from the presses between the beginning of the Long Parliament and the return of Charles II. Besides its 22,158 printed works, however, it consisted of less than 'one hundred several manuscripts that were never printed, most of them on the king's side, which no man durst venture to publish without endangering his ruine'.[132] Nevertheless, these years apart, manuscript remained the safest vehicle for the publishing of controversial opinion and unauthorized news. In 1662, Sir Roger L'Estrange, soon to be the new Surveyor of the Press, described what was probably the normal ratio of script to print as the preferred medium for dangerous material. 'Of libells some are only written, others printed; and those in manuscript are comonly the more seditious and scandalous of

[131] Cranfield, *The Press and Society from Caxton to Northcliffe*, ch. 1; Matthias A. Shaaber, *Some Forerunners of the Newspaper in England, 1476–1622* (Philadelphia, 1929); Laurence Hanson, 'English Newsbooks, 1620–1641', *Library*, fourth ser., 18 (1938), 355–84; Folke Dahl, 'Short Title Catalogue of English Corantos and Newsbooks, 1620–1642', *Library*, fourth ser., 19 (1939), 44–98; Joseph Frank, *The Beginnings of the English Newspaper, 1620–1660* (Cambridge, Mass., 1961); *Catalogue of the Pamphlets, Books, Newspapers, and Manuscripts . . . collected by George Thomason*; Nigel Smith, *Literature and Revolution in England, 1640–1660* (New Haven, 1994), pt. 1; Siebert, *Freedom of the Press in England*, pt. 4; Fraser, *The Intelligence of the Secretaries of State*, 122; R. B. Walker, 'The Newspaper Press in the Reign of William III', *Historical Journal*, 17 (1974), 691–709.

[132] PRO, SP29/26/91. On the impact of print in these years see, for example, *Cavalier and Puritan: Ballads and Broadsides Illustrating the Period of the Great Rebellion, 1640–1660*, ed. Hyder E. Rollins (New York, 1923); Christopher Hill, *The World Turned Upside Down: Radical Ideas during the English Revolution* (London, 1972); Bernard Capp, *Astrology and the Popular Press: English Almanacs, 1500–1800* (London, 1979), 72–88; Lois Potter, *Secret Rites and Secret Writing: Royalist Literature, 1641–1660* (Cambridge, 1989); P. W. Thomas, 'The Impact on Literature', in John Morrill (ed.), *The Impact of the English Civil War* (London, 1991), 123–42; James Holstun (ed.), *Pamphlet Wars: Prose in the English Revolution* (London, 1992); Smith, *Literature and Revolution in England*; Freist, *Governed by Opinion*, chs. 3–4.

the two. Besides that they are forty times as many, and by the help of transcripts, well nigh as publick as the other.'[133]

In general, therefore, it was the manuscript separates and newsletters, the handwritten squibs and lampoons, the scribal collections of poems and ballads, which the government had most occasion and most reason to fear. But such material was also the most difficult to police and control, its authors and copiers the hardest to identify. With the press, at least, some degree of systematic regulation was possible. Proclamations and ordinances against the printing of seditious and dangerous books were a constant feature of the sixteenth and seventeenth centuries.[134] The prosecution of people under the laws of sedition also reflects the continued anxiety over this issue during the course of the period. Not only were there those arraigned for the production, distribution, and reception of print but also a growing proportion of men and women arrested for speaking seditious words or spreading false news were doing so in response to a printed text which they had read or heard.

It is clear that many of people's attitudes and opinions were conditioned or provoked by what they knew from printed sources. One text with which everyone was thoroughly familiar was the Bible and this provided the ideas, images, and vocabulary out of which to fashion ideas on politics, as on all other subjects. In the years leading up to the Civil War there is evidence that many adopted the justifications for opposition to Charles I which puritan preachers and other dissenting voices taught them to find in the Scriptures. Thus, in March 1636 a Northamptonshire petty chapman, John Lewes, was arrested for having opined on his travels that 'the kinge was noe better then the begger (as he heard preachers say out of the Byble, or as it was written in his Byble) except he discharges his callinge as he ought. Nay he was worse then the begger and his case shalbe more miserable.' Three years later, a London carpenter, George

---

[133] PRO, SP29/51/10i. L'Estrange made the same point before a House of Lords committee in November 1675: HMC, *9th Report, Part II* (London, 1884), 66. On the continued importance of manuscript circulation throughout this period, see J. W. Saunders, 'The Stigma of Print: A Note on the Social Bases of Tudor Poetry', *Essays in Criticism*, 1 (1951), 139–64; W. J. Cameron, 'A Late Seventeenth-Century Scriptorium', *Renaissance and Modern Studies*, 7 (1963), 25–52; *Poems on Affairs of State*, i, ed. deF. Lord, xxxvii–xlii; D. F. McKenzie, 'Speech-Manuscript-Print', in Dave Oliphant and Robin Bradford (eds.), *New Directions in Textual Studies* (Austin, Tex., 1990), esp. 93–9; Love, *Scribal Publication in Seventeenth-Century England.*

[134] For examples of such injunctions, see *APC, 1547–50*, 421; *APC, 1552–54*, 365; *APC, 1554–56*, 245; *APC, 1575–77*, 107–8; *APC, 1586–87*, 322; *APC, 1588*, 128–9; *APC, 1600–1*, 266; *APC, 1617–19*, 38; HMC, *9th Report, Part II*, 76; HMC, *13th Report, Appendix, Part IV*, 121, 332; PRO, SP12/92/26; SP12/235/81; SP12/284/67; PRO, SP16/449/26; SP16/484/57; SP16/515/106; PRO, SP18/181/110; SP18/219/41; PRO, SP29/16/60; SP29/51/6–10; SP29/78/96; SP29/378/35i.

Goodwin, was down at Rye in Sussex when he found himself before the mayor for saying in public that 'King James, neglecting to do justice, lost his right to the kingdom and King Charles going on in the same courses is an usurper and saith that if he had his right he should enjoy the kingdom. His ground for this is that in Ecclesiastes, that better is poore and a wise child then an old and folish king.'[135]

In August 1639 one of the biggest topics of conversation was naturally the rebellion which had just broken out north of the border over the attempt to impose the English prayer book on Scotland. When, during a discussion among locals in Ashby Magna, Leicestershire, John Owenbie was asked 'what newes he heard concerninge the Scottish warres, and what the cause thereof was', he explained that the Scots justified their resistance by citing 'the 5 of Jer. and the last verse and the 5th chapter of the first epistle of St Peter and the 2 and 3 verses'. He also offered the prescient observation that 'he had read manie histories but he never heard of anie where the beginninge of difference betwixt the kinge and his subiects were grounded upon religion but they ended in open rebellion . . .'. A year later, Edward Neale of Shelley in Essex, commenting on the recent storming of Lambeth Palace by London apprentices, predicted that 'they would shortly rise in the countrie and then the first houses they would pull downe should be the houses of those that tooke part with the bisshopps. And the said Neale did alledge that place of Jeremiah c: 22, ver. 6 and 7.'[136]

As cheap printed materials became even more readily available during the seventeenth century, the evidence suggests that other kinds of literature were also serving as the prompt or inspiration for dangerous opinions. Thus a 'small book', or cheap pamphlet, was being read at an alehouse in Evesham, Worcestershire, on Friday 5 March 1624. It was an apparently now lost piece of government propaganda written by the popular author Nicholas Breton, and one of the many tracts penned to mark the safe return of Prince Charles and the duke of Buckingham from their expedition to Spain in October 1623. On the day in question, John Brent, from near Wolverhampton, said to be 'a comon carryer of letters betwene recusants', called in at Richard Moore's where he found John Tysoe, yeoman, together with the host who was reading this work. Upon enquiry, Moore 'shewed him the said book, the same being a smalle booke lately written by one Nicholas Britten and intitaled *Great Britain's*

---

[135] PRO, SP16/317/16; HMC, *13th Report, Appendix, Part IV*, 208. For the influence of the Bible on contemporary thought, see Christopher Hill, *The English Bible and the Seventeenth-Century Revolution* (London, 1993).

[136] PRO, SP16/430/10iii; SP16/468/139. On the first of these cases see also Freist, *Governed by Opinion*, 260–5.

*Thankfulness to God for our Peaceable King and the Happy Return of Prince Charles*'. Moore extolled its contents, 'taking occasion to praise and magnifie God for the said prince's return and for God's blessing on this kingdom by the king and prince in the inioyning of the gospell theareuppon'. Brent's reaction indicates that Catholics did not necessarily share in the mood of national euphoria which this incident had provoked, for 'in shewe of dislike of such' he asserted that he would rather have the king of Spain as his ruler.[137]

Broadside ballads could incite similar outbursts. In October 1640 a party playing at cards at the widow Black's in St Martin's Lane had a laugh when one of the company 'produced a ballad lately printed concerning two Welchmen, the which he said he had sent into Scotland with other letters where it would make very good sport, and in a geering manner wished he had but the Nout's head to send away with it, for that would make sport indeede'. When asked whom he meant by 'the Nout', he replied, 'the archbishop of Canterbury'.[138] Almanacs made their impact in this sense, too. In November 1682, Edward Mathews, a painter from Surrey, was in trouble for saying that the king had only six months to live, something he claimed to know from a highly unlikely source, a nativity cast by the popular Tory almanac writer John Gadbury.[139]

The records of sedition also provide fragmentary glimpses of the way in which printed news might enter common circulation and fashion popular opinion. Thus, in June 1625 a publication informing the people of their new monarch's progress was clearly being discussed in King's Lynn and around East Anglia. At Wisbech Henry Denne, a cordwainer, went into the shop of his colleague, William Eaton, on Wednesday 8 June. There he saw Robert Byrbacke at work and said to him 'that he could tell him newes'. '"What news?"' asked Byrbacke, to which Denne replied that Charles I was no more. At this Eaton 'told him that he had seene a book at Linne wherin he reade how that the king was gone to Greenwich'.

---

[137] PRO, SP14/160/73i. This is either an unknown work by Breton or else a misattribution of one of the many pamphlets that were written on this subject, such as: John Taylor, *Prince Charles his Welcome from Spaine* (London, 1623); Anon., *The Joyfull Returne, of the Most Illustrious Prince, Charles* (London, 1623). For a discussion of the literature provoked by this episode, see David Cressy, *Bonfires and Bells: National Memory and the Protestant Calendar in Elizabethan and Early Stuart England* (London, 1989), ch. 6.

[138] PRO, SP16/469/95, 470/33. The ballad may well have been Martin Parker's *Britaines Honour: In the Two Valiant Welchmen, who Fought against Fifteene Thousand Scots* (1640). For the text, see C. H. Firth, 'Ballads on the Bishops' Wars, 1638–40', *Scottish Historical Review*, 3 (1906), 266–8; *Cavalier and Puritan*, ed. Rollins, 89–94; this incident is discussed in Freist, *Governed by Opinion*, 255–60.

[139] PRO, SP29/428/35. See Capp, *Astrology and the Popular Press*, 93.

"'I thanke God it is not as it was reported"', replied Denne, "'for it is reported that the king is dead"'.' Denne then told James Thompson, labourer, that the king had been 'made away within theise three dayes'; Thompson, in turn, told Richard Tyllney and John Stanion.[140]

A good example of the distribution of such printed material is afforded by the dissemination of the newsbooks and pamphlets from Scotland during 1640 in which apologists for the prayer book rebellion attempted to justify their action and raise support in the south. On 13 March the government issued a proclamation against the 'late sondry base, false and libellous discourses and pamphletts, as well manuscripts as in printe, [which] have bene sente from Scotlande and other partes of his majesties dominions and spreade and published in diverse places of this kingdon of England, especially in the city of London . . .'. They were soon circulating in the inns and taverns of the capital and providing a major topic of conversation among their patrons. Thus in August, for example, a letter which 'did import ill newes to the Englishe nation comytted by the Scootes' was circulating at a tavern in Broad Street and the issue was being hotly discussed at Mrs Streeter's in Drury Lane and the Red Lion in Bishopsgate Street.[141]

But it is clear that they circulated out of London and around the country very quickly in that same month of August 1640, disseminated in the packs of carriers and traders and via the network of inns and taverns nationwide. Thus on the 11th Robert Abbot, a Cambridge chandler, received 'certaine printed pamphlets and discourses concerning the intentions of the armye of the kingdome of Scotland which had bin sent to him from London'. They were delivered 'by a common carryer named Powell' and left at his house 'under the forme of a packet of parcells bundled up in paper' containing a total of 'six little books'. These 'pamphlets and discourses' were probably the same as the 'certain bookes sent out of Scotland' which were travelling with Edward Cole, a clothier from Suffolk, and were heard to 'rattle in his pocket'. He was to be found advertising them at the White Hart in Bocking, Essex, and trying to distribute them among a company of soldiers billeted at Braintree where he had various copies concealed about the churchyard. They included a broadside entitled *Information from the Scottish Nation, to all the True English, Concerning the Present Expedition*. At the same time, it was the talk both at the Red Lion

---

[140] PRO, SP16/3/53i–v.
[141] PRO, SP16/449/26; SP16/466/91–92i, 466/115–16; SP16/464/31; SP16/464/51, 465/31–2, 466/93, 466/112–14, 467/14–15.

and the Swan in Kettering, Northamptonshire, that the invading Scots were coming for the heads of Laud and Strafford, after a local parson let it be known 'that he had letters from the Scotts armie to that purpose'. Meanwhile, at Lewes in Sussex a draper discovered a copy of the twelve-page pamphlet *The Intentions of the Armie of the Kingdome of Scotland Declared to their Brethren of England* which he handed in to a justice of the peace.[142]

Carriers and traders were clearly responsible for bringing many of these pamphlets and broadsides down from the north in the first place. Thus an Irishman, Erasmus Astley, was arrested at Worcester during August in possession of 'a booke intituled *The Short Declaracon of the Kirke of Scotland*' which he confessed to picking up 'in Scotland about halfe a yeare since'. Soon after, one of the bailiffs of Ipswich got hold of 'a printed information from the Scottish nation, which was originallie found and taken upp verie latelie att Newcastle (by a seaman of this towne) where . . . diverse of them were scattered abroad'. It contained 'a dangerous invitation to the Inglishe to joyne with them in there rebellions'. In October Joseph Woodgate, a London tailor, was on his way back from Scotland when he lodged overnight at the Red Lion in Brickhill, Bedfordshire. There he got chatting to the parson of Church Lawford, Warwickshire, and showed him his recent acquisitions, 'a booke which was *The Second Declaracon or Justificacon of the Scotts Coming into England* and another written by one Udall longe since and nowe newlie reprinted'. He would have divulged more had not the parson spoken up against the Scots. The next night, however, Woodgate had reached Holwell, near Hitchin in Hertfordshire, and there he met the local minister to whom he showed 'the petitions of the lordes of England and of the rebells of Scotland'.[143]

After the Restoration, evidence for the influence of print on the information which people received and the opinions which they expressed becomes even more plentiful. Just as with manuscript libels, the records of sedition demonstrate the extent to which printed material was scattered abroad in the London streets and fluttered in the breeze as it was pinned up at the Royal Exchange, at Westminster Hall, and on doors and walls throughout the city. In December 1675, for example, there was a

---

[142] PRO, SP16/464/57; SP16/464/79, 464/79i, 465/43; SP16/465/33, 465/44–45; SP16/465/60, 465/86.

[143] PRO, SP16/465/46; SP16/466/48; SP16/470/10, 470/12. The 'booke' which Woodgate showed at the Red Lion was probably *The Lawfulnesse of our Expedition into England Manifested*, a seven-page pamphlet 'printed at Edinburgh by Robert Bryson' and 'to be sold at his shop at the sign of Jonah': for a copy see PRO, SP16/469/87.

libel 'hung upon the horse in Cheapside' which proclaimed that Tangier would be sold to the French. A patron at the Palsgrave's Head divulged its contents to the assembled company on being asked '"What news?"' In February 1677 a printed ballad, *Vox Popili, or Faire Warning to Every Member of the Late Parliament*, was found pinned up on the gate at Westminster Hall. John Nayler, a bricklayer, noticed it but claimed that as 'he could neither read nor write, he thought it had been a bill about a house to let'. In May 1680 large numbers of a libel entitled *A Letter to a Person of Honour Concerning the Black Box* were found scattered at the Royal Exchange, prior to it being dispersed around the country.[144]

Taverns remained a crucial venue for the distribution of seditious pamphlets and prints. In April 1673, for example, a popish priest was reported broadcasting an 'idle ridiculous paper' prejudicial to the government: he 'read it openly at the Castle taverne at Eltham and a person present got a copy of it'. At another London tavern in July 1678 Samuell Packer chanced upon a copy of 'a pamphlet entitled *The Growth of Popery*', found 'in his seat upon the table'. He took it to 'Leach's the citty stationer' where he asked for it to be stitched up and delivered to him at the King's Head. The apprehension of Packer soon led to the house of Jenckes, a linen draper, by the Royal Exchange where were found 'behind a great looking glass severall pamphlets, particularly *Harrington's Case* and in his clossett *Brown's Case*'. In March 1683 a woollen draper found a printed pamphlet of eight pages entitled *A Political Catechism* at the Angel and Crown tavern near St Benet Fenchurch.[145]

By this time, the coffee house was also a major outlet for the distribution of news and political polemic of all kinds in print. As early as February 1662 Sir Roger L'Estrange had been well aware that 'the principall and professed dealers' in scandalous libels against the government, whether in manuscript or print, were 'observed to be some certain stationers and coffee-men, and that a great part of their profit depends upon this kinde of trade'. He recommended then that all coffee sellers should be regulated so as to guard against this but it was not until the end of 1675 that the order to suppress them was issued, to 'prevent and hinder all scandalous papers, books, or libells concerning the government or the publick matters' from being left in them 'to be there read or perused or divulged'. Just as with newsletters, many coffee masters enhanced their business not only by purveying such texts but also by transcribing and

---

[144] PRO, SP29/375/194; HMC, *9th Report, Part II*, 70; PRO, SP29/413/118–19. For other examples of material being posted up, see PRO, SP29/82/71; SP29/407/95; SP29/419/93.

[145] PRO, SP29/335/40; SP29/405/122, 405/135; SP29/423/10i.

even writing them. Not long after the proclamation of 1675, for example, William Peate, master of a coffee house in Sheer Lane, and Thomas Jon, keeper of a tavern near the Falcon stairs in Southwark, were, together with Thomas Jenkinson, under suspicion as the authors and copiers of libels. In 1684, John Heyrick, master of the Protestant coffee house in St Sepulcher's, Middlesex, was found guilty of writing and displaying 'an infamous libell' against the king, the government, and Sir Roger L'Estrange in particular; soon afterwards he was in trouble again for having 'invented and contrived a second scandall worse then the former against the same worthy person'.[146]

It was in the 1670s, thought Roger North, that coffee houses 'began to be direct seminaries of sedition and offices for the dispatch of lying'. In May 1679 Parliament allowed the Licensing Act of 1662 to expire, with the consequence, it was said, that 'there came out every day such swarms of impudent licentious libels upon all sorts of persons, and upon all subjects, printed, as the like was never known'.[147] Even before this, however, cases of printed pamphlets being read, distributed, and discussed in London coffee houses become frequent in the records. During 1675, for example, the anti-episcopal tract *A Letter from a Person of Quality to his Friend in the Country*, possibly written by John Locke, was said to be 'in all the coffee houses'. Mary White, 'at a coffee-house behind the Exchange' bought three dozen copies at 1*s.* each from Katherine Knight, 'a hawking woman who carried books about'. She kept at least six of them and sold a large number on to Mrs Jackson in Charterhouse Lane.[148]

The following year, *The Long Parliament Dissolved* was circulating in just this way. In March 1677 George Evans confessed to having seen it 'in a coffee-house, in the hands of one King, an upholsterer, who told him he had bought it of John Hancock, senior', said to have been a trader in such material since 1642. Hancock refused to sell one to Evans 'saying it was a prohibited book, and everyone was not to be trusted with it'. Similarly, in February 1678 a 'certaine seditious and scandalous pamphlet called *Harrington's Case*' was found at the Rainbow coffee house near Temple Bar where one patron was seen to 'pull the pamphlet out of his pocket'

---

[146] PRO, SP29/51/10i; SP29/376/80; SP29/378/40; SP29/378/76, 378/79; *Middlesex County Records*, ed. Jeaffreson, iv. 243–4. Cf. *Towzer Discover'd: Or a New Ballade on an Old Dog that Writes Strange-Lee* (Printed for J. B., London, 1683).

[147] *Poems on Affairs of State*, i, ed. deF. Lord, xxxviii; *Poems on Affairs of State*, ii, ed. Mengel, xxix.

[148] Pincus, '"Coffee Politicians Does Create"', 828; HMC, *9th Report, Part II*, 66; *Middlesex County Records*, ed. Jeaffreson, iv. 66–9. Women were often the hawkers of such wares. A list of 44 mercury-hawkers in London drawn up about 1668 included 31 women: PRO, SP29/251/196. See the engraving of a female seller of the *London Gazette* in *The Criers and Hawkers of London: Engravings and Drawings by Marcellus Laroon*, ed. Sean Shesgreen (Aldershot, 1990), 187, and cf. 101, 151.

and show it to his neighbour. In June of that year two men were discovered in 'the coffee house at the sign of the Black Boy in Cardinal's Cap
Alley, near Lombard Street' reading 'a printed book'. This and another
'printed paper' were apparently brought there by one Smith, a bookseller
in Cornhill.[149]

In January 1679 a printed tract, *Mr Prance's Discoursies of the Plott and Sir
Edmond Berry Godfrey's Murder*, was discovered circulating in Preston's coffee house, and during 1680 'a sheete a printing entitled *A Letter to a Person
of Honour Concerning the Black Box*' was also being passed around the city's
coffee men, just as it had been posted up at the Exchange. In June of that
year it was equally possible to find a paper containing derogatory articles
against the duke of York at Richard's in Threadneedle Street, or a dangerous pamphlet 'in form of a letter beginning *My Dear Friend*' at the
Amsterdam coffee house. In the spring of 1681 another of the many libels
against the duke, *The Character of a Popish Successor Compleate*, was in circulation, about which its alleged author 'did whisper in every coffee house'. In
1683 a search was again made of the Amsterdam coffee house for the libel
by the 'notorious papist' Edward Fitzharris, *The True Englishman Speaking
Plain English*.[150]

In the provinces, meanwhile, the coffee house was becoming just as
active as a purveyor of print to the widest audiences. At Hereford in the
late 1670s a libellous verse entitled *A Public Vindication of Paul Foley, esq., to
be Left at the Coffee House with the Letters* was typical of the dangerous material which prompted action by civic leaders. In January 1681 there was an
order to suppress the coffee house of William Pearce at Warminster,
Wiltshire, as he 'hath of late made it his dayly practice to expose to the
view of the inhabitants divers seditious pamphlets and libells against the
government now established in both Church and State'. Apparently it did
little good since in the spring of 1683 the Warminster coffee house, and
that in Devizes plus many others across the western counties, were
reported to be hotbeds of subversive talk against the government. It
was also from a 'Pearce's coffee house' that a group of Baptists in
Devon were plotting to restore a republican regime in the summer of
1682: among the many seditious pamphlets which they received were

[149] HMC, *9th Report, Part II*, 70; PRO, SP29/401/22; SP29/404/236.

[150] PRO, SP29/411/36; SP29/413/118–19, 414/55i; SP29/413/169; SP29/415/165;
SP29/433/140. On the murder of Sir Edmund Berry Godfrey, the alleged involvement of Miles
Prance, and the publications occasioned by the affair, see *Poems on Affairs of State*, ii, ed. Mengel,
3–11. On Fitzharris's libel, see *Poems on Affairs of State*, iii, ed. Schless, 465 n. For comment on the
satirical print in London coffee houses in 1689–90, see Edinburgh University Library MS,
La. III. 545, fo. 115ᵛ.

*Vox et Lacrimae Anglorum, Vox Populi,* and *Matters of Fact in the Present Election of Sherriffs and the Miscarriages of the Lord Mayor and others Briefly Described.* Meanwhile, in Chester a seditious paper was being read at Alderman Wilcock's coffee house, just as ballads were being sung in the streets, at the time of the duke of Monmouth's visit to the city in September 1682. Mrs Burry at the Dolphin in Chichester, Sussex, was in trouble during August of 1689 when a printed *Letter from a Friend in the City to a Friend in the Country,* considered to be dangerous, was sent to her for public show.[151]

Given the distribution of news and propaganda, both in manuscript and print, through the coffee houses, it is not surprising that so many cases of seditious speeches should be reported as having taken place within them. Increasingly coffee houses became the sites where people met to discuss current affairs, to express their views on the political situation and even to plot against the government.[152] Ultimately, the coffee house provides the most vivid illustration of the way in which the written word could act as a stimulus and an inspiration to oral exchange. These new institutions were the most active centres of gossip and discussion precisely because they were the most dynamic market places for script and print.

The circulation of rumour and news demonstrates the sheer vitality of oral exchange in early modern England. People at all social levels and in every part of the country found out information by talking to others and by listening. Even today, much of our intelligence and gossip is received in this way and a large part of it still relies upon whom we know or happen to meet. It is hardly surprising, then, that word of mouth should remain as important a part of news gathering at the end of the seventeenth century as it had been at the beginning of the sixteenth. And some of the fabulous beliefs generated by an active grapevine, such as frenzied panics about the threat of imagined enemies or fantastic prophecies about the return of sleeping heroes, remained as much a feature of the late Stuart period as they had been of the early Tudor one.

---

[151] HMC, *13th Report, Appendix, Part IV,* 349; *Records of the County of Wiltshire,* ed. Cunnington, 266; PRO, SP29/427/23; SP29/420/36; SP29/420/67; *CSPD, 1689–90,* 216. For the Monmouth ballads in Chester: PRO, SP29/420/66, 420/81; for an example of the kind, see *Young Jemmy: An Excellent New Ballad, to an Excellent New Tune* (Printed for Alexander Banks, London, 1681).

[152] For examples of seditious conversations, rumours, and plots in coffee houses, see PRO, SP29/47/118; SP29/95/56; SP29/101/16; SP29/360/18; SP29/376/138; SP29/378/76, 378/79; SP29/391/45; SP29/394/175; SP29/400/199i; SP29/404/237; SP29/415/178; SP29/417/51; SP29/427/23; SP29/428/26i, 428/27.

Yet, these two centuries also experienced important changes in the anatomy of communication and witnessed a thorough restructuring of the underpinnings of much oral exchange. Well before this period, of course, government edicts had circulated in written form, letters between official bodies and among private individuals had carried news, and political songs had been committed to paper for mass distribution. But during the sixteenth and seventeenth centuries, developments in professional journalism, the emergence of a postal service, and the commercialization of printing, all played a part in stimulating an ever increasing appetite for news and opinion. By the end of the period, institutions such as coffee houses were providing new sites for reading and offered a whole range of outlets for the production, distribution, and reception of the written word (see Plate 17).

Even in the late 1630s the best means which people had of finding out what was happening at court or in Europe was to go to London, seek out the Royal Exchange, and ask a diplomat or a merchant. By the late 1670s, however, they could go to any one of over a hundred coffee houses in the capital, or the scores of others in towns throughout the country, and read all about such things for themselves in a newsletter or in the *Gazette*. And at the same time they might also read or hear any number of more uncensored and polemical pamphlets or libels which covered the coffee seller's tables and walls. The implications of this, in terms of levels of general awareness, political sophistication, and popular involvement in the affairs of the realm, were enormous. Throughout this period, the governors of Church and State repeatedly warned 'the vulgar' against busying their heads with talk of politics, for such things were above them and none of their concern. By the end of the seventeenth century such warnings were being drowned out by a chorus of people reading aloud, asking for news, and expressing opinion.

# Conclusion

A NOW well-established consensus about the evolution of English society in the sixteenth and seventeenth centuries has emerged, which runs broadly as follows. Thanks to a cluster of developments, which include substantial demographic growth, a much brisker land market after the dissolution of the monasteries, consequent price inflation, and commercialization of the economy at every level, the social order became much more variegated and complex in this period. In particular, there grew a significantly larger and more self-conscious middle rank, comprising market-oriented farmers, those engaged in services and the professions, merchants, and retailers. As a result, the gulf between the incomes, wealth, and lifestyles of these 'middling sorts of people' and the mass of labouring poor beneath them became palpably more pronounced than ever before.

Coincidentally, these processes of economic and social change were underscored by a number of cultural and intellectual developments. The Reformation, it is often claimed, introduced a Protestant religion which, particularly in its most Calvinistic forms, had greater purchase amongst the bible-reading middling ranks than it did with the majority of the illiterate population. At the same time, considerable expansion in formal education, which tended to be socially selective in its reach, drove a qualitative wedge between the literate, bookish world of the upper and middle orders and the residual oral culture of the majority. 'Literacy' and 'illiteracy', therefore, became one of the great cleavages which underpinned social differences and defined social relations.

This rather dichotomous view, of the dominant literate sphere of the minority and the traditional oral environment of the masses, has a long history. The conceptual construction of a binary opposition between 'oral' and 'written' tradition goes back to the early modern period itself and to the ideological debates occasioned by the Reformation. From the beginning, and for centuries thereafter, Protestant apologists would identify an essential difference between their Church and that of Rome around this issue. Whereas the Catholics, it was insisted, based their doctrine on the 'unwritten traditions' of man, as elaborated by church fathers over the centuries, the Reformed faith claimed to derive its authority solely from the written word of God, as contained in the Scriptures.[1] When the study of popular culture, or 'popular antiquities', first began in the later eighteenth century, the peculiar customs and beliefs of the common people were conceived of within this framework, as survivals from 'the smoking ruins of popery' curiously preserved in oral tradition. Because the masses were illiterate, they had perpetuated rites and ceremonies which had long been 'erazed by public authority from the written word' and from the lives of those with access to it. The folkloric and antiquarian imagination of the nineteenth century did much to confirm and elaborate this view which sat well with the expectations and perceptions of the urban middle classes. Its legacy dominates perceptions of the period even today.[2]

Indeed, the great flowering of research into social history over the last generation has tended to confirm this conception at every point. In demonstrating the significant growth in the number of schools during the sixteenth and seventeenth centuries, for example, it has emphasized the partial nature of formal education. Institutions of higher learning, such as the grammar schools, naturally drew their pupils from the upper and mid-dling ranks and excluded girls. But even petty schools and other places of primary instruction were more open to the children whose parents could afford to be without their labour and presented more of an opportunity for sons than for daughters. In tandem with this, research into literacy levels has ratified this picture of social and gender differences. By calculating the percentage of men and women capable of writing their name on a document, as opposed merely to making a mark, figures for 'literacy' have been computed, based on the assumption that signing betrays a relatively fluent reader. The resulting statistics appear to indicate, once again, how much more likely to be literate were the upper and middling ranks than the lower orders, and the great advantage which urban dwellers had over rural, and men over women, in this respect.[3]

---

[1] This opinion can be followed in Alexander Alane, *Of the Auctorite of the Word of God against the Bisshop of London* (Strassburg, 1544?); Richard Hooker, *Of the Laws of Ecclesiastical Polity*, ed. A. S. McGrade (Cambridge, 1989), 110–11; BL, Harleian MS, 6839, fos. 161–4; Joseph Hall, *The Olde Religion* (London, 1628), 156–8, 167–8; John Evelyn, *The History of Religion*, ed. R. M. Evanson (2 vols., London, 1850), i. 437–40, ii. 273–7; John Tillotson, *The Rule of Faith* (London, 1666); BL, Additional MS, 25279.

[2] John Brand, *Observations on Popular Antiquities* (Newcastle, 1777), iv; and see pp. 6–8 above.

[3] See the discussion and references cited on pp. 16–19 above.

Thus, the latest scholarship has demonstrated the educationally under-privileged status of the lower orders in general and of women in particular, and the figures for literacy levels appear to endorse the impression that such groups were on the fringes of, or altogether outside, literate culture. As a result, there has been little basis upon which to contradict the long-held impression that the majority of people, especially in rural areas, had only oblique contact with the written word either in manuscript or print. Even in the nineteenth century, agricultural labourers and their families are often depicted as still operating in a world little touched by reading matter and literary influences. Hardy's image of Mrs Durbeyfield with her 'lumber of superstitions, folk-lore, dialect, and orally transmitted ballads' lingers on as an abiding impression of country folk even in the late Victorian period.[4]

But the assumptions which underpin all of these findings are essentially misplaced. As a guide to basic literacy levels, the composition of educational establishments is of only partial relevance. The medieval evidence indicates that the majority of elementary instruction went on within the home during the Middle Ages and had little to do with formal institutions.[5] Although one of the distinguishing features of the sixteenth and seventeenth centuries was the considerable growth in the number of local and parochial schools, the point remains valid for the early modern period. Basic reading ability continued to be learned from mothers or other family members within the domestic environment. Girls acquired the skill as well as boys and, indeed, it was part of the preparation for their own educative duties as future raisers of children.

It follows from this that the ability to write a signature on a document is no reliable guide to reading ability at this time. This method of calculating 'literacy' was first proposed in the nineteenth century, by which time elementary education was becoming widespread, the technology associated with writing had changed significantly, and there was a much closer correlation between the ability to sign and the ability to read. But in the medieval and early modern periods there was no such connection between these skills, which remained quite separate. In early modern England, most people were able to achieve competence in understanding the vernacular language in print without ever having the opportunity, or the need, to wield a pen. The statistics which we have for 'literacy' levels are thus huge underestimates of basic reading ability in general, and

---

[4] See pp. 7–8 above.

[5] M. T. Clanchy, *From Memory to Written Record: England, 1066–1307* (2nd edn., Oxford, 1993), 15–16.

female capability in particular.[6] The remarks of contemporaries about 'the illiterate', or 'the illiterate multitude' must be treated with a high degree of caution. To many commentators, 'illiteracy' referred to the inability to read Latin, while it was also a term frequently levelled at those who could not write. Equally, it could apply to people who were unable to decipher one of the various forms of handwriting then in use, or else it might simply denote verbal infelicity. It does not necessarily imply anything about the ability to understand a simple printed text in English, as it would today. Significantly, an outsider, the French emigré, Misson, observed at the end of the seventeenth century that 'there is hardly the meanest peasant in England but what can read'.[7]

Thus the dichotomy between the 'literate' and the 'illiterate', so often invoked by contemporaries and now used by historians as a basis upon which to construct models of social and cultural difference, is largely misleading. It does not need to be emphasised, of course, that people operated on vastly different levels of intellectual sophistication in this as in any other society, and there was enormous variety both in types of reading matter and in levels of comprehension. But the issue of basic reading ability is not, by this period, the crucial divide.

Early modern England was, therefore, a much more 'literate' environment than has ever been fully appreciated. It was also a much more 'literary' one than has yet been generally accepted. The fact that something like four million broadside ballads were produced in the second half of the sixteenth century alone, and that an Elizabethan preacher could find them in the cottages of poor husbandmen in rural Suffolk, gives some idea of just how ubiquitous the printed page was, even in the Tudor period.[8] So far as the seventeenth century is concerned, the full extent of the quantity and distribution of cheap printed material has yet to be thoroughly established. It is certain, however, that given the continued growth in broadside ballad output, the advent of the chapbook and the newsbook, the development of the political pamphlet, and the ever greater use of the presses for all manner of ephemeral publication, the amount of

---

[6] See the comments in Margaret Spufford, 'First Steps in Literacy: The Reading and Writing Experiences of the Humblest Seventeenth-Century Spiritual Autobiographers', *Social History*, 4 (1979), 414; T. C. Smout, 'Born Again in Cambuslang: New Evidence on Popular Religion and Literacy in Eighteenth-Century Scotland', *Past and Present*, 97 (1982), 121–3; J. Hoeppner Moran, 'Literacy and Education in Northern England, 1350–1550: A Methodological Inquiry', *Northern History*, 17 (1981), 8; Keith Thomas, 'The Meaning of Literacy in Early Modern England', in Gerd Baumann (ed.), *The Written Word: Literacy in Transition* (Oxford, 1986), 102–3.

[7] *M. Misson's Memoirs and Observations in his Travels over England. With some Account of Scotland and Ireland*, trans. John Ozell (London, 1719), 17.

[8] Tessa Watt, *Cheap Print and Popular Piety, 1550–1640* (Cambridge, 1991), 11–12.

literature in circulation expanded exponentially. The catalogue of the
stationer, George Thomason, suggests the dimensions of just one
aspect of this production in London during the extraordinary decades of
mid-century.[9]

What impresses the historian of the oral traditions of this period,
which provide such vivid insight into the world view of the majority, is the
extent to which they were indebted to the written word, either very
directly or else through innumerable intermediaries. Long before 1500,
centuries of manuscript circulation, as well as preaching, minstrelsy, and
drama, had thoroughly infused the vernacular repertoire with literary
influences. Thereafter, however, the immense proliferation of both the
handwritten and printed word would determine fundamentally the
nature of popular culture in all its dimensions. One of the fascinating and
defining characteristics of English society in the early modern period is
the way in which oral, scribal, and printed media fed in and out of each
other as part of a dynamic process of reciprocal interaction and mutual
infusion.

In almost every aspect of contemporary culture, the permeation of the
popular vernacular stock by learned and literary sources is evident. The
very language itself, for example, was transformed as a consequence of
the exchange of ideas and texts across Europe during the Renaissance.
The huge influx of 'loan words' considerably changed the nature of both
written and spoken English. It also helped to throw into relief the many
local languages which were slower to adapt than that of London and the
court and were coming to be known as 'dialects' by the third quarter of
the sixteenth century. In the long run, however, no one was immune from
the influence of linguistic change and the hegemony of 'received' pronunciation and authorized vocabulary came to be felt, to a greater or less
extent, in every part of the country and among all social groups.

Equally, the publication of classical dicta and Latin tags in their thousands demonstrates the adoption and naturalization of material fed into
common circulation by the printing press. To the *Adages* of Erasmus, in
particular, we owe hundreds of the still familiar clichés of daily discourse.
The longevity of much proverbial wisdom, its currency across many
nations, and its perpetuation in written tradition as well as spoken,

---

[9] *Catalogue of the Pamphlets, Books, Newspapers, and Manuscripts Relating to the Civil War, the
Commonwealth, and Restoration, Collected by George Thomason, 1640–1661* (2 vols., London, 1908). For
some suggestive works, see Bernard Capp, *Astrology and the Popular Press: English Almanacs
1500–1800* (London, 1979); Margaret Spufford, *Small Books and Pleasant Histories: Popular Fiction and
its Readership in Seventeenth-Century England* (London, 1981); Antony Griffiths, *The Print in Stuart
Britain 1603–1689* (London, 1998).

learned discourse as well as popular, evidences a certain universality in moral values, prescribed codes of conduct, and human aspirations. At the same time, however, proverbs can seem inconsistent and contradictory unless set in context. Only from the specific circumstances in which they are used do they derive their meaning and when these are established it becomes clear that they could be employed in wholly different ways and have very different meanings within society.

The impact of cheap print on popular culture can be observed very clearly in the influence which it had on other staple products of oral tradition. The lullabies which parents and nurses sang to their charges, the verses which children chanted in the streets, and much edification and entertainment delivered around the winter evening fireside came to be informed and determined by the broadsides and pamphlets which rolled from the presses. Many of the jokes, riddles, and stories told in this period seeped into circulation via the printed page. About one-quarter of the nursery rhymes still in common use today are believed to date from the seventeenth century, demonstrating the way in which ballads and songs produced ostensibly for adult audiences were appropriated and adapted by the young and learned by rote.

Even in the anecdotes and remembrances of local folklore the influence of print is detectable. So much of what Victorian collectors would later seize upon as the products of an unmediated oral tradition of the people turns out to derive from the print culture of the early modern period. That so many artefacts and monuments around the country came to be given some connection with King Arthur, for example, can be directly attributed to the cult status which the British hero achieved under the Tudor regime and to the dissemination of his legend in story and song, drama and ritual. Equally, it was in the wake of the widespread printing of the *Gest of Robyn Hode*, and later of the many broadside ballads celebrating the deeds of the famous outlaw, that place names and landmarks nationwide were suddenly invented to bask in his glory by association. The significant developments in antiquarian writings over these two centuries added to more obviously popular works in providing the source of learned fictions which were absorbed into parochial tradition. There they would remain, eventually to be dismissed, when scholarly opinion no longer endorsed them, as 'vulgar errors'.

In other spheres, too, the written word was restructuring the nature of spoken tradition and communication. In many areas of economic, social, and cultural life, forms of expression which had always remained largely unwritten were coming to be enshrined in text and, in turn, the contents of these texts passed back into the oral realm. The transmuting of local customs, from series of conventions governed by practice and experience into sets of regulations locked in binding agreements, provides a graphic example of this process at work. Custom had always been a supremely oral phenomenon, something which almost by definition evaded transcription. That so many manors and boroughs, liberties and franchises had seen their customs documented by the end of the seventeenth century is evidence of a significant transition from memory to record within local society. The codification of what amounted to ritual ways of living and ancient systems of remembering put an end to one of the last purely oral dimensions of economic life in England.

It might also be imagined that there were few aspects of contemporary communication less likely to be committed to paper than the kind of doggerel verses, crude in form, crude in content, which people extemporized in their alehouses for the purpose of broadcasting neighbourhood gossip or humiliating opponents. Even this most scurrilous aspect of parish-pump politics, however, often took on a literary dimension. Although gaining access to the materials and the scribal services necessary to make copies of such compositions could be difficult, the effort was clearly considered to be worthwhile. The perceived utility of conveying something as fundamentally oral as a short song or squib about a local individual in textual form demonstrates just how deeply the written word and its varied uses had entered into popular consciousness. At the same time, it suggests, even in the provincial communities of the early seventeenth century, an audience which was sufficiently capable of reading crabbed handwriting to justify the effort of publicity through this means. Few phenomena demonstrate so powerfully just what a literary environment England had become by this time.

Scurrilous verse and scandalous gossip about parochial figures was not the only kind of topical comment to find its way into writing. News of much wider import and concerning national leaders also circulated throughout local society in the form of manuscript 'libels', even in the early sixteenth century. Indeed, many of the wildest rumours and most outrageous stories which periodically convulsed the nation over the course of these two centuries were the products of written prophecies, private missives, or professional newsletters, rather than merely the fruits of the oral grapevine. In these circumstances, as in others, writing did not undermine circulation by word of mouth, but rather fuelled and elaborated it. By the mid-seventeenth century such material was also appearing in print in unprecedented quantities, fanning the flames of misinformation and raising the levels of popular panic. But print also augmented and eventually expanded the manuscript tradition of critical comment aimed at governments and their ministers. Printed attacks on the person of the monarch, ridicule of royal officials, and opposition to the policies of the crown all provided fodder for the seditious conversations of people at large. This was to have the profoundest of political consequences and would ultimately transform the nature of public opinion in England.

The conclusion to be drawn from all of this evidence is that the written word, in both manuscript and print, penetrated to a far deeper level in society and circulated in much greater quantities than was once imagined. This was both cause and effect of the fact that many more people than has ever been suspected could read it to some degree for themselves. Ironically, by approaching early modern England from the perspective of its oral culture, this book has helped to demonstrate just what a literate and textually orientated society it was.

# BIBLIOGRAPHY

MANUSCRIPT SOURCES

*Bodleian Library, Oxford*

*Ashmole MS*

36–7 (Verses of Scotch bagpiper)
48 (Ballad book of Richard Sheale, mid-16th cent.)
244 (Simon Forman, 'Of Giantes', 1610)
784 (Ashmole's 'Journey into the Fens 1657')
816 (Verses containing technical terms of Derbyshire miners)
1788 (Aubrey's account of Dee)

*Aubrey MS*

1 ('The Naturall Historie of Wiltshire, 1685. Part I')
2 ('The Naturall Historie of Wiltshire, 1685. Part II')
3 ('Hypomnemata Antiquaria. An Essay towards the Description of the North Division of Wiltshire')
5 ('An Interpretation of Villare Anglicanum')

*Sancroft MS*

130 (Commonplace book of William Sancroft)

*Western MS*

Eng. Lang. e. 4. (Samuel Pegge, 'Alphabet of Kenticisms', 'Derbycisms', 'Proverbs and Proverbial Sayings', 'A Glossary explaining certain Oaths and Exclamations')
Eng. Lang. e. 6. (Andrew Clark, 'Notes of English words quoted as found in MSS. or in conversation with country-folks', 1912)
Welsh f. 4. (Collection of proverbial sentences)
Willis 2 (Antiquities collected by Brown Willis of Bucks)

*British Library, London*

*Additional MS*

6027 (fos. 82–83, John Norden, Survey of Ottery St Mary, Devon, 1617)
6223 (F[rancis] Taverner, 'The History and Antiquities of Hexton, in the County of Hertford', transcribed with additions by E[dward] Steele, 1713)
10309 ('Characters and Poems', c.1630)
15917 (Thomas Stavely, 'The History, and Antiquitys, of the Ancient Town, and once Citty of Leicester', 1679)

19990 ('A Brief Collection of the Antiquities of the Castell and Towne of Dover')

22623 (George Purefoy, 'The Description of Mylford Haven', 1595)

23963 ('A Description of the Towne of Dunwich', 1590)

24539 (Joseph Hunter, 'An Alphabetical Catalogue of . . . the Vernacular Language of Hallamshire', 1821)

24891 (Thomas Rowleie, 'A Discorse on Brystowe' transcribed with additions by Thomas Chatterton)

25279 (F.S., 'Scripture and Tradition')

27879 (Ballad book owned by Thomas Percy)

28013 (Proverbs collected by Henry Oxenden)

28640 (Commonplace book of the Revd John Rous)

31853 (John Norden, 'A C'horographicall Description', 1595)

32530 (Roger North, 'Of Etimology')

34141 (Ralph Bigland, 'Collections for Lincolnshire', 1780s)

38599 (Commonplace book of the Shanne Family of Methley, co. York)

38855 (Hodgkin Papers, vol. x. 'Illustrations of Social History, 1573–1843')

42508 (John Norden, Surveys of Hertfordshire manors, 1603)

*Cottonian MS*

Julius F. VI. (Historical and Topographical Collections, temp. Eliz. I and Jas. I)

*Egerton MS*

2223 (Customary of Taunton and Taunton Dean, Somerset, 1647)

2231 (Early 19th-cent. copies of John Aubrey's letters, from Bodleian originals)

2578 (Sir Thomas Widdrington, 'Analecta Eboracensia: Or some Remayns of the Auncient City of York', 1670s?)

2868 (James Raine, 'Glossary of the Northumbrian Dialect', begun 1854)

*Harleian MS*

965 (Richard Symonds, 'Notes on Churches in the Counties of Oxfordshire, Worcestershire and Berkshire', 1644)

1026 (Memorandum Book of Justinian Pagitt, lawyer, c.1633)

2118 ('Yorkshire Pedegrees', partly by the third Randle Holme, temp. Chas. I)

2119 ('Cheshire Pedegrees', partly by the third Randle Holme, temp. Chas. I)

2127 (Collection of 'Songs and Sonnets', 17th cent.)

6726 (Collections Relating to Herefordshire, 1655)

6766 (fos. 192–212, Silas Taylor, 'The History of the County of Hereford')

6768 (Extracts from John Layer's MS Description of Cambridgeshire, c.1639)

6829 ('Antiquities of the County of Lincoln')

6839 (Fragment of Discourse concerning Tradition, early 17th cent.)

6866 (fos. 73–81, 'A Relation of a Conference', at York House in 1626)

7017 (fos. 83–132, 'Fragments of Elegancies, Proverbs, Formulaic Form of Speaking')

(fos. 241–49, 'A Geographicall Descritpion of Brecknockshire')

(fos. 251–59, 'The History of Brecknock')

*Lansdowne MS*

210 (fo. 80ᵛ, 'The saying of old husbend men', temp. Mary Tudor)

231 (John Aubrey, 'Remains of Gentilisme and Judaisme', 1687–9)

620 ('Reports of the Starr-Chamber Cases. From Pasch. I, Car. 1 to Hill. 3, Car. 1 inclusive')

639 (Isaac Cotton, 'The Course and Manner of Prosecucon of Causes in the Highe Court of Starchamber', 1622)

674 (Notebook of Thomas Davies, 1618–30)

701 (Commonplace book, 17th cent.)

890 (Abraham de la Pryme, 'The History, Antiquities, and Descriptions of the Town and County of Kingston upon Hull')

896 (Collections chiefly relating to Beverley, East Riding)

897 (Abraham de la Pryme, 'The History and Antiquities of the Town and Parish of Hatfield near Doncaster in Yorkshire')

898 (fos. 42–48, Abraham de la Pryme's account of Doncaster)

1033 (White Kennett, 'Etymological Collections of English Words and Provincial Expressions')

1039 (White Kennett, 'History of Customs')

*Sloane MS*

241 (Sir Robert Cotton, 'A Brief Description of the World. A Description of England. The Names and Arms of all the Nobility . . .')

384 (Collection of Jests and Witty Sayings, 17th cent)

542 (Miscellaneous Poems)

1322 (Robert Hegge, 'The Legend of St Cuthbert with the Antiquities of the Church of Durham', 1628?)

1489 (Collection of Jests and Anecdotes, 1627)

1899 (Thomas Browne, 'Account of his Journey into Kent with Dr Plot, 1693')

1911–1913 (fos. 195–7, continuation of above)

2628 (Commonplace book, early 17th cent.)

2789 (fos. 2–7, 'Memorandum of a tour through the Western Counties, temp. Chas. II)

3111 (fo. 2ʳ, Rhymes for a widow to recover her lands, 17th cent.)

### Cambridgeshire Record Office, Cambridge

126/M88, M89, M90 (Notes on disputes at Whittlesey, temp. Chas. I)

258/M22 (Notes on disputes at Over, 16th and 17th cent)

399/E6 (Copy of composition between lord and tenants of Chesterton, 1577)

L3/17/3 (Copy of composition between lord and tenants of Milton, 1591)

P109/28/4, 28/5, 28/6 (Notes on disputes at Littleport, 17th cent)

### Cambridge University Library

Ely Diocesan Records
B/2/20 (Office Act Book, 1600–6)

B/2/21 (Office Act Book, 1600–6)
B/2/24 (Office Act Book, 1606–7)

*Cumbria Record Office, Carlisle*

D Lons/W1/14 (Sir John Lowther's Memorandum Book, 1677–89)

*Edinburgh University Library*

*Lang MS*

La. III. 467 (John Maxwell, commonplace book, 1580s)
La. III. 545 (Robert Kirk, 'Sermons, Conferences, Men's Opinions of the Late
   Transactions, with a Description of London, ann. 1689')

*Essex Record Office, Chelmsford*

Typescript Calendar of Essex Session Rolls, 1536–1714 (26 vols.)

*Folger Shakespeare Library, Washington DC*

Va. 308 ('A Lancashire Tale'; 'A Yorkshire Tale'; 'Clavis')

*Hampshire Record Office, Winchester*

44M69/G3/159 (John Newbolt, 'Report on Counterfeiters', 1615)

*Harvard University, Houghton Library*

fMS. Eng. 1084 ('Camera Stellata: Reportes of the Starrchamber, Pasche Primo
   Caroli Regis')

*Harvard University, Law School Library*

LMS. 1128 ('Reports of Cases in the Star Chamber during the Reign of K. Charles I')

*Huntington Library, San Marino, California*

*Ellesmere MS*

233 (Lord Ellesmere v. the copyholders of Great Gaddesdon)
1145 (George Owen, 'The Description of Milford Haven', 1595)
2728 (Hole v. Williams et al., 1607)
2733 (Earl of Lincoln v. Dymoke et al.)
2739 (Ellesmere's notes on 'scandalum magnatum')
2740 ('Scandals with their sentences')
5956 (Lambe v. Wheatley et al., 1607)

*Hastings MS*

Legal Box 5 (9) (Pestell v. Johnson, *c.*1632)

## Magdalen College Library, Oxford

I. 7. 21 (MS notes by Dr J. Cotton in John Ray, *A Collection of English Words* (2nd edn., London, 1691))

## Nottinghamshire Record Office, Nottingham

M461–M463 ('Transcriptions of Proceedings of the Court of the Archdeaconry of Nottingham: 1565–1675', 3 vols.)

## Nottingham University Library

Southwell Archdeaconry Records

LB 220 (Depositions, 1600–5)
LB 221 (Depositions, 1606–10)
LB 222 (Depositions, 1611–15)
LB 223 (Depositions, 1616–20)
LB 224 (Depositions, 1621–5)
LB 225 (Depositions, 1626–8, 1630)

## Oxfordshire Record Office, Oxford

Oxford Diocesan Papers

c. 22 (Deposition Book, Unidentified Court, 1592–3)
c. 23 (Deposition Book, Unidentified Court, 1594–6)
c. 24 (Deposition Book, Vicar General's Court, 1603–6)
c. 25 (Deposition Book, Unidentified Court, 1609–16)
d. 16 (Deposition Book, Vicar General's Court, 1589–93)

## Public Record Office, London

ASSI35/1–67 (Home Circuit Assizes, Indictments, 1558–1625)
ASSI45/1–26 (Northern Circuit Assizes, Depositions, 1613–1760)
PL27/1 (Palatinate of Lancaster, Depositions, 1663–90)
E126/1–8 (Court of Exchequer, Books of Decrees, James I to Charles II)
E134 (Court of Exchequer, Depositions by Commission, Elizabeth I to James II)
STAC8 (Court of Star Chamber Proceedings, James I)
SP12 (State Papers Domestic, Elizabeth I)
SP14 (State Papers Domestic, James I)
SP15 (State Papers Domestic, Addenda, Elizabeth I and James I)
SP16 (State Papers Domestic, Charles I)
SP18 (State Papers Domestic, Interregnum, 1649–60)
SP29 (State Papers Domestic, Charles II)

*Wren Library, Trinity College, Cambridge*

Adv. d. 1. 7 (Interleaved MS notes, perhaps by John Ray or else by Jacob (James) Duport, in a copy of John Ray, *A Collection of English Proverbs* (Cambridge, 1670))

PRINTED PRIMARY SOURCES

*The Acts of the High Commission Court within the Diocese of Durham*, ed. W. H. D. Longstaffe (Surtees Society, 34, Durham, 1858).

*Acts of the Privy Council of England, 1542–1631* (46 vols., London, 1890–1964).

ADAMS, THOMAS, *The Workes of Tho: Adams* (London, 1629).

—— *A Commentary or, Exposition upon the Divine Second Epistle Generall, Written by the Blessed Apostle St. Peter* (London, 1633).

ADY, THOMAS, *A Perfect Discovery of Witches* (London, 1661).

AIKIN, JOHN, *A Description of the Country from Thirty to Forty Miles Round Manchester* (London, 1795).

ALANE, ALEXANDER, *Of the Auctorite of the Word of God against the Bisshop of London* (Strassburg, 1544?).

*The Antiquarian Repertory: A Miscellany Intended to Preserve and Illustrate Several Valuable Remains of Old Times*, ed. Francis Grose (4 vols., London, 1775–84).

*The Archdeacon's Court: Liber Actorum, 1584*, ed. E. R. C. Brinkworth (2 vols., Oxfordshire Record Society, 23–4, Oxford, 1942–6).

ASCHAM, ROGER, *Toxophilus: The Schole of Shootinge* (London, 1545).

—— *The Scholemaster* (London, 1570).

ASHMOLE, ELIAS, *Elias Ashmole (1617–1692): His Autobiographical and Historical Notes, his Correspondence, and other Contemporary Sources Relating to his Life and Work*, ed. C. H. Josten (Oxford, 1966).

ATKYNS, SIR ROBERT, *The Ancient and Present State of Glocestershire* (2nd edn., London, 1768).

AUBREY, JOHN, *The Natural History and Antiquities of the County of Surrey: Begun in the Year 1673* (5 vols., London, 1718–19).

—— *The Natural History of Wiltshire*, ed. John Britton (London, 1847).

—— *Wiltshire: The Topographical Collections of John Aubrey, F.R.S., A.D. 1659–70*, ed. J. E. Jackson (Devizes, 1862).

—— *Brief Lives*, ed. Andrew Clark (2 vols., Oxford, 1898).

—— *John Aubrey: Three Prose Works*, ed. John Buchanan-Brown (Fontwell, 1972).

—— *Aubrey on Education*, ed. J. E. Stephens (London, 1972).

—— *Monumenta Britannica*, ed. John Fowles and Rodney Legg (Sherborne, 1980–2).

B., R., *Adagia Scotica, or A Collection of Scotch Proverbs and Proverbial Phrases* (London, 1668).

BACON, FRANCIS, *The Works of Francis Bacon*, ed. James Spedding, Robert Leslie Ellis, and Douglas Denon Heath (7 vols., London, 1857–9).

BACON, NATHANIELL, *The Annalls of Ipswiche: The Lawes, Customes and Government of the Same*, ed. William H. Richardson (Ipswich, 1884).

*The Bagford Ballads*, ed. J. W. Ebsworth (Ballad Society, Hertford, 1878).

BAILEY, NATHAN, *Universal Etymological English Dictionary* (London, 1721).

BALDWYN, WILLIAM, *A Treatise of Morall Phylosophie, Contaynyng the Sayinges of the Wyse* (London, 1547).

*Ballads from Manuscripts*, ed. F. J. Furnivall (2 vols., London, 1868–73).

BAMFORD, SAMUEL, *Early Days* (London, 1849).

BARCLAY, ALEXANDER, *The Ship of Fools*, ed. T. H. Jamieson (2 vols., Edinburgh, 1874).

BARET, JOHN, *An Alvearie or Triple Dictionarie, in Englishe, Latin, and French* (London, 1573).

BASKERVILLE, THOMAS, 'Thomas Baskerville's Journeys in England, Temp. Car. II', in Historical Manuscripts Commission, *Thirteenth Report, Appendix, Part II* (London, 1893), 263–314.

BAX, RICHARD, 'Notes and Extracts from the Account-Book of Richard Bax, a Surrey Yeoman (kept between 1648–1662)', ed. Alfred Ridley Bax, in G. L. Apperson (ed.), *Gleanings after Time* (London, 1907), 205–21.

BAXTER, RICHARD, *Gildas Salvianus; The Reformed Pastor* (London, 1656).

—— *The Poor Man's Family Book* (London, 1674).

—— *The Certainty of the Worlds of Spirits* (London, 1691).

—— 'The Reverend Richard Baxter's Last Treatise', ed. Frederick J. Powicke, *Bulletin of the John Rylands Library*, 10 (1926), 163–218.

—— *The Autobiography of Richard Baxter*, ed. N. H. Keeble (Everyman edn., London, 1985).

BEDWELL, WILHELM, *A Brief Description of the Towne of Tottenham Highcrosse in Middlesex* (London, 1631).

BEST, HENRY, *The Farming and Memorandum Books of Henry Best of Elmswell, 1642*, ed. Donald Woodward (British Academy, Records of Social and Economic History, new ser., 8, London, 1984).

BEWICK, THOMAS, *A Memoir of Thomas Bewick Written by Himself*, ed. Iain Bain (Oxford, 1975).

*Bishop Percy's Folio Manuscript*, ed. J. W. Hales and F. J. Furnivall (3 vols., London, 1867–8).

BLACKSTONE, SIR WILLIAM, *Commentaries on the Laws of England* (4 vols., London, 1765–9).

BLAU, ROBERT, *Libamina Junioribus Philologis Degustanda, or the Locutions of the Latine Tongue* (Edinburgh, 1702).

BLOMEFIELD, FRANCIS, and PARKIN, CHARLES, *An Essay towards a Topographical History of the County of Norfolk* (5 vols., Fersfield, 1739–75).

BLOUNT, THOMAS, *The Academie of Eloquence* (London, 1654).

—— *Glossographia: Or a Dictionary Interpreting all such Hard Words* (London, 1656).

—— *Fragmenta Antiquitatis: Antient Tenures of Land, and Jocular Customs of some Mannors* (London, 1679).

BOETHIUS, HECTOR, *The Hystory and Chroniklis of Scotland* (Edinburgh, 1540?).

*The Booke of Merrie Riddles* (London, 1617).

*A Booke of Merrie Riddles* (London, 1631).

*Books of Examinations and Depositions, 1570–1594*, ed. G. H. Hamilton and E. R. Aubrey (Southampton Record Society, Southampton, 1914).

BORDE, ANDREW, *Hereafter foloweth a Compendyous Regyment or a Dyetary of Helth, made in Mou[n]tpyllier* (London, 1542).

—— *The Fyrst Boke of the Introduction of Knowledge* (1542; London, 1555?).

BOSWELL, JAMES, *The Life of Samuel Johnson* (2 vols., Everyman edn., 1906).

BOURNE, HENRY, *Antiquitates Vulgares; Or, the Antiquities of the Common People* (Newcastle, 1725).

—— *The History of Newcastle upon Tyne* (Newcastle, 1736).

BOVET, RICHARD, *Pandaemonium, or the Devil's Cloyster* (London, 1684).

BOWND, NICHOLAS, *The Doctrine of the Sabbath Plainely Layde Forth* (London, 1595).

BOYLE, ROBERT, *The Works of the Honourable Robert Boyle*, ed. Thomas Birch (6 vols., London, 1772).

BRAND, JOHN, *Observations on Popular Antiquities* (Newcastle, 1777).

—— *Observations on the Popular Antiquities of Great Britain*, ed. Sir Henry Ellis (3 vols., London, 1849).

—— *The History and Antiquities of the Town and County of the Town of Newcastle upon Tyne* (2 vols., London, 1789).

BRATHWAIT, RICHARD, *Whimzies: Or, a New Cast of Characters* (London, 1631).

BRERETON, SIR WILLIAM, *Travels in Holland, the United Provinces, England, Scotland and Ireland, 1634–1635*, ed. Edward Hawkins (Chetham Society, 1, London, 1844).

BRETON, NICHOLAS, *The Works in Verse and Prose of Nicholas Breton*, ed. A. B. Grosart (2 vols., Edinburgh, 1879).

BRINSLEY, JOHN, *Ludus Literarius: Or, The Grammar Schoole* (London, 1612).

—— *Pueriles Confabulatiunculae: Or Childrens Dialogues* (London, 1617).

Broadside Ballad Collections, Bodleian Library, Oxford.

BROME, JAMES, *Travels over England, Scotland and Wales* (London, 1700).

BROWNE, EDWARD, 'Journal of a Tour in Derbyshire', in *Sir Thomas Browne's Works*, ed. Simon Wilkin (4 vols., London, 1835–6), i. 22–42.

BROWNE, THOMAS, *The Works of Sir Thomas Browne*, ed. Geoffrey Keynes (4 vols., London, 1928; repr. 1964).

BRYSKETT, LODOWICK, *A Discovrse of Civill Life* (London, 1606).

BUCKINGHAM, DUKE OF, *Poems and Songs Relating to George Villiers, Duke of Buckingham*, ed. F. W. Fairholt (Percy Society, 29, London, 1850).

BULLEIN, WILLIAM, *A Dialogue bothe Pleasaunt and Pietifull wherein is a Godlie Regiment against the Fever Pestilence* (London, 1564).

BULLOKAR, JOHN, *An English Expositor* (London, 1616).

BULLOKAR, WILLIAM, *Bullokars Booke at Large, for the Amendment of Orthographie for English Speech* (London, 1580).

BUNYAN, JOHN, *The Pilgrim's Progress*, ed. J. B. Wharey and Roger Sharrock (Oxford, 1960).

—— *Grace Abounding to the Chief of Sinners*, ed. Roger Sharrock (Oxford, 1962).

BURTON, HENRY, *A Divine Tragedy* (London, 1641).

BURTON, ROBERT, *The Anatomy of Melancholy*, ed. Holbrook Jackson (3 vols., Everyman edn., London, 1932).

BURTON, WILLIAM, *The Description of Leicester Shire* (London, 1622).

BUTCHER, RICHARD, *The Survey and Antiquitie of the Towne of Stamford, in the County of Lincolne* (London, 1646).

BUTLER, CHARLES, *The English Grammar* (Oxford, 1633).

BYNG, JOHN, *The Torrington Diaries*, ed. C. Bruyn Andrews (4 vols., London, 1970).

CAIUS, JOHN, *The Works of John Caius, M.D.*, ed. E. S. Roberts (Cambridge, 1912).

*Calendar of Assize Records*, ed. J. S. Cockburn (10 vols., London, 1975–82).

*Calendar of State Papers, Domestic Series, 1547–1704* (92 vols., London, 1856–1924).

CALTHROPE, CHARLES, *The Relation betweene the Lord of a Mannor and the Coppy-Holder his Tenant* (London, 1635).

CAMDEN, WILLIAM, *Remaines, Concerning Britaine* (2nd edn., London, 1614).

—— *Britannia*, ed. Edmund Gibson (London, 1695).

CAPELL, EDWARD, *Notes and Various Readings to Shakespeare* (3 vols., London, 1775).

CARE, HENRY, *The Tutor to True English* (London, 1687).

CAREW, RICHARD, *The Survey of Cornwall* (London, 1602).

—— 'The Excellencie of the English Tongue', in William Camden, *Remaines, Concerning Britaine* (2nd edn., London, 1614), 36–44.

CARMICHAELL, JAMES, *The James Carmichaell Collection of Proverbs in Scots*, ed. M. L. Anderson (Edinburgh, 1957).

CARTER, SAMUEL, *Lex Custumaria: Or, a Treatise of Copy-hold Estates* (2nd edn., London, 1701).

CASAUBON, MERIC, *A Treatise Proving Spirits, Witches and Supernatural Operations* (London, 1672).

[CASE, JOHN?], *The Praise of Mvsicke* (Oxford, 1586).

*Cavalier and Puritan: Ballads and Broadsides Illustrating the Period of the Great Rebellion 1640–1660*, ed. Hyder E. Rollins (New York, 1923).

CAWDREY, ROBERT, *A Table Alphabeticall* (London, 1604).

CAXTON, WILLIAM, *The Prologues and Epilogues of William Caxton*, ed. W. J. B. Crotch (Early English Text Society, orig. ser., 176, London, 1928).

CHAPMAN, GEORGE, *The Works of George Chapman: Plays*, ed. R. H. Shepherd (London, 1874).

CHAPPLE, WILLIAM, *A Review of Part of Risdon's Survey of Devon* (Exeter, 1785).

CHAUCER, GEOFFREY, *The Riverside Chaucer*, ed. Larry D. Benson (3rd edn., Boston, Mass., 1987).

CHAUNCY, SIR HENRY, *The Historical Antiquities of Hertfordshire* (London, 1700).

CHESTERFIELD, LORD, *The Letters of the Earl of Chesterfield to his Son* (2 vols., London, 1774).

CHILDREY, JOSHUA, *Britannia Baconica: Or, the Natural Rarities of England, Scotland, and Wales* (London, 1660).

*The City Law* (London, 1647).

CLARE, JOHN, *The Shepherd's Calendar*, ed. Eric Robinson and Geoffrey Summerfield (Oxford, 1964).

—— *John Clare's Autobiographical Writings*, ed. Eric Robinson (Oxford, 1983).

CLARKE, JOHN, *Paroemiologia Anglo-Latina in Usum Scholarum Concinnata* (London, 1639).

CLEMENT, FRANCIS, *The Petie Schole* (London, 1587).

COBBETT, WILLIAM, *Rural Rides* (2 vols., Everyman edn., London, n.d.).

*The Cobler of Caunterburie* (London, 1590).

COCKERAM, HENRY, *The English Dictionarie* (London, 1623).

CODRINGTON, ROBERT, *A Collection of Many Select, and Excellent Proverbs out of Several Languages* (London, 1672).

COE, WILLIAM, 'The Diary of William Coe of Mildenhall, Suffolk. A.D. 1680–1729', *East Anglian*, new ser., 11–12 (1906–8).

COGAN, THOMAS, *The Haven of Health* (London, 1612).

COKE, SIR EDWARD, *The Compleate Copy-Holder* (London, 1641).

COKER [JOHN], *A Survey of Dorsetshire* (London, 1732).

COLES, ELISHA, *The Compleat English Schoolmaster* (London, 1674).

—— *An English Dictionary* (London, 1676).

*A Collection of Curious Discourses Written by Eminent Antiquaries*, ed. Thomas Hearne (2nd edn., 2 vols., London, 1771).

*A Collection of Highland Rites and Customes Copied by Edward Lhuyd from the Manuscript of the Rev James Kirkwood (1650–1709) and Annotated by him with the Aid of the Rev John Beaton*, ed. J. L. Campbell (Folklore Society, Cambridge, 1975).

*A Collection of Letters Illustrative of the Progress of Science in England from the Reign of Queen Elizabeth to that of Charles II*, ed. J. O. Halliwell (London, 1841).

*A Collection of Pieces in the Dialect of Zummerzet*, ed. J. O. Halliwell (London, 1843).

COLLIER, JOHN, *The Miscellaneous Works of Tim Bobbin, Esq. Containing his View of the Lancashire Dialect* (London, 1775).

COMENIUS, JOHANN AMOS, *Orbis Sensualium Pictus*, trans. Charles Hoole (London, 1659).

'Common Rights at Cottenham and Stretham in Cambridgeshire', ed. W. Cunningham, in *Camden Miscellany*, xii (Camden Society, third ser., 18, London, 1910), 169–289.

*The Complaynt of Scotlande*, ed. J. A. H. Murray (Early English Text Society, extra ser., 17, London, 1872).

COOPER, ANTHONY ASHLEY, *Sensus Communis: An Essay on the Freedom of Wit and Humour* (London, 1709).

COOPER, CHRISTOPHER, *The English Teacher* (London, 1687).

COOPER, THOMAS, *Thesavrvs Lingvae Romanae et Britannicae* (London, 1565).

COOTE, EDMUND, *The English Schoole-Maister* (London, 1596).

CORNWALLIS, SIR WILLIAM, *Essayes*, ed. D. C. Allen (Baltimore, 1946).

CORYATE, THOMAS, *Coryats Crudities* (London, 1611).

COTGRAVE, JOHN, *The English Treasury of Wit and Language* (London, 1655).

COTGRAVE, RANDLE, *A Dictionarie of the French and English Tongves* (London, 1611).

COTTA, JOHN, *A Short Discoverie of the Unobserved Dangers of Severall Sorts of Ignorant and Unconsiderate Practisers of Physicke in England* (London, 1612).

*The Country-mans New Common-Wealth: Being an Exact Epitome of Many Witty Sentences, Pithy Sayings, Quaint Observations, both Divine and Morall* (London, 1647).

*The Court Rolls of the Manor of Wakefield from October 1639 to September 1640*, ed. C. M. Fraser and Kenneth Emsley (Yorkshire Archaeological Society, Leeds, 1977).

*The Court Rolls of the Manor of Wakefield from October 1664 to September 1665*, ed. C. M. Fraser and Kenneth Emsley (Yorkshire Archaeological Society, Leeds, 1986).

COVERDALE, MILES, *Goostly Psalmes and Spirituall Songes Drawen out of the Holy Scripture* (London, 1535?).

COWELL, JOHN, *The Interpreter: Or Booke Containing the Signification of Words* (Cambridge, 1607).

COWPER, WILLIAM, *The Poems of William Cowper*, ed. John D. Baird and Charles Ryskamp (2 vols., Oxford, 1980).

*Critical Essays of the Seventeenth Century*, ed. J. E. Spingarn (3 vols., Oxford, 1908).

CROMPTON, RICHARD, *Star Chamber Cases* (London, 1630).

CULLUM, SIR JOHN, *The History and Antiquities of Hawsted, and Hardwick, in the County of Suffolk* (2nd edn., London, 1813).

DAINES, SIMON, *Orthoepia Anglicana* (London, 1640).

DAVIES, JOHN, *The Complete Works of John Davies of Hereford*, ed. A. B. Grosart (2 vols., Edinburgh, 1878).

DAYE, ANGEL, *The English Secretorie* (London, 1586).

DEERING, CHARLES, *Nottingham Vetus et Nova: Or an Historical Account of the Ancient and Present State of the Town of Nottingham* (Nottingham, 1751).

DEFOE, DANIEL, *The Great Law of Subordination Consider'd* (London, 1724).

——— *A System of Magick; Or, a History of the Black Art* (London, 1727).

——— *A Tour thro' the Whole Island of Great Britain*, ed. G. D. H. Cole (London, 1927).

DEKKER, THOMAS, *Villanies Discouered by Lanthorne and Candle-light* (London, 1616).

DELAMOTHE G., *The Treasvre of the French Tovng* (London, 1592).

DELONEY, THOMAS, *The Gentle Craft* (London, 1637).

*The Demau[n]des Joyous* (London, 1511).

DENT, ARTHUR, *The Plaine Mans Path-way to Heauen* (London, 1601).

DENTON, JOHN, *An Accompt of the Most Considerable Estates and Families in the County of Cumberland*, ed. R. S. Ferguson (Cumberland and Westmorland Antiquarian and Archaeological Society, 2, Kendal, 1887).

*Depositions and Other Ecclesiastical Proceedings from the Courts of Durham, extending from 1311 to the Reign of Elizabeth*, ed. James Raine (Surtees Society, 21, London, 1845).

*Depositions from the Castle of York relating to offences committed in the Northern Counties in the Seventeenth Century*, ed. James Raine (Surtees Society, 40, Durham, 1861).

'Depositions taken before the Mayor and Aldermen of Norwich, 1549–1567', ed. Walter Rye, *Norfolk and Norwich Archaeological Society*, 2 (1905), 1–96.

[DEVEREUX, ROBERT], *The Wyll of the Deuyll, and Last Testament* (London, 1548?).

*The Dicts and Sayings of the Philosophers*, ed. Curt F. Buhler (Early English Text Society, orig. ser., 211, London, 1941).

*Dobsons Drie Bobbes: A Story of Sixteenth-Century Durham*, ed. E. A. Horsman (Oxford, 1955).

DOD, JOHN, *Old Mr Dod's Sayings* (London, 1667).

DODSWORTH, ROGER, *Yorkshire Church Notes, 1619–1631*, ed. J. W. Clay (Yorkshire Archaeological Society, record ser., 34, 1904).

DRAXE, THOMAS, *Bibliotheca Scholastica Instrvctissima* (London, 1616).

DRAYTON, MICHAEL, *The Works of Michael Drayton*, ed. J. William Hebel (5 vols., Oxford, 1931–41).

DRYDEN, JOHN, *Essays of John Dryden*, ed. W. P. Ker (2 vols., Oxford, 1900).

DUGDALE, SIR WILLIAM, *The Antiquities of Warwickshire* (London, 1656).

—— *The History of Imbanking and Drayning* (London, 1662).

DYCHE, THOMAS, *A Guide to the English Tongue in Two Parts* (London, 1707).

DYKES, OSWALD, *English Proverbs with Moral Reflexions* (2nd edn., London, 1709).

EACHARD, JOHN, *The Grounds and Occasions of the Contempt of the Clergy and Religion Enquired into* (London, 1670).

EARLE, JOHN, *Micro-cosmographie: Or, a Peece of the World Discovered; in Essayes and Characters* (London, 1628).

*Early Travellers in Scotland*, ed. P. Hume Brown (Edinburgh, 1891).

EGLISHAM, GEORGE, *The Forerunner of Revenge* (Franckfort, 1626).

*Elizabethan Critical Essays*, ed. G. Gregory Smith (2 vols., Oxford, 1904).

ELYOT, SIR THOMAS, *The Boke Named the Gouernour* (London, 1531).

—— *The Dictionary* (London, 1538).

*England as seen by Foreigners in the Days of Elizabeth and James the First*, ed. William Brenchley Rye (London, 1865).

*English Family Life, 1576–1716: An Anthology from Diaries*, ed. Ralph Houlbrooke (Oxford, 1988).

*The English Reports* (176 vols., Edinburgh, 1900–30).

*Episcopal Visitation Returns for Cambridgeshire: Matthew Wren, Bishop of Ely, 1638–1665*, ed. W. M. Palmer (Cambridge, 1930).

ERASMUS, DESIDERIUS, *Dicta Sapientu[m]: The Sayenges of the Wyse Me[n] of Grece in Latin with the Englysshe Folowyng* (London, 1527?).

—— *Apophthegmes*, trans. Nicholas Udall (London, 1542).

—— *Adagia in Latine and English*, trans. Bartholomew Robertson (London, 1621).

—— *The Colloquies or Familiar Discourses of Desiderius Erasmus of Roterdam*, trans. H. M. (London, 1671).

ERDESWICKE, SAMPSON, *A Survey of Staffordshire* (London, 1723).

EVELYN, JOHN, *Acetaria: A Discourse of Sallets* (London, 1699).

—— *The History of Religion*, ed. R. M. Evanson (2 vols., London, 1850).

—— *The Diary of John Evelyn*, ed. E. S. de Beer (6 vols., Oxford, 1955).

'Exmoor Courtship', and 'An Exmoor Scolding', *Gentleman's Magazine*, 16 (1746), 297–300 and 352–5.

'Extracts from the Act Books of the Archdeacons of Nottingham', ed. R. F. B. Hodgkinson, *Transactions of the Thoroton Society*, 29 (1925), 19–67; 30 (1926), 11–57; 31 (1927), 108–53.

'Extracts from the Records of the Wiltshire Quarter Sessions', ed. R. W. Merriman, *Wiltshire Archaeological and Natural History Magazine*, 20 (1882), 322–341; 21 (1884), 75–121; 22 (1885), 1–38, 212–31.

EYRE, ADAM, *A Dyurnall, or Catalogue of all my Accions and Expences from the 1st of January, 1646[7]*, ed. H. J. Morehouse (Surtees Society, 65, Durham, 1877).

*Fergusson's Scottish Proverbs from the Original Print of 1641 Together with a Larger Manuscript Collection*, ed. Erskine Beveridge (Scottish Text Society, new ser., 15, Edinburgh, 1924).

FERNE, JOHN, *The Blazon of Gentrie* (London, 1586).

FERRAND, JACQUES, *Epotomania, or A Treatise Discoursing of the Essence, Causes, . . . and Cure of Love, or Erotique Melancholy* (Oxford, 1640).

FIENNES, CELIA, *The Journeys of Celia Fiennes*, ed. Christopher Morris (London, 1947).

*A Fifteenth-Century School Book from a Manuscript in the British Museum (MS. Arundel 249)*, ed. William Nelson (Oxford, 1956).

FISHER, R. B., *A Practical Treatise on Copyhold Tenure* (London, 1794).

FITZHERBERT, SIR ANTHONY, *The Book of Husbandry*, ed. W. W. Skeat (English Dialect Society, 37, London, 1882).

FLECKNOE, RICHARD, *The Diarium, or Journall: Divided into 12. Jornadas* (London, 1656).

FLEMING, SIR DANIEL, *Description of the County of Westmorland*, ed. G. F. Duckett (Cumberland and Westmorland Antiquarian and Archaeological Society, 1, Kendal, 1882).

—— *Description of the County of Cumberland*, ed. R. S. Ferguson (Cumberland and Westmorland Antiquarian and Archaeological Society, 3, Kendal, 1889).

FLORIO, JOHN, *Florio His Firste Fruites* (London, 1578).

—— *Florios Second Frvtes* (London, 1591).

—— *A Worlde of Wordes, or Most Copious, and Exact Dictionarie in Italian and English* (London, 1598).

FOTHERBY, MARTIN, *Atheomastix: Clearing Foure Truthes, against Atheists and Infidels* (London, 1622).

FOX, GEORGE, *The Journal of George Fox*, ed. John L. Nickalls (Cambridge, 1952).

FOXE, JOHN, *Acts and Monuments*, ed. S. R. Cattley (8 vols., London, 1837–41).

*Fragments of an Early Fourteenth-Century Guy of Warwick*, ed. Maldwyn Mills and Daniel Huws (Medium Aevum Monographs, new ser., 4, Oxford, 1974).

FULLER, THOMAS, *The Holy State* (Cambridge, 1642).

—— *The History of the Worthies of England* (London, 1662).

FULLER MD, THOMAS, *Gnomologia: Adagies and Proverbs, Wise Sentences and Witty Sayings, Ancient and Modern, Foreign and British* (London, 1732).

FULWOOD, WILLIAM, *The Enimie of Idlenesse* (London, 1568).

'Furse of Moreshead: A Family Record of the Sixteenth Century', ed. H. J. Carpenter, *Report and Transactions of the Devonshire Association*, 26 (1894), 168–84.

GARDEN, JAMES, 'Professor James Garden's Letters to John Aubrey, 1692–1695', ed. Cosmo A. Gordon, in *The Miscellany of the Third Spalding Club*, iii (Aberdeen, 1960), 1–56.

*Gazophylacium Anglicanum: Containing the Derivation of English Words* (London, 1689).

*The Gentleman's Magazine Library: Being a Classified Collection of the Chief Contents of 'The Gentleman's Magazine' from 1731 to 1868*, ed. G. L. Gomme (3 vols., London, 1883–5).

GERARD, JOHN, *The Herball or General Historie of Plantes*, ed. Thomas Johnson (London, 1633).

GERARD, THOMAS, *The Particular Description of the County of Somerset*, ed. E. H. Bates (Somerset Record Society, 15, London, 1900).

GIFFORD, GEORGE, *A Discourse of the Subtill Practices of Deuilles by Witches and Sorcerers* (London, 1587).

—— *A Dialogue Concerning Witches and Witchcraftes* (London, 1593).

GIL, ALEXANDER, *Logonomia Anglica: Qva Gentis Sermo Facilivs Addiscitvr* (London, 1619).

GLANVILL, JOSEPH, *An Essay Concerning Preaching* (London, 1678).

—— *Saducismus Triumphatus: Or Full and Plain Evidence Concerning Witches and Apparitions* (2nd edn., London, 1682).

*The Golden Legend*, trans. William Grainger Ryan (2 vols., Princeton, 1993).

GOLDSMITH, OLIVER, *The Bee and Other Essays* (Oxford, 1914).

GOODMAN, JOHN, *Winter-Evening Conference between Neighbours* (2nd edn., London, 1684).

GOUGE, THOMAS, *The Young Man's Guide* (London, 1670).

GOUGH, RICHARD, *The History of Myddle*, ed. David Hey (Harmondsworth, 1981).

GREENE, ROBERT, *The Life and Complete Works in Prose and Verse of Robert Greene*, ed. A. B. Grosart (15 vols., London, 1881–6).

GROSE, FRANCIS, *A Classical Dictionary of the Vulgar Tongue* (London, 1785).

—— *A Provincial Glossary with a Collection of Local Proverbs and Popular Superstitions* (London, 1787).

H., J., *Two Essays of Love and Marriage* (London, 1657).

HABINGTON, THOMAS, *A Survey of Worcestershire*, ed. John Amphlett (2 vols., Worcestershire Historical Society, Oxford, 1895–9).

HAKLUYT, RICHARD, *The Principal Navigations, Voyages, Traffiques and Discoveries of the English Nation*, ed. Jack Beeching (Harmondsworth, 1972).

HALL, JOSEPH, *The Olde Religion* (London, 1628).

HARMAN, THOMAS, *A Caueat for Commen Cvrsetors Vvlgarely Called Vagabones* (London, 1567).

HARRISON, WILLIAM, *The Description of England*, ed. Georges Edelen (Ithaca, NY, 1968).

HARRISON, WILLIAM, *The Difference of Hearers* (London, 1614).

HART, JOHN, *An Orthographie* (London, 1569).

—— *A Methode or Comfortable Beginning* (London, 1570).

HARVEY, JOHN, *A Discoursive Probleme Concerning Prophesies* (London, 1588).

HAWARDE, JOHN, *Les Reportes del Cases in Camera Stellata, 1593 to 1609,* ed. W. P. Baildon (London, 1894).

HEAD, RICHARD, *The Canting Academy* (London, 1673).

HEARNE, THOMAS, *The Remains of Thomas Hearne,* ed. John Buchanan-Brown (London, 1966).

HERBERT, GEORGE, *The Works of George Herbert,* ed. F. E. Hutchinson (Oxford, 1941).

*Hertford County Records,* ed. W. J. Hardy (6 vols., Hertford, 1905–30).

HEYWOOD, JOHN, *A Dialogue Conteinyng the Number in Effect of all the Prouerbes in the Englishe Tongue* (London, 1546).

—— *John Heywood's 'A Dialogue of Proverbs',* ed. Rudolph E. Habenicht (Berkeley and Los Angeles, 1963).

HEYWOOD, OLIVER, *The Rev. Oliver Heywood, B.A., 1630–1702: His Autobiography, Diaries, Anecdote and Event Books,* ed. J. Horsfall Turner (4 vols., Brighouse, 1882–5).

HEYWOOD, THOMAS, *The Dramatic Works of Thomas Heywood* (6 vols., London, 1874).

HILL, RICHARD, *Songs, Carols, and other Miscellaneous Poems, from the Balliol MS. 354, Richard Hill's Commonplace-Book,* ed. Roman Dyboski (Early English Text Society, orig. ser., 101, London, 1907).

HISTORICAL MANUSCRIPTS COMMISSION, *Third Report* (London, 1872).

—— *Fourth Report* (London, 1874).

—— *Fifth Report* (London, 1876).

—— *Ninth Report, Part II* (London, 1884).

—— *Tenth Report, Appendix, Part IV* (London, 1885).

—— *Eleventh Report, Appendix, Part VII* (London, 1888).

—— *Twelfth Report, Appendix, Part IV* (London, 1888).

—— *Thirteenth Report, Appendix, Part IV* (London, 1892).

—— *Thirteenth Report, Appendix, Part II* (London, 1893).

—— *Fourteenth Report, Appendix, Part VIII* (London, 1895).

—— *Fifteenth Report, Appendix, Part X* (London, 1899).

—— *Various Collections,* vol. i (London, 1901).

—— *Various Collections,* vol. iv (London, 1907).

—— *Various Collections,* vol. vii (London, 1914).

—— *Report on the Records of the City of Exeter,* ed. J. H. Wylie (London, 1916).

*The History and Antiquities of Glastonbury,* ed. Thomas Hearne (Oxford, 1722).

HOBBES, THOMAS, *Leviathan,* ed. Richard Tuck (Cambridge, 1991).

HOLCROFT, THOMAS, *Memoirs of the Late Thomas Holcroft, Written by Himself* (3 vols. London, 1816).

HOLINSHED, RAPHAEL, *Holinshed's Chronicles of England, Scotland and Ireland* (6 vols., London, 1807–8).

HOLLINGWORTH, RICHARD, *Mancuniensis; Or, an History of the Towne of Manchester* (Manchester, 1839).

HOLLYBAND, CLAUDIUS, *The Frenche Littleton* (London, 1576).

HOLME, RANDLE, *The Academy of Armoury* (London, 1688).

'The Holme Riddles (MS. Harl. 1960)', ed. Frederick Tupper, *Publications of the Modern Language Association*, 18 (1903), 211–72.

HOLMES, NATHANIEL, *The Peasants Price of Spirituall Liberty* (London, 1642).

HOOKER, JOHN, *The Description of the Citie of Excester*, ed. W. J. Harte, J. W. Schopp, and H. Tapley-Soper (Devon and Cornwall Record Society, Exeter, 1919).

HOOKER, RICHARD, *Of the Laws of Ecclesiastical Polity*, ed. A. S. McGrade (Cambridge, 1989).

HOOLE, CHARLES, *Childrens Talke, English and Latin* (London, 1659).

—— *A New Discovery of the Old Art of Teaching Schoole* (London, 1660).

HORMAN, WILLIAM, *Vulgaria* (London, 1519).

HOSKYNS, JOHN, *The Life, Letters, and Writings of John Hoskyns, 1566–1638*, ed. L. B. Osborn (New Haven, 1937).

HOUGHTON, THOMAS, *Rara Avis in Terris: Or the Compleat Miner* (London, 1681).

HOWARD, HENRY, *A Defensatiue against the Poyson of Supposed Prophesies* (London, 1583).

HOWELL, JAMES, *Proverbs, or, Old Sayed Sawes and Adages* (London, 1659).

HUDSON, WILLIAM, 'A Treatise of the Court of Star Chamber', *Collectanea Juridica: Consisting of Tracts Relative to the Law and Constitution*, ed. F. Hargrave (2 vols., London, 1791–2), ii. 1–240.

HULOET, RICHARD, *Abcedarivm Anglico-Latinvm* (London, 1552).

HUNT, THOMAS, *Libellus Orthographicus: Or, the Diligent School Boy's Directory* (London, 1661).

HUTCHINS, JOHN, *The History and Antiquities of the County of Dorset* (2 vols., London, 1774).

HUTCHINSON, FRANCIS, *An Historical Essay Concerning Witchcraft* (London, 1718).

HUTCHINSON, WILLIAM, *A View of Northumberland* (2 vols., Newcastle, 1778).

*Illustrations of the Fairy Mythology of 'A Midsummer Night's Dream'*, ed. J. O. Halliwell (London, 1845).

*Inedited Tracts: Illustrating the Manners, Opinions, and Occupations of Englishmen during the Sixteenth and Seventeenth Centuries*, ed. W. C. Hazlitt (Roxburghe Library, London, 1868).

*In God's Name: Examples of Preaching in England from the Act of Supremacy to the Act of Uniformity 1534–1662*, ed. John Chandos (London, 1971).

INMAN, FRANCIS, *A Light vnto the Vnlearned* (London, 1622).

IZACKE, RICHARD, *Antiquities of the City of Exeter* (London, 1677).

JACKSON, THOMAS, *A Treatise Containing the Originall of Vnbeliefe* (London, 1625).

JAMES VI & I, *Daemonologie, in Forme of a Dialogue* (Edinburgh, 1597).

—— *A Covnter-Blaste to Tobacco* (London, 1604).

—— *Flores Regij: Or, Proverbes and Aphorismes, Divine and Morall . . . Collected by J. L. S.* (London, 1627).

JOHNSON, SAMUEL, *A Dictionary of the English Language* (2 vols., London, 1755).

JONSON, BEN, *The Works of Ben Jonson*, ed. C. H. Herford and Percy Simpson (11 vols., Oxford, 1925–52).

JOSSELIN, RALPH, *The Diary of Ralph Josselin, 1616–1683*, ed. Alan Macfarlane (British Academy, Records of Social and Economic History, new ser., 3, London, 1976).

JULIUS, PHILIP, 'Diary of the Journey of Philip Julius, Duke of Stettin-Pomerania, through England in the Year 1602', ed. Gottfried von Bülow, *Transactions of the Royal Historical Society*, new ser., 6 (1892), 1–67.

KELLY, JAMES, *A Complete Collection of Scottish Proverbs, Explained and Made Intelligible to the English Reader* (London, 1721).

KEMPE, WILLIAM, *The Education of Children in Learning* (London, 1588).

KENNETT, WHITE, *Parochial Antiquities Attempted in the History of Ambrosden, Burcester, and Other Adjacent Parts in the Counties of Oxford and Bucks* (Oxford, 1695).

KENRICK, WILLIAM, *A Rhetorical Grammar of the English Language* (London, 1784).

*Kentish Sources: VI Crime and Punishment*, ed. E. Melling (Maidstone, 1969).

K[ERSEY], J[OHN], *New English Dictionary* (London, 1702).

KINDER, PHILIP, 'Historie of Darby-Shire', ed. W. G. D. Fletcher, *Reliquary*, 22 (1881–2), 17–24, 97–101, 181–4, 197–200, and 23 (1882–3), 9–10.

KING, DANIEL, *The Vale-Royall of England: Or, the County Palatine of Chester Illustrated* (London, 1656).

KIRK, ROBERT, *The Secret Common-Wealth and a Short Treatise of Charms and Spels*, ed. Stewart Sanderson (Folklore Society, Cambridge, 1976).

LAMBARDE, WILLIAM, *A Perambulation of Kent: Conteining the Description, Hystorie, and Customes of that Shyre* (London, 1576).

*Lancashire Quarter Sessions Records, 1590–1606*, ed. James Tait (Chetham Society, new ser., 77, Manchester, 1917).

LANEHAM, ROBERT, *A Letter* (London, 1575).

LATIMER, HUGH, *Sermons by Hugh Latimer*, ed. G. E. Corrie (Parker Society, Cambridge, 1844).

LEIGH, CHARLES, *The Natural History of Lancashire, Cheshire, and the Peak, in Derbyshire* (Oxford, 1700).

LEIGH, EDWARD, *Analecta de XII. Primus Caesaribus* (2nd edn., London, 1647).

LELAND, JOHN, *The Itinerary of John Leland in or about the Years, 1535–1543*, ed. Lucy Toulmin Smith (5 vols., London, 1906–10).

LE STRANGE, SIR NICHOLAS, *'Merry Passages and Jeasts': A Manuscript Jestbook of Sir Nicholas Le Strange (1603–1655)*, ed. H. F. Lippincott (Salzburg, 1974).

*Letters and Papers, Foreign and Domestic, of the Reign of Henry VIII*, ed. J. S. Brewer and James Gairdner (21 vols., London, 1862–1910).

LEVINS, PETER, *Manipulus Vocabulorum* (London, 1570).

LEWIS, JOHN, *The History and Antiquities Ecclesiastical and Civil of the Isle of Tenet in Kent* (London, 1723).

LEYCESTER, SIR PETER, *Historical Antiquities, in Two Books* (London, 1673).

LHWYD, EDWARD, *Life and Letters of Edward Lhwyd*, vol. xiv of *Early Science in Oxford*, ed. R. T. Gunther (Oxford, 1945).

LIDDELL, HENRY, *The Letters of Henry Liddell to William Cotesworth*, ed. J. M. Ellis (Surtees Society, 197, Durham, 1987).

LING, NICHOLAS, *Politeuphuia: Wits Common Wealth* (London, 1597).

LOCKE, JOHN, *Some Thoughts Concerning Education*, ed. J. W. and J. S. Yolton (Oxford, 1989).

LOWE, ROGER, *The Diary of Roger Lowe of Ashton-in-Makerfield, Lancashire, 1663–74*, ed. William L. Sachse (London, 1938).

LUPTON, DONALD, *London and the Countrey Carbonadoed and Quartred into Severall Characters* (London, 1632).

LUPTON, THOMAS, *A Thousand Notable Things, of Sundry Sortes* (London, 1579).

LYE, THOMAS, *The Childs Delight* (London, 1671).

LYLY, JOHN, *The Complete Works of John Lyly*, ed. R. W. Bond (3 vols., Oxford, 1902).

MACHELL, THOMAS, *Antiquary on Horseback: The First Publication of the Collections of the Rev. Thos. Machell, Chaplain to King Charles II, towards a History of the Barony of Kendal*, ed. Jane M. Ewbank (Cumberland and Westmorland Antiquarian and Archaeological Society, extra ser., 19, Kendal, 1963).

MACHYN, HENRY, *The Diary of Henry Machyn, Citizen and Merchant-Taylor of London, from A.D. 1550 to A.D. 1563*, ed. John Gough Nichols (Camden Society, first ser., 42, London, 1848).

MANLOVE, EDWARD, *The Liberties and Cvstomes of the Lead-Mines within the Wapentake of Wirksworth in the County of Derby* (London, 1653).

MANNINGHAM, JOHN, *The Diary of John Manningham of the Middle Temple, 1602–1603*, ed. Robert Parker Sorlien (Hanover, NH, 1976).

MANSHIP, HENRY, *A Booke of the Foundacion and Antiquitye of the Towne of Greate Yermouthe*, ed. Charles John Palmer (Great Yarmouth, 1847).

MANSHIP, HENRY, jnr., *The History of Great Yarmouth*, ed. Charles John Palmer (Great Yarmouth, 1854).

MANWAYRING, SIR HENRY, *The Sea-mans Dictionary* (London, 1644).

MAPLET, JOHN, *A Greene Forest, or a Naturall Historie* (London, 1567).

MAPLETOFT, JOHN, *Select Proverbs* (London, 1707).

MARBECK, JOHN, *A Booke of Notes and Common Places* (London, 1581).

MARKHAM, GERVASE, *Countrey Contentments, in Two Bookes* (London, 1615).

—— *The English Husbandman* (London, 1635).

MARSHALL, WILLIAM, *The Rural Economy of Yorkshire* (2 vols., London, 1788).

—— *The Rural Economy of Gloucestershire* (2 vols., London, 1789).

—— *The Rural Economy of Norfolk* (2nd edn., 2 vols., London, 1795).

MARTIN, MARTIN, *A Description of the Western Islands of Scotland circa 1695* (Glasgow, 1884).

MARTINDALE, ADAM, *The Life of Adam Martindale Written by Himself*, ed. Richard Parkinson (Chetham Society, 4, London, 1845).

MASSINGER, PHILIP, *The Plays and Poems of Philip Massinger*, ed. Philip Edwards and Colin Gibson (5 vols., Oxford, 1976).

MELTON, JOHN, *Astrologaster, or, The Figvre-Caster* (London, 1620).

*Mendip Mining Laws and Forest Bounds*, ed. J. W. Gough (Somerset Record Society, 45, Frome, 1931).

MERES, FRANCIS, *Witts Academy: A Treasurie of Goulden Sentences, Similies and Examples. Set Forth Cheefely for the Benefitt of Young Schollers* (1598; London, 1636).

MERITON, GEORGE, *The Praise of York-Shire Ale* (3rd edn., York, 1697).

*Middlesex County Records*, ed. J. C. Jeaffreson (4 vols., Middlesex County Records Society, London, 1886–92).

*Middlesex Sessions Records*, ed. William Le Hardy (4 vols., London, 1935–41).

MIDDLETON, THOMAS, *The Witch*, ed. W. W. Greg and F. P. Wilson (Malone Society Reprints, Oxford, 1950).

MIEGE, GUY, *A New Dictionary French and English with another English and French* (London, 1677).

MILTON, JOHN, *The History of Britain*, ed. G. P. Krapp, in *The Works of John Milton* (18 vols., New York, 1931–8), x. 1–325.

MINSHEU, JOHN, *A Spanish Grammar* (London, 1599).

—— *Pleasant and Delightfvll Dialogves in Spanish and English* (London, 1599).

*M. Misson's Memoirs and Observations in his Travels over England: With some Account of Scotland and Ireland*, trans. John Ozell (London, 1719).

MONMOUTH, GEOFFREY OF, *The Historia Regum Britanniae of Geoffrey of Monmouth*, ed. Acton Griscom (London, 1929).

MONTAIGNE, MICHEL DE, *The Essayes or Morall, Politike and Millitarie Discourses*, trans. John Florio (London, 1603).

MORTON, JOHN, *The Natural History of Northamptonshire* (London, 1712).

MORYSON, FYNES, *An Itinerary Containing his Ten Yeeres Travell* (4 vols., Glasgow, 1907–8).

*Mother Bunch's Closet Newly Broke Open* (1685; London?, 1715).

MUFFETT, THOMAS, *Healths Improvement*, ed. Christopher Bennet (London, 1655).

MULCASTER, RICHARD, *Positions wherein those Primitive Circumstances be Examined, which are Necessarie for the Training up of Children* (London, 1581).

—— *The First Part of the Elementarie which Entreateth Chefelie of the Right Writing of our English Tung* (London, 1582).

MUNDY, PETER, *The Travels of Peter Mundy, in Europe and Asia, 1608–1667*, ed. Sir Richard Carnac Temple and Lavinia Mary Anstey (5 vols. in 6, Hakluyt Society, second ser., 17, 35, 45, 46, 55, 78, Cambridge, 1907; London, 1914–36).

NASH, TREADWAY, *Collections for the History of Worcestershire* (2 vols., London, 1781–2).

NASHE, THOMAS, *The Works of Thomas Nashe*, ed. R. B. McKerrow, rev. F. P. Wilson (5 vols., Oxford, 1958).

*A New Canting Dictionary* (London, 1725).

NEWCOME, HENRY, *The Autobiography of Henry Newcome, M.A.*, ed. Richard Parkinson (2 vols., Chetham Society, 26–7, Manchester, 1852).

NEEDHAM, MARCHAMONT, *A Discourse Concerning Schools and School-Masters* (London, 1663).

*Nine Specimens of English Dialects*, ed. W. W. Skeat (English Dialect Society, 76, London, 1896).

NORDEN, JOHN, *The Surveyors Dialogue* (London, 1610).

NORTH, ROGER, *The Lives of the Norths*, ed. Augustus Jessopp (3 vols., London, 1890).

*North Riding Quarter Sessions Records*, ed. J. C. Atkinson (8 vols., North Riding Record Society, London, 1884–90).

'Notes from two Court Books of the City of Norwich, from 1666–1688', ed. Walter Rye, *Norfolk and Norwich Archaeological Society*, 2 (1905), 97–205.

NOWELL, LAURENCE, *Laurence Nowell's Vocabularium Saxonicum*, ed. Albert H. Marckwardt (Ann Arbor, 1952).

*Old English Ballads 1553–1625*, ed. Hyder E. Rollins (Cambridge, 1920).

OSBORNE, DOROTHY, *Letters to Sir William Temple*, ed. Kenneth Parker (Harmondsworth, 1987).

OVERBURY, SIR THOMAS, *New and Choise Characters* (London, 1615).

OWEN, GEORGE, *The Description of Pembrokeshire*, ed. Dillwyn Miles (Llandysul, 1994).

PALMER, SAMUEL, *Moral Essays on Some of the Most Curious and Significant English, Scotch and Foreign Proverbs* (London, 1710).

PALSGRAVE, JOHN, *The Comedy of Acolastus Translated from the Latin of Fullonius by John Palsgrave*, ed. P. L. Carver (Early English Text Society, orig. ser., 202, London, 1937).

PARKINSON, JOHN, *Paradisi in Sole Paradisus Terrestris* (London, 1629).

PARROT, HENRY, *The Mastive, or Young-Whelpe of the Olde-Dogge* (London, 1615).

PEACHAM, HENRY, *The Garden of Eloquence* (London, 1577).

PEACHAM, HENRY, *The Complete Gentleman, The Truth of Our Times, and The Art of Living in London*, ed. Virgil B. Heltzel (Ithaca, NY, 1962).

PEELE, GEORGE, *The Famous Chronicle of King Edward the First, Sirnamed Edward Longshankes* (London, 1593).

—— *The Old Wiues Tale* (London, 1595).

PEGGE, SAMUEL, 'An Alphabet of Kenticisms', in *Original Glossaries*, ed. W. W. Skeat (English Dialect Society, 12, London, 1876), 9–78.

—— *Two Collections of Derbicisms*, ed. W. W. Skeat and Thomas Hallam (English Dialect Society, 78, London, 1896).

PEGGE, SAMUEL, *Anecdotes of the English Language: Chiefly Regarding the Local Dialect of London and its Environs* (2nd edn., London, 1814).

PEPYS, SAMUEL, *The Diary of Samuel Pepys*, ed. Robert Latham and William Matthews (11 vols., London, 1970–83).

*The Pepys Ballads*, ed. W. G. Day (5 vols., Cambridge, 1987).

PERCY, THOMAS, *Reliques of Ancient English Poetry* (3 vols., London, 1765).

PERKINS, WILLIAM, *A Discourse of the Damned Art of Witchcraft* (Cambridge, 1608).

PHILLIPS, EDWARD, *The Mysteries of Love and Eloquence* (London, 1658).

—— *The New World of English Words* (London, 1658).

*The Pinder of Wakefield*, ed. E. A. Horsman (Liverpool, 1956).

PINNOCK, WILLIAM, *The History and Topography of Huntingdonshire* (London, 1822).

PLATTER, THOMAS, *Thomas Platter's Travels in England, 1599,* ed. Clare Williams (London, 1937).

PLOT, ROBERT, *The Natural History of Oxford-shire* (Oxford, 1677).

—— *The Natural History of Stafford-Shire* (Oxford, 1686).

POCOCKE, RICHARD, *The Travels through England of Dr. Richard Pococke,* ed. James Joel Cartright (2 vols., Camden Society, new ser., 42–4, London, 1888–9).

*Poems on Affairs of State: Augustan Satirical Verse, 1660–1714,* gen. ed. George deF. Lord (7 vols., New Haven, 1963–75).

PORTER, HENRY, *The Pleasant History of the Two Angry Women of Abington* (London, 1599).

PRIMROSE, JAMES, *Popular Errours: Or the Errours of the People in Physick,* trans. Robert Wittie (London, 1651).

PRYME, ABRAHAM DE LA, *The Diary of Abraham de la Pryme, the Yorkshire Antiquary,* ed. Charles Jackson (Surtees Society, 54, Durham, 1869–70).

PUTTENHAM, GEORGE, *The Arte of English Poesie* (London, 1589).

*Quarter Sessions Records for the County of Somerset,* ed. E. H. Bates (4 vols., Somerset Record Society, 23, 24, 28, 34, 1907–19).

*Quarter Sessions Records with other Records of the Justices of the Peace for the County Palatine of Chester, 1559–1760,* ed. J. H. E. Bennett and J. C. Dewhurst (Record Society of Lancashire and Cheshire, 94, Chester, 1940).

R., N., *Proverbs English, French, Dutch, Italian, and Spanish: All Englished and Alphabetically Digested* (London, 1659).

RAINOLDE, RICHARD, *A Booke Called the Foundacion of Rhetorike* (London, 1563).

RAVENSCROFT, THOMAS, *Melismata: Musicall Phansies, Fitting the Court, Citie, and Countrey Humours* (London, 1611).

RAWDON, MARMADUKE, *The Life of Marmaduke Rawdon of York,* ed. Robert Davies (Camden Society, first ser., 85, London, 1863).

RAY, JOHN, *A Collection of English Proverbs* (Cambridge, 1670; 2nd edn., 1678).

—— *A Collection of English Words, Not Generally Used, with their Significations and Original* (London, 1674; 2nd edn., 1691).

—— *The Correspondence of John Ray,* ed. Edwin Lankester (London, 1848).

*Records of Early English Drama: Cambridge,* ed. Alan H. Nelson (Toronto, 1989); *Chester,* ed. Lawrence M. Clopper (Toronto, 1979); *Coventry,* ed. R. W. Ingram (Toronto, 1981); *Cumberland, Westmorland, Gloucestershire,* ed. Audrey Douglas and Peter Greenfield (Toronto, 1986); *Devon,* ed. John M. Wasson (Toronto, 1986); *Herefordshire, Worcestershire,* ed. David N. Klausner (Toronto, 1990); *Lancashire,* ed. David George (Toronto, 1991); *Newcastle upon Tyne,* ed. J. J. Anderson (Toronto, 1982); *Norwich, 1540–1642,* ed. David Galloway (Toronto, 1984); *Shropshire,* ed. J. A. B. Somerset (Toronto, 1994); *York,* ed. Alexandra F. Johnston and Margaret Rogerson (Toronto, 1979).

*Records of the County of Wiltshire being Extracts from the Quarter Sessions Great Rolls of the Seventeenth Century,* ed. B. H. Cunnington (Devizes, 1932).

*Records Relating to the Barony of Kendal,* ed. J. F. Curwen (3 vols., Cumberland and Westmorland Antiquarian and Archaeological Society, record ser., 4–6, Kendal, 1923–6).

REGIUS, URBANUS, *A Co[m]parison betwene the Olde Learnynge and the Newe*, trans. William Turner (Southwark, 1537).

*A Relation of a Short Survey of 26 Counties Observed in a Seven Weeks Journey*, ed. L. G. Wickham Legg (London, 1904).

'A Relation of a Short Survey of the Western Counties', ed. L. G. Wickham Legg, in *Camden Miscellany*, xvi (Camden Society, third ser., 52, London, 1936).

RELPH, JOSIAH, *A Miscellany of Poems, Consisting of Original Poems . . . in the Cumberland Dialect* (Glasgow, 1747).

*Reports of Cases in the Courts of Star Chamber and High Commission*, ed. S. R. Gardiner (Camden Society, new ser., 39, London, 1886).

*Reprinted Glossaries*, ed. W. W. Skeat (4 vols., English Dialect Society, 1–4, London, 1873–9).

*Reprints of Rare Tracts and Imprints of Antient Manuscripts, &c. Chiefly Illustrative of the History of the Northern Counties*, ed. M. A. Richardson (7 vols., Newcastle, 1843–9).

REYCE, ROBERT, *Suffolk in the XVIIth Century: The Breviary of Suffolk by Robert Reyce, 1618*, ed. Lord Francis Hervey (London, 1902).

REYNER, EDWARD, *Rules for the Government of the Tongue* (London, 1656).

RHODES, JOHN, *The Countrie Mans Comfort or Religious Recreations, Fitte for all Well-Disposed Persons* (1588; rev. edn., London, 1637).

*The Riddles of the Exeter Book*, ed. Frederick Tupper (Boston, Mass., 1910).

RISDON, TRISTRAM, *The Chorographical Description or Survey of the County of Devon* (London, 1811).

*Rites of Durham*, ed. J. T. Fowler (Surtees Society, 107, Durham, 1903).

ROBERTS, ALEXANDER, *A Treatise of Witchcraft* (London, 1616).

ROBINSON, ROBERT, *The Art of Pronunciation* (London, 1617).

*Round about our Coal Fire, or Christmas Entertainments* (1734; London, 1740).

ROUS, JOHN, *Historia Regum Angliae*, ed. Thomas Hearne (2nd edn., Oxford, 1745).

ROUS, JOHN, *Diary of John Rous, Incumbent of Santon Downham, Suffolk, from 1625 to 1642*, ed. Mary Anne Everett Green (Camden Society, first ser., 66, London, 1856).

ROWE, NICHOLAS, 'Some Account of the Life, &c. of Mr. William Shakespear', in *The Works of Mr. William Shakespear*, ed. Rowe (6 vols., London, 1709), i. i–xl.

ROWLANDS, SAMUEL, *The Letting of Hvmovrs Blood in the Head-Vaine* (London, 1600).

*The Roxburghe Ballads*, ed. W. Chappell and J. W. Ebsworth (9 vols., Ballad Society, London, 1871–99).

RUGG, THOMAS, *The Diurnal of Thomas Rugg, 1659–1661*, ed. William L. Sachse (Camden Society, third ser., 91, London, 1961).

*Rump: Or an Exact Collection of the Choycest Poems and Songs Relating to the Late Times*, ed. H. B[rome] and H. M[arsh] (London, 1662).

SALMON, N[ATHANIEL], *The History of Hertfordshire* (London, 1728).

SANCROFT, WILLIAM, *Modern Policies, Taken from Machiavel, Borgia, and Other Choice Authors* (4th edn., London, 1653).

SANDFORD, EDMUND, *A Cursory Relation of all the Antiquities and Familyes in Cumberland*, ed. R. S. Ferguson (Cumberland and Westmorland Antiquarian and Archaeological Society, 4, Kendal, 1890).

SANFORD, JOHN, *An Entrance to the Spanish Tongve* (London, 1611).

SANFORDE, JAMES, *The Garden of Pleasure* (London, 1573).

SCOT, REGINALD, *The Discouerie of Witchcraft* (London, 1584).

*The Seconde Tome of Homelyes* (London, 1563).

SELDEN, JOHN, *Table Talk of John Selden*, ed. Sir Frederick Pollock (London, 1927).

*A Series of Precedents and Proceedings in Criminal Causes, Extending from the Year 1475 to 1640; Extracted from Act-Books of Ecclesiastical Courts in the Diocese of London*, ed. W. H. Hale (London, 1847).

SHAKESPEARE, WILLIAM, *The Complete Works of William Shakespeare*, ed. Gary Taylor and Stanley Wells (Oxford, 1987).

*Shakespeare Jest-Books*, ed. W. C. Hazlitt (3 vols., London, 1864).

SHEPARD, THOMAS, *Theses Sabbaticae* (London, 1655).

SHERIDAN, THOMAS, *A Course of Lectures on Elocution* (London, 1762).

SHERRY, RICHARD, *A Treatise of the Figures of Grammer and Rhetorike* (London, 1555).

*The Shirburn Ballads, 1585–1616*, ed. Andrew Clark (Oxford, 1907).

SIDNEY, SIR PHILIP, *The Countess of Pembroke's Arcadia*, ed. Jean Robertson (Oxford, 1973).

SKINNER, STEPHEN, *Etymologicon Linguae Anglicanae* (London, 1671).

SMITH, JOHN, *The Sea-Mans Grammar* (London, 1653).

SMITH, SIR THOMAS, *De Recta et Emendata Lingvae Anglicae Scriptione, Dialogus* (London, 1568).

SMYTH, JOHN, *The Berkeley Manuscripts*, ed. Sir John Maclean (3 vols., Gloucester, 1883–5).

*Social England Illustrated: A Collection of XVIIth Century Tracts*, ed. Andrew Lang (London, 1903).

*Somerset Assize Orders, 1629–1640*, ed. T. G. Barnes (Somerset Record Society, 65, Frome, 1959).

SOMNER, WILLIAM, *The Antiquities of Canterbury* (London, 1640).

*Songs and Ballads, with Other Short Poems, Chiefly of the Reign of Philip and Mary*, ed. Thomas Wright (London, 1860).

*The South English Legendary*, ed. Charlotte D'Evelyn and Anna J. Mill (2 vols., Early English Text Society, 235–6, London, 1956).

*The Spectator*, ed. Donald F. Bond (5 vols., Oxford, 1965).

SPELMAN, SIR HENRY, 'Incenia: Sive Norfolciae Descriptio Topographica', in *Reliquiae Spelmannianae* (Oxford, 1698), 133–62.

—— *The History and Fate of Sacrilege* (London, 1698).

SPENCER, JOHN, *Kaina Kai Palaia: Things New and Old* (London, 1658).

SPENSER, EDMUND, *Poetical Works*, ed. J. C. Smith and E. De Selincourt (Oxford, 1912).

SPRAT, THOMAS, *The History of the Royal-Society of London* (London, 1667).

*The Staffordshire Quarter Sessions Rolls, 1581–1606*, ed. S. A. H. Burne (5 vols., William Salt Archaeological Society, Kendal, 1931–40).

STAMPOY, PAPPITY, *A Collection of Scotch Proverbs* (London, 1663).

STANIHURST, RICHARD, 'A Treatise Conteining a Plaine and Perfect Description of Ireland', in *Holinshed's Chronicles of England, Scotland and Ireland* (6 vols., London, 1807–8), vi.

*Statutes of the Realm* (11 vols., London, 1810–24).

STEPNEY, WILLIAM, *The Spanish Schoole-master* (London, 1591).

STOW, JOHN, *A Survey of London*, ed. C. L. Kingsford (2 vols., Oxford, 1908).

STUART, GEORGE, *A Joco-Serious Discourse: In Two Dialogues between a Northumberland-Gentleman and his Tenant a Scotchman, both Old Cavaliers* (London, 1686).

*Stuart Royal Proclamations: Volume I*, ed. J. F. Larkin and P. L. Hughes (Oxford, 1973).

STUKELEY, WILLIAM, *Itinerarium Curiosum* (London, 1724; 2nd edn., 2 vols., 1776).

—— *Stonehenge: A Temple Restor'd to the Druids* (London, 1740).

—— *Abury: A Temple of the British Druids* (London, 1743).

—— *The Family Memoirs of the Rev. William Stukeley, M.D.*, ed. W. C. Lukis (3 vols., Surtees Society, 73, 76, 80, Durham, 1882–7).

*Surrey Quarter Sessions Records: Order Book and Sessions Rolls, 1659–1666*, ed. Dorothy L. Powell and Hilary Jenkinson (3 vols., Surrey Record Society, 35, 36, 39, London, 1934–8).

SWIFT, JONATHAN, *A Proposal for Correcting, Improving and Ascertaining the English Tongue* (London, 1712).

—— *A Complete Collection of Genteel and Ingenious Conversation* (London, 1738).

*The Tatler*, ed. Donald F. Bond (3 vols., Oxford, 1987).

TAVERNER, RICHARD, *Proverbes or Adagies with Newe Addicions Gathered out of the Chiliades of Erasmus* (London, 1539; 1552).

TAYLOR, JOHN, *Wit and Mirth* (1626; London, 1628).

—— *The Carriers Cosmography* (London, 1637).

TAYLOR, JOSEPH, *A Journey to Edenborough in Scotland*, ed. William Cowan (Edinburgh, 1903).

THORESBY, RALPH, *Ducatus Leodiensis: Or, the Topography of the Ancient and Populous Town and Parish of Leedes* (London, 1715).

—— *The Diary of Ralph Thoresby, F.R.S.*, ed. Joseph Hunter (2 vols., London, 1830).

THORNTON, ALICE, *The Autobiography of Mrs Alice Thornton, of East Newton, Co. York*, ed. Charles Jackson (Surtees Society, 62, Durham, 1875).

THOROTON, ROBERT, *The Antiquities of Nottinghamshire* (London, 1677).

—— *The Antiquities of Nottinghamshire*, ed. John Throsby (3 vols., Nottingham, 1790–6).

*Three Centuries of Derbyshire Annals, as Illustrated by the Records of the Quarter Sessions of the County of Derby, from Queen Elizabeth to Queen Victoria*, ed. J. C. Cox (2 vols., London, 1890).

TILLOTSON, JOHN, *The Rule of Faith* (London, 1666).

TODD, HUGH, *Account of the City and Diocese of Carlisle*, ed. R. S. Ferguson (Cumberland and Westmorland Antiquarian and Archaeological Society, 5, Kendal, 1890).

*The Topographer and Genealogist*, ed. John Gough Nichols (3 vols., London, 1846–58).

TORRIANO, GIOVANNI, *Select Italian Proverbs* (Cambridge, 1642).

TRESCOT, THOMAS, *The Zealous Magistrate* (London, 1642).

TRYON, THOMAS, *A New Method of Educating Children* (London, 1695).

*Tudor Parish Documents of the Diocese of York*, ed. J. S. Purvis (Cambridge, 1948).

*Tudor Royal Proclamations*, ed. P. L. Hughes and J. F. Larkin (3 vols., New Haven, 1964–9).

*Tudor Treatises*, ed. A. G. Dickens (Yorkshire Archaeological Society, 125, Wakefield, 1959).

TURBERVILLE, GEORGE, *The Booke of Faulconrie or Hauking* (London, 1575).

TURNER, WILLIAM, *Libellus De Re Herbaria Nouus: In Quo Herbarum Aliquot Nomina Greca, Latina, & Anglica Habes* (London, 1538).

TURNER, WILLIAM, *The First and Second Partes of the Herbal of William Turner* (London, 1568).

TUSSER, THOMAS, *Five Hundred Points of Good Husbandry*, ed. Geoffrey Grigson (Oxford, 1984).

*Two Collections of Derbicisms*, ed. W. W. Skeat (English Dialect Society, 78, London, 1896).

*The Union-Proverb* (London, 1708).

URE, DAVID, *The History of Rutherglen and East-Kilbride* (Glasgow, 1793).

VERSTEGAN, RICHARD, *A Restitution of Decayed Intelligence* (Antwerp, 1605).

*The Vulgaria of John Stanbridge and the Vulgaria of Robert Whittinton*, ed. Beatrice White (Early English Text Society, orig. ser., 187, London, 1932).

WALKER, JOHN, *A Critical Pronouncing Dictionary* (London, 1791).

WALKER, OBADIAH, *Of Education, Especially of Young Gentlemen* (London, 1673).

WALKER, WILLIAM, *Paroemiologia Anglo-Latina* (London, 1672).

—— *Idiomatologia Anglo-Latina* (3rd edn., London, 1680).

WALTON, IZAAK, *The Lives of Doctor John Donne, Sir Henry Wotton, Mr Richard Hooker, Mr George Herbert and Doctor Robert Sanderson*, ed. Vernon Blackburn (London, 1895).

—— *The Complete Angler* (Everyman edn., London, 1906).

WARD, JOHN, *Diary of the Rev. John Ward, A.M., Vicar of Stratford-upon-Avon, Extending from 1648 to 1679*, ed. Charles Severn (London, 1839).

WARD, NED, *The London Spy: The Vanities and Vices of the Town Exposed to View*, ed. Arthur L. Hayward (London, 1927).

WARD, SAMUEL, *A Collection of such Sermons and Treatises as have been Written and Published by Samuel Ward* (London, 1636).

*Warwick County Records*, ed. S. C. Ratcliffe and H. C. Johnson (9 vols., Warwick, 1935–64).

WASE, CHRISTOPHER, *Considerations Concerning Free-Schools, as Settled in England* (Oxford, 1678).

WATKINS, CHARLES, *Treatise on Copyholds* (London, 1797).

WATSON, JOHN, *The History and Antiquities of the Parish of Halifax, in Yorkshire* (London, 1775).

WEBBE, JOSEPH, *Pueriles Confabulatiunculae, or Childrens Talke* (London, 1627).

WEBSTER, JOHN, *The Displaying of Supposed Witchcraft* (London, 1677).

WEEVER, JOHN, *Ancient Funerall Monuments* (London, 1631).

*West Riding Sessions Records*, ed. John Lister (2 vols., Yorkshire Archaeological Society, Leeds, 1888–1915).

WESTCOTE, THOMAS, *A View of Devonshire in 1630*, ed. George Oliver and Pitman Jones (Exeter, 1845).

*Western Circuit Assize Orders 1629–1648: A Calendar*, ed. J. S. Cockburn (Camden Society, fourth ser., 17, London, 1976).

WHEELER, ANN, *The Westmorland Dialect, in Three Familiar Dialogues* (Kendal, 1790).

WHETSTONE, GEORGE, 'English Pronvnciation: Or a Shorte Introdvction and Waye to the English Speache', in his *The Honovrable Repvtation of a Sovldier* (Leyden, 1586), 73–103.

WHITEWAY, WILLIAM, *William Whiteway of Dorchester: His Diary, 1618 to 1635* (Dorset Record Society, 12, Dorchester, 1991).

WHYTHORNE, THOMAS, *The Autobiography of Thomas Whythorne*, ed. James M. Osborn (Oxford, 1961).

WIDLEY, GEORGE, *The Doctrine of the Sabbath* (London, 1604).

WILLIS, BROWNE, *An History of the Mitred Parliamentary Abbies and Conventual Cathedral Churches* (2 vols., London, 1718–19).

WILSON, THOMAS, *The Arte of Rhetorique*, ed. G. H. Mair (Oxford, 1909).

W[INSTANLEY], W[ILLIAM], *The New Help to Discourse* (London, 1669).

WITHALS, JOHN, *A Dictionary in English and Latine; Devised for the Capacitie of Children, and Young Beginners* (London, 1634).

WODROEPHE, JOHN, *The Spared Hovres of a Sovldier in his Travels: Or the True Marrowe of the French Tongue* (London, 1623).

WOOD, ANTHONY, 'Survey of the Antiquities of the City of Oxford', Composed in 1661–6, by Anthony Wood, ed. Andrew Clark (3 vols., Oxford Historical Society, 15, 17, 37, Oxford, 1889–99).

—— *The Life and Times of Anthony Wood, Antiquary, of Oxford, 1632–1695, Described by Himself*, ed. Andrew Clark (5 vols., Oxford Historical Society, 19, 21, 26, 30, 40, Oxford, 1891–1900).

—— *Parochial Collections Made by Anthony à Wood, M.A. and Richard Rawlinson, D.C.L., F.R.S.*, ed. F. N. Davis (3 vols., Oxfordshire Record Society, 2, 4, 11, Oxford, 1920–9).

*Worcestershire County Records: Calendar of the Quarter Sessions Papers*, ed. J. W. Willis Bund (2 vols., Worcester, 1900).

WOOD, WILLIAM, *New Englands Prospect* (London, 1634).

WORCESTRE, WILLIAM, *Itineraries*, ed. John H. Harvey (Oxford, 1969).

WORLIDGE, JOHN, *Systema Agriculturae: The Mystery of Husbandry Discovered* (London, 1669).

WRIGHT, JAMES, *The History and Antiquities of the County of Rutland* (London, 1684).
YONGE, WALTER, *Diary of Walter Yonge, Esq.*, ed. George Roberts (Camden Society, first ser., 41, London, 1848).
*York Civic Records*, ed. Angelo Raine (8 vols., Yorkshire Archaeological Society, Wakefield, 1939–53).

SELECT SECONDARY SOURCES

ABRAHAMS, ROGER D., 'Introductory Remarks to a Rhetorical Theory of Floklore', *Journal of American Folklore*, 81 (1968), 143–58.
—— 'Proverbs and Proverbial Expressions', in Richard M. Dorson (ed.), *Folklore and Folklife: An Introduction* (Chicago, 1972), 117–27.
ADDY, SIDNEY O., *Household Tales with Other Traditional Remains Collected in the Counties of York, Lincoln, Derby, and Nottingham* (London, 1895).
ANGLO, SYDNEY, 'The *British History* in Early Tudor Propaganda', *Bulletin of the John Rylands Library*, 44 (1961–2), 17–48.
APPLEBY, ANDREW B., 'Agrarian Capitalism or Seigneurial Reaction? The Northwest of England, 1500–1700', *American Historical Review*, 80 (1975), 574–94.
ARENA, E. O., and DUNDES, ALAN, 'Proverbs and the Ethnography of Speaking Folklore', *American Anthropologist*, 66/6 (1964), 70–85.
ASHTON, JOHN, *Chapbooks of the Eighteenth Century* (London, 1882).
ASTON, MARGARET, 'Lollardy and Literacy', in her *Lollards and Reformers: Images and Literacy in Late Medieval Religion* (London, 1984), 193–217.
—— *England's Iconoclasts* (Oxford, 1988).
AUSTEN, BRIAN, *English Provincial Posts, 1633–1840: A Study Based on Kent Examples* (London, 1978).
BAKHTIN, MIKHAIL, *Rabelais and his World*, trans. Helene Iswolsky (Cambridge, Mass., 1965).
BALDWIN, T. W., *William Shakspere's Small Latine and Lesse Greeke* (2 vols., Urbana, Ill., 1944).
BALFOUR, M. C., and THOMAS, NORTHCOTE W., *Examples of Printed Folklore Concerning Northumberland* (Folklore Society, London, 1904).
BARBER, CHARLES, *Early Modern English* (London, 1976).
BARBER, C. L., *Shakespeare's Festive Comedy: A Study of Dramatic Form and its Relation to Social Custom* (Princeton, 1959).
BARNES, T. G., 'Star-Chamber Mythology', *American Journal of Legal History*, 5 (1961), 1–11.
—— 'Due Process and Slow Process in the Late Elizabethan and Early Stuart Star Chamber', *American Journal of Legal History*, 6 (1962), 221–49 and 315–46.
—— 'Star Chamber and the Sophistication of the Criminal Law', *Criminal Law Review* (1977), 316–26.
—— 'Star Chamber Litigants and their Counsel, 1596–1641', in J. H. Baker (ed.), *Legal Records and the Historian* (London, 1978), 7–28.

—— et al. (eds.), *List and Index to the Proceedings in Star Chamber for the Reign of James I, 1603–25, in the Public Record Office, London, Class STAC8* (3 vols., Chicago, 1975).

BARRY, JONATHAN, 'Popular Culture in Seventeenth-Century Bristol', in Reay (ed.), *Popular Culture in Seventeenth-Century England*, 59–90.

—— 'Literacy and Literature in Popular Culture: Reading and Writing in Historical Perspective', in Harris (ed.), *Popular Culture in England*, 69–94.

BASKERVILL, C. R., *The Elizabethan Jig and Related Song Drama* (Chicago, 1929).

BATHO, GORDON, 'Landlords in England', in Thirsk (ed.), *The Agrarian History of England and Wales*, iv: *1500–1640*, 256–306.

BELLAMY, JOHN, *The Tudor Law of Treason: An Introduction* (London, 1979).

BELLANY, ALASTAIR, '"Raylinge Rymes and Vaunting Verse": Libellous Politics in Early Stuart England, 1603–1628', in Kevin Sharpe and Peter Lake (eds.), *Politics and Culture in Early Stuart England* (Basingstoke, 1994), 285–310.

—— 'A Poem on the Archbishop's Hearse: Puritanism, Libel, and Sedition after the Hampton Court Conference, *Journal of British Studies*, 34 (1995), 137–64.

BENNETT, H. S., *English Books and Readers, 1475–1640* (3 vols., Cambridge, 1965–70).

BENNETT, JOAN, 'An Aspect of the Evolution of Seventeenth-Century Prose', *Review of English Studies*, 17 (1941), 281–97.

BIRRELL, JEAN, 'Common Rights in the Medieval Forest: Disputes and Conflicts in the Thirteenth Century', *Past and Present*, 117 (1987), 22–49.

BLACK, W. G., *Folk Medicine; A Chapter in the History of Culture* (Folklore Society, London, 1883).

BLANK, PAULA, *Broken English: Dialects and the Politics of Language in Renaissance Writings* (London, 1996).

BOLTON, W. F. (ed.), *The English Language: Essays by English and American Men of Letters, 1490–1839* (Cambridge, 1966).

BOND, DONALD F., 'English Legal Proverbs', *Publications of the Modern Language Association*, 51 (1936), 921–35.

BORSAY, PETER, *The English Urban Renaissance: Culture and Society in the Provincial Town, 1660–1770* (Oxford, 1989).

BREWER, JOHN, and STYLES, JOHN (eds.), *An Ungovernable People: The English and their Law in the Seventeenth and Eighteenth Centuries* (London, 1980).

BRIGGS, K. M., *The Anatomy of Puck: An Examination of Fairy Beliefs among Shakespeare's Contemporaries and Successors* (London, 1959).

—— *A Dictionary of British Folk-Tales in the English Language* (4 vols., London, 1970).

BRINKWORTH, E. R. C., *Shakespeare and the Bawdy Court of Stratford* (London, 1972).

BRITTEN, JAMES, *Old Country and Farming Words* (English Dialect Society, 30, London, 1880).

BROCKETT, J. T., *A Glossary of North Country Words in Use* (2nd edn., Newcastle, 1829).

BROOK, G. L., *A History of the English Language* (London, 1958).

BROOK, G. L., *English Dialects* (London, 1963).

BROOKS, C. W., *Pettyfoggers and Vipers of the Commonwealth: The 'Lower Branch' of the Legal Profession in Early Modern England* (Cambridge, 1986).

BRYSON, ANNA, *From Courtesy to Civility: Changing Codes of Conduct in Early Modern England* (Oxford, 1998).

BRYSON, W. H., *The Equity Side of the Exchequer* (Cambridge, 1975).

BUCHAN, DAVID, *The Ballad and the Folk* (London, 1972).

BURKE, PETER, *Popular Culture in Early Modern Europe* (London, 1978).

—— 'Introduction', in Burke and Porter (eds.), *The Social History of Language*, 1–20.

—— and PORTER, ROY (eds.), *The Social History of Language* (Cambridge, 1987).

BURKE, U. R., *Spanish Salt: A Collection of all the Proverbs which are to be Found in Don Quixote* (London, 1877).

BURNE, CHARLOTTE S., and JACKSON, GEORGINA F., *Shropshire Folk-Lore: A Sheaf of Gleanings* (London, 1883).

BUSHAWAY, BOB, *By Rite: Custom, Ceremony and Community in England, 1700–1880* (London, 1982).

CAMERON, W. J., 'A Late Seventeenth-Century Scriptorium', *Renaissance and Modern Studies*, 7 (1963), 25–52.

CAMPBELL, J. L., and THOMSON, DERICK, *Edward Lhuyd in the Scottish Highlands, 1699–1700* (Oxford, 1963).

CAMPBELL, MILDRED, *The English Yeoman under Elizabeth and the Early Stuarts* (London, 1960).

CAPP, BERNARD, *Astrology and the Popular Press: English Almanacs, 1500–1800* (London, 1979).

—— 'Popular Literature', in Reay (ed.), *Popular Culture in Seventeenth-Century England*, 198–243.

CHAMBERS, E. K., *The Mediaeval Stage* (2 vols., Oxford, 1903).

—— *The Elizabethan Stage* (4 vols., Oxford, 1923).

—— *English Literature at the Close of the Middle Ages* (Oxford, 1945).

CHAPPELL, W., *Popular Music of the Olden Time* (London, 1859).

CHARLTON, KENNETH, *Education in Renaissance England* (London, 1965).

—— '"Not Publike onely but also Private and Domesticall": Mothers and Familial Education in Pre-Industrial England', *History of Education*, 17 (1988), 1–20.

—— 'Mothers as Educative Agents in Pre-Industrial England', *History of Education*, 23 (1994), 129–56.

CHARTIER, ROGER (ed.), *The Culture of Print: Power and the Uses of Print in Early Modern Europe*, trans. L. G. Cochrane (Cambridge, 1989).

CHARTRES, JOHN, and HEY DAVID (eds.), *English Rural Society, 1500–1800* (Cambridge, 1990).

CHAYTOR, H. J., *From Script to Print: An Introduction to Medieval Vernacular Literature* (Cambridge, 1945).

CLANCHY, M. T., 'Remembering the Past and the Good Old Law', *History*, 55 (1970), 165–76.

—— 'Learning to Read in the Middle Ages and the Role of Mothers', in Greg Brooks and A. K. Pugh (eds.), *Studies in the History of Reading* (Reading, 1984), 33–9.

—— *From Memory to Written Record: England, 1066–1307* (2nd edn., Oxford, 1993).

CLARK, PETER, 'The Ownership of Books in England, 1560–1640: The Example of some Kentish Townsfolk', in Lawrence Stone (ed.), *Schooling and Society: Studies in the History of Education* (Baltimore, 1976), 95–111.

—— *English Provincial Society from the Reformation to the Revolution: Religion, Politics and Society in Kent, 1500–1640* (Hassocks, 1977).

—— *The English Alehouse: A Social History, 1200–1830* (London, 1983).

—— 'Migrants in the City: The Process of Social Adaptation in English Towns 1500–1800', in Peter Clark and David Souden (eds.), *Migration and Society in Early Modern England* (London, 1987), 267–91.

CLAY, CHRISTOPHER, 'Landlords and Estate Management in England, 1640–1750', in Christopher Clay (ed.), *Rural Society: Landowners, Peasants and Labourers, 1500–1750* (Cambridge, 1990), 246–378.

CLIFTON, ROBIN, 'The Popular Fear of Catholics during the English Revolution', *Past and Present*, 52 (1971), 23–55.

—— *The Last Popular Rebellion: The Western Rising of 1685* (London, 1984).

COGSWELL, THOMAS, 'The Politics of Propaganda: Charles I and the People in the 1620s', *Journal of British Studies*, 29 (1990), 187–215.

—— 'Underground Verse and the Transformation of Early Stuart Political Culture', in Susan Amussen and Mark Kishlansky (eds.), *Political Culture and Cultural Politics in Early Modern England* (Manchester, 1995), 277–300.

COLLINSON, PATRICK, *The Elizabethan Puritan Movement* (London, 1967).

—— *The Religion of Protestants: The Church in English Society, 1559–1625* (Oxford, 1982).

—— *The Birthpangs of Protestant England: Religious and Cultural Change in the Sixteenth and Seventeenth Centuries* (Basingstoke, 1988).

—— 'Ecclesiastical Vitriol: Religious Satire in the 1590s and the Invention of Puritanism', in John Guy (ed.), *The Reign of Elizabeth I: Court and Culture in the Last Decade* (Cambridge, 1995), 150–70.

CONNERTON, PAUL, *How Societies Remember* (Cambridge, 1989).

COSS, P. R., 'Aspects of Cultural Diffusion in Medieval England: The Early Romances, Local Society and Robin Hood', *Past and Present*, 108 (1985), 35–79.

COTTLE, BASIL, *The Triumph of English, 1350–1400* (London, 1969).

CRAIGIE, WILLIAM A. (ed.), *The Critique of Pure English from Caxton to Smollett* (Oxford, 1946).

CRANE, RONALD S., 'The Vogue of Guy of Warwick from the Close of the Middle Ages to the Romantic Revival', *Publications of the Modern Language Association*, 30 (1915), 125–94.

CRANFIELD, G. A., *The Press and Society from Caxton to Northcliffe* (London, 1978).

CRAWFORD, CHARLES, *Collectanea: First Series* (Stratford-on-Avon, 1906).

—— *Collectanea: Second Series* (Stratford-on-Avon, 1907).

CRESSY, DAVID, *Literacy and the Social Order: Reading and Writing in Tudor and Stuart England* (Cambridge, 1980).

CROFT, PAULINE, 'The Reputation of Robert Cecil: Libels, Political Opinion and Popular Awareness in the Early Seventeenth Century', *Transactions of the Royal Historical Society*, sixth ser., 1 (1991), 43–69.

CROFTS, J., *Packhorse, Waggon and Post: Land Carriage and Communications under the Tudors and Stuarts* (London, 1967).

CROSBY, RUTH, 'Oral Delivery in the Middle Ages', *Speculum*, 11 (1936), 88–110.

CROW, JOHN, 'Some Jacobean Catch-Phrases and Some Light on Thomas Bretnor', in Herbert Davis and Helen Gardner (eds.), *Elizabethan and Jacobean Studies Presented to Frank Percy Wilson* (Oxford, 1959), 250–78.

CUST, RICHARD, 'News and Politics in Early Seventeenth-Century England', *Past and Present*, 112 (1986), 60–90.

—— 'Honour and Politics in Early Stuart England: The Case of Beaumont v. Hastings', *Past and Present*, 149 (1995), 57–94.

DAHL, FOLKE, 'Short Title Catalogue of English Corantos and Newsbooks, 1620–1642', *Library*, fourth ser., 19 (1939), 44–98.

DAVIES, CONSTANCE, *English Pronunciation from the Fifteenth to the Eighteenth Centuries* (London, 1934).

DAVIES, HORTON, *Like Angels from a Cloud: The English Metaphysical Preachers, 1588–1645* (San Marino, Calif., 1986).

DAVIS, NATALIE ZEMON, *Society and Culture in Early Modern France* (Stanford, Calif., 1975).

DEACON, GEORGE, *John Clare and the Folk Tradition* (London, 1983).

DENHAM, M. A., *A Collection of Proverbs and Popular Sayings, Relating to the Seasons, the Weather, and Agricultural Pursuits; Gathered Chiefly from Oral Tradition* (Percy Society, 20, London, 1846).

*The Denham Tracts*, ed. James Hardy (2 vols., Folklore Society, London, 1892–5).

DENT, R. W., *Shakespeare's Proverbial Language: An Index* (Berkeley and Los Angeles, 1981).

DILLEY, ROBERT S., 'The Cumberland Court Leet and Use of the Common Lands', *Transactions of the Cumberland and Westmorland Antiquarian and Archaeological Society*, new ser., 67 (1967), 125–51.

D'ISRAELI, ISAAC, 'The Philosophy of Proverbs', in his *A Second Series of Curiosities of Literature* (3 vols., London, 1823), i. 414–80.

DOBSON, E. J., 'Early Modern Standard English', *Transactions of the Philological Society* (1955), 25–54.

—— *English Pronunciation, 1500–1700* (2nd edn., 2 vols., Oxford, 1969).

DORSON, RICHARD M., *The British Folklorists: A History* (London, 1968).

DOUGLAS, DAVID C., *English Scholars, 1660–1730* (2nd edn., London, 1951).

DUFFY, EAMON, *The Stripping of the Altars: Traditional Religion in England, c.1400–c.1580* (New Haven, 1992).

DUNDES, ALAN, 'On the Structure of the Proverb', *Proverbium*, 25 (1975), 961–73.

EISENSTEIN, ELZABETH L., *The Printing Press as an Agent of Change: Communications and Cultural Transformations in Early-Modern Europe* (2 vols., Cambridge, 1979).

ELLIOTT, RALPH W. V., 'Isaac Newton as Phonetician', *Modern Language Review*, 49 (1954), 5–12.

ELLIOTT, V. B., 'Single Women in the London Marriage Market: Age, Status and Mobility, 1598–1619', in R. B. Outhwaite (ed.), *Marriage and Society: Studies in the Social History of Marriage* (London, 1981), 81–100.

ELLIS, ALEXANDER J., *On Early English Pronunciation* (5 vols., London, 1869–89).

ELTON, G. R., *Police and Police: The Enforcement of the Reformation in the Age of Thomas Cromwell* (Cambridge, 1972).

EMMISON, F. G., *Elizabethan Life: Disorder* (Chelmsford, 1970).

—— *Elizabethan Life: Morals and the Church Courts* (Chelmsford, 1973).

—— *Elizabethan Life: Home, Work and Land* (Chelmsford, 1976).

EVANS, A. J., 'The Rollright Stones and their Folk-Lore', *Folk-Lore*, 6 (1895), 6–51.

EVERITT, ALAN, 'Farm Labourers', in Thirsk (ed.), *The Agrarian History of England and Wales*, iv. 396–465.

—— 'The Marketing of Agricultural Produce', in Thirsk (ed.), *The Agrarian History of England and Wales*, iv. 466–592.

—— 'The English Urban Inn, 1560–1760', in Alan Everitt (ed.), *Perspectives in English Urban History* (London, 1973), 91–137.

—— 'River and Wold: Reflections on the Historical Origin of Regions and Pays', *Journal of Historical Geography*, 3 (1977), 1–19.

—— 'Country, County and Town: Patterns of Regional Evolution in England', *Transactions of the Royal Historical Society*, fifth ser., 29 (1979), 78–108.

EWEN, C. L'ESTRANGE, *Witchcraft in the Star Chamber* (n. pl., 1938).

FAITH, ROSAMOND, 'The Class Struggle in Fourteenth-Century England', in Raphael Samuel (ed.), *People's History and Socialist Theory* (London, 1981), 50–60.

FEBVRE, LUCIEN, and MARTIN, HENRI-JEAN, *The Coming of the Book: The Impact of Printing, 1450–1800*, trans. David Gerard (London, 1976).

FENTRESS, JAMES, and WICKHAM, CHRIS, *Social Memory* (Oxford, 1992).

FINNEGAN, RUTH, 'Literacy Versus Non-Literacy: The Great Divide?', in Robin Horton and Ruth Finnegan (eds.), *Modes of Thought: Essays on Thinking in Western and Non-Western Societies* (London, 1973), 112–44.

—— *Oral Poetry: Its Nature, Significance and Social Context* (Cambridge, 1977).

—— *Literacy and Orality: Studies in the Technology of Communication* (Oxford, 1988).

FIRTH, C. H., 'Ballads on the Bishops' Wars, 1638–40', *Scottish Historical Review*, 3 (1906), 257–73.

—— 'The Ballad History of the Reigns of Henry VII and Henry VIII', *Transactions of the Royal Historical Society*, third ser., 2 (1908), 21–50.

—— 'The Ballad History of the Reigns of the Later Tudors', *Transactions of the Royal Historical Society*, third ser., 3 (1909), 51–124.

—— 'The Ballad History of the Reign of James I', *Transactions of the Royal Historical Society*, third ser., 5 (1911), 21–61.

FIRTH, C. H., 'The Reign of Charles I', *Transactions of the Royal Historical Society*, third ser., 6 (1912), 19–64.

FISCHER, DAVID HACKETT, *Albion's Seed: Four British Folkways in America* (Oxford, 1989).

FISHER, JOHN H., 'Chancery English and the Emergence of Standard Written English in the Fifteenth Century', *Speculum*, 52 (1977), 870–99.

—— 'Caxton and Chancery English', in Robert F. Yeager (ed.), *Fifteenth-Century Studies* (Hamden, Conn., 1984), 161–85.

FISHER, W. R., *The Forest of Essex: Its History, Laws, Administration and Ancient Customs* (London, 1887).

FLETCHER, ANTHONY, and STEVENSON, JOHN (eds.), *Order and Disorder in Early Modern England* (Cambridge, 1985).

*Folklore, Myths and Legends of Britain* (London, 1973).

FORBY, ROBERT, *The Vocabulary of East Anglia* (2 vols., London, 1830).

FOX, LEVI (ed.), *English Historical Scholarship in the Sixteenth and Seventeenth Centuries* (London, 1956).

FRANK, JOSEPH, *The Beginnings of the English Newspaper, 1620–1660* (Cambridge, Mass., 1961).

FRASER, PETER, *The Intelligence of the Secretaries of State and their Monopoly of Licensed News, 1660–1688* (Cambridge, 1956).

FREARSON, M. C., 'The English Corantos of the 1620s' (unpublished Ph.D. dissertation, University of Cambridge, 1993).

FREIST, DAGMAR, *Governed by Opinion: Politics, Religion and the Dynamics of Communication in Stuart London, 1637–1645* (London, 1997).

GIGLIOLI, PIER PAOLO (ed.), *Language and Social Context* (Harmondsworth, 1972).

GOMME, A. B., *The Traditional Games of England, Scotland, and Ireland* (2 vols., London, 1894–8; repr., 1984).

GOODY, JACK (ed.), *Literacy in Traditional Societies* (Cambridge, 1968).

—— *The Domestication of the Savage Mind* (Cambridge, 1977).

—— *The Logic of Writing and the Organization of Society* (Cambridge, 1986).

—— *The Interface between the Written and the Oral* (Cambridge, 1987).

—— and WATT, IAN, 'The Consequences of Literacy' in Goody (ed.), *Literacy in Traditional Societies*, 27–68.

GÖRLACH, MANFRED, *Introduction to Early Modern English* (Cambridge, 1991).

GOUGH, J. W., *The Mines of Mendip* (London, 1967).

GOWING, LAURA, *Domestic Dangers: Women, Words and Sex in Early Modern London* (Oxford, 1996).

GRAFF, HARVEY J., *The Legacies of Literacy* (Bloomington, 1987).

GRAY, C. M., *Copyhold, Equity, and the Common Law* (Cambridge, Mass., 1963).

GREEN, IAN, *The Christian's ABC: Catechisms and Catechizing in England, c.1530–1740* (Oxford, 1996).

GRIFFITHS, ANTONY, *The Print in Stuart Britain 1603–1689* (London, 1998).

GRIFFITHS, PAUL, FOX, ADAM, and HINDLE, STEVE (eds.), *The Experience of Authority in Early Modern England* (Basingstoke, 1996).

GRINSELL, L. V., 'The Legendary History and Folklore of Stonehenge', *Folklore*, 87 (1976), 5–20.

GUTCH, E., *Examples of Printed Folk-Lore Concerning the North Riding of Yorkshire, York and the Ainsty* (Folklore Society, London, 1901).

—— *Examples of Printed Folk-Lore Concerning the East Riding of Yorkshire* (Folklore Society, London, 1912).

—— and PEACOCK, MABEL, *Examples of Printed Folk-Lore Concerning Lincolnshire* (Folklore Society, London, 1908).

GUY, J. A., *The Court of Star Chamber and its Records to the Reign of Elizabeth I* (Public Record Office Handbooks, 21, London, 1985).

HABERMAS, JÜRGEN, *The Structural Transformation of the Public Sphere: An Inquiry into a Category of Bourgeois Society*, trans. Thomas Burger (1962; Cambridge, Mass., 1989).

HALDANE, A. R. B., *Three Centuries of Scottish Posts: An Historical Survey to 1836* (Edinburgh, 1971).

HALLIWELL, J. O., *The Nursery Rhymes of England, Collected Principally from Oral Tradition* (Percy Society, 4, London, 1842) and (5th edn., London, 1853).

—— *An Historical Sketch of the Provincial Dialects of England* (London, 1847).

—— *Descriptive Notices of Popular English Histories* (Percy Society, 23, London, 1848).

—— *Popular Rhymes and Nursery Tales* (London, 1849).

—— *Dictionary of Archaic Words* (London, 1850).

HAMBURGER, PHILIP, 'The Development of the Law of Seditious Libel and the Control of the Press', *Stanford Law Review*, 37 (1984–5), 661–765.

HANSON, LAURENCE, 'English Newsbooks, 1620–1641', *Library*, fourth ser., 18 (1938), 355–84.

HARDY, THOMAS, *The Mayor of Casterbridge* (1886; New Wessex edn., London, 1974).

—— *Tess of the d'Urbervilles* (1891; New Wessex edn., London, 1974).

HARRIS, TIM, *London Crowds in the Reign of Charles II: Propaganda and Politics from the Restoration until the Exclusion Crisis* (Cambridge, 1987).

—— (ed.), *Popular Culture in England, c.1500–1850* (Basingstoke, 1995).

HART, CYRIL E., *The Commoners of Dean Forest* (Gloucester, 1951).

—— *The Free Miners of the Royal Forest of Dean and the Hundred of St. Briavels* (Gloucester, 1953).

HAZLITT, W. C., *Tenures of Land and Customs of Manors* (London, 1874).

HENDERSON, ANDREW, *Scottish Proverbs* (Edinburgh, 1832).

HENIGE, DAVID, *The Chronology of Oral Tradition* (Oxford, 1974).

—— *Oral Historiography* (London, 1982).

HESELTINE, JANET E., 'Introduction', in W. G. Smith, *The Oxford Dictionary of English Proverbs* (Oxford, 1935), vii–xxviii.

HESLOP, OLIVER, *Northumberland Words: A Glossary of Words Used in the County of Northumberland and on Tyneside* (2 vols., English Dialect Society, 66, London, 1892).

HILL, CHRISTOPHER, *The World Turned Upside Down: Radical Ideas during the English Revolution* (London, 1972).

HILL, J. W. F., *Tudor and Stuart Lincoln* (Cambridge, 1956).

HINDLE, STEVE, 'The Shaming of Margaret Knowsley: Gender, Gossip and the Experience of Authority in Early Modern England', *Continuity and Change*, 9 (1994), 391–419.

HOLDEN, WILLIAM P., *Anti-Puritan Satire, 1572–1642* (New Haven, 1954).

HOLDSWORTH, W. S., *A History of English Law* (17 vols., London, 1903–72).

—— 'Defamation in the Sixteenth and Seventeenth Centuries', *Law Quarterly Review*, 40 (1924), 302–15, 397–412, and 41 (1925), 13–31.

HOLMES, CLIVE, 'Drainers and Fenmen: The Problem of Popular Political Consciousness in the Seventeenth Century', in Fletcher and Stevenson (eds.), *Order and Disorder in Early Modern England*, 166–95.

HOLT, J. C., *Robin Hood* (2nd edn., London, 1989).

HOMANS, G. C., *English Villagers of the Thirteenth Century* (Cambridge, Mass., 1941).

HONE, WILLIAM, *The Every-Day Book* (2 vols., London, 1825–7).

HOUSTON, R. A., *Scottish Literacy and the Scottish Identity: Illiteracy and Society in Scotland and Northern England, 1600–1800* (Cambridge, 1985).

HOYLE, R. W. (ed.), *The Estates of the English Crown, 1558–1640* (Cambridge, 1992).

HUDSON, ANNE, *The Premature Reformation: Wycliffite Texts and Lollard History* (Oxford, 1988).

HUDSON, KENNETH, 'Shakespeare's Use of Colloquial Language', in Kenneth Muir (ed.), *Shakespeare Survey*, 23 (Cambridge, 1970), 39–48.

HUGHES, ANN, 'Religion and Society in Statford upon Avon, 1619–38', *Midland History*, 19 (1994), 58–84.

HUGHES, EDWARD, *North Country Life in the Eighteenth Century: The North East, 1700–1750* (Oxford, 1952).

HULME, HILDA M., 'Derbyshire Dialect in the Seventeenth Century', *Journal of the Derbyshire Archaeological Society*, new ser., 15 (1941), 88–103.

HUNT, ROBERT, *Popular Romances of the West of England* (2 vols., London, 1865).

HUNT, WILLIAM, *The Puritan Moment: The Coming of Revolution in an English County* (Cambridge, Mass., 1983).

HUNTER, G. K., 'The Marking of *Sententiae* in Elizabethan Printed Plays, Poems and Romances', *Library*, fifth ser., 6 (1951), 171–88.

HUNTER, MICHAEL, *John Aubrey and the Realm of Learning* (London, 1975).

HUTTON, RONALD, *The Rise and Fall of Merry England: The Ritual Year, 1400–1700* (Oxford, 1994).

—— *The Stations of the Sun: A History of the Ritual Year in Britain* (Oxford, 1996).

INGRAM, MARTIN, 'Ridings, Rough Music and Mocking Rhymes in Early Modern England' in Reay (ed.), *Popular Culture in Seventeenth-Century England*, 166–197.

—— *Church Courts, Sex and Marriage in England, 1570–1640* (Cambridge, 1987).

JARRELL, MACKIE L., 'The Proverbs in Swift's *Polite Conversation*', *Huntington Library Quarterly*, 20/1 (1956), 15–38.

JOHNSON, WALTER, *Folk Memory: Or the Continuity of British Archaeology* (Oxford, 1908).

JOHNSTONE, PHILIP MAINWARING, 'Mural Paintings in Houses: With Special Reference to Recent Discoveries at Stratford-on-Avon and Oxford', *Journal of the British Archaeological Association*, new ser., 37 (1932), 75–100.

JONES, JAMES H., 'Commonplace and Memorization in the Oral Tradition of English and Scottish Popular Ballads', *Journal of American Folklore*, 74 (1961), 97–112.

JONES, RICHARD FOSTER, *The Seventeenth Century: Studies in the History of English Thought and Literature from Bacon to Pope* (Sanford, Calif., 1951).

—— *The Triumph of the English Language* (Stanford, Calif., 1953).

JONES, W. J., 'A Note on the Demise of Manorial Jurisdiction: The Impact of Chancery', *American Journal of Legal History*, 10 (1966), 297–318.

—— *The Elizabethan Court of Chancery* (Oxford, 1967).

KAYE, J. M., 'Libel and Slander-Two Torts or One?', *Law Quarterly Review*, 91 (1975), 524–39.

KENDRICK, T. D., *British Antiquity* (London, 1950).

KERRIDGE, ERIC, *Agrarian Problems in the Sixteenth Century and after* (London, 1969).

KINGSFORD, C. L., *English Historical Literature in the Fifteenth Century* (Oxford, 1913).

KIRSHENBLATT-GIMBLETT, BARBARA, 'Toward a Theory of Proverb Meaning', *Proverbium*, 22 (1973), 821–27.

KNIGHTS, L. C., *Drama and Society in the Age of Jonson* (London, 1937).

KÖKERITZ, HELGE, 'Shakespeare's Use of Dialect', *Transactions of the Yorkshire Dialect Society*, 60 (1951), 10–25.

LAQUEUR, T. W., 'The Cultural Origins of Popular Literacy in England, 1500–1850', *Oxford Review of Education*, 2 (1976), 255–75.

LARWOOD, JACOB, and HOTTEN, JOHN CAMDEN, *The History of Signboards, from the Earliest Times to the Present Day* (2nd edn., London, 1866).

LECHNER, JOAN MARIE, *Renaissance Concepts of the Commonplaces* (New York, 1962).

LEVY, F. J., 'How Information Spread among the Gentry, 1550–1640', *Journal of British Studies*, 21/2 (1982), 11–34.

LILLYWHITE, BRYANT, *London Coffee Houses* (London, 1963).

LINDLEY, KEITH, *Fenland Riots and the English Revolution* (London, 1982).

LOVE, HAROLD, *Scribal Publication in Seventeenth-Century England* (Oxford, 1993).

MACAULAY, T. B., *The History of England*, ed. Hugh Trevor-Roper (Harmondsworth, 1979).

MACCULLOCH, DIARMAID, 'Kett's Rebellion in Context', *Past and Present*, 84 (1979), 36–59.

MACDERMOT, EDWARD T., *The History of the Forest of Exmoor* (1911; rev. edn., Newton Abbot, 1973).

MCINTOSH, M. K., *A Community Transformed: The Manor and Liberty of Havering, 1500–1620* (Cambridge, 1991).

McKENZIE, D. F., *Oral Culture, Literacy and Print in Early New Zealand: The Treaty of Waitangi* (Wellington, 1985).

—— 'Speech-Manuscript-Print', in Dave Oliphant and Robin Bradford (eds.), *New Directions in Textual Studies* (Austin, Tex., 1990), 87–109.

MAGEE, BRIAN, 'The Protestant Wind: Some Aspects of the Revolution of 1688', *Month*, 177/922 (1941), 334–43.

MALCOLMSON, R. W., '"A Set of Ungovernable People": The Kingswood Colliers in the Eighteenth Century', in Brewer and Styles (eds.), *An Ungovernable People*, 85–127.

MANNING, ROGER B., 'The Origins of the Doctrine of Sedition', *Albion*, 12 (1980), 99–121.

—— *Village Revolts: Social Protest and Popular Disturbances in England, 1509–1640* (Oxford, 1988).

MARCKWARDT, ALBERT H., 'An Unnoted Source of English Dialect Vocabulary', *Journal of English and Germanic Philology*, 46 (1947), 177–82.

MARTIN, MORRIS, 'The Case of the Missing Woodcuts', *Print Quarterly*, 4 (1987), 343–61.

MATTHEWS, WILLIAM, *Cockney Past and Present* (London, 1938).

—— 'South Western Dialect in the Early Modern Period', *Neophilologus*, 24 (1939), 193–209.

MITCHELL, W. F., *English Pulpit Oratory from Andrewes to Tillotson* (London, 1932).

MORAN, J. HOEPPNER, 'Literacy and Education in Northern England, 1350–1550: A Methodological Inquiry', *Northern History*, 17 (1981), 1–23.

—— *The Growth of English Schooling, 1340–1548: Learning, Literacy, and Laicization in Pre-Reformation York Diocese* (Princeton, 1985).

MOTHERWELL, WILLIAM, 'Preface', to Henderson, *Scottish Proverbs*, vii–lxxxvii.

MUGGLESTONE, LYNDA, '*Talking Proper*': *The Rise of Accent as Social Symbol* (Oxford, 1995).

NEESON, J. M., *Commoners: Common Right, Enclosure and Social Change in England, 1700–1820* (Cambridge, 1993).

NEUBURG, VICTOR E., *Popular Literature: A History and a Guide* (London, 1977).

NORTHALL, G. F., *English Folk-Rhymes* (London, 1892).

—— *Folk-phrases of Four Counties (Glouc., Staff., Warw., Worc.,) Gathered from Unpublished MSS. and Oral Tradition* (English Dialect Society, 73, London, 1894).

OBELKEVICH, JAMES, 'Proverbs and Social History', in Burke and Porter (eds.), *The Social History of Language*, 43–72.

O'CONOR, NORREYS JEPHSON, *Godes Peace and the Queenes: Vicissitudes of a House, 1539–1615* (London, 1934).

O'DAY, ROSEMARY, *Education and Society, 1500–1800: The Social Foundations of Education in Early Modern Britain* (London, 1982).

OFFER, R., 'Two Mining Account Books from Farnley Colliery, 1690–1720', *Transactions of the Yorkshire Dialect Society*, 5/34 (1933), 9–28.

OHLGREN, THOMAS H. (ed.), *Medieval Outlaws: Ten Tales in Modern English* (Stroud, 1998).

ONG, WALTER J., 'Oral Residue in Tudor Prose Style', *Publications of the Modern Language Association*, 80 (1965), 145–54.

—— *Orality and Literacy: The Technologizing of the Word* (London, 1982).

OPIE, IONA, and OPIE, PETER, *The Oxford Dictionary of Nursery Rhymes* (Oxford, 1951).

—— *The Lore and Language of Schoolchildren* (Oxford, 1959).

—— *The Classic Fairy Tales* (Oxford, 1974).

—— and TATEM, MOIRA, *A Dictionary of Superstitions* (Oxford, 1989).

ORME, NICHOLAS, *English Schools in the Middle Ages* (London, 1973).

—— *Education and Society in Medieval and Renaissance England* (London, 1989).

—— 'The Culture of Children in Medieval England', *Past and Present*, 148 (1995), 48–88.

OWST, G. R., *Literature and Pulpit in Medieval England* (2nd edn., Oxford, 1961).

PALLISER, D. M., 'Civic Mentality and the Environment in Tudor York', *Northern History*, 18 (1982), 78–115.

PANTIN, W. A., 'A Medieval Collection of Latin and English Proverbs and Riddles, from the Rylands Latin MS. 394', *Bulletin of the John Rylands Library*, 14 (1930), 81–114.

PARKINSON, THOMAS, *Yorkshire Legends and Traditions* (2 vols., London, 1888–9).

PARTRIDGE, A. C., *Orthography in Shakespeare and Elizabethan Drama* (London, 1964).

PETTIT, P. A. J., *The Royal Forests of Northamptonshire: A Study in their Economy, 1558–1714* (Northamptonshire Record Society, Gateshead, 1968).

PHILLIPS, MARGARET MANN, *The 'Adages' of Erasmus: A Study with Translations* (Cambridge, 1964).

PHYTHIAN-ADAMS, CHARLES, 'Ceremony and the Citizen: The Communal Year at Coventry 1450–1550', in Peter Clark and Paul Slack (eds.), *Crisis and Order in English Towns, 1500–1700* (London, 1972), 57–85.

—— *Re-thinking English Local History* (Occasional Papers in English Local History, Leicester, 1987).

PINCUS, STEVE, '"Coffee Politicians Does Create": Coffeehouses and Restoration Political Culture', *Journal of Modern History*, 67 (1995), 807–34.

PORTER, ENID, *Cambridgeshire Customs and Folklore* (London, 1969).

POWELL, ANTHONY, *John Aubrey and his Friends* (London, 1948).

PRIDE, J. B., and HOLMES, J. (eds.), *Sociolinguistics* (Harmondsworth, 1972).

RAVEN, C. E., *English Naturalists from Neckam to Ray* (Cambridge, 1947).

—— *John Ray: Naturalist* (2nd edn., Cambridge, 1950).

READER, FRANCIS W., 'Wall-Paintings of the Sixteenth and Early Seventeenth Centuries Recently Discovered in Bosworth House, Wendover, Bucks', *Archaeological Journal*, 87 (1930), 71–97.

—— 'Tudor Mural Paintings in Lesser Houses in Bucks', *Archaeological Journal*, 89 (1932), 116–73.

—— 'Tudor Domestic Wall-Paintings', *Archaeological Journal*, 92 (1935), 243–86.

—— 'Tudor Domestic Wall-Painting, Part II', *Archaeological Journal*, 93 (1936), 220–62.

REAY, BARRY, 'Popular Literature in Seventeenth-Century England', *Journal of Peasant Studies*, 10 (1983), 243–49.

—— (ed.), *Popular Culture in Seventeenth-Century England* (London, 1985).

—— 'Introduction: Popular Culture in Early Modern England', in Reay (ed.), *Popular Culture in Seventeenth-Century England*, 1–30.

ROBERTSON, JEAN, *The Art of Letter Writing: An Essay on the Handbooks Published in England During the Sixteenth and Seventeenth Centuries* (London, 1942).

ROBINSON, HOWARD, *The British Post Office: A History* (Princeton, 1948).

ROLLINS, HYDER E., 'The Black-Letter Broadside Ballad', *Publications of the Modern Language Association*, 34 (1919), 258–339.

—— 'Concerning Bodleian MS. Ashmole 48', *Modern Language Notes*, 34 (1919), 340–51.

—— 'An Analytical Index to the Ballad Entries (1557–1709) in the Register of the Company of Stationers of London', *Studies in Philology*, 21 (1924), 1–324.

ROLLISON, DAVID, 'The Bourgeois Soul of John Smyth of Nibley', *Social History*, 12 (1987), 308–30.

—— *The Local Origins of Modern Society: Gloucestershire, 1500–1800* (London, 1992).

ROSS, ANNE, 'Severed Heads in Wells: An Aspect of the Well Cult', *Scottish Studies*, 6 (1962), 31–48.

ROSS, RICHARD, 'The Memorial Culture of Early Modern English Lawyers: Memory as Keyword, Shelter, and Identity, 1560–1640', *Yale Journal of Law and the Humanities*, 10 (1998), 229–326.

SACHSE, WILLIAM L., 'The Mob and the Revolution of 1688', *Journal of British Studies*, 4 (1964), 23–40.

SALMON, VIVIAN, 'Language-Planning in Seventeenth-Century England: Its Context and Aims', in C. E. Bazell et al. (eds.), *In Memory of J. R. Firth* (London, 1966), 370–97.

SAMAHA, JOEL, 'Gleanings from Local Criminal-Court Records: Sedition amongst the "Inarticulate" in Elizabethan Essex', *Journal of Social History*, 8/4 (1975), 61–79.

SAUNDERS, J. W., 'The Stigma of Print: A Note on the Social Bases of Tudor Poetry', *Essays in Criticism*, 1 (1951), 139–64.

SCHOELL, FRANK L., 'G. Chapman's Commonplace Book', *Modern Philology*, 17 (1919–20), 199–218.

SCHOENBAUM, S., *Shakespeare's Lives* (2nd edn., Oxford, 1991).

SCHOFIELD, R. S., 'The Measurement of Literacy in Pre-Industrial England', in Goody (ed.), *Literacy in Traditional Societies*, 311–25.

SCOTT, JAMES C., *Domination and the Arts of Resistance: Hidden Transcripts* (New Haven, 1990).

SCOTT, SIR WALTER, *Minstrelsy of the Scottish Border*, ed. Thomas Henderson (London, 1931).

SCRIBNER, R. W., 'Oral Culture and the Diffusion of Reformation Ideas', *History of European Ideas*, 5 (1984), 237–56.

SHAABER, MATTHIAS A., *Some Forerunners of the Newspaper in England, 1476–1622* (Philadelphia, 1929).

SHAKLEE, MARGARET, 'The Rise of Standard English', in Timothy Shopen and Joseph M. Williams (eds.), *Standards and Dialects in English* (Cambridge, Mass., 1980), 33–62.

SHAPIN, STEVEN, *A Social History of Truth: Civility and Science in Seventeenth-Century England* (Chicago, 1994).

SHARP, BUCHANAN, *In Contempt of All Authority: Rural Artisans and Riot in the West of England, 1586–1660* (Berkeley and Los Angeles, 1980).

—— 'Popular Political Opinion in England, 1660–1685', *History of European Ideas*, 10 (1989), 13–29.

SHARPE, J. A., *Defamation and Sexual Slander in Early Modern England: The Church Courts at York* (Borthwick Papers, 58, York, 1980).

—— *Early Modern England: A Social History, 1550–1760* (2nd edn., London, 1997).

SHAW-LEFEVRE, G. J., LORD EVERSLEY, *Commons, Forests and Footpaths* (London, 1910).

SIEBERT, F. S., *Freedom of the Press in England, 1476–1776* (Urbana, Ill., 1952).

SIMON, JOAN, *Education and Society in Tudor England* (Cambridge, 1966).

SIMPSON, CLAUDE M., *The British Broadside Ballad and its Music* (New Brunswick, NJ, 1966).

SIMPSON, JACQUELINE, 'The Local Legend: A Product of Popular Culture', *Rural History*, 2 (1991), 25–35.

SIMPSON, JOHN, and SPEAKE, JENNIFER, *The Concise Oxford Dictionary of Proverbs* (3rd edn., Oxford, 1998).

SISSON, C. J., *Lost Plays of Shakespeare's Age* (Cambridge, 1936).

—— and ZACHRISSON, R. E., 'New Materials for the Study of Tudor and Stuart English', *Studia Neophilologica*, 3 (1930), 101–15.

SKEAT, W. W., *Early English Proverbs Chiefly of the Thirteenth and Fourteenth Centuries* (Oxford, 1910).

—— *English Dialects from the Eighth Century to the Present Day* (Cambridge, 1911).

SKINNER, QUENTIN, *Reason and Rhetoric in the Philosophy of Hobbes* (Cambridge, 1996).

SLACK, PAUL, 'Mirrors of Health and Treasures of Poor Men: The Uses of the Vernacular Medical Literature of Tudor England', in Charles Webster (ed.), *Health, Medicine and Mortality in the Sixteenth Century* (Cambridge, 1979), 237–73.

SMITH, ALAN, 'The Image of Cromwell in Folklore and Tradition', *Folklore*, 79 (1968), 17–39.

SMITH, CHARLES G., *Spenser's Proverb Lore* (Cambridge, Mass., 1970).

SMITH, JOHN RUSSELL, *A Bibliographical List of the Works that have been Published towards Illustrating the Provincial Dialects of England* (London, 1839).

SMITH, NIGEL, *Literature and Revolution in England, 1640–1660* (New Haven, 1994).

SMOUT, T. C., 'Born Again at Cambuslang: New Evidence on Popular Religion and Literacy in Eighteenth-Century Scotland', *Past and Present*, 97 (1982), 114–27.

SPUFFORD, MARGARET, *Contrasting Communities: English Villagers in the Sixteenth and Seventeenth Centuries* (Cambridge, 1974).

—— 'First Steps in Literacy: The Reading and Writing Experiences of the Humblest Seventeenth-Century Spiritual Autobiographers', *Social History*, 4 (1979), 407–35.

—— *Small Books and Pleasant Histories: Popular Fiction and its Readership in Seventeenth-Century England* (London, 1981).

—— (ed.), *The World of Rural Dissenters, 1520–1725* (Cambridge, 1995).

—— 'Women Teaching Reading to Poor Children in the Sixteenth and Seventeenth Centuries', in Mary Hilton, Morag Styles, and Victor Watson (eds.), *Opening the Nursery Door: Reading, Writing and Childhood 1600–1900* (London, 1997), 47–62.

STARNES, DE WITT T., and NOYES, GERTRUDE E., *The English Dictionary from Cawdrey to Johnson, 1604–1755* (Chapel Hill, NC, 1946).

STEPHEN, J. F., *A History of the Criminal Law of England* (3 vols., London, 1883).

STONE, LAWRENCE, 'The Educational Revolution in England, 1560–1640', *Past and Present*, 28 (1964), 41–80.

—— *The Crisis of the Aristocracy 1558–1641* (Oxford, 1965).

STREET, B. V., *Literacy in Theory and Practice* (Cambridge, 1984).

STRETTON, TIM, 'Women, Custom and Equity in the Court of Requests', in Jenny Kermode and Garthine Walker (eds.), *Women, Crime and the Courts in Early Modern England* (London, 1994), 170–89.

TATE, W. E., *The Parish Chest: A Study of the Records of Parochial Administration in England* (3rd edn., Cambridge, 1969).

TATLOCK, J. S. P., *The Legendary History of Britain: Geoffrey of Monmouth's Historia Regum Britanniae and its Early Vernacular Versions* (Berkeley and Los Angeles, 1950).

TAWNEY, R. H., *The Agrarian Problem in the Sixteenth Century* (London, 1912).

TAYLOR, ARCHER, *The Proverb* (Cambridge, Mass., 1931).

—— *English Riddles from Oral Tradition* (Berkeley, Calif., 1951).

—— *Selected Writings on Proverbs*, ed. Wolfgang Mieder (Helsinki, 1975).

TAYLOR, RUPERT, *The Political Prophecy in England* (New York, 1911).

THIRSK, JOAN (ed.), *The Agrarian History of England and Wales*, iv: *1500–1640* (Cambridge, 1967).

THOMAS, KEITH, *Religion and the Decline of Magic: Studies in Popular Beliefs in Sixteenth- and Seventeenth-Century England* (London, 1971).

—— 'Age and Authority in Early Modern England', *Proceedings of the British Academy*, 62 (1976), 205–48.

—— 'The Place of Laughter in Tudor and Stuart England', *Times Literary Supplement* (21 Jan. 1977), 77–81.

—— *Man and the Natural World: Changing Attitudes in England, 1500–1800* (London, 1983).

—— *The Perception of the Past in Early Modern England* (Creighton Trust Lecture, London, 1984).

—— 'The Meaning of Literacy in Early Modern England', in Gerd Baumann (ed.), *The Written Word: Literacy in Transition* (Oxford, 1986), 97–131.

—— 'Numeracy in Early Modern England', *Transactions of the Royal Historical Society*, fifth ser., 37 (1987), 103–32.

—— 'Children in Early Modern England', in Gillian Avery and Julia Briggs (eds.), *Children and their Books* (Oxford, 1989), 45–77.

THOMAS, ROSALIND, *Oral Tradition and Written Record in Classical Athens* (Cambridge, 1989).

THOMASON, GEORGE, *Catalogue of the Pamphlets, Books, Newspapers, and Manuscripts Relating to the Civil War, the Commonwealth, and Restoration, Collected by George Thomason, 1640–1661* (2 vols., London, 1908).

THOMPSON, E. P., 'Anthropology and the Discipline of Historical Context', *Midland History*, 1/3 (1972), 41–55.

—— 'The Crime of Anonymity', in Douglas Hay et al., *Albion's Fatal Tree: Crime and Society in Eighteenth-Century England* (London, 1975), 255–344.

—— *Whigs and Hunters: The Origin of the Black Act* (London, 1975).

—— 'The Grid of Inheritance: A Comment', in Jack Goody, Joan Thirsk, and E. P. Thompson (eds.), *Family and Inheritance: Rural Society in Western Europe, 1200–1800* (Cambridge, 1976), 328–60.

—— *Customs in Common* (London, 1991).

—— 'History and Anthropology', repr. in his *Persons and Polemics* (London, 1994), 202–27.

THOMSON, R. S., 'The Development of the Broadside Ballad Trade and its Influence upon the Transmission of English Folksongs' (unpublished Ph.D. dissertation, University of Cambridge, 1974).

THORNLEY, ISOBEL D., 'Treason by Words in the Fifteenth Century', *English Historical Review*, 32 (1917), 556–61.

TILLEY, MORRIS PALMER, *Elizabethan Proverb Lore in Lyly's 'Euphues' and in Pettie's 'Petite Pallace' with Parallels from Shakespeare* (New York, 1926).

—— *A Dictionary of the Proverbs in England in the Sixteenth and Seventeenth Centuries* (Ann Arbor, 1950).

TOLKIEN, J. R. R., 'Chaucer as a Philologist: The Reeve's Tale', *Transactions of the Philological Society* (1934), 1–70.

TONGUE, R. L., and BRIGGS, K. M., *Somerset Folklore* (Folklore Society, London, 1965).

TRUDGILL, PETER, *Sociolinguistics: An Introduction* (Harmondsworth, 1974).

TUCK, RICHARD, 'Civil Conflict in School and Town, 1500–1700', in Brian Mains and Anthony Tuck (eds.), *Royal Grammar School Newcastle upon Tyne: A History of the School in its Community* (Stocksfield, 1986), 1–38.

UNDERDOWN, DAVID, *Revel, Riot, and Rebellion: Popular Politics and Culture in England, 1603–1660* (Oxford, 1985).

—— 'The Taming of the Scold: The Enforcement of Patriarchal Authority in Early Modern England,' in Fletcher and Stevenson (eds.), *Order and Disorder in Early Modern England*, 116–36.

—— *Fire from Heaven: Life in an English Town in the Seventeenth Century* (London, 1992).

UNDERDOWN, DAVID, 'Regional Cultures? Local Variations in Popular Culture during the Early Modern Period', in Harris (ed.), *Popular Culture in England*, 28–47.

VANSINA, JAN, *Oral Tradition: A Study in Historical Methodology*, trans. H. M. Wright (London, 1965).

—— *Oral Tradition as History* (London, 1985).

VINCENT, DAVID, 'The Decline of the Oral Tradition in Popular Culture', in Robert D. Storch (ed.), *Popular Culture and Custom in Nineteenth-Century England* (London, 1982), 20–47.

—— *Literacy and Popular Culture: England, 1750–1914* (Cambridge, 1989).

VINCENT, W. A. L., *The Grammar Schools: Their Continuing Tradition, 1660–1714* (London, 1969).

WAKELIN, MARTYN F., *English Dialects: An Introduction* (rev. edn., London, 1977).

—— 'Significant Spellings in the St Ives Borough Accounts', *Neophilologus*, 57 (1973), 284–6.

—— 'Evidence for Spoken Regional English in the Sixteenth Century', *Revista Canaria De Estudios Ingleses*, 5 (1982), 1–25.

WALKER, J., 'The Censorship of the Press during the Reign of Charles II', *History*, new ser., 35 (1950), 219–38.

WALLER, P. J., 'Democracy and Dialect, Speech and Class', in P. J. Waller (ed.), *Politics and Social Change in Modern Britain* (Brighton, 1987), 1–33.

WALTER, JOHN, 'Grain Riots and Popular Attitudes to the Law: Maldon and the Crisis of 1629', in Brewer and Styles (eds.), *An Ungovernable People*, 47–84.

—— 'A "Rising of the People"? The Oxfordshire Rising of 1596', *Past and Present*, 107 (1985), 90–143.

WATSON, FOSTER, *The Grammar Schools to 1660: Their Curriculum and Practice* (Cambridge, 1908).

WATT, TESSA, *Cheap Print and Popular Piety, 1550–1640* (Cambridge, 1991).

WEBER, EUGEN, *Peasants into Frenchmen: The Modernization of Rural France, 1870–1914* (Stanford, Calif., 1976).

WESTWOOD, JENNIFER, *Albion: A Guide to Legendary Britain* (London, 1985).

WHITING, B. J., 'Proverbial Material in the Popular Ballad', *Journal of American Folklore*, 47 (1934), 22–44.

—— *Chaucer's Use of Proverbs* (Cambridge, Mass., 1934).

—— *Proverbs, Sentences and Proverbial Phrases from English Writings mainly before 1500* (Cambridge, Mass, 1968).

WIENER, CAROL Z., 'The Beleaguered Isle: A Study of Elizabethan and Early Jacobean Anti-Catholicism', *Past and Present*, 51 (1971), 27–62.

WILLIAMS, JOSEPH M., '"O! When Degree is Shak'd": Sixteenth-Century Anticipations of Some Modern Attitudes Toward Usage', in T. M. Machan and C. T. Scott (eds.), *English in its Social Contexts: Essays in Historical Sociolinguistics* (Oxford, 1992), 69–101.

WILSON, F. P., 'English Proverbs and Dictionaries of Proverbs', *Library*, second ser., 26 (1945–6), 51–71.

—— *Shakespearian and Other Studies*, ed. Helen Gardner (Oxford, 1969).

—— *The Oxford Dictionary of English Proverbs* (3rd edn., Oxford, 1970).

WOOD, ANDY, 'Custom, Identity and Resistance: English Free Miners and their Law *c.*1550–1800', in Griffiths, Fox and Hindle (eds.), *The Experience of Authority in Early Modern England*, 249–85.

WOOLF, D. R., 'Speech, Text and Time: The Sense of Hearing and the Sense of the Past in Renaissance England', *Albion*, 18 (1986), 159–93.

—— 'The "Common Voice": History, Folklore and Oral Tradition in Early Modern England', *Past and Present*, 120 (1988), 26–52.

—— 'Of Danes and Giants: Popular Beliefs about the Past in Early Modern England', *Dalhousie Review*, 71 (1991), 166–209.

WRIGHT, A. R., *British Calendar Customs: England*, ed. T. E. Lones (3 vols., Folklore Society, London, 1936–40).

WRIGHT, ELIZABETH MARY, *Rustic Speech and Folk-Lore* (Oxford, 1913).

WRIGHT, JOSEPH (ed.), *The English Dialect Dictionary* (6 vols., London, 1898–1905).

WRIGHT, LOUIS B., *Middle-Class Culture in Elizabethan England* (Chapel Hill, NC, 1935).

WRIGHTSON, KEITH, *English Society, 1580–1680* (London, 1982).

—— '"Sorts of People" in Tudor and Stuart England', in Jonathan Barry and Christopher Brooks (eds.), *The Middling Sort of People: Culture, Society and Politics in England, 1550–1800* (Basingstoke, 1994), 28–51.

—— and LEVINE, DAVID, *Poverty and Piety in an English Village: Terling, 1525–1700* (2nd edn., Oxford, 1995).

WRIGLEY, E. A., 'A Simple Model of London's Importance in Changing English Society and Economy 1650–1750', *Past and Present*, 37 (1967), 44–70.

WURZBACH, NATASCHA, *The Rise of the English Street Ballad, 1550–1650* (Cambridge, 1990).

WYLD, HENRY CECIL, *A History of Modern Colloquial English* (3rd edn., Oxford, 1936).

ZELL, MICHAEL, 'Fixing the Custom of the Manor: Slindon, West Sussex, 1568', *Sussex Archaeological Collections*, 122 (1984), 101–6.

# INDEX